Big Business in Mining and Petroleum

The International Library of Critical Writings in Business History

Series Editor: Geoffrey Jones
Professor of Business History,
University of Reading

Big Business in Mining and Petroleum

Edited by

Christopher Schmitz

Lecturer in Modern History
University of St Andrews, Scotland

THE INTERNATIONAL LIBRARY OF CRITICAL WRITINGS IN BUSINESS HISTORY

An Elgar Reference Collection

Published by
Edward Elgar Publishing Limited
Gower House
Croft Road
Aldershot
Hants GU11 3HR
England

Edward Elgar Publishing Company
Old Post Road
Brookfield
Vermont 05036
USA

British Library Cataloguing in Publication Data
Big Business in Mining and Petroleum. –
(International Library of Critical
Writings in Business History; Vol. 10)
  I. Schmitz, Christopher J. II. Series
  338.47622

Library of Congress Cataloguing in Publication Data
Big business in mining and petroleum / edited by Christopher Schmitz.
      p. cm. — (International library of critical writings in
  business history; 10) (An Elgar reference collection)
    Includes bibliographical references and index.
    1. Mineral industries—History. 2. Petroleum industry and trade–
–History. 3. International business enterprises—History.
  4. International trade—History. 5. Big business—History.
  I. Schmitz, Christopher, 1950–   . II. Series. III. Series: An
  Elgar reference collection.
  HD9506.A2842   1995
  338.2'09—dc20   94–42439
                                                                            CIP

ISBN 1 85898 048 8

Printed in Great Britain by Galliard (Printers) Ltd, Great Yarmouth

Contents

Acknowledgements

The editor and publishers wish to thank the following who have kindly given permission for the use of copyright material.

Australian Economic History Review for article: Peter Richardson (1987), 'The Origins and Development of the Collins House Group, 1915–1951', *Australian Economic History Review*, **XXVII** (1), 3–29.

Alexander Dow for his own article: (1984), 'Finance and Foreign Control in Canadian Base Metal Mining, 1918–1955', *Economic History Review*, 2nd series, **XXXVII**, 54–67.

Butterworth Heineman Ltd for article: Marian Radetzki (1989), 'The Role of State Owned Enterprises in the International Metal Mining Industry', *Resources Policy*, **XV**, 45–57.

Economic History Association and Cambridge University Press for articles: Ralph W. Hidy (1952), 'The Standard Oil Company (New Jersey)', *Journal of Economic History*, **XII**, 411–24; Richard J. Barker (1966), 'French Entrepreneurship During the Restoration: The Record of a Single Firm, the Anzin Mining Company', *Journal of Economic History*, **XXI**, 161–78.

Frank Cass & Co Ltd for article: Charles Harvey and Jon Press (1990), 'The City and International Mining, 1870–1914', *Business History*, **XXXII**, 98–119.

Harvard Business School Publishing for articles: Noel H. Pugach (1971), 'Standard Oil and Petroleum Development in Early Republican China', *Business History Review*, **XLV** (4), 452–73; William Graebner (1973), 'Great Expectations: The Search for Order in Bituminous Coal, 1890–1917', *Business History Review*, **XLVIII**, 49–72; Bernard W.E. Alford and Charles E. Harvey (1980), 'Copperbelt Merger: The Formation of the Rhokana Corporation, 1930–1932', *Business History Review*, **LIV**, 330–58.

Harvard University Press for excerpts: Raymond Vernon (1983), 'The World Oil Market in Transition', in *Two Hungry Giants: The United States and Japan in the Quest for Oil and Ores*, 19–37; Raymond Vernon (1983), 'Japan's Institutions and Practices', in *Two Hungry Giants: The United States and Japan in the Quest for Oil and Ores*, 82–106.

Macmillan Press Ltd for the excerpts: Geoffrey Jones (1981), 'The British in Foreign Oilfields', in *The State and the Emergence of the British Oil Industry*, 47–84; William Ashworth (1991), 'Coal', in *The State in Business, 1945 to mid 1980s*, 91–103.

Pitman Publishing for the excerpt: Ervin Hexner (1946), 'Aluminum', 'Tin', 'Zinc', 'Diamonds', 'Petroleum', in *International Cartels*, 216–21, 238–54, 256–62.

Princeton University Press for excerpt: Theodore H. Moran (1974), 'From Chileanization to Nationalization: Success and Revenge in the Movement Away from *Dependencia*, in *Multinational Corporations and the Politics of Dependence: Copper in Chile*, 119–52.

Reed Consumer Books Ltd for excerpt: T.A.B. Corley (1988), 'Towards Joint Venture 1949–54', in *A History of the Burmah Oil Company, volume II: 1924–66*, 171–99.

Resources for the Future for excerpts: Orris C. Herfindahl (1959), 'Price Manipulation – 1870 to World War I', in *Copper Costs and Prices: 1870–1957*, 70–91; Raymond F. Mikesell (1971), 'Conflict in Foreign Investor–Host Country Relations: A Preliminary Analysis', in *Foreign Investment in the Petroleum and Mineral Industries*, 29–55; Raymond F. Mikesell (1971), 'Bethlehem's Joint Venture in Brazilian Manganese', in *Foreign Investment in the Petroleum and Mineral Industries*, 365–8.

Peter Richardson and Jean-Jacques Van Helten for their own article: (1984), 'The Development of the South African Gold-Mining Industry, 1895–1918', *Economic History Review*, 2nd series, **XXXVII** (3), 319–40.

Routledge for excerpt: Raymond F. Mikesell and John W. Whitney (1987), 'An Overview of the World Mining Industry', in *The World Mining Industry: Investment Strategy and Public Policy*, 1–29.

Royal Institute of International Affairs for excerpt: Phillip Crowson (1983), 'Non-Fuel Mineral Procurement Policies', in Nobutoshi Akao (ed.), *Japan's Economic Security: Resources as a Factor in Foreign Policy*, 145–67.

Twentieth Century Fund for excerpt: Louis Lister (1960), 'Coal: Concerted Practices', in *Europe's Coal and Steel Community: An Experiment in Economic Union*, 251–81.

University of Arizona for excerpt: Thomas R. Navin (1978), 'Pollution, Politics and Proven Reserves', in *Copper Mining and Management*, 97–109, 371.

Every effort has been made to trace all the copyright holders but if any have been inadvertently overlooked the publishers will be pleased to make the necessary arrangement at the first opportunity.

In addition the publishers wish to thank the Library of the London School of Economics and Political Science, the Marshall Library of Economics, Cambridge University and the Photographic Unit of the University of London Library for their assistance in obtaining these articles.

Introduction

The exploitation of mineral resources has been an international industry through a considerable part of human history. There is evidence that copper trading flourished in the Mediterranean world as far back as the thirteenth century BC, while tin from Cornwall and Spain was being exported to the Middle East by about 1000 BC. Mining was also almost certainly the ancient world's biggest business; the massive complex of silver-lead mines at Laurion, in Greece, employed at least 20,000 men in 413 BC (Shepherd, 1993; 74, 115, 338), while numerous Roman mines in Spain and other parts of their empire were worked on a scarcely less impressive scale. From the earliest phases of human civilization, the practical difficulties associated with locating mineral deposits, often in remote or inhospitable environments, coupled with the technical problems and financial implications involved in exploiting them, meant that there was a strong momentum towards large-scale enterprise, and frequently entailing state intervention. Such was the case in late sixteenth-century England, when statutory monopolies were established, and German technical experts were imported, to produce strategically important copper and brass products for the nation's munitions industry (Donald, 1961). By the nineteenth and twentieth centuries, similar technical and financial constraints ensured that the mineral industries remained amongst the world's largest industrial organizations. At the same time, the accelerating pace of global industrialization resulted in a rapidly expanding market for fuel and non-fuel minerals. World mine production of copper, for example, rose from around 60,000 tonnes a year in the mid-1850s to 9 billion tonnes by the end of the 1980s, and crude petroleum output growing from less than 50 million tonnes in 1905 to just under 3 billion tonnes a year in the late 1980s (Schmitz, 1979; 64; Venn, 1986; 8; British Geological Survey, 1990; 18, 50).

This collection of readings aims to provide a reference tool for international business historians, particularly in order to redress a long-standing imbalance in the literature, which has tended to analyse corporate growth largely in terms of the experience of manufacturing industry (Schmitz, 1993; 11). If it is possible to identify a general theme emerging from the research represented in this volume, it appears to be that the mining and petroleum industries have certain characteristics which differentiate them from other industries, in particular, geological factors which most obviously dictate the location of operations, as well as strongly influencing the technological and organizational parameters within which the enterprises function. In relation to mining – although the point applies equally to the oil industry – Mikesell and Whitney argue, 'orebodies are where you find them. Unlike manufacturing, marketing, or service industries, mine location is determined by geology. This explains why mining firms were the first modern nonfinancial multinational corporations. Large mining firms send teams of geologists all over the world to locate new sources of minerals' (Mikesell and Whitney, 1987; 30). The consequent spread of mineral and petroleum production into many of the earth's wilderness regions, as well as to less developed nations, has also ensured that these industries have experienced increasing and unusually sensitive environmental and political constraints during the course of the twentieth century.

Defining the business organizations which are the subject of this volume is not entirely a straightforward matter since they tend to have evolved in a variety of ways and from a number of different directions. This is particularly the case with what are generally termed 'mining' companies in the literature. Sometimes, like RTZ or Newmont, these started life as ore-producers, before integrating forwards (often after a considerable passage of time) into smelting, refining or semi-fabrication. Others, like ASARCO or AMAX (American Metal) started as smelters or refiners, before integrating backwards into mining. Yet more, like Metallgesellschaft, have remained principally metals trading firms throughout their lives, but have, at various times, diversified into different areas of minerals exploration, mining, smelting and refining. Consequently, the definition of mining firms proposed by Mikesell and Whitney (Chapter 1), is extremely valuable in providing a manageable and generally applicable framework with which to approach the industry. They set the parameters of their own study by suggesting that 'mining' includes the production of 'the major metals from the exploration and mining stages to the processing stage from which they are normally marketed for use in manufacturing'. Their study includes coal, iron ores, ferroalloys (for example nickel and chromium), and the non-ferrous metals (such as aluminium, copper, gold and zinc). However, they exclude the aluminium refining or iron and steel industries beyond the ore-producing stage, largely because they argue these would require large-scale studies in themselves. For similar reasons, these latter activities are only briefly alluded to in some of the papers included in this collection. In contrast to mining firms, petroleum firms are rather more easily delineated since the largest amongst them are much more frequently vertically integrated through the four main stages in the industry: crude production, refining, transportation and marketing, although, like mining, there has been some variation in their growth patterns.

The position occupied by mining and petroleum companies amongst the world's largest industrial firms of the twentieth century is outlined in Table 1. Amongst other things, this indicates a continuing momentum towards larger-scale enterprise, particularly in the petroleum industry where the total turnover of the top twelve firms almost doubled (in 1992 prices) from around $290 billion in 1956, to $570 billion in 1992, a rise reflected in the continued high global rankings of oil companies. In contrast, mining firms in general slipped significantly in the table. The continuing importance of American firms is apparent, although there are indications that this dominance was weakening by the 1990s, especially in the mining sector. At the same time, the absence of Japanese enterprises amongst the ranks of the largest oil and mining corporations, even in 1992, is perhaps significant. Later twentieth-century state intervention in mining and petroleum – if on the retreat in some economies – is also evident in organizations like Elf Aquitaine, PDVSA, British Coal and Zambia Industrial and Mining. A degree of long-term stability in the industry leadership of many of the major oil firms is equally noteworthy, most obviously Exxon (which started life as Standard Oil of New Jersey) and the Royal Dutch–Shell group, whilst within the mining sector firms like RTZ (Rio Tinto) and De Beers have succeeded in maintaining a prominent profile since the early twentieth century, despite intervening vicissitudes. All these observations clearly raise important questions about the nature of corporate growth in mining and oil, as well as the changing nature of world markets for these commodities, and many of these issues are addressed in the papers included in this collection.

Mikesell and Whitney, in their overview of the world mining industry (Chapter 1), comment

Table 1   The Largest Petroleum and Mining Companies in the World, 1912–1992
(market capitalization 1912; turnover 1956, 1992, $ millions; and world ranking
amongst all industrial firms)

1912		1956		1992	
Petroleum Companies					
1 Standard Oil (NJ)	390 (2)	Standard Oil (NJ)	7127 (2)	Exxon	103 547 (2)
2 Shell	91 (25)	Royal Dutch-Shell	6500 (3)	Royal Dutch-Shell	98 935 (4)
3 Standard Oil (Indiana)	88 (26)	Socony-Mobil	2750 (8)	British Petroleum	59 216 (11)
4 Standard Oil (NY)	73 (31)	Gulf	2340 (14)	Mobil	57 389 (13)
5 Standard Oil (Calif.)	71 (33)	Texas Co.	2046 (16)	ENI	40 366 (21)
6 Prairie Oil & Gas	50 (51)	British Petroleum	2021 (17)	Elf Aquitaine	39 718 (22)
7 Burmah Oil	38 (63)	Standard Oil (Indiana)	1890 (19)	Chevron	38 523 (24)
8 Mexican Petroleum	37 (66)	Shell Union	1365 (21)	Texaco	37 130 (27)
9 Texas Co.	29 (81)	Standard Oil (Calif.)	1453 (23)	Total	26 142 (45)
10 Atlantic Refining	26 (93)	Sinclair Oil	1180 (30)	Amoco	25 543 (46)
11 Vacuum Oil	26 (95)	Phillips Petroleum	1033 (37)	PDVSA	21 375 (56)
12 Royal Dutch	23 (107)	Sun Oil	731 (60)	Pemex	21 293 (57)
Mining Companies					
1 Anaconda	178 (5)	National Coal Board	2483 (10)	Ruhrkohle	15 712 (81)
2 De Beers	158 (12)	Anaconda	749 (55)	British Coal	7 082 (219)
3 Rio Tinto	143 (13)	American Metal	667 (67)	RTZ	5 888 (258)
4 Utah Copper	95 (22)	ASARCO	593 (77)	CRA	3 875 (370)
5 Phelps Dodge	95 (23)	Kennecott	567 (84)	De Beers	3 667 (392)
6 ASARCO	92 (24)	International Nickel	445 (110)	Zambia Ind & Min	3 043 (457)
7 Rand Mines	65 (39)	Phelps Dodge	419 (113)	Codelco-Chile	3 017 (462)
8 Crown Mines	63 (40)				
9 International Nickel	57 (44)				
10 Calumet & Hecla	51 (49)				
11 Cons. Gold Fields	47 (52)				
12 Harpener Bergbau	45 (53)				

Sources: 1912 ranking by stock market valuation. Schmitz, 1993; 30; Schmitz, unpublished paper. 'The World's Largest Industrial Companies of 1912'. 1956, 1992 rankings by gross sales, *Fortune*. 'Fortune Global 500', (1957), (1993). Royal Dutch, 1912, represents nominal capitalization. A major omission in Fortune magazine's listing for 1956 was the British state-owned National Coal Board; its turnover for that year is taken from Ashworth (1986; 683), and the rankings in the original Fortune list adjusted accordingly.

on its high degree of concentration of ownership and control in the hands of a relatively small number of multinational firms, most of which are privately owned. They also indicate that big business in mining is evident in another sense: in the concentration of the bulk of output for many minerals in a relatively small number of very large-scale individual mines. This, in turn, introduces a complex of geological and technical factors which add a high degree of uncertainty, and cost, to the exploration and set-up stages of such operations: a modern open-pit copper mine, with associated milling and smelting facilities, perhaps involving an initial outlay running to a billion dollars or more. At the same time, Mikesell and Whitney join a long line of writers, such as Orris Herfindahl (Chapter 10), in stressing the essentially competitive nature of world markets in almost all minerals, despite the apparent tendency towards oligopoly in this sector. The consequent volatility of mineral prices has presented producers, over at least the past two centuries, with an additional degree of uncertainty, of a kind virtually unknown in manufacturing industry.

Raymond Vernon's review of the international oil market (Chapter 2) suggests that similar constraints have been present in this industry, and that oil companies have been 'continuously engaged in a search to hold down their risks' and inject an element of stability into their operating environment. This quest took various forms, but typically involved experiments with cartels or, more successful in the long run, strategies of vertical integration coupled with the refining of organizational capabilities. Such policies have helped giant oil firms like Exxon and Royal Dutch–Shell dominate their industry through most of the twentieth century but, as Vernon indicates, the market share of the seven major producers (the 'seven sisters') fell from 98 to 24 per cent between 1950 and 1979 and this, coupled with the enduring weakness of OPEC (the Organization of Petroleum Exporting Countries), leads him towards a pessimistic view of future world oil market stability.

Raymond Mikesell rounds out the introductory section of this volume by providing a survey (Chapter 3) of a particularly contentious aspect of corporate growth in the extractive industries – the frequently troubled relationship between multinational enterprises and host nations. He approaches this with the belief that it is necessary to break away from what he sees as the over-simplifying approaches in many accounts, which tend to dwell on 'foreign exploitation' or the investment-restricting impact of socialism. However, after attempting to set out the potential parameters for 'meaningful bargaining' in a theoretical context, he rather pessimistically concludes that conflict is probably unavoidable, but that agreement and conciliation should be attainable through the application of 'joint maximizing solutions', if these can possibly be identified.

The fact that big business in general – in the guise of cartels, large-scale integrated firms or multinational enterprise – is not uniquely a product of the twentieth century, is now well established in the literature (Wilkins, 1970; 199–217; Schmitz, 1986; 16–22). This is especially true of the mining industry where, as already suggested, a unique combination of locational and technical problems, coupled with inherently unpredictable markets, meant that various forms of business concentration were apparent far earlier than the more widespread, later nineteenth-century drift towards large-scale enterprise in railways, public utilities and manufacturing. As G.C. Allen's classic essay (Chapter 4) demonstrates, British copper producers in the late eighteenth century were encouraged to form a joint marketing organization, with the enormous capitalization, for the time, of £0.5 million (around $2.5 million), in an attempt to control output and prices. In common with numerous occasions during the following two centuries, a new supply of relatively cheaply-won ores (in this case from Welsh open-pit mines) had destabilized the market and resulted in a rapid collapse in prices. However, despite the involvement of most leading members of the industry, this combination found itself increasingly unable to control the situation, with debt-funded stocks rising, and imports being sucked into Britain by artificially high prices. In writing his paper in the early 1920s, Allen found a 'curious parallel to that of many recent combinations' and, indeed, the inherent weakness of the Cornish Metal Company of 1785–92 was closely mirrored in the unfortunate experiences of subsequent copper cartels, as discussed in Herfindahl's paper (Chapter 10). Whilst Allen's copper combination was created and managed by a diverse group of businessmen – miners, smelters and equipment suppliers – it was generally more common for large-scale firms before the mid-nineteenth century to be closely owned and controlled by family groups, and one such example in the extractive sector was the Anzin Mining Company. As Barker discusses in his paper (Chapter 5), this firm dominated the French coal mining industry in the early nineteenth century, employing as many as 6,000 workers in its pits by the 1830s, and had a share capitalization equivalent to about $7 million in 1832. Despite being owned by a limited number of investors – most notably the politically-powerful Périer banking family – this enterprise does not quite conform to a once commonly held view of managerially conservative French family-dominated firms. Instead, the Périers took a lead in promoting major reforms of the Anzin company's organization in the early 1820s, and took it through a period of technological innovation and vertical integration which consolidated its position as one of Europe's leading coal producers of the period. Numerous other examples could be given of the early growth of big business in mining, all of which would serve to underline the points made by Allen's and Barker's papers, that very many of the features of twentieth-century business organization in the extractive sector, as well as many of the problems encountered by such enterprises, were anticipated in developments which took place well before the mid-nineteenth century.

Nevertheless, a variety of factors combined to produce an unprecedentedly rapid increase in business concentration in many areas of the world's mining and petroleum industries in the later nineteenth and twentieth centuries. The third section of this anthology contains a number of papers illustrating this theme, and starts with an examination, by Schmitz, of the rise of big business in the copper industry between the 1870s and 1920s (Chapter 6). Although specific to one, albeit dominant, part of the mining sector, many of the issues raised in this article apply with equal force to other areas of mineral extraction and processing; in particular the momentum towards large-scale enterprise induced by the inevitable trend towards the exploitation of increasingly large-scale but correspondingly lower grade mineral deposits. One point made in this paper, that organizational changes in mining allowed the emergence of 'permanent' mining houses – in contrast to the regime of notoriously speculative and short-lived mining enterprises which dominated previous perceptions of the industry – is echoed in the essay by Richardson and Van Helten (Chapter 7). Their study of South African gold mining demonstrates that the long-term mining programmes of the leading companies were encouraged, in large part, by the Rand's distinctive reefs of gold-bearing conglomerate, which could be delineated and exploited in a much more predictable way than the types of gold deposit more commonly located in other parts of the world. They also discuss the rise to prominence of organizations like the Werner Beit group and Consolidated Gold Fields, the way in which the former came to dominate the Rand through a series of mergers between 1906 and 1911, and how both were deeply implicated in the ill-fated Jameson conspiracy of 1895–6, which attempted to wrest the Transvaal from the Boers and into the sphere of British colonial control.

Peter Richardson's article (Chapter 8) extends the theme of evolving mining investment houses by demonstrating the extent to which a constellation of business interests, which had its origins in the Australian lead–zinc industry, spread out to dominate many areas of that country's business system from the 1920s onwards. There is also an imperial dimension in this paper, rather like the previous one, with Richardson underlining the way in which the Collins House Group originally emerged as a war-time response to the heavy involvement of German interests in the Australian metals trade in the years prior to 1914. Subsequent strategy was also driven, in part, by a perceived need to combat the multinational spread of American mining firms in the interwar period, a theme which is developed by Alford and Harvey, in their article on the formation of the Rhokana Corporation (Chapter 9). This merger of leading interests on the Northern Rhodesia copperbelt in 1930 was jointly sponsored by the British-based Rio Tinto company and Rhodesian Anglo-American, part of South Africa's leading mining group, initially to forestall major investment in the region by the American Smelting and Refining Company (ASARCO). Alford and Harvey analyse the complex motives behind this episode and conclude that formal merger theory offers relatively little in the way of explanation; instead they stress the importance of the political pressures involved, as well as the specific advantages which the two sponsoring groups sought in the arrangement.

A broader approach to the history of organizational change in mining and petroleum – specifically pooling and cartel arrangements – is provided in the next two selections, by Herfindahl (Chapter 10) and Hexner (Chapter 11). These review, respectively, market-fixing arrangements in the copper industry between the 1860s and the First World War, and a variety of international cartels in the aluminium, tin, zinc, diamond and petroleum markets before the Second World War. Herfindahl's primary conclusion was that, with the exception of an American producers' sales pool in the 1870s, attempts to control the copper market have generally been doomed to failure – most spectacularly the French syndicate of 1887–89 – given what he saw as the essentially competitive nature of the market for this and similar primary commodities. He also highlights the difficulty, for contemporaries as well as later scholars, of establishing whether pools were in operation in given periods, given the inherent tendency to secrecy amongst the parties to these agreements. Hexner found a mixed record amongst the cartels he studied, the most successful being the international diamond cartel, controlled since at least the 1930s by the De Beers organization – aided and abetted in various ways by the policies of the South African state. A political dimension also loomed large in international petroleum agreements, with diplomacy exercising great influence on marketing in an otherwise privately-organized international trade, according to Hexner. At the same time, he implied, the varying fortunes of aluminium, tin and zinc cartels largely reflected the nature of the product: those in tin were generally the most effective, since production was not only highly geographically concentrated, but was also very much controlled within two colonial spheres, those of Britain and the Netherlands. Aluminium and zinc cartels were rather less successful, in part because their production was more widely diffused throughout the world.

The United States was, in many senses, the major breeding ground for organizational change in business in the century after the 1860s, and the mining and petroleum industries were no exceptions to this pattern. In her paper on the American lead industry (Chapter 12), Elizabeth May suggests how tariff policy and geology interacted to mould the nature of corporate growth, and led to the dominance of major producers like the St Joseph Lead Company and the Guggenheim family controlled ASARCO. As far as oil is concerned, Ralph Hidy's essay (Chapter 13) represents a classic study of pioneering organizational change in the world's largest oil company, and stands as a prologue to the much fuller account published in 1955 in Ralph and Muriel Hidy's volume, *Pioneering in Big Business, 1882–1911: History of*

Standard Oil Company (New Jersey). In an argument which is now a central strand in Alfred D. Chandler's highly influential history of American business, *The Visible Hand* (1977), Hidy suggested that John D. Rockefeller and his managerial team skilfully crafted a vertically-integrated organization which aimed at maximizing long-term growth, rather than short-term profit, as well as working towards the steady coordination of through-put from crude oil production to final consumer. In this way, although firms in other industries, such as Du Pont and General Motors, were later to assume the mantle of leading organizational innovators in American business, Standard of New Jersey, as Hidy convincingly argues, 'constituted the first successful attempt to organize and operate, on a massive scale, the production and distribution of goods other than services'.

The one significant exception to the pattern of rapidly increasing business concentration in mining in the pre-Second World War era, in the United States and elsewhere, was the coal industry. As the next group of papers, by Graebner (Chapter 14), Lister (Chapter 15) and Ashworth (Chapter 16) illustrate, the pre-Second World War industry tended to be represented by a multitude of competing colliery firms, except in Germany where the coal industry was heavily cartelized from the 1890s onwards, or was vertically integrated within large-scale iron and steel enterprises. This position was considerably modified after 1945 with a wave of coal nationalizations, most notably in Britain and France. Short of such direct intervention, as Graebner implies, the coal industry generally suffered from conditions which were inherently disadvantageous to business concentration or market control. In particular, geological and technical factors mean that coal deposits are far more widely dispersed through the world and are normally far more easily worked than other minerals, so the coal industry has always tended to have lower barriers to entry than other kinds of mining. Graebner catalogues the indifferent history of attempts to escape the rigours of excessive competition in the American coal market into the 1920s, while Lister provides an outline of similar attempts within the European coal industry, before more coordinated action became possible within the framework of the European Coal and Steel Community, and the European Economic Community, in the 1950s and 1960s. Ashworth's brief review of the British coal industry under state ownership since 1947 demonstrates how, in many ways, it has suffered from excessive political interference, being required to operate under constantly changing and generally onerous financial and marketing constraints. In these terms, and against a background of an increasingly competitive world coal market, it is hardly surprising that British Coal (formerly the National Coal Board) contracted drastically between the late 1940s and the late 1980s – its workforce falling to a seventh of its original level and its output being halved. By 1994, it might be added, the decline had become even more pronounced, as what remained of British Coal stood on the brink of being returned to private ownership.

As the twentieth century has progressed, political pressures in general have tended to increase on large-scale mining and petroleum firms, both in their domestic markets and within the international arena. The latter has almost certainly been most keenly felt in respect of the nationalization programmes which occurred in many nations, particularly in the less developed world, during the 1960s and 1970s. However, as Radetzki argues (Chapter 17), this trend appears to have come to an end by the 1980s, partly as a result of the greater perceived inefficiency of such state-run concerns and because nationalization often ruptured existing international vertical links within the industry – thus arguably increasing transaction costs for the affected enterprises. He also suggests that this trend was strongly encouraged in the first place by factors that, once again, are unique to the mineral industries; the obvious inability of multinational firms physically to move mineral deposits meant that there could be far-reaching state intervention without a risk that the parent might move the activity, as might happen with manufacturing subsidiaries. Other, and perhaps equally worrying, developments for mining and oil company executives since the 1950s, have been the twin problems of increasing environmental concern and anxieties about future availability of economically-recoverable natural resources. Navin's article (Chapter 18) addresses both these issues, with particular reference to the recent experience of the copper industry within the United States. He demonstrates that in the wake of the pioneering Paley Commission of 1952, both themes have inter-twined, and have meant that copper company executives have repeatedly been forced, rather reluctantly, to enter the political arena, in order to negotiate terms of compliance with environmental legislation or to debate resource conservation issues – and this was no easy matter, especially for top management in firms like Anaconda, which had long held a reputation for obsessive secrecy.

The fourth and final section of this anthology contains papers which examine the implications of foreign direct investment (FDI) in the mining and petroleum industries since the late nineteenth century, and more especially, the relationships between multinational enterprise (MNE) and host nations. There has been, for some time, a rapidly growing literature on MNE and FDI in general, and this allows us to set out, with certain necessary reservations, the broad parameters of international investment in the extractive and mineral processing industries. As far as the United States is concerned, its total FDI in mining (including smelting) and oil (extraction and refining) rose from around $219 million in 1897, to $2.57 billion in 1929, and $27.9 billion in 1970 (in current prices), representing around 35 to 40 per cent of all American-sourced FDI through this period (Wilkins, 1970; 110; Wilkins, 1974; 182–3, 330). The dominance of American FDI in oil and mining in 1970 is suggested by another set of estimates which gives the equivalent figure for Britain as $4.6 billion, Japan as $1.1 billion and the German Federal Republic as just $0.42 billion (Franko, 1976; 48); although, as the first two papers in this section (Chapters 19 and 20) imply, British FDI was undoubtedly far more influential in these sectors at an earlier stage in the twentieth century. More recent systematic estimates than those for 1970 are difficult to locate and, in any case, all such figures must be treated with some degree of circumspection. As one survey of world mining investment has cautioned: 'Statistics on the volume and distribution of foreign investment in mining are limited, difficult to interpret, and generally out of date because of the rash of nationalization, especially in Latin America' (Bosson and Varon, 1977; 46).

A metropolitan perspective of mining and petroleum FDI, from the point of view of the pre-First World War British capital market, is provided by Charles Harvey and Jon Press (Chapter 19) and Geoffrey Jones (Chapter 20). These papers indicate the vitality and global significance of British-sourced FDI in the half-century before 1914, when perhaps as many as 8,000 or 9,000 individual mining firms were formed for all kinds of foreign mining in every corner of the globe, and many hundreds more oil ventures for operations ranging as far afield as Russia, Iraq, Burma and Mexico. The vast majority of these were single-objective enterprises – what Mira Wilkins has termed 'free-standing companies', to distinguish them from classic multi-operation MNE – and they appear to have suffered from an excessively high failure rate. This led numerous authors, including Harvey and Press, and Jones, to conclude that most of these firms had very weak managerial structures. However, both these papers highlight the significance of informal networks of promoters, engineers, financiers, lawyers and investors, in British capital markets in this period. Harvey and Press convincingly argue that the City of London represented 'a large, vital, multi-functional cluster of organizations' which, in providing an interlocking network of promotional activities, can be seen as a risk-minimizing strategy. In this way, British multinational enterprise in the extractive sector arguably built more upon external economies of scale than its American or continental European counterparts. However, foreign mining and oil ventures remained amongst the highest risk forms of investment and, despite the success stories outlined by Harvey and Press, and Jones, such as Rand Mines or Shell, there were many more which failed through bad geological advice, local political troubles or a host of other difficulties. Jones also demonstrates how oil companies, in an excess of competitive zeal, suffered from repeated attempts to 'blacken' one another, encouraging a long-standing, negative public perception of them – effectively epitomizing the unacceptable face of international capitalism.

The political dimension to international investment in the mineral and petroleum industries is prominent in the next group of articles in this collection. Pugach (Chapter 21) discusses the commercial rivalries which led Standard Oil of New York (SOCONY) to negotiate exploration rights in China on the eve of the First World War. However, despite considerable assistance from the US State and Commerce Departments (not always welcomed by SOCONY), the proposed joint-venture with the Chinese government was a failure, due to both the inexperienced and often tactless attitudes of the American firm and, perhaps more significant, what Pugach describes as the duplicity and underlying xenophobia which characterized the Chinese approach to negotiations.

Whilst American FDI was finding its way into distant areas like Asia in the early twentieth century, the vast bulk was directed in what Mira Wilkins (1970) has figuratively described as a 'spillover' into adjoining Canada and Latin America. Dow (Chapter 22) examines the impact of foreign mining investment within the former economy, particularly that coming from the United States, and suggests that traditional anxieties about foreign dominance in less developed nations should not mask the fact that comparable emotions can arise in a high-income society, with a similar culture, like Canada. He also outlines the way in which political pressures resulted in partial repatriation of key American-founded enterprises, most notably International Nickel in the late 1920s. The extract from Moran's study of American investment in Chilean copper (Chapter 23) illustrates the more commonly presented paradigm of American investment in a less developed economy. He traces the way in which moves to nationalize the main American copper companies operating in Chile were started in the 1960s, and brought to fruition under the ill-fated President Salvadore Allende in 1971. Perhaps most interesting is his examination of why the responses to the threat of nationalization by the two major firms affected – Anaconda and Kennecott – differed so radically.

The chapter from the second volume of Corley's history of the Burmah Oil Company (Chapter 24) depicts the way in which this particular British petroleum multinational responded to the granting of political independence to Burma in 1948. After a period of tortuous negotiations, which lasted from 1949 until 1954, a fairly amicable joint-venture agreement was reached between the company, which had been working the Burmese oilfields since 1886, and the national government. One problem had been the somewhat unpredictable nature of Burmese politics but, rather surprisingly, as Corley shows, the main stumbling block was the generally uncooperative attitude of both Labour and Conservative governments back in

Britain. In contrast with the uncertain experiences of SOCONY in China, Anaconda and Kennecott in Chile, and Burmah Oil in Burma, the leading American steel firm, Bethlehem, was able to invest in Brazil in the years after 1949 in a rather painless way, as Mikesell points out in his short paper (Chapter 25). Its joint-venture agreement with private Brazilian interests gained it access to some of the world's most promising manganese deposits, while the Brazilians, he suggests, benefited from the funding and technical expertise that Bethlehem was able to bring them. Thus, he implies, it stands as a model of how best-practice FDI should be arranged.

The global importance of leading South African gold and diamond mining firms like De Beers, Rand Mines, Crown Mines and Consolidated Gold Fields in the pre-1914 era is apparent from Table 1, as is the continuing importance of De Beers into the 1990s. Nevertheless, as Duncan Innes forcefully argues (Chapter 26), the true significance of South African corporate control in world mining (as well as other areas of industry) has long been concealed behind the nebulous structure of interlocking enterprises created, and still dominated, by succeeding members of the Oppenheimer family. He demonstrates that a network of interlocking corporate structures, built around the powerful Anglo-American group of companies, had come to control as many as 250 mining companies operating in at least 22 countries by 1976, as well as some 73 assorted industrial and financial concerns. This, he argues, has made the Anglo-American group, however diffuse the nature of its organization, one of the biggest multinational investors in the world.

The final three selections in this anthology relate to Japanese enterprise in the world's mining and petroleum industries. All are underpinned by the basic fact that this rapidly expanding economy of the later twentieth century has few indigenous mineral resources, and so has long been forced to acquire a considerable part of these abroad. Elizabeth Schumpeter's paper (Chapter 27), drawn from a massive monograph on Japan's economy, published in America the year before the outbreak of the Pacific war, details the extent to which Japanese firms became involved in the exploitation of the mineral resources of Manchuria, annexed by the Japanese army in 1931. Most of the leading Japanese 'zaibatsu' (industrial–financial combines), including Mitsui, Mitsubishi and Sumitomo, were involved in this process, working in particular through the agency of the Japanese government-controlled South Manchuria Railway Company, to develop the region's extensive coal and iron deposits. Schumpeter makes it clear that the Japanese state was heavily involved in all these ventures, reflecting the strategic importance of securing scarce fuels and metals.

A continuing, proactive role for the state in post-war Japan's mineral procurement policies is emphasized in Raymond Vernon's paper (Chapter 28). He outlines the variety of ways in which Japanese firms have been encouraged, in large measure under the aegis of the influential Ministry of International Trade and Investment (MITI), to invest in international mining and oil ventures, often when pure commercial considerations might have dictated otherwise, as in the case of Mitsui's reluctant involvement in an Iranian petrochemical venture. Such themes are continued in the article by Phillip Crowson, an economist employed by RTZ (Chapter 29). He further suggests that, in common with virtually all leading industrial nations, Japan has had no coherent mineral procurement policy, but rather, an *ad hoc* set of responses to its increasingly pressing need for imported fuels and industrial raw materials. He also underlines the fact that Japan has tended to import crude ores and concentrates, rather than refined metals which, amongst other things, has retained the higher value-added end of metals refining and fabrication within the domestic economy. Another point of significance in this final paper is its highlighting of particular Japanese FDI methods – in part mirroring those of German firms like Metallgesellschaft – whereby, in addition to orthodox joint-ventures, its firms have also provided loan finance to foreign mining enterprises, against long-term sales contracts.

These papers collectively address many issues which have been central to discussion of corporate change in the extractive and mineral processing industries over the past century or more, as well as related issues in mining and petroleum technology and international primary commodity markets. What this collection is unable to do, is to provide more than a few case studies of the growth of individual firms in these industries. However, such a task has been admirably accomplished by the ongoing *International Directory of Company Histories* project, the fourth volume of which (Hast, 1991) contains brief historical sketches of 72 leading companies in the mining and metals sector, as well as an identical number of leading petroleum firms – in both cases covering nationalized as well as private-sector enterprises. It is hoped, in conclusion, that this set of papers may act not only as a guide to what has been achieved to date in this particular field of scholarship, but also as a stimulus to further research on the development of business enterprise in the world's mining and oil industries.

References

Ashworth, William (1986), *The History of the British Coal Industry, vol. 5. 1946–1982: The Nationalized Industry* (Oxford: Clarendon Press).

Bosson, Rex and Varon, Benison (1977), *The Mining Industry and the Developing Countries* (New York: World Bank–Oxford University Press).

British Geological Survey (1990), *World Mineral Production 1985–89: Preliminary Statistics* (London: HMSO).

Chandler, Alfred D. Jr. (1977), *The Visible Hand: The Managerial Revolution in American Business* (Cambridge MA: Harvard University Press).

Donald, M.B. (1961), *Elizabethan Monopolies: The History of the Company of Mineral and Battery Works from 1565 to 1604* (Edinburgh: Oliver & Boyd).

Franko, Lawrence (1976), *The European Multinationals: A Renewed Challenge to American and British Big Business* (London–New York: Harper & Row).

Hast, Adele (ed.) (1991), *International Directory of Company Histories*, volume IV (Chicago–London: St James Press).

Hidy, Ralph W. and Hidy, Muriel E. (1955), *Pioneering in Big Business, 1882–1911: History of Standard Oil Company (New Jersey)* (New York: Harper).

Mikesell, Raymond F. and Whitney, John W. (1987), *The World Mining Industry: Investment Strategy and Public Policy* (Boston–London: Allen & Unwin).

Schmitz, Christopher J. (1979), *World Non-Ferrous Metal Production and Prices, 1700–1976* (London: Frank Cass).

Schmitz, Christopher J. (1993), *The Growth of Big Business in the United States and Western Europe, 1850–1939* (Basingstoke: Macmillan).

Shepherd, R. (1993), *Ancient Mining* (London–New York: Elsevier).

Venn, Fiona (1986), *Oil Diplomacy in the Twentieth Century* (Basingstoke: Macmillan).

Wilkins, Mira (1970), *The Emergence of Multinational Enterprise: American Business Abroad from the Colonial Era to 1914* (Cambridge MA: Harvard University Press).

Wilkins, Mira (1974), *The Maturing of Multinational Enterprise: American Business Abroad from 1914 to 1970* (Cambridge MA: Harvard University Press).

Part I
Theoretical Perspectives
and Industry Surveys

[1]

1

An Overview of the World Mining Industry

General Characteristics

The mining industry is defined in various ways, depending upon what materials are covered and the degree of processing of the materials extracted from the earth. According to the broadest definition, mining includes discovering, extracting and processing of all non-renewable resources up to the point at which they are used as inputs for fabricating or for producing energy. This broad definition includes the energy minerals such as coal, petroleum and natural gas; refined or processed metals such as copper, steel and the ferroalloys; and nonminerals such as diamonds, phosphate and potash. A much narrower definition of mining includes only crude or nonprocessed mine products, such as mineral ores and coal, and excludes petroleum and natural gas. In this study we deal mainly with the major metals from the exploration and mining stages to the processing stage from which they are normally marketed for use in manufacturing. The major metals include iron and the ferroalloys (nickel, manganese, chromium and molybdenum); and the nonferrous metals (aluminum, copper, lead, gold, silver, tin and zinc). However, we shall not deal with the iron and steel industry beyond the iron ore mining stage or with the aluminum industry beyond the bauxite mining stage since these industries would require large studies in themselves.

The production of metals involves several stages that are generally carried on by large mining firms, although small mining operations may engage in the initial stage. The first stage is exploration of areas identified by geological reports as possessing potential mineral resources. Modern exploration methods are quite sophisticated and include geological, geochemical and geophysical investigation; three-dimensional sampling by core drilling or other methods; laboratory analyses, including ore treatment, concentration, and recovery tests;

2   THE WORLD MINING INDUSTRY

and economic appraisal. The objective is to discover and evaluate an orebody that can be economically exploited.

Geochemical exploration is used to measure the chemical properties of the area surrounding the deposit in order to delineate abnormal chemical patterns that may be related to potentially economic mineral deposits. Geophysical investigations employ electronic equipment that can detect subtle contrasts in such physical properties as specific gravity, electrical conductivity, heat conductivity, seismic velocity and magnetic susceptibility. Where much of the bedrock is concealed, telegeologic or remote sensing techniques measure various geologic properties from aircraft or satellites. Exploration is commonly carried on by teams of specialists that include geologists, geochemists and geophysicists. There are different levels of exploration beginning with regional geologic mapping of areas up to 50,000 square km (20,000 square miles) and ending with intensive investigations of orebodies by means of numerous drillings to obtain bulk samples which are then metallurgically tested to determine the dimensions and character of the orebody.

If the results of exploration activities suggest that an economical deposit has been found, the second stage is conducting a feasibility study which involves engineering and economic evaluations of the mining project. It is on the basis of this study that companies decide whether to go ahead with a mining project; the study may also be reviewed by prospective lenders. The feasibility study for a large mining project may be quite costly, running to $25 million or more in some cases. The total cost of exploration and the feasibility study for a large mine may run to $50 million or more. It is uncertain whether a profitable mine will be constructed until all the stages have been completed. In the initial exploration stage, several million dollars may be spent with less than a 10 per cent chance of a successful outcome.

The third stage is the construction of the mine, the metallurgical plant, and infrastructure. There are two basic types of operations to extract mineral ores: open-pit or surface mining, and underground mining. An open-pit mine is largely a quarrying operation that handles a large volume of material. Such mining involves drilling and blasting the ore and hauling it out of the pit in large trucks with capacities ranging up to 200 tons, or in ore trains. The ore is hauled to crushers and then to the metallurgical plant. In underground mining, shafts are dug into ore deposits below the surface, from which ore is drilled, blasted and removed through underground passages to the surface. Iron, bauxite and copper ores are extracted by means of open-pit mining, while lead, zinc, silver and gold are largely extracted by underground mining. There are also some underground copper mines. Economies of scale in open-pit mining permit the mining of relatively low-grade ores. As much as 100,000 tons of ore per day containing less than 1 per cent metal are extracted in the larger open-pit operations. Higher ore grades are necessary for underground mining to be profitable.

Large mines involve huge capital outlays running to a billion dollars or more. The mining complexes usually include beneficiation or concentration of ores for production of concentrates with 25 per cent or higher metal content. In the case of copper, large mine complexes include plants for smelting copper or for producing copper metal by hydrometallurgical methods, but in the case of other metals such as gold, lead, zinc, tin and iron, metal is produced in separate plants which may or may not be owned by the mining company. The degree of processing that usually takes place at the mine differs widely among metals, but refining the product for marketing to fabricators nearly always takes place in separate plants that refine the products of several mines.

Since mines tend to be located in mountains, deserts, or jungles and away from developed areas, infrastructure is often a substantial proportion of capital cost. It is frequently necessary to provide sources of power and water, as well as highways, railroads and port facilities. In addition the mining company may be responsible for constructing living quarters for workers and their families and for providing education and other public services required by the mining community. In developing countries especially, it is usually necessary to provide a training program for the nationals who work in the mine.

The Importance of World Production of Minerals

Table 1.1 shows 1985 world mine production (metal content) of twenty-two nonfuel minerals together with the *reserve base* (measured reserves that can be economically produced plus marginal reserves and some subeconomic resources that may be economically produced in the future).[1] The relative importance of each of these minerals in the world economy must be determined by the value of annual production based on market prices. The reserve base provides a rough indication of the number of years a mineral can be produced at current levels of output and in most cases the reserve base is sufficient to support current annual production for a number of decades. While consumption is increasing for each of these minerals, the reserve base is constantly being expanded by the discovery of new resources. For most minerals the rate of increase in the reserve base has been greater than the rate of increase in annual production.

4   THE WORLD MINING INDUSTRY

Table 1.1   *World Mine Production and Reserve Base, 1985ᵃ*

	Production		Reserve base	
Bauxite	76,300	mt	23,200,000	mt
Chromite	10,600	st	7,500,000	st
Cobalt	35,100	st	9,200,000	st
Columbium	29,000	thousand lb	9,100,000	thousand lb
Copper	7,805	mt	525,000	mt
Diamonds (industrial)	37.8	million carats	990	million carats
Gold	47.0	million troy oz	1,450	million troy oz
Ilmenite	4,615	thousand st	734,000	thousand st
Iron ore	799	million st	98,000	million st
Lead	3,350	mt	143,000	mt
Manganese	25,800	st	12,000,000	st
Mercury	188,000	76-lb flasks	7,200,000	76-lb flasks
Molybdenum	209,500	thousand lb	25,950,000	thousand lb
Nickel	821,000	st	111,000,000	st
Platinum group	7,400	thousand troy oz	1,200,000	thousand troy oz
Rutile	392	thousand st	133,400	thousand st
Silver	394	million troy oz	10,800	million troy oz
Tantalum	710	thousand lb	76,000	thousand lb
Tin	201,000	mt	3,000,000	mt
Tungsten	45,100	mt	3,460,000	mt
Vanadium	71,000	thousand lb	36,500,000	thousand lb
Zinc	6,560	thousand mt	300,000	thousand mt

ᵃ estimated
Note: mt = metric ton; st = short ton
Source: Bureau of Mines, *Mineral Commodity Summaries 1986*, Washington, DC: US Department of Interior, 1986.

The total value of world crude mineral production in 1978 has been estimated by F. G. Callot at about $479 billion, of which 67 per cent represented petroleum and natural gas; 18 per cent coal and lignite; 10 per cent metals; and 4 per cent nonmetals.[2] The 1978 value of mine production of forty-five major nonfuel minerals was estimated at $62 billion, of which 46 per cent was produced in developed countries; 25 per cent in developing countries; and 29 per cent in communist countries (mainly the Soviet Bloc and China).

Except for a few developing countries whose export incomes are mainly derived from nonfuel mineral production, mine production of nonfuel minerals represents a very small percentage of GNP. For the developed countries, the mine value of nonfuel minerals produced represented only 0.4 per cent of the aggregate of these countries' GNP, and for the developing countries about 0.8 per cent of GNP (Callot, 1981, p. 27).[3] The value of mine production of metals in the

OVERVIEW 5

USA in 1980 (based on the recoverable metal content of the ores) was $8.9 billion, or 0.3 per cent of US GNP. However, these low percentages of GNP do not indicate the importance of nonfuel minerals in the world's economy since without them industrial production would soon come to a halt.

Table 1.2 shows the 1978 value of world mine production of twenty of the most important nonfuel minerals ranked by value of mine production. The mine value of the twenty minerals was $5.5 billion, or about 90 per cent of the total value of world mine production of nonfuel minerals. Between 1978 and 1984 world mine production of metals declined by about 3 per cent and the combined real price index of the ten most important minerals declined by about 9 per cent. Therefore, the 1984 value of world mine production of the twenty nonfuel minerals was probably less than $50 billion in 1978 prices.

Table 1.2 *World Production of Major Crude Minerals in 1978* (billions of dollars)

Mineral	Value	Ranking
Iron	$11.6	1
Copper	8.6	2
Gold	7.5	3
Phosphates	3.0	4
Tin	2.5	5
Potash	2.5	6
Diamonds	2.0	7
Lead	2.0	8
Zinc	1.0	9
Asbestos	1.9	10
Silver	1.8	11
Bauxite	1.6	12
Nickel	1.5	13
Sulphur	1.3	14
Platinum	1.2	15
Molybdenum	1.0	16
Manganese	0.9	17
Kaolin	0.8	18
Tungsten	0.8	19
Chromite	0.6	20
Others	7.0	
Total	$62.0	

Source: F. G. Callot, "World Mineral Production and Consumption in 1978", *Resources Policy*, March 1981, p. 16.

6   THE WORLD MINING INDUSTRY

*Distribution of the Value of Nonfuel Minerals Production
by Major Country and Region in 1978*

Table 1.3 shows the ranking by value output and percentage of total
value output of nonfuel minerals for twenty countries that accounted
for virtually all nonfuel mine production in 1978. It will be observed
that the leading producer is the USSR, which produced 32 per cent
more crude nonfuel minerals by value than the USA, ranked second;
South Africa, Canada and Australia ranked third, fourth and fifth
respectively, and the combined value of mine output of nonfuel
minerals of these three countries exceeded that of the USSR. If
comparable data were available for 1984, they would undoubtedly
show that both the USSR and the three countries named above
increased their value output relative to that of the USA. Only two
Western European countries, France and West Germany, are listed
in Table 1.3 and both rank below Poland. It is somewhat surprising to
note that developing countries together (excluding China) produced
only 13.7 per cent of the total value output of crude nonfuel minerals

Table 1.3   *Major World Producers of Nonfuel Minerals Ranked by
Value of Mine Output, 1978* (billions of dollars)

Country	Value	%	Ranking
USSR	$12.9	20.7	1
USA	8.8	14.1	2
South Africa	6.8	11.0	3
Canada	4.4	7.2	4
Australia	3.1	4.9	5
China	2.6	4.1	6
Chile	1.5	2.4	7
Brazil	1.4	2.2	8
Peru	1.0	1.6	9
India	1.0	1.5	10
Mexico	0.9	1.5	11
Zaire	0.9	1.4	12
Poland	0.9	1.4	13
France	0.8	1.3	14
Zambia	0.8	1.2	15
Malaysia	0.7	1.2	16
Morocco	0.7	1.1	17
West Germany (FRG)	0.6	1.0	18
Philippines	0.5	0.8	19
Japan	0.5	0.8	20
Others	0.1		

Source: F. G. Callot, "World Mineral Production and Consumption in 1978",
Resources Policy, March 1981, p. 26.

OVERVIEW 7

as contrasted with 40.3 per cent for developed countries (including South Africa), and 26.2 per cent for the communist countries (including China).[4]

Table 1.4 shows the leading world producers of twenty-two major nonfuel minerals in 1985. It will be observed that the USA was among the five largest producers of eight of these minerals (copper, gold, iron ore, lead, mercury, molybdenum, silver and zinc), while the USSR was among the five largest producers of fifteen of these minerals. Moreover, the USSR ranked first or second in ten of these minerals, while the USA was first or second in only three (copper, lead and molybdenum). The importance of Australia, Canada and South Africa as leading producers of several of these commodities is worth noting. South Africa is among the first five leading producers for chromite, gold and manganese; Australia among the first five producers of bauxite, lead, zinc and nickel; while Canada is among the first five producers of copper, gold, lead, nickel and zinc.

The industrial countries of North America, Western Europe and Japan consume over 80 per cent of nonfuel minerals produced in the non-communist world, while the largest non-communist producers of thirteen of the twenty-two minerals listed in Table 1.4 are in the developing countries, plus South Africa. In 1985 developed countries produced the largest share of mine output of titanium (ilmenite and rutile), lead, mercury, molybdenum, nickel and zinc, and a substantial (but not majority) portion of bauxite, copper, iron ore, silver, tantalum, tungsten and vanadium. Developed countries also produced the bulk of the *refined* copper, ferromanganese, steel and other processed minerals, but a large proportion of the mine raw materials for these products comes from developing countries plus South Africa. Developing countries plus South Africa hold larger shares of the reserves of most important nonfuel minerals than developed countries. Moreover, the developing countries' share of world resources from which additional reserves will eventually be established by increased exploration is substantially larger than that of the developed countries.

Production and reserves of several important minerals are heavily concentrated in South Africa and the Central African countries of Gabon, Zaire, Zambia and Zimbabwe. These minerals include chromium, cobalt, industrial diamonds, gold, manganese, the platinum group metals (platinum and palladium) and vanadium. Tin production is heavily concentrated in the Far Eastern countries of Malaysia, Indonesia and Thailand. Production of bauxite, copper, iron ore, lead, nickel and zinc are more widely distributed geographically, with substantial production in both developed and developing countries.

Table 1.4 *Leading World Producers of Selected Nonfuel Mine Products, 1985*

Product	Major country producers
Bauxite	Australia, 35%; Guinea, 16%; Brazil, 8%; Jamaica, 7%; USSR, 6%
Chromite	South Africa, 31%; USSR, 31%; Albania, 9%; Turkey, 7%; India, 5%; Zimbabwe, 5%
Cobalt	Zaire, 51%; Zambia, 14%; USSR, 9%; Canada, 6%; Cuba, 5%
Columbium	Brazil, 83%; Canada, 17%
Copper	Chile, 17%; USA, 13%; Canada, 9%; USSR, 8%; Zaire, 7%
Diamonds (indus.)	Zaire, 35%; Botswana, 18%; USSR, 17%; South Africa, 15%; Australia, 7%
Gold	South Africa, 47%; USSR, 19%; Canada, 6%; USA, 5%; Australia, 4%
Ilmenite	Australia, 19%; Canada, 18%; Norway, 15%; USSR, 11%; South Africa, 10%
Iron ore	USSR, 30%; Australia, 16%; USA, 12%; Canada, 12%; Brazil, 8%
Lead	Australia, 14%; USA, 12%; Canada, 8%; Mexico, 6%; Peru, 6%
Manganese	USSR, 43%; South Africa, 15%; Brazil, 9%; Gabon, 9%
Mercury	USSR, 34%; Spain, 23%; Algeria, 12%; USA, 8%
Molybdenum	USA, 51%; Chile, 17%; Canada, 7%; Peru, 5%; Mexico, 4%
Nickel	USSR, 24%; Canada, 24%; Australia, 10%; Indonesia, 9%; New Caledonia, 9%
Platinum group	USSR, 50%; South Africa, 43%; Canada, 5%
Rutile	Australia, 51%; Sierra Leone, 26%; South Africa, 16%
Silver	Mexico, 16%; Peru, 14%; USSR, 12%; USA, 11%; Canada, 10%
Tantalum	Thailand, 35%; Australia, 25%; Brazil, 25%
Tin	Malaysia, 20%; USSR, 17%; Thailand, 10%; Indonesia, 10%; Bolivia, 9%
Tungsten	China, 30%; USSR, 20%; South Korea, 6%; Australia, 4%
Vanadium	South Africa, 42%; USSR, 31%; China, 17%
Zinc	Canada, 18%; Australia, 11%; Peru, 9%; Mexico, 5%; USA, 4%

Source: Bureau of Mines, *Mineral Commodity Summaries 1986*, Washington, DC: US Department of Interior, 1986, p. 89.

Concentration of Ownership and Control

Ownership and control of world mining is heavily concentrated in a small number of multinational mining firms (most of which are privately owned) and in state mining enterprises (SMEs). There are thousands of small, privately owned mining firms in the developed countries and in some of the major Latin American mining countries, such as Brazil, Chile, Mexico and Peru. However, small mines produce less than 25 per cent of world output and their activities tend to be concentrated in gold, silver, diamonds and other precious stones, and in types of mining where economies of scale are less important. The vast bulk of the world's output of bauxite, copper, iron ore, manganese, molybdenum and nickel is produced by large-scale operations in mines costing over $50 million. A substantial amount of gold, silver and platinum is produced as byproducts of large-scale copper and copper-nickel mining. Small- and medium-sized mines account for about 75 per cent of the output of chromite and tungsten in the market economy countries, over half of the output of lead and zinc, and nearly 30 per cent of the tin production (Leaming, 1983, pp. 64–5).

Prior to the 1960s, the bulk of the mining capacities of developing countries were owned by multinational mining firms. The wave of expropriations in Africa and Latin America during the 1960s and 1970s brought a large portion of bauxite, copper, iron ore and tin producing capacity under control of SMEs. In some countries, such as Brazil, SMEs came to dominate the national mining industry without expropriation of mining firms; while in Mexico mixed private domestic and state ownership replaced foreign ownership. By the early 1980s SMEs controlled nearly 65 per cent of the copper mining capacity of developing countries; multinational mining firms controlled less than 25 per cent; and the remainder was under private domestic control. In iron ore, nearly three-fourths of the output of developing countries was in the hands of SMEs, with perhaps no more than 10 per cent under effective control by multinationals, and the remainder was controlled by private domestic enterprise. In the case of tin, about half of Third World output is controlled by SMEs and the remainder divided between private domestic enterprises and multinationals. However, the bulk of Third World output of bauxite and nickel mining is effectively controlled by multinational companies. SMEs in Brazil, Ghana, Guinea and Jamaica own substantial interests in bauxite mines in partnership with multinational aluminum companies, but the multinationals provide the management and purchase most of the output.

Despite the expropriation of mining properties in developing countries, large multinational mining firms continue to own and control a substantial share of metal producing capacity in the non-communist world. These multinational firms are relatively few in number and have their headquarters in the USA, Canada, Australia, South Africa, or one of the Western European countries. The major multinational firms listed in Appendix Table 1.1a produce metals in both developed and developing countries. Most of these companies produce more than one metal or nonmetal mineral; most are integrated through the stages of production from mining to refining the metal, while a few of them (such as German and Japanese companies) confine their operations largely to smelting and refining of metals. The most important US multinational mining firms in terms of metal production are AMAX, Anaconda (Arco), ASARCO (American Smelting and Refining Company), Alcoa, Newmont, Kennecott (Standard Oil of Ohio), US Steel, Phelps Dodge, Kaiser Aluminum & Chemical, Exxon and St Joe Minerals (Fluor Corporation). Three British Firms, Rio Tinto Zinc (RTZ), Consolidated Gold Fields and Selection Trust (subsidiary of British Petroleum), produce a wide range of metals in a number of developed and developing countries. RTZ controlled assets in excess of $9 billion in 1982 and its subsidiaries accounted for the second largest volume of copper production of any corporate group in the world and are among the five largest producers of bauxite, zinc and tin. There are several major Canadian multinationals, including INCO (the world's largest nickel producer) and Alcan (one of the world's largest aluminum producers). Two Australian multinationals, Broken Hill Pty and Conzinc Rio Tinto of Australia (CRA), a subsidiary of RTZ, have substantial mining operations in the Asia-Pacific region. Anglo-American of South Africa (AAC) produces a wide range of minerals with investments throughout the world.

The companies listed in Appendix Table 1.1a account for well over half the non-communist world output of gold, bauxite-alumina-aluminum, nickel, molybdenum, diamonds, lead and zinc; over 40 per cent of the copper output; and a substantial portion of the world's output of iron ore, manganese, tungsten, chromium, vanadium, platinum-palladium, tin and a number of other metals. Although these companies have a substantial share of the nonfuel mineral output of developing countries, the largest share of their mining assets are in developed countries, including the USA, Canada, South Africa, Australia and Western Europe. Many of these multinational firms also hold minority equity interests in joint ventures with SMEs in developing countries, and in many cases two or more multinationals will have an equity interest in the same operating company. Finally, many of these multinational firms are major producers of petroleum, coal and uranium, as well as nonfuel minerals.

OVERVIEW 11

Six large integrated aluminum companies produced about 60 per cent of the non-communist world's aluminum output in 1980 and several are integrated into fabrication. The six largest producers of nickel accounted for about 70 per cent of the non-communist world's output of refined nickel or ferronickel. The largest multinational producers of tin, lead and zinc produce about half the non-communist world's refined output of each of these metals; while the largest multinational firms producing copper accounted for over one-third of the non-communist world's production of refined copper.

Entry of US Petroleum Companies
The financial structure of the world mining industry has been affected by the entry of large petroleum (or other nonmining) firms into metal mining during the last decade. This entry has taken the form of mergers between older multinational mining firms and large US petroleum firms, and of the direct entry of petroleum firms into metal mining. Examples of the former include the merger of Anaconda with Arco; of Kennecott Copper with Standard Oil of Ohio; of Freeport Minerals with McMoRan; and of St Joe Minerals with Fluor Corporation. Exxon and Standard Oil of Indiana, through its subsidiary Amoco Minerals, have established new mining operations in the USA and abroad. For example, Exxon owns and operates the large Disputada copper mine in Chile, while Amoco Minerals is a major partner in the Ok Tedi gold/copper mine in Papua New Guinea (PNG).

These firms that now control a substantial portion of the world mining industry have large amounts of capital to invest in contrast to the traditional mining firms whose financial resources in recent years have been reduced by low profits. This is especially significant in view of the high capital costs for modern mines. On the other hand, petroleum and other large companies that have recently entered the mining business are unlikely to continue to invest in mining unless profits are comparable with those in other industries. The new entrants have less dedication to exploration and expansion of their share of world output of particular metals than the traditional mining firms that possess a highly specialized group of geologists and mine managers. Moreover, an important purpose of some of the mergers was to acquire the undeveloped orebodies of the traditional mining firms as a means of resource asset diversification, since it is cheaper and less risky to buy ore reserves than to find them. This could have an adverse effect on exploration both in the USA and abroad.

12   THE WORLD MINING INDUSTRY

Trends in Production, Consumption and Real Prices of Major Metals

World production and consumption of metals are sensitive to changes in the rates of growth of real GNP in the industrial countries. The average annual increase in the United Nations (UN) Index of World Metal Production was 5.1 per cent for the 1953–63 period and 5.7 per cent for the 1963–73 period, but declined to 0.2 per cent for the 1973–80 period. For the market economies the rate of growth in the index of metal production declined from 4.5 per cent per annum in the 1953–63 period to 3.7 per cent in the 1963–73 period, and became negative in the 1973–80 period (see Table 1.5).

From 1945 to the early 1970s, world demand for metals grew rapidly, paralleling the rapid growth of real GNP in the industrial countries. However, the rate of real GNP growth in the industrial economies declined from an annual average of 5.1 per cent during the 1960–73 period to 2.5 per cent during the 1973–80 period, with a further decline during the world recession beginning in 1981.

The average annual rate of growth in consumption of eight major minerals (weighted by value of consumption) in the non-communist countries declined from 6.4 per cent in the 1961–70 period to 2.4 per cent in the 1970–80 period. The average annual rate of growth in consumption of copper declined from 3.9 per cent to 2.5 per cent;

Table 1.5   *Average Annual Rates of Growth in World Production of Metals (in percentages)*

	1953–63	*1963–73*	*1973–80*
World[a]	5.1*	5.7	0.2
All market economies	4.5	3.7	−0.4
Developed[b]	4.7	3.2	−1.1
Developing[c]	4.1	5.0	0.9
Centrally planned economies[d]	11.5	13.0	2.5

* = based on the period 1955–63
[a] Excludes China, Mongolia, Democratic People's Republic of Korea, Democratic Republic of Vietnam, and Albania.
[b] Includes northern North America, Europe (excluding Eastern Europe), Australia, Israel, Japan, New Zealand and South Africa.
[c] Includes Caribbean, Central and South America, Africa (except South Africa), Asian Middle East, and East and South-East Asia (except Israel and Japan).
[d] Includes Bulgaria, Czechoslovakia, East Germany (GDR), Hungary, Poland, Romania and USSR.
Note: Based on the UN Metals Production Index which includes iron ore and thirty nonferrous metals, including gold, bauxite, chromium, cobalt, lead, manganese, mercury, molybdenum, nickel, platinum, silver, tantalum, tin, tungsten, uranium and zinc.
Source: United Nations, *Monthly Bulletin of Statistics*, New York: United Nations, various issues.

OVERVIEW   13

Table 1.6   *Consumption Growth in Nonfuel Minerals in the Market
Economies, 1961–70, 1970–80 and 1980–95 (Projected) (per cent per
annum)*

	1961–70	1970–80	Projected[A] 1980–95	Projected[B] 1983–2000
Copper[a]	3.9	2.5	2.6	2.7
Tin[a]	0.4	−0.8	0.2	1.0
Nickel[a]	7.6	2.2	2.4	2.9
Lead[a]	4.3	2.1	3.2	1.8
Zinc[a]	4.5	1.3	3.1	2.0
Aluminum[a]	9.9	4.3	3.9	4.0
Iron ore	5.4	0.8	2.5	2.4
Manganese ore[b]	8.6	1.8	3.0	n.a.
Average[c]	6.4	2.4	2.9	n.a.

[A]   World Bank
[B]   US Bureau of Mines
[a]   Refined metal includes secondary material
[b]   Manganese content basis
[c]   Weighted by the value of consumption in industrial and developing countries in 1980
n.a. = not available
Source: World Bank, 1983, p. 87; and Bureau of Mines, 1986b.

iron ore from 5.4 per cent to 0.8 per cent; and aluminum from 9.9
per cent to 4.3 per cent (see Table 1.6). The projected rates of growth
in consumption of most of the eight minerals for 1980–95 shown in
Table 1.6 are somewhat higher than the actual rates during the
1970–80 period, but are well below the actual rates of growth for the
1961–70 period. The consumption growth projections made by the
World Bank and the US Bureau of Mines (BOM) shown in Table 1.6
differ as a consequence of the use of different projection periods and
of different methodologies by the two agencies. Some investigators
regard the consumption growth projections for at least some metals
as too high. For example, a World Bank staff study projects the
annual rate of growth in copper consumption between 1984 and 1995
at 1.3 per cent per year (Takeuchi, Strongman, Maeda (1986), p. 117).

   The decline in rates of growth in world consumption of minerals
has been due to a combination of lower rates of growth in GNP in the
industrial countries and a shift in the composition of consumption in
favor of services. The latter trend is likely to continue in industrial
countries, but in developing countries the rates of growth in demand
for commodities with a high metal content, e.g. automobiles and
refrigerators, are likely to be relatively high. In addition, new
materials technology has led to conservation in the use of certain
metals and to the substitution of nonmetallic materials (e.g. optical
fibers) for metals.

14   THE WORLD MINING INDUSTRY

The structural decline in demand for minerals during the 1970s, together with the cyclical decline during the 1981–3 recession, created a condition of world overcapacity in metals in the late 1970s and early 1980s. This led to a sharp fall in real prices of metals. Actually, there has been a long-term downward trend in real prices of most metals since the mid-1960s. Figure 1.1 shows movements in the combined (weighted) index of prices of ten major metals and minerals – copper, tin, nickel, bauxite, aluminum, iron ore, manganese ore, lead, zinc and phosphate rock – for the 1950–85 period in both current and constant 1981 dollars. The average index of prices (in 1981 dollars) in 1980–85 was 66 per cent of the average for the 1950–2 period; 59 per cent of the average for 1964–6; and 50 per cent below the average for 1972–4 (World Bank, 1986, p. 11). Thus not only were average mineral prices (in constant dollars) in 1980–5 at their lowest level in more than thirty years, but the trend has been downward since 1964–6.

There is considerable evidence that the real cost of producing metals, including capital costs of creating new capacity, has risen relative to most metal prices, and that in 1982–5 the prices of major minerals did not cover the full economic costs of production for most mines. Over the longer run, full economic costs must be reflected in higher prices if the metals industry is to replace existing capital equipment and depleted reserves, and expand capacity to meet long-run growth in demand for the products. For these reasons real prices of metals are almost certain to rise above the levels of the early 1980s. When metal prices will rise depends in considerable measure on the elimination of world overcapacity in most metals. A World Bank staff study of January 1986 forecasts the combined (weighted) index of prices (in constant dollars) of ten major metals and minerals in 1995 at 82 (1979–82 = 100), a level slightly lower than the average index for 1982–5 (World Bank, 1986, p. 11). Although this may be too pessimistic, it implies that overcapacity in the metals industries will exist for at least another decade. How much prices will rise when consumer demand and capacity are again in equilibrium will depend upon the marginal economic costs of expanding capacity or the full economic costs of the last unit of additional capacity required to meet consumer demand. Such projections are difficult to make because both capital and operating costs have been changing rapidly in recent years. A 1983 study by the BOM estimates that a copper price of $1.25 to $1.50 (in 1981 dollars) would be necessary to cover full economic costs of producing copper at the 1981 world level. This is more than twice the average price in 1985 (Rosenkranz, Boyle and Porter, 1983, p. 28). Other investigators believe that sufficient additional capacity to meet copper demand in the 1990s will be

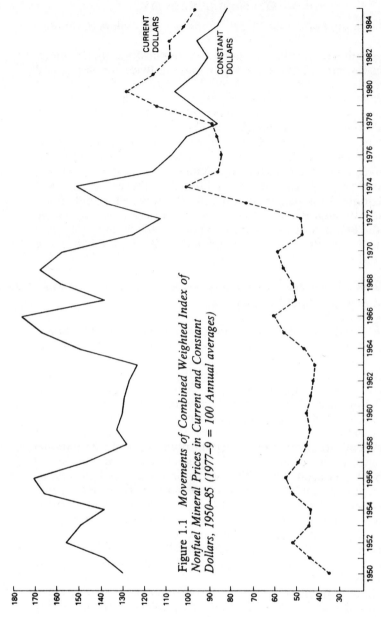

Figure 1.1 *Movements of Combined Weighted Index of Nonfuel Mineral Prices in Current and Constant Dollars, 1950–85 (1977–9 = 100 Annual averages)*

Note: The commodities in the index weighted by 1977–9 export values are: copper, tin, nickel, bauxite, aluminum, iron ore, manganese ore, lead, zinc and phosphate rock.
Source: World Bank, *Half-Yearly Revision of Commodity Price Forecasts and Quarterly Review of Commodity Markets for December 1985*, Washington, DC: World Bank, January 1986.

16   THE WORLD MINING INDUSTRY

provided at a price of about $1 per pound in 1985 dollars (Crowson, 1983).

Although the real costs per pound of duplicating all the metal producing capacity in existence today may be twice the per pound cost of creating new capacity in the 1970s, a substantial portion of existing capacity will be producing metals well into the next century. The per unit cost of additional capacity required to meet the demand for metals during the remainder of this century will not be the average cost of duplicating existing capacity, but the per unit cost of expanding capacity by the lowest cost producers. Moreover, technological developments are continually taking place that reduce per unit costs of new capacity. Therefore, it is difficult to forecast the prices of metals required to induce sufficient capacity growth to meet future demands. Although it seems likely that real prices must rise above those in the first half of the 1980s, it appears unlikely that real prices will rise to the levels of the 1960s and early 1970s by the end of the present century.

Market Structure and Competition

Despite a high degree of concentration of production, world markets for minerals are generally quite competitive and most metal prices are subject to a high degree of fluctuation over the business cycle. Most major metals are traded on commodity exchanges – the London Metal Exchange (LME) or the New York Commodity Exchange (COMEX) or both. Although the volume of trade in metals on the LME and COMEX is relatively small compared to total trade in metals, quotations on these exchanges govern the contract prices between metal producers and buyers in domestic and international markets. In recent years growing competition from developing countries has reduced the ability of major mining and processing firms to maintain 'producer' prices in sales to their customers. There are also merchant markets in virtually all metals, which provide alternative sources of supply for buyers and outlets for small producers. In periods of declining demand and short supply, prices in the merchant markets may differ substantially from producer prices quoted by the other integrated suppliers of copper, nickel, zinc and other metals.

SMEs in developing countries tend to maintain capacity in periods of declining demand and sell all they can produce at world market prices, while producers in the USA, Canada and certain other developed countries have sought to maintain prices by reducing output in line with demand. For example, US copper producers reduced production by more than a third from 1981 to 1984 in response to the decline in the price of copper, while Chile's SME, Corporacion Nacional del Cobre (CODELCO), expanded copper output.

There are no commodity exchanges or well-organized markets for bauxite, iron ore, or for other ores and concentrates. Most of the output of iron ore and bauxite is both controlled and consumed by the integrated aluminum and steel companies. There is, however, a substantial amount of trade in copper, lead and zinc concentrates produced by companies without smelting or refining capacities. Concentrates are usually sold under long-term contracts at prices related to the world price of the metal less the processing costs, or the concentrates may be processed on a toll or fee basis, with ownership of the metal remaining with the seller.

The Adequacy of Mineral Reserves

Despite the doomsday forecasts of depletion of nonfuel mineral resources, or their scarcity in relation to growing demand during the present century, there appear to be ample resources for meeting the projected growth in demand well into the twenty-first century. Over the past half-century continuous exploration aided by technological advances has increased reserves of most nonfuel minerals more rapidly than they have been depleted, and much of the earth's surface has not been adequately explored by modern methods. The development of seabed minerals could conceivably provide ample supplies of copper, nickel, manganese, cobalt and other minerals for many generations to come.

Over the past two decades two developments have changed the outlook for the availability of nonfuel minerals. One has been the sharp decrease in the rate of growth in world demand for metals since the mid-1960s. The second has been the rapid advances in technology for (1) the production of minerals from lower ore grades without a significant rise in costs; and (2) the substitution of materials that are exceedingly abundant in the earth's crust, such as clays, for less abundant ones. Aluminum can be made from clays rather than bauxite; optic fibers made of sand can replace copper in communications; new ceramic materials made from clay have the potential to replace metals in engine blocks; and alloys made of nickel can replace cobalt in jet engines. There is a growing consensus that a scarcity of nonfuel minerals is unlikely to constitute a limitation on world economic growth, at least to 2030 (Manners, 1981, pp. 1–20). However, this optimistic assessment depends upon (1) the maintenance

18   THE WORLD MINING INDUSTRY

of relatively free markets for minerals; (2) the availability of mineral resources on land and under the ocean for exploration and development; and (3) a continuation of current rates of technological progress.

Import Dependence on Nonfuel Minerals

All nations are to some degree dependent on imports of nonfuel minerals. In the USA and Western Europe the degree of dependence on imports has increased with the exhaustion of higher grade ores of traditional industrial metals, such as copper, iron ore, lead, zinc and tin, and with the introduction of new metals, such as aluminum, chromium, cobalt, columbium, tantalum, titanium and vanadium, into the industrial process during the twentieth century. Import dependence increases not only with shifts in demand relative to domestic sources of supply, but with the discovery and development of cheaper sources in other countries. Thus while the USA is potentially self-sufficient in copper and iron ore, a portion of its requirements of these commodities is imported from foreign sources. In the early 1920s the USA was self-sufficient in bauxite for producing aluminum, but as the aluminum industry expanded and cheaper sources of bauxite were developed in other countries, the USA became dependent on imports for the vast bulk of its bauxite requirements.

Figure 1.2 shows US net import reliance on selected minerals and metals as a percentage of consumption in 1981, while Figure 1.3 shows net import reliance for the European Economic Community (EEC), Japan and the USSR in 1980. According to these charts, the USSR is significantly reliant on imports for only a few minerals, but unlike the market economy countries, it tends to strive for self-sufficiency with little regard for the relationship between world prices and domestic production costs.

Recycling and the use of scrap materials as inputs for the production of metals tend to reduce import dependence. Secondary recovery constitutes an important source of supply for certain metals. This source is limited by the cost of collecting and processing scrap, and for most metals this source cannot be counted on to provide more than 10 to 15 per cent of supply. However, a much higher proportion of supplies of copper, steel and aluminum is provided by scrap.

Import dependence is sometimes confused with vulnerability of supply of minerals. Foreign supplies of most nonfuel minerals are available except in the case of an all-out war in which large areas of the world are engaged in military conflict or transportation routes are

Figure 1.2 *US Net Import Reliance on Selected Minerals and Metals*

MINERALS AND METALS	NET IMPORT RELIANCE AS A PERCENTAGE OF APPARENT CONSUMPTION	MAJOR FOREIGN SOURCES (1977–80)
Columbium	100	Brazil, Canada, Thailand
Diamond (industrial stones)	100	Ireland, Rep. of South Africa, Belg–Lux, UK
Graphite (natural)	100	Mexico, Rep. of Korea, Madagascar, USSR
Mica (sheet)	100	India, Brazil, Madagascar
Strontium	100	Mexico
Manganese	98	Rep. of South Africa, Gabon, France, Brazil
Bauxite & alumina	94	Jamaica, Australia, Guinea, Surinam
Cobalt	91	Zaire, Belg–Lux, Zambia, Finland
Tantalum	91	Thailand, Canada, Malaysia, Brazil.
Chromium	90	Rep. of South Africa, Philippines, USSR, Finland.
Fluorspar	85	Mexico, Rep. of South Africa, Spain, Italy
Platinum group metals	85	Rep. of South Africa, USSR, UK
Asbestos	80	Canada, Rep. of South Africa
Tin	80	Malaysia, Thailand, Bolivia, Indonesia
Nickel	72	Canada, Norway, Botswana, Australia
Potash	68	Canada, Israel
Zinc	67	Canada, Mexico, Spain, Australia
Cadmium	63	Canada, Australia, Mexico, Belg–Lux
Tungsten	52	Canada, Bolivia, People's Rep. of China, Thailand
Antimony	51	Rep. of South Africa, Bolivia, People's Rep. of China, Mexico
Silver	50	Canada, Mexico, Peru, UK
Selenium	49	Canada, Japan, Yugoslavia
Barium	43	Peru, People's Rep. of China, Ireland, Morocco, Chile
Titanium (ilmenite)	43	Australia, Canada, Rep. of South Africa
Vanadium	42	Rep. of South Africa, Chile, Canada
Mercury	39	Spain, Algeria, Japan, Italy
Gypsum	37	Canada, Mexico, Jamaica
Iron ore	28	Canada, Venezuela, Brazil, Liberia
Iron & steel	19	Japan, Europe, Canada
Lead	10	Canada, Mexico, Peru
Gold	7	Canada, USSR, Switzerland
Sulfur	7	Canada, Mexico
Copper	5	Chile, Canada, Peru, Zambia

Note: US net import reliance on selected minerals and metals as a percentage of consumption, 1981. Sources shown are points of shipment to the USA and are not necessarily the initial sources of the materials. Net import reliance = imports − exports + adjustments for government and industry stock changes. Apparent consumption = US primary + secondary production + net import reliance. Substantial quantities of rutile, rhenium and zircon are imported, but data are withheld to avoid disclosing proprietary information. Import-export data from the US Bureau of Mines.

Source: Paul R. Portney (ed.), *Natural Resource Policy*, Baltimore, Md: Johns Hopkins University Press, for Resources for the Future, 1982, p. 75.

Figure 1.3   *Net Import Reliance on Selected Minerals and Metals*

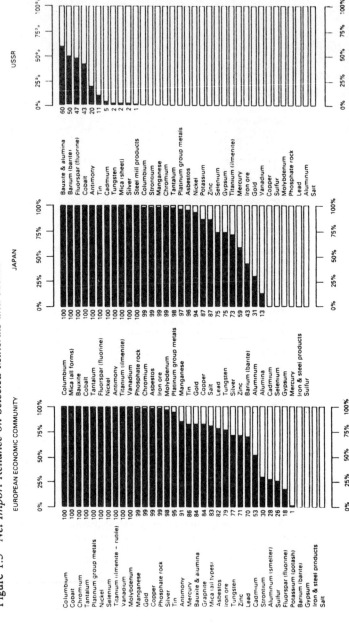

Note: Net import reliance on selected minerals and metals as a percentage of consumption, 1980. The European Economic Community in 1980 included Belgium, Denmark, France, West Germany (FRG), Eire, Italy, Luxemburg, the Netherlands and the United Kingdom. The trade in columbium, tantalum and vanadium is reported together for the EEC. Data for potassium, strontium and graphite are not available for Japan.

Source: Paul R. Portney (ed.), *Natural Resource Policy*, Baltimore, Md: Johns Hopkins University Press, for Resources for the Future. 1982, p. 101.

disrupted. Vulnerability of supplies to disruption during peacetime exists only for a few minerals where production is highly concentrated in a few countries, as is the case with cobalt (Zaire) and with chromium, manganese and platinum-palladium (South Africa).

International trade in nonfuel minerals is exceedingly important to hold down raw material costs in the industrial countries. Fortunately, such trade is relatively free of tariffs and quotas as compared with trade in agricultural and manufactured products. Since a large proportion of nonfuel mineral resources is found in developing countries, the flow of capital and transfer of skills and management to developing countries is exceedingly important for expanding world supplies of mineral products.

Principal Mining Industry Problems and Public Policy Issues

Three categories of problems affecting the world mining industry are addressed in this book. The first concerns problems created by changes in the structure of the mining industry during the past twenty-five years. The second concerns relations between the mining industry and governments, which often reflect conflicts between a variety of social interests on the one hand and the economic interests of the privately owned mining sector on the other. The third category consists of international problems involving both conflict and cooperation at a governmental level.

Structure of the World Mining Industry

The principal change in structure in the world mining industry during the past twenty-five years has been the growth of SMEs from producing a small percentage of the mine output of market economies to producing a substantial percentage in a number of major metals. The growth of SMEs has affected the competitive structure of the world mining industry in three important ways. First, cost elements of SMEs differ from those for privately owned mining firms. Second, the objectives and considerations governing investment decisions of SMEs differ from those of private enterprises. Third, production and marketing strategies of state enterprises tend to be less sensitive to cyclical declines in market demand and price than is the case with privately owned mines.

Most of the large mines owned by SMEs were initially acquired by expropriation of foreign-owned properties for which compensation was paid at a fraction of replacement value. This was true for mining properties in Bolivia, Chile, Guyana, Peru, Venezuela, Zaire and Zambia, among others. In such cases the SMEs began operations

22   THE WORLD MINING INDUSTRY

virtually free of debt and thus avoided the high interest costs incurred
by privately owned mines. Moreover, the large additions to capacities
of SMEs in the 1970s and early 1980s were mainly financed by low-
interest foreign loans arranged by their governments. These external
loans were sometimes provided by international development financing
institutions, such as the World Bank and the Inter-American
Development Bank, but in most cases the external funds were raised
in the private international financial markets with a government
guarantee. These capacity expansions financed by low-cost foreign
loans are in part responsible for worldwide overcapacity in important
metals such as copper and iron ore. In addition to low-cost financing,
SMEs have cost advantages over private firms in the form of lower
taxes and government provision of infrastructure, such as highways,
ports and power, that must usually be supplied directly by privately
owned mining firms.

Investment decisions by SMEs are often made on the basis of
promoting employment and regional development or of increasing
foreign exchange earnings for the country rather than on the basis of
relative profit-earning opportunities. SMEs are also not subject to the
same financial and political risk considerations as foreign private
enterprises. Some SMEs have been developed mainly to supply the
domestic market in place of imports which are restricted by means of
tariffs or quotas. Any excess of domestic production over domestic
requirements is sold abroad, often at prices well below costs.

When the vast bulk of the world's metals was produced by
multinational firms, downward adjustments in production took place
with cyclical declines in consumption and product prices. However,
SMEs tend to be insensitive to price declines in their production and
market strategies for two reasons. First, labor costs in developing
countries are more a fixed cost because of termination pay regulations
and government policies to maintain employment. Second, state
enterprises generally seek to maintain exchange earnings in the face
of low prices despite the fact that their current receipts may not cover
total foreign exchange and domestic currency costs. Privately owned
mines in developing countries are also under government pressure to
maintain employment. In addition, foreign-owned mines in developing
countries have been financed with a high proportion of external debt
so that production must be maintained to service debt. Even Western
European governments deter mining companies from shutting down
or reducing employment in periods of low prices.[5]

The existence of a large segment of the world mining industry in
which investment and production/marketing decisions are made more
on the basis of government policy objectives than on the basis of
private profit maximization has made investment decision-making in

OVERVIEW 23

the private mining industry exceedingly difficult. Comparative cost advantage and projections of world demand and supply balance no longer serve as reasonably reliable guides for decisions to invest in new capacity. Nonmarket factors, such as subsidized loan financing and a variety of governmental operating subsidies, greatly distort mining costs among countries. SMEs in a number of copper producing countries, including Chile, Peru, Zaire and Zambia, hold large undeveloped orebodies which they plan to exploit as soon as financing can be provided, but they are unlikely to be guided by the projected long-run global demand for and supply of copper. Cyclical fluctuations in mineral prices are exacerbated by the failure of SMEs to adjust output to demand conditions, thereby greatly increasing risks for private investors. Finally, political risks of foreign investment in developing countries have increased, even where such investment is welcome.

Government Mining Policies and Regulations in Developed Countries
Any reader of current mining journals will be impressed by the amount of space devoted to government policies and regulations or proposed regulations that affect the mining industry. Governments have a strong national security interest in the mining industry and the industry has strong support from politicians representing the mining regions of the country. In recent years mining operations in developed countries have come into conflict with a number of environmental interests, including the preservation of public lands for recreational use and ecological balance, and the maintenance of uncontaminated air, water, soil and landscape. Although this conflict between mining and environmentalists first surfaced in developed countries, it has spread rapidly to developing countries as well. Some recent mining contracts between multinational companies and host governments contain rules on environmental contamination that are as strict as comparable mining regulations in developed countries.

The US mining industry is faced with serious problems in meeting environmental regulations, particularly with respect to sulfur dioxide (SO_2) emissions of smelters, and these problems may increase with the imposition of new regulations designed to deal with sulfur sources of acid rain. Compliance with environmental regulations involves large capital expenditures and higher operating costs, which affect the international competitive position of the domestic industry. Other developed countries have comparable SO_2 emission standards, but their administration appears to be less burdensome on the industry than that in the USA.

In most countries outside the USA and Canada, mining industries have been recipients of a variety of government subsidies and

24   THE WORLD MINING INDUSTRY

domestic markets have been protected by import restrictions. However, the USA has low tariffs and no quota restrictions on primary metals. The US mining industry argues that subsidies on foreign production plus the importance of a strong domestic industry for national defense reasons justify government measures to assist the domestic industry. But the US mining industry has had much less success in lobbying for import controls on minerals than have the more labor-intensive industries such as the textiles. The USA does have antidumping and countervailing duty laws, and there is a real possibility that nonferrous metal imports may be subject to the same types of restrictions, including voluntary export restrictions, that have been applied to steel.

National security concerns for vulnerability to import disruption of strategic minerals have been an important element in US minerals policy, much more so than in other developed countries. Although the USA has resorted mainly to stockpiling imported minerals for dealing with potential import disruption, there exists a strong movement in this country to subsidize the production of relatively low-grade deposits of cobalt, chromium and platinum-palladium for this purpose.

International Mineral Issues
There are a number of international mineral issues in which the world mining industry has a vital interest. Given the competition in mineral products between developed and developing countries, it is not surprising that many of these issues have arisen from differences in organizational structure and strategies between the mining industries in developed and developing countries. One issue has to do with international financial assistance to the mining industries of developing countries. US and Canadian firms argue that such assistance subsidizes the operations of their competitors in the developing countries and the US government has recently opposed loans in support of mining projects in such countries.

Another issue concerns proposals to organize international commodity agreements in copper, iron ore, bauxite and other metals for the purpose of influencing world prices. For more than two decades the governments of Third World countries have sought through the United Nations Conference on Trade and Development (UNCTAD) to negotiate such arrangements, while both private mining interests and governments of developed countries have been generally cool to international agreements for controlling world prices of minerals.

The negotiation of the Law of the Sea Treaty (LOST) brought into conflict the positions of the USA and certain other developed countries with those of Third World countries regarding the control

OVERVIEW 25

of exploration and development of manganese nodules on the ocean floors. Consortia of US and other developed country mining enterprises have spent hundreds of millions of dollars investigating this source of minerals for eventual development by multinational mining companies, while Third World countries insist that these resources belong to all countries and that exploitation should be governed by an international organization. Also, countries producing substantial amounts of land-based nickel (Canada) and cobalt (Zaire) have a special interest in preventing the mining of manganese nodules from flooding world markets for these minerals.

Finally, the world mining industry has an interest in the formulation of international trade rules governing world trade in minerals. There is considerable danger that trade in nonferrous metals may become subject to the kind of market-sharing arrangements that have characterized trade in steel products. Uncertainties regarding the outcome of these international issues add to the difficulties of investment decisions on mining projects for firms in both developed and developing countries.

Notes

1 Resources in the reserve base include measured reserves plus indicated producible resources for which information is not sufficient for reserve classification. See Bureau of Mines, 1986a, pp. 182–5.
2 Callot (1981) estimated values at the first stage of normal product marketing, i.e. crude oil (not refined products) and concentrates (not refined metals). For the main metals (except iron ore), values represent a certain percentage of the value of the metal content of the ores. Building and construction materials such as sand, gravel and stone were excluded.
3 Because the real prices of most major nonfuel minerals were lower in 1978 than in most years during the 1970s and early 1980s, these percentages were slightly higher in other recent years.
4 The World Bank includes South Africa as a developed, but not an industrial, country and classifies China as a developing country. UN documents usually include both China and South Africa in the developing country category. Some statistical sources put both the Soviet Bloc countries and China together with certain other countries in the category of 'planned economy' countries. In this book South Africa is included as a developed country and China as a communist country.
5 For a discussion of the effects of government policies and large indebtedness on mining operations see Stobart (1984, pp. 259–66).

Appendix Table 1.1a

Major Multinational Firms Producing Nonfuel Minerals, 1980

Firm	Location of Principal Mining Investments:[d]	Principal Nonfuel Minerals	Total assets (billions of dollars)
US Companies:[b]			
AMAX	USA, Australia, Canada, Zambia. Botswana. South Africa, Philippines, Indonesia. Papua New Guinea. UK, Mexico, Dominican Republic	Molybdenum, copper. iron ore. lead. zinc. nickel. tungsten. silver. aluminum	5.1
Aluminum Co. of America (Alcoa)	USA, Guinea, Australia, Jamaica. Dominican Republic, Brazil, Surinam, Mexico	Bauxite, alumina, aluminum	6.0
Anaconda (sub. of Atlantic Richfield)[a]	USA, Mexico, Australia, Chile. Jamaica	Copper, silver, gold. zinc, aluminum, nickel. molybdenum	21.6
ASARCO (American Smelting & Refining Co.)[a]	USA, Mexico, Australia, Peru, Canada	Copper, silver, lead, zinc, gold. molybdenum	2.2
Amoco (sub. of Standard Oil of Indiana)	USA. Canada. Australia, Papua New Guinea	Copper, molybdenum. other metals	24.3
Exxon[a]	USA, Canada, Spain, Chile, Australia	Copper, other base metals	62.3
Freeport-McMoRan	USA, Indonesia, Canada	Sulfur. gold, copper, nickel	1.7
Getty Oil[a]	USA, Australia, Canada, Chile	Copper, other base metals	9.9
Hanna Mining	USA, Canada, Brazil, Guatemala	Iron ore, nickel, bauxite, alumina. aluminum	0.5
Kaiser Aluminum & Chemical	USA, Jamaica, Canada, Australia, New Caledonia, Ghana, Western Europe, Bahrain	Bauxite, alumina, aluminum, nickel	3.6
Kennecott (sub. of Standard Oil of Ohio)[a]	USA, Canada, Australia, Mexico	Copper, molybdenum, gold, silver, lead, zinc, ilmenite	16.0
Newmont Mining	USA, Canada, Peru, South Africa, Chile, Indonesia, Philippines	Iron ore, cobalt, silver, gold, copper, nickel, lithium, molybdenum, vanadium	1.9

Firm	*Location:*	*Minerals*	*Total assets*
Phelps Dodge	USA, Canada, Peru, South Africa	Copper, silver, gold, palladium	2.0
Reynolds Metals	USA, Jamaica, Haiti, Canada, Brazil, Philippines, Ghana	Bauxite, alumina, aluminum, fluorspar	3.3
St Joe Minerals (sub. of Fluor Corp.)[a]	USA, Chile, Australia, Peru, Argentina	Lead, zinc, gold, copper, iron ore, silver	4.7
US Steel	USA, Canada, South Africa, Gabon	Iron ore, manganese, zinc	19.4
Australian Companies:[c]			
Broken Hill Pty (BHP)	Australia, Papua New Guinea, Indonesia	Iron ore, copper, tin, lead, zinc, gold, alumina, aluminum, manganese	6.9
Conzinc Rio Tinto (CRA) (sub. of Rio Tinto Zinc, UK)	Australia, Papua New Guinea, Malaysia	Copper, zinc, tin, gold, lead	4.5
Belgian Companies:[c]			
Union Minière	Belgium, Canada, Brazil, USA, Mexico, Spain	Copper, zinc, silver, gold, platinum-palladium	n.a.
Canadian Companies:[c]			
INCO	Canada, USA, Indonesia, Guatemala, Australia, Brazil, New Caledonia, Mexico, Philippines	Nickel. copper, gold, silver, platinum-palladium, cobalt, magnetite	3.4
Cominco	Canada, Australia, USA, Greenland, Japan, Philippines, Western Europe	Lead, zinc, silver, gold	2.7
Noranda Mines	Canada, USA, Australia	Copper, gold, silver, lead, molybdenum, cobalt	4.6
Falconbridge Nickel	Canada, Norway, Dominican Republic	Nickel. copper, cobalt, iron ore, gold. silver	1.1
Aluminum Co. of Canada (Alcan)	Canada, Brazil, Jamaica, Guinea	Bauxite. alumina, aluminum	6.6

Continued overleaf

Firm	Location:	Minerals	Total assets
French Companies:[c]			
Pechiney-Ugine Kuhlman (owned by French govt)	France, Greece, Guinea, Australia, Spain, Netherlands, Canada, Cameroon	Bauxite, alumina, iron ore, aluminum	4.5
Le Nickel-SLN (sub. of Elf Aquitaine (owned by French govt)	France, New Caledonia, Cameroon	Nickel	n.a.
IMETAL	France and other Western European countries, Brazil, Morocco, Peru, Australia	Zinc, lead, silver, copper, other metals	1.7
German Companies:[c]			
Metallgesellschaft AG	Germany, Australia, Canada	Lead, zinc, tin, tungsten	1.8
Preussag	Germany, Canada	Zinc, lead, copper, silver, mercury	1.3
Japanese Companies:[c]			
Mitsubishi Metal Corp.	Japan, Australia, Canada, Peru, USA	Copper, nickel, silver, gold, tin	1.5
Netherlands Companies:[c]			
Billiton International Metals (sub. of Royal Dutch Petroleum)	Netherlands, Australia, Canada, Brazil, Surinam, Indonesia, Thailand, Peru, Western Europe, Colombia	Copper, nickel, tin, bauxite, tungsten, zinc, molybdenum	15.5
Patino NV	Netherlands, Canada, Brazil, New Caledonia, Australia, Malaysia, Nigeria	Tin, nickel, cobalt, lithium	0.2
South African Companies:[c]			
Anglo-American Corp. (AAC)	South Africa, USA, Canada, Botswana, Brazil, Zambia, Swaziland, Zimbabwe, Western Europe, Australia	Copper, nickel, iron ore, platinum, manganese, tin, tungsten, diamonds, chromium, silver, zinc, vanadium, gold	4.1

Firm	Location:	Minerals	Total assets
DeBeers Consolidated Mines	South Africa, Botswana, Namibia, Mexico, Lesotho	Diamonds	4.8
Swedish Companies:[c]			
Granges International	Sweden, Liberia, Canada, Saudi Arabia	Iron ore, phosphates	1.2
Swiss Companies:[c]			
Swiss Aluminum Ltd (Alusuisse)	Switzerland, Australia, Canada, USA, Sierra Leone, New Zealand, Guinea	Bauxite, alumina, aluminum, fluorspar, lead, zinc, copper, phosphates	5.0
United Kingdom Companies:[c]			
Rio Tinto Zinc (RTZ)	UK, Australia, Papua New Guinea, South Africa, Canada, Indonesia, Spain, Zimbabwe, Panama, New Zealand	Copper, lead, zinc, iron ore, alumina, aluminum, bauxite, silver	9.0
Consolidated Gold Fields	South Africa, Australia, USA, Philippines, Papua New Guinea, UK	Gold, copper, iron ore, platinum, silver, tin, ilmenite, titanium	2.1
Selection Trust (sub. of British Petroleum)[a]	South Africa, Australia, USA, Sierra Leone	Copper, iron ore, gold, other metals	42.5

[a] Bulk of assets in petroleum or other industries outside nonfuel minerals
[b] Information on US assets taken from *Moody's Industrial Manual*, New York: Moody's Investors Service, 1983 (1982 figures)
[c] Information on foreign company assets taken from *Moody's International Manual*, New York: Moody's Investors Service, 1982 (1981 figures) and "International 500," *Fortune*, August 22, 1983 (1982 figures)
[d] *Engineering and Mining Journal International Directory of Mining*, New York: McGraw-Hill, 1981, and company annual reports for location and minerals

References

Bureau of Mines (1986a), "Minerals in the World Economy," preprint from *Minerals Yearbook 1984* (Washington, DC: US Department of Interior).

Bureau of Mines (1986b), *Mineral Commodity Summaries, 1986* (Washington, DC: US Department of Interior).

Callot, F. G. (1981), "World Mineral Production and Consumption in 1978," *Resources Policy*, March, pp. 15–28. This article is an abridged version of a comprehensive report by F. G. Callot in the French journal, *Annales des Mines*, November/December 1980.

Crowson, Philip (1983), "Aspects of Copper Supply: Past and Future," *CIPEC Quarterly Review* (Paris: Intergovernmental Council of Copper Exporting Countries), January–March, pp. 38–47.

Leaming, George F. (1983), paper presented at Second International Symposium on Small Mine Economics and Expansion, Helsinki; paper summarized in article entitled "Second Small Mine Symposium Held in Helsinki," *World Mining*, October.

Manners, Gerald (1981), "Our Planet's Resources," *The Geographical Journal*, vol. 147, part I, March.

Rosenkranz, R. D., Boyle, Jr., E. H., Porter, K. E. (1983), *Copper Availability– Market Economy Countries: A Minerals Availability Program Appraisal* (Washington, DC: US Department of Interior, information circular 8930).

Stobart, Christopher (1984), "The Effects of Government Involvement on the Economics of the Base Metals Industry," *Natural Resources Forum*, July, pp. 259–66.

Takeuchi, K., Strongman, J., Maeda, S. (1986), *The World Copper Industry: Its Changing Structure and Future Prospects*, Staff Commodity Working Paper no. 15 (Washington, DC: World Bank), November.

World Bank (1983), *The Outlook for Primary Commodities*, Staff Commodity Working Paper no. 9 (Washington, DC: World Bank).

World Bank (1986), *Half-Yearly Revision of Commodity Price Forecasts and Quarterly Review of Commodity Markets for December 1985* (Washington, DC: World Bank), January.

[2]

2

THE WORLD
OIL MARKET
IN
TRANSITION

With Japan importing practically all its crude oil from foreign sources and the United States importing a third of its requirements from abroad, the two countries have a major stake in the future evolution of the world oil market. At the same time, accounting together for over half the world's consumption of crude oil and oil products outside the communist countries, each also has a strong interest in the policies and practices of the other in such markets.

The world oil market has been rapidly taking on new characteristics whose implications run very deep. In general, the dominance of U.S.-based firms in those markets has been on the decline and other institutions have filled the vacuum. Taken by itself, that trend says very little about the likelihood of conflict or about the opportunities for cooperation between the two countries. A closer look at the process of change is needed in order to detect its implications for the future.

The Rise and Fall of the International Oil Companies

Stability by agreement. From the oil industry's beginnings over a century ago, the U.S. firms that led the industry and the handful of rivals with whom they shared the world's markets were continuously engaged in a search to hold down their risks. The reasons for the emphasis on stability were evident. This has been an industry that has demanded large lumpy commitments from its entrepreneurs—com-

20 TWO HUNGRY GIANTS

mitments such as those required to develop an oil field or to build a refinery. Once the commitments were made, operation of the productive facility has entailed high fixed costs, so that small variations in price or in output have had a relatively powerful effect on profits. At the same tme, the short-term elasticities of both supply and demand have been very low. When prices have changed, demand and supply have been slow to respond, so that the price could move a considerable distance before it was checked by market forces.

From their earliest days, therefore, the big oil companies looked on unregulated oil markets with a special sense of unease. It was largely this uneasiness that led the two or three leading U.S. firms in 1928 to join their competitors in the Middle East in creating the world oil cartel of 1928. From the viewpoint of the U.S. firms, the operations of their British, Dutch, and French rivals — along with the sporadic sales of the newly established Soviet Union — represented a strong threat to the stability of world markets. Responding to that threat, the leading multinational oil companies put in place a control structure that succeeded in stabilizing the world oil market for over a decade, until the outbreak of World War II put an end to the arrangement.

The experience of those years of relative tranquillity in the oil market suggests some of the difficulties that must be overcome in order to stabilize the market for a commodity such as oil. At that time, the number of sellers in international markets was comparatively small; three or four companies controlled 90 percent of the oil moving in international trade. Yet remarkably elaborate arrangements were required to keep these three or four companies moving in step. One set of arrangements was directed to ensuring that the world's oil production did not exceed the amount that the oil companies thought they could sell at a price satisfactory to them. Another set of arrangements was fashioned to ensure that each of the participants in the market could be relied on to limit its competition, so that the price structure would not be impaired.

As one element in the system of production control, the major international oil companies entered into the so-called red-line agreement, an agreement that created a partnership among them in the Middle East. By itself, the agreement could not have led to the control of production all over the world. To achieve that objective, the participants had to be sure that compatible restraints would be applied to production in other important centers, such as Venezuela and the United States. These links were in fact achieved, but not without considerable effort on the part of the oil majors. The U.S. restraints were put in place during the early 1930s by a system of state-directed proration schemes.[1] The Venezuelan restraints were assured by a system of interlocking ownerships that involved the principal firms participating in the Middle East agreement. The other key agreement of 1928, the "as is" agreement, was designed to provide the necessary assurance against destabilizing competition. This was an agreement in principle among the company heads to freeze their respective shares in each of the markets in which they were selling their products. To be operational, however, the agreement required extensive elaborations market by market, often requiring a specification of shares for each selling enterprise product by product and channel by channel.[2]

Perhaps the most complex structure to be put in place in the 1930s, however, was a pricing mechanism for oil and its products — a mechanism whose role would be understood and acknowledged by all the leading sellers.[3] Because the market price of crude oil was always very much higher than the cost of production for a considerable part of the total supply, the risk of an outbreak of price cutting was usually high. At the same time, it was not easy for any seller immediately to detect a case of price cutting by rivals. The various grades and types of crude oil and their numerous products came from many different sources and were sold in scores of different markets. Accordingly, some very clear and easily administered pricing conventions were required if price rivalry was to be avoided. Such conventions could build the confidence of the various sellers in the predictability of their rivals' behavior and could reduce the risk that different sellers might unintentionally offer their wares at different prices in the same market. Moreover, a price structure of that sort could discourage buyers from playing off sellers against one another and from shopping for bargains, thus adding to the security of the control system.

The exact provisions of the price structure of that period are no longer very important.[4] Like OPEC's efforts of the 1970s and 1980s, the system demanded that its participants have access to some key price for crude oil, a price that none of the participants was in a position to control unilaterally. Such a price was provided in the 1930s by a private publication, *Platt's Oilgram*, which regularly published a figure purporting to represent the price of crude oil available for sale to independent buyers free on board (f.o.b.) U.S. ports in the Gulf of Mexico. From the viewpoint of the sellers, that price had one attractive

22   TWO HUNGRY GIANTS

feature that the OPEC market prices of a later era would not share: the prices of *Platt's Oilgram* were formed in the U.S. market, where supply was under the careful month-to-month scrutiny and control of state proration boards who were empowered to fix production limits.

The establishment of a signal price, however, was only a small first step in the creation of a stable system. Oil could come from several different sources; the challenge was to develop a pricing system that did not inadvertently create price competition in any important market. The principal market for oil from the Gulf ports at the time was the U.S. east coast. Accordingly, the first object of any such system was to ensure that oil coming from other sources, notably Venezuela and nearby Caribbean sources, would not be landed at a lower price in the east coast ports. To achieve that objective, the oil companies that were shipping from the Caribbean area took to quoting an f.o.b. price at their Caribbean shipping points which would land their oil in New York at the same price as oil delivered from the Gulf ports to New York. The Caribbean f.o.b. price having been established, the price in any European market was calculated by beginning with the f.o.b. Caribbean price and adding the appropriate ocean freight to the designated European market. The resulting price, it is important to observe, would be charged in that market for oil from all sources, whether from the Caribbean, the Middle East, or the Dutch East Indies.

These calculations, of course, were based on the assumption that all important sellers in the world would fall in with the prescribed pricing practices. Moreover, the system could work only if sellers used approximately the same freight costs in order to calculate the final price appropriate for given destinations. In the absence of some uniform practice in calculating freight costs, such an outcome would have been impossible, inasmuch as the oil was freighted under a variety of different arrangements. For instance, a considerable part of the oil was carried on tankers owned by the sellers themselves, while the rest was carried on ships under chartering contracts of many different sorts. To provide the necessary guide to freight cost changes, the price quotations generated by the London chartering market proved indispensable.

Systems of this sort must not only be universal: they must also constantly be adapted to the changing conditions of the market. In the case of oil, that fact was evident by the close of World War II, as the major oil companies rapidly expanded their production from the relatively low-cost sources of the Persian Gulf. With production from

THE WORLD OIL MARKET IN TRANSITION 23

that area becoming a major source of supply, the practice of charging higher prices in the more easterly markets — higher prices for oil delivered to Syria, for instance, than for oil delivered to Greece — eventually became an unsustainable anomaly, an anomaly that was dangerous for the stability of the market. Bitter protests from the British navy, a major customer in the area, provided the immediate occasion for a change. A few years later, pressures from the U.S. government, which by then was buying large quantities of oil for the European Recovery Program, pushed the oil companies further toward quoting a Persian Gulf price.

The nature of the change that the international oil companies adopted served to highlight one source of their flexibility that would distinguish them sharply from national governments and from their state-owned enterprises. The international oil companies were producers of oil from many different places in the globe. For them, the overriding objective was to maintain a stable global system, not to maximize the advantages of any one area over any other. Accordingly, they were quite capable of contemplating changes in their joint arrangements that tipped the balance of advantage from one area to another, secure in the knowledge that their own operations covered both the advantaged and the disadvantaged areas.

The Persian Gulf price that emerged in the latter 1940s was linked to the prices quoted by *Platt's Oilgram* for Gulf of Mexico oil in such a way as to avoid conflict between supplies from the world's two main sources of oil. Given the production capacity of the Persian Gulf oil fields at the time, the oil companies could define the market area that the Persian Gulf oil would serve. That area being more or less determined, the Persian Gulf price was set to generate a delivered price at the boundary of its market area that was equal to oil delivered to the same boundary from the Gulf of Mexico. In the beginning, when the production of the Persian Gulf area was still relatively small, that boundary fell by common consent in the area of Greece; but as the major oil companies expanded their Middle East production, the boundary moved rapidly westward to Italy, then to Britain — and then, by 1950, to the east coast of the United States.

The appearance of Middle East oil in U.S. markets triggered a series of events that eventually brought an end to the unified system for the control of the world's oil markets. And without such unity, maintaining effective control over world prices became much more difficult.

24   TWO HUNGRY GIANTS

The events that demonstrated the crucial importance of global unity, however, took some decades to unfold.

With the appearance of Middle East oil in the U.S. market, domestic producers whose facilities were confined to the United States had to confront the fact that the importing firms were obtaining the oil at very low prices, far lower than those of U.S. supplies. The appearance of that oil was threatening the position of U.S. producers in their home markets. At the same time, the influence of the state regulatory agencies over the U.S. market was being undermined. The obvious policy response, which the U.S. developed in the 1950s, was to break the U.S. market away from world markets by imposing import restrictions.

With the imposition of import restrictions in the United States, however, the control of the international oil companies over world markets was weakened. A world in which *Platt's Oilgram* and London charter rates determined prices everywhere was a comparatively safe and sheltered world. Insofar as any political forces could determine the Platt prices, they were the regulatory commissions of the various states of the United States; and those commissions were prepared to hear fully and sympathetically any views that the U.S. oil industry wished to express on the subject. With Persian Gulf prices being quoted independently of prices in the Gulf of Mexico, the international oil companies were more vulnerable to the demands of the governments in oil-exporting countries that those prices should be raised.

Stability by alliance and integration. The stability of the system fashioned by the international companies, however, rested not only on its universal reach but also on the ability of each of the enterprises to forge vertical and horizontal links that diversified its sources of crude oil and its markets. In this respect, too, the international companies differed from the state-owned enterprises that would ultimately dispossess them from some of their activities.

To build up their vertical and horizontal links, companies commonly created consortia and partnerships among themselves at various stages of the business. The red-line agreement had, of course, stimulated that approach among the producers in the Middle East. But many important partnerships were developed outside the area.[5] And the suspension of the red-line agreement after World War II did not end the practice of forging such partnerships. During the 1950s and part of the 1960s, the widespread networks that these links created had the effect of reducing the vulnerability of individual firms to the negotiating pressures of governments. These links gave the companies a capacity to make the needed adjustments in order to deal with short-term shocks in the channels of supply, such as the shut-down of the Suez Canal during the 1956 Israeli-Egyptian war.[6]

The vertical structure of each of the enterprises was also a prominent feature of their organization. Each of the leading international oil companies owned or controlled not only the producing oilfields but also most of the refineries on which their business relied; even the tankers and distribution facilities that they employed were usually tied down under long-term arrangements.[7] Such vertical linkages had numerous advantages, which have been fully described in other sources. Some of these advantages would apply to any industry that shared the characteristics of the oil industry — that is, an industry in which the barriers to entry were high, in which the fixed costs of operation were substantial, and in which the environment was full of uncertainties.[8] In these circumstances, any participant that was not vertically integrated faced risks of variation in the sale of the product that were particularly high, and financial consequences from such variation that were especially costly.

In the case of the crude oil industry, all these conditions strongly applied. But there were special conditions in that industry as well, which made vertical integration particularly attractive for the firms involved.[9] The highest barriers to entry lay at the crude production level, where the difficulties of negotiating with host governments and the high risks of exploration for newcomer firms posed particularly formidable obstacles. The refining business offered barriers as well, but these were easier to overcome inasmuch as most refineries at the time were located in the consuming countries. And the distribution business presented even less formidable entry problems.

The strategic problem for the crude oil producers, therefore — an especially serious problem in times of easy supply — was to maintain a distribution system large enough to keep their wells operating at profitable levels. Stated differently, it was in the interests of the majors to curb independent distributors lest their presence tempt sellers of oil products to maintain their volumes by cutting their prices. Downstream entrants could be curbed if the crude oil prices charged to related subsidiaries and to independent third parties were kept relatively high, so high as to compel the refinery and distribution facilities to operate at a loss. That, in fact, appeared to be the policy of

26   TWO HUNGRY GIANTS

the major oil companies through the 1950s and much of the 1960s. But soon thereafter, despite all the safeguards, their control over prices broke down.

The oligopoly's decline. The kind of world oil market that Japan and the United States are likely to face in the future will obviously be profoundly different in some critical respects from the market they have faced in decades past. A central question will be the role that is to be played by the principal oil-exporting countries. That role could greatly affect the chances of conflict or the opportunities for cooperation between the two countries. Speculation of that sort is bound to begin with OPEC.

Objective opinions on the potential of OPEC are hard to come by: nearly every such view has been colored by the position and interests of the observer.[10] On my reading of the evidence, OPEC has always lacked some of the essential ingredients for an effective control mechanism. Its members have been too numerous, with too many differing perceptions of their collective priorities; composed of national governments, the organization has been barred from altering the benefits flowing to any national area relative to any other; and its reach has been much less than global, excluding notably the United States, the North Sea, and Mexico.

The decline of the control of the majors during the 1960s, therefore, left a vacuum that OPEC could not fill. Some of the reasons for the decline of the international oil companies were fairly evident. One was the extraordinary improvements in international travel and communication, improvements that allowed the oil-exporting countries to train large numbers of officials and technicians in the West or to acquire Western expertise through foreign advisers. With foreign advisers' help, for instance, Libya adopted a law governing oil concessions that was a model of legal sophistication. Under its provisions, Libya tended to favor foreign concessionaires that had no alternative sources of foreign oil, a preference that was to greatly enhance the country's bargaining power during the 1960s.

At least as important a cause of the decline in the power of the international oil companies, however, was the sharp increase in the number of private oil companies engaged in foreign production and sale. As was noted earlier, the number of firms that were producing oil in Africa and the Middle East increased rapidly during the 1950s and 1960s. American independents such as Getty Oil, Occidental Oil, and

Marathon Oil, developed substantial producing stakes in North Africa and the Middle East. This was the period, too, in which a Japanese independent, the Arabian Oil Company, made its entry into the Kuwait neutral zone, and in which Azienda Generale Italiana Petroli (AGIP) obtained a foothold in Iran. Table 2.1 reflects the swift change in the structure of the market during this period.

Table 2.1. Crude oil production, by ownership, 1950–1979 (in percent).[a]

	1950	1957	1966	1970	1979
Seven majors	98.2	89.0	78.2	68.9	23.9
Other international oil companies	1.8	11.0	21.8	22.7	7.4
Producing country oil companies	b	b	b	8.4	68.7
Total	100.0	100.0	100.0	100.0	100.0

a. Excluding crude oil produced in the United States and the communist countries.

b. Negligible.

Sources: Adapted from Brian Levy, "World Oil Marketing in Transition," *International Organization* 36, no. 1 (Winter 1982): 117. Also based on M. A. Adelman, *The World Petroleum Market* (Baltimore: Johns Hopkins University Press, 1972), pp. 80–81; Shell Briefing Service, *The Changing World of Oil Supply,* June 1980, p. 7; and the 1970 and 1979 annual reports of leading oil companies.

One sign of the decline in market control during the 1950s and 1960s was the pronounced reduction in the profit margins of the major oil companies. Part of the squeeze came from the fact that the governments of the oil-exporting countries seized the occasion repeatedly to demand a larger share of the majors' profits in the sale of crude oil.[11] Part came from the independents' offering their oil products in Western Europe and elsewhere at depressed prices. Accordingly, from a level of about 80 cents per barrel in the early 1950s, the majors' net profits per barrel fell to 53 cents in 1960 and 32 cents in 1972.[12] At first, the declining profit margins were more than offset by increases in the volume of sales. But by the latter 1960s, it began to appear that sales increases could not be counted on much longer to offset the declining profit margins. The multinationals were in trouble.

The weakening of the oligopoly could be laid not only to the rising role of the independent oil companies but also to the emergence of another group noted in Table 2.1, the oil companies of the producing

28 TWO HUNGRY GIANTS

countries themselves. Practically all of these enterprises were state-owned. A few located in the more industrialized countries, such as British National Oil Company and Norway's Statoil, were created from scratch as operating companies. But those in the developing countries were usually created and enlarged by successive acts of expropriation, which step by step shoved aside foreign-owned companies that had been operating in the preempted areas. As a rule, the activities taken on by these state-owned enterprises followed a regular pattern. Very early, they assumed the role of bargaining agents for their respective governments and took over management of some of the local distribution and refining activities. Later, some moved into the more demanding activities of exploration, exploitation, and exportation.[13] By the early 1980s, a dozen or more of these firms had to be counted as significant participants in the international oil trade.

The crisis that erupted in the fall of 1973 can be looked on either as a grand coda signaling the end of the era in which the international oil companies controlled the oil market, or as the overture to a new regime not yet defined. Elements of both existed. Even at that late date, the international oil companies still were distributing a very considerable share of oil that moved in international trade. But their control over prices, which had been weakening for a decade or more before the 1973 episode, was unambiguously ended at that time. It would take another five years and another crisis — that generated by the Iranian revolution and Iran's war with Iraq in 1978 and 1979 — to establish the fact that the international oil companies no longer controlled a considerable portion of the channels of distribution.

The Transition

The formation of prices. An unambiguous signal that the oil companies had lost control over the international price of oil occurred in the fall of 1973, during the Israeli-Egyptian war, when the open-market price for oil suddenly went soaring from a little under $3 per barrel to about $10.50.[14] Well before that time, the big multinational networks had begun to send signals to independent buyers (so-called third-party buyers) that such buyers could no longer depend on the multinationals as reliable sources of supply. In a pinch, it was clear, the multinationals would serve their own networks first. The high-priced spot oil market that developed in the 1973 crisis, therefore, was

THE WORLD OIL MARKET IN TRANSITION 29

typically the result of deals outside the multinational networks, between state-owned oil companies that were beginning to move into international distribution and panicked buyers such as public utilities, chemical companies, and independent refiners.

At this stage, however, most of the oil from OPEC countries continued to move through the channels of the multinationals rather than the spot market. As long as the posted prices of the oil-exporting countries remained unchanged, the cost of that oil to the companies was not affected. In the fall of 1973, however, following the breathtaking rise in spot prices, the OPEC countries decided unilaterally to raise their posted prices, thereby sharply increasing the cost of crude oil to the multinationals.

What followed in the years from 1973 to 1978 was consistent with the picture of a somewhat unruly oligopoly, composed of a dominant member (Saudi Arabia), a dozen followers barely prepared to acknowledge its leadership, and a large outer circle of producers pricing under the shelter of the oligopoly. It was clear at this stage that the majors had lost control of prices, but not at all clear what organizing force had taken its place. By any measure, prices were more variable during these years than in the years before 1973. Part of the movement was due to changes in the official OPEC price; part was due to the fact that some of the oil-exporting countries, casting an eye on prevailing spot prices, refused to be bound by contract prices and contract quantities previously agreed upon with buyers; but part was due to the fact that each of the producing countries felt even more free than in the past to tinker with its royalty rates, its tax rates, and its other terms of sale. At times, the tinkering was intended to increase the country's revenues. At times, too, some of the oligopoly's members appeared to be engaged in trying to increase their share of the market, a tactic especially dangerous for the stability of the oligopoly. These frequent adjustments, which were typically uncoordinated between countries, continually altered the net costs to buyers, as well as the differences in such costs between different classes of buyers.

The periodic meeting of OPEC after 1973 were largely devoted to trying to keep its members from going their separate ways. Up to that time, however, the implacable antagonisms between Saudi Arabia and Iraq, Iraq and Iran, Iran and Saudi Arabia, and Libya and the conservative Arab oil exporters, coupled with the remoteness of Nigeria, Venezuela, and Indonesia, had prevented the development of the com-

30 TWO HUNGRY GIANTS

mon sense of tolerance that effective oligopolies require of their participants. When oil supplies temporarily tightened or when supplies hung heavy over the market, the various sellers typically struck off on their own.[15] There were times when OPEC efforts seemed briefly to reduce the disparate trends, but at other times the efforts failed. We will never know exactly how the OPEC countries would have behaved in that period if OPEC itself had not existed; but their behavior can easily be explained without much reference to the role of OPEC. In any event, the experience of those years emphasized the difficulties of agreeing on either price ceilings or price floors in a market composed of several dozen sellers with widely disparate motivations selling several dozen different grades of oil in several dozen different countries.

By the time of the 1978 crisis, users of oil around the world had grown accustomed to the fact that oil of a given grade offered in any market no longer had a single price. There were bargains to be had for the assiduous shopper and premiums to be paid by the unwary one; there were, in short, strong incentives for any buyer to learn about the market. Figure 2.1 portrays schematically the kind of pattern that was being generated by the market, a pattern that generated a dis-

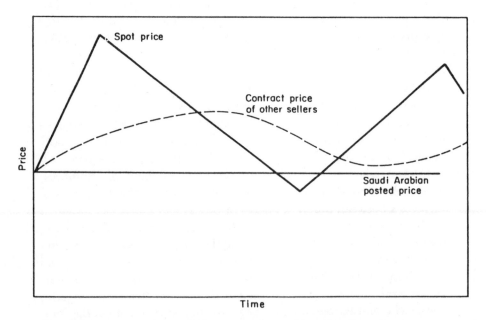

Figure 2.1. Patterns of price behavior in the world crude oil market.

concertingly wide range of prices for a given grade of oil at a given moment from different sources. The events of the 1978 crisis emphasized the fact that the multinational oil companies no longer could guarantee stability either of supply or of price to their customers. Countries such as Japan that were cut off from the supply lines of some of the major oil companies at that time were not losing much in the way of security.

After the 1978 crisis, the continuation of variations in the market price of oil suggested that the pricing problems of OPEC were persisting. In 1981 and again in 1982, after considerable effort, OPEC came to some agreement on posted prices; indeed, the 1982 agreement even included a commitment for the first time to put a lid on production.

Nevertheless, the conditions for maintaining an effective agreement among the sellers were even less propitious than they had been in the 1970s, as some of them confronted compelling pressures to increase their foreign exchange earnings.[16]

The channels of distribution. By the early 1980s, the role of the state-owned companies in the international distribution of oil had grown sufficiently so that one could begin to see some concrete evidence with which to appraise their specific strengths and weaknesses. On the basis of that evidence, it was beginning to appear that such enterprises would have difficulty in maintaining some measure of control over world markets analogous to the earlier control of multinational enterprises.

As Table 2.2 on page 32 indicates, the state-owned enterprises of the oil-exporting countries were selling over 40 percent of the world's oil by the end of the 1970s, leaving a greatly curtailed sphere of operation for the multinationals. Even Saudi Arabia, linked to Western markets by the formidable networks of Aramco's four U.S. partners, was marketing about 30 percent of its oil directly through its state-owned oil company.[17] To be sure, some of the expansion of the state-owned enterprises was not threatening to the core of the multinationals' activities because it entailed nothing more than a takeover of the sales that the multinational firms had been making to independent refiners and distributors. But eventually the state-owned enterprises began cutting into the muscle of the multinationals' operations. Between 1973 and the end of the decade, the multinationals experienced a decline on the order of 7 million barrels daily within their own vertical chains of refineries, petrochemical plants, and gasoline stations.[18]

Nevertheless, the state-owned enterprises had not begun building

32 TWO HUNGRY GIANTS

Table 2.2. Marketing channels of internationally traded oil for the period 1950–1979 (in percent).

	1950	1957	1966	1973	1976	1979
Marketing by international oil companies:						
Interaffiliate transfers	92.8	82.4	80.0	69.6	59.1	46.6
Third-party sales	7.2	17.6	20.0	22.5	16.3	11.2
Direct marketing by producer countries	a	a	a	7.9	24.6	42.2
Total	100.0	100.0	100.0	100.0	100.0	100.0

a. Negligible.
Sources: Brian Levy, "World Oil Marketing in Transition," *International Organization* 36, no. 1 (Winter 1982): 121; *Petroleum Intelligence Weekly* 19, no. 8 (February 25, 1980): 4.

rival chains of their own in international markets. Instead, they were relying on a variety of independent buyers to absorb their oil. Now and then, one of the established international oil firms entered into an open-market deal with a state-owned enterprise; by 1980 the majors were buying over 10 percent of their own crude oil on the open market. More commonly, the buyers were firms engaged in refining and distributing oil in their own national markets, which formerly had acquired their crude oil from the large international firms. In some cases, the national firms that were importing oil proved to be state-owned, such as Petrobras in Brazil or Hispanoil in Spain. Indeed, some of the state-owned sellers of oil, such as those in Venezuela, Nigeria, and Saudi Arabia, pursued an explicit policy of favoring state-owned buyers.[19] At one point, Saudi Arabia conditioned its sale of oil to Denmark with the provision that Denmark create a state-owned distribution company.[20] And in 1982 the Saudi Arabian state-owned exporter announced that it would sell only to buyers officially designated by the importing countries.[21]

Some of the direct sales by state-owned enterprises were made on the spot market as isolated tanker shipments; all told, that kind of sale amounted to one or two million barrels daily. Most sales were made under contracts that stipulated some stated quantity to be shipped over a period of several months. These longer-run commitments sometimes were arranged as part of an even larger framework in which governments undertook to supply and acquire very large quantities of oil. In

THE WORLD OIL MARKET IN TRANSITION   33

1978, for instance, the Japanese government negotiated with Mexico just such a framework, which entailed the financing of petrochemical plants, rail lines, and port facilities, as well as large-scale loans to Mexican borrowers; in return, the Japanese could look forward to sales over the long term that might eventually reach 300,000 barrels per day.[22] At about the same time, Mexico undertook similar broad-ranging deals with France, Brazil, and several other countries.

Arrangements of this sort, however, often failed to provide anything like the degree of security that buyers or sellers were seeking. In 1980, for example, in spite of the framework accord, Mexico cut back sharply on shipments to Japan. And when France refused to accept a price increase for Mexican oil late in 1981, Mexico threatened to cut off France's participation in subway, steel, and automobile projects in Mexico.[23]

The firm-to-firm contracts issued by state-owned enterprises, as it turned out, also proved fragile. As noted earlier, when prices stiffened, sellers repeatedly refused to perform pursuant to such contracts.[24] Before 1973, in the era when multinational oil companies controlled the market, buyers could respond to such a contingency by trying to develop and control their own upstream supplies. But by 1980 that possibility rarely existed, except perhaps in the United States.

For any enterprise whose fortunes depended on a steady supply of oil, therefore, the markets of the early 1980s were seen as high-risk markets. Various efforts were afoot to try to reduce those risks. For instance, in the early 1980s public markets were established in New York and London to provide a market for dealing in oil futures; a market of that sort, it was hoped, might provide a means of buffering buyers and sellers against uncertainty. But early reports on the functioning of that market were not very encouraging.[25] And experiences with other such markets, such as the London Metals Exchange markets in copper, suggested that these facilities would do little to contribute to market stability and might even have a contrary effect by attracting destabilizing speculation.

Nor did it seem likely that the inventory policies of the intermediary firms in the oil business would provide a new source of stability. At times, such firms drew on their inventories to supply a tight market; but at other times, they seemed to be building up their inventories for speculative profits.[26] Some ameliorating factors, to be sure, were slightly blunting the threat of price instability. Official stockpiles had

34   TWO HUNGRY GIANTS

Table 2.3. Capital and exploration expenditures on crude oil and natural gas by the world petroleum industry, 1964–1980.[a]

	1964–1968		1969–1973		1974–1978		1979–1980	
	Amount (in millions of dollars)	Percent	Amount (in millions of dollars)	Percent	Amount (in millions of dollars)	Percent	Amount (in millions of dollars)	Percent
United States	19,425	67.5	24,850	58.8	65,595	53.2	56,500	53.4
Other Western Hemisphere countries	4,560	15.9	7,200	17.0	17,830	14.5	18,300	17.3
Western Europe	925	3.2	3,000	7.1	21,425	17.4	17,700	16.7
Middle East	1,375	4.8	2,400	5.7	6,825	5.5	4,150	3.9
Other	2,485	8.6	4,800	11.4	11,600	9.4	9,150	8.7
Total	28,770	100.0	42,250	100.0	123,275	100.0	105,800	100.0

a. Excludes communist areas.

Source: Chase Manhattan Bank, Energy Economics Division, "Capital Investments of the World Petroleum Industry," annual brochure, all issues 1964 to 1980.

grown somewhat, especially among the OECD countries. But by and large, the sense of insecurity among users was high.

One trend from which users could take some comfort was the shift in the geographical location of the capital and exploration expenditures being made by the world's oil industry in the production of crude oil and gas. As Table 2.3 shows, that pattern shifted after the 1973 crisis. The long-term trend in the relative decline of the United States was checked. Western Europe's position, based mainly on North Sea activity, rose considerably. The area that lost substantially in relative position was the Middle East, of course. To be sure, the geographical shift in development expenditures represented no guarantee that production would shift to the same degree. But from the users' viewpoint, the shift offered the prospect of some increased measure of security in the medium term.

Besides, by the early 1980s there were already some signs that the added efforts of producers to bring in oil from safe areas was beginning to have some considerable effects on the patterns of current production. In 1973 the thirteen OPEC countries had accounted for about 67 percent of the world's crude oil production outside the communist countries. By 1981, however, their contribution had dropped to 50 percent, lower than it had been since the early 1960s. And the prospective figure for 1982, assuming they adhered to their agreed production ceiling, would decline further to about 40 percent. The margins of influence and margins of safety for the OPEC countries, although still very large, were considerably reduced.

From the viewpoint of some of the oil-exporting countries, the resurgence of development activities in various "safe" areas of the world suggested that their own postions might prove more precarious in the course of time. Accordingly, they began to explore measures to protect such positions. In their efforts to reduce their reliance on the multinationals, practically all major oil-exporting countries had very early developed plans for building downstream facilities (oil refineries and petrochemical plants) on their own home territory, and for assembling their own tanker fleets.[27] That strategy, however, was more relevant for periods of shortage than for periods of surplus. In shortage, it freed the oil exporters from any reliance on the refining and distributing facilities of the multinationals and placed the exporters in a position of denying the multinationals any share of the extraordinary profits available in such periods. In surplus, however, the oil exporters still had to face the risk that their products might be displaced in importing countries, either by official restrictions on imports or by the competitive offerings of others.

Worries of this sort, when coupled with the needs of the oil exporters for help in acquiring the requisite technology and management to run their enterprises, probably explain why the oil-exporting countries were often willing to bring foreign partners ino the new refineries and petrochemical complexes that they were setting up on their home soil.[28] Links between state-owned enterprises and foreign oil companies appeared throughout the world, in many different forms: sometimes in joint ventures, sometimes in long-term service contracts, sometimes in more ambiguous relationships. In some instances the new partnerships were with the very multinationals that they had dispossessed from crude oil operations. Exxon, for instance, developed new links with Venezuela; Gulf Oil and British Petroleum retained ties with Kuwait; and Mobil moved into various downstream operations with Saudi Arabia.

The oil exporters were still faced, however, with the need to obtain more secure assurances of their ability, in the event of surplus, to protect their competitive positions in foreign markets. Neither OPEC's

36   TWO HUNGRY GIANTS

muscle nor long-term contractual arrangements nor the creation of processing facilities on their own soil seemed likely to provide the requisite
assurances. Another kind of strategy still remained to each of the state-
owned enterprises, one that the multinational enterprises themselves
had favored in years gone by. This was for each state-owned enterprise
to acquire its own refineries and distribution facilities in the markets of
the importing countries.

The beginnings of such a strategy had already been visible before the
revolution that toppled the shah in Iran, when the National Iranian Oil
Company (NIOC) began to acquire distribution facilities abroad; in
joint ventures with private firms or with other state-owned enterprises
NIOC acquired downstream facilities in India, South Africa, and Sene-
gal. Meanwhile, the state-owned enterprise of Abu Dhabi made similar
arrangements in Pakistan, as did Mexico's Petroleos Mexicanos in Spain.
The tendency picked up momentum in the 1980s, as the Kuwait Petroleum Company acquired interests in various refining and engineering
facilities in the United States.[29]

It was uncertain, however, whether arrangements of that sort would go
very far. In some respects, state-owned enterprises were more limited in
their choice of strategies than private multinational enterprises. When the
strategy entailed investment in foreign countries, state-owned enterprises
had to be responsive to the commands of their governments. Some governments would find it hard to authorize downstream investment by the
state-owned enterprises in oil-importing countries; the Mexican and Venezuelan governments, for instance, would have great difficulty in auth-
orizing such investments in the U.S. market. Moreover, despite the fact
that state-owned British Petroleum, Elf-Aquitaine, and AGIP managed
to make heavy investments in foreign markets, it was not at all clear that
downstream investments on a significant scale by state-owned oil companies from the OPEC countries would share the same kind of welcome.

The Prospects

Despite the efforts of buyers and sellers to reintroduce some measure
of stability in the market, therefore, the likelihood of continued instability is fairly high. On the supply side, variations in price have done
little to evoke stabilizing reactions. In the short run, price increases
have not expanded supply nor have price declines reduced it; the
marginal costs of oil and oil products to major suppliers are so low

THE WORLD OIL MARKET IN TRANSITION 37

relative to the market price as to be irrelevant to price determinations. On the demand side, price elasticities in the short run have also been very low.

Nor is the market likely to develop stability by agreement among the participants. Although OPEC is attempting valiantly to fill the breach, its success seems unlikely. The number of sellers in the market appears too large, their interests too disparate. Each state-owned enterprise is in some degree a creature of its government; many governments are unwilling to tie themselves to the elaborate long-term agreements that would be needed to bring stability to the market; and even if they were, it seems altogether unlikely that the participants could develop the level of mutual trust required of the participants in a successful oligopoly.

Gaining stability through long-term bilateral agreements, as some buying and selling countries hope to do, seems equally chimerical. Such agreements have proved fragile under pressure, whether from the pressure of spot prices or from the pressure of political frictions.

Japan and the United States, therefore, seem to be confronting international oil markets that differ in two key respects from the markets of earlier decades. First, the threat of price instability appears much greater than in the past. Second, the degree of concentration among the sellers is lower and their policies more loosely coordinated. In later chapters, these changes will be discussed in terms of the reactions of the United States and Japan, in an effort to determine their implications. For the present, however, we turn to the hard minerals to learn whether analogous developments have occurred in those markets.

For notes to accompany this chapter please see page 673.

Excerpt from *Foreign Investment in the Petroleum and Mineral Industries*, 29–55.

CHAPTER 2

CONFLICT IN FOREIGN INVESTOR–HOST COUNTRY RELATIONS: A PRELIMINARY ANALYSIS

Raymond F. Mikesell

The case studies included in this book give many examples of conflict between foreign investors, on one hand, and host governments and labor organizations, on the other. Popular accounts of these conflicts oversimplify the issues and emphasize the irrational elements—irrational in the sense of not being relevant to the economic issues involved; for example, charges of socialism or of foreign exploitation. Thus the issues on which meaningful bargaining takes place, the elements in bargaining strength, and the complex nature of conflict itself are not revealed. While the type of conflict with which we are concerned is capable of rational analysis and the range of possible or likely solutions can be assessed, the outcome of the "game" does not ordinarily admit to formal mathematical solution as in the case of stylized problems in game theory.

NATURE OF THE CONFLICTS ARISING OUT OF FOREIGN INVESTMENTS IN MINERALS AND PETROLEUM

Before attempting an analysis of certain categories of conflict, I will review briefly the major types of conflict that arise out of rela-

tions between foreign mineral and petroleum companies and host governments. Conflict of the kind with which we are concerned does not occur until a foreign investor has made a financial commitment and has been successful in discovering and developing resources. The initial agreement (if such exists) regulating the terms of entry involves bargaining between the foreign buyer and the seller of the concession (or other contractual agreement for the exploitation of resources). If there is competition among several foreign company bidders, the concession might go to the highest bidder, taking into account the various conditions of the contract. However, this is wholly a matter of marketplace bargaining. Once a substantial investment has been made and has proved successful, conflict may arise over the taxes and other payments to the government that affect the net earnings of the company, the amounts of net earnings that may be repatriated, the area that has been explored by the company and in which it is permitted to produce, the prices charged for the product, the level of output, the prices paid by the company for domestic goods and

Note: Many of the ideas expressed in this chapter were suggested by an unpublished paper written by William P. McGreevey, University of California, Berkeley.

services, the exchange rate applicable to local currency purchases, and the employment of domestic goods and services (including labor) as against foreign goods and services in company operations. In addition to conflict with the national government, there may be conflicts with domestic labor unions over remuneration and conditions of employment and with state or municipal governments or quasi-government agencies regarding a variety of matters important to operations. Examples of most of these issues will be found in the case studies; our concern in this chapter is with formulating a framework of analysis for certain broad categories of conflict.

We may divide conflict involving a foreign resource company and the host government broadly into three categories: issues related to (1) the division of total net revenues from operations between the foreign company and the host government; (2) the control of export prices, output, and other conditions affecting the level of total revenues; and (3) the domestic impact of foreign company operations. A fourth category of issues is related to the legal form of control of the resource operations themselves—e.g., the percentage of foreign ownership, nationalization with a foreign management contract, etc.— but these issues have more to do with the resolution of conflict. Thus, the issue of control over various aspects of resource exploitation may be resolved by one of a variety of legal forms of operation. Moreover, the legal form of control may have more political than economic or operational significance.

The main emphasis of this chapter will be on the first and second categories of issues: those relating to the division of net revenues, and those relating to export pricing and the level of output as they affect total revenues. The latter, which have become increasingly important in recent years, involve two types of situations (or some combination of them). First, the host country and the foreign company may have different views with respect to the maximization of returns from the production of resources. These arise from differences in outlook relating to long-run prices or from the application of different rates of discount

to future revenues.[1] The government may want to limit the rate of exploitation in order to conserve reserves for future production or it may expect that the long-term trend in prices will be upward, or at least not downward. The companies, in turn, may want to maintain their share of the world market by expanding output in relation to demand or by reducing prices to meet foreign competition. Alternatively, the companies may want to maintain prices at the cost of larger exports while the government may want to expand exports. This general type of situation, in which the foreign company and the host government entertain different views with respect to the optimum policy for maximizing total revenues over time, may be distinguished from the second situation. In this, the interests of the foreign company and the host country diverge with respect to the desirability of maximizing total revenues (regardless of the time path). For example, the foreign company may want to keep prices low for sales to its affiliates in other countries since the higher the price (and total returns), the larger the amount of total revenues which must be shared with the host government. The foreign company may also want to limit output from a relatively high-cost source of supply in meeting its marketing commitments abroad in favor of lower-cost alternative sources, or it may for security reasons desire to conserve its potential supplies in politically safe areas.

Where the basic interests of the foreign company diverge from those of the host government with respect to total revenues, the situation becomes exceedingly complex since not only is the conflict concerned with the division of the revenues, but the protagonists do not have a common interest in maximizing the total revenues to be divided. In such cases, the issue of control becomes more important than that of the sharing of the revenues. The issue of control may also become important in the first situation—

---

[1] One might expect that the discount rate for a developing country would be higher than that for an international company (aside from the risk element); however, officials of developing countries rarely think in these terms.

where the company and the government have divergent views with respect to the method of maximizing revenues over time or to the time path of the revenue stream. However, in such cases there is greater scope for accommodation through the achievement of a common evaluation of world demand and supply conditions.

The area of conflict over domestic impact, including the purchases of domestic goods and services and domestic processing of materials, involves both economic and political factors. When government revenues are determined as a share of total net revenue, higher production costs reduce the government's take. The government may, nevertheless, find it politically expedient to side with labor in a dispute over wages. On the other hand, the country may realize long-run economic gains from a larger volume of domestic purchases by the foreign companies even if domestic prices are higher than import costs. Host governments may demand that resource companies process minerals rather than ship ores, but the companies may resist such demands even where domestic processing of materials may offer substantial cost advantages.[2] The case studies provide examples of settlements of disputes over taxes and other matters in which agreement to construct processing facilities constituted a part of the final resolution of the conflict.

Legal and Institutional Setting for Conflict

In most cases, foreign companies operating in minerals and petroleum enter the host country on the basis of a concession agreement covering royalties, taxes, and other payments to the government, together with certain conditions of operation. In other cases, foreign companies come in under general minerals legislation and acquire mineral rights by the purchase of domestic firms or by acquisition from governmental agencies in accordance with general legal and administra-

tive procedures. Conflict may arise from action by the government in changing, or threatening to change, the conditions of the initial contract or by calling for a renegotiation of the initial contract. Alternatively, it may arise from the imposition of taxes and other conditions affecting company operations not explicitly covered by the contract. In many cases, the general mineral laws under which a company enters the country are changed and, in some instances, guarantees to investors provided under these laws are revoked by subsequent legislation. Frequently sovereign states do not regard themselves as bound by any contract or by previous laws and constitutional provisions in force at the time a foreign investment was made. Governments may also decide that contracts made by a previous government are unconstitutional, and these decisions may or may not be upheld in the courts. Disputes between the government and the foreign companies may take place at various administrative levels within the government, and the final resolution may be left to the chief of state or, in many cases, to court decisions reached only after many years of litigation. In a few cases, where the host government agrees, disputes are taken to the UN Court of International Justice or are decided by arbitration. Also, the government of the foreign investor frequently plays a role in a dispute, particularly where expropriation or contract annulment is threatened, and the United States, at least, has powerful sanctions which it may use, or threaten to use, against the host government in the event of expropriation without adequate compensation.

In this chapter we shall not be concerned with the legal and administrative framework nor with the appeals to the sanctity of contracts or property rights nor with legal justice and international morality. Nevertheless, these factors do constitute important constraints in the resolution of conflicts, the force of which differs greatly from country to country. In Castro's Cuba, they are nil, but in a country like Brazil, which is anxious to attract foreign investment and public loans and eager to maintain an image of constitutional and

---

[2] Frequently companies do not want to process minerals or refine petroleum locally because overseas customers have their own refineries. In addition, import duties tend to be high on processed materials and low or nonexistent on raw materials.

responsible government, the legal restraints on government action in conflicts with foreign investors are exceedingly important.

Options in Disputes

Except as limited by internal legal restraints on government administration, governments can require companies to pay higher taxes, raise wages and fringe benefits, negotiate foreign sales at prescribed minimum prices, expand output (so long as additional external capital is not required), or sell to certain consumers such as the Communist countries.[3] Governments also have the sovereign right to take over the properties and operations of the foreign investors. The only absolute options open to foreign investors are refusal to provide their managerial and technical services and the international marketing outlets over which they have control, and refusal to bring additional capital into the host country. They may withdraw from the country but have no absolute right to take their capital with them. In practice, however, foreign companies do have and exercise other options. They may refuse to reinvest any profits or depreciation and depletion allowances which they are permitted by law to repatriate. They also may curtail operations and sales in a variety of ways that will affect total revenues in order to reduce their losses, or perhaps to pressure the host country into meeting their demands. Moreover, a multinational company may compensate for losses sustained by restricting operations in one country through expanding output from alternative sources of supply in other areas of the world.

External Influences

Aiding the foreign company in conflicts relating to contract violations or threats of

expropriation by the host government are the government of the foreign investor, the international assistance agencies, and the international financial community. The U.S. government has characteristically supported U.S. companies in their disputes with foreign governments. While direct military intervention has been discarded as a means of protecting the economic interests of the United States, U.S. power can be brought to bear in different ways. A recent example is the amendment to the Foreign Assistance Act of 1961 which requires that foreign aid be terminated in any country which has expropriated U.S. owned property, nullified existing contracts, or imposed taxes or other conditions having the effect of expropriation without prompt and full compensation.[4] Thus the threat of losing U.S. aid was tied directly into the issue between companies and governments.

Although international assistance agencies such as the World Bank group, the International Monetary Fund, and the Inter-American Development Bank are not required by their charters to refuse assistance to governments that expropriate foreign investments, they are committed to encouraging private foreign investment and have been known to deny their largess to countries following "unsound" international financial policies. More broadly, the general international financial community upon which developing countries are dependent for import credits and for the refinancing of external indebtedness is bound to react unfavorably to expropriation and nullification of contracts in the absence of a mutually satisfactory financial settlement. Thus, because of the heavy dependence of nearly all developing countries on external aid and private credits, host governments are under a severe constraint in resorting to actions which constitute legal or de facto expropriation. Moreover, in the case of export industries, the government might find itself barred by international action from

[3] Officials of U.S. companies may be constrained from selling certain commodities to Communist countries in conformance with similar regulations applying to companies located in the United States. While this kind of extraterritoriality on the part of the U.S. government has been protested by many foreign countries, including Canada, U.S. officials of foreign companies are in fact subject to such legal restraints by the U.S. government.

[4] Foreign Assistance Act of 1961, sec. 620 (c); subsec. (e) was added by the Foreign Assistance Act of 1962 and amended by the Foreign Assistance Acts of 1963 and 1964. Subsec. (e) spells out the procedures for determining full value.

selling the products of an expropriated investment in world markets.

Another external factor that affects conflict is the character of the international market for the product. Not only is the world market price subject to fluctuation, but the volume of output of the country and the marketing policies and practices of the foreign investor (or that of the host government itself when it assumes a measure of control over prices and marketing) have an effect upon world price, since world markets for petroleum and most minerals are far from perfectly competitive. Not only may the foreign investor sell a portion of his output to affiliates, but there may be collusion with other international firms or with foreign governments with respect to the prices. The producing countries themselves, notably in petroleum but also in other commodities such as copper, engage in collaborative action in order to influence the world market price. Moreover, to an increasing degree the governments of the producing countries are organizing their own companies to produce and market petroleum and other commodities, often in competition with private concession holders in their own country. Finally, large consuming countries, such as the United States, have an influence on world prices through price and import controls and through the administration of the U.S. antitrust laws. These external factors greatly affect the bargaining process between governments and foreign investors since, as has been noted, conflict is not concerned solely with the share of the total net revenues or rents but is also related to the size of the revenue from the export of the product.

CONFLICT OVER THE SHARES OF THE RENT

Conflict between companies and governments over the shares in total net revenue from resource operations occurs because surpluses over cost arise either from supply scarcities—such as those associated with the natural resources or the technical and man-

agerial skills possessed by the companies— or from imperfections in the markets for the factors of production or the products. In this discussion, I shall refer to any surplus above the current expenditures necessary to produce output as rent. As will be noted later on, however, there are several types and sources of rents. If each factor of production were paid (on a current basis) the equilibrium price for its service, there could be no conflict. Thus, if the government of the host country sold its resources in the world market; let contracts for the supply of capital, management, and technical services required for producing resources on the basis of competitive bidding; and renegotiated the contracts every year, no conflict over rents would arise.[5] However, this would not constitute direct foreign investment but simply the lending of capital and the selling of services at market prices. This situation differs from that in which a long-term investment is made by the foreign investor. Unless the foreign investor expected to receive a share of the rent over and above current payments to the factors of production, including the going rate of return on capital, he would not have made the investment. The government, however, as the owner of the scarce natural resources also expects a substantial share of the rent, and the labor unions which monopolize the domestic labor supply, often with the aid of political power, may expect a share of the rent in the form of returns higher than the going wage for the type of labor provided.

Companies producing resources sometimes sell their products in world markets and sometimes sell to their own processing or marketing affiliates (or both), depending upon the structure of the industry. For purposes of analysis, I shall assume initially that the producing firms sell the product in a world market, although the market may be imperfect in the sense that marginal revenue is less than average revenue; i.e., larger sales can only be made at a lower price. I shall also

---

[5] Where the foreign company producing the resource also purchases the output, there could be conflict over the price unless there was a mutually recognized world price.

assume that the producing firm is maximizing with respect to the price received in the world market.[6] These assumptions will be modified later on in this chapter.

Sources of Rent from Supply Scarcities

In his *Principles of Economics,* Alfred Marshall distinguished three kinds of rent, all of which are relevant to our problem: (1) *pure rent,* which he defined as the return to a factor that could not, even in the long run, be increased in supply; (2) *quasi-rent,* which is differentiated from pure rent as a return to a factor that could not be increased in supply in the short run, but that could be increased in the long run; and (3) the rent of natural ability.[7] Marshall saw pure rent as a return to the natural qualities and state of land made scarce in "old" countries, but the concept is applicable to minerals in the subsoil in all countries. Investments in fixed capital assets in the form of plant and equipment could not be withdrawn in the short run (except at a substantial loss); once plants were built and machinery put in place, all payments above variable cost were to be regarded as quasi-rents. Returns from the specialized technical and managerial resources possessed by international mining and petroleum firms over and above the prevailing market prices for the services of the managers and technicians might be regarded as analogous to Marshall's concept of "rent of ability." Thus, Marshall distinguished for us a long-period rent usually associated with land, quasi-rents to fixed capital assets such as equipment and buildings, and extraordinary returns to the specialized knowledge and experience which constitute important resources of large mining and petroleum firms.

All three kinds of rent exist as a floating surplus above the required payments for the factors of production. They are created by the inherent supply conditions for these factors of production. The supply scarcities include: the land in which the minerals are found, together with the cost of geological surveys and exploration that have been invested in the land; certain development expenditures that do not depreciate and that, like land, give rise to pure rent; reproducible structures and equipment that depreciate over time and must be replaced; and the technology and managerial skills that are to some degree monopolized by international producing firms. The rents arising from the technical knowledge and skills of the foreign companies are built into the initial supply prices of the specialized resources of these firms and are determined by what they can earn in other producing areas in association with fixed capital investment. While these supply prices must be covered in calculations entering into the decision of the foreign company to invest in an area, once these resources are committed, together with capital investment in fixed assets, they cannot readily be withdrawn without loss since they are essential to continued operations and will be supplied so long as revenues are in excess of current expenditures. Since the technical and managerial services are in effect joint costs with the capital investment, the rents associated with their initial supply prices are a part of the quasi-rents derived from capital investment in reproducible assets.

All of these rents must come from the surplus generated from the difference between gross revenues from the sale of the products and the current expenditures for the productive factors. Except under the terms of an agreement among the claimants, which terms are always subject to change, there is no inherent system whereby the rents are allocated among the various claimants, since the rents are by their very nature surpluses above the required payments for current output. Not even depreciation allowances constitute an assured prior claim on the total surplus

[6] Where an international firm has alternative supply sources for sales to its own affiliates, we may think of its marketing requirements as the market and each producing area as a separate source of supply. The market price might be regarded as being determined by the prices of the products sold to the ultimate consumers plus the cost of processing or refining, marketing, etc., including normal profits.

[7] Marshall, *Principles of Economics* (London: Macmillan, 1898), pp. 476–503.

available for distribution, and such allowances are frequently an important element in the conflict between companies and the host government. Moreover, fluctuations in gross revenues in relation to current costs arising from changes in market prices and other factors often give rise to violent fluctuations in the total surplus. There may also be periods during which gross revenues do not cover current costs, but firms may go on producing in the expectation that surpluses will be earned later on.

The Role of Risk

Companies usually justify the existence of exceptionally high returns on a particular investment in terms of the high risk involved in the extractive industries. They point to cases of millions of dollars invested in geological surveys and exploration from which the companies have received no returns, and argue that these unsuccessful investments must be balanced against high returns from the successful ones. The host governments, however, tend to look only at the level of company earnings from those investments that have proved to be successful and argue that these earnings should constitute no more than a reasonable return on invested capital.

In order to attract capital to an area which has not been explored, the contract or concession agreement must allow for a return appropriate to the estimated risk involved. Most contracts or concessions today are let on a competitive bid basis. Corporations apply estimated probabilities to risk and return variables before submitting their bids. A bid for a concession may involve an initial price to be paid for the concession and, if taxes and other conditions have not been standardized by the host country, the bid may include special tax agreements, bonus arrangements, and other conditions. Risk calculations also allow, or should allow, for the possibility that the host country will subsequently alter the terms of the contract to obtain a larger share. Presumably the greater the risk in relation to the expectation of gains, the higher

will be the supply price of capital in a competitive bid situation.[8]

Once an investment has been made which proves to be a bonanza, the returns necessary to induce (or retain) capital investment into the concession area drop sharply. So long as the successful bidder for the concession can both retain the entire concession and the original terms, he makes large monopoly profits which are analogous to rents. Hence the returns on his capital are now well above the current supply price of capital for investment in the high-yielding concession area. The host country may seek to capture all or part of this rent for itself by increased taxation or by reducing the concession area and making more advantageous contracts with other foreign producing firms for developing a portion of the original concession area.[9] The rent claimed by both the government and the foreign company arises basically from the monopoly positions with respect to the resources held by the two parties. The host country owns the resources, but the foreign company has a monopoly by virtue of its concession contract which provides a return higher than the current supply price of capital (including risk and rent of ability) *after* the investment has proved successful. The amount of the rent fluctuates with the price of the product, the current supply prices of the other productive factors including capital, and the productivity of the operation.[10] The supply price of capital fluctuates with risk but, as we have noted, the risk element is substantially higher in the case of capital required for the initial development of the concession than in the case of capital

[8] Companies may not be completely rational with respect to intermediate term benefit-cost calculations; they may bid higher than seems warranted in order to increase the proportion of world reserves which they control or to prevent their competitors from doing so. Large firms are generally more interested in long-term growth than in short- or intermediate-term profits.

[9] Both of these methods have been employed by Saudi Arabia, Iraq, and other petroleum-producing countries.

[10] By virtue of their control of scarce technical and managerial skills, the long-run prices of other productive factors owned by the companies include rent of ability. However, once these factors are committed along with fixed capital investment, their supply prices decline to the current payments to the factors.

needed once the venture shows promise of yielding high returns. Thus we must differentiate between two types of capital involving two levels of risk.[11] For any particular investment, only the risk element in the current supply price of capital is relevant. Any amount received by the foreign investor above this derives from the control of the natural resources.[12]

The above analysis raises the question of how foreign companies are compensated for the risk involved in the initial investments, assuming that after the investments are made and have proven successful the supply curve for capital shifts because of the reduced risk element. The answer lies in the expectation of the companies that they will receive a portion of the rent generated by the natural resources after they have been successfully developed and not simply a return based on the lower-risk supply price of capital after the operation has begun to yield high returns. Obviously, if host governments would only permit the companies to earn a return based on the supply price of capital *after* mines and oil fields proved to be successful, high-risk capital investments would not be made. Hence the companies must be promised a share of rent attributable to resources as defined here. But the host government is not likely to yield a large share of this rent indefinitely, and it will shortly seek to revise the terms of the contract in line with the current rather than the original supply price of capital. Herein lies the fundamental basis for conflict over the rents arising from the natural resources. However, the companies continue to supply high-risk capital because they have been gen-

erally successful in capturing enough of the rent to compensate them for their high risk.[13]

This analysis of risk has an important bearing on the concept of exploitation and on the idea that foreign companies should earn only the going rate of return on capital plus an allowance for risk. Such expressions are found in recent resolutions of the Organization of Petroleum Exporting Countries (OPEC)[14] and also in statements by economists. For example, Edith Penrose defines exploitation as "the use of superior economic or political power by foreign interests to prevent a country from making the most profitable use of its own resources." She goes on to say,

> There is no reason . . . why the oil companies should earn greater profits than is necessary to induce them to continue investing in the industry and to compensate them for their initial risks. In other words, if excess profits are to be earned, a producing country can complain of exploitation to the extent to which it is unable to obtain them for itself because of the superior bargaining power of the oil company; if it could obtain them, the use of its resources would thereby become more profitable to the country.[15]

However, the rate of return that is derived from resource operations, and which is necessary to induce companies to continue investing in a country once petroleum has been found in large quantities, differs substantially from that necessary to induce and to undertake high-risk investments in unexplored areas. There is simply no way to measure the proper compensation for risk under these circumstances. While greater competition in international petroleum reduces the overall returns of the petroleum

[11] Actually, many levels of risk are involved in investment in a particular concession area. For example, the opening up of mines or the drilling of wells in a new field within the concession area will involve greater risk than would similar investment in the old fields but a greater risk would be involved in the initial investment before any portion of the concession area was proved.

[12] It may also be noted that the yield (rent) from natural resources after they have been successfully developed is far higher than before as a consequence of the risk capital invested in their exploration. A part of this higher yield might be regarded as a return on the risk investment, but the entire return is in the nature of rent. In fact, there is no return on resources without some capital investment having taken place.

[13] Risk is a cost and not a part of rent; but once an investment is made, all returns over and above current outlays take on the nature of rent.
[14] "Declaratory Statement of Petroleum Policy in Member Countries," Res. XVI.90, *OPEC Bulletin*, August 1968, pp. 1–5.
[15] Penrose, "Profit Sharing Between Producing Countries and Oil Companies in the Middle East," *Economic Journal*, vol. 69 (June 1959), p. 255.

companies, conflict over the rent from the resources will continue.

Quasi-Rents

Once investments have been made and the foreign investor is earning substantial profits the bargaining power shifts in favor of the host country. But the bargaining power of the company in this situation is frequently under-estimated to the detriment of both parties in the conflict. Quasi-rents melt away with time as machinery wears out and new wells must be drilled to replace those which have been depleted. Investment is a continuous flow and even the maintenance of a constant level of output requires a continuous volume of in-vestment. If company profits are squeezed too hard, the company may fail to reinvest any of its profits and even fail to reinvest its depreciation and depletion allowances. Thus, as Chile discovered in the 1950s and as Venezuela discovered more recently, output may fall even with a rising world demand for the product as a consequence of the govern-ment's having absorbed too large a share of the total revenue. The position of the com-panies would be weaker if they did not have the options of (1) supplying their world markets from other sources and (2) gradually reducing their commitment in the host country by withdrawing their capital for more profitable investment elsewhere. To the degree that the capital assets can be with-drawn and employed elsewhere at an equal or higher rate of return, the return on that capital does not constitute rent so far as the particular country is concerned; the return is simply the market price for the factors even though it may represent a monopoly price from the standpoint of the world market. Thus a host government may make a mistake in absorbing a portion of the cur-rent world market return to the factors sup-plied by the foreign investor and not simply the rent or surplus above this return. If the host country wants to expand output and the total rent from its unexploited resources, it will have to offer terms which will attract both new capital and reinvested profits and depreciation. Such returns will need to be at least as high as that readily available to the company in employing its financial and tech-nical resources elsewhere in the world.

The Allocation of Rent from Natural Resources

It would appear that the only rent properly in dispute between the foreign resource com-pany and the host government is that arising from the resources themselves. Unless the foreign company receives a rate of return sufficient to cover depreciation on its invested capital plus normal profits, including an allowance for "relevant" risk, plus rent of ability, it will withdraw its capital and shift its resources to other areas. Such a shift may, of course, take place gradually since it will pay the company to continue operations so long as current revenue exceeds current cost. While the scarce productive factors supplied by the company, including capital and tech-nical and managerial resources, cannot be withdrawn in the short run (except at a loss), they can be withdrawn in the longer run. The natural resources are in a somewhat different category. The land usually has no alternative uses of comparable value, and the supply can-not be increased except by large additional expenditures of capital and technology where additional reserves may be suspected. How-ever, in most cases resources of comparable value are available or are likely to be found in other areas of the world. Thus, the rent from any particular resource is always in jeopardy from the expansion of supply elsewhere.

What claims can be made on the rent arising from scarce natural resources? The government of the host country usually holds title to the minerals and the subsoil. The foreign company that discovered the deposits believes it should be richly rewarded by extraordinary profits from its concession as a proper compensation for risk. However, the returns to the company permitted by the original contract may exceed by a substantial amount that required to cover risk, rent of ability, and normal profits required to attract capital after the initial high-risk investment has been made, so that what the successful foreign company receives is a portion of the rent arising from the natural resources by reason of its exclusive concession. In addition to the company and the host government, domestic labor or the owners of other productive factors may demand a portion of the rent by reason of their monopoly position. However, there is no way to evaluate the various claims on the rent of the natural resources. Initially, the allocation is established by agreement among the claimants, but agreements are always subject to dispute and renegotiation.

The Temporal Evolution of Claims on Rent

The allocation of the rent from natural resources reflects the bargaining positions of the claimants, but these positions shift over time. The initial allocation is made by the concession agreement or contract between the foreign company and the host government and, while the agreements may run for half a century or more—they tend to be somewhat shorter now—it is generally recognized that they are subject to renegotiation from time to time, and the outcome of these renegotiations reflects shifts in the bargaining power of the claimants.

Why should a country which thinks it holds substantial mineral wealth in the ground ever agree to concession contracts with international companies? Could it not develop the resources itself and thus capture all the rents produced by the exploitation of the resources? Nationalists in some countries have argued that the government could and should develop its own resources. Political parties in Argentina and Chile, for example, have long argued that nationals should develop their country's resources, and Mexico has believed since the 1930s that it could best achieve resource development with domestic capital and talent. Despite these examples, two elements must enter into consideration. First, there is no assurance before a shaft is bored or a hole is drilled that minerals or oil actually exist

beneath the surface. The very unpredictability of the outcome of an expensive investment of capital makes it most unappetizing to a government which is capital-poor. Second, the international companies have certain skills (and try actively to monopolize them either through their enormous size or control of patents and the skilled labor force) which can command a rent of natural ability. At least at the moment before drilling or boring begins, the utility functions of the government and the company are likely to be decidedly different: the company is a risk taker and the government by necessity must be a risk avoider. These conditions lead to contractual arrangements in which the parties will have specified claims on the revenue from a product which may or may not come into existence. Initially, the government is bound to believe that something is better than nothing, that resources undeveloped are of no use whatever; and that, if developed with the help of an outside company that is prepared to accept the risk, any return is a positive gain. At the same time, the foreign company is prepared to undertake operations if the expected return is at least as great as that which would be earned in any other part of the world or in any other activity that it might undertake with comparable risk. It is only after production begins and large rents accrue to the foreign company that conditions for conflict occur. Well before that time, however, legal claims have been established.

Consider the evolution of a mining enterprise. It begins with expectations on the part of the government and the foreign entrepreneur that are most unclear. However, the government has nothing and is prepared to yield a part of its sovereignty; i.e., grant a concession to the foreigner in return for the promise of a small share of the gain. Once the mine is proved, substantial investments by the foreigner will take place in the form of railroads, pipelines, port facilities, and of machinery for the removal of overburden as in open-pit copper mining. After several years have passed, investments have been made, and the state realizes that whatever legal arrangements it may have made, it can change them. For example, in the case of Chile, taxes paid by the Braden Company were less than 1 percent of gross sales value over the period 1913–24. During the period 1930–39, the Chilean government took less than 6 percent of the value of copper production. After 1939, the government's share began to rise rapidly until it reached nearly 64 percent in 1953 (see chapter 16). This evolution can be related to changing bargaining positions of the government and the companies[16] as well as to the change in the economic policies of the government.

An important element that enters into bargaining power on the side of the government is the domestic political situation. In many of the less developed countries, the advent of political pluralism and the first signs of interest-group politics have enhanced the political power of populist parties. Such parties came into power in Brazil in the 1930s with Vargas, in Chile with Ibáñez in 1950, in Venezuela with Betancourt in 1958, and in Argentina with Perón in 1945. These parties are galvanized by support from center and leftist parties into taking a stiff attitude in bargaining over the share of the rents with foreign enterprise. Moreover, foreign enterprise often resisted such governments less strongly because they feared that resistance would bring to power an even more left-leaning government. Also, as developing countries grow in wealth and economic capability, their ability to take over and operate technically advanced enterprises increases and nationalization becomes a more feasible option.

As a consequence of the political developments in populist governments, the growth of the industry itself generates increased bargaining power for the government. As the foreign-controlled industry becomes more important in the economy, it becomes an object of attack by political forces opposing the government in power. This process also works

through the growth and strengthening of labor unions. Since the early 1950s, Bolivian tin miners have provided a sustained revolutionary force. Only through a complicated client arrangement between oil workers' unions and political parties has the revolutionary potential of Venezuelan oil workers been dissipated. In other cases, workers in the export activities provide the main force in favor of bringing a larger share to governments in the host countries.

This process has an important indirect mechanism as well. The threat of what in the literature of game theory is called a "warfare solution" brings the companies to accept a less favorable share than might otherwise be the case. The combination of a populist government in power, militant trade unions, and a socialist party with a prospect of coming to power is bound to make a foreign company more "reasonable" in reacting to government demands.

At a further point in time, the bargaining position of the host country may be strengthened by the possibility of successful exploitation of its resources by national companies, or by joint ventures with other foreign firms, or by the negotiation of more favorable contracts or concession agreements with other foreign firms. The original concessionaire will have proved the existence of reserves within a large concession area and thus greatly reduced the risk of additional investment in the same or adjacent areas. Moreover, the original concessionaire is usually required to relinquish substantial portions of the original concession over the life of the contract. During his period of operation, the original concessionaire has trained a large number of domestic workers, supervisory personnel, and even managers who are available to run the enterprise should it become nationalized. While the host country may still not have all of the skills and experience necessary to operate a resource industry on its own and will usually lack access to world markets for the products, it may be able to find willing partners among the growing number of private independent petroleum or mineral firms or national petroleum firms in developed

---

[16] For an interesting discussion of this process see Raymond Vernon, "Long-Term Trends in Concession Contracts," *Proceedings of the American Society of International Law*, Sixty-first Annual Meeting (Washington, 1967), pp. 81–89.

countries that are eager to join with the host government in exploiting its resources. Thus, increased competition in the supply of specialized factors needed for resource exploitation and marketing, which were once the almost exclusive preserve of a few international companies, reduces the long-run supply prices of these factors. If the original concessionaire is to remain in the country, it must be willing to adjust its share of the rent to reflect these new competitive conditions.

A PARTIAL THEORY OF BARGAINING

In the resource industries, the spread between current or variable costs of producing a given output and the price at which that output is sold is generally quite broad. Moreover, the marginal cost of production (excluding taxes) is frequently far below the market price. Total rent, defined as the difference between total revenue and current expenses (excluding taxes), is therefore likely to constitute a large share of total revenue. Since there are no fixed rules for sharing this rent among the various claimants once the host government decides to insist on contract renegotiation, a wide area for bargaining exists. However, two points must be borne in mind. First, even in the short run, the company would find it desirable to reduce output if marginal revenue were less than its marginal cost, including taxes, or if the excess of marginal revenue over marginal cost, including taxes, would be larger if the company supplied a larger share of its market from an alternative source.[17] Second, in the longer run, the company can gradually withdraw its

capital and other productive factors if net returns are less than these factors could earn elsewhere. Thus, the total rent from the production of the resources is not independent of the shares. In addition, the company might decide to withdraw from operations even though it could continue to earn a net return over current outlays because if it gave in to the demands of the host government its contracts in other areas might be jeopardized.

The Bilateral Monopoly Case as an Illustration of Conflict

The bargaining situation in which the total amount of rent to be shared is not independent of the relative shares may be illustrated (by analogy) by referring to the bilateral monopoly model in figure 1.[18] The monopsonist (buyer) is purchasing a service or commodity required in producing goods for sale in an imperfect market. The buyer's demand curve for this service or commodity is given by his marginal revenue product curve, D. Barring an agreement on a joint maximizing solution at OP, the price of the service or commodity is indeterminate between OP' and OP''. At price OP' and quantity OQ', the monopsonist (buyer) will be maximizing his profits ($P'WZY$). At the price OP'' and quantity OQ'', the monopolist (seller) will be making maximum profits ($RMNP''$). In the joint maximizing case, total profits, RXY, are divided between the buyer and the seller in a manner determined by the slope of the buyer's marginal revenue product curve and the seller's marginal cost curve. (In the model it is assumed that there are no fixed costs.)

In the absence of a long-run agreement that continues to be honored by the conflicting parties, there will be constant dispute over whether the shared profits should move more favorably toward one or the other of the parties. It should be noted that the aggregate amount of profits is not fixed but changes with the share of each party. Joint profits are

[17] As will be discussed in chapter 3, the form of taxation will affect the short-run adjustment in output to a change in taxes. If taxation is based on a percentage of total net profits, an increase in taxes is less likely to affect output in the short run. (However, if the company has alternative sources of supply for its markets, any reduction in earnings might lead it to reduce output in the area of reduced earnings in favor of output from other areas.) On the other hand, if taxes are a fixed amount per unit of output or if they are based on posted prices rather than on realized prices, they become a part of unit costs. Such taxes may raise the marginal costs in higher-cost mines or oil fields to a level which exceeds marginal revenue, with the result that output will be cut back.

[18] For an analysis of bilateral monopoly, see George J. Stigler, *The Theory of Price* (New York: Macmillan, 1961), pp. 240–41.

maximized at price *OP* and quantity *OQ*,
since at *OP* the supply price (or marginal
cost of the seller) will equal the marginal
revenue product (*MRP*) to the buyer. But
demand for the factor or commodity equal to
OQ could not be achieved except by special
agreement between the parties since neither
party maximizes his profits at that point.
Either party by itself, assuming that it had
the bargaining strength, would always be able
to increase its profits through further use of
its monopoly (monopsony) power. But in so
doing, it would increase its absolute share at
the expense not only of its partner but of the
total amount of profits to be shared.

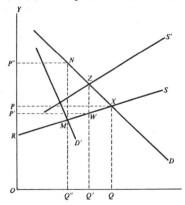

Figure 1.

    S = Seller's marginal cost (supply) curve, and
          buyer's average cost curve
    S' = Buyer's marginal cost curve
    D = Buyer's marginal revenue product (demand)
          curve, and seller's average revenue curve
    D' = Seller's marginal revenue curve
    OP = Joint profit-maximizing price
    OQ = Joint profit-maximizing output
    OP' = Buyer's profit-maximizing price
    OQ' = Buyer's profit-maximizing output
    OP* = Seller's profit-maximizing price
    OQ* = Seller's profit-maximizing output

The purpose of the above analysis is to
illustrate a situation in which the outcome of
conflict over the shares of total profits is
indeterminate, but the outcome affects the
size of the total profits to be shared. This
situation is quite common in the type of conflict we are studying; namely, that between
a foreign company and a host government.

However, we cannot actually apply our
bilateral monopoly illustration to the parameters relevant to the determination of output and the sharing of the rents in a conflict
situation facing a foreign company and a host
government (or labor union). Marginal costs
to the host country are not actually involved
when a host government bargains with a
foreign company over the rent from the exploitation of lands. Also, the "price" the
company is paying to the host country for
the use of the mineral lands may not be a
variable unit price but a share of the total
profits or rent. Nevertheless, we may assume
that the foreign company is selling the product in an imperfect market (hence a declining marginal revenue product curve), and that
its output will be influenced over time by the
taxes, wages, and other costs the company
must pay. In the short run, the producer
frequently has the option of meeting his
marketing requirements from other sources
or of failing to maintain or expand his world
market share by means of price competition.
In the longer run, he may expand capacity by
additional investment, or permit capacity to
decline by failing to replace worn-out equipment or to drill new wells to replace depleted
ones. The effects of increased taxes and factor
costs on output and investment in capacity
are well illustrated in the case studies dealing
with Chilean copper (chapter 16) and Venezuelan petroleum (chapters 5 and 6). In any
conflict situation involving a host country
and a foreign resource company, we must
take account of time in analyzing conditions
for a joint maximizing solution.

Under what conditions would either party
to a conflict be content with a joint maximizing solution, since at this point he may not
be maximizing his profits or rent? In other
words, why might a company or host government refrain from pushing its advantage to
the point at which an increase in its net revenue was obtained at the cost of a decline in
total revenue? We must first establish whether
the company (or those who control it) has an
interest in maximizing its own net revenue,
since an affiliate of an integrated firm may be

operated from the standpoint of maximizing the after-tax profits of the integrated firm, possibly at the expense of the net revenue of the producing affiliate. If we assume that the private company is seeking to maximize its own profits with respect to its *own* marginal revenue and marginal cost curves, it should have an interest in maximizing total net revenues (profits before taxes) so long as taxes take the form of a percentage of before-tax revenues. This would, of course, not be true in the case of taxes on the volume of output unless marginal production costs were falling throughout the relevant range. In any case, a company is not going to have a short-run interest in producing at a point where marginal cost exceeds marginal revenue after allowing for taxes. A producing affiliate of an integrated company might cut back output if alternative sources yielded a higher after-tax profit per unit of output, even though marginal revenue exceeded marginal cost. On the other hand, the host government might not have an interest in maximizing total revenue or output if it believed it could raise its tax take by increasing taxes to the point at which the company would be forced to reduce output (to avoid operating at a point at which marginal cost exceeded marginal revenue) or to refrain from making investments; e.g., drilling new wells as old ones are depleted in order to maintain output.

Nevertheless, a government or a company might be constrained from taking such actions to achieve a temporary increase in net revenues. By means of a series of retaliatory actions, each of which had the effect of reducing the total net revenue to be shared, each party might be able to harm the other. What might be good bargaining strategy in the short run may prove to be poor policy in the longer run. Moreover, the host government must be continually aware that the future level of investment of a company will be determined by its present and prospective profits.[19] A com-

pany, on the other hand, is aware that dissatisfaction with its policies will lead to demands for various types of controls, expropriation, or an invitation to other foreign firms to enter the country.

Conflict and Game Theory

The conflict that we are discussing must be differentiated from the two-person, zero-sum games which have proved, because of their determinacy, to be of great analytical interest to mathematicians interested in game theory. In the zero-sum case, the total prize is independent of the shares won by the contestants; the situations we are considering are in the category of two-person, nonzero-sum games. Because the total amount of rent or profit available for sharing depends upon the actions of the parties in seeking to increase their share, rational conduct requires that conflict be combined with accommodation or coordination. The distinction between zero-sum games and the type of conflict we are considering is analyzed by Thomas Schelling in his book *The Strategy of Conflict*.

> On the strategy of pure conflict—the zero-sum games—*game theory* has yielded important insight and advice. But on the strategy of action where conflict is mixed with mutual dependence—the nonzero-sum games involved in wars and threats of war, strikes, negotiations, criminal deterrence, class war, race war, price war, and blackmail; maneuvering in a bureaucracy or in a traffic jam; and the coercion of one's own children—traditional game theory has not yielded comparable insight or advice. These are the "games" in which, though the element of conflict provides the dramatic interest, mutual dependence is part of the logical structure and demands some

---

[19] It is important to take into account the rate of social value productivity in the host country in comparing present gains—say, from higher taxation—against future losses from reduced foreign investment. Let us assume that the social rate of discount in a developing country is 15 percent. Suppose the country decided that, if it increased taxes on the foreign resource company, it would gain an additional $1 million per year for five years, but that as a consequence the company would reduce its investment and thereafter the government would lose $1 million per year in potential revenues. The present value of the additional revenue for five years is $3.34 million, while the present value of what is lost forever is $3.32 million.

kind of collaboration or mutual accommodation—tacit, if not explicit—even if only
in the avoidance of mutual disaster. There
are also games in which, though secrecy
may play a strategic role, there is some
essential need for the signaling of intentions and the meeting of minds. Finally,
there are games in which what one player
can do to avert mutual damage affects what
another player *will* do to avert it, so that
it is not always an advantage to possess
initiative, knowledge, or freedom of
choice.[20]

Schelling points out that relatively few nonzero-sum games admit to formal mathematical
solution. However, the bargaining area within
which solutions are possible can be determined on the basis of information about the
setting of the conflict situation. For example,
if the governments of most of the other petroleum-producing countries have negotiated
contracts whereby the government gets 50
percent of the net profits, a government demanding contract renegotiation is unlikely to
settle for less. On the other hand, a company
with investments in other countries may
threaten to withdraw from operations if it is
forced to take only 25 percent of the profits,
since by doing so it would jeopardize its 50
percent take elsewhere. If both parties to the
conflict are aware of these limits, which if
exceeded would force drastic action by one
party or the other leading to the elimination
or substantial curtailment of total revenue,
the dimensions of the area of negotiated
settlement can be determined.

In the process of conflict and coordination
between foreign investors and companies, we
have a situation which is neither pure conflict
nor pure coordination. The participants in
the game are opponents, but since their
mutual action determines total profits and
each other's absolute share of total profits
(no matter what their relative shares), they
have important common interests. They are
not partners, for their interests do diverge in

[20] Schelling, *The Strategy of Conflict* (London: Oxford
University Press, 1963), p. 83.

important respects. Nonetheless, they cannot
ignore the possibility of mutual benefit and
harm. Both company and government have
strong interests in maintaining a high and
growing level of revenue even though they
cannot agree wholly on the sharing of it.
While each party is seeking to maximize his
share, rational behavior requires each to favor
a movement toward joint profit maximization.

An important element in the bargaining
process and in the determination of bargaining power is the degree of flexibility of the
partners. Flexibility is an advantage because
the government may offer terms that provide
both security and freedom of operations to
the concessionaire over a reasonable length
of time combined with a rate of return to
the company just sufficient to induce the
investment. The alternative without such flexibility might be less security and freedom but
a higher rate of return to the company to
allow for greater risk. In a country with a
militant nationalist group, however, the government may be strictly limited as to the
degree of freedom and assurance of contractual conditions it can offer. As a consequence,
the government may have to offer the company a higher guaranteed return and assume
a larger share of the risk than would otherwise be the case. For example, Argentina
during the Frondizi period (1958–63) found
itself restricted to negotiating drilling and
exploitation contracts that greatly limited the
freedom of the companies but that required
the government to bear a large share of the
risks involved in both producing and transporting the oil to domestic markets (see
chapter 7). On the other hand, as Schelling
noted, inflexibility may sometimes prove to
be an advantage to one of the parties to a
conflict. When the terms a government can
offer are limited by political constraints, the
government might very well wrest more favorable terms from the foreign company than
would otherwise be the case, simply because
the company realizes that the government
cannot go further in bargaining and still remain in power. For example, the American

copper companies knew that the alternative to the Frei Chileanization program was expropriation, and the companies had more flexibility than the government in offering solutions to avoid mutual damage.

Bargaining would be far less complex and the outcome more readily predictable if each party could estimate confidently the intentions and the relative bargaining strength of his opponent. Part of the surface conflict may be regarded as an effort to gauge the strength of the opponent; but even with such explorations there may still be considerable doubt on each side about the acceptability of various offers, how a given proposal will be countered, and what action might provoke an extreme reaction from the other side. With perfect knowledge, the area within which serious negotiations could take place would be generally recognized and solutions could perhaps be more readily achieved. On the other hand, lags in perception of changes in bargaining power tend to heighten the conflict. Thus, as a firm with both a large commitment and large profits perceives that its bargaining power is reduced, it should react more magnanimously to the demands of the host country. By the same token, governments should recognize the options of foreign investors during periods when large new investments are being contemplated.

CONFLICT AND THE MARKET FOR THE PRODUCT

Much of the foregoing analysis of conflict over the shares of rents is based on the assumption that the firm maximized with respect to the world market demand for the product. In integrated firms in which producing affiliates sell wholly or largely to processing or marketing affiliates, profits are maximized for the operations of the integrated firm and not necessarily for the affiliate in an individual producing country. Intrafirm pricing policies may not be based on a world market price, but may instead reflect a desire to concentrate profits in one affiliate or another, to minimize taxes, to avoid restrictions on transfers of profits, or other reasons. Thus a petroleum firm may want to concentrate profits in producing affiliates because of depletion allowances at the extractive stage. Also, if it has a monopoly position in sales to certain independent refineries in competition with its own refineries, a high price for crude oil or minerals puts the independent refineries at a disadvantage. On the other hand, if taxes on net profits are high at the extractive stage relative to taxes at other stages in an integrated operation, prices established for the resources may be low. Firms may also differentiate with respect to price between customers. For many years, the international petroleum companies have established "posted prices" for Middle East petroleum (initially as a device for controlling competition in sales to Western Europe and other areas), but they have sold at discounts from the posted prices when necessary to meet competition. Chilean copper has been sold at one price to U.S. firms and at another price in Western Europe (see chapter 15).

The existence of integrated firms and of imperfect markets for petroleum and minerals has resulted in serious conflict between the foreign companies and the host governments over pricing policies. The host governments have an interest in the maintenance of high prices since the bulk of their revenues are derived from taxes on net earnings of the producing companies. In petroleum (and in the past in Chilean copper), host governments have required the companies to calculate net revenues for tax purposes on the basis of posted or reference prices which may be substantially higher than prices actually realized by firms in sales to customers. However, realized prices for intrafirm sales are largely a matter of accounting practice.[21] The governments of the petroleum-producing countries acting through OPEC have sought to maintain world prices of petroleum by

[21] One means of calculating realized (or "netback") prices for an integrated firm is to subtract the cost of transportation, refining, and marketing from the price of the refined or processed product paid by the ultimate consumer.

requiring adherence to posted prices or reference prices for tax calculations and by preventing a decrease in posted prices. Direct attempts have also been made to prevent granting of discounts from the posted price (see chapters 5 and 9). There is also evidence of collusive action among the governments of the copper-producing countries for maintaining world market prices (see chapter 15).

Given the low marginal cost of production for petroleum[22] and for certain minerals, and given the low elasticity of world demand for these commodities,[23] it is certainly to the interest of the producing countries and companies alike to avoid open price competition. Nevertheless, the various producing areas are in competition with one another. They want to maintain prices and yet each producing country wants to expand its output, an expansion which is necessarily at the expense of other producing areas. Some governments of petroleum-producing countries—e.g., Iran—have put pressure on the companies to expand production and marketing of their petroleum. Other countries have negotiated additional contracts with companies other than the original concession holder for expanding output, and some have formed their own national petroleum companies, usually as joint ventures with foreign companies. These arrangements, together with the development of petroleum fields in other countries both by the large international companies and by the independents, have undermined the international price structure for petroleum established by the major international oil companies. Thus far, the governments of the petroleum-producing countries have not engaged directly in marketing to any significant degree; marketing is usually handled through the partners in joint ventures with the national companies, some of which are government-owned integrated companies in the developed countries. While the

national petroleum companies maintain the fiction of selling only at posted prices, price competition undoubtedly occurs in downstream operations. Competition has squeezed the profits of the large international petroleum companies since tax calculations continue to be based on posted prices that have not been changed for years, and OPEC members have been successful in compelling the companies to eliminate allowances off the posted price for purposes of tax calculations (see chapters 5 and 9).

The after-tax rate of returns on net worth from petroleum production in the Eastern Hemisphere for seven international petroleum companies was only 11.3 percent in 1966 as against 18.7 percent in 1957, and the rate of return on net worth to these companies has been below the rate of return for U.S. manufacturing companies since 1963. Downstream earnings of the petroleum companies have also been declining.[24] On the other hand, per-barrel payments as well as total payments to the governments of the producing countries have been rising steadily since 1960. This has occurred in spite of widespread discounts off posted prices in sales by the producing companies and increased competition in product markets at all levels. Further increases in taxes and/or further decreases in realized prices may eventually drive company earnings to or below the supply price of development capital for the highest cost producing areas. This would lead to a reduction in output and of rents in those producing countries where company earnings are lowest because of relatively high taxes, or of high production costs, or both. Lower output in some producing areas will, however, tend to stem the decline in oil prices.

Can it be argued that, in the light of the low marginal costs of production relative to crude prices, the high taxes imposed by the host governments in petroleum have helped to prevent world oil prices from plummeting toward marginal production costs? There is

---

[22] M. A. Adelman has estimated the producing-developing cost of Middle East oil at 20 cents per barrel, including a 20 percent return on capital; this is only about one-tenth the open market price of crude oil in 1968.

[23] For some minerals, such as copper, the elasticity of substitution may be fairly high so that the maximum price in the short run is by no means the optimal long-run price.

[24] *Eastern Hemisphere Rides the Storm*, Petroleum Department, First National City Bank of New York, January 1968.

much to be said for this position. Two decades ago, the major oil companies could maintain world oil prices through a variety of cartel practices; since then their control of the world oil market has declined substantially, and open market prices continue to sag.[25] Given the competition in petroleum that exists today, what would crude oil prices be if the host governments had not captured a substantial share of the total rent? Would not much more capital have been attracted to the world petroleum industry in the absence of the substantial increases in taxes imposed by the host governments since the 1940s? In the absence of monopoly elements in the production of petroleum, the rents from petroleum resources should have fallen with the tremendous increase in oil reserves since World War II—from about 70 billion barrels in 1947 to about 400 billion barrels in 1967.[26] During the past twenty years, a substantial share of the rents from petroleum resources have been shifted from the companies to the host governments, although the companies have earned very good returns on their investments. Before too long, the companies may be earning little more than the supply price of development capital. In fact, OPEC's recently announced policy is to reduce the net earnings of the companies to a level no higher than necessary to attract the private capital, and to renegotiate the financial provisions of the contracts whenever profits rise above this necessary level.[27]

Whether crude oil prices will continue to fall will depend in large measure upon the ability of the producing countries to curtail output. However, once crude oil prices fall to the point at which earnings of the companies decline below the supply price of capital, a further decline in prices must inevitably reduce the rent per unit of output accruing to the host governments. This is especially significant in view of the announced policies of the producing countries to control production and marketing.[28]

Conflict over the Volume of Production

Where integrated firms have several sources of supply for meeting their requirements in markets which they control, conflict may occur over how much will be supplied from a particular source. Companies will have an interest in supplying from the cheapest source or in equating marginal cost with marginal revenue (including allowance for taxes) on the basis of their aggregate supply and demand functions. Thus the amount of the product to come from any particular affiliate would be determined by a combination of marginal production costs, taxes, transport costs, and any special factors such as security of supply. However, in petroleum at least, efforts have been made by OPEC to standardize taxation as well as to avoid open price competition, so that differences in taxation may not provide a means by which, say, higher-cost producing countries might compete for markets with lower-cost areas. This means that the basis for a rational allocation of output from the various producing areas must lie in relative costs of production. Thus, relative cost would be the basis for output allocation for an integrated firm with several sources of supply for the markets which it controlled, provided the firm is permitted to control its several outputs from the standpoint of profit maximization.

However, resource firms do not always have a free hand in allocating output, and disputes between companies and host governments with respect to rates of production are quite common.[29] (See, for example, the ac-

[25] As of 1968, open market prices of Middle East crude oil were approximately 30 percent below posted prices—the prices that were representative of realized prices before 1960.

[26] Where net returns from resource exploitation are increased by market control over the returns which would occur under competitive conditions, the difference should be regarded as monopoly profit rather than as rent on the resources.

[27] "Resolutions of the XVIth Conference, Vienna, June 24-25, 1968," *OPEC Bulletin*, August 1968; res. XVI.90, p. 4.

[28] *Ibid.*

[29] A high official of OPEC has informed the author that individual disputes between petroleum companies and the host governments concerning the volume of production by the companies have probably been one of the most important, if not the most important, areas of conflict. However, unlike disputes relating to taxation, disputes over production are largely carried on behind the scenes with little publicity.

count of the dispute between Iran and the Oil Consortium in chapter 10.) But disputes over the level of output in individual countries go beyond relations between the foreign investor and the host government since an increase in the output of one producing country is likely to be largely at the expense of the output of another country. Moreover, this may well involve affiliates of the same company operating in different producing areas, a situation not uncommon in the petroleum industry. An important bargaining weapon in the hands of the host governments in such conflicts may be the negotiation of contracts with other companies for the production and marketing of resource materials in competition with both the older concessionaires and other producing countries. As noted in chapters 9 and 10, the formation of national oil companies with foreign partners has been quite common in the Middle East; Venezuela is planning to follow a similar practice (see chapter 5).

OPEC has been acutely aware of the problem of production and marketing since conflicts in this area are in large measure a form of competition among the producing countries themselves and tend to undermine the international price structure for petroleum. As noted in chapter 9, some OPEC members have sought to establish and enforce production quotas among members, but others, including Saudi Arabia, have been rather cool to the idea.[30] A resolution was passed at the fourteenth conference of OPEC in November 1967 that "reaffirms its conviction that a Joint Production Program is an effective instrument for the pursuit of the Organization's fundamental objectives of stabilizing and maintaining crude and product prices at equitable levels, and instructs the Economic Commission to undertake a comprehensive study in depth with a view to perfecting an economically practical system for the Program implementation. . . ."[31] However, at the time of

writing, OPEC was having little success in achieving a production control program.[32]

To be effective, a production allocation program would have to include the output of the national petroleum companies as well as that of the foreign private companies. Any petroleum production agreement would be faced with many of the same problems that are encountered by the International Coffee Agreement and similar agreements based on export quotas. If quotas were determined on the basis of historical shares, lower-cost producing areas would not have an advantage in the future over higher-cost areas. There would also be the problem of determining quotas for new producing countries and of inducing them to join the production allocation program. Finally, members of the agreement would constantly be seeking a revision of their quotas as a consequence, for example, of a discovery of new petroleum fields. It should be said, however, that a commodity agreement in petroleum would be easier to implement than one in coffee or sugar, where a domestic surplus cannot be avoided simply by shutting off a valve. It is less likely, however, that the importing countries will cooperate in the case of petroleum.

Under an international petroleum agreement in which taxes are more or less standardized among producing areas and output regulated by quotas, individual producing companies could not maximize total net revenues with respect to their own cost and demand functions. Presumably, aggregate quotas would be established with a view to maximizing aggregate gross revenue. However, there would still be room for conflict between the companies and the host governments. In countries with relatively high costs, private companies might not produce the country's quota or might not expand investment sufficiently to increase output in line with the annual increase in quotas, preferring instead to

---

[30] In fact, quotas were established in the early 1960s, but generally they were not observed.

[31] OPEC, *1967 Review and Record* (Vienna, 1968), pp. 12–13.

[32] Early in July 1968 OPEC held a conference with a view to the establishment of production controls. According to press accounts, the conference failed to reach any agreement on this issue which, perhaps more than any, involves direct competition among the members for shares in a relatively fixed income. See "La OPEP También Fracaso en Formular Programa de Producción," *El Nacional* (Caracas), 7 July 1968.

meet more of their marketing requirements from lower-cost sources. The host government might counter by raising the output of the national oil company, and the private companies might seek to acquire concessions in countries not under the quota. On the other hand, both the companies and the host governments might gain from an arrangement which prevented oil prices from declining toward marginal costs. Bargaining is easier over a large pie than over a small one.

COORDINATION

While conflict may be inevitable and continuous, there is a strong basis for coordination both in order to avoid warfare in which both parties incur losses and because there may be a common interest in maximizing total rent over a given time path. The proximate conditions for the existence of a common interest in maximizing total net receipts or rent are rather exacting: that both the company and the host government expect to share in any increase in the total rent and each party is convinced that any action which reduces total rent will reduce his return. Conversely, neither party expects to gain from a reduction in total rent, or lose from an increase in total rent. These conditions frequently do not exist. For example, if the demand for the product of the firm is elastic and unit costs are declining with increased output, rent could be increased by expanding output and lowering prices. But if the foreign investor is required to pay profit-sharing taxes to the government based on a fixed or posted price, he may not choose to lower prices since his absolute (and relative) share of the rent might actually decline with an increase in total net revenues or rent. To cite another example, the host government might be able to exact a larger absolute share of the rent by raising taxes which in turn would require the company to reduce output of marginal mines or oil fields. On the other hand, we have already noted that integrated firms are interested in maximizing after-tax profits of

the parent firm and not the before-tax net revenues of individual producing affiliates. Instead they may deliberately sacrifice net earnings in one affiliate in favor of larger earnings for another. However, the longer-run consequences of such actions on the part of either the host government or the foreign company may be harmful not only to total net revenue but to the absolute returns of both. Taxes which force a curtailment of output will jeopardize new investment and in the long run may result in a withdrawal of existing capital investment as well. Action on the part of the companies that curtails total net revenue is likely to lead to a variety of demands and counteractions on the part of the host government that may restrict the ability of the company to compete for certain markets and hence lead to a further curtailment of total net revenue.

This suggests that a fruitful area for coordination between the host government and the foreign investor would be the establishment of rules of the game whereby neither party would take action, or force the other party to take action (in order to avoid a reduction in his return), that would reduce total net revenue below the maximum level that can be achieved with the current volume of investment or fixed factors employed. Given the constraint of joint maximization, there might still be room for conflict over the relative shares of the rent, and the outcome would depend upon the bargaining positions of the parties as related to new investment.

The existence of multinational firms seeking to maximize the profits of the parent firm rather than of affiliates operating in individual countries makes it difficult to apply the joint maximizing rule suggested above. In principle, the joint maximizing rule would require the individual producing affiliate to maximize its profits with respect to its own marginal cost and marginal revenue functions, and to operate in competition with other affiliates of the same firm at the same stage of production. However, the marginal revenue function becomes indeterminate in a situation in which an affiliate of an international firm is selling mainly to downstream affiliates which may be buying from other producing affiliates as well. The international firm is by its very nature seeking to maximize total profits from all of its operations and is usually operating at all stages in an oligopolistic market.

Despite the conceptual and practical difficulties in applying the joint maximizing principle to situations involving integrated multinational firms, producing countries are insisting that companies operating under their laws have an obligation to maximize profits or, more broadly, total net revenues before taxes, rather than operate solely in the interest of maximizing the after-tax profits of the multinational firm. This has been the basis for demands on the part of host countries to control pricing, production, and marketing policies of foreign-owned companies. International companies may object to this principle as being incompatible with their raison d'être. But host governments, in demanding a voice in the control of the pricing and other policies of the producing company, are in effect insisting that this principle be adopted. Host governments are concerned that they may be exploited as a consequence of the downstream operations of the companies over which they have no control. As a consequence, host countries often adopt taxation and other policies that may result in reducing both total net revenues of the affiliate and their own revenues either immediately or in the long run.

While no formula will provide an automatic solution to all of the problems of pricing and production allocation under the circumstances described here, an agreed framework of general rules could facilitate the resolution of conflicts in accordance with the joint maximizing principle. As will be discussed later on, joint maximization must be related to a specific level of investment, since the output from a given resource base will depend upon investment in fixed structures such as mines and producing wells. The following are suggested as illustrative of rules that might be established for joint maximization with respect to a given level of investment.

1. The company and host government should jointly establish a price or prices for the various grades of the raw material or crude oil that represent the best approximation to the open market price.[33] Also there should be sufficient price flexibility to enable the producing affiliates to meet market competition.

2. Companies should not deliberately shift sources of supply to other producing areas in order to increase their after-tax profits unless the host government has raised taxes to the point at which marginal cost exceeds marginal revenue to the foreign investor. In the short run, adjustments of output from various supply sources within the integrated firm in response to changes in total market demand might be made on a proportional basis, again so long as marginal cost was less than marginal revenue. In the longer run, however, adjustments in output would reflect changes in capacity as governed by the level of investment.

3. The host government should not enforce pricing or production policies that would make it unprofitable for a company to expand (or maintain) output with its present fixed capital resources. This means that the host government should not raise taxes to the point at which marginal cost exceeds marginal revenue to the firm, given the agreed price established for revenue and tax calculations.

Let us now explore how the illustrative rules indicated above might be applied to each of several affiliates of an international firm operating in different producing countries. We may begin by asking how output would be allocated among the several producing affiliates if there were no taxes, assuming a unitary price for the product that may be

[33] Where no universally recognized open market price exists, or where the open market price is relevant for only a small portion of total sales (as in the case of petroleum), netback prices might be calculated as an approximation to the open market price. Netback prices of crude oil could be established by subtracting from the final product prices the various downstream costs including transportation, refining, and marketing, with an allowance for return on capital. In an unpublished memorandum, M. A. Adelman has shown that netback prices of Middle East crude oil tend to move in line with open market prices.

either a competitive world market price or a price established by the international firm with a view to equating marginal revenue with marginal cost. If it is a freely competitive price, each affiliate would produce at the point where marginal cost equals price. The joint maximizing principle would require that the level of taxation would not result in a cutback of output of any affiliate so long as marginal production cost plus the tax on the marginal unit of output did not exceed price or marginal revenue. This condition would be satisfied by a percentage net profits tax. However, petroleum and most minerals are sold in monopolistic markets in which price is usually well above marginal cost. In this case and in the absence of taxes, output among the affiliates would be allocated so that the difference between the unitary price established by the international firm and marginal production cost would be equal for each affiliate. If any affiliate produced more than this critical output, the net revenue of the international firm and of the other affiliates taken together would be less than the maximum.

Now let us assume that each affiliate pays a net profits tax. Other things being equal, the international firm will allocate output so as to equalize the difference between the price and the marginal cost, including the tax on the last unit of output. Thus the international firm would seek to equalize for each affiliate after-tax earnings on marginal output, E', or

$$E' = P - C' - t(P - C')$$

where P is the price, C' is the marginal production cost, and t is the rate of tax on net profits.

What the joint maximizing rule suggests is that the international firm should operate on the principle of allocating output among its affiliates on the basis of equalizing $P - C'$ so long as marginal production cost plus the tax on the marginal unit does not exceed price.[34]

[34] This would not occur so long as the only tax was a tax on net profits, since $P - C'$ must always be greater than $t(P - C')$. However, this would not necessarily be true if there were unit taxes on output in addition to the net profits tax.

The host government, on the other hand, would be conforming to the joint maximizing principle if the tax system avoided a situation in which marginal production cost plus the total tax on marginal output was greater than price. If all producing countries had a uniform net profits tax (and no other taxes), output would be allocated on the basis of the marginal production cost of the affiliate, except to the degree that security of supply was an important factor. However, this could mean zero output for producing affiliates with relatively high marginal production costs throughout the relevant range of output. They could not, for example, reduce their tax rates as a means of offsetting their cost disadvantage. This is exactly the intent of OPEC's principle of unifying tax systems in member countries.

Under the short-run joint maximizing rule suggested above, the level of taxes and the level of net returns to the company would continue to govern investment decisions, including the reinvestment of profits and depreciation and depletion allowances. (The method of calculating net returns for this purpose would have to be left to the company.) Thus, for example, the foreign investor will not be interested in reinvesting profits and depreciation allowances for a larger output unless he receives additional earnings over and above the world market rate of return on the capital and other resources made available, including an allowance for risk and rent of ability. Hence, for example, the investor may, over time, shift some resources out of Venezuela and into North Africa because he can earn a larger return on these resources there either because of lower production costs or lower taxes or both. This shift might take place through a failure to reinvest depreciation and depletion allowances even though the foreign investor continued to maximize total net returns from existing capital investment.

The element of coordination for securing mutual advantage particularly comes to the fore in the area of pricing. Perfectly competitive markets do not exist either for the principal minerals moving in international trade or for petroleum. An oligopolist must pursue a profit maximizing strategy which is difficult to achieve; it is much more difficult for a foreign company and a host government selling their product in an oligopolistic market who find themselves in opposition over other questions. Sound strategy must be concerned not only with short-term advantage but also with the long-run demand for the product. For example, some copper specialists have expressed concern that the Chilean government's Copper Corporation will seek to push prices so high that many copper users will switch to alternative metals, principally aluminum.

The increasing role of host governments in the control of pricing and marketing policies of foreign resource companies may appear as a source of conflict when they take over functions that traditionally the foreign investors have reserved for themselves. Actually, this trend has opened up an important field for coordination. Should we view the activities of OPEC solely in terms of a group of governments organized to bargain more effectively with the foreign companies in their conflict over the share of the total revenues, or may not OPEC in part be regarded as a mechanism for maintaining prices to the advantage of both the international oil companies and producing countries in an international market where marginal costs are only a fraction of market prices? On the other hand, the entry into the market of a number of national petroleum-producing companies in the Middle East may be reducing total revenues from petroleum production. Their activities may very well thwart the efforts of OPEC in achieving joint profit maximization unless OPEC is successful in enforcing a system of production controls. The copper producing countries have only recently become sufficiently organized to attempt a coordinated effort among themselves and with the four or five major companies, the latter with a much longer history of collusion.[35] May not the new

---

[35] For a history of cartelization, overt and covert, in the American copper industry, see O. C. Herfindahl, *Copper Costs and Prices, 1870–1957* (Baltimore: The Johns Hopkins Press for Resources for the Future, 1959).

government-foreign investor partnerships in Chilean copper provide a vehicle for joint maximization?

SOLUTIONS TO DISPUTES

We turn finally to a discussion of the actual and possible solutions to the problems discussed. A solution is the actual outcome of any particular dispute between a host government and a foreign company. As such, it is a complicated combination of factor prices, government revenue shares, company profits, and all the other elements of dispute between the relevant bargaining entities. Once a new profit-sharing agreement has been signed, a tax guarantee adopted, or a pricing policy decided upon, a solution has been reached—however temporary it may be. The parties to the dispute have measured each other's bargaining power in the relevant setting and found that obtaining more is not possible and getting less unnecessary.

We may adopt the threefold classification of (1) warfare, (2) joint maximization, and (3) intermediate solutions.

1. *Warfare solutions* are the two extremes of expropriation-nationalization and voluntary foreign company withdrawal. Warfare solutions in the form of expropriation or a cessation of operations by the company usually yield less satisfactory returns to both parties to the conflict than any of a range of joint maximizing solutions. Unless the country has available or has access to the specialized resources and marketing outlets required for modern extractive operations, the host government is unlikely to gain more by expropriation than it would receive by accepting the maximum share of the revenue the foreign company is willing to grant it through negotiation. Moreover, scarce capital resources would be required to compensate the owners, since few developing countries could afford to jeopardize their international credit standing by an act of expropriation without satisfactory compensation.

The minimum share that the company would demand as a condition for not terminating its operations involves more complicated issues. In some cases, the company might find it worthwhile to accede to the demands of the government for a larger share so long as the company received something more than its current cost including depreciation and depletion. It could then gradually withdraw its investment by not reinvesting its depreciation and depletion allowances. However, by agreeing to the demands of the host government, a company might undermine its tax status in investments in other areas so that it might decide to cease operations if its share were reduced significantly below that provided in contracts with other countries. Also, the company's net return might be higher by supplying all of its markets from other areas and shutting down production entirely in the country in question if its net earnings declined beyond a certain level.[36] However, the desire for diversification of supply sources in the interest of security of supply might preclude such a decision.

Whatever the outcome of such calculations, the threat of expropriation or withdrawal has a role to play in the bargaining process. Just as nations threaten warfare in which both parties must inevitably lose in terms of welfare broadly conceived, so also do parties to economic conflict threaten warfare solutions in order to exercise, or at least to test, their bargaining strength. In addition, noneconomic factors, such as national pride or "standing on legal rights," provide an important explanation for warfare solutions.

It is certainly conceivable that, over time, the domestic ability to produce the mineral product could grow to such a point that the "rent of ability" claimed by the foreign company would wither away. The Mexicans have proved in recent years that they can run an integrated domestic oil industry; Petrobras in Brazil, a government-controlled company, is making significant progress toward meeting Brazil's internal requirements for petroleum.

[36] It has been suggested that private oil companies might profit more from buying their oil from nationally owned companies in competition with one another and by making their profits in downstream operations.

It is entirely possible that in some minerals and petroleum-producing activities the "majors" can now be dispensed with. To the extent that this is true, the threat of nationalization becomes more credible. Something similar has happened in international petroleum as a consequence of the activities of French, Italian, and Japanese companies in entering into joint ventures with state-owned companies for the exploitation of concessions in Iran, Iraq, Saudi Arabia, and other areas in recent years (see chapter 9). These activities have reduced the supply prices of the specialized resources for producing petroleum that were formerly monopolized by the large international companies and, in addition, have helped to lower the share of the rent from the natural resources going to external capital.

2. *Joint maximization solutions* are those which imply that one party to the conflict does not improve his satisfaction in a manner that reduces the total amount of satisfaction; these solutions are consistent with maximum total net revenue or rent. Joint maximization of total net revenues may be considered from three standpoints. First, there is the maximization of total revenues (before local taxes) from the employment of the existing fixed factors, including the investment commitment by the foreign company and the reserves under its control. Second, joint maximization may also be regarded from the standpoint of maximizing the total revenue from the known and potential reserves in a particular concession. This would require that the foreign investor expand his investment up to the point at which total net revenues (before local taxes) are maximized. A third type of maximization of total revenues would be that from the total existing and potential reserves of a commodity in the entire country. This might involve more than one foreign company or joint venture and would depend largely upon the policy of the government in granting additional concessions.

Joint maximization under any of the three concepts will depend upon the division of the shares of the revenues between the host government and the foreign company or companics. Under the first concept of joint maximization, the returns to the foreign company must be sufficient to induce it to maximize revenue from its existing investment, but without necessarily reinvesting depreciation and depletion allowances. It should not have an incentive to shift supply to alternative sources or a disincentive to compete in foreign markets which it could supply with a resulting increase in total net revenue because the company could not make a profit or would incur a loss. Under the second concept of joint maximization, returns to the company must be equal to the opportunity cost of capital in other producing countries in order to remove any incentive to disinvest through failure to reinvest depreciation allowances. Investment must be carried on at a level sufficient to drill new wells as old ones are depleted, dig new mine shafts as some become exhausted, replace worn-out machinery, etc. In order to induce an expansion of net investment required to exploit fully the reserves in the concession, the company may require higher returns to compensate for added risk, together with some assurance of the stability of that return, which must be at least as high as that available in the best alternative employment of the company's resources in investments involving comparable risk.[37] Finally, if a country is going to be able to induce new investments in new concessions in areas which are unexplored, it may have to offer a return which will cover the additional risks. This does not necessarily mean that companies obtaining the new concessions might not be willing to acquire them at the same or even lower returns than those received by the old concessionaire. For example, in the Middle East, new companies have acquired concessions under less favorable terms than those of old concessionaires. While this development has undoubtedly strengthened the bargaining position of the host governments vis-à-vis the old concession-

aires, the latter, mainly the major international oil companies, have affiliates with large markets and have alternative sources of supplying these markets. Hence, market outlets play an important role in the bargaining strength of the company.

3. *Intermediate solutions* are those which result in something less than maximum total net revenue or rent from the amount of fixed factors currently employed. Intermediate solutions are quite common. In these, one party or the other does not receive a sufficiently large share of the total net revenues to work for the maximization of the total revenue. Companies may cut back on output in favor of output from alternative sources in meeting market demand, or may fail to expand output with the growth of the external market. This is frequently accompanied by disinvestment or the failure to expand net investment for maximizing revenues from the resources under the control of the company. The host government may also establish export prices that are not consistent with the maximization of revenue either from the existing investment or from a larger investment. Also, host governments may be unwilling to relinquish additional concessions or may withdraw parts of a concession already granted. Concession policies, however, are frequently related to the desire for conservation or to the desire to reserve certain areas for state development at some time in the future. Usually, such procedures are not based on a careful calculation of the present value of the returns from alternative policies. In some cases, however, nations are willing to relinquish access to additional reserves under arrangements, such as joint ventures or service contracts, that provide the state with an additional degree of control and perhaps a larger share of the rent as well.

The case studies presented in this book include numerous examples of conflict situations and of a variety of solutions. Clearly, in the case of Chilean copper during the 1950s and early 1960s and in Venezuelan petroleum in recent years, the host countries have imposed levels of taxation which have violated the

---

[37] The rate of return required by a company to make additional net investments may be no higher than that required to induce it to reinvest depreciation and depletion allowances. However, the company may require an assurance of tax stability.

principle of joint maximization in the short run and have reduced investment in the long run. The increasing level of taxation in the Middle East undoubtedly was a factor in encouraging companies to develop reserves in North Africa, although security of supply and competition for reserves among the companies undoubtedly played a role. The recent tendency of countries in the Middle East to develop reserves by the formation of joint ventures and to market in competition with the private petroleum companies may well reduce total revenues as a consequence of pressure on prices. Whether it also will reduce net revenues of the governments remains to be seen. The events leading up to the formation of the joint ventures in Chilean copper and Mexican sulphur illustrate the complex issues in conflicts relating to control that government–foreign investor partnerships have been established to solve. The success of these arrangements in dealing with these issues is yet to be determined.

SUMMARY

1. By their nature, mineral and petroleum production arrangements are productive of conflict. Rents of several kinds are created by the act of production; by almost any concession system prior claims would be established to them, and, given any substantial profitability, one party would eventually begin to feel cheated. Necessarily, it is the host country that develops this feeling and seeks to assuage it by raising the domestic share of profits at the expense of the share of the foreign enterprise.

2. Conflict and the evolving claims of government and company have a dynamic logic. Being committed with fixed capital investments, the company can no longer choose to leave if its initial claims are altered, except at a substantial loss. Thus some few years after investments have been made, the pressure to increase the government's share will grow— and be met by the company. The foreign investor's bargaining power is improved by his

option to reinvest profits and depreciation allowances and to bring in new capital for additional concessions, though in general the older the concession, or the more "committed" the company, the larger is the share of total rents the government can expect to get.

3. When large new investments are being contemplated, the tables are turned on the host government. Now it must compete with all other possible areas open to foreign companies for investments and it must offer an expected profitability to the foreign company as great as that the company could get at any other site. The moment of new investment is the moment of greatest bargaining strength for the company. However, this advantage may be offset by the willingness of other firms to bid for new concessions in promising areas where they are available.

4. The existence of "third parties," such as labor unions and national populist parties, enhances the possibility and credibility of threats of expropriation. However, these threats are countered by the dependence of developing countries upon external public and private capital. Only governments of the extreme left will ignore this external dependence, including the specialized resources of the foreign investor. However, the fear of the emergence of Castro-type governments has undoubtedly served as a bargaining weapon in the hands of moderate governments in conflicts with foreign investors.

5. Generally speaking, both the host country and the foreign company have a common interest in achieving a joint maximizing solution. Joint maximization poses difficult problems in the case of producing affiliates of integrated multinational firms. These problems can be dealt with only by means of open or tacit recognition of certain rules of the game. Joint maximizing solutions may be viewed from the standpoint of maximizing total net revenues on the basis of the fixed factors currently employed or from the standpoint of the total known and potential reserves available to the foreign company under its concession agreement. The former requires

a share of the revenue to the company sufficient to induce it to maintain a level of output
that will maximize total net revenue on the
basis of market demand, given its fixed investment commitment. The latter type of maximization would require continuous investment.
Both reinvestment of depreciation and depletion and net new investment will require a
return at least as high as that available to the
firm in the best alternative employment of
the company's resources in investments of
comparable risk. There is the further possibility of maximizing revenues from the total
known and potential reserves of the country,
but this involves the resource policies of the
country and the decision to grant new concessions.

6. While conflict is unavoidable, so also is
accommodation and cooperation if the parties
are to promote their common interest. Rational behavior requires the players in the
game to seek joint maximizing solutions in
which the size of the pie is not reduced by
the scramble over the portions.

Part II
Early Development of Cartels and Large Firms

[4]

AN EIGHTEENTH-CENTURY COMBINATION IN THE COPPER-MINING INDUSTRY

THE history of the combination among the producers of copper between the years 1785 and 1792 is interesting, not only because its form affords us an early example of a modern type of combination, but also because its development during the seven years of its existence presents a curious parallel to that of many recent combinations. A short description of the course of events in the copper-mining industry during the years which immediately preceded the formation of the combine will be sufficient to indicate the causes which brought it about, and will in addition show the way in which Boulton & Watt [1] became so intimately connected with the industry. That connection, as will be seen, was fraught with the most serious consequences.

About 1780 there were two main producing centres of copper ore in this country, Cornwall and Anglesea. They were bitter competitors, and the conditions under which copper was mined in the two counties were so different as to deserve notice. While the two mines of Anglesea (the Paris and Mona Mines) were recent discoveries and were worked at small expense, most of the numerous Cornish mines were deep and in continual danger of becoming water-logged.[2] Copper mining in Cornwall would in fact have been an almost impossible undertaking, if there had been no pumping engines to free the mines from water, and throughout the eighteenth century Savery's and Newcomen's engines had been employed for that purpose. By the '70's, however, these were proving inefficient and very expensive to work, owing to the increasing depths of the mines, and it seems

---

[1] Most of the material for this essay has been obtained from the Boulton & Watt MSS. in the Birmingham Public Library. The letters, which Boulton wrote to his partner, while the former was in Cornwall, have proved the chief source of information. As the correspondence is for the most part unclassified, it has been impossible in some cases to give as exact references as might be wished. A box labelled *Cornish Letters* contains the greater part of the information given here about the Cornish Metal Company, including a valuable account in outline of its activities up to 1787; but there is among the MSS. a large amount of material, to which it is impossible to refer with any degree of precision.

[2] Hunt, *British Mining;* and *The Journal of the Royal Geological Society of Cornwall*, Vol. III.

probable that it was only the appearance of Watt's engine
which saved the mines from complete extinction. In 1777
his engines were introduced into Cornwall, and were adapted
by most of the mining companies of " adventurers." [1] A considerable saving in the cost of coal and a much greater efficiency
in working resulted. This reduction in the cost of producing
the ore gave a stimulus to Cornish mining, and the revival of
old mines and the opening of many new ones came as a direct
consequence. The result was an increase in the supply of copper
in the '80's, which, being unaccompanied by any appreciable
increase in demand, brought about a fall in price,[2] which again
reduced the mines to their previous unprofitable position. It is
in this connection that Boulton and Watt came to exercise an
important influence on the future history of the industry. As
they relied for their income, not only on the sale of their engines,
but also on the monthly dues or " savings" paid to them by
those adventurers who had made use of their patent, this fall
in price, which rendered probable the abandonment of many
of the mines, threatened Boulton and Watt with a loss of their
patent dues.[3] Since, moreover, at this time the Cornish mines
provided practically the only market for their engines, the ruin
of the industry would have brought disaster on the partners.
Realising that the mines must be kept going at all costs, Boulton
at first attempted to encourage the adventurers to continue to
work the mines by taking shares in them [4]—a practice which
was followed by the other contractors to the mines,[5] whose
interests were in many respects coincident with those of Boulton
and Watt. Although the latter lost money by these investments, they more than recompensed themselves for such losses
by the profits on their engine business. Boulton soon found,
however, that this method would be inadequate to prevent the
mines from ceasing to work, for during the early '80's their
position became desperate. His next step, therefore, was an
attempt to improve the management of the mines, and he used
his power as a shareholder to destroy the waste and inefficiency,
of which there were many glaring instances in the mine administration.[6] More interesting, however, were his attempts to
reorganise the copper trade on its marketing side, attempts
which led ultimately to the formation of the combine of 1785.

    [1] Boulton & Watt MSS., *An Account of the Benefits of Watt's Engines to
Cornwall, July 13th,* 1795.
    [2] *Ibid., Boulton to Watt, Nov. 24th,* 1780.   [3] *Ibid., October* 1782.
    [4] *Ibid., July* 1781.   [5] *Ibid., George Fox to Watt, January 29th,* 1784.
    [6] *Ibid., Boulton to Watt, August 22nd,* 1785.

The nature of the problem which Boulton set himself to solve was twofold. Firstly, it was essential that the relation between the Cornish adventurers and the various smelting companies should be changed; and, secondly, the competition between Cornwall and its rival Anglesea had to be restricted. There is no space here to consider the curious methods by which the Cornish ores were disposed of during the eighteenth century to the Welsh smelters, who marketed them. It suffices to say that during the '70's and early '80's the ores were purchased at " ticketings " by eleven different smelting companies.[1]   " These companies were perpetually contending with each other as well as with Anglesea, and the method of combating each other was by lowering the price of copper, which generally produced a proportionate effect in the price of ores, to the great detriment of the miners." [2]   It seems that at this time the prices which the adventurers received from the smelters for the ores were even lower than the depressed state of the copper market warranted, and the miners were unable to hold out for higher prices, partly because they were disunited, and partly owing to the fact that their capital was small when compared with the great expense of working the mines.[3]   This meant that they relied on the proceeds of each monthly sale to enable them to meet the expenses of the following month, and they were, there-fore, not in a position to refuse the low prices which the smelters offered.   Thus the trade was wholly in the power of the smelting companies, and Boulton realised that the miners' fortunes could never improve while this method of marketing their produce was maintained.   In his attempt to wrest the control of the copper trade from the smelters, Boulton was supported by Thomas Williams, the manager of the two Anglesea mines, who had no cause to love the smelting companies, since they were his bitter competitors. It may be noted that the Anglesea miners, although they were at one time " oppressed by the copper companies " as Cornwall was, had taken steps to set up smelting works of their own and to market their copper themselves.[4] They were especially successful in developing the foreign markets.[5] The increase of Anglesea's production at this time was even greater than that of Cornwall's.   In 1778, Anglesea produced

[1] Hunt, *British Mining, Letter from Thomas Williams to Lord Uxbridge, August 6th,* 1785.

[2] Boulton & Watt MSS., Account of Cornish Metal Company among *Cornish Letters,* c. 1787.

[3] *Ibid.*

[4] Boulton & Watt MSS., *Boulton to Watt, June 10th,* 1785.   [5] *Ibid.*

1200 tons of copper compared with its rival's 3000 tons; in 1785 the respective amounts obtained at the two centres were 3000 tons and 4400 tons.[1] In these circumstances there can be no wonder that the market was glutted, and that both centres suffered from mutual competition. Between 1780 and 1785 both Boulton and Williams had suggested many schemes to the Cornish adventurers, by which the latter might free themselves from the smelters' control and come to some agreement with Anglesea for the purpose of maintaining a high level of prices.[2] It was not till 1785 that these proposals began to receive general support in Cornwall, but in the autumn of that year a thorough reorganisation of the copper trade on its marketing side was effected.

The initiators of the " copper revolution," as it was called, realised that if the Cornish miners were to control the smelting and marketing of their ores, fresh capital would have to be introduced into the industry, and a new organisation set up, which could co-ordinate the activities of the numerous mines. To this end the Cornish Metal Company was established on September 1st, 1785, with a nominal capital of £500,000, £130,000 of which was immediately subscribed.[3] A large proportion of this, it may be noted, was advanced by Boulton and his friends, and by the other contractors to the mining companies. The objects of the Metal Company, it was stated, were " to keep up the price of copper ores at a proper standard and to contract for the smelting of all ores as should best promote the interests of the mines." [4] The Company agreed to buy all the ores raised in Cornwall from September 1st, 1785, to September 1st, 1792, and to sell the copper in a metallic state. The associated miners of Cornwall, for their part, agreed to sell all their ores to the Company at such prices as should be fixed by the Governor and by the thirty-six directors, two-thirds of whom were to be nominated by the miners. They also guaranteed to the subscribers to the Company's capital interest at the rate of eight per cent. per annum.[5] Thus after September 1785 Cornwall possessed a central selling agency, which bore a close resemblance to the modern Kartel, and which controlled the marketing of all the ores raised in the county. It was now in a position to

---

[1] Hunt, *British Mining.*
[2] Boulton & Watt MSS., *Boulton to Watt, October,* 1782; and Hunt, *British Mining, Letter from Williams to Lord Uxbridge, August 6th,* 1785.
[3] Boulton & Watt MSS., *Cornish Letters.*
[4] *Ibid., Resolution of Meeting of Lords and Adventurers, July 22nd,* 1785.
[5] *Ibid.*

come to some agreement with Anglesea, by which prices could be maintained at a high level to the benefit of all copper producers.

According to the price agreement between the Cornish Metal Company and Anglesea a minimum price for all the copper produced by the two centres was fixed, and from this price both parties bound themselves not to depart under a penalty of £100,000. Cornwall's share of the total sales was to be three-fifths, while that of Anglesea was fixed at two-fifths.[1] It is to be remarked, however, that no attempt was made at the time to set any limit to the total amount of production. By this agreement it was also stipulated that, after the ore had been smelted, the metal was to be sent for sale to warehouses at London, Birmingham, Bristol and Liverpool. Anglesea was given the right of serving Liverpool, Cornwall that of supplying the Bristol consumers; while both at Birmingham and London there was to be a general warehouse, to which both centres were to send their copper. Each party was required to present the other with weekly accounts of its sales, and five merchants were to be appointed " to govern and direct the trade for the mutual benefit of each party." The operation of the contract was to begin in May 1786, after which date the price of copper was to be £86 a ton.[2] This price, it seems, was about £12 higher than that which had ruled in May 1785; and it was thought that high prices could in the future be paid for Cornish ores, that Boulton & Watt's engine dues would be secured, and that large profits would be gained by all who were concerned in the copper industry.

The optimism which greeted the formation of this combination was, however, hardly justified by its results. Just as the introduction of Watt's engines had first brought salvation to the miners, but later had resulted in the full weight of their burdens being restored, so the prosperity which accompanied the Metal Company in its first few months of life was productive of forces which ultimately led to disaster. The formation of the combine brought about an immediate rise in the price of copper,[3] and this fact, together with the knowledge that the price would be £86 a ton after the next May, caused the directors of the Metal Company to be generous in the prices at which they bought ores from the miners. This increase in the price of ores " threw a temporary gleam of sunshine on the miners

---

[1] Boulton & Watt MSS., *Cornish Letters.*   [2] *Ibid.*
[3] *Ibid., Boulton to Watt, July 10th,* 1785.

and encouraged them to erect new engines in deep mines at great expense." [1] The result was that a greater quantity of ore began to be produced than the Metal Company could dispose of in a metallic state, and so a stock of unsaleable copper soon began to accumulate.[2]

It was not, however, the excessive production which alone caused this accumulation of copper. The stocks of this metal in the hands of some of the old smelting companies were " much greater than had been computed "; while certain other mining companies, which possessed rich mines and large stocks of copper, had not been included within the price association. Their production was stimulated by the high prices which ruled at this time, and they and the smelting companies sold copper considerably under the price stipulated by the agreement between Cornwall and Anglesea.[3] By 1787, moreover, foreign copper from Hungary, Sweden and Holland began to flow into England, as well as into the foreign markets which Cornwall and Anglesea had previously supplied. One instance is well worth mentioning. A quantity of unrefined copper, " which had lain for years at Cadiz while low prices were to be had," was bought by an English firm, shipped to this country, refined, and sold under the price fixed by the agreement.[4]

It is worth remarking that the possibility of foreign competition had been foreseen by the promoters of the combination, even before the danger had become immediate, for in March 1786 there was an unsuccessful attempt to induce the Swedish copper producers to enter into the price association.[5]

The effect of this competition on the fortunes of the combination may best be realised by a consideration of the Metal Company's accounts which were presented in October 1787. By this time practically the whole of the Company's capital was represented by a stock of copper in its warehouses,[6] although an additional subscription of £11,000 had been raised a few months before. The Company, moreover, was deeply in debt. When it had found that its initial capital had been insufficient to enable its contract with the miners to be carried out, owing to lack of sales, recourse was had to a temporary form of loan.[7] A contract was made between the Company and the smelters, by which the latter, instead of receiving a fixed sum for smelting,

---

[1] Boulton & Watt MSS., *Cornish Letters.*   [2] *Ibid.*   [3] *Ibid.*   [4] *Ibid.*

[5] *Ibid., Wilson to Boulton & Watt, March 3rd,* 1786.

[6] *Ibid., Boulton to Watt, October 11th,* 1787; *Boulton to Wedgewood, October 15th,* 1787.

[7] *Ibid., Cornish Letters.*

agreed to pay for the ores, when delivered to them by the Company. These ores, though in the possession of the smelting houses, were still to be considered the property of the Company, and were really a security for a loan advanced to it. At the end of the " regulated time of smelting ores " the copper was to be returned to the Metal Company, which then repaid to the smelters the money advanced and interest at the rate of eight per cent. Although this method was only meant to be a temporary expedient for raising money, in actual fact more and more advances had to be obtained from the smelters, so that by 1787 these advances had become practically permanent loans and amounted to £228,500. This sum was secured by 2677 tons of copper in the smelters' possession, while in the Company's own warehouses were 4027 tons. The total value of the whole stock was over half a million pounds.[1]

At the Company's meeting in October 1787 it was estimated that this stock was at least equal to a two years' supply, and so it was declared that the Company would have to deduct from the prices paid to the miners for their ores a sum equal to two years' interest on the capital invested in their purchase.[2] It was evident that this would make the burden on the miners intolerable. A few small mines had already been stopped and all were losing by this time. A further reduction would complete the ruin of the industry.

Moreover, disputes with Anglesea had before this time broken out. Since Williams was a skilful salesman, he had managed to obtain the principal sales for his own mines, and Cornwall was unable to make up its due proportion of the total sales. Williams, however, refused to restrict his sales in any degree—to the wrath of the Cornishmen.[3]

Boulton saw clearly enough that the only possible way of preventing the ruin both of the Metal Company and of the miners was to secure a restriction of produce. This course he strongly urged on the adventurers during the autumn of 1787, but for some time without effect.[4] Mutual jealousies among the adventurers made it impossible for a decision to be arrived at as to which mines should be closed, but another and more potent reason prevented the Cornishmen from adopting his plan. The adventurers were frightened of the working miners. The latter, on hearing of the probable cessation of work in some

---

[1] Boulton & Watt MSS., *Boulton to Watt, October 11th*, 1787.   [2] *Ibid.*
[3] *Ibid., March 3rd*, 1787; *and June 15th*, 1787.
[4] *Ibid., Cornish Letters.*

mines, had revolted and attacked Truro, where the Company's
offices were situated.[1]   The mob was dispersed only with great
difficulty, and " no mine dared give up " [2] for fear of another
riot.   If the mines stopped, moreover, considerable numbers
of miners would be thrown out of work.   As these " could not
in that county get their bread by any other means, they would
prove an intolerable burden to the parishes to which they
belonged." [3]   So the adventurers informed Boulton that " they
might as well sink their money in employing the poor as maintain them without working."

The state of the Company's finances, together with the fact
that Anglesea had sold more than her fair share of copper,
induced the miners at the meeting in October 1787 to decide to
break their agreements both with the Metal Company and with
Anglesea, and to revert to the old methods of sale.   In order
to prevent the Company from further depressing the market
by attempting to sell its huge stock, the miners agreed to pay
the subscribers £17,000 a year for five years provided that the
Company did not sell more than 1300 tons of copper a year.[4]
The result of this breach of the contract was disastrous.   Anglesea
immediately lowered the price of its copper, which still more
reduced the sales of Cornish copper,[5] and it seemed that Cornwall was now doomed as a copper-producing centre.

This renewal of competition was disliked, however, by
Anglesea almost as much as by Cornwall, and before the end
of the year another agreement was made, by which the Cornish
Metal Company's position was re-established and its contract
with Anglesea renewed with modifications.[6]   In this new contract
attempts were made to avoid the defects of the former combination; but prolonged negotiations were necessary before the
following terms were accepted by both parties.   In order to
avoid mutual suspicions and breaches in the agreement, it was
decided to place the sale of all the copper produced in Cornwall
and Anglesea in one hand until September 1792.   Thomas
Williams was made the joint agent of the two centres.   He was
to reside at London, to direct the course of the trade from there,
and, in return, to receive a commission of two per cent. on the
amount of the sales.[7]   The price of copper was to be fixed at
joint quarterly meetings at London; but, to avoid the danger

[1] Boulton & Watt MSS., *Boulton to Watt, October 8th,* 1787.
[2] *Ibid., October 11th,* 1787.   [3] *Ibid., Cornish Letters.*
[4] *Ibid., Boulton to Watt, October 11th,* 1787.   [5] *Ibid., Cornish Letters.*
[6] *Ibid., Boulton to Watt, November 8th,* 1787.   [7] *Ibid., February 20th,* 1788.

of unforeseen competition, there was to be a certain amount of elasticity in the price. It was also stipulated that both Cornwall and Anglesea should restrict the production of copper to 3000 tons each per annum, and, although for 1788 Cornwall was to be allowed to sell twice as much as Anglesea, in subsequent years the sales were to be equal. The price of copper, moreover, was reduced to £80 a ton.

One very significant suggestion, which received much support about this time, is worth noticing. It was that a Bill should be introduced into Parliament to bind the contracting parties, and that " five commissioners should be appointed by this Act to see it put into execution, and to be ultimate arbiters in all disputes." [1] Although there was much talk about this Act, it does not seem evident that Parliamentary sanction was actually sought for the new combination.

It was chiefly due to the efforts of Boulton and of Williams that the agreements had been resuscitated, and during the early months of 1788 they used their influence in the trade to enforce a restriction of output, which was so necessary for the success of the combination. Only with utmost difficulty, however, could the Cornish adventurers be prevailed upon to give up their mines or reduce their production.[2] Although several mines stopped working in 1788 owing to their heavy losses, the Metal Company found it necessary to bring about a further decrease by granting " a compensation to such mines " as would discontinue working, " equal to 40s. for every ton of copper annually produced." [3] It was not, however, till October 1789, after the cessation of several large mines,[4] that the desired reduction had been brought about, and that the Metal Company could dispose of any part of its enormous stock which had been accumulating up to that date.

Although the Metal Company had been saved from complete ruin, the position of all those concerned in the copper-mining industry was in 1789 still very serious. The Company was burdened with huge stocks, and could not, therefore, afford to give reasonable prices for the ores.[5] For this reason nearly all the mining companies of Cornwall were losing money.[6] The merchants who supplied them with materials had to consent

---

[1] Boulton & Watt MSS., *Cornish Letters.*
[2] *Ibid.*, *Boulton to Fox, January 30th*, 1788.
[3] *Ibid.*, *Minute of a Metal Company Committee Meeting, February 28th*, 1788.
[4] *Ibid.*, *An Account of the Benefits of Watt's Engines to Cornwall, July 13th*, 1795.
[5] *Ibid.*, *Cornish Letters.*   [6] *Ibid.*, *Boulton to Watt, October 5th*, 1789.

to a reduction on their bills, and Boulton & Watt were unable
to obtain the payments of their engine dues from many of the
mines. Where the mines had stopped working the partners'
loss was, of course, permanent. Among the labouring miners
the direst poverty and distress were the fruits of the Metal
Company's failure. The reduction in the " get " of ore, and
in its price meant that thousands were thrown out of work or
reduced to starvation wages. Among these miners at this time
" the spirit of violence was upon the ferment." [1] When it was
decided to close one mine in the autumn of 1789, they " intimated
a visit to take down the greatest house in Truro." [2] The mine
did not close ! For some time past all that Boulton had been
able to suggest as a remedy was that " Mr. Pitt " should " send
orders for 3000 tons of copper," or, as an alternative, " a press
gang." There seemed, in fact, no possibility of getting rid of
the huge stock, by which the Metal Company was burdened,
and yet its sale was the only means by which the prices paid
for the ores could be raised.

The next year, however, Cornwall was saved as if by a miracle.
The great store of copper ore in Anglesea, which had been mined
so cheaply, was by 1790 becoming exhausted.[3] Its decay was
apparently quite unexpected by those interested in the Cornish
mines, for Boulton often declared, just before this time, that
Williams' ultimate aim was to supply the whole of the copper
market, and that his alliance with Cornwall was merely a temporary policy to keep up prices until he could do so.

This decline in Anglesea's production enabled the Metal
Company to dispose of some of its surplus stock during 1790,
and so to give considerably higher prices for the ores.[4] Yet,
in spite of the improvement in the situation, the burden of the
stock, which amounted in 1790 to 5500 tons of copper, valued
at £400,000, lay heavy on the adventurers. Several of them
began selling to the excluded smelting companies, which, having
no dead stock, could offer higher prices for the ores than the
Metal Company could.[5] In order to induce the adventurers to
keep to their contracts and to maintain the combination intact,
Williams in July 1790 offered to smelt the ores at the Anglesea
works " upon lower terms than is in the power of the old

[1] Boulton & Watt MSS., *Boulton to Watt, October 5th,* 1789.   [2] *Ibid.*
[3] Joseph Carne, *A Paper in the Journal of the Royal Geological Society of
Cornwall.*
[4] Boulton & Watt MSS., *Cornish Letters.*
[5] *Ibid., Circular Letter from Williams to the Cornish Copper Miners, July 9th,*
1790.

companies." [1] He declared that the market at that time would take only 6500 tons of copper, but he was prepared to allow Cornwall to supply 4000 tons of this to Anglesea's 2500 tons. He also offered to the shareholders of the Metal Company a douceur of $2\frac{1}{4}$ per cent. on their capital in order to induce them to keep the Company in existence beyond the date fixed for its dissolution. By this means he hoped to retain a control over the copper trade even after Anglesea had been reduced to impotence as a producing centre. The result of the entire scheme is doubtful; but it is certain that he was not successful in his attempt to prolong the life of the Company, for it came to an end early in 1792.[2]

By that time the Metal Company's position had enormously improved. It had sold the whole of its stock; it had wiped off its debts; and by March 1792 it possessed practically intact its subscribed capital.[3] This achievement was only possible, as one writer says, because " the reduced produce of the mines of Anglesea, in conjunction with the ruin of several Cornish mines, had the effect of raising the price of copper from £80, at which it stood in 1790, to £90, which was its price in 1791." [4] By 1792 copper stood at £100 a ton.[5] Thus the Metal Company was able to get rid of its stock at a high price on a market from which its most dangerous competitor had been removed. The clause in the price agreement that the sales of both Cornwall and Anglesea should be equal after 1788 was, of course, ignored, when Anglesea proved unable to supply its quota.

It might be thought that the Cornish production of copper would have rapidly increased after 1790; but this did not immediately occur. The explanation is to be found in the fact that, once the mines had been closed, it was always a long and expensive business to set them to work again. Extensive floods, moreover, which occurred in 1791, made any such attempt useless.[6] Thus all favoured the Metal Company, when once its fortunes had changed.

It is curious to notice that Boulton was by no means so pleased with the improvement as might have been expected. His interests by 1790 had undergone a change. Before that date they had been, in the main, linked with those of the producers

[1] Boulton & Watt MSS., *Circular Letter from Williams to the Cornish Copper Miners, July 9th,* 1790.

[2] *Ibid., Accounts of Cornish Metal Company, March 1st,* 1792.   [3] *Ibid.*

[4] Joseph Carne, *Journal of the Royal Geological Society of Cornwall.*

[5] Hunt, *British Mining.*

[6] Boulton & Watt MSS., *Boulton to Watt, March 26th,* 1791.

of copper; afterwards he became more interested in the copper industry as a consumer. This was due to the development of his coining business, which he had begun when the price of copper was low, and which had been stimulated by the large purchases of copper that he had made in 1788 from the Metal Company, in order to relieve it of part of its stock.[1] After 1790, while other markets for Watt's engines were developing, and while Cornwall was, therefore, no longer of such vital interest to the partners as it once had been, Boulton's coining business was beginning to assume considerable proportions. So it can be understood that the rise in the price of copper became a very serious matter for him, now that the centre of his interests had shifted. Thus Boulton, who had striven so hard to form a combination to put up prices, was now hit very hard by the organisation which he had himself created. Possibly it was owing to his influence that the Company came to an end in March 1792, even before the expiration of its contract with the Cornish miners.

From this time onwards the demand for copper rapidly increased as a result of the extension of manufactures in England, and of the growth of the navy during the French war. In spite of the great increase in the " get " of ore after 1792, and although the old methods of sale were reverted to, prices rose almost without interruption until the end of the century.[2] This, of course, rendered any attempt to renew the combination unnecessary, nor was any such attempt made after the Cornish Metal Company had been dissolved.

G. C. ALLEN

---

[1] Smiles, *Lives of Boulton & Watt;* also, Boulton & Watt MSS., *Boulton to Watt, March 26th,* 1791.

[2] Hunt, *British Mining.*

[5]

French Entrepreneurship During the Restoration: The Record of a Single Firm, the Anzin Mining Company *

IN THIS paper, which examines the business operations of the Anzin Mining Company during the Restoration, the record of a single firm has been used to assess recent interpretations of the nature of French entrepreneurship in the nineteenth century. These interpretations portray French industry in its formative period developing around "small units, small volume, and small horizons." [1] "Cautious management, obsolescent plants, and high profits" have been cited as main features which came to characterize the business operations of even the largest firms.[2] It has been pointed out also that maximization of profits was not a fundamental aim of the French entrepreneur, nor did he indulge in the competitive business practices common to American industrial development.[3] In France, security and continuity of the firm were as important to the entrepreneur as profits, and the acquired rights of the small or marginal firm were respected and preserved. The family character of most French enterprises has been emphasized in explanation of these phenomena.[4] Close identification of family name and family honor with business holdings prescribed a minimizing of risks in the family firm, as well as consideration for the welfare of other family enterprises. Finally, in order to allow these conditions to endure, French entrepreneurs favored a high protective tariff.

The extent to which the business operations of the Anzin Mining Company during 1815–1830 substantiate these interpretations is examined below. An intensive study of the record of this important firm

* Research for the present article was made possible by a United States Government Grant under Public Law 584, 79th Congress (Fulbright Act).

[1] John E. Sawyer, "The Entrepreneur and the Social Order: France and the United States," in William Miller (ed.), *Men in Business* (Cambridge: Harvard University Press, 1952), p. 14.

[2] David S. Landes, "French Entrepreneurship and Industrial Growth in the Nineteenth Century," *Journal of Economic History*, IX (May 1949), 49.

[3] *Ibid.*, pp. 48–50; Sawyer, "The Entrepreneur and the Social Order," p. 17. See also David S. Landes, "French Business and the Businessman: A Social and Cultural Analysis," in Edward M. Earle (ed.), *Modern France* (Princeton: Princeton University Press, 1951), pp. 348–49; A. H. Cole, "An Approach to the Study of Entrepreneurship," *Journal of Economic History*, VI (Supplement 1946), 8–9.

[4] Landes, "French Entrepreneurship," pp. 52–54.

became possible when the minutes of the board of directors were made available after World War II.[5]

II

During the Restoration the Anzin Mining Company was the most important coal mining firm in northern France. By 1830 its mining concession in the Department of Nord, between the Scarpe and Escaut Rivers, stretched through twelve communes, from Condé and Valenciennes near the Belgian frontier in the east toward Douai and as far as the Aniche mining concession in the west.[6] By then the annual extraction of coal by the firm, which ordinarily amounted to about one quarter of the total French production, was almost 400,000 tons. The only larger coal producing region in France was the Loire valley, where coal extraction in 1831 was 654,210 tons.[7]

Most of the coal extracted by the Anzin company was used by towns located relatively near to the mines themselves, such as Lille, Arras, Douai, St. Omer, Lens. However, Anzin coal was shipped by barge to Dunkerque, and thence to ports along the coast of France as far as Bordeaux and La Rochelle; a small amount reached Paris by way of the Oise River and the Canal of St. Quentin; and coal from company pits at Fresnes was exported to Belgium, where it was much preferred by manufacturers at Tournay for the calcination of lime.[8]

The characteristics of its product and the location of its mining concession were problems for the Anzin company. A large proportion of the company's coal, especially that from pits at Fresnes and Vieux-Condé, was high grade anthracite. It was a hard, dry coal, capable of producing an intense, constant heat. Still, at a time when industry in France was just beginning to switch from wood to coal, this circumstance placed the company at a disadvantage. For use in forges, for

[5] National Archives, 49 AQ 1–5 (microfilm), "Copie des déliberations de la Régie de la Compagnie des Mines d'Anzin, 1757–1920."

[6] See "Renseignements sur la compagnie propriétaire des mines d'Anzin, Raismes, Fresnes, Vieux-Condé, Denain, Abscon, et sur les droits et péages exorbitants et injustes perçus sur les houilles ou charbon de terre de la Belgique. . . ." MS. (1833), 19 pp., in National Archives, F12 2534A. Henceforth cited as "Renseignements sur les mines d'Anzin."

[7] See J. Berard, "Produit des mines de houille du Royaume pour l'exercise 1831," MS. (March 21, 1832), in National Archives, F12 2534A.

[8] See Jacques Renard, *Réponse de la Compagnie des mines de Charbon d'Anzin, Raismes, et Vieux-Condé aux pétitions de quelques fabricans des Départements du Nord, et de quelques associés dans les mines de la Belgique, qui demandent la réduction à 11 centimes du droit de 33 centimes perçu à l'entrée en France des charbons des Pays-Bas* (Anzin, December 12, 1821), 36 pp., in National Archives, AD XIII 14. Henceforth cited as *Renard Report*.

The Anzin Mining Company   163

driving steam engines, and for general heating purposes, most French consumers favored more easily ignited bituminous coals, called *houilles flambantes.*[9] The older pits at Anzin yielded bituminous coal, but by 1815 these were becoming depleted and progressively more difficult and dangerous to work. An extension of the vein of coal worked at Anzin was discovered at Abscon (1822) and Denain (1828), but extraction there was delayed for years because of the need first to drain a subterranean lake, "Le Torrent."[10] Also, while the vein was relatively close to the surface of the earth in Belgium, near Mons and Liege, it became deeper as it ran west into France. Such conditions slowed the work at Denain especially, and at Abscon and Anzin they increased expenses for drainage and for timbering underground passageways and galleries.[11]

Difficulties such as these were important in explaining why the company's cost for extraction was greater than that for other regions. According to Marck Jennings, the company's general agent after 1827, extraction costs were customarily 3 to 4 francs per ton at Newcastle, 5 to 6 francs at Mons, and 7 to 8 francs for the Loire valley.[12] In a special report to the directors in 1826, Casimir Périer calculated the cost for Anzin at 8.9 francs per ton during 1821–1822 and 7.9 francs during 1823–1825.[13] Jennings himself, writing in 1832 at the time of the government inquiry into the French coal industry, reported that the cost then varied between 8 to 9 francs.[14] The average cost of extraction for Anzin coal, which amounted to 40 to 50 per cent of its sale price, was thus higher than the 5 to 6 francs cited by most contemporary critics of the company.

The cost of extraction included the major expense of employing between 4,500 and 6,000 workers, whose average salary was 1 franc, 50 centimes per day, and for whom the company undertook to provide whether business was good or bad.[15] Not included in this cost, however,

---

[9] See C. Migneron, "Réponse aux questions posées à l'occasion de l'enquête sur les houilles," MS. (February 15, 1833), in National Archives, F12 2534A.

[10] Casimir Périer, "Rapport fait à la Régie par Casimir Périer," (Saint-Vaast, June 15, 1826), in National Archives, 49 AQ 1. Henceforth cited as *Périer Report.*

[11] *Périer Report; Renard Report.*

[12] Marck Jennings, *Réponse aux questions à faire résoudre par l'enquête sur les houilles* (Paris, December 8, 1832), in National Archives, F12 2534A. Henceforth cited as *Jennings Report.*

[13] *Périer Report.*

[14] *Jennings Report.*

[15] This average cost, for miners at the vein, remained rather constant from 1811 to 1833. The only notable change was made in 1824, when wages were increased by 20 centimes for workers in pits at Anzin. See National Archives, 49 AQ 1 (September 20, 1824; June 27, 1833).

were the many extra expenses incurred by the firm as a result of the paternalistic benefits it provided for its employees. For example, in cases of death or accident at the mines the company indemnified the families or persons involved, and it established an elaborate pension plan for retired workers. The company was unusual in that it also housed most of its employees, provided them with free medical care, and built schools for their children. The Périer brothers, who were directors of the company and who interested themselves in new experiments in education, established a school for *"enseignement mutuel"* at Anzin in 1817;[16] and in 1825 they arranged for company workers to take night school instruction in geometry and mechanical arts, using lessons compiled by Charles Dupin.[17] In all, the directors estimated that these and other benefits cost the company 25 centimes per day for each worker.[18]

Among other additional expenses was an annual concession payment due the government in accordance with the law on mines of April 21, 1810. In 1831 this payment of 5 per cent on the net profit of the company amounted to 52,910 francs.[19] And finally, although this was not strictly an element of cost, the company gave considerable attention to the accumulation of a reserve fund for use in times of crisis.[20]

Yet, in spite of all the problems and expenses, the firm's extraction of coal rose rather steadily during the first half of the Restoration, reaching 379,251 tons in 1821 (Chart 1), or approximately 100,000 tons above the highest level of production under the Empire.[21] For reasons to be noted later, both production and sales of coal declined temporarily after 1821, but by 1825 the firm's business had improved and, according to Vuillemin,[22] production rose to 392,800 tons in 1830. Moreover, throughout the Restoration, the gross profit of the firm (income

[16] *Ibid.* (March 6, 1817); Joseph DeGérando, "Éloge de M. Scipion Périer," *Bulletin de la société d'encouragement pour l'industrie nationale* (52 vols., Paris, 1802–1853), XX (1821), 125.

[17] See Charles Dupin, "Exposé fait à la Société d'encouragement sur les progrès dus nouvel enseignement de la géometrie et de la mécanique, appliquées aux arts et métiers, en faveur de la classe industrielle," *Bulletin de la société d'encouragement pour l'industrie nationale*, XXIV (1825), 374–80.

[18] Nationl Archives, 49 AQ 1 (June 27, 1833).

[19] See "Relevé général des contributions directes de 1831, payées par la Compagnie propriétaire des mines d'Anzin. . . ." (November 7, 1832), in National Archives, C 1252, dossier Joseph Périer.

[20] *Périer Report.* See also Louis Reybaud, *Le fer et la houille* (Paris: Michel Levy frères, 1874), p. 176.

[21] See A. de Saint-Léger, *Les mines d'Anzin et d'Aniche pendant la Révolution* (4 vols.; Paris: Lib. Ernest Leroux, 1939), I, part 1, xliv.

[22] Emile Vuillemin, *Le bassin houiller du Pas-de-Calais* (3 vols.; Lille: Danel, 1880–84), II, 343.

The Anzin Mining Company 165

from coal sales minus cost of extraction) remained high, at about 40 to 50 per cent. The firm itself never disclosed precise figures, but it can be estimated that gross profit ranged between one and two million francs during 1815–1820, and from two to three million francs during 1821–1832.[23] Such large profits permitted the directors to declare remakably high dividends, which were maintained even during periods of declining coal sales (Chart 1).

Chart 1

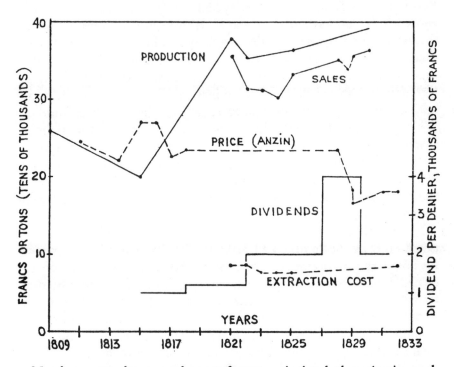

Northern merchants and manufacturers insisted that Anzin coal prices were kept too high and that, consequently, the company's profits were exorbitant. It was said that, although the cost of extraction for the company decreased during 1815–1830, the company raised rather than lowered its prices for coal. Actually, it would appear that extraction costs were always high for the company, and declined only slightly after 1823 (Chart 1). As for Anzin coal prices, company policy did keep

[23] For contemporary estimates, see "Renseignements sur les mines d'Anzin"; A. Pichault de la Martinière, *Mémoire sur la nécessité de modifier la législation des douanes en général, et, en particulier, les lois sur les houilles* (Paris, c. 1833), p. 21, in National Archives, F12 2534B.

these as high as possible, but significant reductions were made in 1816 and again in May and October 1829 (Chart 1). The reduction in 1816 was probably related in part to the tariff law of that year, while the 1829 reductions were ordered to stimulate sales.[24] The price of coal from Fresnes and Vieux-Condé was generally 2 to 3 francs per ton lower than Anzin coal, although at times, as in 1829, prices were made the same for coals from all company pits.

The family character of the Anzin company accounted for the high profit-high dividend policy practiced by its directors. Throughout the Revolution and Empire the company had been preserved as a very small and exclusive association of investors, who negotiated mostly among themselves for possession of the company's rather limited number of shares (that is, 24 *sols,* divided into 288 *deniers*), and who expected a high return on their investment.[25] By the Restoration, only thirty to forty families owned shares in the mines, and only exceptionally were sales allowed to individuals who were not members of these families. When such sales did occur, the company usually exercised its right to purchase the shares from the buyer. The shares were then either retired or re-sold to members of the society. Actually, the high price of shares discouraged outside investment in the company: for example, 35,000 francs per *denier* in 1816; 60,764 francs in 1823; 90,700 francs in 1828; 120,000 francs in 1832.

In proportion to their interests in the firm, shareholders might be called upon by the company to make up deficits or to advance money for necessary improvements in the mines. Yet, a unique feature of the company was that no annual general assemblies of the shareholders were held to decide upon policies or to elect officers. Control of the mines was left in the hands of six directors, representing families who held the largest blocks of shares. During the period 1815–1821 the principal directors were Scipion Périer, Jacques Désandrouin, Louis Thief-fries, César and Joseph Taffin, and Count Gilles Hocquart; and during the years 1821–1832, Casimir and Joseph Périer, Joseph and Hyacinthe Taffin, Count Hocquart, Jacques Renard, and Prince Ernest d'Aren-berg.[26]

These directorships were perpetuated within a very few families. The influential Périer family may be used as an example. Their interests and

24 National Archives, 49 AQ 1 (October 16, 1829).

25 See Saint-Léger, *Les mines d'Anzin,* I, part 1.

26 Prince Ernest d'Arenberg, owner of rich forest lands near Raismes, became a director in September 1821, following Désandrouin's death. Count Hocquart replaced Augustin Sabatier (d. 1813) in September 1817.

The Anzin Mining Company 167

directorship in the mines dated from the financial reorganization of the company in 1795, at which time Claude Périer, a wealthy banker from Grenoble, acquired 27½ *deniers*.[27] After Claude Périer's death in 1801, his shares were divided among his eight sons and two daughters, but the control of these interests passed into the hands of two of the sons, Scipion and Casimir, who in 1805 became a director and assistant director of the mines, respectively.[28] Casimir Périer, the most famous member of the family (he was Premier and Minister of Interior of France in 1831–1832), headed the company after Scipion died in April 1821.[29] Joseph Périer, another brother, became an assistant director in the same year. In 1832, after Casimir's death, Joseph Périer became a director, and Casimir's son Auguste was named assistant director.[30] Thus five Périers representing three generations were prominent in directing the affairs of the company.

The influential position of the Périers in the company was ensured not only by their accumulation of a large block of shares, but also through the special services they performed in banking, business, and politics. The company, for example, preferred to conduct money affairs as discreetly as possible, without unnecessary publicity regarding such things as its investment in government bonds *(rentes)*, sales or transfers of shares, or loans made by the company to individual shareholders. The Périer bank in Paris, which became the financial house of the company, could be entrusted with matters such as these.[31] Then too, after 1818 the Périers owned the famous machine shops of Jacques Périer at Chaillot, near Paris, which supplied the company's steam engines and other mining equipment.[32] In addition, the Périers also had

[27] Saint-Léger, *Les mines d'Anzin*, I, part 1, 45–46, 51–52. See Francois Vermale, *Le père de Casimir Périer, 1743–1801* (Grenoble: B. Arthaud, 1935).

[28] See Archives of the Municipal Library of Grenoble, R 90564, "Liquidation de la succession de M. Claude Périer"; National Archives, 49 AQ 1 (May 20, 1834); Saint-Léger, *Les mines d'Anzin*, I, part 1, 89.

[29] National Archives, 49 AQ 1 (May 3, 1821).

[30] *Ibid.* (July 15, 1832).

[31] The bank was founded in April-May, 1801, by Casimir and Scipion Périer, Henry Flory, and William Sabatier. Flory and Sabatier remained with the bank until 1807. Joseph Périer became a partner in 1822. The bank had three accounts with the Anzin company: one for expenditures; a special account for the Dames de Fontenelles, who were shareholders; and an account for the company's reserve fund. See Notarial Archives (Minutier Centrale, Paris), Étude Bezier, LXVIII (845), Notoriété concernant Périer frères, 20 octobre 1825; National Archives, 49 AQ 1 (June 21, 1827).

[32] Notarial Archives, Étude Prud'homme, CVIII, Répertoire 24, Dépôt de vente, par Jacques-Constantin Périer à Scipion Périer, de l'établissement de Chaillot, 30 novembre 1822; DeGérando, "Éloge de M. Scipion Périer," p. 120. (Neither Jacques-Constantin Périer, 1742–1818, nor his brother, Auguste-Charles Périer, were related in any way to the Périer family discussed in this paper.)

important contacts in Paris with high-ranking government officials and with leading businessmen and scientists. Until his death in 1821, Scipion Périer was a member of such bodies as the Council General on Manufactures, an advisory council attached to the Ministry of Interior. The three brothers—Scipion, Casimir, and Joseph—succeeded one another as members of the important Chamber of Commerce of Paris; and they participated in the valuable work of the Society for the Encouragement of National Industry. Finally, Casimir Périer was also prominent as a member of the Chamber of Deputies during 1817–1831, and became Premier in 1831–1832. More than the other Anzin directors, these varied activities of the Périer brothers provided opportunities to guide or to protect the affairs of their firm.

A particular instance in which the Périers used their influence to safeguard the interests of the firm illustrates one of the basic policies of the Anzin directors during the Restoration, tariff protection. For the Anzin company, the main coal tariff of the Restoration was that of April 28, 1816, which raised the duty on Belgian coal entering France by way of the Department of Nord from 11 to 33 centimes per 100 Kg (1.0 to 2.9 francs per ton). This tariff, which the Anzin directors fought to maintain, gave the company enough of an advantage over Belgian coal prices to make its position nearly monopolistic. Commercial users of coal in the Department of Nord were especially bitter because the tariff favored the Anzin company at their expense. For the Departments of Meuse, Moselle, and Ardennes, which the Anzin company did not supply, the tariff set duties of only 15 centimes.

In 1817, Count Jean-Antoine Chaptal, who was then President of the Society for the Encouragement of National Industry, voiced strong objections to the tariff of 1816. Chaptal published a lengthy memoir in which he reproved the policies of the Anzin company, and in which he proposed a uniform tariff on coal of not more than 10 centimes all along the northeastern frontier of France.[33] Since Chaptal was considered by his contemporaries as an authority on the needs of French industry, the memoir provoked the government to order a serious re-examination of the coal tariff. In January 1818, Count Chabrol de Crouzol, the undersecretary at the Ministry of Interior, instructed the Council General on Manufactures to study the matter and to advise the ministry as soon

[33] Jean-Antoine Chaptal, *Observations sur les commerce des houilles ou charbons de terre Belge en France, sur la cherté de ce combustible, et sur les moyens d'en faire diminuer le prix* (Paris, 1817), 79 pp., in National Archives, F12 2474A.

The Anzin Mining Company   169

as possible.[34] The Council, in turn, organized a special committee to review Chaptal's proposal.[35] The chairman of this committee was, oddly enough, Scipion Périer, whose directorship at the Anzin company naturally prejudiced his views in favor of the tariff.

Scipion Périer's defense of the tariff before the committee was calculated to show, first, that neither the tariff nor his company could be blamed for the high price of coal in northern France, and, second, that considerations other than the self-interest of the Anzin mines lay behind his company's policy.[36] Thus Scipion pointed out that the slight rise in the price of Anzin coal in 1817 (Chart 1) was in no way related to the tariff. His company, he said, had spent large sums relieving unemployment at the mines in that year, and therefore felt justified in recuperating the loss by a price increase. The high price of coal in France in general, he continued, was not a consequence of the tariff, but resulted from shipping costs (local tolls on rivers and canals, government navigation fees) and city coal taxes. Paris, for example, taxed coal at almost 7 francs per ton (a rate nearly equal to the cost of extraction at Anzin, and more than double the tariff on Belgian coal).[37] Scipion then stated that his firm could withstand a tariff reduction. The Anzin company, he said, prospered mainly by reason of its excellent administration. However, he added that there was more at stake than the prosperity of the Anzin mines alone: [38]

. . . the Anzin company, having withstood the competition of coals from Mons during the entire period of the union of Belgium and France, could still withstand it if the duty was reduced and the charge for entry by the Escaut was at the same rate as for the Meuse. But he (i.e., Scipion Périer) observes that several mines have been opened recently in the Department of Nord. He believes that an increase in the duty on entry by the Escaut is necessary to encourage the development of their business. And he fears that the reduction of the duty on entry all along the frontier . . . will be extremely harmful to coal mines of the Midi, which have had great losses, and which, not having sufficient markets, would have to expand these to Paris and Rouen.

In this defense of the tariff, Scipion Périer's protection of the interests of smaller mining companies in northern France (for example, Aniche,

[34] National Archives, F12 195, Procès-verbaux du Conseil des Fabriques et Manufactures, January 29, 1818.

[35] *Ibid*. (January 29, 1818; February 21, 1818).

[36] *Ibid*. (February 9 and 19, 1818).

[37] See Joseph Périer, *Rapport à la Chambre de Commerce de Paris sur la navigation intérieure et sur l'approvisionnement de la capitale en charbon de terre* (Paris, April 1826).

[38] National Archives, F12 195 (February 9, 1818).

Litry, Auberchicourt, Ardinghen) is particularly noteworthy, and he was not altogether insincere in his concern for their welfare. During the Restoration, his company did not expand its concession in the Department of Nord at the expense of smaller mining firms. In 1819–1820, for example, Scipion Périer and the other directors considered acquiring the nearby Aniche mines, but decided against such a move.[89] As will be seen, the Anzin directors had reason to believe that their own concession was sizable enough.

Scipion Périer's defensive technique of pointing out the many problems involved in any proposal for tariff reduction was successful. The Council General on Manufactures, in fact, after listening to testimony from representatives of mines in the Loire Valley and from merchants from Mons, concluded finally that the issue was so complex that the best policy was to leave things as they were, except that the tariff might be lowered for the Departments of Meuse, Moselle, and Ardennes.[40] The law of April 21, 1818, which reduced the duty on coal entering France by the Meuse River from 15 to 10 centimes, reflected this decision of the Council.

The only further modification of the tariff during the Restoration was the law of June 7, 1820, which granted a reduction for the Department of Moselle. The tariff was skillfully defended in the Chamber of Deputies by Casimir Périer.[41] The Anzin company also found valuable allies in the Count de Saint-Cricq, who was Director General of Customs (1814–1824), and Louis Becquey, the Director General of Roads, Bridges, and Mines (1818–1830).[42] These officials were impressed by the argument that the tariff did not keep coal from Belgium out of France. On the contrary, toward the end of the Restoration imports increased until by 1830 they exceeded the total production of the Anzin mines.[43] Moreover, a further argument against lowering the French tariff was the much higher Belgian duty on coal of 1 franc, 78 centimes per 100 Kg, imposed in 1814; in 1822 Belgium placed a special duty of 1 franc, 48 centimes on coal from Fresnes, which was exempt under the earlier law.

[89] National Archives, 49 AQ 1 (September 9, 1819; March 9, 1820). See also Bertrand Gille, *Recherches sur la formation de la grande entreprise capitaliste (1815–1848)* (Paris; S.E.V.P.E.N., 1959), pp. 62–64.

[40] National Archives, F12 195 (February 26, 1818).

[41] See, for example, *Archives parlementaires de 1800 à 1860. Recueil complet des débats législatifs et politiques des chambres françaises* (2nd Series, Paris, 1862), XXVII, 438–39.

[42] *Ibid.*, XXVII, 440.

[43] Ministère du Commerce et des Travaux Publics. Conseil Supérieur de Commerce, *Enquête sur les houilles, 1832* (Paris, 1833), pp. 23–24.

The Anzin Mining Company 171

Because of the Belgian tariff of 1822, Anzin officials eventually asked the French government to consider tariff retaliation. In May 1824, in a letter to the Director General of Customs, who was then Viscount Castelbajac, Jacques Renard proposed that the tariff on Belgian coal should be doubled. The Anzin company, wrote Renard, would refrain from increasing its coal prices for as long as the duty was in force.[44] Renard's proposal, however, was too radical for government officials. By this date, rather than tamper further with the tariff, they preferred to concentrate on plans for improving navigation and reducing tolls on rivers and canals, with a view toward lowering shipping costs.

Tariff protection was of great concern to the Anzin directors because of the high profit-high dividend policy of their family-structured firm. This did not mean, however, that after 1816 the directors took advantage of the tariff by expanding their firm's production of coal as far as possible. On the contrary, in the period 1815–1821, the directors did not attempt to increase coal production beyond the limitations of their existing plant. Old pits were exploited as they always had been, and machinery installed during the early years of the Empire was continued in use. A modest, ineffectual attempt was made in 1816 to drain *"Le Torrent"* by the use of a windmill;[45] but otherwise little was done to augment the company's supply of Anzin-type coal. The directors were actually uncertain whether extraction of this type of coal could ever be increased, in part because no effort had ever been made to investigate thoroughly the real potentialities of the company's concession.[46] Instead, after March 1817, customers were encouraged to order anthracite coal from Fresnes and Vieux-Condé.[47] Thus, at least during 1815–1821, the Anzin company did not maximize production or profits.

It would be an exaggeration to say that the firm was allowed to coast along solely because of the margin of security won by the tariff of 1816. More important, the firm's limited production of coal reflected the generally poor economic-business environment of the early Restoration.[48] The economic dislocations and business uncertainties caused by the fall of Napoleon and the re-establishment of the Bourbon monarchy; the crisis of 1816–1817; the slow mechanization of French in-

[44] National Archives, F12 193 (5), Procès-verbaux du Bureau du Commerce et des Colonies, May 19, 1824.
[45] National Archives, 49 AQ 1 (March 8, 1816).
[46] *Périer Report.*
[47] National Archives, 49 AQ 1 (March 6, 1817).
[48] See Gille, *Recherches sur la formation de la grande entreprise,* pp. 23–33; G. Bertier de Sauvigny, *La Restauration* (Paris: Flammarion, 1955), pp. 269–316.

dustry; the inadequacies of France's internal transportation system—such factors as these undoubtedly convinced the directors that expansion of their plant would be unwise.

In view of the poor economic-business environment of the early Restoration, the Anzin directors cannot be too seriously criticized for the fact that, in 1820–1821, the firm suddenly found itself unprepared to meet an increased demand for coal. Its supplies of anthracite coal from Fresnes and Vieux-Condé remained sufficient, but the demand for Anzin-type coal increased to a level which the company was unable to supply. To make matters worse, loading facilities along the Escaut River, which had been poor previously, were now completely inadequate. No provision had been made for stocking supplies of coal along the river's edge. Coal had to be brought directly from the mines to a small number of docks, where some barges had to wait for three or four months before they could be loaded. A situation of favoritism and bribery arose, and resulted in much ill will toward the company.[49]

Under these conditions the business of the company began to decline. Sales of coal decreased by 39,000 tons between 1821 and 1822 (Chart 1). Merchants who were unable to obtain either the type or amount of coal ordered by their customers began to deal with Belgian firms. Even those merchants who remained loyal to the Anzin company complained of the poor quality of its coal, and there were charges that the company deceived its clients by mixing its coals.[50] Then, in 1822, another misfortune occurred: Belgium imposed its tariff on coal from Fresnes. The Anzin directors began to fear that they would have to dip into the company's reserve fund, ". . . *cette arche de salut de nos établissements pour les temps difficiles.*"[51]

The continued decline in business, growing complaints from merchants and manufacturers, the retaliatory Belgian tariff, and probably, in 1821, the succession of Casimir Périer to the post of his deceased brother Scipion, shook the company out of its complacency and provoked a thoroughgoing and expensive overhaul of its obsolescent plant and lax administration. The first action taken by Casimir Périer and the other directors was to order economies. They began by selling most of the company's horses and wagons and all of its coal barges. Henceforth, private contractors were employed for hauling and ship-

[49] *Périer Report; Renard Report.*
[50] *Renard Report.*
[51] *Périer Report.*

The Anzin Mining Company 173

ping.[52] Next, warehouses were inventoried and 400,000 francs worth of supplies (most of which had been ordered unnecessarily) were sold.[53] The use of oil for lighting purposes at the mines was investigated, found to be more economical, and substituted for candles.[54]

Economies were also made in the payroll. For example, positions as company guards which had been created for older workers were abolished. For miners at the vein the rate of pay remained the same (one franc, fifty centimes per day), but the work load was calculated more closely to provide that each worker extracted enough coal each day to compensate for the cost of medical care and other benefits supplied by the company.[55] Such economies were sufficient to cover an increase in the company's pension payments caused by numerous forced retirements, as well as to provide for a raise in wages ordered in 1824 for miners who risked working over four hundred meters below ground in Anzin pits.[56]

The directors also turned to the improvement of their plant. They noted, for example, that steam engines built for the firm during the Empire were uneconomical; that the system in use for heating boilers was wasteful; and that the operators of the machines, who were most often older employees waiting for retirement, were unnecessarily careless.[57] One of the first measures taken to remedy this situation was the replacement of the superannuated machine attendants by younger men. The directors also ordered the conversion of boiler fire-pots for the use of inferior grades of coal, and steps were taken to improve the heating system of boilers in general. Finally, between 1822 and 1826, almost all old steam engines were replaced by new, two cylinder, high pressure engines patented in France by Humphrey Edwards.[58] At first the company attempted to construct the new engines in its own machine shops, but this proved to be too expensive. Beginning in 1822 the machines were ordered from the Périer-owned Chaillot works, where Edwards had become a partner. In 1826, Casimir Périer reported expenditures by the Anzin company of 457,186 francs for new

[52] National Archives, 49 AQ 1 (May 4, 1822).
[53] *Ibid.* (September 28, 1822).
[54] *Ibid.* (March 13, 1823).
[55] *Ibid.* (September 25, 1823).
[56] *Ibid.* (September 20, 1824).
[57] *Périer Report.*
[58] National Archives, 49 AQ 1 (May 4, 1822; June 21, 1827). For other references to Edwards, see *Bulletin de la société d'encouragement pour l'industrie nationale*, XIV (1815), 297; XVI (1817), 267-30; XVII (1818), 169-74, 365-86.

174   *Richard J. Barker*

steam engines and for the repair of old ones. But he noted also that, since the new engines used only one third as much coal, the company saved about 43,000 francs in operating expenses during 1823–1826.[59]

The company also initiated the first real exploration of its concession. The first major success was the discovery of Anzin-type coal at Abscon in 1822. Six years later an even richer bed of this coal was reached in an experimental pit at Denain. These finds were a boost for the morale of the company, but as seen earlier there still remained the problem of testing various methods for draining underground water deposits and for casing mine shafts and galleries against the shifting sandy subsoil which prevailed in the area. It was not until 1826 that *"Le Torrent"* was brought under control, and even then it was not completely drained.[60]

Meanwhile, to win back the favor of coal merchants and consumers, the company hired salesmen and gave discounts on large orders of coal. In 1824, the directors authorized their general agent to help merchants compete with Belgian coal by granting them extended credit (up to one year) and, if necessary, by reducing the price of medium-size coal by 5 per cent.[61] In 1825, for example, Carlier, Mirland & Company of Dunkerque was given a discount of almost three francs on every ton of Anzin coal supplied to the Royal French Navy, on condition that they ordered at least 3,300 tons of coal each year at regular prices.[62] Earlier, in 1822, in order to offset the retaliatory Belgian tariff, the company reduced the price of coal from Fresnes by 10 per cent for consumers in Belgium.[63]

The company also improved its services by enlarging its loading facilities on the Escaut River. By 1826, fifteen to twenty barges could be served at one time at Anzin. Moreover, the directors began to give closer attention to the problems involved in shipping coal via rivers and canals. In 1820, in order to secure a voice in supervising the upkeep of the Canal of Sensée, which connected the Escaut and Scarpe Rivers, the directors invested 50,000 francs in the company then constructing the canal.[64] Even more important to the company was the Canal of St. Quentin, connecting the Escaut and Somme River basins, and the Canal of Crozat, which joined the Somme and Oise Rivers. Although

[59] *Périer Report.*
[60] *Périer Report.*
[61] National Archives, 49 AQ 1 (May 20, 1824).
[62] *Ibid.* (April 11, 1825).
[63] *Ibid.* (May 4, 1822).
[64] *Ibid.* (September 7, 1820).

The Anzin Mining Company   175

constructed in 1801–1810, this vital link in the canal system of north-eastern France was unsuitable for navigation during the greater part of each year.[65] In 1823, therefore, Casimir Périer was authorized to see to the establishment of a coal depot on the Oise River to assure that coal shipments to Paris would not be interrupted at times when the canals were closed for repairs.[66] Later, in 1827, when the job of improving and operating the two canals was given to Augustin Honorez & Company, the Anzin directors invested one million francs in the project. When Honorez's company was reorganized as a *société en commandite* in 1833 (4,000 shares at 1,000 francs) the Anzin company owned 986, or about one quarter of the shares.[67]

Finally, to complete this survey of the measures taken by Casimir Périer and the other directors to place their firm on a more solid footing, it should be noted that after 1822 even the much vaunted administration of the mines received a thorough reorganization. Partly this was a result of the changeover made in the exploitation of the company's concession. But it is clear too that the directors found that a good deal of laxness, inefficiency, and even cupidity had developed at the mines. The maintenance department in particular came in for much criticism. Mine shafts and galleries had been allowed to deteriorate, buildings were poorly constructed, foundations for steam engines were unsafe, and replacement parts for company machinery were lacking. Evidently, the chief of the department, in collusion with purchasing agents and merchants, had ordered unnecessary supplies at large discounts, and pocketed the profits.[68]

The general shake-up that resulted at the mines can be better imagined than described. Lax employees were dismissed, special inspectors and overseers were appointed, the accounting system was perfected, inventories were held, and company offices at Anzin, Fresnes, and Vieux-Condé were ordered to submit more frequent and more accurate reports to the general agent.[69] After 1822 the administration of the mines at Fresnes and Vieux-Condé was united; and in 1825 the administration at Anzin was divided into two *sous-directions*.[70] Of special importance was the organization of a *"Comité de Conférences*

[65] See Ministère de l'Intérieur, *Situation au 31 mars 1830 des canaux et autres ouvrages entrepris en vertu des lois des 20 juin et 5 août 1821. . . .*(Paris, 1830).
[66] National Archives, 49 AQ 1 (November 13, 1823).
[67] *Ibid.* (June 21, 1827; May 20, 1834).
[68] *Ibid.* (September 28, 1822).
[69] *Ibid.* (September 28, 1822 et seq.).
[70] *Ibid.* (May 4, 1822; September 16, 1825).

176   *Richard J. Barker*

d'Administration," presided over by the general agent. This committee, composed of all important company officials, was ordered to meet three times each month and to submit its reports to the directors. The committee was instituted to give more coordination to the work being carried out at the mines. It also served to instruct the general agent and to give him more personal contact with other company officials.[71] At the same time, the prestige and authority of the general agent was increased. After 1824 company officials were fined heavily when orders from the directors, which were passed on by the general agent, were not carried out in the time limit specified.[72]

In this modernization of the Anzin company after 1821, one detects the determination and inspiration of a strong personality at work. This role was filled by Casimir Périer, who guided the affairs of the firm after Scipion's death in 1821. Although Casimir had many other obligations, business as well as political, he presided over board meetings at Saint-Vaast regularly from March 1821 to March 1823, during the time the firm underwent major reorganization. In this same period, special meetings of the board were also held in Paris, where Casimir resided, and where he headed the firm's branch office.[73] Casimir Périer's report to the directors in June 1826 shows the thoroughness of his knowledge of his firm's affairs.

The Anzin company thus weathered successfully what was in fact the most serious crisis it faced during the Restoration. At the same time, however, the crisis exposed a firm with outdated equipment, limited production, poor service, and lax administration. Scipion Périer's prideful statement in 1818 regarding the excellent administration of the mines was thus unfounded. His argument that the tariff was needed to protect the business of small mining companies in northern France was touching, but events proved that, at least before 1821, the tariff also helped the Anzin company to maintain limited production and high profits. After 1821 the tariff was less effective in keeping Belgian coal out of France, and the Anzin company was forced to take positive action to meet increased competition. It should be noted that the company's position was never desperate. Necessary improvements at the mines were financed through increased reinvestment of earnings, and evidently without recourse to the company's special reserve fund.

[71] *Ibid.* (September 10, 1827).
[72] *Ibid.* (September 20, 1824).
[73] *Ibid.* (October 28, 1828).

The Anzin Mining Company   177

Indeed, dividends were nearly doubled in 1822, and remained at that high level throughout the period of declining sales.

By 1825 the business of the company showed considerable improvement. However, competition with Belgium continued strong, and the company had lost many of its established markets. Also, beginning in 1826 French industry entered upon a period of increasing business stagnation. By 1828 a business depression developed which, merging as it did finally with the Revolution of 1830 in France, did not end until 1832. Throughout the remainder of the Restoration, therefore, in order to offset a necessary reduction in its coal prices in 1828, the newly-renovated and reorganized Anzin company continued to demand, and to receive, tariff protection. The tariff on coal entering France by the Department of Nord was not lowered until 1835, when it was reduced by one half.[74] The Anzin company strengthened its own position in 1828 by staging an elaborate reception at Anzin for Charles X.[75] Casimir Périer and the other directors took care to point out to the king and government officials that their firm would soon be able to provide for the needs of all industries and other consumers of coal in the north of France. Although such extensive service was the stated goal of the company at the time, it was never achieved.

III

In conclusion, the Anzin Mining Company during the Restoration was a closely held family firm, managed by a self-perpetuating board of six directors who practiced a policy of high prices, high profits, high dividends, and tariff protection. During 1815–1821 the firm's management was exceedingly cautious. Maximization of profits was not attempted in this period since the firm's extraction of coal was raised only to the limit that its existing plant would permit. The directors contemplated sharing markets in northern France with smaller mining firms, and cited the welfare of these firms as a factor necessitating continued tariff protection. Tariff protection also allowed the directors to keep coal prices high, and thus to continue to pay high dividends and add to their firm's emergency reserve fund. These phenomena confirm recent interpretations of French entrepreneurship in the nineteenth century. However, it is suggested that the firm's limited extrac-

[74] Ordinances of October 10 and December 28, 1835; law of Juiy 2, 1836.

[75] Regarding this affair, see the interesting anonymous memoir in National Archives, F12 2534A, dossier "Houilles, Lille," s.d. (1833?).

178   *Richard J. Barker*

tion of coal during 1815–1821 was a consequence mainly of the poor economic-business environment of the early Restoration rather than a deliberate, continuing policy on the part of the directors. After 1821, when demand for coal increased in France, Casimir Périer and the other directors ordered a thorough reorganization and renovation of their enterprise. A serious attempt was made to maximize production of Anzin-type coal. The firm's production did not increase dramatically after 1821, but this was a result of difficulties encountered in exploiting new finds of coal at Abscon and Denain. After about 1825 the modernized firm did begin to expand to a new level of production, and the directors broadened their goal to include all consumers of coal in northern France. It would appear, therefore, that with a proper business environment and motivation the Anzin company operated forcefully and efficiently, accepted the necessity for technological change, and expanded its business horizons. While the record of the Anzin company from 1815 to 1821 follows the pattern suggested as typical of French entrepreneurship, the characterization should be broadened to include flexibility of action during favorable circumstances.

RICHARD J. BARKER, *Montclair State College*

Part III
Technology, Markets, Cartels and Corporations

[6]

Economic History Review, 2nd ser. XXXIX, 3 (1986), pp. 392-410

The Rise of Big Business in the World Copper Industry 1870-1930[1]

By CHRISTOPHER SCHMITZ

By any measure, the world copper industry between the 1870s and the 1920s was characterised by the growth of large corporations. Assessed in terms of market share, the extent of vertical integration, or the accumulation of capital, the leading producers appear to have increasingly dominated the industry. By 1929, the capital assets of the leading United States copper firms alone stood in the region of $1·5 billion, while the leading four firms in the industry (also American) controlled more than 50 per cent of world production. This, coupled with the growing presence of multinationals like Anaconda, Kennecott, and Rio Tinto in Latin America and Africa, led to continuing fears being expressed about the monopoly position of these enterprises.

Recent research on the rise of the large-scale business corporation has reorientated analysis away from monopoly profit motives and more in the direction of responses to market imperfections, coupled with technological imperatives. In particular the work of Alfred Chandler and Oliver Williamson has emphasized the role of the large firm as an efficiency instrument, internalizing functions previously performed by the market.[2] Increasingly, from this viewpoint, resource allocation and intermediate product exchange would be conducted within firms in order to minimize the transaction costs of using the market price mechanism.[3]

Chandler and Williamson in large measure derive their generalizations from the experience of manufacturing industry. Consequently, the growth of big business in the copper industry provides a valuable opportunity to assess recent theories of corporate growth in relation to extractive industry. It is the contention of this paper that technological pressures, rather than transactional considerations, have been more significant in the mining and smelting sectors than Williamson might allow, even though the refining and fabricating sectors of the copper industry probably conform more closely to his views.[4] It is possible to show that in the mining industry the rise of big business resulted

[1] Earlier versions of this paper were delivered at La Trobe University, the University of Leeds and the International Mining History Conference, University of Melbourne, 1985. I am grateful for numerous comments from participants at these meetings; also for advice from Roger Burt over a longer period of time.
[2] A. D. Chandler, *The Visible Hand: The Managerial Revolution in American Business* (Cambridge, Mass. 1977); O. E. Williamson, *Markets and Hierarchies: Analysis and Antitrust Implications* (New York, 1975); O. E. Williamson, 'The Modern Corporation: Origins, Evolution, Attributes', *Journal of Economic Literature*, XIX (1981), pp. 1537-68.
[3] L. Hannah, *The Rise of the Corporate Economy* (2nd edn. 1983), p. 3.
[4] Williamson, *Markets and Hierarchies*, pp. 2-4, 60-1, 82-6.

from the logic implied by a series of geological and technological considerations.

I

The extent of business concentration in the copper industry after 1870 can
be assessed at a number of levels. First of all, the size of firms as represented
by their capital assets suggests a strong momentum towards large-scale activity.
Allowing for data deficiencies which make it difficult to construct comparable
long-term indicators of asset growth, it is possible to contrast the size of
leading firms in the mid-nineteenth century with those of later periods. The
leading copper firm in Cornwall and Devon (the world's main producing area
until 1857) was Devon Great Consols. In January 1866, when it stood just
before a long period of decline, this mine had a market valuation equivalent
to $2.98 million.[5] In contrast, the market valuation of the issued stock of
Calumet & Hecla, the leading U.S. (and at times leading world) producer to
1883, grew from a median point of $4·9 million in 1870, to $10·6 million in
1874 and $23 million in 1880.[6] Thereafter the growth of industry capital can
be measured in broad terms by reference to Table 1.

The trend towards the growth of large firms accelerated after 1869, when
a new tariff in the United States heavily increased duties on imported copper.[7]
Behind the shelter of this legislation, the Lake Michigan producers, particularly Calumet & Hecla, rapidly increased their market share, while maintaining domestic prices by dumping copper overseas.[8] During the 1870s Calumet &
Hecla accounted for around 52 per cent of United States output, and dominated
the domestic American market until the early 1880s, when mining at Butte,
Montana commenced on a large scale. A savage price war through the 1880s
led to the emergence of the Butte producers, led by the Anaconda and
Boston & Montana firms, as market leaders.[9] Outside the rapidly growing
and protected American market, few copper firms grew to substantial size
before the 1930s. In Spain, the Rio Tinto and Tharsis companies, working
large low-grade ore-bodies, commanded nominal assets which, together, stood
in the region of about $22 million in the late 1880s.[10] Until 1900, the
other major producing regions, Chile, Germany, Australia, and Japan were
characterized by firms with far smaller capital assets than the leading firms in
the United States. Even with the spread of investment capital into large-scale
mining prospects in Russia, Chile, Katanga, and Northern Rhodesia, between
1900 and 1939, the scale of capitalization of non-U.S. copper firms still lagged
far behind that of firms like Anaconda.[11] Apart from any question of capital

[5] G. C. Goodridge, 'Devon Great Consols', *Transactions of the Devonshire Association*, xcvi (1964), pp.
228-68.

[6] W. B. Gates, *Michigan Copper and Boston Dollars* (Harvard, 1951) pp. 224-7.

[7] F. W. Taussig, *Tariff History of the United States* (New York, 8th edn. 1931), pp. 219-21.

[8] O. C. Herfindahl, *Copper Costs and Prices, 1870-1957* (Baltimore, 1959), pp. 70-2, 246; Gates, *Michigan
Copper*, pp. 39-63.

[9] K. R. Toole, 'The Anaconda Copper Mining Company: A Price War and a Copper Corner', *Pacific
Northwestern Quarterly*, XL (1949), pp. 312-29.

[10] W. R. Skinner, *Mining Manual for 1887* (1887), pp. 376, 435.

[11] By 1937, the largest non-U.S. copper firm was the Rhodesian Anglo American-Nchanga Consolidated-
Rhokana group, with combined assets of $87·4 million.

Table 1. *Leading Corporations in the Copper Industry, 1898-1929*

	1898	1909	1919	1929
United States (assets in $m)*				
Anaconda	52·5	170·2	254·2	680·6
United Copper		50·0		
Greene Cananea		15·0	61·1	
Chile Copper			155·5	
ASARCO		118·6	215·3	241·0
Calumet & Hecla	57·0	57·8	100·0	87·0
Copper Range		40·9	19·9	9·3
Phelps Dodge		49·4	247·3	124·7
Greenwater Copper		34·0		
Kennecott Copper			135·6	337·8
Guggenheim Exploration		36·9		
Utah Copper		25·0	83·8	
United Kingdom ($m equivalent)				
Rio Tinto	19·1	22·5	23·1	39·9
Caucasus Copper		11·1		
Great Cobar		8·5	9·0	
Rhodesian Anglo-American				17·0
Roan Antelope				6·1
Japan ($m equivalent)				
Sumitomo			75·4	69·6
Mitsubishi Mining	7·5	7·5	15·1	46·4
Furukawa		2·5	10·0	10·4
Belgium ($m equivalent)				
Union Minière		1·9	1·5	24·5
du Haut Katanga				
Australia ($m equivalent)				
Mount Lyell	4·4	7·0	6·3	12·1
Chillagoe	7·3	5·3	5·7	
Mount Elliott		3·6	6·1	8·5

* Assets equal nominal capitalization plus debenture issues. Anaconda 1898 includes assets of wholly owned subsidiaries; 1909 includes assets of Amalgamated Copper Co. Calumet & Hecla 1898 represents median market valuation of issued stock; on the same basis 1909 is $64m. Chillagoe 1898 represents assets of Chillagoe Mining & Railway Co. Ltd.

Sources: *Stock Exchange Year Book* (1895-1948); W. G. Skinner, *Mining Manual* (1887-1930); R. L. Nash, *Australasian Joint-Stock Companies Yearbook* (Sydney, 1899-1913); A. D. H. Kaplan, *Big Business in a Competitive System* (Washington, 1954), pp. 145-9.

markets or institutional factors favouring a higher degree of business concentration in the United States than elsewhere, from the early 1880s onwards the United States was both the world's leading producer and consumer of copper.[12] The high degree to which United States copper producers operated within a domestic market, at times relatively unaffected by world market forces, undoubtedly aided their growth.

The increasing size of the leading firms was paralleled by the growth in their market shares. On trend, from the 1880s to the late 1920s the leading four firms increased their share of world mine output from around a third to over a half (Table 2). After 1930, when the United States leadership of the industry faced a growing challenge from the African copperbelt, the extent of market control by the top firms declined. In the sphere of smelting and

[12] In 1883 the U.S. overtook Chile as the world's leading mine producer of copper, a position it maintained until the late 1970s. During the period 1892-1929 the U.S. accounted for 50-65 per cent of world output and some 35-45 per cent of total consumption; Metallgesellschaft A-G, *Metal Statistics* (Frankfurt-am-Main, 1894-1937).

BIG BUSINESS AND COPPER, 1870-1930   395

Table 2. *Mine Production of the Eight Leading World Copper*
Firms as a Percentage of World Output, 1890-1935

Rank of firm:	1890	1900	1912	1923	1928	1935
First	11·0	15·9	15·5	21·2	21·1	16·9
Second	10·5	7·4	11·3	19·0	19·5	13·4
Third	9·8	7·1	8·0	6·2	6·5	7·7
Fourth	8·2	3·8	4·0	4·4	5·9	7·5
Fifth	5·8	3·7	3·1	3·5	3·5	6·6
Sixth	3·8	3·2	2·4	3·3	3·4	5·6
Seventh	2·2	2·3	2·1	3·2	3·1	4·3
Eighth	1·8	2·2	2·0	2·9	2·6	2·7
Firms 1-4	39·5	34·2	38·8	50·8	53·0	45·5
Firms 5-8	13·6	11·4	9·6	12·9	12·6	19·2
Firms 1-8	53·1	45·6	48·4	63·7	65·6	64·7
Coeff. C*	0·045	0·041	0·047	0·091	0·094	0·068

* Coeff. C = Herfindahl's coefficient of industry concentration, calculated from the shares of the top eight firms.
    Sources: 1890, R. P. Rothwell, ed. *Mineral Industry, 1893* (New York, 1894), pp. 236-48; *Mineral Resources of the United States, 1894* (Washington, 1895), pp. 33-58.
    1900, T. R. Navin, *Copper Mining and Management* (Tucson, 1978), p. 396.
    1912-35, O. C. Herfindahl, *Copper Costs and Prices, 1870-1957* (Baltimore, 1959), pp. 165-7.

refining, where capital costs and economies of scale were greater than in mining, the control of the leading firms was even more pronounced. In 1911, the United Metals Selling Co. group (including Anaconda-Amalgamated, the Lake mines, the Arizona Copper Co. and Greene-Cananea) controlled 31 per cent of United States and 22 per cent of world refinery output. The American Smelting and Refining Co. (ASARCO) group (including Utah, Nevada Consols, Ray, and Cerro de Pasco) controlled 24 and 17 per cent respectively, while Phelps Dodge (with its Arizona mines) controlled 13 and 9 per cent.[13] With these three United States groups controlling some 48 per cent of world capacity, two German groups, the American Metal Co. (Metallgesellschaft) and Aron Hirsch und Sohn, between them controlled a further 13 per cent. In 1921, after rapid war-time expansion, the leading three United States firms controlled 74 per cent of world refining capacity, while the American Metal Co. (transferred from German to United States control in 1917) controlled another 8 per cent, and Japanese refineries a further 8 per cent.[14] By 1926 total United States capacity had contracted to around 50 per cent of the world level and following major refinery construction in Europe, Africa, and Canada, to 36 per cent in 1932.[15]

The increased size and growing market share of the leading copper firms arose partly through internal growth, but largely through merger activity. In the United States the three leading groups in the industry, Anaconda, ASARCO-Kennecott, and Phelps Dodge, all grew rapidly from the late 1890s by an active process of horizontal and vertical integration. Indeed, particularly during the great merger movement of 1898-1902,[16] at a time of rapid expansion

[13] *Mining Magazine,* v (1911), p. 464.
[14] R. Allen, *Copper Ores* (1923), pp. 18-19.
[15] W. Y. Elliott et al. *International Control in the Non-Ferrous Metals* (New York, 1937), p. 479.
[16] N. Lamoreaux, *The Great Merger Movement in American Business, 1895-1904* (Cambridge, 1985), pp. 1-5, 155; R. L. Nelson, *Merger Movements in American Industry, 1895-1956* (Princeton, 1959), pp. 71-105, 129-38, 144-53.

396 CHRISTOPHER SCHMITZ

in electrical technology and demand for copper, these giant firms increasingly seemed to epitomize the leading edge of the trust movement.

ASARCO was incorporated in April 1899 with a capital of $115 million, bringing together a number of trans-Mississippi lead smelters. Promoted by interests which included the copper-broking Lewisohn brothers of New York and Henry H. Rogers of the Standard Oil Co., by 1901 it had come largely under the influence of the Guggenheim family. With the construction of a plant at Garfield, Utah, in 1907 ASARCO entered copper smelting, in competition with Anaconda. Thereafter its interests in copper mining and smelting grew steadily. In 1904 the Guggenheims staked a claim in the development of the first of a new generation of giant, low-grade (porphyry) copper mines, with the incorporation of the Utah Copper Co. The Guggenheim Exploration Co. (1899) also pioneered the development of two large Chilean porphyry deposits, at Braden (El Teniente) and Chuquicamata (the latter being sold to Anaconda 1923-29). In 1907 the Guggenheims sold most of their ASARCO stock and in 1915 the main part of the Guggenheims' own copper interests were consolidated into the Kennecott Copper Co. (including Utah, Nevada, Ray, Chino, and Braden). Vertical integration continued with the acquisition of firms like the Alaska Steamship Co. and in 1929 the Chase Co., a leading fabricator. By 1937 Kennecott was the largest United States copper producer, with around 36 per cent of domestic mine production.[17]

From its origins at Butte, Montana in the mid-1870s, the Anaconda Company came to represent the prime example of large-scale, integrated enterprise in the world copper industry by 1929 (Figure 1). Through the 1890s it integrated horizontally into adjacent claims at Butte and vertically into timber, water, transportation, smelting and refining concerns. Its greatest spurt of corporate growth occurred during the great merger boom at the turn of the century, when the giant Amalgamated Copper Co. was floated, in April 1899, with an initial capital of $75 million (increased in 1901 to $155 million), in order to consolidate a large number of mining, smelting and refining interests.[18] The Amalgamated Copper Co., promoted by a powerful combination of Standard Oil interests (H. H. Rogers, J. D. Ryan and William G. Rockefeller) allied with the Lewisohn-Bigelow group and the National City Bank, at once dominated the United States and world copper markets through a complex corporate network. Throughout the life of the Amalgamated Co., Anaconda remained at the heart of the structure. On the liquidation of the former, in June 1915, Anaconda (having already absorbed many of the Amalgamated enterprises in 1910-15) assumed full control. Thereafter, through the 1920s, with capital assets passing half a billion dollars, the corporation made major acquisitions overseas, for instance obtaining in 1923 a majority stake in Chuquicamata, Chile, the world's largest copper mine. It also consolidated its integration into fabrication in 1922, with the purchase for $45 million of the American Brass Co.

Outside the United States, the network of control between copper firms

[17] D. Lynch, *The Concentration of Economic Power* (New York, 1946), p. 135.
[18] F. E. Richter, 'The Copper Mining Industry in the United States, 1845-1925', *Quarterly Journal of Economics*, XLI (1927), pp. 236-91, 684-717; 'The Amalgamated Copper Company: A Closed Episode in Corporation Finance', *Qu. J. Econ.* XXX (1915-16), pp. 387-407.

BIG BUSINESS AND COPPER, 1870-1930   397

Figure 1. *Anaconda: Corporate Growth, 1875-1929*

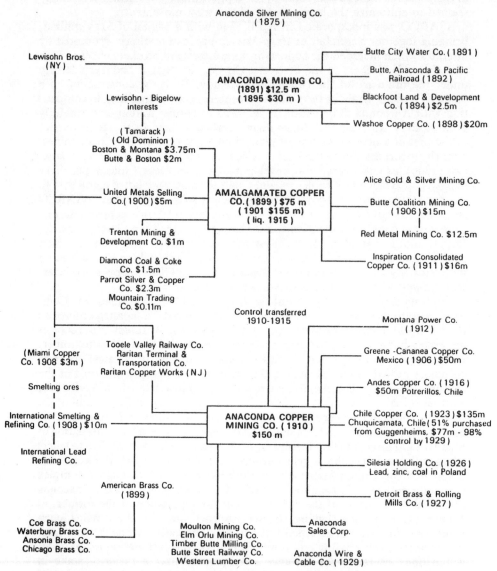

Sources: Stock Exchange Year Book (1913-48); W. G. Skinner, *Mining Manual* (1896-1949); I. F. Marcosson, *Anaconda* (New York, 1957); F. E. Richter, 'The Amalgamated Copper Company: A Closed Episode in Corporation Finance', *Qu. J. Econ.*, XXX (1915-16), pp. 387-407. Tamarack was absorbed by Calumet & Hecla in 1917 and Old Dominion was increasingly associated with Phelps Dodge after 1918.

398   CHRISTOPHER SCHMITZ

generally occurred through less obvious channels. The London and Paris Rothschilds, for instance, held a large interest in Rio Tinto and other Iberian producers from the late 1880s, effectively owned the Boleo mine in Mexico from 1885, and in 1895 exercised an option to buy 25 per cent of the Anaconda stock for $7·5 million (although this interest was soon sold).[19] A number of German firms, including Metallgesellschaft, Aron Hirsch und Sohn, and Beer Sondheimer, also commanded diffuse networks of control through many areas of the world's mining and metal-trading businesses before 1914. The most prominent of these, Metallgesellschaft, operated through a number of major subsidiaries such as the American Metal Co. (1887) and the Australian Metal Co. (1898).

Whilst subject to variation, the profits of the major copper corporations were generally large up to 1930. By the end of that year total accumulated dividends from United States copper companies stood at $2,317 million.[20] Despite the impressive growth and profitability of big business in the world copper industry in the 60 years to 1930, it can be argued that that growth cannot be fully understood simply in terms of attempts to control the market. It is vital to set against the appearance of market domination the fact that the leading companies seem to have been increasingly unable to set prices and control supply for more than a few short-lived periods. Amongst primary commodity prices, those for copper are particularly unstable and through the period 1870 to 1939 were becoming more volatile on trend.[21] The question of price stability and the nature of the price system itself will be considered below. Meanwhile, business concentration in the copper industry, if not following directly from market control, should be approached in the context of the technological and resource-base complex within which this industry was set.

II

The economic exploitation of copper minerals over at least the past two centuries has followed a broad pattern of mining progressively leaner ores from increasingly large individual deposits. This has arisen through a combination of shallow, relatively easily won vein deposits, such as those in Cornwall, becoming exhausted by the later nineteenth century and the contemporaneous development of cost-cutting technology in mining, concentrating, and smelting processes. The decline in average ore grades (Table 3) has been paralleled by shifts in the major types of ore-body being exploited. In geological terms,

---

[19] *Engineering & Mining Journal* (Sept. 1895), p. 294; (Oct. 1895), p. 389; (June 1896), p. 561. The British and French Rothschilds together held 30·8 per cent of the issued ordinary capital of Rio Tinto in 1905, rising to 36·2 per cent in 1929; C. Harvey, *The Rio Tinto Company, 1873-1954* (Penzance, 1981), p. 110; B. W. E. Alford and C. E. Harvey, 'Copper Merger: The Formation of the Rhokana Corporation, 1930-32', *Business History Review*, LIV (1980), p. 338.

[20] Annual returns of North American mining company dividends, in *Eng. & Min. J.* (1908-31).

[21] From the early nineteenth century, the coefficient of variation for the London price of standard grade copper (electrolytic wirebars from 1915) shows a clear trend of increasing instability; 1840-9 the C. V. was 5·7, 1870-9 it was 13·3, 1900-9 17·1, 1930-9 22·5, and by the 1960s was 36·6. For the period 1870-99, J. R. Hanson II, 'Export Instability in Historical Perspective: Further Results', *Journal of Economic History*, XL (1980), pp. 17-23, suggests that in a group of 18 primary commodities only beef and coffee prices were, overall, more volatile than copper prices.

BIG BUSINESS AND COPPER, 1870-1930   399

Table 3. *Declining Copper Ore Grades, 1800-1930*
(*per cent copper*)

1800	9·27	average yield English ores
1850	7·84	average yield English ores
1870-85	6·56	average yield English ores
1886-1905	2·96	average yield Calumet & Helca ores
1906	2·50	average yield United States ores
1915	1·66	average yield United States ores
1925	1·54	average yield United States ores
1930	1·43	average yield United States ores

Source: W. Y. Elliott et. al. *International Control in the Non-ferrous Metals* (New York, 1937), p. 374.

there are three main forms of copper ore-body: massive sulphide,[22] strata-bound, and porphyry deposits. Massive sulphide deposits, usually found in veins or infillings in sedimentary and volcanic rocks, typically have a high-grade metal content (around 4 to 20 per cent copper in the period up to 1939), but with a few exceptions are relatively limited in extent (containing from several thousand to several million tonnes of ore) and almost always have a well defined cut-off point where they meet the non ore-bearing, or "country" rock. Due to their accessibility and ease of working, especially where subject to secondary enrichment and oxidization,[23] vein deposits of this type provided the major source of copper mined until the early twentieth century, for example from the mines of Cornwall and Devon, and of Butte, Montana. Strata-bound deposits are less common than massive sulphides but form generally medium to large bodies (ranging from around a million to 250 million tonnes of ore, commonly averaging 3 to 6 per cent copper, up to 1939). The Kupferscheifer worked in the Mansfield mines of Germany and the stratiform deposits of the African copperbelt are the best examples of this type which, like massive sulphides, tend to have a fairly well defined cut-off against barren country rock. Finally, there are the low-grade "porphyry" deposits (typically running at about 0·45 to 2·5 per cent copper), which are commonly very large (from 100 to 2,000 million tonnes of ore in the 1930s). These huge, low-grade, disseminated orebodies are not usually distinguished by a sharp cut-off between payable ore and barren rock, but rather large tracts of ground in which there is a gradation from relatively high-grade mineralization to material well below the economic definition of payable ore (in the 1930s a cut-off point of about 0·7 per cent copper). This gradation is of significance both in respect of theories concerning the relationship between ore grade and size of orebodies and in the technology required to exploit these deposits.

In general terms it is apparent that there is a fairly strong negative correlation between ore grade and size of deposit. Data relating to 87 leading copper mines/prospects up to 1930-1 have been assembled and the average grade plotted against total copper content (defined as past production plus, in the case of mines/prospects in operation 1930-1, projected reserves).[24] This

[22] Massive, not in the sense of large scale, but in the strict geological sense of discrete mineral aggregations.

[23] Weathering of original (sulphide) ores, by atmospheric action and percolating groundwater, can concentrate the copper content in an enriched zone, and render them easier to smelt.

[24] Regression analysis of the data (where G = average percentage grade and T = copper tonnage in orebody) yields the following results:

$$\log. T = 3.73937 - 2.8948 \log. G \qquad r^2 = 0.5943$$
$$\quad\;\; (0.19252) \quad\;\; (0.25074)$$

Full details of the data set may be obtained from the author.

indicates (Figure 2) that certain broad groupings of mines/ore-bodies were exploited between the early nineteenth century and the 1930s. First, the Cornwall and Devon group consisted of relatively small but high grade mines, working principally between about 1800 and 1870, within the overall limits of about 4·5 to 12 per cent copper in ore-bodies containing up to 50 thousand tonnes of copper. The next group is a high-grade Australian group, including mines in South Australia and Queensland, worked mainly between the 1840s and 1870s, at about 17 to 22 per cent copper and containing 13,000 to 52,000 tonnes of copper. A scattering of points with a trend towards lower grades and higher volume deposits then represents mines working into the early twentieth century. Two major groupings complete the picture; the stratiform African copperbelt deposits, being opened up between 1907 and 1930, with grades of from 3·3 to 7·5 per cent and reserves of around 2·3 to 14 million tonnes of copper, and the important porphyry group, represented by 12 mines in 1931 (nine in the United States and three in Chile). These ranged in grade from 0·95 per cent (Miami, Arizona) to 2·18 per cent (El Teniente, Chile) and in terms of deposit size at 1931, from 450 thousand tonnes (Copper Queen, Arizona) to 22·5 million tonnes (Chuquicamata, Chile). Also plotted is a pyritic sub-group, represented by large, low-grade deposits in Iberia and at Mount Lyell in Tasmania, which are not porphyries but which contained on average less than three per cent copper.

Although there are localized exceptions to this model, such as the copper district of northern Michigan, where the larger deposits tended to exhibit higher grades,[25] in general, as mining companies have moved towards exploiting lower grade ores (as they increasingly must), then they have encountered disproportionately larger scale ore-bodies. This is particularly true of the porphyry coppers where a geological proposition known as Lasky's Law suggests that where there is a gradation from relatively rich to relatively low grade material in a deposit, the tonnage of ore increases geometrically as grade decreases arithmetically.[26] This is illustrated (Figure 2) by the example of Bingham mine in Utah, which moves through time (1899 to 1970) towards a lower grade and higher tonnage. Amongst non-porphyries, where there is a sharper cut-off from ore to barren rock, the relationship appears to be less clear although in general it would appear to hold true, for example with the Anaconda mine at Butte from 1907 to 1964.

III

The implications of this relationship during the last century have been profound. Not only has more of the world's supply of new copper had to come from lower grade and larger bodies of ore, but also mining companies

---

[25] W. S. White, 'The Native-Copper Deposits of Northern Michigan', in J. D. Ridge, ed. *Ore Deposits in the United States, 1933-1967* (New York, 1968), I, pp. 306-7.
[26] S. G. Lasky, 'How Tonnage and Grade Relations Help Predict Ore Reserves', *Eng. & Min. J.* (April 1950), pp. 81-5.

Figure 2. *Major Copper Deposits, 1800-1931: Grade and Tonnage*

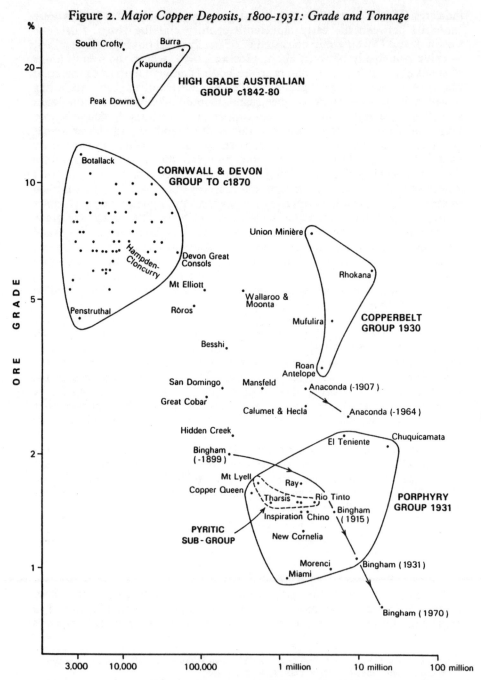

have had to finance larger-scale and more capital-intensive projects, each of which has tended to yield its return over longer periods of time, thus further increasing the true cost of finance. This trend was clearly emerging even in the second half of the nineteenth century, as larger-scale ore-bodies were encountered in the mines of the western United States and the pyritic deposits of Iberia and Tasmania. However, the trend was sharply accelerated by the growing prominence of the huge porphyry deposits, opened up after 1904 (by 1928 these contributed around 40 per cent of annual world mine production[27]), and by the development of the Northern Rhodesian stratiform deposits in the late 1920s.

As early as the 1870s, the opening up of a larger ore-bodies required a new scale of finance. In Spain, the Rio Tinto mines with their estimated 200 million tonnes of ore were purchased in 1873 by a consortium of British and German investors for £3·85 million, with further initial investment required (for example on a railway) to the extent of around £2 million. To cover this outlay the company had to commence working on a large scale and by 1884 was the leading copper producer in the world, processing over a million tonnes of ore a year.[28] Capital investment in Spain was, however, limited (compared with the United States) by the generally labour-intensive nature of the operations. In Tasmania in the early 1890s, the Mount Lyell Co. was opening up a huge pyritic orebody, which prompted the normally flamboyant chairman, Bowes Kelly, to counsel the 1894 A.G.M. that while production of rich silver ores had produced high returns "it is necessary that shareholders should always remember that the enduring and lasting value of the mine, from which we expect regular dividends in the future to come, exists in the enormous mass of low grade ore".[29] A similar sentiment, that the working of large-scale ore-bodies must go hand in hand with long-term and large-scale capitalization, was expressed in 1895 by Marcus Daly, chairman of the Anaconda Mining Co, on the occasion of increasing its capital from $12·5 million to $30 million:[30]

> The policy of the Company from the beginning has been not so much to realize immediate returns as it has been to try to lay the foundation for a long life of activity and usefulness. For this purpose, the profits of the Company have been expended in the enlargement and betterment of the plant until today, in its remodelled, reconstructed, and completed state, it stands without a peer among the copper producers of the world. It can be truthfully said that in all the history of copper mining, no enterprise on so large a scale was ever before projected.

When Daly had first become interested in Anaconda in 1880, he quickly appreciated the need for heavy capital investment, in order to compete with the Michigan mines which were nearer the markets of the eastern seaboard and which dominated the United States copper market. Only a large through-put would ensure sufficiently low unit production costs and to achieve this he had to convince his backers, J. B. A. Haggin, G. Hearst and L. Tevis, to provide an initial personal investment of $4 million. At first "the magnitude

[27] A. B. Parsons, *The Porphyry Coppers* (New York, 1933), p. 6.
[28] Harvey, *Rio Tinto*, pp. 18-35; S. G. Checkland, *The Mines of Tharsis* (1967), pp. 113-5.
[29] University of Melbourne Archives, Mount Lyell Mining & Railway Co. Papers, 2/5/1, minutes of A.G.M. 29 Nov. 1894.
[30] I. F. Marcosson, *Anaconda* (New York, 1957), pp. 88-9.

BIG BUSINESS AND COPPER, 1870-1930   403

of Daly's plan took Hearst's breath away",[31] but within a decade the scale was justified as Anaconda took the leadership of the domestic industry from Calumet & Hecla.

The background to rising capital costs in mining in general, lay with the continual need for technological change. As mines worked deeper and tackled larger and lower-grade ore deposits, the traditional skills of miners had to be supplemented by rock-drills, explosives, ventilation, and improved underground haulage, whilst at the surface better milling techniques, capable of handling larger volumes of ore, had to be implemented.[32] In addition, as the world's mining frontier passed to new regions in the late nineteenth century, mines came to be established in increasingly remote areas, with high costs of labour, power, and materials. The cost of shipping the product to an increasingly distant market, as well as necessitating higher investment on transport infrastructure, also encouraged more mines to integrate vertically into smelting capacity, since this effectively reduced the cost of shipping each unit of metal. With the development of the porphyry copper deposits after 1904, the trend towards higher levels of capital investment and the impetus to large-scale business activity was accelerated, not only because of the huge initial investments required but also the lengthened time scale over which those investments would be realized. In addition, longer lead times were often

Table 4. *Porphyry and Non-porphyry Copper Producers, 1912-16*

	Ore Reserves, million tonnes	Ore grade, per cent	Ore costs per ton ($)	Years' life
1. *Non-porphyries*				
Cape Copper (S)[13]	0·162	4·6		2
Namaqua Copper (S)[16]	0·051	7·1	4·47	3
Hampden-Cloncurry (A)[16]	0·299	6·9	21·54	3
Great Cobar (A)[12]	2·74	2·5		8
Mount Lyell (A)[14]	3·12	2·4	7·00	10
Mount Morgan (A)[14]	3·13	4·2	11·94	10
Mount Elliott (A)[12]	0·455	12·3	27·70	12
2. *Porphyries*				
Nevada Cons. (U)[15]	50·5	1·48	1·67	17
Miami (U)[14]	35·1	0·95	1·88	32
Ray (U)[13]	78·4	1·65	2·38	33
Utah (U)[13]	268·0	1·07	1·60	35
Chino (U)[15]	90·0	1·40	1·84	38
El Teniente (C)[16]	113·7	2·50		78
Chuquicamata (C)[16]	700·0	2·12	2·11	87
Inspiration (U)[15]	97·1	1·40	1·98	125

Notes: Superscript = year data refer to. Years' life = current rate of output/ore reserves. Differences in computing ore costs in original sources suggest caution in their interpretation.

Locations: A, Australia; C, Chile; S, South Africa; U, United States.

Sources: *Mineral Industry* (1911-18); R. Allen, *Copper Ores* (1923); A. B. Parsons, *The Porphyry Coppers* (New York, 1933); J. E. Carne, *The Copper-mining Industry. . . in New South Wales* (Sydney, 2nd. ed. 1908); Queensland Mines Dept. *Annual Report* (Brisbane, 1912-17); Mount Lyell Mining & Railway Co. papers (University of Melbourne Archives).

[31] Toole, 'Anaconda Copper', p. 315; M. P. Malone, *The Battle for Butte: Mining and Politics on the Northern Frontier, 1864-1906* (Seattle, 1981), pp. 22-53.
[32] For detailed discussion of improvements in mining, milling, and smelting techniques see, A. B. Parsons, ed. *Seventy-five Years of Progress in the Mineral Industry, 1871-1946* (New York, 1947), pp. 1-161, 199-222; H. Barger and S. H. Schurr, *The Mining Industries, 1899-1939: Output, Employment and Productivity* (New York, 1944), pp. 105-41, 222-39.

necessary before projects would start making a return. At Chuquicamata, the Guggenheims spent a reported $50 million between 1912 and 1922, opening up the world's largest copper deposit.[33] A comparison of two groups of porphyry and non-porphyry mines around 1911-16 (Table 4) suggests the nature of the difference between their expected life spans, as well as highlighting some differences in their cost structures.

Lower costs in exploiting porphyries resulted from the economies of scale arising through developments in both mining and milling techniques. The majority of porphyries were worked as open-cuts, borrowing blasting and steam-shovel stripping techniques from Michigan iron-ore mining. Where underground mining of porphyries were made necessary by the nature of the orebody, such as at Miami and El Teniente, block caving techniques were employed. The net effect of both these was to replace selective by non-selective methods of mining, in which all material in the mineralized area was removed, waste as well as metallic ore. In the vein mines of Cornwall, Australia, and the United States the skilled "hard-rock" miner had a central role in the ore-winning process and much of the work-culture of mining revolved around his skills in following a tortuous and often deceptive lode. Excavator and truck drivers displaced the skilled miner and through the 1920s further economies were achieved through using increasingly large earth movers. As early as 1915 some marked differences existed in the costs of working copper ores by non-selective (open-cut and caving) methods, compared with traditional stoping methods (Table 5).

Table 5. *Estimated Mining Costs and Labour Productivity for Selective and Non-Selective Mining Methods, 1915*

	Average cost per ton ore ($)	Tons ore per man-shift
Open-cut mines	0·31	24·69
Caving	0·52	12·74
Open stopes	1·25	6·84
Shrinkage stopes	2·68	6·02
Square-set timbering	4·83	1·55

Source: C. W. Wright, *Mining Methods and Costs at Metal Mines in the United States*, United States Bureau of Mines Information Circular 6503 (Washington, 1931), cited by T. J. Hoover, *The Economics of Mining Non-ferrous Metals* (Stanford, 1933), pp. 138-9.

Complementing the move to non-selective mining was a revolution in milling techniques principally brought about by the application of flotation to copper ores. This process was first tried with these ores at Butte in 1912 and by 1915 had been introduced at Inspiration and El Teniente. Its success there soon led to its being generally adopted by porphyry producers and moved one mining engineer to comment in 1932 that "the oil flotation process . . . has meant more to the copper industry, in so far as increased recoveries and reduced costs are concerned, than any other single factor in the past twenty years".[34] Downstream in the production process, advances in smelting and refining moved this part of the industry nearer continuous

[33] Parsons, *Porphyry Coppers*, p. 93; Elliot et. al. *International Control*, p. 404.
[34] P. Yeatman, *Choice of Methods in Mining and Metallurgy* (New York, 1932), cited in D. W. Fuerstenau, ed. *Froth Flotation: Fiftieth Anniversary Volume* (New York, 1962), p. 21.

operation (for instance by the growing practice after 1890 of leaving the semi-finished copper matte in the furnace while it was recharged), at the same time reducing costs by larger scale working.[35] The net effect of all these technological changes, and one which reflected the impetus to big business in the United States industry, was its capital-output ratio, which increased markedly on trend from 0·76:1 in 1870 to 2·46:1 in 1919 (in 1929 prices).[36] The opportunity cost of not having adopted these technologies is suggested by one calculation that all the copper produced in the United States in 1929-30, by the methods known in 1912-15, would have cost an average 12·7 cents a pound rather than the actual cost of 6·06 cents.[37]

The opening up of porphyry and large stratiform deposits also increased the impetus to longer term planning and larger scale capitalization in the industry, inasmuch as they could be fairly accurately delineated with a minimum of exploration activity. With just a few exploratory drill holes, deposits such as Inspiration, Ray, or Roan Antelope, could be fully assessed in advance of any mining activity. This is in sharp contrast to vein mining where great uncertainty attached to any forward planning. Indeed, it could be argued that "permanent" mining corporations, that have become so prominent in the world mineral industry since the end of the nineteenth century, have largely grown out of particular mining areas where a high degree of forward planning was possible. The Rand banket reef, the massive lodes at Anaconda, or the low-grade ores of Spain and Chile, provided a more stable long-term environment for their respective companies and led to the steady growth of houses like Consolidated Goldfields, Rio Tinto Zinc, Anaconda, and Kennecott. For the first time, capitalist enterprise in metal mining could compete with manufacturing industry in terms of financial planning and long-term growth. The longer-term strategy of such mining corporations would also be encouraged, according to Chandler, by the formation of a managerial hierarchy that itself became "a source of permanence, power, and continued growth".[38] In this way, firms such as Anaconda were induced to maintain continuous exploration programmes, to ensure future mining projects of sufficient scale to match their asset growth.

IV

Whilst economies of scale have propelled successful copper companies towards a larger scale of operations, they have also been prompted towards vertical integration, particularly downstream into refining and then into fabricating, by the desire to instill a degree of control into unstable markets for their products. As Chandler and Williamson have indicated, the internalization of intermediate product exchange within one firm can provide great

---

[35] Between 1890 and 1906 the smelting furnaces at Anaconda were expanded from 50 feet in length (capacity 122 tons/24 hrs) to 116 feet (270 tons/24 hrs), whilst fuel/ore ratios improved from 1:2·75 to 1:4·19; W. H. Dennis, *A Hundred Years of Metallurgy* (1963), p. 135.

[36] I. Borenstein, *Capital and Output Trends in Mining Industries, 1870-1948* (New York, 1954), p. 36.

[37] Parsons, *Porphyry Coppers*, pp. 13-16; in 1929, equivalent to a gross saving of $132 million on U.S. domestic copper production.

[38] Chandler, *Visible Hand*, p. 8.

advantages over the use of competitive market modes of contracting. Contractual uncertainties are avoided and transactions costs minimized, and in the words of Williamson, "the parties to an internal exchange are less able to appropriate subgroup gains, at the expense of the overall organization".[39]

The move into fabrication owes much to the greater value-added that accrues there compared with the earlier stages of production and with the lesser degree of volatility in prices for semi-manufactured products. For example, in the period 1912-13, the mean monthly New York price for ingot electrolytic copper was 15·88 cents a pound compared with a price of 21·88 cents for sheet copper (the latter thus enjoying a premium of 38 per cent over the raw metal). At the same time, the price of electrolytic copper fluctuated more widely than for sheet.[40] These facts no doubt helped prompt Anaconda to move into fabrication in 1922 with the acquisition of the American Brass Co, the leading United States fabricator. On the occasion of the merger, the Anaconda chairman J. D. Ryan commented:[41]

> The time has come when we cannot compete in the industry if we control only one stage of the business. Anaconda is not now able to operate its mines at a steady and economical rate. We have had high prices during periods of scarcity and low prices during periods of depression. . . . We believe that great benefits will arise by reason of the proposed merger. The raw material supply will be assured at steady prices . . . . In this way, from the mine to consumer, there can be one just and fair profit, and the industry will be stabilized.

One consequence of moving into refining was an immense increase in capital requirements, not only to equip the plants but for financing the stock of copper necessarily tied up in the process. Because of their high set-up and running costs, only ten electrolytic refineries were built in the United States up to 1911.[42] One report in 1908 suggested that the value of copper tied up in the electrolytic vats (representing a capacity of 400 thousand tonnes per annum) was around 50 thousand tonnes, valued at about $14·5 million.[43] Only firms the size of Anaconda or ASARCO could afford to finance this order of fixed capital.

The impression therefore emerges that the growth of big business in the copper industry owes much to a combination of geological and technological factors, in conjuction with market pressures, all of which have conspired to impel large mining and smelting companies to become even larger. This was in order to be able to finance, in a stable planning environment, the scale of operations necessary to sustain the growth in the world's demand for this raw material.

V

In recent years, the work of Chandler and Williamson has transformed the approach to the study of big business and the relationships between markets

[39] Ibid. pp. 6-7; Williamson, *Markets and Hierarchies*, p. 29.
[40] The coefficients of variation of monthly prices 1912-13 for electrolytic and sheet copper were, respectively, 7·92 and 5·59.
[41] Marcosson, *Anaconda*, pp. 175-6.
[42] T. R. Navin, *Copper Mining and Management* (Tucson, 1978), pp. 65-6.
[43] *Australian Mining Standard*, 23 Sept. 1908, pp. 357-8.

BIG BUSINESS AND COPPER, 1870-1930   407

and firms.[44] In particular, the concept of transactions costs has allowed a fundamental re-evaluation of the process of vertical integration. Assuming that the market mechanism of neo-classical economics is only used by firms at a cost (in essence the transactional costs of gathering market information, of advertising and contracting), the pressure will be to internalize these functions within the firm, where it is economical to do so.[45] This in turn has only been permitted by, and has encouraged, the development of new forms of managerial organization as detailed by Chandler.[46]

The transactions costs incurred by the copper industry in using the market mechanism have always been high. In common with other primary commodity markets, that for copper is subject to a high degree of instability, due in large measure to short-run inelasticities of demand and supply.[47] This resulted in pressure towards oligopolistic business forms and market controls even before 1870, as copper producers sought to reduce the uncertainties and costs attendant on contracting in ever fluctuating market conditions.[48] However, market control before 1870 rarely, if ever, entailed attempts at vertical integration. Not only, as Chandler has pointed out, did the slow growth of managerial divisionalization outside railway enterprises hinder this development before the 1870s, but also, it is argued here, in the case of the copper industry, vertical integration was promoted strongly by the move towards larger scale ore deposits, often increasingly remote from major markets. Once integration from mining to smelting was effected by such firms as Anaconda, then the transactions costs motive to integrate into refining and fabrication could assume larger proportions.

If big business in the copper industry has arisen mainly through the trend towards larger ore deposits, coupled with the pressures of an inherently unstable market, there still remains the question of whether these large corporations have had any significant effect in reducing price competition. There is a well established body of literature which credits such companies as Anaconda and Kennecott with having exercised some considerable degree of oligopoly power through the present century.[49] It can be argued, however, that there have been effective limits to such power. These arise from a combination of the short-run inelasticity of demand and supply (and hence the volatility of prices), the relatively weak barriers to industry entry, and the

---

[44] See, for example, S. J. Nicholas, 'Agency Contracts, Institutional Modes, and the Transition to Foreign Direct Investment by British Multinationals before 1939', *J. Econ. Hist.* XLIII (1983), pp. 675-86; Y. Suzuki, 'The Formation of Management Structure in Japanese Industrials, 1920-40', *Business History*, XXVII (1985), pp. 259-82; D. C. North, 'Transaction Costs in History', *Journal of European Economic History*, 14 (1985), pp. 557-76.

[45] Williamson, *Markets and Hierarchies*, pp. 29-51.

[46] Chandler, *Visible Hand*, pp. 1-6, 9-10, 240 ff.

[47] R. F. Mikesell, *The World Copper Industry: Structure and Economic Analysis* (Baltimore, 1979), pp. 154-7.

[48] R. R. Toomey, *Vivian and Sons, 1809-1924: A Study of the Firm in the Copper and Related Industries* (1985), pp. 312-46. An alternative response from the 1870s was the increasing use of hedging contracts on the London Metal Exchange, to reduce contractual uncertainties within a competitive market context; Economist Intelligence Unit, *The London Metal Exchange* (1958), pp. 21-2, 26-48, 65-9.

[49] D. Mezger, *Copper in the World Economy* (1980), p. 44, argues "the price of copper on the world market cannot be derived from usual notions of the relationship of supply and demand", while up to 1934 another source contends that "the years 1923 to 1926 make up the only period which we can class as 'normal' (competitive) in the history of copper since 1913"; Elliott et al. *International Control*, p. 427.

high propensity to substitution in the medium term, and the international nature of the market for copper coupled with the dual pricing system that prevails.

There is a considerable weight of evidence in recent studies that in anything but the short term, competitive price models provide the best explanation of the functioning of the world copper market.[50] The dual pricing system itself assumes great significance in these models. That is, whilst the majority of copper traded since the late nineteenth century has been sold under contract by the major producers (particularly in the United States), there remains a vigorous and influential free market, primarily centred on the London Metal Exchange. Since 1877 the LME has offered a forum for trading in physical copper (and more importantly in copper futures), which enables daily prices to be generated which are widely held to reflect the current balance of supply and demand in the world market, even though it only handles a fraction of world supply.[51] Studies such as those of Felgran show that not only have producer prices tended to follow those of the free market but that the former have not shown any particular tendency towards greater stability, except where they have been held considerably below market prices.[52]

In past periods of high prices brought about through market manipulation by leading producer groups, most notably the Secretan corner of 1887-9 and the Amalgamated pool of 1899-1900, the evidence suggests that alternative sources of supply from scrap copper and small, independent mines soon helped undermine their control. During 1929-30, when the American producers' combine, Copper Exporters' Inc. tried to hold the price at nearly 18 cents a pound in the face of world depression, the main result appears to have been the rapid development of the Northern Rhodesian copperbelt.[53] Also, by the 1930s, aluminium was becoming a viable substitute for copper in many areas of consumption. Despite the high costs of establishing large-scale mining and smelting/refining capacity, it is clear that the barriers to entry in the industry are weak. Even in the short run there is evidence that high prices will stimulate large numbers of small mines to commence production (reinforcing flows of scrap on to the market).[54] In the longer term, even high-cost operations like those of the Rhodesian copperbelt mines can be stimulated to undertake development.

As far as predatory price-cutting aimed at restricting competition is concerned, there is little evidence that this was practised to any significant degree before the 1950s, unless one excepts the vicious price war of the mid-1880s between Calumet & Hecla and Anaconda, which had the more specific aim of

[50] B. R. Stewardson, 'The Nature of Competition in the World Market for Refined Copper', *Economic Record*, 46 (1970), pp. 169-81; S. D. Felgran, 'Producer Prices Versus Market Prices in the World Copper Industry' (unpublished Ph.D. thesis, Yale University, 1982), pp. 35-6, 58-61; E. C. Hwa, 'Price Determination in Several International Primary Commodity Markets: A Structural Analysis', *International Monetary Fund Staff Papers*, XXVI (1979), pp. 157-88.
[51] Mikesell, *World Copper Industry*, pp. 81-93; R. Gibson-Jarvie, *The London Metal Exchange* (1976).
[52] Felgran, thesis, pp. 35-6, 58-61.
[53] Elliott et al. *International Control*, p. 67.
[54] C. J. Schmitz, 'Small is Sometimes Beautiful: Advantages of the Micro-project in the Australian Copper Industry, 1953-81', *Camborne School of Mines Journal*, 83 (1983), pp. 29-33. The growing role of scrap in the U.S. market is clear; in 1910-24 this was 22·8 per cent of consumption, rising to 33·3 per cent 1925-39; C. J. Schmitz, *World Non-ferrous Metal and Prices, 1700-1976* (1979), p. 34.

bringing down the new Butte producer. Indeed, during the 1920s the eventually disastrous build-up of excess capacity in the world copper industry was largely brought about because the leading producers failed to restrict the entry of new capacity by price cutting. The scope that large mining corporations has for cutting prices is also severely limited due to their continually moving towards larger-scale and more capital-intensive operations. With the marked trend to higher volume, lower grade ore-bodies and by integration into smelting and refining, the capital charge to each unit of production is increased, and with less elastic capital costs, supply becomes less elastic.[55] In certain circumstances such producers may even be tempted to increase output against falling prices, to maintain revenue, suggesting the possibility of a backward-sloping supply curve.

In the late 1950s Orris Herfindahl undertook a study of past price and market behaviour in the copper industry, in order to answer questions about the long-term cost and depletion of non-renewable resources. He concluded that, with a few exceptions, such was the long-run competitive nature of the world (and United States) copper market, that prices could be taken as a proxy for costs. He argued that "since the turn of the century, there have been no periods of collusion that produced price increases as large as those brought about by Secretan and Amalgamated".[56] In fact, since 1913 the copper industry has been dominated by a secular downturn in deflated prices.

Table 6. *London Metal Exchange Copper Prices, 1870-1939*
Standard grades, £ per metric tonne, in current and at 1913 prices

	current prices	1913 prices
1870-9	78·06	67·88
1880-9	60·25	66·21
1890-9	53·42	68·49
1900-9	70·86	82·40
1910-14	66·36	68·41
1915-19	115·60	59·28
1920-9	73·40	43·69
1930-9	43·77	42·09

Source: C. J. Schmitz, *World Non-ferrous Metal Production and Prices, 1700-1976* (1979), pp. 270-2.

A comparison of current and deflated prices (Table 6) suggests that, as far as copper is concerned, the supposed price depression of the last quarter of the nineteenth century is largely a myth, but that a pronounced price fall, in real terms, began during the First World War and continued up to the Second. It is against this background that attempts to control the market by successive American-led producers' groups after 1919 must be measured.

Significantly, comparison between the deflated prices which successive market corners achieved shows a similar steady downward trend. In terms of 1913 prices, the Secretan corner topped out at around £93·67 a tonne (on the London market), while the Amalgamated pool reached £86·75, and the 1929 price plateau of the Copper Exporters' Inc. only represented the equivalent of £61·80.[57] Thus were all attempts at market control and price fixing trapped

[55] Elliott et al. *International Control*, pp. 430-2.
[56] Herfindahl, *Copper Costs*, p. 154.
[57] This despite Copper Exporters' Inc. controlling some 63·5 per cent of world output 1926-9; ibid. p. 124.

410   CHRISTOPHER SCHMITZ

within the long-term dynamic of technological and organizational change
which inexorably reduced costs and prices. Increasing economies of scale in
conjunction with the transactional economies enjoyed by vertically integrated
firms, as emphasized by the Chandler and Willamson models, resulted in
declining real costs. These were, in turn, largely translated into declining real
prices, with little evidence of sustained super-normal profits being made by
the leading producers. In all, Herfindahl concluded that "there is a body of
opinion that tends to credit the copper industry with a degree of monopoly
power that it does not have".[58] The continued instability of copper markets
from 1870 to 1930 and beyond was at one and the same time a sign that market
control was not readily attainable and signalled a strong incentive to further
vertical integration for producers.

University of St Andrews

[58] Ibid. p. 10.

[7]

THE
ECONOMIC HISTORY
REVIEW

SECOND SERIES, VOLUME XXXVII, No. 3, AUGUST 1984

SURVEYS AND SPECULATIONS, XXIII

The Development of the South African Gold-Mining Industry, 1895-1918

By PETER RICHARDSON and JEAN-JACQUES VAN HELTEN

The second half of the nineteenth century was the great era of gold discoveries. Between 1849 and 1898 a regular series of strikes was made in north America, Australasia, southern Africa, and Asiatic Russia. The gold rushes began in California in 1849. Two years later attention focused on the British colonies of New South Wales and Victoria in south-eastern Australia. In the following two decades, Australasia continued to be the main source of new gold, with discoveries in New Zealand in the 1860s and Queensland in the 1870s. In the 1880s, southern Africa became the magnet for the diggers: first in the eastern Transvaal at Barberton, then on the Witwatersrand in 1886. In the final decade of the century, it was north America and Australia once again which sustained the gold frontier: in 1893 "the golden mile" at Kalgoorlie in the Western Australian desert threatened for a time to outbid even the riches of the South African Rand, whilst in the frozen wastes of the Klondyke and Alaska gold prospectors endured almost unimaginable hardships in what was to prove the last of the classic rushes.[1] Less spectacular, but no less important, was the steady development of the Russian gold-mining industry throughout this period, spreading eastward from the Ural mountains to the Yenisei, the Lena, and the Amur rivers to cover much of Siberia.[2]

The economic consequences of these discoveries were dramatic. The increase in gold production paved the way for a currency revolution of international dimensions. In 1851 the annual value of new gold output was $(US) 67m. By

[1] W. P. Morrell, *The Gold Rushes*, (2nd ed., 1968), pp. 74-118, 200-313, 374-411; G. Blainey, *The Rush that Never Ended: A History of Australian Mining*, (Melbourne, 3rd ed., 1978), pp. 5-104, 161-208; P. Vilar, *A History of Gold and Money, 1450-1920* (1976), pp. 319-31; see also W. R. Ingalls, 'Chronology of the Gold and Silver Industry, 1442-1892', *Mineral Industry, Its Statistics, Technology and Trade*, I (1893), pp. 225-31.

[2] Morrell, *The Gold Rushes*, pp. 43-73; Olga Crisp, ed. *Studies in the Russian Economy before 1914* (1976), passim.

320   PETER RICHARDSON AND JEAN-JACQUES VAN HELTEN

1899, this figure had increased to $(US) 311·5m. At the same time there had been a relative decline in the output of newly mined silver. In the period 1848-1860, the production ratio of silver to gold fell from 16:1 to 4:1; despite a rise thereafter, silver never regained the pre-eminence it had once possessed.[3] These changes in the output of gold and silver provided the material basis for the adoption of a gold exchange standard by the countries of the industrializing world. Between 1850 and 1896, most of the major trading nations of Europe, together with the Russian Empire and the United States, followed the earlier English example and finally abandoned silver as the basis of their currency; thereafter, the value of their money was expressed in terms of gold.[4] At a time of expanding world trade, the move toward a single international currency system was assisted by the expansion of gold production which resulted from these discoveries.[5]

Urbanism and immigration also followed in the wake of the larger gold discoveries. The population of California, for example, rose from 14,000 to 250,000 between 1849 and 1852.[6] Between 1895 and 1898, there was a net outward migration of 75,500 United Kingdon citizens to South African ports as a result of the economic expansion generated by the Witwatersrand gold fields.[7] Gold rush towns grew with similar speed. San Francisco was a city of 35,000 inhabitants within three years of the opening of the diggings there.[8] The expansion of Melbourne in Victoria as a result of gold was almost as rapid, rising from 29,000 to 123,000 in a single decade.[9] Johannesburg supported a white population of 25,000 in 1889, a figure which nearly quadrupled in the following decade.[10]

The discovery in 1886 of the Witwatersrand gold fields in the South African Republic was arguably the most important of all of these famous nineteenth-century discoveries. The gold mines of South Africa have supplied an increasingly large proportion of the world's newly mined gold. As early as the first decade of this century, the Transvaal colony, within which lay the Witwatersrand and several other minor gold fields, was the largest single producer of gold in the world.[11] However, the impact of the Witwatersrand discoveries was greater than a consideration of its place in total world production reveals. Its regional impact was also profound, not least because the

[3] W. R. Ingalls, 'Gold Production and Commodity Prices', *Mineral Industry*, XVII (1908), p. 416; R. P. Rothwell, 'The World's Production of Gold and Silver', *Mineral Industry*, I (1893), p. 211.

[4] M. de Cecco, *Money and Empire: The International Gold Standard, 1890-1914* (Oxford, 1974), pp. 39-61.

[5] A. G. Ford, *The Gold Standard, 1880-1914: Britain and Argentina* (1962), p. 26; see also D. Innes, 'Capitalism and Gold', *Capital and Class*, 14 (1981), pp. 10-14; J. J. Van-Helten, 'Empire and High Finance: South Africa and the International Gold Standard, 1890-1914', *Journal of African History*, 23 (1982), pp. 529-48.

[6] E. J. Hobsbawm, *The Age of Capital, 1848-1875* (1977), pp. 79-80.

[7] P. Richardson and J. J. Van-Helten, 'The Gold-Mining Industry in the Transvaal, 1886-99' in P. Warwick, ed. *The South African War: The Anglo-Boer War, 1899-1902* (1980), p. 21.

[8] Hobsbawm, *Age of Capital*, p. 79.

[9] G. Davidson, *The Rise and Fall of Marvellous Melbourne* (Melbourne, 1979), p. 6.

[10] K. F. Bellairs, *The Witwatersrand Gold Fields: A Trip to Johannesburg and Back* (1889), p. 33, quoted in D. H. Houghton and J. Dagut, eds. *Source Material on the South African Economy, 1860-1970*, I, *1860-1899* (Cape Town, 1972), p. 302; for later figures on the growth of Johannesburg, see C. Van Onselen, *Studies in the Social and Economic History of the Witwatersrand*, I, *New Babylon* (1982), p. 2.

[11] Ingalls, 'Gold Production and Commodity Prices', p. 424: by 1908 the Transvaal produced 30% of the world's output of gold.

discovery of the Witwatersrand formed part of what is sometimes called "the mineral revolution" in southern Africa. The finding of gold on a large scale in the Transvaal was preceded in 1870 by the discovery of what was then the largest source of diamonds in the world at Kimberley in Griqualand West. The gold discoveries also coincided with the discovery of large deposits of coal in the Transvaal and the neighbouring Natal colony.[12] This tripartite transformation in the productive capacity of the region changed the whole political and economic constellation of South Africa. The development of industrial capitalism in the region was markedly accelerated, whilst the long era of dispossession of independent African chiefdoms was finally completed, paving the way for the mobilization of large numbers of African labourers to provide cheap labour for this industrial revolution.[13]

As a major cause of these changes, the gold-mining industry found itself at the centre of successive controversies involving the South African Republic and British imperial authorities, culminating in the Jameson Raid of 1895 and the Anglo-Boer war in 1899. The industry itself was described by contemporaries as monopolistic and politically partial in these disputes, an opinion which has been repeated by historians on many subsequent occasions. In this article we propose to contribute to this continuing controversy, paying attention to one particular aspect, the changing economic structure of the gold-mining industry itself. The argument is divided into three parts. The first, which embraces sections I and II, surveys the arguments which have been developed to explain the significance of the emergence of deep-level mining on the Rand. In the second part, which covers sections III to IV, we attempt to show the limitations of this debate and the erroneous conclusions that it has generated. We then posit an alternative explanation of corporate behaviour based on little-studied aspects of the history of Rand mining. In sections V and VI, we outline the contribution that this re-examination can make to the debate about the development of capitalist relations in the Witwatersrand mining industry. Finally, section VII offers a brief survey of our main findings.

I

In the context of mining history, the importance of the Witwatersrand was emphasized by one particular feature which marked it off as qualitatively different from anything that had preceded it. As Lehfeldt wrote nearly sixty years ago:

> With the development of this field gold mining came for the first time into the normal economic categories. Alluvial and quartz mining elsewhere has always been so speculative that no clear connexion between costs of production and return could be predicted of it, but on the Rand gold mining is an industry rather than a gamble,

[12] On the diamond discoveries, see R. Turrell, 'Kimberley: Labour and Compounds, 1871 to 1888' in S. Marks and R. Rathbone, eds. *Industrialization and Social Change in South Africa: African Class Formation, Culture and Consciousness, 1870-1930* (1982), pp. 45-76. On the mineral revolution in general see C. W. de Kiewiet, *A History of South Africa Social and Economic* (1941), pp. 115-20: D. Hobart Houghton, 'Economic Development', in M. Wilson and L. Thompson, eds. *The Oxford History of South Africa*, II, *South Africa, 1870-1966* (1975), pp. 10-22.

[13] For a recent review of the very extensive literature on this area see Marks and Rathbone's 'Introduction' to *Industrialization and Social Change in South Africa*, esp. pp. 9-17.

and the economic results, not perhaps of a single mine, but of the field are calculable.[14]

The key to an understanding of this statement lies in an appreciation of the fact that the Witwatersrand had itself been transformed from a field of outcrop workings to one where deep-level mining was the order of the day. The development of the deep-levels derived from the realization that the reefs, or beds of gold-bearing conglomerate, descended southward at a flattening angle of dip at right angles to the strike of the outcrop. In 1889-90, anticipating benefits from this phenomenon

> shrewd promoters occupied ground on the southern side of the outcrop companies. Consequently [by] 1894, the field had two rows of mines running parallel across country. The original row of mines was called the outcrop mines, and the second or more southerly row of mines was called the 'deep-levels', and in places there was the nucleus of another row of mines (named second row deeps) searching for reefs at even greater depths.[15]

The outcrop companies remained, for more than a decade thereafter, the linchpin of production on the field, although they represented a constantly declining proportion of output and dividends as deep-level mines came into production and the older and smaller outcrops were exhausted. Thus, in 1888, 97·9 per cent of all dividends came from companies working down to 1,000 feet. By 1898, this figure had declined to 4·6 per cent and by 1913 it was as low as 4·1 per cent. By contrast, 30·1 per cent of all dividends in 1913 came from mines working between 300 and 4,000 feet.[16]

The origins of this important transformation in the nature of the Rand mines has, not surprisingly, been subjected to very close scrutiny by historians and has become the subject of, at times, impassioned debate. By common consent, this debate began in 1965 in the pages of this journal, when Geoffrey Blainey made his now celebrated call to historians to examine the material base of the political action taken by a conspiratorial group of mineowners in Jameson's ill-fated attempt to overthrow the Boer government in 1895. In so doing, Blainey drew attention to one of the fundamental facts of the Witwatersrand at that time, "a distinction between outcrop and deep mines [which] seems vital for understanding the motives of the Rand capitalists . . . . All but a few companies can be safely classed as either deep-level or outcrop companies." In Blainey's view, "the Jameson Raid . . . was essentially the revolt of the two big companies that were heirs to the treasures and problems of the deep-levels."[17]

As Donald Denoon has recently remarked:

> There was general delight at Blainey's fireworks. The present writer [Denoon] seized upon the divergent economic interests of deep-level and outcrop gold mines to help explain divisions within the Transvaal British community after the war; Dr Ian Phimister developed Blainey's analysis of Cecil Rhodes's economic interests to illuminate Rhodesian history; and the magisterial *Oxford History of South Africa* incorporated his analysis within the liberal summation of South African history.[18]

[14] Quoted in S. H. Frankel, 'Fifty Years on the Rand', *Economist*, 19 Sept. 1936, p. 523.

[15] G. Blainey, 'Lost Causes of the Jameson Raid', *Econ. Hist. Rev.*, 2nd ser., XVIII (1965), p. 353.

[16] S. H. Frankel, *Capital Investment in Africa: Its Course and Effects* (1938), Table 13, p. 85.

[17] Blainey, 'Lost Causes of the Jameson Raid', pp. 354, 364.

[18] D. Denoon, 'Capital and Capitalists in the Transvaal in the 1890s and 1900s', *Historical Journal*, 23 (1980), pp. 111-12; the works to which Denoon referred were: D. Denoon, ' 'Capitalist Influence' and the

SOUTH AFRICAN GOLD   323

The delight to which Denoon referred might have been general but it was by
no means universal. The initial attack on Blainey's thesis came from two
historians. First, Robert Kubicek pointed out that, though the distinction
between outcrop and deep-level mines was indeed a valid one at the level of
production, the structure of *ownership* which prevailed on the Rand in the
1890s was a more important feature of the various groups of mining finance
houses which, even at this early stage, dominated the Rand gold mines:

> The capital needs and structures of the several financial groups engaged in gold-
> mining operations on the Rand varied considerably. The Wernher Beit complex
> had already access to a variety of dependable sources of continental capital which
> it used carefully and very successfully in both outcrop and deep-level operations.
> Gold Fields, though much less ably and soundly managed, had realized a large
> profit in getting out of outcrops which it used to move into deep-levels . . . . But
> neither it nor Wernher Beit were in 1895 as vulnerable financially as their main
> competitors. The groups controlled by Barnato, Robinson and Farrar had engaged
> in speculative ventures which not only fleeced the investing public . . . but which
> also left their respective financial establishments in an exposed position. All three,
> though they had interests in producing outcrop companies, were engaged, if not
> overextended, in floating new outcrop or deep-level ventures. The Albu and Goerz
> interests, backed by German banks, and therefore possessed of a more secure capital
> base, were in 1895 just in the process of becoming firmly established through the
> reconstruction of outcrop companies and acquiring deep-level claims.[19]

The second attack came from Arthur Mawby. Like Kubicek, Mawby rejected
Blainey's distinction between outcrop and deep-level companies and emphasized the ownership profile of the various groups:

> . . . The distinction between outcrop and deep-level mining houses is untenable.
> Eckstein's and Consolidated Gold Fields were simply the *first* mining houses to
> move into deep-level mining. As it became obvious during the later 1890s that the
> future of gold mining lay in deep-levels, so most mining groups acquired deep-
> level holdings.[20]

Mawby went further, however, and attacked the economic basis of the distinction which Blainey and his supporters had drawn beween outcrop and deep-
level companies:

> The theory's greatest weakness, however, is the implication that the only significant
> variable in mining economics was the cost of operations . . . . The theory . . .
> overlooks the most important variable in Rand mining economics—the variations
> in the quality of the gold reef, and thus in the amount of gold contained in any
> given amount of rock.[21]

Although Mawby came close at this point to rejecting any distinction between
outcrop and deep-level companies, it is clear from the earlier quotation above

Transvaal Government During the Crown Colony Period, 1900-1906', *Hist. Jour.* XI (1968), pp. 301-31;
I. R. Phimister, 'Rhodes, Rhodesia and the Rand', *Journal of Southern African Studies*, I (1974), pp. 74-
90; L. Thompson, 'Great Britain and the Afrikaner Republics, 1870-1899' and 'The Compromise of Union'
in *The Oxford History of South Africa*, II, pp. 309, 314 and 335.
   [19] R. V. Kubicek, 'The Randlords in 1895: A Reassessment', *Journal of British Studies*, XI (1972), pp.
101-2.
   [20] A. A. Mawby, 'Capital Government and Politics in the Transvaal, 1900-7: A Revision and a Reversion',
Hist. Jour., XVII (1974), p. 392.
   [21] Ibid. p. 389.

324 PETER RICHARDSON AND JEAN-JACQUES VAN HELTEN

that he did in fact accept that it was valid at the level of production rather than of ownership.

The force of the arguments advanced by Kubicek and Mawby was later acknowledged by Richard Mendelsohn in an important restatement of the debate. Whilst he reiterated, as have all who have written since Blainey, the fundamental importance of the distinction between the types of producing mine in the 1890s, he also found that the

> critics' conclusion that the boundary between deep-level and outcrop ownership was blurred needs some qualification. It does not particularly apply to . . . The Gold Fields Company, which had made use of the share market boom of 1894/5 to liquidate its outcrop holdings . . . . As regards Wernher Beit, its deep-levels were of greater strategic importance to it than its outcrops. The deeps were relied upon to provide the firm's profits long after its outcrops were worked out.[22]

In this modest restatement of the outcrop/deep-level distinction at the level of ownership, Mendelsohn was careful to acknowledge that Blainey's contrast between the financial stability of the conspirators' firms and the instability of the non-conspirators' firms was too stark. At the same time, he distinguished more clearly than Kubicek or Mawby had between the conspirators, Wernher Beit, Gold Fields and Farrar/Anglo-French, and the other groups:

> The chief difference between firms inside and those outside the conspiracy was that the former were committed by 1895 to long-range mining programmes while the latter were either preoccupied with stock-jobbing or were content with modest holding operations. This meant that the conspirators stood to gain far more over the long-term than the rest from the replacement of a self-willed and frequently obstructive Boer government by one more easily manipulated by the mining industry.[23]

II

The treatment of deep-level production after the war of 1899-1902 has been less detailed, but no less controversial. Donald Denoon was the first historian to try and project Blainey's argument forward into the period of British rule in the Transvaal:

> By the reconstruction period [1900-1907] the new deep-level mines had gained the upper hand both in the Chamber [of Mines] and in relations with Government; but the newly poor outcrops were still rich enough and angry enough to create difficulties.[24]

Denoon reiterated this argument in slightly more detail in his book, *A Grand Illusion*, but failed, as Mawby has pointed out, to extend his analysis much further.[25] For his part, Mawby was content to echo Kubicek in claiming that the outcrop/deep-level distinction as applied to the mining finance houses was no more valid after the war than before it:

[22] R. Mendelsohn, 'Blainey and the Jameson Raid: The Debate Renewed', *Jour. South. African Stud.*, VI (1980), p. 160.
[23] Ibid. p. 170.
[24] Denoon, ''Capitalist Influence' and the Transvaal Government', p. 320.
[25] D. Denoon, *A Grand Illusion: The Failure of Imperial Policy in the Transvaal Colony During the Period of Reconstruction* (1973), p. 191.

A consideration of the directorships of the deep-level mines of the Rand for 1904, shows, in the first place, that *all* major gold-mining houses (other than Robinson's), and also some lesser gold-mining groups, were represented on the boards of, and thus had important interests in, deep-level mines which they did not control. It shows, in the second place, that all major gold-mining houses (other than Robinson's) and also some of the lesser groups, controlled deep-level gold-mining companies. And it shows, in the third place, that all major mining companies held outcrop mining interests during the period under discussion.[26]

More recently, Shula Marks and Stanley Trapido have attempted to inject some of the subtlety of Mendelsohn's restatement of the pre-war period into the discussion about the reconstruction period. In a perceptive and wide-ranging article about the nature of the South African state, they suggested that the overwhelming power of the Wernher Beit group of mining companies was evidence of continuing differences of commitment to long-term mining programmes in the postwar period. Although Marks and Trapido indicated that some of these differences derived from the vast spread of the Wernher Beit investments outside the mining industry in South Africa, they clearly stated that commitment to long-term mining was influenced primarily by considerations within the productive section of the industry itself.[27]

In a review of the debate published two years after Marks and Trapido's article, Denoon returned to the charges levelled against him by Kubicek and Mawby. Although he did not consider the implication of Marks and Trapido's point, he tacitly accepted Mawby's argument that his stark contrast between outcrop and deep-level groups had not stood up to analysis. In summarizing the period between the Jameson Raid and the end of the Anglo-Boer war he wote:

> [Between 1895 and 1902] mining expanded enormously, and involved increasing numbers of men in wage labour. Two share booms occurred, one in 1899 and another in 1902. Kubicek has shown how some groups used the 1895 boom to restructure and rationalize their holdings, and it seems *prima facie* very likely that other groups used the later booms to alter their interests in pursuit of long-term profits. The successful development of deep-level mines, even in the difficult circumstances of Kruger's republic, may well have encouraged groups of companies to edge towards deep-level development.[28]

This may well be true; but, even if the contrast between outcrop and deep-level groups cannot be sustained, it does not necessarily follow that there were no other, equally significant, differences between the mining houses. As Marks and Trapido have observed, such differences derived from the variable value and productive capacity of different mines, whether or not they were outcrop or deep-level concerns. This contrasts strongly with a later work by Kubicek which seeks to explain the differences between the various groups on grounds such as the nationality of their major partners, their different sources of capital and different financial development strategies, whilst virtually ignoring the question of differing productive capacity of the holdings of the finance houses.[29]

[26] Mawby, 'Capital, Government and Politics in the Transvaal', pp. 391-2.
[27] S. Marks and S. Trapido, 'Lord Milner and the South African State', *History Workshop Journal*, 8 (1979), pp. 58-60.
[28] Denoon, 'Capital and Capitalists in the Transvaal', p. 119.
[29] R. V. Kubicek, *Economic Imperialism in Theory and Practice: The Case of South African Gold-Mining Finance, 1886-1914* (Durham, N.C., 1979), pp. 195-6; for the review mentioned see S. Marks, 'Scrambling for Africa', *Jour. African Hist.*, 23 (1982), pp. 111-12.

326   PETER RICHARDSON AND JEAN-JACQUES VAN HELTEN

In the remainder of this article we wish to explore some of the potentials and limitations of this extension of the debate.

III

Neither Mendelsohn nor Marks and Trapido examined in any detail the "long-range mining programmes" to which they referred. Had they done so, they would have discovered that, in the decade after the Boer War, these program-mes were by no means synonymous with deep-level production. Thus, it is clear that the undoubted productive supremacy of Wernher Beit was based on its rich inheritance of outcrop and first-row deep-levels. The two Wernher Beit groups, Rand Mines and H. Eckstein, controlled seven of the best outcrop companies on the rich central section of the Rand and had control over, or were "largely interested" in, ten out of the thirteen first-row deep-level companies lying on the dip of the central outcrops. The great majority of these first-row deeps were at the beginning of their productive life in 1902.[30] No other group at the time had such a large collection of mines under its control; more importantly, no other group had such a good balance in its producing mines between short-life high dividend payers (i.e. good outcrops) and longer-life deep-levels that were at the beginning of their profitable life. The only other group in 1902 to come anywhere near Rand Mines/Eckstein in the number of producing companies was the Johannesburg Consolidated Investment Corporation [J.C.I.]. But the life expectancy and quality of its outcrops failed to match those of its rival, whilst its deep-levels were smaller in number and were concentrated in the broken and poorer sections of the Central Rand.[31] In this respect, then, there can be little doubt that distinctions within the industry to which Marks and Trapido drew attention were justified. These distinctions derived from a well-balanced and long-term production programme based upon an astute juxtaposition of outcrop and deep-level concerns.

Essentially, the development strategy involved bringing new properties to a state of productive readiness to replace mines brought into production at an earlier time and nearing the end of their profitable lives. After 1902, it is clear that the developing mines along the Witwatersrand were essentially deep-level companies, many of which were classified as second- or third-row deeps. For example, in 1908 *The Economist* summarized the development profile of the Central Rand in the following terms:

> the rich mines . . ., called the outcrops, are being rapidly exhausted, and in a few years familiar dividend payers will cease to pay. Their places will, however, be taken by the deep-levels of the first, second and third grade [i.e. rows] . . . . The future of the Rand depends upon its deep-levels, and the latter, in their turn, will depend for their success upon economical working.[32]

[30] *Economist*, 17 May 1902, p. 773.
[31] *Report received from Mr. M. Birchenough the Special Commissioner Appointed by the Board of Trade to Inquire and Report upon the Present Position and Future Prospects of British Trade in South Africa, 1904*, (P.P. 1904, LXI), p. 17; a full breakdown of the different contributions of the major groups to the actual production on the Rand is given in Kubicek, *Economic Imperialism*, p. 54.
[32] *Economist*, 25 Jan. 1908, pp. 155-6.

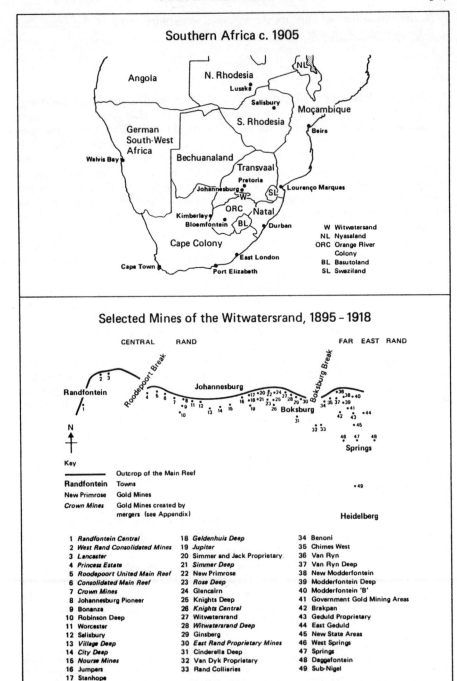

Southern Africa c. 1905

W   Witwatersrand
NL   Nyasaland
ORC   Orange River Colony
BL   Basutoland
SL   Swaziland

Selected Mines of the Witwatersrand, 1895–1918

CENTRAL   RAND   FAR   EAST   RAND

Key

————	Outcrop of the Main Reef
Randfontein	Towns
New Primrose	Gold Mines
Crown Mines	Gold Mines created by mergers (see Appendix)

1 Randfontein Central	18 Geldenhuis Deep	34 Benoni
2 West Rand Consolidated Mines	19 Jupiter	35 Chimes West
3 Lancaster	20 Simmer and Jack Proprietary.	36 Van Ryn
4 Princess Estate	21 Simmer Deep	37 Van Ryn Deep
5 Roodepoort United Main Reef	22 New Primrose	38 New Modderfontein
6 Consolidated Main Reef	23 Rose Deep	39 Modderfontein Deep
7 Crown Mines	24 Glencairn	40 Modderfontein 'B'
8 Johannesburg Pioneer	25 Knights Deep	41 Government Gold Mining Areas
9 Bonanza	26 Knights Central	42 Brakpan
10 Robinson Deep	27 Witwatersrand	43 Geduld Proprietary
11 Worcester	28 Witwatersrand Deep	44 East Geduld
12 Salisbury	29 Ginsberg	45 New State Areas
13 Village Deep	30 East Rand Proprietary Mines	46 West Springs
14 City Deep	31 Cinderella Deep	47 Springs
15 Nourse Mines	32 Van Dyk Proprietary	48 Daggafontein
16 Jumpers	33 Rand Collieries	49 Sub-Nigel
17 Stanhope		

In this respect there was much less difference between the major groups, than in the area of their productive capacity. At the end of the Boer War, Rand Mines/Eckstein between them had five non-producing companies directly under their control: the Village Deep, the Robinson Central Deep, the South Nourse company, the Modderfontein Extension and the New Modderfontein companies. This compared with no less than twenty-one producing companies in the same year.[33] Two other groups, singled out by Mendelsohn but not considered by Marks and Trapido (the Consolidated Gold Fields Company and the Farrar/Anglo-French Exploration group) also had a healthy balance between producing and developing deep-level properties. In 1902, Goldfields had only two producing mines—the Robinson Deep and the Simmer and Jack Proprietary—together with a clutch of eleven deep-levels, mainly second-row properties approaching the productive stage at varying speeds. Similarly, the Farrar/Anglo-French Exploration group had only four producing mines but nine developing deep-level companies in its predominantly East Rand holdings.[34] Two other groups, A. Goerz & Co. and S. Neumann, also showed a healthy distribution of assets between producing and developing properties, though their portfolios were distributed over larger areas of the West Rand and the as-yet unproven East Rand.[35]

IV

Given the overwhelming trend towards deep-level mining in these development programmes on the Central Rand, it is not surprising that, in the course of the third decade of active mining on the Witwatersrand, the once predominant form of outcrop production began to fade from the scene with increasing rapidity. With the passing of the outcrop mines, the phase of "mixed" production drew to a close. In part, this was the result of simple exhaustion of payable reserves in many outcrop-claim areas. Thus, within five years of re-commencing production after the War, the Johannesburg Pioneer, Stanhope, and the Worcester companies all went out of production.[36] In 1908 the Eckstein-controlled Bonanza mine went into liquidation after a "life of exceptional prosperity".[37] In 1912 the Salisbury mine, which had produced continuously since 1887 (except for the period of the War), also disappeared, having distributed £248,823 in dividends.[38] Other failing outcrops were used to finance new investment or to provide capital goods for other companies into which they were absorbed. Thus, in 1908 profits from the old Jumpers gold mine began to be diverted to finance the development of new mines— the Chimes West and Benoni companies—on the East Rand.[39] In 1909, the

[33] *British Trade in South Africa* (P.P. 1904, LXI), p. 17.
[34] Kubicek, *Economic Imperialism*, p. 109; *Economist*, 31 May 1902, p. 846; *S.A. Trade Report, 1904*, p. 17.
[35] Kubicek, *Economic Imperialism*, pp. 144-5, 148-9.
[36] *Economist*, 10 May 1902, p. 732; *Mineral Industry*, XVII (1908), p. 398 and XXI (1912), p. 379.
[37] *Mineral Industry*, XVII (1908), p. 398.
[38] *Mineral Industry*, XXI (1912), p. 379.
[39] *Mineral Industry*, XVII (1908), p. 404.

"almost exhausted" Crown Reef was absorbed into Crown Mines Ltd. to provide mill infrastructure rather than the assets of a developed mine.[40]

However, there was another important reason for the disappearance of the outcrop/deep-level distinction in these years. As the Appendix indicates, all the groups then operating were affected by a major wave of mergers on the Central Rand between 1906 and 1911. This movement effectively ended any lingering distinction between outcrop and deep-level mines, and it also created substantially larger claim areas and a smaller number of producing mines with greatly enlarged stamping capacities. Thus, in the year which began in September 1909 the number of producing mines fell from 68 to 59 as a direct result of this policy, eliminating such famous outcrop and deep-level names as the Crown Reef, Langlaagte Deep, Robinson Central Deep, Geldenhuis Estate, Jumpers Deep, and four Randfontein companies.[41]

There were four motives behind this transformation. First, there was the need to reduce costs as a direct result of the irregularity of the ore values found in small productive units. As Lionel Phillips of Wernher Beit explained to his fellow partner F. Eckstein:

> The conditions of mining during the last few years have gone through a considerable transition. In the old days, and with small appliances, the object was to get a high grade, and in those days faith in the regularity of the gold deposition in the sedimentary deposits here was too great. It was quite true that nowhere in the world before has been found such a wonderfully even distribution of the metal taken over a large area; but the more we work the mines the more evident it becomes that over small distances the deposit is most erratic. This being the case, the old habit of working a rich narrow streak must, as it has already done, give place to working larger and larger bodies . . . .[42]

Secondly, there were "the obvious advantages of economy which should be possible to a group of mines brought together under one control".[43] Thirdly, there were the advantages of reinforcing existing assets rather than involving companies in the uncertainty associated with risky exploration ventures, such as the Far East Rand. This can be seen by examining the extent to which Rand Mines/Eckstein shied away from risk-taking. Both companies took a particularly prominent part in the merger movement which swept across the Central Rand between 1906 and 1911. The key year for the Wernher Beit companies was 1908/9. The Appendix shows that no less than six major mergers in this year involved this group, out of which grew extensions to the Village Deep, City Deep, Nourse Mines, Geldenhuis Deep and the Rose Deep, and a wholly new mine, the Crown Mines. These changes involved the disappearance of twenty-two separate mining concerns. In addition, in November 1909 Rand Mines Ltd. acquired the whole of the claim property of Rand Mines Deep Ltd.

As the chairman of Rand Mines Ltd., R. W. Schumacher, observed at the AGM, "the whole year [i.e. 1909] has been one of strengthening and

[40] *Economist*, 7 May 1910, p. 1033, Report of the chairman's speech and proceedings at 15th AGM of Rand Mines Ltd.

[41] *Mineral Industry*, XIX (1910), pp. 275-6.

[42] Phillips to Eckstein, 2 Mar. 1908, in M. Fraser and A. Jeeves, *All that Glittered: Selected Correspondence of Lionel Phillips, 1890-1924* (Cape Town, 1977), p. 185.

[43] *Economist*, 15 Sept. 1906, p. 1507.

330   PETER RICHARDSON AND JEAN-JACQUES VAN HELTEN

consolidating our assets and of making provision for the future . . . ."[44] This policy of reinforcing existing assets rather than seeking out new higher risk business was also reflected in the group's acquisition of a controlling interest in East Rand Proprietary Mines [E.R.P.M.] in 1911, formerly controlled by the Farrer/Anglo-French Exploration group,[45] and in the acquisition of the mines controlled by S. Neumann and Co. in 1916.[46]

Finally, there was the pressing need to find new sources of working capital as a result of the prolonged downturn in the market for South African mining shares which followed the collapse of the 1902-3 share boom.[47] The consequences of this period of capital starvation were profound, as W. Fischer Wilkinson, the Transvaal correspondent of the influential New York journal, *The Mineral Industry* explained:

> In some cases the deep-level areas, which have been amalgamated with producing mines immediately above them, have belonged to companies which have either exhausted their working capital, or not had sufficient funds to bring them into the producing stage. The mining houses which controlled them expressed their inability to obtain the necessary capital from their shareholders, or the public, and were not prepared to finance these companies from their own funds. The Simmer Deep, the City Deep, the Knights Central, the Jupiter and the East Rand amalgamations may be quoted as examples of consolidation brought about largely for financial reasons . . . . The position at the commencement of 1908 was that many deep-level companies were in a desperate financial condition. Their funds were exhausted, or insufficient to bring them to the producing stage. Fresh capital was wanted, and it was not obtainable, and it was evident that even if fresh capital were obtained it would be a long time before these properties would be able to pay dividends. The adoption of the policy of amalgamation saved the situation. By consolidating with the producing companies the necessity of raising fresh capital was avoided. The shareholders in the deep-mines became partners in the dividends of the producing mines, giving in return their ground and whatever cash assets they happened to possess. The producing mines received as compensation for the increase in their capital the prospect of an extended life and were enabled with the funds supplied by the deep-mines to work on a large scale and consequently at a reduced cost of working.[48]

V

Long-range mining programmes involved prospecting for new gold-bearing ground. In the period 1902-18 this too highlighted the growing commitment of all groups to deep-level mining. At this time, in marked contrast to the prewar period, the greatest opportunities lay, not in deep-level ground of the Central and West Rand, but on the eastward extension of the Main Reef series known as the Far East Rand. These gold-bearing formations occurred on a wide area of ground which ran from Modderfontein to Springs and more

[44] *Economist*, 7 May 1910, p. 1032-4, Report of chairman's speech and proceedings at 15th AGM of Rand Mines Ltd.

[45] Phillips to Eckstein, 18 Dec. 1911, in Fraser and Jeeves, *All that Glittered*, pp. 254-6.

[46] Phillips to Wallers, 16 Dec. 1916, in Fraser and Jeeves, *All that Glittered*, pp. 297-9.

[47] S. H. Frankel, *Investment and the Return to Equity Capital in the South African Gold-Mining Industry, 1887-1965: An International Comparison* (Oxford, 1967), pp. 17-22; see also Kubicek, *Economic Imperialism*, pp. 22-9.

[48] *Mineral Industry*, XVII (1908), pp. 401-2.

intermittently on to Nigel and Heidelberg. In 1912 the American *Engineering and Mining Journal* claimed without undue exaggeration that "up to a few years ago this area, with the exception of one or two established mines, was looked upon with some disfavour as being highly speculative and much poorer than the main portion of the Witwatersrand. It has now become alive with expansion and progress."[49] This "expansion and progress" supported nine producing mines by 1914, operating at a gross profit of 12s. 11d. per ton. This compared with 43 producing mines on the Central Rand operating at an average profit of 8s. 5d. per ton. By 1918 the number of producing companies on the Far East Rand had risen to 11, whilst those on the Central Rand had fallen to 38. In addition the average profitability of Far East companies had risen to 16s. 3d. per ton whilst companies on the central Rand had fallen to 3s. 9d. per ton. By 1919, 70 per cent of total distributed dividends were coming from the Far East Rand. "This increasing difference in the profitability of mines on the two fields . . . was achieved through a rising revenue per ton and a lower increase of working costs per ton of Far East Rand mines compared with those on the Central Rand."[50]

In one important respect the gold deposits of the Far East Rand differed substantially from those of the Central Rand: they were usually overlaid with deposits of coal.[51] On the farms of Geduld, Springs, de Rietfontein, Daggafontein, Brakpan, Schapenrust, and Witpoortje this meant that collieries preceded gold mines, and that, when developed as gold mines, these were deep-level operations. Only on the more northerly and earlier-developed of the East Rand farms of Modderfontein and Kleinfontein was the familiar outcrop of the Central Rand to be found.[52]

Examination of the changing balance of power between the groups, as shown by the extent of their commitment to the deep-levels of the Far East Rand, gives a picture of the post-1902 mining industry that is radically different from that drawn by Marks and Trapido, or for that matter by Mendelsohn. There seems little doubt that some of the most substantial investment and profits in the post-war era were made, not by the groups that had secured good deep-level ground in the 1890s, but by those that had failed to secure a lien on these richer properties of the Central Rand.

The two groups with a considerable amount of German capital, the General Mining and Finance Corporation and A. Goerz & Co., not only displayed a modest spread of investment between producing and developing mines on the Central Rand, but secured valuable properties on the East Rand which they were actively bringing into production by the time the Anglo-Boer War came to an end. General Mining had three properties that lay on the East Rand, Rand Collieries, the Van Ryn mine, and the Cindarella Deep, which lay on the deep-level dip of the E.R.P.M.[53] Goerz & Co., on the other hand, was

[49] Quoted in *Mineral Industry*, XXI (1912), p. 381.
[50] D. Innes, 'The Mining Industry in the Context of South Africa's Economic Development, 1910-1940' in *Collected Papers of the Institute of Commonwealth Studies (University of London), The Societies of Southern Africa in the 19th and 20th Centuries*, 7 (1975-6), p. 143.
[51] A. P. Cartwright, *The Gold Miners* (Cape Town, 1962), p. 177.
[52] Ibid. pp. 178-9.
[53] Kubicek, *Economic Imperialism*, pp. 144-6; Mawby, 'Capital, Government and Politics', p. 392, n. 17.

arguably the real pioneer of the Far East Rand, having secured options before the war of 1899-1902 on the farms of Modderfontein 167, Geduld, and Witpoortje from which were to emerge the Modderfontein Deep Level, Van Dyk Proprietary, and Geduld Proprietary Mines, and later East Geduld. These companies were to prove, after much trial and tribulation, "the foundations of the fortunes of the group that was to become the Union Corporation Ltd. . . . [although] it was only in December 1914 that Geduld [Proprietary] declared a maiden dividend of five per cent."[54]

Perhaps the most dramatic reversal of fortune amongst the old groups was that associated with J.C.I. At the end of the war of 1899-1902 the affairs of the group were in a bad way, having suffered considerably in the mining crash of 1895-6, the war itself, and the failure of Carl Hanau's Coronation Syndicate. Nevertheless, by judicious use of profits, particularly from three rich outcrop companies, the Ginsberg, Glencairn and the New Primrose, together with the selective sale of other outcrop assets, J.C.I. was able to push ahead with the development of its deep-level properties (the Witwatersrand and the Van Ryn Deep).[55] Between 1910 and 1918 this situation was further transformed, first by the acquisition of two ultimately rich Far East Rand properties— Government Gold Mining Areas (Modderfontein) Consolidated Ltd. in 1910 and New State Areas in 1918—and secondly by the purchase in 1917 of the mines of the J. B. Robinson group.[56]

If the changing fortunes of the older groups were mirrored in their commitment to the Far East Rand, this was even truer of another group which came to prominence solely on the strength of its holding on the Far East Rand, the Consolidated Mines Selection Co. Ltd. [C.M.S.]. This company had held mineral rights on the Far East Rand since the end of the nineteenth century and was actively associated with development of Brakpan and Springs mines.[57] Through the latter company, the C.M.S. was also closely involved with another group having "substantial mineral rights in the area", the Transvaal Coal Trust. By 1916, C.M.S. had managed to secure control of the Transvaal Coal Trust, and in order to secure further expansion in the area of the Far East Rand it promoted the Anglo-American Corporation in 1917.[58] With the rapid addition of the West Springs and the Daggafontein mines to the group's portfolio, it became "one of the big financial houses of the Rand".[59]

By contrast, the three expansion-orientated groups of the 1890s, the Wernher Beit companies, Consolidated Gold Fields, and Farrar/Anglo-French were much more cautious in exploiting the possibilities of the Far East Rand. Wernher Beit companies initially took a prominent part in the exploration and development of the East Rand. Through the New Modderfontein Gold Mine Co. and later the Modderfontein 'B' Co., the group first appeared to match the exploratory drive of the C.M.S. and the Goerz Group. Indeed,

[54] Cartwright, *The Gold Miners*, pp. 177-8; Kubicek, *Economic Imperialism*, pp. 148-50.
[55] Kubicek, *Economic Imperialism*, pp. 122-5, 197.
[56] Cartwright, *The Gold Miners*, pp. 180-3, 187; Fraser and Jeeves, *All that Glittered*, pp. 216, 282-3.
[57] *Economist*, 30 Oct. 1909, p. 881, Report of the chairman's speech and proceedings of AGM of Consolidated Mines Selection Co. Ltd., 29 Oct. 1909; W. Skinner, *The Mining Manual for 1908* (1909), pp. 258-9.
[58] Innes, 'The Mining Industry', pp. 143-4.
[59] Cartwright, *The Gold Miners*, p. 194.

SOUTH AFRICAN GOLD   333

development went ahead so fast on Wernher Beit's two Modderfontein properties that both were producing by 1912, and by the middle of the First World
War had become the stars in an otherwise lacklustre portfolio of low-grade
companies.[60] However, the evidence suggests that, with the change in the
mineral law initiated by the introduction of the mining-lease system under
the new gold law of 1908, Wernher Beit's initiative began to falter.[61] Thus,
in the same year Lionel Phillips, a partner in the firm of H. Eckstein, wrote
that

> cutting up the area [government held land in the Far East Rand] in the manner
> proposed, robs the whole scheme of its glamour and makes each individual property
> more speculative. Some of them will no doubt be very good and others possibly so
> low grade as to be only just payable . . . . There is certainly more risk where the
> fortunes of a company will be dependent upon any one given area only.[62]

The consequence of this attitude was that in a rival bid with J.C.I. for the
area subsequently known as Government Gold Mining Areas (Modderfontein)
Consolidated Ltd., Rand Mines underpriced their offer and lost out to their
rivals.[63] Given these developments, it is not surprising that Alan Jeeves and
Maryna Fraser concluded in their book *All that Glittered* that "by 1910 . . .
in the critical area of new business, the initiative had begun to pass to others."[64]
    Not that Rand Mines was alone in its tardiness in accepting the challenge
of the mining-lease system on the East Rand. The General Mining and Finance
Corporation was also offered the same ground and was similarly reluctant to
tender.[65] However, the failure of Rand Mines to take up the challenge of
these new business opportunities casts some doubt on the extent of their
commitment to long-term mining programmes beyond that enshrined in the
relatively safe areas of productive first-row deep-levels and the outcrop areas
of the farm Modderfontein. Even before the Union of South Africa came into
being, it seems that the Wernher Beit companies had become a force for
conservatism, in stark contrast to their behaviour in the 1890s. The consequences of this change were to be revealed much more clearly when Wernher
Beit's successor company, Central Mining and Investment Corporation Ltd.,
found itself in 1917-8 "largely excluded from the most significant business
available on the Rand since 1909".[66]
    Consolidated Goldfields and Anglo-French Exploration showed no more
radical commitment to the Far East Rand than did Wernher Beit. Both
Goldfields and Farrars showed a modest interest in the possibilities of joint
ventures with Rand Mines/Eckstein under the new round of mining leases in
1917/8, but both were more content to develop and improve their existing

    [60] Fraser and Jeeves, *All that Glittered*, p. 282.
    [61] This system was established under the Gold Law of 1908, Transvaal Act No. 35 of 1908, which was
made a Union Statute after 1910. Under Act No. 30 of 1918, the Mining Leases Board was made a statutory
body. "It is, in effect, a method of leasing the right to exploit gold resources to the highest bidder. The
system also assumes that areas shall be large enough, and in other ways suitable for what is in the opinion
of the Government Mining Engineer a workable mining proposition": Frankel, *Capital Investment in
Africa*, p. 104.
    [62] Phillips to Eckstein, 26 Oct. 1908, in Fraser and Jeeves, *All that Glittered*, p. 198.
    [63] Phillips to Wernher, 24 Dec. 1909, in Fraser and Jeeves, *All that Glittered*, p. 202.
    [64] Fraser and Jeeves, *All that Glittered*, p. 13.
    [65] Cartwright, *The Gold Miners*, p. 182.
    [66] Fraser and Jeeves, *All that Glittered*, p. 284.

334   PETER RICHARDSON AND JEAN-JACQUES VAN HELTEN

assets on the Central Rand. As we have seen, at the end of the war of 1899-1902 the Goldfields company had only two producing mines, together with a number of developing second-row deep-levels on the Central Rand, and two important properties in the Nigel district beyond the proven end of the Far East Rand.[67] Between 1902 and 1914, the company broadened its productive base considerably, bringing into production all of its second-row deeps on the Central Rand, and, after much expense, the ultimately very profitable Sub-Nigel company. At the same time, Goldfields pioneered some of the most successful cost-cutting schemes associated with the mergers of 1906-11, consolidating its deep-level holdings into five large blocks of claims known as the Robinson Deep, the Simmer and Jack Proprietary, the Simmer Deep, the Jupiter, and the Knights Deep.[68] The Farrar/Anglo-French Exploration group's efforts were more limited. Its most successful venture throughout this period continued to be the producing mines of the New Kleinfontein group.[69] The formation in 1908 of the giant E.R.P.M. out of eight producing and developing companies was a disaster for the group, and financial mismanagement by George Farrar led to a loss of overall control.[70] Production difficulties continued to plague this new giant mine for a considerable time after the coup against Farrar in 1911, although it ultimately proved to be a great profit earner.[71] After 1912, the group confined itself to appreciable blocks of shares in ten mines along the Central Rand.[72]

VI

This shift to predominantly deep-level mining after 1902, as exemplified in both the amalgamations of the Central Rand and the opening of the Far East Rand, had significant consequences. The productive base of the industry was transformed. Large-scale industrial organization and financial criteria became the predominant forms of operation. Between 1906 and 1910, the main period of the amalgamation movement, the tonnage milled rose from 16,366,829 tons to 24,837,259 tons, whilst the number of stamps working increased from 8,200 to 9,205.[73] The average output per stamp per 24 hours increased at this time from 5.34 tons to 7.19 tons, largely as a result of heavier stamps and the introduction of tube mills, which, within this five-year period, had increased from 2 to 181.[74] At the same time, the average claim area of mines in existence increased from 287 in 1898 to 663 in 1910 and to 973 in 1920, partly as a consequence of amalgamation but also because of the larger claim areas of the companies operating on the Far East Rand.[75] Between 1895 and 1914 the average yearly grade of ore milled fell from 10·091 dwts per ton to 6·263 dwts per ton.[76] Not surprisingly, the internal rate of net return on invested capital

[67] Kubicek, *Economic Imperialism*, pp. 108-10.
[68] Consolidated Gold Fields of South Africa Ltd., *The Gold Fields, 1887-1937* (1937), p. 80.
[69] Skinner, *The Mining Manual for 1906-1912*, passim.
[70] Kubicek, *Economic Imperialism*, pp. 135-9.
[71] Cartwright, *The Gold Miners*, p. 267.
[72] Kubicek, *Economic Imperialism*, p. 139.
[73] R. R. Mabson, *The Statist's Mines of the Transvaal, 1906-1910* (1906-1910), Table 5.
[74] *Mineral Industry*, XIX (1910), p. 276.
[75] Frankel, 'Fifty Years on the Rand', p. 524. A 'claim area' was approximately 1·44 acres.
[76] Frankel, *Investment and Return to Equity Capital*, Table 6, p. 28.

SOUTH AFRICAN GOLD   335

fell quite sharply, from 8·5 per cent in the period 1887-1903 to 2·1 per cent in the period 1887-1914.[77] However, the aggregate gross *total* of working profits was very substantially enlarged as working costs were ruthlessly trimmed. Average gross profits for all mines on the Witwatersrand rose from £2,799,360 at an average value per ton of 16·28s. in 1902, to £11,216,105 at an average value of 10·50s. per ton in 1910.[78]

At the level of company organization there was a growing institutionalization of function formerly associated with individual speculators and syndicates. The impetus towards a recognizably corporate group structure had begun in the 1890s with the formation of companies such as Rand Mines Ltd. (1893), the General Mining and Finance Corporation (1895) and A. Goerz and Co. (1897). However, in the period after the war there was a marked acceleration in the movement to rationalize many of the assets of companies inherited from purchases of earlier promoters. This can be seen most clearly in the series of administrative reorganizations beween 1905 and 1911 which led to the creation of the Central Mining and Investment Corporation, and in the series of mergers and takeovers between 1895 and 1905 involving the private interests of the Barnato and Joel families, which led to the reorganization of J.C.I.[79]

These alterations in the productive base of the mining industry heralded another change of long-term historical importance: the increasing ability of the industry to finance part of its capital requirements from internally-generated funds. Unfortunately, we do no have enough figures to enable us to make direct comparisons, but the main trend is clear. In the period before the Anglo-Boer War, appropriations from revenue of companies existing at the end of 1932 amounted to £5,783,437. In the period 1903-14, this amount almost trebled to £17,124,779. During the same period cash subscriptions to all companies in the form of equity capital (the only major form of capital investment at this stage) declined from £44,489,756 for the period 1887-1902, to £29,932,947 in the period 1903-14. These changes were substantial enough in themselves, but in the difficult times of the First World War and after, the continuation of this trend meant that appropriations from revenue for companies which survived until 1932 were greater by £6,909,326 than the cash subscription to *all* companies in the same period.[80]

These figures for dividend payment and internally-generated capital throw doubt on Kubicek's recent conclusions that the business strategies of the various "international entrepreneurs" who controlled the destinies of the Rand mining finance houses had the effect of preventing the "industry from developing its full potential as a steady provider of substantial dividends".[81] By failing to consider the implications of the transformation in the productive base of the industry between 1895 and 1918, Kubicek has emphasized the *speculative* element in the industry long after it had ceased to be the main

---

[77] Ibid. Table 5, p. 27.

[78] P. Richardson, *Chinese Mine Labour in the Transvaal* (1982), Table A:12, p. 202.

[79] For the emergence of Central Mining see Fraser and Jeeves, *All that Glittered*, pp. 10-12; on J.C.I. see Skinner, *The Mining Manual for 1908*, pp. 348-50.

[80] These figures are drawn from Frankel, *Capital Investment in Africa*, Table 14, p. 95 (Cash subscriptions to *all* companies) and Table 15, pp. 96-7 (Appropriations from revenue of companies existing at the end of 1932).

[81] Kubicek, *Economic Imperialism*, p. 197.

336   PETER RICHARDSON AND JEAN-JACQUES VAN HELTEN

source of either profit or new capital. By the First World War, productive mining and sound new developments had come to provide the base for a steady aggregation of profits and had reduced the companies' dependence upon fluctuating supplies of new working capital from abroad. However, despite the increasing ability of the industry to generate its own working capital as a result of these changes, it could not free itself from reliance on foreign capital to develop wholly new areas of mining ground. This can be clearly seen in the decision by C.M.S. Ltd. to seek American financial support for its Far East Rand expansions in 1917.[82] In the circumstances after 1913, this dependence remained obscured by the relatively small amount of average annual capital subscribed to the industry from abroad. As Frankel has commented:

> At various times during this period [i.e. 1913-1932] a considerable number of mines were being 'nursed' by the parent groups from current profits . . . the industry was practically forced to maintain itself on the basis of its capital resources and was in fact largely based on the last great expansion boom of 1908-10, when a sum exceeding £14 millions of new capital was invested in the industry.[83]

This review of the long-term accumulation strategies of the various groups between 1902 and 1918 suggests that current research has obscured some important behavioural and structural changes in the Witwatersrand mining industry. In the first place, by ignoring the implications of the development of the Far East Rand and the merger movement, it has failed to draw attention to the growing conservatism of Wernher Beit, Consolidated Goldfields, and Farrar/Anglo-French, all of which profited from deep-level development on the Central Rand. Second, it has failed to appreciate the extent to which the outcrop/deep-level distinction retained its relevance at the level of production well into the third decade of mining. Moreover, it has not emphasized the extent to which all groups became deep-level producers thereafter and that the key to their differences lay in the variable quality of the claim areas on the Central Rand and in the extent of their commitment to the newer areas of mining ground on the Far East Rand. Finally, by ignoring the importance of the Far East Rand in this period, it has made unintelligible the veritable revolution in the balance of power amongst the groups which became evident during the First World War. The sharply augmented power of J.C.I., A. Goerz and Co., and C.M.S. at the expense of the more conservative groups derived largely from the Far East Rand and suggests that the causes of this process deserve greater attention than they have so far received from historians.

These changes also have implications for our understanding of the nature of capitalist enterprise in the Witwatersrand mining industry. Several attempts have been made recently to analyze the system of production which emerged in this period. Since the mid-1970s there has been a concerted effort to come to terms with a feature of the industry which J. A. Hobson observed as early as 1894: its highly concentrated ownership structure.[84] Thus, in 1976, F. A. Johnstone argued that, in contrast to the truly monopolistic Kimberley

---

[82] T. Gregory, *Ernest Oppenheimer and the Economic Development of Southern Africa* (1962), pp. 75-108; for a more recent and quite different account see D. Innes, 'Monopoly Capitalism and Imperialism in South Africa: The Role of the Anglo-American Group' (Unpublished Univ. of Sussex D. Phil. Thesis, 1980).

[83] Frankel, 'Fifty Years on the Rand', p. 524.

[84] J. A. Hobson, *The Evolution of Modern Capitalism. A Study of Machine Production*, 4th ed. (1926), p. 267.

diamond-mining industry, the Transvaal gold mines displayed "an oligopolist
but highly centralized structure of ownership and control".[85] Robert Davies
has argued that the mining industry in the period between 1900 and 1924 "can
be identified as being, in the first quarter of the twentieth century, in its phase
of transition from competitive to monopoly capitalism". This involved changes
in "the relations of production" which sought to gain "the advantages of large
scale socialized production".[86] Similarly, Duncan Innes has argued that
monopoly capitalist relations of production can be identified in the Witwatersrand mining industry by 1917 and that they derived from the necessity of
controlling critical variables in the cost profile of the mines.[87] Shula Marks
has been more specific, citing "Werhner Beit & Co. as the most centralized
and effectively monopolistic of the mining houses".[88] Only Kubicek has stood
out against this trend, arguing that monopolistic tendencies within the gold-
mining industry were in decline after 1900, but he based his conclusions on
the erroneous deduction that European capital was beating a retreat from the
industry after the Anglo-Boer War.[89]

Although we cannot go into this debate in detail, it is clear that the notion
of monopoly capitalism used by these writers rests upon the identification of
a range of structural and behavioural patterns amongst the various mining
groups. First, there was a decline in competitive relations between the groups,
accompanied by a tendency towards an increasingly restricted number of
sellers of the end-product. Secondly, there was an enlargement of the scale
of production through the concentration and centralization of capital. Thirdly,
there was an interpenetration of banking with industrial capital.[90] The twin
processes of Far East Rand development and Central Rand mergers which we
have identified as the routes to predominantly deep-level production on the
Witwatersrand raise interesting questions in this context. As a direct result of
these changes, our analysis has confirmed that there was a trend towards a
restricted number of mining groups together with an enlargement of the scale
of production as a direct result of the amalgamation of existing capital in
producing mines and the takeover of the assets of some groups by others
(centralization). We have also noted the absolute increase in the scale of profits
extracted (concentration) and the interpenetration of finance and industrial
capital.[91]

[85] F. A. Johnstone, *Class, Race and Gold: A Study of Class Relations and Racial Discrimination in South
Africa* (1976), p. 14.
[86] R. H. Davies, *Capital, State and White Labour in South Africa, 1900-1960: An Historical Materialist
Analysis of Class Formation and Class Relations* (New Jersey, 1979), pp. 46-7.
[87] Innes, 'Monopoly Capitalism and Imperialism in South Africa', pp. 108 ff.
[88] Marks, 'Scrambling for Africa', p. 108.
[89] Kubicek, *Economic Imperialism*, pp. 197-8.
[90] The notion of monopoly capitalism upon which this debate is based can be traced in the following
works: K. Marx, *Capital: A Critique of Political Economy, Vol. I* (Harmondsworth, 1976), p. 777; Marx,
Capital, Vol. III (Harmondsworth, 1981), pp. 567-9; V. I. Lenin, *Imperialism: The Highest Stage of
Capitalism* (Peking, 1973); R. Hilferding, *Finance Capital: A Study of the Latest Phase of Capitalist
Development* (1981); P. Sweezy, *The Theory of Capitalist Development: Principals of Marxian Political
Economy* (1942), pp. 254-307; P. Baran and P. Sweezy, *Monopoly Capital: An Essay on the American
Economic and Social Order* (1968); H. Braverman, *Labour and Monopoly Capital: The Degradation of Work
in the Twentieth Century* (1974); G. Arrighi, *The Geometry of Imperialism: The Limits of Hobson's Paradigm*
(1978); N. Poulantzas, *Classes in Contemporary Capitalism* (1975), pp. 109-51; E. Mandel, *Late Capitalism*
(1978), pp. 523-61; B. Warren, *Imperialism: Pioneer of Capitalism* (1980), pp. 57-65.
[91] For a further discussion of this point see J.-J. Van Helten, 'British and European Economic Investment
in the Transvaal with Specific Reference to the Witwatersrand Goldfields and District, 1886-1910'
(unpublished University of London Ph.D. thesis, 1981), pp. 88-131, 302-3, 314, 316-24; and J.-J. Van
Helten, 'Mining and Imperialism', *Jour. South. African Stud.*, VI (1980), pp. 230-5.

338   PETER RICHARDSON AND JEAN-JACQUES VAN HELTEN

VII

It is important, finally, to offer a precise statement of the claims we have made. Our focus upon the differing routes to deep-level mining after 1902, and the important implication that this has upon our understanding of corporate behaviour, should not be allowed to obscure our support of Blainey's original finding that this process pre-dated the war of 1899-1902. However, given that deep-level mining did not immediately replace outcrop mining and that the two forms co-existed and finally blended with each other, no simple equation between deep-level production and monopoly capitalism can be said to have existed before 1914. Our concentration upon the transformation of productive enterprise upon the Witwatersrand should not disguise the fact that other important pressures had a material impact upon the development of this highly centralized and concentrated form of capitalism. Both before and after the Boer War, state policies in the field of labour, mineral law and infrastructural development, technological changes, and the activities of European financial institutions all played a crucial part in this process. In short, what emerges from our survey is striking confirmation that changes in the nature of capitalist mineral production were protracted and derived from a variety of responses to pressures on profitability. These, in turn, have had a lasting impact upon the reproduction and expansion of capital.

This impact can be seen by looking at the central question of monopoly capitalism in the context of declining competition amongst the mining groups. A complex picture emerges from our survey. On the one hand we have confirmed, elsewhere, Innes's view that collusion in the areas of technology and labour did increase markedly at this time, despite intermittent outbreaks of competition.[92] Furthermore, despite the absence of collusion in the area of product pricing, there can be no doubt that the need to control costs increased during the period 1895-1918 as large-scale low grade production became widespread.[93] However, in one critical area, that of access to mineral-bearing ground, competition not only persisted but intensified.[94] As a corollary of this, the groups also continued to compete for new capital to fund these ventures.

This conclusion is not particularly surprising. The secrecy with which purchases of mining ground and mineral leases was conducted in the 1890s (the original deep-levels) and in the 1930s (the Far West Rand)[95] indicates that the acquisition of these claims was the life blood of the process of capital accumulation. Failure to secure potentially productive assets was ultimately a sentence of death for mining concerns. Collusion in this area of activity, as

[92] Richardson and Van Helten, 'The Gold Mining Industry in the Transvaal', pp. 31-4; P. Richardson and J.-J. Van Helten, 'Labour in the South African Gold-Mining Industry, 1886-1914', in Marks and Rathbone, *Industrialization and Social Change in South Africa*, pp. 88-91; see also A. Jeeves, 'The Control of Migratory Labour on the South African Gold Mines in the Era of Kruger and Milner', *Jour. South. African Stud.*, II (1975), pp. 19-29.

[93] As Gregory has observed of the period of the gold standard "because gold had, and continues to have, an unlimited market for any quantity that can be produced, there was no need, and there is no need, to attempt to limit the supply in accordance with market conditions": *Ernest Oppenheimer and the Economic Development of Southern Africa*, pp. 15-16.

[94] This feature was also noted in F. Wilson, *Labour in the South African Gold Mines, 1911-1969* (Cambridge, 1972), p. 33.

[95] Blainey, 'Lost Causes of the Jameson Raid', p. 353; Cartwright, *The Gold Miners*, pp. 241-8.

the policy of Rand Mines, Consolidated Gold Fields, and Farrars on the East
Rand indicates, was only a second-best option, once the chance of super-
profits, which derived from exclusive ownership or control, had been lost.
However, once brought into production, these assets could best be made
profitable by the benefits of collusion especially in the area of labour costs,
stores and technology. Not that competition was eliminated in this way. The
search for new means of production was unceasing because the extraction of
minerals involved the exploitation of wasting assets. Thus, capital accumulation in Rand mining was a continuing process of competition *and* collusion in
which competition for access to new means of production played a fundamental
role. It was these *two* elements which supported an expanded scale of production, controlled by a small but changing number of mining finance houses,
with a "highly centralized structure of ownership and control".[96]

University of Melbourne
Institute of Commonwealth Studies, London.

[96] In this sense the history of mining on the Witwatersrand tends to give empirical support to Semmler's
timely reminder that 'fewer units of capital does not imply decreased competition and decreased rivalry',
see W. Semmler, 'Theories of Competition and Monopoly', *Capital and Class*, 18 (1982), p. 110.

Appendix

Principal Amalgamations on the Central Rand, 1906-11

Year	Name of New Company	Companies Absorbed	Controlling Group
1906	Simmer Deep	South Geldenhuis Deep South Rose Deep Rand Victoria Mines Rand Victoria East Simmer and Jack East	Consolidated Gold Fields of South Africa
1907	Jupiter	Jupiter Simmer and Jack West	Consolidated Gold Fields of South Africa
1907	West Rand Consolidated Mines	West Rand Mines Violet	General Mining and Finance Corporation
1907	Randfontein Central	Block "A" Randfontein Mynpacht Randfontein West Randfontein	J. B. Robinson
1908	East Rand Proprietary Mines	Angelo Driefontein Consolidated New Comet New Blue Sky Cindarella Cason Angelo Deep Driefontein Deep (pt.) H.F. Co. Hercules and Sundry Claims	Farrar/Anglo-French Exploration Co.
1908	City Deep	City Deep South City South Wolhuter Wolhuter Deep Farm of Klipriviersberg	Wernher Beit/Eckstein

340   PETER RICHARDSON AND JEAN-JACQUES VAN HELTEN

Year	Name of New Company	Companies Absorbed	Controlling Group
1908	Village Deep	Village Deep Turf Mines	Wernher Beit/Eckstein
1908	Nourse Mines	Henry Nourse } Nourse Mines Nourse Deep } (1905) South Nourse }	Wernher Beit/Eckstein
1908	Witwatersrand Deep	Witwatersrand Deep Driefontein Deep (125 claims)	S. Neumann & Co.
1908	Knights Central	Knights Central South Knights	S. Neumann & Co.
1909	Roodepoort Utd. Main Reef	Roodepoort Utd. Roodepoort Gold Mine Co.	General Mining and Finance Corporation
1909	Crown Mines	Crown Reef Crown Deep Paarl Central Langlaagte Deep Robinson Central Deep South Rand Gold Mine Co. Central Deep New Vierfontein Mines South Langlaagte South Deeps	Wernher Beit/Eckstein
1909	Geldenhuis Deep	Geldenhuis Estate Geldenhuis Deep Jumpers Deep	Wernher Beit/Eckstein
1909	Rose Deep	Rose Deep Glen Deep	Wernher Beit/Eckstein
1909	Randfontein Central	Randfontein Central Ferguson Randfontein Van Hulsteyn Randfontein Johnston Randfontein	J. B. Robinson
1909	Randfontein South	Robinson Randfontein Porges Randfontein South Randfontein North Randfontein Stubbs Randfontein	J. B. Robinson
1909	Lancaster	Lancaster Lancaster West	A. Goerz & Co.
1909	Consolidated Main Reef	Consolidated Main Reef Main Reef East Main Reef Deep	S. Neumann & Co.
1911	Randfontein Central	Randfontein Central Randfontein South	J. B. Robinson
1911	Princess Estate	Princess Estate West Roodepoort Gold Mine Roodepoort Central Deep	S. Neumann & Co.

Sources: The Mineral Industry for 1906-1911 (New York, 1907-12); Fraser and Jeeves, *All that Glittered*, pp. 392-402; W. Skinner, *The Mining Manual for 1906-1912* (1907-13).

[8]

[1987]

Excerpt from *Australian Economic History Review*, 1987, **XXVII**, (1), 3–29.

PETER RICHARDSON

THE ORIGINS AND DEVELOPMENT OF THE
COLLINS HOUSE GROUP, 1915-1951*

Introduction

'In some respects Collins House resembles the devil... Everyone has heard the name of his Satanic majesty. Everyone suspects his vast influence upon their affairs. Yet few have seen him: few could describe accurately his features; even fewer have transacted business with him.'[1]

The importance of the Collins House Group (CHG) is, it seems, an accepted fact of life in Australian business, journalist, political and academic circles. For instance, in 1961 the *Australian Financial Review* claimed that Collins House was 'the most prolific parent of industrial

*The material collected in this article forms part of a wider investigation into the history of the Collins House Group of mining and metallurgical companies sponsored by the Australian Corporate History Programme of the University of Melbourne. The support of the Programme is gratefully acknowledged. The findings of this investigation are to be published under the title *The Collins House Group, 1915-1951* by Allen & Unwin Australia Pty. Ltd., in 1987. All companies material cited or quoted in this paper is private copyright, and reproduced with permission of the companies concerned. The following abbreviations are used in these notes:

AA   Australian Archives, Canberra Repository
AMG   Archives of Metallgesellschaft AG, Frankfurt/Main, West Germany
BHAS   Records of the Broken Hill Associated Smelters Pty. Ltd. in MUA
BHS   Records of the Broken Hill South Co. Ltd. in MUA
BPP   British Parliamentary Papers
BT   Records of the Board of Trade, in PRO
CO   Records of the Colonial Office, in PRO
CAPD   Commonwealth of Australia Parliamentary Debates
CAPP   Commonwealth of Australia Parliamentary Papers
Cmd   Command Papers, in BPP.
GBR   Records of Gibbs Bright & Co., in MUA.
MLMR   Records of the Mount Lyell Mining and Railway Co. Ltd. in MUA
MUA   Melbourne University Archives
NBH   Records of North Broken Hill Ltd. in MUA
PRO   Public Record Office, Kew, England.
WMC   Records of the Western Mining Corporation Ltd. in MUA.
WSRP   Papers of W. S. Robinson in MUA.

[1] *Australian Financial Review*, 28 November 1961, p. 6; this feeling about the elusive quality of the CHG was echoed by R. W. Connell in his book, *Ruling Class, Ruling Culture. Studies of Conflict, Power and Hegemony in Australian Life* (London 1977), p. 74; 'It is indeed a little difficult to say where the 'group' begins and ends.'

Peter Richardson

enterprises Australia has ever seen'.[2] Similarly, Geoffrey Tebbuth of the *Herald* claimed in 1970 that Collins House was synonymous 'in and out of politics and commerce with deeply entrenched financial and industrial power and business acumen'.[3] In the same year Harold Bell, the then Economic Adviser to the AMP Society, told the 36th Summer School of the Australian Institute of Political Science that although Australia was markedly deficient in 'great financial complexes' akin to those of Japan, West Germany and South Africa, where 'great industrial groupings tend to pivot around one of the large banks', Collins House represented 'the nearest approach we have had to some groupings of this kind'.[4]

Elements of this position can be found in arguments presented from both sides of the Australian political spectrum. Amongst organized and non-aligned elements of the left, Collins House has long had a reputation as one of the most important centres of monopoly power in the newly emerging world of corporate wealth. Beginning with the writings of J. N. Rawlings, A. P. Warren, Len Fox, L. Aarons and Brian Fitzpatrick in the 1930s, this view had its greatest prominence in the period between the Second World War and the early sixties. For example, at the 1948 Congress of the Communist Party of Australia, Collins House was declared to be the 'chief centre of reaction in Australia . . .' which dominated 'the economic and political life of our country and people'.[5] Similar opinions circulated in some right wing circles, especially in the Country Party in the 1940s and 1950s. Thus, Country Party member for the Federal seat of Richmond in New South Wales, Hubert Anthony, declared during the House of Representatives second reading debate on the Aluminium Industry Bill in November 1944 that Collins House was one of a few 'interested or sinister groups which are exercising influence upon the Government'.[6]

Historians and social scientists have tended to reflect the essence of these views very closely. Thus, for Geoffrey Blainey, Collins House was 'the Australian synonym for industrial power' and 'the home of the most

---

[2] *Australian Financial Review*, 28 November 1961, p. 6.
[3] Quoted in S. Encel, *Equality and Authority. A Study of Class, Status and Power in Australia* (Melbourne 1970), p. 381.
[4] Harold Bell, 'The Large Corporation in Australia' in Australian Institute of Political Science, *Big Business in Australia* (Sydney 1970), p. 41.
[5] A comprehensive review of this literature and the associated decisions of the Communist Party of Australia's Annual Conferences on Collins House can be found in Richard A. Kuhn, 'Paradise on the Instalment Plan. The Economic Thought of the Australian Labor Movement Between the Depression and the Long Boom' (University of Sydney Ph.D. Thesis, 1985), pp. 397–404; perhaps the best known of the products of this school of thought was E. W. Campbell, *The Sixty Families Who Own Australia* (Sydney 1963).
[6] CAPD, Vol. 180 (1944), p. 2354. Speech by Mr. Hubert Anthony on the Second Reading of the Aluminium Industry Bill, 29 November 1944. W. S. Robinson vigorously denied these charges, see MUA/WSRP: Correspondence Files, A–B: Robinson to Evatt, 8 December 1944.

Collins House Group, 1915–1951

influential group of financiers between the wars'.[7] Ian Hore-Lacy, in his edited version of W.H. Courbould's memoirs, likewise identified Mount Isa Mines as the only 'major Australian mining group today without Collins House antecedents'.[8] Peter Cochrane echoed these views when he wrote:

> Two mining groups dominated manufacturing development through-out the period between the wars. These were Anglo-Australian groups in which British capital predominated. The first was an alliance of lead-zinc interests which became known as Collins House; the second, the iron and steel manufacturer Broken Hill Proprietary.[9]

Similarly, Connell in his book *Ruling Class, Ruling Culture* identified BHP and Collins House as 'the two major industrial complexes of the interwar period'.[10] This view can also be found in Connell's collaborative work with Irving, *Class Structure in Australian History.*[11]

Given this wide concensus on the importance of Collins House, it is a remarkable fact that there is still no major published work on this corporate group. There are a small number of histories of individual companies associated with Collins House, largely in the genre of self-congratulatory centenary studies.[12] There are memoirs of those associated with Collins House, although these are often reticent about the relationship between the companies which form the Group.[13] There is also

---

[7] Geoffrey Blainey, *The Rush That Never Ended. A History of Australian Mining*, 3rd edition (Melbourne 1978), pp. 278 and 281.

[8] I. Hore-Lacy (ed.), *Broken Hill to Mount Isa. The Mining Odessey of W. H. Courbould* (Melbourne 1981), p. 191.

[9] Peter Cochrane, *Industrialization and Dependence. Australia's Road to Economic Development* (Brisbane 1980), p. 76.

[10] Connell, *Ruling Class*, p. 69.

[11] R. W. Connell and T. H. Irving, *Class Structure in Australian History. Documents, Narrative and Argument* (Melbourne 1980), p. 271.

[12] See, for example, M. H. Ellis, *Metal Manufactures Ltd: A Golden Jubilee History* (Sydney 1966); EZ Industries Ltd., *EZ Review: 50 Years of Progress* (Hobart 1966); Zinc Corporation Ltd., *The First Fifty Years* (Melbourne 1956); A. Heintz, *The Fabulous Hill* (Melbourne 1957).

[13] One of the more notorious of these is W. G. Meudell, *The Pleasant Career of a Spendthrift* (London 1929), which dealt at some length with, *inter alia*, the career of W. L. Baillieu. The storm of indignation which this book produced on publication led to its withdrawal and subsequent much amended republication in 1936 under the title *The Pleasant Career of a Spendthrift and his Later Reflections*. Examples of the extent of the changes made by Meudell can be found in Encel, *Equality and Authority*, pp. 379–81, footnotes 8–12 and M. Cannon, *The Land Boomers* (Melbourne 1967) pp. 64–5. Another prominent member of Collins House, W. S. Robinson, had his edited memoirs published posthumously under the title, G. Blainey (ed.), *If I Remember Rightly. The Memoirs of W. S. Robinson, 1876–1963* (Melbourne 1967). Robinson never made reference directly to the CHG in his memoirs, although he did acknowledge the existence of 'the associated companies in Australia and the United Kingdom' (p. 202). However, G. Lindsay Clark in his memoirs entitled *Built on Gold. Recollections of Western Mining* (Melbourne 1983), p. 3, specifically recognised the existence of the CHG.

Peter Richardson

a considerable amount of biographical material, though much of it sketchy and impressionistic, and there are illuminating, if short, passages, in more general economic histories of the period.[14] This generally low level of historical treatment is in contrast to the available work on Broken Hill itself, whence so much of the wealth of the Group derived.[15] This article is a preliminary attempt to redress this imbalance.

II

The CHG takes its name from the building of the same title situated at 360–366 Collins Street in the financial district of Melbourne. Built in 1911 and owned until 1960 by a small group of companies representing the Baillieu family interests, Collins House became the headquarters for a bewildering array of companies.[16] Although all occupants of Collins House remained tenants of legally separate companies throughout the period covered by this paper, they were attracted to this location by the twin advantages of ease of communication and common interests in the mining, smelting, metallurgical and chemical industries.

Despite this uniformity, not all occupants of the building could be held to be members of an indentifiable group as such. Thus, between 1913 and 1924, Collins House served as the Australian headquarters of the Cape Explosives Co. Ltd. This company, a subsidiary of the De Beers Consolidated Diamond Mines Ltd., whilst working with leading members of Collins House, could not be classified as a member of a Group in any meaningful sense.[17] Similarly, the Mount Lyell Mining

[14] See, for example, Cannon, *Land Boomers*, pp. 131–38 for the early career of W. L. Baillieu; for other material on W. L. Baillieu see J. Poynter, 'William Lawrence Baillieu' in B. Nairn and G. Serle (eds.), *Australian Dictionary of Biography [ADB], Volume 7: 1891–1939* (Melbourne 1979), pp. 138–45; see also J. Kennett, 'Sir Colin Fraser' in *ADB, Vol. 8: 1891–1939*, pp. 576–7; R. Davenport-Hines, 'Clive Latham Baillieu' in D. Jeremy (ed.), *Dictionary of Business Biography: Vol. 11* (London 1984), pp. 96–99; portraits of Sir Herbert Gepp and Sir Walter Massy-Greene can be found in C. D. Kemp, *Big Businessmen. Four Biographical Essays* (Melbourne 1960), pp. 13–140; material on another early associate of the Collins House enterprises can be found in the encyclopaedic work by George Nash, *The Life of Herbert Hoover. The Engineer, 1874–1914* (New York 1983), pp. 348–370. The only systematic and detailed treatment of the CHG is unpublished, see John Kennett, 'The Collins House Group' (Monash University, M.Econ. Thesis, 1983).
[15] On Broken Hill in general see George Farwell, *Down Argent Street* (Sydney 1948); G. Blainey, *The Rise of Broken Hill* (Melbourne 1968); B. Hardy, *West of the Darling* (Brisbane 1969); B. Kennedy, *Silver, Sin and Sixpenny Ale: A Social History of Broken Hill, 1883–1921* (Melbourne 1978); O. H. Woodward, *A Review of the Broken Hill Lead-Silver-Zinc Industry*, 2nd edition (Sydney 1965).
[16] G. Serle, *John Monash. A Biography* (Melbourne 1982), p. 179; details of the ownership of Collins House can be traced in MUA/NBH: 2nd. Accession/Deeds, Agreements etc., leases between North Broken Hill Ltd. and various companies dated 5 February 1912 — 30 September 1960.
[17] Peter Richardson, 'Nobels and the Australian Mining Industry, 1907–1925', *Business History*, Vol. XXVI, No. 2 (1984), p. 176.

6

Collins House Group, 1915–1951

and Railway Co. Ltd. (MLMR) a lessee of parts of Collins House backing onto Little Collins Street, for a long time had friendlier links with BHP than the CHG. This was the case despite the existence of a substantial shareholding by the MLMR in the Group sponsored Electrolytic Zinc Co. of Australasia Ltd. (EZ) after 1920, and in a Group associated company, Metal Manufactures Ltd. (MM) after 1916.[18]

Tenancy of Collins House was thus only a necessary part of any definition of the Group. Additional, stronger links can also be identified to provide the sense of collaborative association and common focus implicit in any group. These links have their origin in the silver-lead-zinc mines of Broken Hill in the far west of New South Wales, and the smelting, refining and marketing interests connected with them. One family, the Melbourne-based Baillieus, are of particular importance in this context. The Baillieu family had been associated with one of the Broken Hill mines, the North Broken Hill Co. NL (NBH), for several years before the construction of Collins House. In 1902, W.L. Baillieu, a Melbourne financier with investments in property, banking, mines and brewing, had managed to secure a controlling interest in the Victoria Cross mine on the northern end of the line of lode at Broken Hill.[19] In 1904 this company was taken over by the NBH, and Baillieu became an important and influential member of the board from 1905.[20] An index of his influence can be found in the decision to transfer the head office of the company from 352 Collins Street to Collins House in 1912.[21]

The Baillieu's were also associated with the floating of another Broken Hill company which was to form the core of the CHG, the Zinc Corporation Ltd. (ZC), founded in 1905.[22] Originally a zinc treatment company employing the flotation method of separating zinc from the other minerals in the ore, ZC became a mining company as well in 1911 when it took over the Broken Hill South Blocks Co. Ltd.[23] Although a London-registered company after 1911, ZC co-operated closely with a range of Australian controlled companies because of its dependence upon their output and tailings dumps for a considerable, if diminishing, proportion

[18] For the details of these shareholdings see MUA/WSRP, Correspondence Files: A–B, Prospectus of EZ, 9 October 1920 and MUA/MLMR/SC:107, Lumsden to W. L. Baillieu, 21 July 1916; the origin of the coolness between MLMR and CHG seems to have been the former's refusal to take up shares in the reconstructed ER&S, see MUA/MLMR/SC:107 Bowes Kelly to Attorney-General, 3 August 1916. On BHP/MLMR relations see G. Blainey, *The Peaks of Lyell*, 3rd edition (Melbourne 1967), pp. 53–68.
[19] *If I Remember Rightly*, pp. 41–2.
[20] *Ibid*, see also W. Skinner, *The Mining Manual for 1906* (London 1906), p. 133 and *The Statist*, 7 April 1906, pp. 628–9.
[21] MUA/NBH: 2nd Accession Deeds, Agreements etc: Lease dated 5 February 1912 between NBH and the Central Proprietary Ltd.
[22] Skinner, *Mining Manual for 1906*, p. 187; PRO/BT 31/11281/86277, Certification of Incorporation of the Zinc Corporation Ltd., 26 October 1905.
[23] *Annual Report of the Zinc Corporation Ltd. 31 December 1911*, p. 5.

Peter Richardson

of its raw materials supplies. One such company was the Broken Hill South Co. NL (BHS), a Melbourne-based company with strong Adelaide connections, dating back to 1893. BHS was a major supplier of zinc tailings to the ZC in the period 1906-1912.[24] However, BHS also had important links with the NBH and the Baillieu interests through another zinc treatment company, the Amalgamated Zinc (De Bavay's) Ltd. (AZ), founded in 1909 to take over the enterprise known as De Bavay's Treatment Co. Ltd. of Melbourne. AZ in turn had close connections with the Baillieu and Latham brewing interests as a result of the utilization of techniques pioneered in fermentation in experiments in ore separation. Like the ZC, AZ was also dependent upon the mines for its raw material supplies and drew heavily upon the tailings dumps and current output of NBH and BHS to secure its long-term future.[25] Through links such as these, the basis of a more active and wide ranging co-operation based on common interests grew up amongst the four companies, NBH, BHS, ZC and AZ. The transfer of the head offices of these companies, or Australian office in the case of the ZC, to Collins House following the move of NBH in 1912 was both a part and a symbol of this process.[26]

Between 1915 and 1939 these three long-life mining companies and treatment operations based in Collins House developed this association to provide the economic and material basis for a non-ferrous metal Group of international importance. From the wealth of these companies, consciously and deliberately acting together, was created a co-operative monopoly of silver-lead-zinc production at Broken Hill in the interwar years. In 1915 NBH, BHS and ZC established the co-operatively owned Broken Hill Associated Smelters (BHAS) by providing capital sufficient to buy out 78 per cent of BHP's interest in its Port Pirie lead smelter.[27] Between 1916 and 1921, the three same companies, in conjunction with AZ, also provided the capital to develop on a commercial basis zinc smelting by electrolysis, using hydro-electricity, under the auspices of the EZ at Risdon in Tasmania.[28] Between 1923 and 1929, the three mining companies also were closely involved in the development of zinc smelting in England, through the National and later the Imperial Smelting Corporation (ISC) at Avonmouth.[29]

As a direct extension of this process of vertical integration, the three

[24] Details of these contracts can be found in MUA/BHS: Prospectus of the Australian Smelting Corporation Ltd., January 1906, in Reports by J. B. Were & Co. on Broken Hill Companies, 1936-37.

[25] MUA/BHS: Prospectus of AZ, 23 October 1909, in Reports by J. B. Were on Broken Hill Companies, etc.

[26] See Skinner, *Mining Manual for 1912, passim.*

[27] MUA/BHAS/1/3/70, Agreement dated 8 May 1915 between BHP, BHS, NBH, and BHAS.

[28] MUA/WSRP, Correspondence Files: A-B, Prospectus of EZ, 9 October 1920.

[29] E. Cocks and B. Walters, *A History of the Zinc Smelting Industry in Britain* (London 1968), pp. 43-73; only ZC subscribed to shares in the National Smelting Corporation in 1923, whilst NBH and BHS subscribed to shares in ISC in 1929, see Table 2.

Collins House Group, 1915-1951

mining companies collaborated in the establishment of a wide range of companies, most of which were wholly owned or controlled. Thus in 1921 the BHAS, on the initiative of its major shareholding supplier companies, BHS, NBH and ZC, established the Australia Ore and Metal Co. Pty. Ltd. to sell its lead overseas.[30] In 1927 the three companies took shares in their major overseas customer and sometime agent for zinc purchases, the British Metal Corporation Ltd. (BMC), and after 1929 in its controlling company, the Amalgamated Metal Corporation Ltd.[31] Similarly, a range of co-operatively owned companies were established with the aim of reducing or controlling production costs on the mines themselves. The first of these was the Barrier Roaster Co. Pty. Ltd., established in 1918. Under this company's direction zinc concentrates from Broken Hill were reduced by roasting to calcines suitable for the treatment by the electrolytic process.[32] This was followed by the founding of Globe Pty. Ltd. in 1919 as a timber buying, and later growing company, and participation in the Broken Hill Co-operative Coal Association in 1924.[33] A much more substantial joint investment was made by these three companies in 1930 with the creation of the Western New South Wales Electric Power Pty. Ltd. to provide electricity and compressed air to the mines.[34]

The collaboration of these three mining companies was further extended by their joint moves into non-ferrous metal fabrication associated with lead and zinc, and related fields of chemical production. Initially, it was the lead market which appeared to offer the biggest opportunities. In 1918, the mining companies subscribed 38 per cent of the initial capital of £145,000 required to establish British Australian Lead Manufacturers Pty. Ltd. (BALM) in collaboration with the British White Lead Convention for the production of pigments and later paints.[35] In 1927-28, a similar combination of Broken Hill companies helped produce the Commonwealth Red Lead and Lithage Co. Ltd., concerned with the production of red lead pigments and lead oxide for battery

[30] MUA/BHAS/3/1, Minutes of the first meeting of Directors of the Australian Ore and Metal Company, 27 April 1921.
[31] *Annual Report of BHS, 30 June 1927*, Schedule of Investments; *Annual Report of NBH, 30 June 1927*, Schedule of Investments; ZC actually took a small shareholding in BMC in 1925, and adjusted its holdings in line with BNH and BHS in 1926-27: see *Annual Reports of ZC, 31 December 1925-27*, Schedule of Investments; on the acquisition of Amalgamated Metal Corporation shares following the merger of BMC and Henry Gardner & Co. Ltd. in 1929, see MUA/NBH: 2nd Acc: SC:20, W. S. Robinson to Sec., NBH, 12 December 1929.
[32] *Annual Report of NBH, 30 June 1918*, Directors' Report.
[33] *Annual Report of NBH for 1919*; MUA/BHS: Publications: *Annual Report of the Broken Hill Co-operative Coal Association Pty. Ltd., 30 June 1947*, Circular to Shareholders, 19 September 1947.
[34] Woodward, *Broken Hill*, pp. 463-4.
[35] G. Blainey, 'History of ICIANZ' (unpublished manuscript 1959), pp. 143-49; D. Rowe, *Lead Manufacturing in Britain. A History* (London 1983), pp. 289-91.

Peter Richardson

production.[36] In 1930 NBH and BHS extended this process still further by purchasing shares in the British lead manufacturers' cartel, Associated Lead Manufacturers, later known as Goodlass, Wall and Lead Industries Ltd.[37]

In the field of the industrial use of zinc, a large part of Australian demand was accounted for by the galvanizing trade. This was divided between the galvanized wire trade, controlled by Lysaght Brothers & Co. Ltd. of Sydney, and the galvanized iron trade, controlled by Ryland Bros. (Aust.) Ltd. Between 1925 and 1935, both of these companies were acquired by BHP.[38] However, in the field of zinc alloy production, particularly brass die moulding, an important interest was acquired by the three mining companies in 1928-29 when the companies purchased, through BHAS, a controlling interest in the Electrolytic Refining and Smelting Co. Ltd. (ER&S) at Port Kembla in New South Wales, and its two subsidiaries, MM and Austral Bronze Ltd. (AB).[39] MM, in conjunction with EZ, also became the vehicle through which the group participated in the Australian aluminium fabricating industry, by providing one third of the capital for the establishment of the Australian Aluminium Co. Pty. Ltd. in 1939.[40] In Britain, through the medium of the ISC, interests in the fabrication of zinc and zinc alloys were also secured in the 1930s, although none of these acquisitions resulted in direct investments by any of the Group companies except the ZC.[41]

These interests in Australian metal fabrication subsequently formed the basis of a further extension of Group investments in the late 1930s, for the purposes of defence. These investments, like much of those in the metal fabrication field, tended to be of a minority rather than controlling nature. Thus, in 1936, the three mining companies participated with BHP, General Motors-Holden, Imperial Chemical Industries Australia and New Zealand Ltd. (ICIANZ) and the P & 0 Steamship Co. Ltd. to found the Commonwealth Aircraft Corporation Ltd. (CAC).[42]

[36] Kennett, 'The Collins House Group', pp. 157-60.
[37] Rowe, *Lead Manufacturing*, pp. 306-8; see also Table 2.
[38] MUA/BHS/1/85/9, Official Transcript of Evidence before the Tariff Board enquiry into Zinc and Spelter, evidence of A. J. C. Bult, 4 March 1934, p. 15; see also CAPP 1934, Tariff Board Report No. 44 on Zinc and Spelter, p. 5; on the acquisition of these two companies by BHP see Helen Hughes, *The Australian Iron and Steel Industry, 1848-1962* (Melbourne 1964), pp. 101-2, 112-13.
[39] MUA/NBH: 2nd Acc: SC:9A: Confidential Memorandum by W. L. Baillieu, W. S. Robinson and C. Fraser on the Acquisition of Certain Assets from the Mount Morgan Co., 24 April 1928.
[40] A. A. Smith (ed.), *40 years On. A History of Alcan in Australia, 1941-1981* (Sydney 1981), p. 7.
[41] Cocks and Walters, *Zinc Smelting*, pp. 74-80.
[42] G. Blainey, *The Steel Master. A Life of Essington Lewis* (Melbourne 1971), pp. 127-31; N. R. Wills, 'The Basic Iron and Steel Industry' in A. Hunter (ed.), *The Economics of Australian Industry. Studies in Environment and Structure* (Melbourne 1963), pp. 239-40.

Collins House Group, 1915–1951

In 1939, NBH and BHS extended this development by taking up shares in BHP's special steel producing company, Commonwealth Steel Ltd.[43]

In the area of chemicals, the Group had interests both as a consumer and a producer. As a consumer of large quantities of mining explosives, the Group sought to collaborate with the only Australian producer after 1924, the British-based Nobel Industries Ltd., later ICIANZ. In 1929, this resulted in the three mining companies and EZ securing preferential rights to a portion of the initial public share issue of ICIANZ.[44] As a producer of chemicals, the Group had a double interest, first as a producer of large quantities of sulphuric acid as a by-product of its smelting activities. In this field both BHAS and EZ had interests, and this formed the basis of the fertilizer merger with ICIANZ and others to produce the Commonwealth Fertilizers and Chemicals Ltd. (CFC) in 1929.[45] Second, as a producer of pigments and lead oxides, the Group had a substantial interest in the paint industry, represented mainly by its share holdings in BALM. However, as a supplier of raw material rather than technology, the Group sought to achieve the collaboration of ICIANZ which had access to the Du Pont company's patents on rival artificial pigments. Consequently, in 1928, the parent company of ICIANZ and Du Pont jointly subscribed 40 per cent of the existing capital of BALM.[46]

In two other areas, both related to mining and its associated industries, the CHG made a significant series of investments. In the field of mineral exploration, the associated mining companies established or participated in three companies, namely the Shale Oil Investigation Pty. Ltd. (1930), Willyama Mining Pty. Ltd. (1934), and the Gold Exploration and Finance Company of Australia Ltd. (CEFCA) (1934). Of these companies, only GEFCA was to be of lasting significance, becoming the holding company of the Western Mining Corporation Ltd. (1933) and Gold Mines of Australia Ltd. (1930).[47] In the field of mineral technology, the Group was intimately associated with the development of the flotation process through three companies, the ZC, AZ, and the Minerals Separation and De Bavay's Processes Australia Pty. Ltd. (MS&DBPA).[48] The latter company, which was founded in 1912, actually predated the collaboration of the First World War, but continued to licence existing developments in flotation technology throughout the interwar period. In fact the com-

[43] D. P. Mellor, *The Role of Science and Industry* (Canberra 1958), pp. 71, 77–79.
[44] W. J. Reader, *Imperial Chemical Industries. A History. Vol. II, The First Quarter Century, 1926–1952* (London 1975), pp. 208 et seq., see also MUA/BHAS/1/134, Todhunter to Shackell, 15 July 1929.
[45] MUA/BHAS/1/134, Shackell and Fraser to NBH, BHS and ZC, 9 August 1929; see also J. R. Poynter, *Russell Grimwade* (Melbourne 1967), pp. 166–7.
[46] MUA/WSRP, Corr: I–M, W. L. Raws to W. S. Robinson, 15 March 1944.
[47] MUA/WMC/8/35/27: Taxation Objections and Company History, Memo by L. Edwards, 22 November 1943; see also Clark, *Built on Gold*, pp. 13–30.
[48] See pages 7–8 above.

Peter Richardson

pany took over all the Australian patents owned and developed by the Minerals Separation Co. Ltd., AZ, and Potter's Sulphide Ore Treatment Co. Ltd.[49] Because of its large shareholding in MS&DBPA, AZ retained a core of distinguished technologists and scientists whose research was to form the basis of what appears to be only genuine diversification of the CHG, the formation of the Associated Pulp and Paper Manufacturers (APPM) in 1936. Faced with the disappearance of its raw material supplies after 1924, as a result of the decision by the NBH and BHS to treat their own output and tailing themselves, the AZ decided to deploy its remaining capital, after the return of its shares in EZ to its shareholders,

Table 1: ANNUAL AVERAGE NUMBER OF MEN EMPLOYED IN CHG MINES AND SMELTERS IN AUSTRALIA, 1915-1939 (for year ending 31 December)

Year	NBH	BHS	ZC	BHAS	EZ Risdon	EZ W. Coast Dist.
1915	886	1259	514	1497	—	—
1916	775	1317	778	N.A.	—	—
1917	816	1269	890	2027	—	—
1918	767	1159	851	2345	375	—
1919	335	1182	823	+1527	322	—
1920	252	441	793	+722	970	N.A.
1921	388	537	473	+551	841	N.A.
1922	563	907	559	1101	894	N.A.
1923	657	1108	638	1384	1282	131
1924	1454	1016	710	1598	1377	158
1925	1477	1099	800	**1650	1029	178
1926	1494	1074	841	1712	1051	N.A.
1927	1651	1088	814	1666	943	184
1928	1502	1113	770	1533	942	341
1929	1529	1075	845	1450	934	447
1930	1296	1054	847	1372	950	337
1931	891	938	787	1116	748	47
1932	901	895	766	975	721	16
1933	958	813	782	970	750	30
1934	1011	843	823	1023	782	43
1935	1071	874	882	1017	830	74
1936	1273	885	986	955	906	318
1937	1567	920	1160	938	1014	398
1938	1768	961	1254	970	1051	492
1939	*+1668	*+969	*+1291	++1009	1120	1120

+ rotation scheme in operation due to Broken Hill Strike and fire at BHAS.
*+ as at 16 June 1939.
** after 1925 BHAS figures are for y/e 30 June in each case.
++ for half year ending 30 June 1939 only.
Sources: South Australia, *Department of Mines: Mining Review*, Nos. 43-71 (1925-1939); New South Wales, *Annual Reports of the Department of Mines, 1915-1938*; Tasmania, *Annual Reports of the Secretary/Director of Mines, 1918-1939*; MUA/ BHAS, Directors Reports, 1915-1939; MUA/NBH, *Annual Report of NBH for y/e 30 June 1939*.

---

[49] Skinner, *Mining Manual for 1919*, pp. 325-6.

Collins House Group, 1915-1951

Table 2: COMMON INVESTMENT HOLDINGS OF CHG MINING COMPANIES, 1938 (by no. of fully paid up £1 ordinary shares, unless otherwise indicated)

Company	Date of Acquisition	No. of Shares issued at acquisition	NBH Shares [June 1938]	BHS Shares [June 1938]	ZC Shares [Dec. 1938]
BHAS	1915	700,000	546,576	446,369	337,055
Barrier Roaster	1918ᵃ	60,000	10,000	10,000	10,000
EZ	1917/20ᵇ	750,000	150,000	50,000	—
BALM	1919	145,000	36,630	36,630	27,473
Globe Pty. Ltd.	1919	36,500	15,000	11,250	10,000
Australian Ore & Metal	1921	10,000ᶜ	500	300	350
BH Co-op Coal Assoc'n	1924	5,000	1,000	600	400
Amalgamated Metalᵈ*	1929	500,000	21,110	21,110	26,388
ER & S (£4,fpu)	1929	53,393	21,357	16,018	16,018
Metal Manufacturesᵉ	1929	33,855	32,194	27,303	27,321
Goodlass, Wall & Lead Industries*	1929	N.A.	11,531	11,531	—
ICIANZ	1929	444,434	22,981	22,981	22,981
ISC*	1929	2,424,987	33,290	55,790	96,500
W'n. NSW Elec. Power (4/- pd.)ᶠ	1930	500,000	180,000	160,000	160,000
Shale Oil Investigs. (16/9d pd.)	1930	37,500	12,500	12,500	12,500
GEFCA* (10/-,fpu)	1934	1,800,000	3,081	8,888	N.A.
Willyama Mining (12/- pd.)	1934	15,000	9,000	8,000	—
APPMᵍ	1936	1,200,000	75,000	75,000	50,000
CAC	1936	700,000	62,500	62,500	50,000

* indicates UK companies, shares quoted in £1 sterling or denominations thereof.
ᵃ balance of the original share issue was taken equally by AZ and EZ.
ᵇ ZC first took 40,000 shares in 1917, and increased its holdings to match NBH and BHS in 1920; ZC sold all its EZ shares in 1924-5; BHS also held 75,000 £1 preference shares in EZ in 1938.
ᶜ 8,745 shares held by BHAS in 1921.
ᵈ These shareholdings derive from share purchases in British Metal Corporation made between 1925 and 1927, which were converted into Amalgamated Metal Shares in 1929 on a 2 for 1 basis.
ᵉ NBH also held 7,414 and BHS 6,286 £1 cumulative pref. shares in MM in 1938.
ᶠ BHS also held 100,000 £1 debentures in W'n. NSW Elec. Power, and NBH 2,782 £50 debentures in 1938.
ᵍ NBH and BHS both held 1,250 £1 deferred ordinary shares each in APPM in 1938.
Note: shares in Metal Manufactures, ER & S and CAC were held in trust by BHAS for the three mining companies.
Sources: *Annual Reports of NBH, BHS for y/e 30 June 1915-38; Annual Reports of ZC for y/e 31 Dec., 1915-38*; MUA/BHAS/3/1: Australian Ore and Metal Co. Ltd., Memorandum by H. L. Shackell, 24 April 1930.

in a new area. The alternative was liquidation.[50] After a series of investigations, the choice settled on by AZ's technical advisers was hardwood paper production. To this end, the company floated Tasmanian Paper Pty. Ltd. in 1926 which, ten years later, became APPM.[51]

[50] *Annual Report of AZ 31 December 1925*, Chairman's Statement to shareholders.
[51] *Annual Report of AZ 31 December 1926; The Bulletin*, 10 March 1927; see also Kennett, 'The Collins House Group', pp. 199-211.

Peter Richardson

Estimating the size and value of the assets created by this long process of expansion is a necessarily difficult and inexact exercise. In terms of employment, the Group's impact was significant in three Australian states, New South Wales, South Australia, and Tasmania, as well as in Britain. Thus the annual average number of men employed in the five major enterprises of the group, NBH, BHS, ZC, BHAS, and EZ, increased from a combined total of 5,497 in 1918 to 6,280 in 1929. Following a contraction in the Depression, expansion in numbers began again in 1934, reaching a combined total of 7,177 in 1939. Of course, these figures considerably underestimate the impact of CHG investments in terms even of Australian employment, as smaller wholly owned or controlled enterprises and other enterprises in which the Group had a large but not a controlling stake are excluded. Valuation of these assets is also problematic as very few of the companies created by the Group were publicly quoted and therefore had no 'market value'. Table 2 gives a chronology of the Group's asset acquisitions, together with details of respective shareholdings at par. In the records of the mines and the other major companies created by the Group, all shares and other holdings in companies are listed at par. Even with this limitation, the figures are impressive. Thus, in 1918 investments at par of BHS, NBH, ZC and AZ totalled £A1,082,470. By 1929, this figure had risen to £A2,195,220. By 1939, the three mining companies alone controlled assets in other companies worth £A3,086,446 at par, the assets of AZ having been returned to the shareholders on the dissolution of the company in 1938. If the investments of the EZ and BHAS companies are added to the above totals, the figures for the three years in question total £A1,114,281, £A2,426,128 and £A4,309,235 respectively. Of course, these figures exclude even the par value of the mines themselves which in 1936-37 had a combined value of £A2,072,261.[52]

III

The answer to why this originally limited and fitful collaboration amongst a select group of mining and treatment companies at Broken Hill became transformed into such a regular, widespread alliance between 1915 and 1939 must begin with the changes which developed in the international base metal mining and metallurgical industries in the two decades prior to the First World War.

During these twenty years the international trade in untreated concentrates, smelted and refined non-ferrous metals, fell very largely under the control of a small group of German companies sometimes known as 'The Trio'. Between 1883 and 1914 three metal trading companies known respectively as Metallgesellschaft AG and Beer, Sondheimer &

[52] Figures calculated from Annual Reports of NBH, BHS and ZC, 1918-1938, and MUA/ BHS,

Collins House Group, 1915–1951

Co., both of Frankfurt am Main, and Aron Hirsch und Sohn of Halberstadt, succeeded separately and jointly in vertically integrating on an international scale the mining, smelting, refining, sale and manufacturing of all the most important non-ferrous metals. In certain key strategic metals with military potential such as lead, zinc, copper and nickel, their control was such as to amount to a preponderant influence upon international prices.[53]

With interests in every continent, the commercial success of these German companies was felt particularly strongly in Australia. German interests predominated in the transportation, smelting, refining and marketing of all three of Australia's economically most important base metals, zinc, lead and copper. It has been estimated that by 1914 virtually the whole output of Australian zinc, with the exception of local consumption and that exported by the English-registered Sulphide Corporation Ltd., was under the control of these German companies through the Spelter Convention.[54]

In addition, with the exception of the lead consumed locally and marketed through BHP, an overwhelming proportion of Australian metallic lead and concentrates was either sold directly to 'The Trio' for consumption by their smelters, or sold to the Metallgesellschaft as sole buying agents for the International Lead Convention which had been formed in 1909.[55] By 1914, NBH, BHS and the ZC all had contracts with one or other members of 'The Trio', for the sale of one or both of these metals.[56] Although a smaller proportion of copper produced in Australia found its way directly into German hands, the very considerable German influence in the American copper industry ensured that a much greater proportion of the profits of this production found its way into these same channels than was immediately apparent.[57] Furthermore, the Mount Morgan Gold Mining Co. Ltd. appointed Aron Hirsch und Sohn as

[53] Robert Liefmann, 'Die internationale Organisation des Frankfurther Metallhandels', *Weltwirtshaftliches Archiv*, Vol. I, No. 1 (1913), pp. 108–22 (a translation of this very important article can be found in PRO/CO 885/25/324 under the title 'The International Organization of the Frankfurt Metal Trade'); see also *The Mining Journal*, 17 July 1915; *The Ironmonger*, 18 March 1916; U.S. Federal Trade Commission, *Report on Co-operation in the American Export Trade*, Vol. I (Washington D.C. 1916), pp. 357–69.

[54] *The Mining Journal*, 17 July 1915; see also Ernest Smith, *The Zinc Industry* (London 1918), pp. 10–43, 148–60.

[55] *The Age*, 22 July 1915, Report of Speech by William Hughes; for a full discussion of the crisis precipitated by Hughes' investigations see Frank Carrigan, 'The Imperial Struggle for Power in the Broken Hill Base-Metal Industry' in E. L. Wheelwright and K. Buckley (eds.), *Essays in the Political Economy of Australian Capitalism*, Vol. 5 (Sydney 1983), pp. 164–86.

[56] PRO/CO 881/15/229/43920, Munro-Ferguson to Bonar Law, 22 September 1915.

[57] AA/CRS/A481/File 3: Memorandum dated 1916 re The Metal Industry: German Domination in Australia, Copper; see also AMG/Informations Bureau: No. 30i: Kupfer Australien: Australian Metal Co. Ltd. to Metallgesellschaft AG, 15 April 1907.

15

Peter Richardson

their world selling agents for the only large-scale custom copper smelter in Australia, the Port Kembla works of ER&S.[58]

The basis of German control was the companies' ability to enter into long-term contracts either for the purchase of untreated concentrates or for the treated metal output. This ability in turn rested upon three very important aspects of the German metal trade. The first was the metal companies' ability to secure subsidized or 'through' freight rates from the mines to the European smelters. The second aspect was the companies' ownership or control of large-scale smelting works in Europe or North America, themselves tied to the trading companies by long-term supply contracts.[59] The third element was the trading companies' ready access to long- and short-term international credits and capital which permitted them to buy in very considerable bulk and invest heavily in the smelting, refining, fabricating and marketing of non-ferrous metals.[60] These three features of the German metal trading houses derived from a common root: their intimate association with large German banks, and through these banks with other large German industrial and commercial concerns.[61]

This elaborate international structure was virtually destroyed by the First World War. In the face of mounting evidence of the strategic implications for the Allied war effort of this effective monopoly, the Australian Commonwealth Government intervened to help break the contractual hold of these German companies over the output of Australian base metals.[62] Under the terms of the Enemy Contracts Annulment Act of 1915, Australian registered companies were freed from any further liability pertaining to their supplying contracts with German companies.[63] English registered companies operating in Australia were not similarly freed until the action brought by Aron Hirsch und Sohn for breach of contract by the ZC had been lost and the High Court decision later confirmed by the Board of Trade under powers vested in the Board by the Trading with the Enemy Acts.[64] The enforced withdrawal of the

[58] PRO/CO/881/15/229/43920, Munro-Ferguson to Bonar Law, 22 September 1915.
[59] For example the Metallbank und Metallurgische Gesellschaft, a foundation of the Metallgesellschaft, held shares of a combined book value of RM 31,291,510.60 in European and American smelting and metal trading companies, see AMG/Informations Bureau: Wilhelm Merton, 'Ein Widerspruch mit Liefmann' (unpublished manuscript 1913), Anlage IV, pp. 52-53.
[60] *Report on Co-operation in the American Export Trade, Vol. 1*, p. 359; a very full report and analysis of these relationships can be found in the decisions of the English Prize Court in the case of the s.s. *Bilbster* (Cargo Ex), reported in *Lloyds List*, 7 October 1915, and the case of the s.s. *Manningtry* (Cargo Ex) in *Lloyds List*, 13 October 1915.
[61] Liefmann, 'Die Internationale Organisation', pp. 116-17.
[62] Ernest Scott, *Australia During the War* (Sydney 1936), pp. 555-58.
[63] Act No. 11 of 1915.
[64] ZC v Aron Hirsch und Sohn, 19 November to 21 December 1915, *All England Law Reports, 1914-15*, pp. 487-96. Statement by Francis Govett to 5th. AGM of ZC, 26 June 1916, in *Financial Times*, 27 June 1916.

Collins House Group, 1915–1951

German metal companies from the Australian market created a vacuum in the Australian mining industry which mining companies at Broken Hill were forced to fill simply to re-establish outlets for the realization of their products. Without this initiative, losses and closure were almost inevitable. However, the scale of operations required was so extensive that no single mine could either meet the capital requirements or supply sufficient raw material to justify the venture. In this way was born the co-operative association of the three leading Broken Hill mines, which was to be known as the CHG. Only by such close collaboration and association could the three companies meet the common need for large amounts of capital, raw material, and new markets.

In some important characteristics, the CHG differed fundamentally from the German companies that it replaced. First, despite its international orientation, the Group was much more restricted in its operations than those of any of the constituent companies of 'The Trio'. The CHG remained a fundamentally Anglo-Australian operation in terms of the sources of its capital, profits and markets, despite its associations with other groups both from within and outside of the British Empire. Second, the Group's major source of capital derived from the profits either of its mining companies or other operations vertically integrated into its productive cycle. By contrast, the German companies had derived increasing amounts of capital from their association with financial institutions together with profits from their operations as metal traders rather than producers.[65] Only in the case of the National Smelting and the ISC, where the role of Lloyds Bank Ltd. was significant in providing investment capital, did the Group have any major association with financial institutions for the provision of capital for one of its projects.[66] Third, whereas the German companies, and particularly the Metallgesellschaft, showed an increasing tendency to raise capital by a combination of financial association and public subscription of capital in companies controlled by the founding house, the CHG relied on neither course to augment its own sources of capital.[67] Whilst generally eschewing publicly subscribed issues of capital to increase the total amount of available funds, the Group increasingly relied upon private subscription of capital from other companies operating in similar markets or with a particular area of expertise to found proprietary or non-listed enterprises to further its operations.

[65] Liefmann, 'Die Internationale Organisation', pp. 113–19; AMG/Informations Bureau: Merton, 'Ein Widerspruch mit Liefmann', *passim*; see also Hans Achinger, *Wilhelm Merton in Seiner Zeit* (Frankfurt/Main 1965), pp. 53–93.

[66] Cocks and Walters, *Zinc Smelting*, pp. 48–50; the English, Scottish and Australian Bank Ltd., and the earlier London Bank of Australia Ltd., had a long standing association with Collins House, although no investment capital was provided by these banks in CHG activities, see D. T. Merrett, *ANZ Bank. A History of the Australia and New Zealand Banking Group Ltd. and its Constituents* (Sydney 1985), p. 200.

[67] Liefman, 'Die Internationale Organisation', pp. 117–18.

17

Peter Richardson

Fourth, the core mining companies of the CHG were not linked directly by any interlocking shareholdings in each other's concern. Such unity as existed derived from an alliance of perceived and acknowledged common interests forged initially at executive level and rooted in a tradition of earlier co-operation, personal friendship and kinship networks.[68] Only subsequently were more formal linkages created. However, prior to 1949 these were only in new and subsidiary organizations, not in the core companies themselves. By contrast, the German companies, particularly the Metallgesellschaft Group, were characterized by a highly leveraged capital structure. Metallgesellschaft AG, Henry R. Merton & Co. Ltd., the American Metal Co., the Metallbank und Metallurgische Gesellschaft all had shareholdings of varying amounts in the central companies of the Group. This created a system of interlocking share-holdings and directorships of a more formal and elaborate type than existed in the case of the CHG.[69]

Yet in two fundamental respects 'The Trio' and the CHG, which largely replaced it, were similar. In the first case, both groups were characterized by a form of organization which resembled a confederation. Both relied, in the last resort, upon means of unity and cohesion which were strikingly different from the multifunctional and multidivisional companies which were beginning to become the predominant form of business organization in Europe and Japan as well as in the United States.[70] In the second case, for both groups the basic means of integration was through interlocking capital ownership, common management and market sharing agreements, rather than a centralized capital and bureaucratic structure.

IV

Why was such an organizational form adopted and why was it retained for so long? In part the answers to these questions must be sought in the circumstances which surrounded the CHG's inception. In the circumstances of the First World War, means had to be found to bring together capital resources, management expertise and raw material supplies in the shortest possible time and on the greatest possible scale. In an environment, both in Britain and in Australia, in which new capital and business organization could not be created through public flotation and subscription to new companies, co-operative collaboration of existing enterprises with sufficient capital was the only means of meeting the

[68] See page 7 above; the significance of networks based on kinship, family and friendship is discussed in J. Scott and C. Griff, *Directors of Industry. The British Corporate Network, 1904-76* (Oxford 1984), pp. 100-27.

[69] *Report on Co-operation in the American Export Trade*, pp. 365-68.

[70] Alfred Chandler, 'The Emergence of Managerial Capitalism', *Business History Review*, 58 (1984), pp. 473-503.

Collins House Group, 1915–1951

situation created by the destruction of the German organization.[71] Further, in the atmosphere of xenophobic nationalism created by the War, limiting the range of participation for security reasons was an additional incentive to create companies with a restricted number of shareholders and customers.[72] Finally, by maintaining existing company structures, and limiting collaboration to subsidiary organizations, risk was much more broadly spread and kept at a distance from the parent organization.

It must also be acknowledged that the long-life mining companies at Broken Hill did not face an overriding imperative to adopt a different form of organization and integration in the years that followed their initial collaboration. Despite differences of mining costs and mine life expectancy, all three companies in the period 1915–39 were faced with a fundamentally similar economic environment. All three companies were, in the last resort, dependent upon the wealth of their mine at Broken Hill for their survival. All three faced identical economic conditions whether in Australia or overseas which placed a premium on co-operation but not necessarily upon unity. Further, all stood to gain from joint vertical integration of their operations through reduction of direct costs and the spread of overheads, through the joint stimulus to demand in home and overseas markets, through the mutual increase of each other's bargaining power in labour and produce markets and the spreading of risk. Yet, none of these advantages were dependent upon more formal means of integration. Indeed, there were serious obstacles to any different form of operation, given this combination of circumstances.

Once created, such patterns of organization and ownership became increasingly difficult and impracticable to change. As each new interest and investment remained the part-property of legally distinct mining companies, each answerable to a broad range of shareholders in Australia and Britain, the valuation of these holdings in any common form remained a constant problem. The solution of merging the parent mining companies into one single entity became less and less possible as the overall value of each operation increased. The capital required by any one company to effect a takeover of the other two became progressively greater and therefore harder to secure or justify. Similarly, any such solution, even if possible in terms of capital resources available, would have given rise to a ruinously expensive scheme of arrangement because of the very high stamp duty and taxation costs involved. These considerations weighed even more heavily because of the Anglo-Australian

---

[71] Statement by Francis Govett to 5th AGM of ZC, 26 June 1916, in *Financial Times*, 27 June 1916.

[72] C. B. Johnstone, 'A History of the Origins, Formation and Development of the Broken Hill Associated Smelters Proprietary Ltd. at Port Pirie, South Australia' (University of Melbourne, Ph.D. thesis, 1982), pp. 243–67.

Peter Richardson

nature of the Group. For these reasons, such Broken Hill takeovers or mergers as did involve NBH, BHS and ZC were limited to much less valuable mining properties. In the interwar period the largest of these was the takeover of the British Broken Hill Pty. Ltd. by NBH in 1923, followed by the Junction Mine in 1929, the Junction North in 1931 and Block 14 in 1942.[73] Similarly the BHS purchased the worked out leases of the Sulphide Corporation in 1940, and Block 10 and BHP companies in 1943.[74] The ZC purchased the non-mining assets of the Sulphide Corporation in 1948.[75]

The alternative form of centralization available to the CHG, through a merger of common interests, was no less difficult. The adjustment and valuation of different interests and the question of control in any merger of this type remained an insuperable obstacle. It was for this reason that the so-called Broken Hill Trust never materialized. First mooted in 1927-28 to coincide with the major expansion of CHG interests associated with the acquisition of ER&S, and its two subsidiaries, MM and AB, the proposed Trust was an attempt to merge mining company shareholdings in a common company with a view to adding additional public capital at a later time. The idea was to leave the mines as separate entities but joint controllers of these investments, or in the event of a change in the balance of shareholdings to avoid giving control to any one company.[76] Difficulties with valuation and forms of control precluded any rapid adoption of the scheme. By the time these had approached a solution the onset of the Depression effectively curtailed any further discussion of the project. In 1939, the proposal was revived in modified form, once again to cope with a spurt of expansion associated with the creation of CAC and APPM, only to be dropped again because of opposition from NBH and the onset of the Second World War.[77] The very changed circumstances of the postwar period precluded any re-opening of the scheme.

However, there were not only negative reasons for adopting this confederate form for the Group's interests. Confederation could also easily accommodate new companies, cope with the demise of old ones and adjust to joint venture agreements without fundamental disruption. Such a form of integration could also permit delicate adjustments and alterations in the relative balance of economic power between the associated companies. Furthermore, such an arrangement facilitated the emergence of more bureaucratized management relations within each company with-

[73] PRO/BT 31/14892/25306, Special Resolution of British BHP Ltd., passed 27 March 1923 and confirmed 11 April 1923.
[74] Woodward, *Broken Hill*, pp. 2-4.
[75] *Annual Report of ZC, 31 December 1948.*
[76] MUA/NBH: 2nd Acc: SC: Broken Hill Finance, Memorandum re Proposed General Investment Trust Co. Ltd., 3 May 1927, enc. in Fraser to Sec., NBH, 5 January 1928.
[77] Kennett, 'The Collins House Group', pp. 228-29.

Collins House Group, 1915-1951

out endangering the overall pattern of relationships. This can be seen clearly in the form of development pursued by the ZC. From the time of its involvement with the National Smelting Corporation in 1923, the ZC was institutionally an Anglo-Australian concern whose range of interests more and more argued for the adoption of the type of management structure akin to that of a multinational corporation. However, the nature of arrangements within the Group were such that a whole range of adjustments between the ZC and the other companies was possible before formal severance from Collins House became necessary for ZC's continued development.

V

The existence of the confederate form of integration within the CHG put a premium upon certain types of integrative structures. Most important in this respect, and fundamental to the whole operation, was the creation of a number of interlocking shareholdings by the mining and metallurgical companies in other separate companies. Originally, the companies participating in this way were NBH, BHS, ZC and AZ. Subsequently, EZ and BHAS were elevated to the status of participating enterprises as was the ISC in England. In the interwar period the Group's most important common shareholdings were found in several types of company. First, there were those companies which were wholly, but jointly, owned subsidiaries such as BHAS, Western New South Wales Electric Power Co. Pty. Ltd., the Globe Timber Co., and the Australian Ore and Metal Co. Second, there were companies in which the Group had substantial common shareholdings which amounted to control. The most important of these companies were APPM, ER&S, MM and AB. Third, there were companies in which the Group had substantial common shareholdings, representation and influences which did not amount to control. The three largest concerns in this category were BALM, ISC and its subsidiary the National Smelting Co. Ltd., and the Australian Aluminium Co. Pty. Ltd. Fourth, there were the minority holdings of financial and strategic market value. Most important in this respect were the Group's shares in ICIANZ, CFC, CAC and the BMC.

This interlocking network of corporately owned shareholding accounts for the formidable pattern of interlocking directorships which further sustained the unity and cohesion of the CHG. The personal links between leading figures of the early CHG, such as W. L. Baillieu, W. S. Robinson, Colin Fraser and J. L. Wharton, which brought the Group into being, became transformed in this context into relationships based on common corporate affiliation and control. One of the most important of these networks of interlocks were those that strengthened the forward and backward linkages of the associated companies.

Peter Richardson

This reflected the pattern of wholly owned companies quite directly. Thus, as in the case of supplies of mining stores and electrical power and compressed air, the interlocks moved vertically backward. They also moved vertically forward to cover consumers such as smelters, refiners and other users of materials involving lead, zinc and copper.[78] These interlocks also moved horizontally to cover associated base and precious metal mines, as in the case of the Mount Read and Roseberry Mines after 1920, Burma Mines after 1923, GEFCA after 1934, and between 1915 and 1927, the Mount Morgan Gold Mining Co.[79] In one important respect, however, these interlocks differed from the interlocking corporate shareholdings which by and large they reflected. This was in the case of the core companies. Throughout the interwar period, there was a high degree of reciprocity of directors between these companies, reflecting the residual importance of the personal linkages which had brought the Group into existence. As was indicated above, these interlocks were not reflected in reciprocal capital ownership.[80]

Directorial interlocks within the Group further reflected shareholding patterns in their relationship with associated industries and competitors in certain branches of manufacturing. This pattern can be seen particularly clearly in the chemical industry where interlocking directorships held by the Group served the dual purpose of retaining leverage over companies like ICIANZ, and ensured co-operation with companies producing superphosphates.[81]

Other CHG interlocks also ensured leverage over sources of bank finance. Collins House directors were found on the boards of Australian and British banks providing financial services to the Group, namely the English, Scottish and Australian Bank and Lloyds Bank Ltd.[82]

Links within the Group were sustained by other formal devices. Of particular importance were the long-term supply agreements which were

[78] For example in 1930, W. S. Robinson was a director of the Australian Ore and Metal Co. Pty. Ltd., Austral Metals Ltd., BMC, ISC, and the National Smelting Co. Ltd.; in addition he was on the London Board of EZ, NBH, and MS&DBPA, and Managing Director of ZC, and BHAS. See Skinner, *The Mining Year Book for 1930*, pp. 49–50, 85, 90, 129, 193, 259, 366, 397, and 695.

[79] In addition to the above W. S. Robinson was, for example, also joint managing director of the Burma Corporation Ltd. (India) which had been registered in London in 1919 to take over Burma Mines Ltd., see Skinner, *Mining Year Book*, pp. 99–100; similarly, W. L. Baillieu in 1919 was on the board of EZ, AZ, BHAS, NBH, Mount Morgan, Mount Elliott, and ZPA, see Skinner, *Mining Manual for 1919*, pp. 12–13, 77–78, 179–86, 338–39, 383 and 602–03.

[80] Thus in 1919, the Deputy Chairman of BHS, William Hyndman, was also Chairman of NBH and on the local Board of the ZC; Thomas Birkbeck was at the same time on the Board of NBH and on the local Board of ZC; Henry Clinton was on the Board of ZC and on the London Board of AZ — a combination also enjoyed by Francis Govett — see Skinner, *Mining Manual for 1919*, pp. 613, 623, 642 and 653.

[81] MUA/BHAS/1/134, Colin Fraser to W. S. Robinson, 13 July 1936; Todhunter to Morrison, 8 March 1929.

[82] A. P. Warren, *The Kingdom of Collins House* (Sydney 1939), pp. 5 and 15.

Collins House Group, 1915–1951

a standard feature of Collins House trading. These agreements covered wholly or partially owned consumers of the Group's mine and smelter output and other large consumers of metal products. The most significant of the 'internal' supply contracts covered the combined Group output of Broken Hill lead concentrates to BHAS. These supplies were controlled under agreements which varied between 50 and 15 years and were particularly favourable to the owner companies, the so-called shareholding supply companies.[83] Another long 'external' supply contract covered the 50-year agreement between the Group's mines and the Zinc Producers Association (ZPA). Established in 1916, this Association became the principal supplier of zinc concentrates under another long-term agreement with the British Government.[84] With the termination of this agreement in 1930, the BHAS form of long-term contract was applied to a direct 15-year agreement between the Group's mines and EZ and the ISC in Britain, and the ZPA dissolved in 1934.[85] Other shorter-term 'external' supply contracts also bound the Group together. During part of the First World War and the whole of the Second for example, the BHAS entered into contracts with the British Government for the joint supply of pig lead for a period covering the duration of hostilities and a period of months thereafter.[86]

These long-term supply contracts were buttressed by a number of market sharing arrangements and agency agreements which further cemented the links within the Group. Within a short time after the cessation of hostilities in World War I, the Group was forced into collaborative agreement with foreign producers of lead and zinc to protect its interests. To undertake the marketing of lead from BHAS, the Group established the Australian Ore and Metal company, whilst in zinc marketing the companies appointed the BMC as agents for their joint London representative, Austral Development. At the same time, joint representation was established in New York through Charles Tennant and Co., a well known metal broker on the London and New York Metal Exchanges.[87] To head off the prospect of American and renewed German competition and even American-German collaboration, the Group went further and

[83] MUA/WSRP, Misc. Subject Files: BHAS: Copies of contracts between ZC and BHAS, 10 June 1915; ZC and BHAS, 13 July 1933, and NBH, BHS and ZC and BHAS, 26 January 1945.
[84] MUA/GBR, A. E. Bright Papers, copy of draft agreement between the Sulphide Corporation Ltd. and ZPA dated June 1916, enclosure in Birkbeck, Yeo & Co. to Broad & Co., 8 June 1916.
[85] MUA/WSRP: Misc. Files: ZPA, Memorandum by A. J. C. Bult on ZPA, 30 November 1948.
[86] Johnstone, 'History of BHAS', pp. 291–92; MUA/WSRP, Misc. Subject Files: Non-Ferrous Metals Control: Report on Contracts with the British Government for the Supply of Lead and Zinc by W. S. Robinson, 6 June 1945.
[87] MUA/WSRP, Misc. Subject Files: Non-Ferrous Metal Control: Confidential Memorandum on External Representation of Australian Industries, 9 October 1944.

Peter Richardson

established a series of agreements with 'friends' for the protection of the Group's outlets. The architect of this policy, W. S. Robinson, described it in the following way:

> The policy I have followed has roughly been to link up the British Empire, France, Belgium and Scandinavian interests, forming practically unbroken lines from Norway to South Africa, and from the United Kingdom to Australasia. In South America, except where Latin sympathies are deep-seated, we can hope to do little against the Americans... In North America, I have linked up the Australian, British and Hudson Bay interest for the purpose of quietly entering into the development of Canada, where the Americans have threatened to take everything.[88]

In 1929, these associations were extended to the international lead cartel and in 1931 to the international zinc cartel. Despite the complete failure of the lead cartel because of its highly proliferated ownership, and the limited success of the zinc cartel, these relationships secured a continuing outlet for the Group's products at a time of severe international overproduction and naturally further cemented relationships within the confederation.[89]

If long-term supply contracts, market sharing and agency agreements were the core of the Group's external representation, they were only part of the scheme of arrangement that held the CHG together in this area. A whole series of government policies, in Britain and Australia, further strengthened these ties, and in the case of the zinc cartel, gave official support for market sharing schemes. Two aspects of the Australian government's trade policy reacted in this way upon the Group. In the field of metal fabrication, the Group benefited from the increasing protection given to the Australian market. This was to be particularly important in the fields of copper and galvanized iron production after 1921.[90] In the field of untreated concentrate production, the adherence of the Commonwealth Government to the terms of the Ottawa Agreement in 1932, ensured a degree of British preference for Australian ores against non-Empire sources.[91]

[88] Robinson to Hughes, 19 April 1920, quoted in Julius Roe, 'Companies, Prices and Pressures: The Broken Hill Strike, 1919–1920' (ANU BA Honours thesis, 1974), pp. 50–51.

[89] MUA/BHAS/1/85/4, Memorandum on Cartel Formation by I. Mikolajczak, 30 October 1934; MUA/BHS, Reports by J. B. Were & Co. on Broken Hill Cos., 1936–37: E.7 EZ; for a full discussion of the international base metal cartels in this period see W. Y. Ellliott, *et al.*, *International Controls in Non-Ferrous Metals* (New York 1937).

[90] CPP 1934, Tariff Board, *Report No. 18 — Copper and Copper Products*, 29 June 1934; Tariff Board, *Report No. 44 — Zinc and Spelter*, 29 June 1934.

[91] Ian Drummond, *Imperial Economic Policy 1917–1939: Studies in Expansion and Protection* (London 1974), pp. 200–02; A. J. Reitsma, *Trade Protection in Australia* (Leiden 1960), pp. 55–56; David L. Glickman, 'The British Imperial Preference System', *Quarterly Journal of Economics*, LXI (1947), pp. 439–70.

24

Collins House Group, 1915–1951

Arrangements adopted by the British government also bore directly on the marketing organization of the Group and placed a premium on its cohesion. The case of the long-term zinc contract negotiated during the First World War was only the best known and most controversial of the arrangements adopted by the British to implement the Empire Base Metals scheme.[92] Active encouragement to develop zinc smelting in Britain after 1917, although not initially favourable to the Group, became much more so after 1923 with the take-over of the National Smelting Corporation.[93] The development of this corporation remained problematic, however, despite this encouragement from official sources. The necessity of placating rival Empire interests in the Base Metals Scheme resulted in output restrictions being imposed upon the corporation after 1939 and the payment of a subvention to the smelters to compensate for lost production.[94] These fluctuations in British policy, with their serious implications for profitability, undoubtedly tended to render co-operation and association even more important, especially so in the unstable economic conditions of the interwar period.[95]

Relations binding the Group together did not end with interlocking shareholdings and directorships, and the marketing arrangements outlined above. Technology also provided a major source of interconnection within the Group. Most significant in this case was MS&DBPA.[96] This company, which was located in Collins House, controlled by Collins House directors and in which AZ had a major shareholding, gave the Group at one stroke a monopoly over all of the most successful flotation patents which had made possible the separation of the lead from zinc in the Broken Hill ores and which had been the foundation for part of the fortunes being earned by the associated companies. Thereafter, the company earned royalty payments on its patents and established a lucrative consulting business on the basis of the technology that it owned. Furthermore, it ensured that the Collins House Group kept abreast of the new developments in this critical field and controlled the emergence of possible competitors.[97]

This example was by no means unique. The Group also secured the dual advantages of collaboration and technological superiority over potential rivals in its development of the electrolytic processes in zinc and

---

[92] A copy of this contract can be found in MUA/GBR, A. E. Bright Papers, 1917–19, Agreement between ZPA and the Board of Trade, dated 12 September 1918.
[93] Cocks and Walters, *Zinc Smelting*, pp. 31–72.
[94] BPP 1939, Cmd. 6028, Import Duties Advisory Committee, *Recommendations of the Import Duties Advisory Committee and Import Duties (Substitution) (No. 2) Order, 1939 (Zinc or Spelter)*, May 1939.
[95] W. S. Robinson, 'The Zinc Problem — The Origin and Development of the Australian Industry', *The Age*, 22 December 1948.
[96] Skinner, *The Mining Manual for 1919*, pp. 325–26.
[97] A full description of the processes covered by this merger can be found in Theordore J. Hoover, *Concentrating Ores by Flotation* (London 1912).

Peter Richardson

copper refining, together with its persistent refinements of the lead smelting and refining processes at BHAS at Port Pirie.[98] Later, with the development of the Imperial Smelting Process in Britain, the critical interrelationship between technology, profits and Group cohesion was again demonstrated.[99]

The companies of the CHG were held together in other ways. Through the institutions of the Broken Hill-based Mine Managers Association and the Melbourne-based Committee of the Barrier Mines, the increasingly dominant Group mines produced a working relationship which affected in the minutest detail the lives of the core companies. Out of this partnership grew the famous Round Table wage bargaining system, which withdrew the companies and employees from the direct purview of the New South Wales Artibration System in 1925.[100] A similar basis for common action was fostered by the ZPA whose directorate was increasingly dominated by the big deep level Group mines. At the end of the Association's life in 1934, only Group mines were supplying any concentrates under the 50 year agreements.[101]

Finally, the associated companies were brought together by a whole range of supporting financial, legal and secretarial services. Collins House was not only the headquarters of mining, manufacturing, and technical companies. It was also home to the legal companies, Pavey, Wilson and Cohen, and Arthur Robinson & Co. Group Australian underwriters, E.L. & C. Baillieu, also worked out of the Collins Street headquarters. Most important of all in this regard was undoubtedly the firm of Edward H. Shackell & Co., later to be known as Secretariat Proprietary Ltd. Throughout the interwar period, this firm doubled as company secretaries and managers for an astonishing array of Group companies. The significance of this arrangement was emphasized by the *Australian Financial Review*:

> What an effective instrument of centralised control it was may be realized from the fact that companies as large and important as, say, Electrolytic Zinc and Associated Pulp and Paper Mills, might not have their employees as business manager, secretary or chief accountant, but officers placed there by Secretariat. As many as 40 goldmining companies — brief meteors, some of them, to be sure — passed through Secretariat. At the height of its influence it was responsible for the management of 56 companies, including such substantial ones as E.Z. and Metal Manufactures.[102]

[98] Johnstone, 'History of BHAS', pp. 450–52; Frank A. Green, *The Port Pirie Smelters* (Melbourne 1977), pp. 14–54.
[99] S. W. K. Morgan, 'The Advent of the Imperial Smelting Process' in Cocks and Walters, *Zinc Smelting*, pp. 161–80.
[100] Kenneth F. Walker, *Australian Industrial Relations Systems* (Melbourne 1970), pp. 178–240.
[101] See footnote 85 above.
[102] *Australian Financial Review*, 30 November 1961, p. 6.

Collins House Group, 1915–1951

VI

Yet even this formidable number of integrative devices was not proof against the emergence of structural weaknesses within the Group. These weaknesses ultimately struck at the very heart of the community of interests upon which the Group was founded, and finally destroyed it. Central to this process was the emergence of divergent interests amongst the mining companies which were the core of the CHG. As long as no single mining company possessed the resources to integrate vertically its own operations, the benefits of co-operation outweighed the costs. This was essentially the case until the late 1930s when the ZC brought into production its newly developed southern leases as the New Broken Hill Consolidated Co. Ltd. in 1936.[103] Under the stimulus of wartime demand, these two companies eventually dwarfed the output of NBH and BHS, and for the first time provided the basis for an integrated system of international zinc production controlled by one company. These developments were the rationale for the creation of the Consolidated Zinc Corporation (CZC) in 1949 by the merger of the ZC and ISC. This development was paralleled by the decision of CZC to establish its own power company at Broken Hill, the Southern Power Corporation Pty. Ltd., its own timber company, the Heron Creek Timber Mills Ltd., and to develop its own simultaneous lead and zinc smelting at the newly acquired Cockle Creek works, formerly owned by the Sulphide Corporation Ltd.[104]

The potential for disruption to Group collaboration by the changing balance of productive power was not confined to zinc. Even before the decision to explore its southern leases was taken by ZC in 1933, that company had shown a progressively upward trend in the output of its lead as well as zinc concentrate production. This gradually began to affect profit sharing arrangements within the BHAS. These had originally been founded upon a formula which took account of both the proportion of original capital subscribed and the proportion of total concentrate production delivered by the shareholding supply companies. Originally this system worked well, but as the balance of output between the three companies began to alter so too did relations between them begin to deteriorate. This development was aggravated by the long-term decline in the productivity of BHS. This had the effect of accelerating the imbalance in the productive capacity of the companies whilst shareholdings remained fixed in their original proportions.[105] By the late 1930s, the long-term deterioration in the BHS prospects was such that the company

---

[103] *Report of Proceedings of 1st AGM of New Broken Hill Consolidated Ltd.*, 20 July 1937.

[104] *Annual Report of CZC, 31 December 1949*, Chairman's Statement.

[105] MUA/WSRP, Corr. Files: A–B, Memorandum on Shareholdings in BHAS by M. L. Baillieu, 30 June 1944.

27

Peter Richardson

sought to defend its revenue and profits by holding onto a share proportion of the BHAS which was substantially out of line with its input
of lead concentrates. After several years of wrangling the situation was
adjusted in 1945. Although the increase in the share capital of the ZC
in BHAS from 25.34 to 50 per cent, and a reduction of BHS capital
from 33.56 to 13.56 per cent, and a reduction in NBH's percentage of
41.10 to 36.44 per cent, seemed like a settlement of the issue, it had
done lasting damage to the association of companies and had in effect
simply confirmed the dominance of ZC without introducing a new basis
for co-operation between the companies.[106]

The collapse of the community of interests based on the Broken Hill
mines, and with them the original CHG, was completed by the considerable changes in the markets for the Group's products after 1945
and the final disappearance of the founding members of the original
senior management. The NBH and BHS, with their greater commitment
to zinc concentrates delivery to EZ and its orientation towards the Australian market, suffered considerably from the retention of price controls
and export restriction after the war. On the other hand, the ZC, and
later CZC with the commitment to the English-based ISC, benefited from
a freer currency and export environment in Britain, especially after 1948
and the devaluation of sterling.[107] The price differential for the same
product which emerged as a result of this, exacerbated differences between
the companies already strained by quarrels over adjustments in productive
capacity at the BHAS.

Discussions amongst senior Collins House management over all these
issues were conducted with the knowledge that the old order was fast
disappearing. As with the material questions underlying the structural
reorganization of the Group, the depletion of management ranks predated
the Second World War. Most important in this respect was the retirement
of W.L. Baillieu in 1932 and his subsequent death in 1936. Equally serious
for the maintenance of these community of personal as well as material
interests was the death of Sir Colin Fraser in 1944. With the retirement
of W.S. Robinson from active management of the ZC in 1946, the demise
of the original triumvirate which had ensured CHG cohesion, even in
times of potential discord and in the absence of legally binding relationships between the mining companies themselves, was complete.[108]
Furthermore, with Robinson's retirement, the potential for discord in
the Group was exacerbated by the removal of an important link between
London and Australian interests. Communication between the Australian

[106] Woodward, *Broken Hill*, pp. 460–63.
[107] Robinson, 'The Zinc Problem'; *Annual Report of CZC Ltd., 31 December 1950*, Statement
by J. R. Govett.
[108] Poynter, 'Baillieu', p. 144; Kennett, 'Fraser', p. 577; *Annual Report of ZC, 31 December
1946*, p. 15.

Collins House Group, 1915–1951

and London companies of the Group became increasingly dominated by a sense of rival nationalism, fostered by ignorance and misunderstanding of respective aims and motives.[109]

All of these developments served to underline the same message: the need for separate rather than co-operative development in the postwar environment, particularly for the CZC. The logical conclusion to all these divergent trends came in 1951, when the wheel came full circle and CZC removed its Australian headquarters from Collins House and established a new one at 95 Collins Street.[110] Henceforth, any notion of a Group of companies in Collins House based on common interests became increasingly difficult to sustain.

Economic History
University of Melbourne

---

[109] Kosmas Tsokhas, *Beyond Dependence. Companies, Labour Processes and Australian Mining* (Melbourne 1986), pp. 37–42.
[110] *Annual Report of CZC, 31 December 1952*, Address of Australian Transfer Office.

By B.W.E. Alford
READER IN ECONOMIC HISTORY
UNIVERSITY OF BRISTOL
AND
C. E. Harvey
LECTURER IN ECONOMIC HISTORY
BRISTOL POLYTECHNIC

Copperbelt Merger: The Formation of the Rhokana Corporation, 1930-1932*

❡ *The concerted actions of giant companies operating on the international stage, notably in mining and petroleum, rival the Schleswig-Holstein question in complexity. In the absence of any clear understanding of the reasons for huge mergers such as that which took place in the southern African copper mining industry at the depth of the Great Depression, rationalizations that reflect Marxist-Leninist simplism and populist paranoia have been popular. Messrs. Alford and Harvey undertake to unravel the reasons for the copper merger, concluding that this merger defies modern, formal merger theory and teaches that there is no substitute for a close study of the motives of "corporate insiders."*

The widespread emergence of big business at the turn of the century was viewed by some observers, most notably by Lenin, as a crucial and late stage in the evolution of capitalism and imperialism. Yet nearly a century has gone by while the scale of business has increased both absolutely and in terms of concentration, and capitalism, if not imperialism, has proved to be an unconscionable time dying. Economic historians and economists, in particular, have identified a number of factors at work in this process, and they have laid special emphasis on developments in markets and technology, and on inter-related changes in business organization and practices that have achieved their highest form to date in the shape of the multi-divisional company.[1]

Business History Review, Vol. LIV, No. 3 (Autumn, 1980). Copyright © The President and Fellows of Harvard College.

* The authors wish to thank Prof. W. Ashworth and an anonymous referee for their comments on an earlier draft of this article. They are, also, particularly indebted to the Rio Tinto-Zinc Corporation for access to the records of the Rio Tinto Company Limited and to Dr. David Avery, Rio Tinto-Zinc company historian, for his help and advice.

[1] The best comprehensive treatment of this subject in an historical context is provided by Alfred D. Chandler Jr., *The Visible Hand: The Managerial Revolution in American Business* (Cambridge, Mass., 1977).

Even so, the causes and consequences of this continued growth in scale are still far from being understood. But while it proves difficult to comprehend the true nature of the new economic Leviathan, at least its growth and size have been carefully measured and, most interestingly, this has revealed that its progress has depended heavily on merger activity.[2] As yet, however, there is little detailed analysis of individual mergers so that it is impossible to judge whether merger activity should be viewed mainly as a response to the opportunities and pressures of market and technological changes, or whether it is, in part at least, the outcome of other business objectives.

The present study, which examines a crucial merger between three companies in the rich Northern Rhodesian Copperbelt in 1930, is offered as a small contribution towards filling this enormous gap in our knowledge of modern economic development. In addition, a cautious attempt will be made to evaluate some of the propositions of current merger theory in the light of this historical evidence. Moreover, indirectly this essay may throw a little light on the much wider issue of the political economy of southern Africa during a formative and fascinating period in its history.

EXPLORATION AND COMPANY PROMOTION

Mineral exploration in Northern Rhodesia gained impetus in the late nineteenth century as a natural extension of mining activities on the Rand.[3] Methods were hit and miss, with individual prospectors roaming the wastelands in search of an El Dorado. Conditions were harsh and success was elusive. But the possibility of buried treasure was a powerful attraction, and from 1906 onwards it became even stronger with the discovery of vast mineral wealth in the Belgian Congo, just over the border from Northern Rhodesia. In that year the *Union Minière du Haut Katanga* was formed; by 1929 it had become one of the world's leading suppliers. Such success was more than enough to stir the interests of hard-headed financiers in London, New York, and Johannesburg. Nevertheless, the technical problems of exploration in Northern Rhodesia remained formidable in comparison with the Congo: there were no

[2] For the U.K. evidence on this, see Leslie Hannah and J.A. Kay, *Concentration in Modern Industry: Theory, Measurement and the U.K. Experience* (London, 1977). The results of this study differ somewhat from other investigations into concentration: see S.J. Prais, *The Evolution of Giant Firms in Britain* (London, 1976).

[3] Full details of the early development of the Copperbelt are to be found in Theodore Gregory, *Ernest Oppenheimer and the Economic Development of Southern Africa* (London, 1962); F.L. Coleman, *The Northern Rhodesian Copperbelt, 1899–1962* (Manchester, 1971); K. Bradley, *Copper Venture* (London, 1952).

ancient workings or frequent copper outcrops to guide the prospector or his supplanter, the mining geologist.

In 1912, however, the British South Africa Company, which held the mineral rights to the whole of Northern Rhodesia, under the British crown, altered its policy of granting individual prospecting licenses to one of granting exclusive prospecting rights to large companies. Between 1922 and 1926 it granted six such concessions totaling 122,000 square miles — an area comparable in size to that of the U.K. Two of these proved successful: the Rhodesian Congo Border Concession (an area of 52,000 square miles) and the N'Kana Concession (1,800 square miles). Originally, both concessions had been granted to a company known as Copper Ventures Ltd., but in 1923 this company floated Rhodesian Congo Border Concession to develop that area, and in 1924 it sold the N'Kana Concession and the N'Kana prospect (otherwise known as the N'Kana claim) to the Bwana M'Kubwa Copper Mining Company Ltd. Subsequently, in 1926, Bwana M'Kubwa sold its rights in the N'Kana Concession to the Selection Trust. It retained the N'Kana claim (where large deposits were proved in 1927) and the right to subscribe 33 per cent of the voting capital to any new operating companies formed to extract ore from the N'Kana concession area.

As it happened, two substantial deposits were soon proved and two operating companies were established — Roan Antelope Copper Mines Ltd. (1927) and Mufulira Copper Mines Ltd. (1930). Moreover, in 1923, the year in which it had been floated, Rhodesian Congo Border Concession (hereafter referred to as RCBC) had discovered further copper ore deposits known as the N'Changa deposits, and in 1926 RCBC floated a company to develop this orebody, to be known as N'Changa Copper Mines Ltd., in which it retained nearly a half share. More exploration revealed that the N'Changa orebody extended into territory still controlled by RCBC. In effect, therefore, RCBC had been able to raise additional capital for the development of N'Changa while retaining financial and physical control over the whole area. Finally, all these developments were subject to the original undertaking given by Copper Ventures Ltd. to the British South Africa Company, which reserved to the latter participating rights and royalty rights on any ore raised.

Behind this flurry of mineral discovery there was a web of financial invention involving British, American, and South African interests. For the moment, however, the important fact is that by 1930 five companies controlled large copper deposits in Northern

Rhodesia: RCBC (1923); N'Changa Copper Mines Ltd. (1926);
Bwana M'Kubwa Copper Mining Company Ltd. (1910), which
since 1924 had a major interest in the N'Kana area; Roan Antelope
Copper Mines Ltd. (1927); Mufulira Copper Mines Ltd. (1930).
The estimated size and quality of their reserves on the eve of the
merger is shown in Table 1.

TABLE 1

THE PROVED AND PROBABLE RESERVES OF THE MAJOR COMPANIES
AS AT THE END OF SEPTEMBER 1930 (SHORT TONS OF 2,000 LB)

Company	Proved ore (m. tons)	% Copper	Probable ore (m. tons)	% Copper	Tons of copper in proved and probable ore
RCBC	47.82	7.3	38.76	8.1	6,630,420
N'Changa	64.28	3.8	21.60	3.8	3,263,440
Bwana M'Kubwa °	70.00	4.0	30.00	4.0	4,000,000
Total (Eventual Merging Companies)	182.10	4.8	90.36	5.7	13,893,860
Roan Antelope	70.00	3.3	30.00	3.3	3,300,000
Mufulira °°	75.00	4.5	25.00	4.5	4,500,000

° N'Kana only.

°° Bwana M'Kubwa held a 30 per cent interest in Mufulira.

Source: Rio Tinto Company Private Archives (R.T.C.): based upon a memorandum by
G. W. Gray headed "Cost of Northern Rhodesian Copper," September 25, 1930.

THE MERGER

The bare facts of the merger between RCBC, N'Changa, and
Bwana M'Kubwa, are that serious negotiations were begun in
1930, and that the outcome was a proposal that RCBC should absorb
the other two companies through an exchange of shares. This was
approved by the RCBC board on December 1, 1930 and by a meeting of the shareholders on December 17. The scheme provided for
an increase in RCBC's authorized capital of £750,000 in £1 shares to
a total of £2 million; of these new shares 676,689 were issued —
550,000 of which were used to acquire the assets of Bwana
M'Kubwa and 126,689 were allotted to the owners of N'Changa in
exchange for their existing shares. A little later, in March 1931, the
company was renamed the Rhokana Corporation.[4]

Having secured the merger by means of share exchanges, its
promoters then issued £4,500,000 7 per cent debentures, at par,

[4] Rio Tinto Company Private Archives (hereafter R.T.C.): "Rhokana Debenture Issue,"
April 20, 1931.

which were convertible to ordinary shares, *pro rata*, at rising prices up to the year 1940. The cash raised by this means was for a development fund that was to be applied primarily for the opening up of the N'Kana mine together with an integrated refinery.

Obviously, the critical factor in the scheme itself was the valuation of the individual companies and this turned on estimates of the potential worth of their ore reserves; an extremely tricky problem and, accordingly, an almost certain source of argument and disagreement. There was one saving factor, however: because the merger was to be on a share-exchange basis, the issue was one of relative and not absolute values, which would have been even more difficult to estimate. In fact, the formula for calculating values was very sophisticated and advanced by contemporary standards: the present worth of each property was estimated as the amount by which the present values of the flow of divisible net returns exceeded the capital investment required to bring the property into full production, if operated independently of the others. Operating costs were assumed to be constant.[5] The final estimates placed before the merger promoters are summarized in Table 2; the experts who produced them were employees of the various companies involved in the merger. RCBC and N'Changa were jointly represented at the negotiations because of RCBC's dominant shareholding in the latter and because the two properties were adjoining. Correspondingly, their valuations were combined.

The raw data on which all these estimates were based were supplied by Dr. J. A. Bancroft, well known as a leading mining expert and consulting geologist to both the Anglo American Corporation and the Rhodesian Anglo American Corporation, as well as being a close associate and *confidante* of the chairman of these companies, Sir Ernest Oppenheimer; the full significance of these connections will become clear a little later.[6] The discrepancies in the estimates arose not from the choice of discount rates or estimates of the capital required to open up and maintain the mines, but from calculations of operating costs. Quite simply, there were few hard facts available. After some tough arguing and bargaining, the estimates of G. W. Gray, technical director of the

---

[5] The rate of discount was taken at 7 per cent throughout the production period with 85 per cent of the gross profit taken as divisible. Each property was assumed to be able to produce 2.1 millions tons of ore per annum for 40 years with 90 per cent of the copper content being recoverable. N'Kana and Mufulira were assumed to come on stream after three years, N'Changa after four years, and RCBC after five years. Further details are available from the authors.

[6] For more details of Bancroft, see Gregory, *Oppenheimer*.

TABLE 2

COMPARATIVE VALUATIONS OF RCBC/N'CHANGA AND BWANA M'KUBWA *

Messrs:	RCBC/N'Changa: Bwana M'Kubwa
Munroe	0.9091 : 1
McNab	0.9852 : 1
Davis	0.9997 : 1
Gray	1.3990 : 1
Actual terms of merger	1.5929 : 1
Yeatman	2.4123 : 1
Adams	7.0685 : 1

* Based on the estimated present worths of their mining interests with copper at £55 per long ton.
Source: R.T.C.: Based on valuations contained in the following reports: H. S. Munroe, "Bwana M'Kubwa Copper Mining Company Limited and Rhodesian Congo Border Concession Limited," undated; A. J. McNab, "Comparative Valuation of Mines," undated; C. R. Davis, "Notes on the Proposed Amalgamation of the Bwana M'Kubwa Copper Mining Company Limited, RCBC and N'Changa," undated; G. W. Gray, "Comparative Valuation of Properties of the Bwana M'Kubwa, R.C.B.C., and N'Changa Properties," October 31, 1930; Pope Yeatman, "Report on the Proposed Amalgamation," undated; and Huntingdon Adams, "Valuation of Bwana M'Kubwa, RCBC and N'Changa Properties," November 5, 1930.

Rio Tinto Company and a member of the N'Changa board, were given greatest weight, though they were not unanimously accepted by the RCBC/N'Changa directorate. There were, however, four main reasons why Gray's results were taken in preference to the others: they offered something of a compromise; a number of the other experts were closely associated with the Rhodesian Anglo American Corporation, which, as will be seen, played a dominant role in the merger; Gray, in contrast with the others, knew all the properties in question; and he provided a detailed and powerful critique of the other reports in comparison with his own.[7]

Gray, did, in fact, produce two valuations based on alternative estimates of world copper prices. At £60 per long ton the division of the new company would have been in the proportions of RCBC 51.2 per cent, N'Changa 8.7 per cent, Bwana M'Kubwa 40.1 per cent. The actual agreement amounted to 52.6 per cent, 8.8 per cent and 38.6 per cent, respectively.

THE PROMOTERS

The Rhokana Corporation was promoted not by the companies themselves but by two international mining companies: Rhodesian

[7] R.T.C.: G.W. Gray, "Notes on Comparative Valuation of Bwana, RCBC, and N'Changa Properties," October 31, 1931.

Anglo American (1928) and the Rio Tinto Company (1873). The former company was under the leadership of Sir Ernest Oppenheimer, who was emerging as the outstanding figure in the economic development of South Africa since Cecil Rhodes, while the latter company was controlled by the London and Paris houses of Rothschilds, under the chairmanship of Sir Auckland Geddes, who had already distinguished himself as an academic, cabinet minister, and diplomat.[8] It must be added that Rhodesian Anglo American was controlled by the Anglo-American Corporation (1917), Oppenheimer's main company through which he had gradually established his ascendency in the South African diamond industry. To understand how these two companies had come together in this enterprise it is necessary to cast back over the previous year or so.

The relationship between the copper companies of the Northern Rhodesian copperbelt became critical at the very beginning of 1929, when the American Smelting and Refining Company (American Smelting) attempted a financial maneuver that, within the space of two years, would have given it control of the N'Changa company.[9] American Smelting was already a very large shareholder in the Rhodesian Selection Trust, a holding company established in 1928 by A. Chester Beatty, who became its chairman, to operate various businesses in Northern Rhodesia.[10] The intricacies of the scheme need not concern us here but the train of developments that it set in motion is of direct relevance.

The American offer prompted an immediate and somewhat startled outcry from various British interests. Sir Edmund Davis, Deputy Chairman of Rhodesian Anglo American and doyen of Rhodesian mining, wrote to Oppenheimer: "If the transaction goes through as represented . . . the American Smelting Company will have pulled off one of the most brilliant deals that have been put through . . . I feel that in the management of the smelting Company must be a number of people who can give me cards and spades in transactions of this kind . . . I do not think I could have thought out such a brilliant deal, and I certainly would not have had the nerve to put it to the owners." [11] Had the Americans

⁸ For details of Oppenheimer's life and career, see Gregory, *Oppenheimer*. For Rio Tinto, see D. Avery, *Not on Queen Victoria's Birthday — the Story of the Rio Tinto Mines* (London, 1974).

⁹ The next few paragraphs rely heavily on Gregory, *Oppenheimer*, 422 *et seq.*

¹⁰ Beatty was originally an American mining expert who subsequently developed a number of major financial interests in mining in southern Africa. He later became a British citizen and Knight of the Realm.

¹¹ Gregory, *Oppenheimer*, 424–425.

succeeded in their audacity it would have meant a significant reduction in British-cum-South African influence in Rhodesia. Oppenheimer, in particular, was dead set against such an eventuality,
and strongly supported the formation of a defensive alliance of
nine British-based companies with large interests in the area, which
then proceeded to block the American bid by putting forward a
counter offer.[12] Furthermore, Davis secured support from Chester
Beatty in respect of certain shareholdings he controlled, a move
that particularly pleased Oppenheimer, as he saw Beatty's and his
own companies as the natural leaders in Northern Rhodesia. In
May 1929, a formal offer from the consortium was accepted by the
N'Changa board.

The immediate effect of this agreement was to provide N'Changa
with the funds it needed for the development of its mining operations, while retaining British/South African control over the company. Indirectly, it secured three further, important advantages for
Oppenheimer: it established Rhodesian Anglo American in the
City of London independently of its parent company, Anglo-
American; it settled a general *modus vivendi* with Beatty; and it
established particularly friendly relations with Rio Tinto. In relation to the last point, Oppenheimer went so far as to contemplate
an amalgamation of British mining interests in Northern Rhodesia,
but then his enthusiasm cooled. Indeed, in May 1930 he became
concerned about the balance of shareholdings between Rio Tinto
and his own company in RCBC and N'Changa and proceeded to
take steps to ensure that this balance was altered to his satisfaction.
In the meantime he made certain of his control of Rhodesian Anglo
American and, in turn, of this company's control of Bwana
M'Kubwa.[13]

In August 1930 Oppenheimer was in London, and by this time
it was becoming clear that the world copper market was deteriorating rapidly. At this point he wrote two memoranda. One
was for his City friends and in it he analyzed Rhodesian Anglo
American's interests in Northern Rhodesia:

(1) It has approximately a 54 per cent interest in Bwana, and as
Bwana has roughly a 30 per cent interest in all Rhodesian Selection
Trust properties in the N'Kana area, Rhodesian Anglo American con-
trols a substantial minority interest in the Chester Beatty group . . .

[12] The companies were British South Africa Company, British Metal Corporation, Johannesburg Consolidated, Rio Tinto, N.M. Rothschild and Sons, Union Corporation, Anglo Metal
Company, Minerals Separation, and Rhodesian Anglo American.
[13] This at least involved him closely with an American company, the Newmont Mining
Corporation of New York, which was an important shareholder in Rhodesian Anglo American.

SOUTHERN AFRICAN COPPER MERGER   337

[and given certain undertakings with the British South Africa Company this could be increased] to about 36 per cent or 37 per cent.

(2) RAA is the largest shareholder in the Rhodesian Congo Border Concession . . and it has established friendly relations with the Rio Tinto Group, which, as a group, has a somewhat larger shareholding than Rhodesian Anglo American.

(3) It controls the various Rhodesian concession companies.

(4) RAA is the biggest individual shareholder in the British South Africa Company.[14]

He went on to point out that the company, and through it Anglo American, were as fully committed to their copper interests as they could afford to be. They had drawn very heavily on their reserves, and Anglo American was heavily and increasingly committed to financing the ominously sagging diamond market, to the extent that he judged it to be substantially "over-invested." [15] His analysis and comments amounted, therefore, to a thinly veiled case for raising capital for further development of the group's diamond and copper interests.

The second document was a long letter from Oppenheimer to Geddes setting out the case for the amalgamation of RCBC, N'Changa, and Bwana M'Kubwa on technical, financial, and political, grounds. For the moment, however, it is important to note that this letter was of a formal nature and was, in fact, read out to a general meeting of shareholders a few months later. It was following this letter that Rhodesian Anglo American and Rio Tinto and its associates agreed to promote the merger. The line up of shareholders is shown in Table 3.

It is important to note that Rothschilds controlled the Rio Tinto company, and the international standing and sheer financial power of this house consequently gave the group an influence out of proportion to its strict paper value.[16] The London and Paris Rothschilds had become involved in Rio Tinto in the late 1880s and in 1929 they held 36.2 per cent of the company's issued ordinary shares; N. M. Rothschild had 21.6 per cent and Rothschild Frères, 14.6 per cent. The remaining shares were spread among very small British and French interests.[17] Rio Tinto was charged with managing the Rothschild holdings in the Copperbelt, and this included their 17-per-cent stake in Minerals Separation, which, combined with the company's 34-per-cent holding, gave Rio Tinto

[14] Gregory, *Oppenheimer*, 433–434.
[15] A euphemism for over-committed.
[16] For details of Rio Tinto's history, see D. Avery, *Not on Queen Victoria's Birthday*.
[17] R.T.C.: File 10-F-38. Calculated from a list of shareholders drawn up in May 1929 on the issue of 50,000 additional ordinary shares.

TABLE 3

COMPARISON OF HOLDINGS BY THE MAJOR GROUPS IN THE RCBC,
N'CHANGA, AND BWANA M'KUBWA COMPANIES AS AT THE END OF
AUGUST 1930 (% OF TOTAL)

	RCBC°			N'CHANGA	BWANA M'KUBWA
	Nominal share value basis		Votes basis	Nominal share value basis	Nominal share value basis
Rhodesian Anglo American	23.9		16.2	0.2	49.5
Rio Tinto Group					
Rio Tinto Company	7.0		8.8	3.6	1.0
Minerals Separation	11.9		10.9	7.3	—
N.M. Rothschild	10.5		11.3	0.3	—
Total		29.4	31.0	11.2	1.0
Anti-merger group		18.9	14.0	0.2	0.6
Other shareholders		27.8	38.8	88.4°°	48.9
		100.0	100.0	100.0	100.0

° The nominal share values and votes basis percentages differ in the case of RCBC because the issued share capital was made up of 49,678 £1 ordinary "A" shares carrying 20 votes each and 700,000 £1 ordinary "B" shares carrying only one vote.

°° RCBC held 43.9 per cent of N'Changa-issued ordinary shares, and this is included in this figure.

Source: R.T.C.: Derived from a document headed "Shareholders' Lists," September 25, 1930.

control of that concern; and as can be seen from Table 3 this was of particular value in relation to control of RCBC.[18]

There were, moreover, certain other factors that made the Rio Tinto group the ideal ally for Oppenheimer. First, the composition of RCBC's share capital, which was crucial to the merger, was particularly favorable to the Rio Tinto group in comparison with Rhodesian Anglo American. Second, a number of RCBC's American shareholders were known to be against any moves towards merger of the three companies and, therefore, as a major shareholder in RCBC and not having an interest in Bwana M'Kubwa, Rio Tinto was likely to be able to pick up the critical additional support needed from other shareholders to gain control of RCBC.[19] Third, the Rio Tinto group had built up an interest in N'Changa

[18] This holding was built up during the 1929 N'Changa affair. Unpublished manuscript supplied by Foseco-Minsep Ltd., "History of Minerals Separation Limited, 1903–1969" (1970). Also, R.T.C.: document headed "List of Investments," dated (as at) August 10, 1930.

[19] The merger was opposed by the American Mayflower Associates (represented by R.E. McConnell) who held 14.3 per cent of RCBC ordinary shares and by the British Union Corporation which held 4.6 per cent of RCBC ordinary shares.

SOUTHERN AFRICAN COPPER MERGER   339

that, when combined with RCBC's holding, would amount to control. Fourth, Rio Tinto had already secured a strong voice in the running of both RCBC and N'Changa: one quarter of RCBC's board were, in effect, Rio Tinto nominees, and Geddes was chairman of its all-important technical committee; and two senior Rio Tinto executives were on the N'Changa board.

Through these channels Oppenheimer and Geddes drew on exclusive and critical technical, financial, and commercial expertise to back their arguments for the merger and to undermine and destroy counter-arguments to their plans. They, and they alone, were in a position to make a careful evaluation of the estimates of the worth of the mines, to which reference has already been made. There was resistance. It was led by Sir Henry Strakosch of the Union Corporation, which had been involved in the N'Changa campaign of two years earlier, and by R.E. McConnell who represented certain American companies. Both were directors of RCBC and Sir Henry, in particular, "was an important City, as well as South African personality, and any opposition on his part and on the part of the companies he represented could not be disregarded." [20] In the event, there was really no contest. The financial press generally was either favorable or neutral, and there was certainly nothing that might now be described as a takeover battle. The promoters backed up their powerful voting position with a forcefully presented case put to the stockholders and the interested public. No one could match their expertise and access to information in this field of mining and, therefore, there could be no effective critical examination of their claims. Indeed, their claims have continued to carry conviction with writers and commentators on the merger and on the development of the Northern Rhodesian copper industry generally.[21] It is essential, therefore, to examine them very closely.

The Public Case

The main spokesman for the promoters was Geddes who, characteristically, enjoyed the limelight and drama of high level business negotiations.[22] In line with Oppenheimer's memorandum, he put forward a five-point argument that economists would now define as the synergic case for the merger. First, it was claimed that

---

[20] Gregory, *Oppenheimer*, 437.
[21] Cf. Gregory, *Oppenheimer*, 422–438; Coleman, *Northern Rhodesian Copperbelt*.
[22] For an insight into the character of Sir Auckland Geddes, see his autobiographical study, *Forging of a Family* (London, 1952).

the three companies acting in combination could mine and smelt ore more efficiently, at given levels of output, than if they operated individually. Some calculations were offered to back up this claim, including one that purported to show how, under one company, the three mines could be equipped for $51 million as against a total of $72.75 million if operated independently.[23] This calculation was made on very simplified assumptions, however, and when the data employed are re-calculated to give alternative rates of return for the mines worked separately or together(and this was a form of appraisal well known to the promoters since it was the method used to estimate the relative values of the mines), the much-vaunted technical savings amounted to no more than 3 per cent — or an internal rate of return of 23 per cent as against 20 per cent.[24] Furthermore, Geddes and Oppenheimer were in possession of a considerable amount of evidence on the structure of the ore bodies and their varying smelting problems, and therefore equipment needs, against which technical economies of the order of 3 per cent were little more than within the margin of error for such estimates. It seems inconceivable that the promoters attached much weight to the claim they made in public. All the more so when it is noted that almost all the technical experts consulted believed that a joint metallurgical complex was not a viable commercial or technical proposition.[25]

The second line of argument centered on managerial efficiency. By mid-1930 the RCBC executive had come to the conclusion that the field organization of the company was "clumsy and cumbersome."[26] There were, fairly clearly, a number of shortcomings in this area and, in particular, the responsibilities of managers were not well defined, and the general manager had proved incapable of supervising such a large undertaking. Amalgamation, claimed Geddes, would provide an opportunity to improve managerial efficiency. Once again, however, the case is not convincing. Deficiencies in management were recognized and understood; their remedy would involve much the same action whether the companies were merged or not. Indeed, it was the intention of the RCBC executive to streamline its organization anyway. To some extent, it is true, it might well have been easier to effect reform within the process of forming a new company, but there could be no question of there

[23] R.T.C.: A.J. McNab, "Comparative Valuation of Mines."
[24] These calculations are available from the authors on request.
[25] Very significantly, Dr. Bancroft, Oppenheimer's close business and technical colleague, was firmly of this view.
[26] R.T.C.: R.M. Preston and G.W. Gray, "Report on Visit to the Company's Property in Rhodesia, August to November 1929."

being a larger pool of talent available to the new company since Rhodesian Anglo American already acted as consulting engineer to all three parties to the merger.

Geddes made finance the third and main element of his argument. It turned on the outcome of extensive and detailed negotiations between RCBC, Bwana M'Kubwa, and various financial interests, among whom by far the most prominent were the banking houses of N.M. Rothschild and Sons of London and Morgan, Grenfell and Company of New York. A tacit agreement had been reached whereby, following the merger, the N'Kana mine would be the first to be brought into production, to be followed by the RCBC mine two or three years later depending on the state of the copper market.[27] In addition, N'Kana would set up a metallurgical plant that would serve all the mines. N'Kana, it was forecast, would come on stream in June 1932. The financial advantages of the arrangements were then spelled out. Construction costs and working capital would amount to £7.4 million, or approximately £4 million less than the amount needed to develop the mines separately. The main savings would result from lower production (which would match market conditions) and from the contribution that N'Kana profits would make towards the capital development of RCBC, thus reducing the need to raise allegedly costly external funds. On top of this, the new company, apparently, would be able to finance itself more cheaply because of its greater security — Rothschilds and Morgan, Grenfell would be prepared to ensure its capital supply by underwriting an issue of £4.5 million, 7 per cent, 20-year convertible debentures issued at par.[28]

No one challenged these claims apart from Strakosch, who disputed the need for immediate finance for N'Kana; though even he did not deny the main thrust of the argument in the longer-term sense.[29] Yet, in retrospect at least, there appear to have been very good grounds for doing so. For a start, no reasons were offered as to why the companies would, independently, have had difficulty in raising capital or as to why the cost of raising it would have been greater than for the joint enterprise. Indeed, Rothschilds already had substantial direct interests in RCBC and N'Changa, while Morgan, Grenfell, through its large holding in Rhodesian Anglo

[27] R.T.C.: R.M. Preston, "Memorandum of Discussion between Messrs. Wetzler, Taylor, Buchanan and Preston," September 11, 1930; R.M. Preston, financial projection headed "Copper Companies Amalgamation: Estimated Cash Requirements to bring Combined RCBC and N'Kana Properties to Treatment of 10,000 tons a day and Period in which Required," November 25, 1930.
[28] R.T.C.: A.C. Geddes, "Address to RCBC Shareholders," December 17, 1930.
[29] Gregory, *Oppenheimer*, 437, n. 35.

American had interests in all three concerns; [30] what better financial support could the companies have had? Beyond this, the enormous potential of the Copperbelt was recognized to the extent of RCBC £1 shares changing hands at £9.25 in November 1930.[31] Why then did Geddes argue this case so strongly?

In immediate terms Geddes was concerned to rebut the main argument advanced by Strakosch and McConnell: that the proposed scheme involved the unacceptable cost of heavy fixed interest payments on debenture capital that was, anyway, an unsound method of financing a mining concern. As has been noted, Strakosch and McConnell made no headway against the powerful forces ranged against them, while at the same time Geddes was able to focus public attention on this aspect of the financial argument to the exclusion of careful questioning of other possible financial consequences of the scheme — for the moment, a point to borne in mind.

Geddes' fourth claim was that the merger would produce big market advantages, a claim that he considered so self-evident as not to require any detailed supporting evidence beyond summarizing Oppenheimer's memorandum to him:

(1) . . . copper is in danger of under consumption, which will be called over-production for a time to be measured in years.

(2) . . . the best way of meeting such a situation in relation to the copper world as it exists today is for the coming production of Rhodesia to be in as few and as strong hands as possible.

(3) . . . the best chance of securing a proper share of the world's supply of copper for the Rhodesian mines is for them to be equipped to meet something more than their probable share of the supply and for that equipment to be under the control of organizations self contained and assured of adequate financial resources.[32]

Certainly the state of the market provided confirmation of these forebodings: the price of electrolytic copper in London had fallen from £76.25 per short ton in 1925 to £55.47 by 1930, while world copper stocks increased from 268,500 short tons to 532,500 short tons between the beginning of 1929 and the end of 1930.[33] Increasing supplies from Rhodesian mines were bound to depress the market further, and the Americans were already threatening tariff protection for domestic suppliers — a tariff that was eventually introduced in 1932.[34] Moreover, it was claimed that a subsidiary market

---

[30] Morgan Grenfell was also nominee for the Newmont Corporation, which had a substantial interest in RAA.

[31] Average for the month calculated from *The Times* daily lists.

[32] R.T.C.: A.C. Geddes, "Address to RCB Shareholders," December 17, 1930.

[33] Metallgesellschaft A.G., *Metal Statistics* (Frankfurt am Main, 1938).

[34] See O.C. Herfindahl, *Copper Costs and Prices, 1870–1957* (Baltimore, 1959).

SOUTHERN AFRICAN COPPER MERGER   343

advantage of the proposed company was its potential monopsony power in factor markets. During 1929, Geddes had declared that the Rhodesian labor problem made it important "to aim at a big commercial organisation to work all the properties." [35] By 1930, however, there was an abundance of labor as a result of tumbling prices in the agricultural sector leading to rising unemployment — a condition that would obviously persist for a considerable time, as Geddes must have known well. [36] Nevertheless, against the worsening world market for copper a merger obviously had a strong appeal. The alternative — some form of market-sharing scheme — was much less attractive since such arrangements generally proved difficult to operate when the going became hard.

Against these considerations, however, Geddes was in possession of detailed calculations on the probable operating costs of RCBC and N'Kana, and these showed convincingly that these mines could remain independently viable if the price of copper were to fall as low as an average of £46 per short ton for the next 40 years! Quite simply, it was the low cost potential of the Rhodesian mines, which derived mainly from unusually high lode factors, that placed them in the front rank of the world industry.

Finally, Geddes emphasized certain "political" benefits that the merger would make possible. Two main issues came under this heading. One concerned relations between the concessionary mining companies and the proprietory British South Africa Company. According to Geddes it would be "immeasurably advantageous [to shareholders in RCBC] to be in the position of partner with, rather than tenant of the Chartered Company," a relationship that would come with the merger, as Chartered had a very large shareholding in Rhodesian Anglo American, and, consequently, it would be strongly in the interest of the Chartered Company to do all in its power to ensure the success of the new concern. [37] But since it was already *effectively* in such a position, through its holdings in Rhodesian Anglo American (not to mention its automatic interest in augmenting its royalty receipts), it is difficult to understand why Geddes bothered to advance such an empty argument, unless he judged at least some shareholders to be so lacking in understanding of RCBC's finances as to be taken in by it.

The other political issue centered on the relations between

---

[35] R.T.C.: C.C. Madden, "Notes of Discussion on Rhodesian Finance at 3 Lombard Street on Wednesday, October 30, 1929," November 8, 1929.

[36] See E.L. Berger, *Labour, Race and Colonial Rule: the Copperbelt from 1924 to Independence* (Oxford, 1974).

[37] R.T.C. — A.C. Geddes, "Address to RCBC Shareholders," December 19, 1930.

Northern and Southern Rhodesia. A general statement on the subject, drafted by Oppenheimer, was widely circulated among members of the merging companies:

> The formation of one large Company would greatly strengthen the posi-
> tion *vis-a-vis* legislation and the Government authorities generally. There
> is a tendency amongst Governments today to intrude themselves into the
> affairs of private enterprises and invariably . . . it is with disastrous
> results. This disposition is probably most accentuated in regard to min-
> ing. . . . This tendency to interfere finds fruitful soil in dissensions
> amongst rival mining enterprises because it provides the Government
> with an excuse to intervene ostensibly with the object of settling those
> differences but really with the aim of controlling the Industry. . . .
> The value of a united front as presented by these Companies . . . ,
> as opposed to individual action and divided council in negotiations with
> the Government, cannot be over estimated.[38]

Oppenheimer was alluding, especially, to the South's campaign
for some form of political union with the North, which was ostensibly based on the idea of the two colonies forming a powerful pro-
Imperial union that would counter the designs of South Africa on
territories to the north of her.[39] The copper companies were extremely skeptical about this declaration, since they saw Southern
Rhodesia as really seeking to get its hands on the mineral wealth
of the Copperbelt. Some form of federation between the two, it
was felt, would render the North a mere appanage of the South
because of the much larger voting power of the latter. The chances
were that among the immediate consequences would be "white-
labor legislation, starvation of Northern Rhodesia in roads, railways
and telegraphs, heavy taxation of the mining industry, and a large
influx of low class Dutch." [40] Undoubtedly, high taxation was seen
as the bigger threat, and fears on this account were raised by the
financial policy of the Colonial Office, which decreed that all local
expenditure should be met from local taxation.

This argument remains convincing among all those put forward
by Geddes, and, as will be suggested a little later, in its broader
implications was of major importance. However, the form in which
it was presented somewhat overstated the case. For one thing, a
merger would only partly achieve the alleged objective, as the
Roan Antelope and Mufulira companies would remain independent.
For another, alternative methods of establishing a united front

---

[38] R.T.C.; E. Oppenheimer to A.C. Geddes, August 19, 1930.
[39] For a general introduction to the political background referred to here, see Eric A.
Walker, *A History of Southern Africa* (London, 1957 edition, revised with corrections,
1959), 607–694.
[40] R.T.C.; R.M. Preston, "Note on the Northern Rhodesian Situation," October 22, 1929.

SOUTHERN AFRICAN COPPER MERGER   345

among mining companies were under discussion. The most favored proposal was one for the establishment of a chamber of mines that would take over certain functions from its individual company members: among other things it would negotiate and deal with matters of taxation, mining legislation, and labor relations.

In sum, we have attempted to expose the case for the merger put to the "outsider" shareholders of RCBC by Geddes as being largely a public relations exercise; unless, of course, it is assumed that Oppenheimer, Geddes, and the Rothschilds believed their own propaganda. From what is known of these men, such a suggestion invites its own disbelief. Moreover, although we have examined the case in detail, it is important to remember that it was put forward by Geddes mainly as a series of assertions that were scarcely challenged by shareholders or the financial press. The obvious question is raised, therefore: what were the real motives for the merger?

COMPANY STRATEGY

As a first step towards unraveling the motives of Rhodesian Anglo American and Rio Tinto in promoting the Rhokana Corporation, it is necessary to examine their longer-term strategies. The Rio Tinto Company had been established in 1873 to develop the rich Rio Tinto mines in Spain.[41] From the 1880s up to World War I it enjoyed high prosperity, though towards the end of this period it became clear that, relatively, it was losing ground among international copper mining companies that were expanding rapidly. By the 1920s the basis of its prosperity was weakening. The copper content of its ore was falling as the lodes were being worked out and this meant that the company's profits depended increasingly on its sales of sulphur and iron, the other two elements contained in pyrites. During the 1920s demand for iron ore was falling relative to supply, and the company's sulphur trade was threatened by the rise of the elemental (Frasch) sulphur industry in the U.S. Despite growing problems within the company, however, changes in management and in strategy had to wait upon one of the most common arbiters of entrepreneurial change: death removed the chairman, Lord Milner, in 1925. It was clear to his successor, Geddes — as it must have been obvious to others in the company for some time — that the need was for diversification of Rio Tinto's mining interests.

Sir Auckland immediately set about this task, and he was con-

41 See Avery, *Not on Queen Victoria's Birthday.*

siderably helped by Rio Tinto's cash reserves, which had been built
up during the halcyon years, even though the company had always
declared handsome dividends. Naturally, he turned his attention to
Northern Rhodesia and began to acquire shares in companies operating there. Then, in early 1929, Rio Tinto eagerly joined the
nine-member consortium formed to beat off the attempted take-
over of N'Changa by American Smelting. During these plots and
counter-plots Rio Tinto and the Rothschilds gained control of
Minerals Separation Ltd. Furthermore, in May 1929 Rio Tinto set
up an investment and general development fund that was financed
by the issue of 500,000 £5 ordinary shares at a premium of £45
(that is, a total of £2¼ million) — a relatively easy operation as the
company's shares were regarded as "blue chip," not least because
of Rothschilds' known involvement in the company.[42] By June it
had acquired 24 per cent of the ordinary share capital of Minerals
Separation (costing £277,000), 4.9 per cent of RCBC (costing
£162,500) and a holding of 65,000 ordinary shares in the British
South Africa Company (costing £127,000).[43] Yet it was still concerned to secure interests in large mines with easily estimated costs
and which involved mining and metallurgical problems that could
be handled by standard technology.

Rio Tinto's holdings in, and representation on, the boards of
RCBC and N'Changa certainly provided it with a good source of
information on Copperbelt mines; in addition, it sent a delegation
of technical experts to investigate the Copperbelt at first hand. One
of its reports in 1929 emphasized that the company's holdings were
not of the best.[44] At the end of the year the main operating companies in Rhodesia were valued, and this revealed clearly that the
company's interests were in the least valuable and most speculative
mines.[45] Moreover, its efforts to secure holdings in richer mines
were thwarted by the fact that in each case the majority of shares
was held by just a few institutional groups who were adamantly
opposed to dilution. This left the alternative of trying to promote
consolidation or amalgamation of companies, and Geddes endeavored to persuade certain American groups to this view in 1929.

[42] R.T.C.: "Report of the Transactions at the Extraordinary General Meeting of Shareholders on May 9, 1929."
[43] R.T.C.: "Rhodesian Properties: Shares held by Rio Tinto Company," June 28, 1929.
[44] R.T.C. : Two main deputations were sent to report on Copperbelt development in
1929. G. Vibert-Douglas, the company's chief geologist, reported directly to Geddes on all
questions between May and September, 1929. Throughout August 1929 Preston and Gray
investigated fully all aspects of Rhodesian mining.
[45] R.T.C.: G.W. Gray to J.N. Buchanan, December 28, 1929, and enclosing a "Comparative Valuation of Roan Antelope, Bwana M'Kubwa, Rhodesian Selection Trust, N'Changa
and RCBC." Previous to this there had been another report from Gray and three from
Douglas: R.T.C. — April 7, April 25, May 25, July 7, July 24.

SOUTHERN AFRICAN COPPER MERGER   347

The plan broke down as a consequence of Rhodesian Anglo American's opposition.[46] So long as Oppenheimer showed no interest in some kind of co-operative undertaking there was little Geddes could do. Nevertheless, he lost no opportunity for placing his company in the limelight, and at its annual general meeting in April 1930 he described his own and his company's role in the American Smelting/N'Changa affair: he had directed a market strategy that had succeeded in defending European, Imperial, and, ultimately, world copper interests against the dire threat of American suzerainty. With the help of mixed metaphors, which had Rio Tinto sailing into strong seas on which the dust finally settled, Sir Auckland explained that he had finally achieved his goal: ". . . no one nation can dominate the Rhodesian field . . . its development is in the hands of companies representing, through their shareholding, practically all the world, American as well as European." [47]

Quite contrary to responding to Rio Tinto's overtures, Oppenheimer became concerned, as has been noted, about its holdings in RCBC and N'Changa, and he gave instructions that Rhodesian Anglo American should increase its holdings by an equivalent of 18 per cent, even though this was at the cost of its cash reserves and of having to place some of its reserve shares on the market together with an issue of loan capital.[48] Moreover, Oppenheimer's chief executives were not in favor of a formal link-up with Rio Tinto because they considered that its interests in Northern Rhodesia were necessarily in line with their own, so that this left it no option but to follow their lead.[49] Yet within four months Oppenheimer's strategy changed sharply and he initiated the discussions that led to the formation of Rhokana. Why?

In attempting to answer this question there is a problem of available evidence. Material in Rio Tinto's archives indirectly throws light on Oppenheimer's policy, but obscurities remain. For direct evidence we have to rely partly on Sir Theodore Gregory's account of the events. Obviously, independent investigation of Rhodesian Anglo American's and Anglo American's archives would be desirable, though given the nature of the evidence provided by Gregory it is doubtful that much more of direct significance would come to light.

[46] R.T.C.: C.C. Madden, "Notes of Discussion on Rhodesian Finance at 3 Lombard Street on Wednesday, 30 October 1929," dated November 8, 1929 (C.C. Madden was personal assistant to Sir Auckland Geddes at the time of the merger negotiations); R.T.C.: J.S. Wetzlar to A.C. Geddes, February 14, 1930, enclosing telegrams of February 13, 1930 from E. Oppenheimer in Johannesburg; R.T.C.: J.N. Buchanan, "Notes on Sir Auckland Geddes Scheme," February 24, 1930.

[47] R.T.C.: Report of the Transactions of the 57th Annual General Meeting, April 14, 1930.

[48] Gregory, *Oppenheimer*, 430–431.

[49] Ibid., 431–433.

Indeed such was — and almost certainly still is — the nature of this kind of international financial diplomacy and maneuvering that crucial parts of negotiations between companies were never solidified into written record. Company relations were highly personalized and laced with intrigue; holding companies and financial consortia were common form in the mining industry in southern Africa. Consequently, it is difficult for the historian to get to grips with underlying factors, but by no means impossible. In this case, at least, it is possible to offer a reasonably complete analysis of the motives leading to the promotion of the Rhokana Corporation.

From late 1929 onwards Oppenheimer's main company, the Anglo American Corporation, experienced increasing pressure on its cash flow and cash reserves. This was caused by a severe fall in international demand for diamonds with the onset of the international depression in 1929.[50] Oppenheimer was chairman of De Beers, the largest diamond marketing company in the world, and De Beers was, in turn, controlled by Anglo American. Much of the fascinating story of diamonds is told by Gregory but, in essence, the problem facing Oppenheimer was how to control the marketing and production of diamonds so as to prevent a complete collapse and disorganization of the diamond market that he and his associates had so assiduously built up over the previous decade. A satisfactory solution proved difficult to achieve, but in any event a primary requirement was cash with which to buy up diamonds coming on the market. Throughout the year 1930 Oppenheimer's companies made enormous financial commitments in this respect; their reward came as stupendous profits during and after World War II when the world became hungry for diamonds. In the immediate term, however, pressure on cash was intense and, among other things, this made it impossible for Oppenheimer to embark on any grandiose schemes in Rhodesia.

For the moment copper affairs were quiet: the Americans had been repulsed, and relations with British companies, especially with Rio Tinto, were very good. Depression in the copper market was providing stability through a kind of stalemate; in this way experience in copper was quite unlike that in diamonds. In another way, however, conditions in the two industries became more alike and in a manner to which Oppenheimer was particularly sensitive. To understand this it is necessary to look again for a moment at developments in the diamond industry.

[50] Gregory, *Oppenheimer*, 160–383. This account could be a little fuller on the detailed financial state of Anglo American, but as a survey and discussion of the diamond industry Gregory's book is impressive.

By 1930 the problem facing the industry was how, and for how long, it could carry large stocks of diamonds, a problem intensified by the knowledge that the existence of large stocks further deterred would-be purchasers. To the complexity of this problem was added the intransigence of the South African government — through the person of the Minister of Mines — which was intent on maintaining its revenue from the diamond industry and, more understandably, extremely concerned about any measure (in particular, about the closure of mines) that would add to the already high unemployment. De Beers effectively controlled the South African diamond industry but was subject to various state mining regulations and the operation of the government itself as a buyer and seller of diamonds.

Apart from these immediate pressures, Oppenheimer was facing a growing challenge to his long-term business strategy, which was to promote the economic development of southern Africa within the sphere of British imperial influence. The challenge came in the form of the sharpening stridency of South African nationalism during the 1920s and the growing enthusiasm in the Rhodesias for some form of self-government.[51] Within South Africa the largely British-dominated business interests were increasingly concerned over the consequences of the growth of *Afrikanerdom*, which was fundamentally opposed to a free labor market and intensely suspicious of the City of London, the center of Imperial finance. Oppenheimer had no doubt as to where, ultimately, this was leading: the exclusion of all British influence from the life of South Africa. Oppenheimer, like his precursor Rhodes, was by no means entirely *homo economicus* in his business life and broader economic thinking. He saw economic development as the powerful civilizing influence in southern Africa, and believed that an essential ingredient of that influence was the preservation of Imperial ties.[52]

Oppenheimer's correspondence with his main business associates leaves no doubt as to his deep fears about the economic and political intentions of the South African government, but it seems doubtful whether this, alone, was sufficiently strong to change his attitude towards the merger of his copper interests with those of Rio Tinto. The situation was difficult but by no means critical. Amidst this political difficulty, however, a significant development occurred: RCBC's copper reserves were proved to be more extensive than previously supposed and were subsequently revalued by

[51] See, in particular, Ralph Horwitz, *The Political Economy of South Africa* (London, 1967); also, Walker, *A History of Southern Africa*.
[52] Gregory, *Oppenheimer*, provides abundant and telling direct evidence, 22, 29 32, 415, 417-418, 444, 595.

Gray, Rio Tinto's technical expert. On a *conservative* basis he recommended that the value of the enterprise should be increased from £4.8 million to £12.2 million.[53] This information was known only to the board of RCBC, which was mainly representative of the large, or "insider," shareholders. Although it cannot be expressly substantiated, it seems certain that such exciting news naturally caused all the interested parties to consider its consequences in relation to the development of the RCBC mine, and for Oppenheimer this would inevitably re-open the question of whether to promote an amalgamation of RCBC, N'Changa, and Bwana M'Kubwa. Clearly, it was essential for Oppenheimer to include not only N'Changa but also Bwana M'Kubwa, because only in this way would the consequent weighting of the capital values of the merging companies in the new company ensure *overall* control for Rhodesian Anglo American.

Even in combination with Oppenheimer's fears about the South African government, it seems doubtful that the prospect of a dominant grip on the Northern Rhodesian Copperbelt was irresistible if it involved heavy financial commitments on the part of his companies. The financial scheme that was, in fact, adopted has already been outlined. Although Oppenheimer is credited with its invention, the intricate subtlety and genius of it suggests that he designed it in close co-operation with the Rothschilds who were masters of such financial alchemy. In addition to the issue of new RCBC shares with which to acquire N'Changa and Bwana M'Kubwa, £4.5 million convertible debentures were issued, as has been noted — £2.5 million underwritten by Rhodesian Anglo American and £2.0 million by Rio Tinto.[54] This was the master stroke. The promoters well knew that the debenture issue would not find much support because the investing public would be aware that interest payments could not be met under the tight financial conditions in the pre-production stage of the new company, and that the likelihood of depressed demand for copper would seriously hamper it for some time to come. Indeed, Rio Tinto instructed J. C. im Thurm and Sons to purchase £2m of Rhokana debentures on its account within a month of the offer to shareholders.[55]

The *Investor's Review* referred scathingly to the terms as "elaborate eyewash," but failed to perceive what would be the result of the underwriting companies being left with the major part of the

[53] R.T.C.: G.W. Gray, "RCBC Position Revised," April 7, 1930.
[54] The Rio Tinto side was handled by J.C. im Thurm and Sons, a stock-brokerage house controlled by the company.
[55] R.T.C.: Letter dated April 8, 1931.

debentures.[56] The full effect occurred in 1932, though it was to be much later before it was commonly understood. In August 1932 Rhokana announced that it could no longer continue to meet its debenture interest payments and offered, instead, a surrender agreement to the major debenture holders, Rhodesian Anglo American and Rio Tinto, whereby the latter were to receive repayment at 120 per cent of the par value of the debentures in £1 ordinary shares at £5 on December 31, 1932. The striking effect of this conversion on the ownership of Rhokana is shown in Table 4.

TABLE 4

EFFECTIVE HOLDINGS OF THE RHODESIAN ANGLO AMERICAN AND RIO TINTO GROUPS IN THE RHOKANA CORPORATION, 1930–32

(% OF ALL ISSUED ORDINARY SHARES)

	As at 31.12.30	As at 17.6.31	As at 23.5.32	As at 31.12.32
Rhodesian Anglo American Group				
R.A.A. Corporation	12.6	12.4	12.4	32.3
Bwana M'Kubwa	38.6	38.6	38.5	22.5
Total	51.2	51.0	50.9	54.8
Rio Tinto Group				
Rio Tinto Company	4.2	7.7	8.3	17.6
Minerals Separation	6.7	5.8	5.4	4.5
N.M. Rothschild	6.3	7.1	8.7	6.6
Total	17.2	20.6	22.4	28.7
Other Shareholders	31.6	28.4	26.7	16.5
	100.0	100.0	100.0	100.0

Source: R.T.C.: For 31.12.30 projected from holdings in N'Changa, RCBC and Bwana M'Kubwa, source as for table 3; for 17.6.31 based upon document headed "Shareholders' List" of the same date; for 23.5.32 based upon document headed "Shareholders in the Rhokana Corporation" of the same date; and for 31.12.32 estimated from details given in an agreement between the Rio Tinto Company, Rhodesian Anglo American, and the Rhokana Corporation headed "Agreement for the Surrender of Debentures," September 17, 1932.

The combined share of Rhokana held by the promoting groups was increased from 68.4 per cent at the time of the merger to 83.5 per cent just two years later. Rhodesian Anglo American had secured control of Rhokana immediately on its formation. But this was by no means all. The terms of the debenture surrender subsequently enabled Oppenheimer to transfer the balance of his group's control from the holding company of Bwana M'Kubwa in

[56] *Investor's Review*, April 18, 1931.

which Rhodesian Anglo American had just over a 50 per cent share, to the latter, and thereby substantially increased its share of the potentially rich RCBC mine. In other words, through the merger Rhodesian Anglo American had used its control of Bwana M'Kubwa to gain control of Rhokana and had then used the debenture conversion to switch a large part of the gain from the "outsider" shareholders in Bwana M'Kubwa to its own "insider" shareholders.[57]

For its part, Rio Tinto had traded a proportion of its holding in RCBC for a share in a much larger enterprise. But after the debenture conversion it virtually regained its original share of RCBC. Correspondingly, its gains were at the "expense" of the "outsider" shareholders in RCBC and N'Changa.

MERGER MOTIVES

Why, then, did the Rhodesian Anglo American and Rio Tinto groups promote this Copperbelt merger? The public case put forward by the promoters has been accepted by other writers on the subject, and it certainly fits quite well with some aspects of merger theory as developed by economists over more recent years.[58] Against this, we have argued that close examination of the evidence reveals this to be unconvincing, to the point of it being inconceivable that the promoters themselves were persuaded by it. Moreover, despite limitations of evidence, it is possible to put forward a convincing alternative explanation.

In immediate terms, the revaluation of RCBC almost certainly caused Oppenheimer to reconsider his attitude towards the original merger proposal made by Rio Tinto. Potentially, it could upset the balance of control over the Copperbelt, and there was even a likelihood of the RCBC property being worth considerably more. Rhodesian Anglo American owned under one quarter of this rich asset and once news of its value leaked out it could well act as a stimulant to the appetites of other mining interests — particularly American ones — which could only mean increased uncertainty in the whole area.

In itself, however, this does not explain why Oppenheimer went

---

[57] Put another way, before the merger Rhodesian Anglo American held 23.9 per cent of RCBC (or 16.2 per cent of its voting capital). At the merger this was increased to 32 per cent (12.6 per cent plus just over a half share in Bwana M'Kubwa). By December 31, 1932 its share was 44 per cent (32.3 per cent plus just over a half share in Bwana M'Kubwa). In 1935 Rhodesian Anglo American made an offer to the remaining "outsider" shareholders in Bwana, and 92 per cent by value accepted. This enabled the Company to acquire the remaining shares by legal right, and Bwana M'Kubwa went into voluntary liquidation.

[58] Cf., Coleman, *Northern Rhodesian Copperbelt*; Gregory, *Oppenheimer*.

for this particular merger. After all, the position of his companies in southern Africa was now pre-eminent, and although Anglo American was experiencing growing difficulties in diamond mining and marketing, somewhat ironically these problems served to strengthen Oppenheimer's business leadership; in fact, they enabled Oppenheimer finally to establish his personal ascendancy over Edmund Davis and Chester Beatty. Davis, in particular, had for long been regarded as the father of Rhodesian mining and he enjoyed "high prestige in the City of London as a living link with Cecil Rhodes and the heroic days of Empire building in Central Africa." [59] Accordingly, a contributory factor in Oppenheimer's unwillingness to go ahead with the merger proposal in 1929 had been his feeling that he might encounter opposition from the City of London. By 1930 the initiative was clearly with Oppenheimer and in purely financial terms he could have sought to control Northern Rhodesian mining industry through a link-up with American finance, though this inevitably meant some form of merger, since any attempt to acquire control of RCBC through direct share purchase would have run into the twin problems of the unwillingness of existing holders to sell and rapidly rising share prices.

To have joined with American interests, however, would have conflicted fundamentally with his firmly expressed desire to promote the economic development of southern Africa within the broader sphere of British political and economic influence, a purpose involving strongly held political belief as much as a desire to secure ultimate financial advantage. The growing nationalism of the South African government, which was making itself increasingly felt in economic life, served to sharpen these sensitivities at a critical moment. Equally, to this aim was added the powerful attraction of the large potential financial gains to be made from the particular form of merger that was being proposed. The South African adventurer was emerging as an Imperial pro-consul, a process in which political conviction and financial self interest could be perfectly fused.

Rio Tinto was, therefore, the obvious ally. It controlled nearly one-third of RCBC's voting capital, it was a British company, and Oppenheimer had already established good relations with it. Much less obvious and well known to the public was the indirect but close financial relationship that existed between the two companies through the banking house of N.M. Rothschild. Apart from con-

---

[59] Gregory, *Oppenheimer*, 407–408. Davis, who was well into his sixties by this time, was a much older man than Oppenheimer who was 49 in 1929.

trolling Rio Tinto and its interests, Rothschilds had been a long-
time financial adviser and supporter of Oppenheimer in his rise
to power in the diamond industry. Correspondingly, as has been
noted, there seems little doubt that Rothschilds played a critical
role in the negotiations and financial scheming that made promotion of the Rhokana Corporation potentially so lucrative, though
the closest documentation of this activity available to the historian
is in the form of records of frequent luncheon and dinner dates and
meetings in well known London clubs. For its part, Rio Tinto's reward was to achieve its objective of regaining its place among the
leading international mining houses. Moreover, like Rhodesian
Anglo American, it succeeded in converting underwriting guarantees into a large stake in the richest known copper mining area in
the world.

Rhokana was registered in Britain, it had a predominantly British board, and Geddes became its first chairman. From the outset,
however, Rhokana's policies were largely determined by Rhodesian
Anglo American for its own advantage and that of its parent,
Anglo American. Considerations of technical, managerial, or financial efficiency were not primary considerations in the years that led
up to World War II; they were matters for secondary attention
against Oppenheimer's broader interests in southern Africa. Marketing problems there certainly were — much bigger, indeed, than the
promoters had anticipated because of the unexpected length and
depth of the decline in world industrial activity. Even so, control of
Rhokana made little difference to the positions of Rhodesian Anglo
American and Rio Tinto in the negotiations that led to agreements
between the major international copper mining companies for controlling output.[60] As to the political factor — which in our view was
a major reason for the merger — somewhat ironically this receded
in importance following a major political re-alignment in South
Africa in 1934. Yet, in truth, it was a double irony. This re-alignment
preserved and polarized the force of *Afrikanerdom* so that it re-
emerged in the ascendancy in 1948, at the very time when Rhokana
was eventually yielding its rich tribute.[61]

Of course, to explain why the merger occurred is not necessarily
to explain how it was able to occur. The crucial and fascinating
fact is that it was made possible by the opportunity given to two
large "insider" shareholders to use their inside knowledge to steal
the march on other shareholders and appropriate the lion's share of

[60] See Gregory, *Oppenheimer*, 440–445.
[61] For the basic details see Walker, *A History of Southern Africa*, 634–637, 769 et seq.;
Horwitz, *The Political Economy of South Africa*, 104–105.

the newly discovered treasure of RCBC. This feature leads directly to our final observations on whether the formation of Rhokana provides any measure of confirmation for modern theories of merger activity.

Rhokana and Merger Theory

An important characteristic of several merger theories is the assumption of the separation of ownership from control, and accordingly they focus attention on the objectives and activities of top management.[62] In the simplest case, managers' personal goals, such as security, prestige, increased income, are associated with the growth and continuity of the firm for which they are responsible. Managers are thus concerned with size maximization, and mergers are seen as a good means of accelerating growth with reasonable safety. Several more complex theories along these lines have been advanced. Among the best known, for example, is that of R. Marris, which suggests that managers seek to maximize sales growth subject to a minimum stock price: as the market value of a firm's shares falls relative to the book value of its net assets, so the possibility of takeover by a "raiding" firm is increased.[63] A second major line of approach has concentrated on examining the advantage of merger to the firms involved, usually distinguished as the "acquiring" and the "acquired." These advantages are assessed in such terms as economies of scale, increased product- and factor-market power, and in relation to such characteristics as size, rate of growth, profitability, stock market rating, and liquidity.

One of the problems involved in reflecting our present study against these theories is that they have been conceived within the context of a post-1945 world, in which the nature of corporate organization in western-type economies has changed a great deal from what it was in the 1930s. But there are other difficulties: these theories are not specified in terms of *international* merger activity; ownership and management were by no means clearly separated in Rhodesian Anglo American and Rio Tinto; the Rhokana merger was not promoted by the merging firms but by two groups of shareholders. It is important to stress this last point since it could be objected that in this case a group of shareholders could be regarded as a surrogate for the firm. Clearly, there was such an identity in

---

[62] A good survey and analysis of merger theory is provided by Sam Aaronovitch and Malcolm C. Sawyer, *Big Business: Theoretical and Empirical Aspects of Concentration and Mergers in the United Kingdom* (London, 1975).

[63] R. Marris, *The Economic Theory of "Managerial" Capitalism* (London, 1964).

Bwana M'Kubwa and N'Changa; but it did not exist in RCBC, which was the key to the merger. The promoters had to secure control of this company in which they were, independently, substantial but still minority shareholders. It was as "insider" shareholders that they came by their exclusive knowledge of the true worth of the company. It was as "insider" shareholders that they had come together to convert substantial interests into control and, within the same act, by means of superlative financial skill, to use that control to secure virtually complete ownership.

Despite these difficulties, indeed, in part because of them, some points of value do emerge from a brief consideration of theoretical issues. Publicly the promoters made claims that fit quite well with the second theoretical approach that has been outlined. Yet close analysis has revealed these claims as being of secondary importance, a finding that is at least in accord with such statistical tests as have been carried out to discover whether claims made in support of mergers are *subsequently* borne out by results.[64]

The formation of Rhokana is interesting, also, in relation to stock market prices. It has been observed by some commentators that fluctuations in merger activity during this period tend to move positively with the level of stock market prices.[65] Quite the reverse is true in this case. Depressed stock markets facilitated the promoters' highly successful debenture conversion scheme. More generally, while merger activity in advanced economies has contributed to the gradual accretion of economic power to large firms, even the largest control only a small fraction of the total national capital stock. In Northern Rhodesia, the Rhokana Corporation achieved a position that gave it a dominance in the determination of the country's economic development.[66] Furthermore, our study contributes indirectly to discussion on the important issue of the impact of the international slump on colonial territories.[67]

To the extent that these comments might be claimed to amount to significant qualifications to merger theory — notwithstanding the difficulties that have been alluded to — it could be objected that the Rhokana merger was *sui generis*, that it was peculiar to the combination of mining, the politics of southern Africa, and the un-

[64] There is a growing literature in this field, and for surveys of it, see T.F. Hogarty; "Profits from Mergers: The Evidence of Fifty Years," *St. John's Law Review*, Special Edition (1975), 44, pp. 317–327; D.C. Mueller, "The Effects of Conglomerate Mergers: A Survey of Empirical Evidence," *Journal of Financial Economics*, forthcoming; M.A. Utton. "On Measuring the Effects of Industrial Mergers," *Scottish Journal of Political Economy*, XXI (February 1974), pp. 13–28.
[65] Hannah and Kay, *Concentration in Modern Industry*, 87.
[66] Cf. this point with A.G. Hopkins, "Imperial Business in Africa: Part II — Interpretations," *Journal of African History*, XVIII (1976), 279.
[67] Cf. A.G. Hopkins, *An Economic History of West Africa* (London, 1973), 237–267.

usual financial conditions of the 1929-32 period. At the outset of this study, however, it was observed that very little detailed evidence and analysis of individual mergers is available and, therefore, it is impossible at this stage to make a case one way or the other in terms of the uniqueness of Rhokana. Nevertheless, if our study is viewed, in part, as an aspect of general multi-national company activity, then we would claim that it is at least very suggestive of the importance of political factors in this area of business strategy. And, to this extent, our study may bear comparison with certain aspects of the earlier development of big business in southern Africa.[68]

More positively, our study does lend support to those who have argued, in relation to formal theories of merger, that much more attention needs to be given to the activities of "insider" shareholders.[69] This was a major ingredient in the promotion of Rhokana. At this same time, this does not lead us to agree with one of the most celebrated commentators on British imperialism: "It may safely be asserted that whenever 'the commercial' is combined with 'the imaginative' in any shape or sort, the latter is exploited by the former."[70] In the Rhokana Corporation, in the eyes of its promoters, the two elements were ideally combined.

[68] Cf. G. Arrighi, *The Political Economy of Rhodesia* (Mouton, The Hague, 1967); John S. Galbraith, *Crown and Charter: The Early Years of the British South Africa Company* (London, 1974).
[69] In particular, Aaronovitch and Sawyer, *Big Business*, 159-164.
[70] J.A. Hobson, *Imperialism: A Study* (London, 1938 edition).

[10]

Excerpt from *Copper Costs and Prices: 1870–1957*, 70–91.

chapter 4 PRICE MANIPULATION—
1870 TO WORLD WAR I

The Michigan Episode, 1870 to the Early Eighties

Copper mining in the Upper Peninsula of Michigan was first pursued vigorously by white men around 1845.[1] Within one decade the output of Lake (i.e., Michigan) copper accounted for well over half the output of the United States, and it reached 86 per cent in the decade 1871–80. During this period, the output of the United States was but a small part of the world total, amounting to 9 per cent in the sixties and 15 per cent in the seventies.

Michigan production came to be strongly dominated by the outputs of the properties merged into the Calumet and Hecla Mining Company in 1871.[2] The output of these properties rose rapidly after 1867, reaching 50 per cent of the U. S. output in 1870, and after the merger remaining slightly over 50 per cent, with the exception of 1877, until 1881. In turn, the output of this company accounted for over 60 per cent of the Lake output in the decade of the seventies.[3]

It was this set of relationships plus a high tariff imposed in 1869 that provided the opportunity for a loose combination of U. S.

[1] See C. Harry Benedict, *Red Metal* (Ann Arbor: University of Michigan Press, 1952), p. 20.

[2] See *ibid.*, pp. 69–76. This company was formed by a consolidation of the Calumet and Hecla companies, which were working adjoining properties, and two smaller companies. The valuations for Hecla and Scott on page 73 of the source cited evidently have been interchanged.

[3] See Table A-1 in the Appendix.

copper producers to multiply profits behind a tariff wall in the seventies and the early eighties.[4] The combination appears to have been effective in restricting domestic sales in the first years of the seventies because copper was exported even though it could have been sold at a higher domestic price. In the next four years or so (about 1875–78), U. S. producers appear to have been on a competitive export basis and were meeting world prices. During the next four years (through 1882, with the possible exception of 1880), the combination was again effective, since the domestic price went above the competitive export price while substantial exports were taking place. The power of the combination seems to have been reduced to little or nothing in 1883 and thereafter. While the data do not permit a completely accurate interpretation of each year's market situation, they do permit a firm conclusion that effective collusion was present in a substantial part of the seventies and early eighties. This conclusion is supported by the observations of contemporary observers, although their comments are not precise enough nor extensive enough to permit a year-by-year interpretation.[5]

In view of the success of the combination in raising the domestic price of copper, the price of Lake copper at New York in these years cannot be taken as an indicator of change in the long-run competitive price. The London GMB[6] price series, corrected for difference in location and quality, is much less likely to have been distorted by successful collusive activities. This series is substituted for the Lake copper series from 1870 to 1883. The substantial difference in many years is clearly apparent.

[4] The assessment of the leading historian of the U. S. copper industry, F. E. Richter, appears to be rather different, although it is not clear from what vantage point he is making his evaluation. He says, ". . . although for a few years it [the tariff] helped to keep domestic copper prices up, certainly in the long run it did little good . . . its original imposition could hardly have been more foolishly timed, as events turned out." See "The Copper-Mining Industry in the United States, 1845–1925," *Quarterly Journal of Economics*, Vol. 41 (1926–27) p. 251. But from the point of view of the U. S. copper producers it is hard to see how this period and its restrictionism could be viewed as anything but a spectacular success.

[5] A more detailed analysis of this period appears in the Appendix.

[6] GMB means good merchantable brands.

72   PERIODS OF UNUSUAL PRICE BEHAVIOR

TABLE 1. *Price of Copper Relative to Wholesale Price Index, 1870–83*[1]

(Cents per pound)

Year	GMB copper, London, adjusted to New York and quality differential[2]	Adjusted Lake copper, New York[3]	Per cent by which adjusted Lake price exceeds adjusted GMB price
1870	21.5¢	24.1¢	12%
1871	22.5	28.7	28
1872	30.7	41.5	35
1873	28.8	33.0	15
1874	26.7	26.8	0
1875	30.4	28.8	−5
1876	29.4	28.8	−2
1877	27.1	27.7	2
1878	25.6	26.5	4
1879	24.8	31.2	26
1880	24.3	32.6	34
1881	23.6	27.9	18
1882	25.3	27.6	9
1883	24.5	24.2	−1

[1] Both series have been multiplied by a constant, .986, designed to bring the Lake price to an electrolytic basis. This ratio is based on the 1900–15 relationship between the New York prices of electrolytic and Lake copper.

[2] The series in *The Mineral Industry, 1893*, Vol. II (New York: Scientific Publishing Company, 1894), p. 260, was converted to gold dollars at mint par and then converted to U. S. currency prices by multiplying by the gold premium for 1870–79. See footnote 1 of Appendix Table A-2 for the source of this series. The U. S. currency price was then divided by the wholesale price index from *Historical Statistics of the United States*, series L 15 (Washington, D. C.: U. S. Government Printing Office, 1949), multiplied by 1.16 to get competitive New York export price (see footnote 2 of Appendix Table A-2 for explanation), and this multiplied by .986 to get electrolytic basis.

[3] Price series is from *Metal Statistics, 1919* (New York: The American Metal Market), p. 227. The series is divided by the wholesale price index (*Historical Statistics of the United States, op. cit.*), and multiplied by .986 to place on electrolytic basis.

Price Manipulation—1870 to World War I 73

Secrétan and Prices during the Eighties

A spectacular growth in copper production in the U. S. northwest began in the early eighties. The years following the entry of western U. S. copper on the market appear to have been years of competitive selling both in the United States and in the world market. Thus C. Kirchhoff, Jr., states that 1881–84 were years of strong competition everywhere.[7] In 1886, the *Engineering and Mining Journal* was bemoaning the state of the copper market.[8] It expressed regret that the U. S. producers had not taken advantage of the tariff wall to agree to put on the home market at a fair figure only as much as it would healthily absorb, and export the remainder. The whole period from 1880 to 1887 was one of falling copper prices coupled with rapidly rising consumption and production, especially in the United States, where output tripled in seven years.[9] World production rose throughout this period of "depression" in the copper industry with the exception of 1886 and 1887,[10] but the rise took place mainly in the United States and Spain. In other places there were declines in production.[11]

In late 1887, the audacious and remarkable Secrétan copper operation began, with the result that the price of copper was raised far above the level it otherwise would have been. The main part of the Secrétan operation was handled by the Société Industrielle et Commerciale des Métaux, a fabricating company headed by M.

[7] *Mineral Resources of the United States, 1883 and 1884* (Washington, D. C.: U. S. Government Printing Office, 1885), p. 322. This basic source for data on minerals was prepared in earlier years by the U. S. Department of the Interior's Geological Survey, later by the Bureau of Mines.

[8] Vol. 41, No. 23 (June 5, 1886), p. 406. The editorial asserts that the Lake combination had brought stable prices, thus promoting trade, and that the old Lake combinations were inaugurated at the request of the manufacturers. No corroboration for this unusual view has been found by the writer of this study.

[9] See *Mineral Resources of the United States, 1900* (GPO, 1901), p. 141.

[10] The period is characterized as one of depression in the copper trade by *Mineral Resources of the United States, 1886* (GPO, 1887), p. 109, and in the issue for *1887* (GPO, 1888), p. 66.

[11] Richter, *op.cit.*, p. 257.

Secrétan. This company made contracts with leading copper producers throughout the world in which the Société agreed to purchase a specified maximum production at a fixed price or, in some contracts, at a fixed price plus a share of the excess of the net profit over the fixed price.[12] Financing for this undertaking was provided by various French banks, including the Comptoir d'Escompte, which went bankrupt in March 1889 when the speculative venture collapsed.

The first contracts were for three years and covered about 64 per cent of the world production of copper. An additional 16 per cent was covered by a separate but co-operating syndicate operation, giving a total control of some 80 per cent.[13] As a consequence of the widespread belief that the Société had acquired a substantial monopoly control, the price of copper rose from some £40 in late 1887 to around twice that amount in the succeeding months.[14] Along with this large rise in price, sales decreased, since many users of copper apparently were dubious of the power of the Société to carry through the operation or found that they could do without their usual volume of purchases.[15] The high price of copper induced an increase in world copper output of about a sixth from 1887 to 1888. Most of this increase came from the United States, whose 1887

---

[12] *Ibid.*, p. 258.

[13] The percentages are calculated from data appearing in *Mineral Resources of the United States, 1887, op.cit.*, p. 67. However, the total world production in this source—275,000 long tons—does not agree with the Merton figure quoted by Richter, *op. cit.*, p. 258. These figures must also be long tons since they agree rather closely with Merton figures appearing in *Mineral Resources of the United States, 1891* (GPO, 1893), p. 101, and in U. S. Department of the Interior, Bureau of Mines, *Summarized Data of Copper Production*, Economic Paper No. 1 (Washington, D. C.: U. S. Government Printing Office, 1928), facing p. 32.

The percentage controlled as calculated from *Mineral Resources of the United States* agrees with the estimated percentage control (80–85 per cent) appearing in *Engineering and Mining Journal*, Vol. 47, No. 2 (January 12, 1889), p. 29.

E. B. Andrews in "The Late Copper Syndicate," *Quarterly Journal of Economics*, Vol. III (July 1889), p. 509, also estimates control at 80–85 per cent.

[14] *The Mineral Industry, 1893*, Vol. II (New York: Scientific Publishing Company, 1894), p. 260.

[15] *Mineral Resources of the United States, 1887, op. cit.*, p. 67, and *Engineering and Mining Journal*, Vol. 49, No. 1 (January 4, 1890), p. 3.

Price Manipulation—1870 to World War I 75

output of 81,000 long tons went to 101,000 in the next year. Outside the Lake district, U. S. output increased by almost a third.[16]

Production increased in firms under contract to the Société, since the maximum production levels in the contracts were above actual levels for 1887. But production also increased in old and new mines outside the controlled group. Mines already operating could afford to push production much higher than before, dead mines took on life, and the United States and other areas saw extensive and intensive prospecting.[17] If these high prices had continued, the increase in output from 1888 to 1889 probably would have been much greater than from 1887 to 1888. In addition, the supply of scrap copper was increasing.

The reluctance of consumers to buy copper and the considerably enlarged production meant somebody was holding greatly enlarged inventories of copper. The holder was the Société, with the financing banks in turn holding "copper warrants." According to Kirchhoff,[18] world stocks of copper were 175,000 tons as against a normal 75,000 tons at the time of the collapse of the Société and the Comptoir d'Escompte in March 1889. That is, stocks constituted about eight to nine months' consumption as against a normal three to four.

In early 1889, the Société began negotiating new contracts with producers which were to cover total outputs for a period of ten years. Some time later, negotiations were in process to reduce output by 20 per cent. These were partly successful, with U. S. producers making a preliminary agreement to suspend deliveries to the Société for two months.[19] But doubt was growing that the price of copper could be maintained at its high level with such high production. The manager of the Comptoir d'Escompte evidently decided the market was about to collapse, for he committed suicide, having induced his institution to advance sums of money on copper in ex-

[16] See *Mineral Resources of the United States, 1891, op. cit.,* p. 101, and for *1900, op. cit.,* p. 142.

[17] See Richter, *op. cit.,* p. 258; *Mineral Resources of the United States, 1887, op. cit.,* p. 68; *Mineral Resources of the United States, 1888* (GPO, 1890), p. 47; and *Engineering and Mining Journal,* Vol. 47, No. 2 (January 12, 1889), p. 29.

[18] See *Mineral Resources of the United States, 1888, op. cit.,* p. 51.

[19] *Engineering and Mining Journal,* Vol. 49, No. 1 (January 4 1890), p. 3.

cess of legally permissible amounts. This was followed by a run on
the bank and subsequently by the suspension of payment by the
Société, whose bankers' guarantees had come mainly from the
Comptoir. Both the Comptoir and the Société were subsequently
liquidated.[20] The failure of the two companies was accompanied by a
halving of the price of copper in London to about £40—the level
from which it had risen only a little more than a year before.

The copper market could not simply resume at the point where it
had been when M. Secrétan came upon the scene, however, for
financial liquidation of the Société and the Comptoir did not reduce
inventories of copper to their normal level. Hence, extensive negotiations took place between the European holders of warehoused
copper (including considerable quantities warehoused in the United
States) and producers over the disposition of the excess stocks.[21]
In September 1889, the bankers made some sales in the United
States that indicated the adoption of an independent policy of rapid
disposition.[22] But this action was stopped when the Anaconda
Copper Mining Company and Calumet and Hecla threatened to
flood the market if the bankers persisted in rapid sale. "Syndicate"
stocks were then disposed of gradually over the next three years or
so. By the beginning of 1890, the *Engineering and Mining Journal*
viewed the U. S. stocks, including foreign-owned, as being at a suit-
ably low level.[23]

How long the market was affected by the bank-held stocks is not
quite clear. Richter says the copper was doled out over a period of
"three or four years,"[24] that is, to the middle of 1892 or 1893. A
"gentleman who is familiar with every department of the copper
industry on both sides of the Atlantic" felt that by late 1892 the

[20] See Andrews, *op. cit.*, p. 513.

[21] The concern of the U. S. firms was enhanced by the fact that the tariff on
copper was reduced in the Tariff Act of 1890. The duty on ore was now 0.5 cent
and on ingots 1.25 cents per pound. See Horval A. Smith, *American Copper
Production*, 72nd Congress, 1st Session, Senate Document No. 58 (Washington,
D. C.: U. S. Government Printing Office, 1932), p. 6.

[22] See *Engineering and Mining Journal*, Vol. 49, No. 1 (January 4, 1890), p. 3,
and Richter, *op. cit.*, p. 259.

[23] Vol. 49, No. 1 (January 4, 1890), p. 3.

[24] Richter, *op. cit.*, p. 259.

warehouse stocks held by nonproducers had just about disappeared and that European stocks of copper were at the lowest feasible working level.[25]

Certainly the prices of 1888 must be excluded from the series that is to indicate changes in long-run cost, and probably more must be. Although 1889 and 1890 prices may not have been greatly different from what they would have been in the absence of the corner, they were still feeling the aftermath both in the presence of the excess stocks and in the pent-up demand that was released several months after the break in price in March of 1889.[26] Even though the warehouse stocks of syndicate copper held by nonproducers were not exhausted until perhaps the fall of 1892, the fact that production continued to increase from 1889 to 1892 means that the force of long-run expansion in demand was quite strong. A situation in which excess stocks slow down the rate of plant expansion is quite different from one where excess stocks not only stop plant expansion but also lower prices and result in unused capacity. Perhaps enough of Secrétan's effect on copper is indicated, therefore, by excluding only 1888–90.

American and European Producers' Associations

In the period between the Secrétan operations and World War I, two associations of copper producers were formed in the United States. The first, the American Producers' Association, was formed in 1892 and continued in operation until 1903. A European Producers' Committee, which included the principal copper mining companies in Spain, Portugal, Germany, the Cape Colony, Mexico, and Austria, was formed simultaneously.[27] The second U. S. group,

[25] *The Mineral Industry, 1892*, Vol. I (New York: Scientific Publishing Company, 1893), pp. 125–27, and 132.

[26] See *Mineral Resources of the United States, 1888, op. cit.,* p. 71.

[27] See U. S. Department of Commerce and Labor, Bureau of the Census, *Mines and Quarries, 1902* (Washington, D. C.: U. S. Government Printing Office, 1904), pp. 490 and 498. See also *Engineering and Mining Journal,* Vol. 89, No. 2 (January 8, 1910), p. 60, and *Mineral Resources of the United States, 1908,* Part I (GPO, 1908), p. 186.

the Copper Producers' Association, was formed in early 1909 and continued in operation until 1915.[28]

These associations undoubtedly were formed with an eye to collective action to restrict production when advantageous. However, the record points to the conclusion that, except in 1892, they were not used directly for this purpose, but instead served mainly as collectors of information. Both the U. S. and European associations formed in 1892 collected, compiled, and exchanged monthly reports on the outputs of the member firms, which included most of the leading firms and many that were quite small. Members of the two associations accounted for about three-fourths of the world output of new copper from 1892 to 1903, with production of the members of the U. S. association running from two to three times the production of the foreign association.[29]

Producers thus were able to find out quickly what the other producers were doing, and face-to-face meetings were possibly more frequent because of the existence of the associations. But the history of collusive actions and attempts at collusion seems to have run along rather independently of the two producers' associations.

THE 1892 AGREEMENT

The first of several attempts to restrict supply did make use of the facilities provided by the producers' associations, however. In 1892, the formation of the American Producers' Association involved a one-year agreement that U. S. production from July 1892 to July 1893 should not exceed 140,000 long tons,[30] and that exports

[28] Adalbert Pabst, *Die Strukturwandlungen der internationalen Kupferwirtschaft und das internationale Kupferkartell* (Berlin: Nem-Verlag G.m.b.H., 1932), p. 47. Data collection continued at least through 1913, for *Metal Statistics, 1919* (New York: American Metal Market), p. 211, contains data for 1909–13 secured from the Copper Producers' Association.

[29] See *Mines and Quarries, 1902, op. cit.*, p. 498.

[30] Production in 1891 was 127,000 long tons according to *Summarized Data of Copper Production, op. cit.* From 1886 to 1891, U. S. production grew at the rate of about 10 per cent per year. Thus, if the quota for July 1892 to July 1893 were to be in line with this past rate of growth it should have been around 15 per cent over calendar 1891 instead of the 10 per cent it actually was.

Price Manipulation—1870 to World War I 79

should not exceed 40,000 long tons.[31] In return, European producers were called on to reduce output by 15 per cent. This was more than they were willing to accept. A reduction of 5 per cent was finally agreed upon.[32]

The *Engineering and Mining Journal* seems to have regarded the agreement as a rather weak restriction on output.[33] In any case, the agreement was observed and quotas were not exceeded, but this observance followed and probably was related to a rather high U. S. output of 86,000 long tons in the first half of 1892. Output in the whole of calendar 1892 was actually 22 per cent over 1891. European production increased by 5 per cent from 1891 to 1892.

It seems doubtful that the 1892 agreement had any important effect on the price of copper. One observer states that the market was "agitated" when the agreement was being negotiated, but this is not apparent in average monthly prices. Output continued to increase from 1891 to 1892 and price continued to decline somewhat more rapidly than wholesale prices were falling. When the agreement expired in July 1893, the U. S. demand had begun to shrink and the agreement was not renewed. Exports in the last half of 1893 were heavy.[34] Output in 1893, both for the United States and for the world, was about 5 per cent below 1892. But before this decline is attributed to the effectiveness of the restrictive agreement, it should be recalled that the price of copper fell 9 per cent relative to the fall in wholesale price index.[35]

[31] *The Mineral Industry, 1892, op. cit.*, p. 123. The agreement was termed an "arrangement of understanding" by this publication since the U. S. producers felt a binding agreement would conflict with the antitrust laws.

[32] *Mineral Resources of the United States, 1892* (GPO, 1893), p. 109.

[33] *The Mineral Industry, 1892, op. cit.* Quotas were set "apparently [at] a point above their possible average working capacity," whatever that jumble of words might mean.

[34] *The Mineral Industry, 1893, op. cit.*, p. 253, and *Mineral Resources of the United States, 1893*, (GPO, 1894), p. 62.

[35] This appraisal of the 1892 agreement differs radically from that of William Gates, who says in *Michigan Copper and Boston Dollars* (Cambridge: Harvard University Press, 1951), p. 83, that it was "the first really effective world copper combination to curtail production." Richter, *op. cit.*, takes no notice of the 1892 agreement in his history of the U. S. copper industry.

80   PERIODS OF UNUSUAL PRICE BEHAVIOR

ATTEMPTS AT AGREEMENT, 1893–95

The copper industry had poor years in 1893 after the panic and in 1894.[36] In late 1893, the principal U. S. producers tried to renew the 1892 agreement on production, but the negotiations failed, "principally on account of some factors making demands which the other producers did not feel warranted in granting."[37] An increased demand and very large fluctuations in the prices of shares in U. S. copper companies developed in 1895. A large part of this activity in the securities market no doubt reflected fears and hopes arising from negotiations between European and U. S. producers around May 1895 to limit U. S. exports to 60,000 tons per year and to reduce European output by 17.5 per cent. Exports in the preceding year had considerably exceeded this amount. Final agreement was announced, whereupon the price of GMB's (London) rose about 10 per cent in three months. The bubble was punctured by the news that one of the largest producers had declined to enter into the agreement after all. Attempts were made later to carry negotiations further, but nothing came of them.[38]

The Amalgamated Episode, 1899–1903

In 1899, Standard Oil interests turned their attention to copper and formed a holding company called the Amalgamated Copper Company. The constituent companies included Anaconda Copper Mining Company, several companies operating at Butte, Montana, and others.[39] With the acquisition in 1901 of the Boston and Montana Mining Company and the Butte and Boston Company,

[36] See *Engineering and Mining Journal*, Vol. 59, No. 1 (January 5, 1895), p. 5.
[37] *Ibid.*
[38] *Engineering and Mining Journal*, Vol. 61, No. 1 (January 4, 1896), p. 5.
[39] See F. E. Richter, "The Amalgamated Copper Company: A Closed Chapter in Corporation Finance," *Quarterly Journal of Economics*, Vol. 30 (1916), p. 387 ff. Amalgamated was dissolved in 1915 and took over the name, in effect, of one of its subsidiaries, the Anaconda Copper Mining Company, and is now known as The Anaconda Company.

Price Manipulation—1870 to World War I 81

Amalgamated controlled about one-fifth of the world production of copper.[40] These two companies were part of the Bigelow-Lewisohn group, which also included two Michigan mines, the Tamarack and the Osceola. This group followed Amalgamated's sales policies both before the 1901 acquisition of the two companies and during that year.[41]

The attempt to restrict output and raise the price of copper was begun in early 1899. Amalgamated instructed its selling agent "not to attempt to force upon the market more than was actually needed for consumption, but to maintain a firm price."[42] In this enterprise, Amalgamated not only had the co-operation of some of the Bigelow group but also of some foreign producers.[43] The price of copper rose immediately from the 11–13 cents of 1898 to about 17–18 cents, where it stayed with only small deviations until December 1901.[44]

The copper producers of the world who were not co-operating made Amalgamated's position increasingly precarious. Gates states that the Michigan companies, except for the Bigelow mines, undersold Amalgamated.[45] From 1898, the year preceding Amalgamated's

[40] *The Mineral Industry, 1902*, Vol. II (published, beginning in 1901, as statistical supplement to *Engineering and Mining Journal*, New York, 1903), p. 202. According to Skelton, however, Amalgamated control after acquisition of the above two companies was about 20 per cent of the *U. S.* output, which would have been only a tenth of world output. See Alex Skelton, "Copper," in William Y. Elliott, *et al.*, *International Control in the Non-Ferrous Metals* (New York: Macmillan, 1937), p. 397. Richter, in "The Copper-Mining Industry in the United States, 1845–1925," *op. cit.*, p. 272, puts Amalgamated control at about one-third or more of U. S. output, which would have been roughly a fifth of world output. John Moody, in *The Truth About the Trusts* (New York: Moody Publishing Company, 1904), p. 4, says the control was "at the present time" (1903 or 1904) 15 per cent of world output. *Mines and Quarries, 1902, op. cit.*, p. 489, states that Amalgamated produced 43 per cent of the U. S. output of copper in 1902, between a fifth and a fourth of world output.

[41] See Gates, *op. cit.*, 86–87, and Skelton, *op. cit.*, p. 397.

[42] *Mines and Quarries, 1902, op. cit.*, p. 500.

[43] Skelton, *op. cit.*, p. 398, states that Amalgamated had the co-operation of "most foreign producers," but this assessment clearly goes too far in view of the fact that foreign output was an important factor in bringing Amalgamated's restriction to an end.

[44] *Mineral Resources of the United States, 1900, op. cit.*, p. 172, and *Mines and Quarries, 1902, op. cit.*, p. 500.

[45] Gates, *op. cit.*, p. 88.

umbrella policy, to 1901, the last year of its restrictive policy, output outside the United States increased by 61,000 tons, or 28 per cent. Within the United States (which was producing 55 per cent of world output), production increased by 38,000 tons (by 14 per cent). The 14 per cent was made up of an increase of 12 per cent in Montana output and an increase of 16 per cent outside of Montana.[46] The steady increase in world production, coupled with reluctance of European buyers to pay the price in 1900 and a slowdown in business activity in Europe in 1901, was accompanied by a decline in exports, a rise in imports, and a rise in inventories held by the co-operating interests.[47] Amalgamated's inventories of refined copper went from 93 million pounds at the end of 1900 to 210 million at the end of 1901.[48]

In these circumstances, Amalgamated concluded it could not hold the price up for the whole industry, whereupon the price declined to about 11 cents in January 1902. There followed an attempt to get the principal producers to restrict production, but the negotiations were unsuccessful.[49] The disintegration of the spirit of co-operation was completed with the demise of the American Producers' Association in 1903 upon the withdrawal of large producing interests, including Amalgamated.[50] The monthly compilation of output statistics therefore ceased.[51]

[46] Montana output, not all of which belonged to Amalgamated, went from 103,000 tons in 1898 to 135,000 in 1900, and then declined to 115,000 tons in 1901. Calculated from *Summarized Data of Copper Production, op. cit.*, and *Mineral Resources of the United States, 1910, Part I*, (GPO, 1911), p. 173.

[47] The excess of the Lake copper price (at New York) over the London price (standard copper) was 0.7 cent from 1896 to 1898. In 1899, the differential went to 1.7 cents and, in 1901, to 2.5 cents.

[48] See *The Mineral Industry, 1902, op. cit.*, pp. 175 and 202, and *Mines and Quarries, 1902, op. cit.*, p. 500.

[49] *The Mineral Industry, 1902, op. cit.*, p. 202.

[50] *Engineering and Mining Journal*, Vol. 77, No. 1 (January 7, 1904), p. 8, and *Mines and Quarries, 1902, op. cit.*, p. 490.

[51] The above picture of collusion and its disintegration does not appear to require modification to take account of the fact that in these years much of the copper output of the United States was sold through a single sales outlet. During 1899, Lewisohn Brothers metal selling agency took over sales of the Amalgamated

Price Manipulation—1870 to World War I   83

If the objective of the three years was the formation of an effective monopoly, Amalgamated's policy must be considered a failure. But, although Amalgamated may have suffered a disaster since the price decline left it with large inventories, the promoters of Amalgamated were not interested solely in the price of copper. The fluctuations in the prices of Amalgamated and other copper company stocks undoubtedly produced handsome rewards for those with superior information on Amalgamated's moves during this period.[52]

1903 to World War I

The history of attempts to influence the price of copper after 1903 is not nearly so clear as for the preceding years. The main items calling for attention are the behavior of the price of copper in the decline in economic activity from September 1902 to August 1904; the very large increase in price from 1904 to 1907 (by 60 per cent) and precipitous fall from 1907 to 1908; and a sharp but smaller rise and fall from 1911 to 1914. Confident assertions by earlier writers that collusive action was responsible for these price increases can be confronted with the contrary view.

---

group. (See Gates, *op. cit.*, p. 86.) The next year, in early 1900, this business was taken over by the newly formed United Metals Selling Company, with Standard Oil men and the two Lewisohns on the board of directors. (See Richter, "The Amalgamated Copper Company: A Closed Chapter in Corporation Finance," *op. cit.*, p. 392.) This company charged from 1.5 to 2.5 per cent commission and sold not only for Amalgamated but for other companies as well. In 1902, for example, its sales amounted to 83 per cent of the U. S. refined copper output. (See *Mines and Quarries, 1902, op. cit.*, p. 490. The company also operated a large refinery at Perth Amboy. Gates, *op. cit.*, p. 87, states that United's sales were about 70 per cent of the U. S. output.) But United Metals and its predecessor rather clearly acted simply as a sales agent without control over quantity or price.

[52] Moody, *op. cit.*, p. 33, quotes the Boston News Bureau as follows: ". . . next to the United States Steel Corporation, more people in the United States have been interested in the Amalgamated Copper speculation, or have been shareholders in its fortunes and its misfortunes than in any other stock ever distributed or promoted in this country."

ALLEGED RESTRICTION BY AMALGAMATED, 1904–05

The first puzzle is provided by C. L. Knight. In the course of explaining that the principal causes of specific cycles in the mine production of copper are cyclical movements in the business activity of copper-consuming countries, he observes that some other factors are involved. One of these other factors he describes as follows:

> The operations of the Amalgamated Copper Company during the first decade of the twentieth century were doubtless the principal factor in preventing a decline in copper prices in 1904 and 1905, when cyclical low points in business conditions occurred in the United States, England, and Germany.[53]

The price of copper had actually risen about 3 cents from 1902 to 1903; but recall that the Amalgamated umbrella broke in early 1902 and that inventories of copper were high at that time. From 1903 to 1904, price declined about a cent and then rose about 3 cents to 1905. Was this actually an example of unusual price behavior which the normal course of events would be unlikely to have produced? "An unprecedented expansion in demand"[54] characterized 1904. While U. S. demand in the first half was off by about 30 per cent, export demand had revived.[55] Growth of consumption was especially great in the second half of the year because of the large requirements of the electrical industries and the Russo-Japanese War. A new and unusual factor was a very large demand for copper by China, and, in addition, production was adversely affected by a strike in the Lake district. But in spite of the strong demand for copper in the latter part of the year, the 1904 average price was below that of 1903. Copper probably fared exceptionally well, however. Note that in the chronology of the National Bureau of Economic Research the trough following the peak of September 1902 did not come until August 1904.

[53] C. L. Knight, *Secular and Cyclical Movements in the Production and Price of Copper* (Philadelphia: University of Pennsylvania Press, 1935), p. 129.

[54] *Mineral Resources of the United States, 1904* (GPO, 1905), p. 221.

[55] *The Mineral Industry, 1904*, statistical supplement to *Engineering and Mining Journal* (New York: 1905), p. 134.

Price Manipulation—1870 to World War I   85

The U.S. copper industry in 1905 enjoyed very strong demand, both from home and foreign demand. In addition, the demand from China went from 10 million pounds in 1904 to 90 million in 1905. Production in the United States was about 900 million pounds. Investment in additional capacity was taking place, but with very strong demand and apparently some transportation difficulties,[56] it is not surprising that the price of copper rose considerably.

The writer concludes, therefore, that Knight's example, selected to illustrate the influence of noncyclical factors on copper prices, is ill-chosen, for it does not appear that any machinations on the part of Amalgamated were involved in the 1904–05 rise in the price of copper. Nor have other opinions agreeing with Knight's suggestion for 1904–05 been found.[57]

ALLEGED POOL OF 1906–07

The rapid rise in the price of copper continued to 1906 but then moved more slowly to 1907.[58] Some writers seem to be confident that a pool—the precise nature of which is not specified—was operating in 1906–07. For example, Skelton asserts flatly that a pool was operating, recognizing, of course, that the exuberant demand for copper did have something to do with the rapid rise in the price of copper.[59] A Federal Trade Commission study on copper asserts at two points that the curtailment of Montana production in 1906 forced the price to 25 cents per pound.[60] On another page,

[56] According to Willard L. Thorp severe freight congestion was experienced in 1905. See *Business Annals* (New York: National Bureau of Economic Research, 1926), p. 3.

[57] This is not the case for the more general and puzzling reference to the first decade of the century, which will be discussed later.

[58] The price of copper in 1904 was 12 cents; in 1905, 16 cents; in 1906, 20 cents; and in 1907, 21 cents.

[59] Skelton, *op. cit.*, p. 398, does not indicate why he was led to conclude that a pool was operating. Elizabeth May, writing in the same volume (William Y. Elliott *et al.*, *op. cit.*), p. 545, on the U. S. copper industry, mentions the 1901 Amalgamated operation but has nothing to say about a pool in 1906–07.

[60] See U. S. Federal Trade Commission, *Report on the Copper Industry* (Washington, D. C.: U. S. Government Printing Office, 1947), pp. 11 and 185.

however, it is asserted that pool operations were in progress in 1906.[61]
Supporting evidence is not given.

Rudulf Lenz, writing in 1910, was also convinced that there was
collusive action in the copper industry in 1906.[62] He recognized that
market conditions for copper were very unusual—that demand was
very strong and that expansion of U. S. supply was hindered by
labor shortage and by shortages of coal, coke, and other supplies resulting from congestion on the railroads. He did not conclude, however, that these abnormal conditions were an adequate explanation
of the price rise in 1906; collective action was an essential part of the
explanation. The main support for this belief was the large share of
smelter output controlled by Amalgamated. According to Lenz, the
company directly controlled 32 per cent of the U. S. output and
indirectly controlled another third. Within the United States,
therefore, it was associated with almost half of the world output.
In addition, it was allied with other companies outside the United
States. Lenz was quite aware, however, of the inadequacy of the
available information on the precise relations among the copper
companies.

As with the alleged 1904–05 episode, there are several writers
who, in the course of compiling a chronological account of events on
the copper market, have failed to note the presence of collusive
action in 1906. Gates, looking at the period through Calumet and
Hecla eyes, makes no mention of collusive action in 1906. The general tenor of his discussion seems to be that the collapse of Amalgamated's 1899–1901 sally, with large new producers opening up in
Arizona, Nevada, and Utah, marked the end of Amalgamated's real
power.[63]

---

[61] *Ibid.*, p. 244.

[62] See Rudulf Lenz, *Der Kupfermarkt unter dem Einflusse der Syndikate und
Trusts* (Berlin: Verlag für Fachliteratur G.m.b.H., 1910), pp. 105–07. In explaining his view of 1906, Lenz uses the rather general term, *Ring*.

[63] See Gates, *op. cit.*, pp. 85–89. So far as smelter output is concerned, however,
Nevada production was negligible until 1906–10. The really large increases be-
tween the two quinquennia of 1896–1900 and 1901–05 came in Arizona and in
Montana, which reached its peak in 1901–05. Utah's absolute increase between
these two five-year periods was much smaller. See *Summarized Data of Copper
Production, op. cit.*, pp. 17–18.

Price Manipulation—1870 to World War I 87

Lutz, in a very brief account of attempts at collusive action in the copper industry, makes no mention of collusive action in 1906, although he does note the formation of the Copper Producers' Association in 1908.[44] Perhaps his failure to mention any collusive action in 1906 should not be regarded as significant, however, since he also fails to note the Amalgamated maneuver of 1899–1901. This was important enough to be included in any survey intended to be complete.

In Pabst's 1932 account of the copper industry and trade the Amalgamated's 1899–1901 episode is also passed over without mention. The events of 1906–07 are referred to only as providing the occasion for the fall in the price of copper out of which came "ein Gentlemen Agreement unter dem Namen Copper Producers Association." He does observe, however, that the course of the price of copper followed closely the course of business activity. This statement suggests the view that change in the volume of business activity adequately accounted for the movement of the price of copper without introducing any element of collusion.[65]

The writer in *Mineral Resources*, in explaining the events of 1906, emphasizes extraordinarily strong demand for copper and disorganization on the supply side. Copper producers were said to be striving to increase output but were hampered by inability to get the labor they wanted to hire and by delayed deliveries of supplies and product because of congestion on the railroads. In the later months of the year, the shortage of coal, coke, and fuel oil in many western states was so pressing that a good many smelters were forced to shut down for short periods until needed supplies arrived.[66]

Demand—both home and export—remained very strong in the first part of 1907. Additional capacity from new mines, abandoned mines, and current producers was coming into operation. The trans-

[44] Hans Lutz, *Das Kupfer als Welthandelsware* (Wurzburg-Aumuhle: Drucherei und Verlag wissenschaftlicher Werke Konrad Triltsch 1939), pp. 34–35.

[65] Pabst, *op. cit.*, p. 47.

[66] See *Mineral Resources of the United States, 1906* (GPO, 1907), p. 377. See also *The Mineral Industry, 1906*, statistical supplement to *Engineering and Mining Journal* (New York: 1907), p. 239.

portation difficulties had been relieved, although the supply of labor was still short.[67]

To the writer, the unusual market conditions in 1906 and early 1907 seem to be adequate to account for the behavior of the price of copper. In the absence of definite information about effective collusive activities,[68] it seems reasonable to attribute the large rise in the price of copper in these years to an unusual course of economic events not associated with collusive activity. The price announcements of Amalgamated probably represented only a barometric action of the most important firm in the industry in a situation where a large price rise would have resulted in any case.

This is also the view of one of the more nearly contemporary observers, F. E. Richter. He ascribes the extraordinary rise in the price of copper to the great rise in demand coupled with the "somewhat feverish condition of industry generally in the years 1905–1907 . . . though charges of manipulation of prices and of 'visible supplies' were common enough."[69]

If this point of view is correct, there is no need to exclude the 1906 experience from this study's price series on the ground that there was collusion. Even so, market conditions, in 1906 especially, were certainly abnormal enough to warrant considering the exclusion of these years from the price record. But since there were no "artificial" restrictions involved, these two years, with their abnormally high prices, have not been excluded.

ATTEMPTED RESTRICTION, 1908 TO WORLD WAR I

There are a number of indications that collusive action was contemplated or attempted between the precipitous price fall of 1907

[67] *Mineral Resources of the United States, 1907, Part I* (GPO, 1908), p. 572.

[68] There is no mention of collusive activity in *Mineral Resources of the United States, 1906* or *1907, op. cit.*, whereas in other years of this period the writers of that review did not hesitate to allude to collusion. Recall also that those writers noted here, with the exception of Lenz, who have asserted that collusion did take place did not support their assertion. Lenz rested his assertion on the important place that Amalgamated held in the market structure, a suggestive but inconclusive fact. Possibly the assertions that collusive activity did exist are representative of conclusions inferred from the behavior of the price of copper.

[69] "The Copper-Mining Industry in the United States, 1845–1925," *op. cit.*, p. 277.

Price Manipulation—1870 to World War I 89

and World War I, but on none of these occasions does the action
appear to have been very successful. In the first part of 1908, several
important producers were restricting output, but this policy apparently rested on an incorrect estimate of the elasticity of output of
the producers who were not co-operating. Restriction was shortly
abandoned and by midyear the leading producers were making a
"normal" output.[70] The formation of the Copper Producers' Association in early 1909, in which all of the leading producers of the
United States were included, has already been mentioned. The
Association's statistical report, the first of which was issued February 10, 1909, included data on the production, export, and domestic consumption of copper.[71]

No convincing evidence has come to the writer's attention to
indicate that the Copper Producers' Association was an instrument
for collusive action. It should be noted, however, that Pabst characterizes this event as "ein Gentlemen Agreement" among Phelps
Dodge Corporation, Calumet and Hecla, American Smelting and
Refining Company, and Amalgamated, under the name Copper
Producers' Association. According to Pabst, the statistical activities
of the Association were supplemented by voluntary limitation of
production which resulted in a reduction of inventories and an
increase in price.[72] But price declined steadily from 1908 to 1911.
It is true that from 1909 to 1910 production outside the United
States increased 10 per cent compared with an increase of 1 per
cent within the United States, and that from 1908 to 1909 production
outside the United States went up by 3 per cent as against 16 per
cent within the United States. From 1908 to 1912, the percentage
increases inside and outside the United States were about the same,
however.[73] The recital of these facts is not conclusive, of course, but
they throw doubt on the view that U. S. producers were restricting
production during these years.

[70] *Mineral Resources of the United States, 1908, Part I, op. cit.,* p. 186.
[71] *Ibid.,* p. 187.
[72] "Voluntary" appears to mean that there was no formal agreement. It is not
clear from Pabst's paragraph whether the alleged curbing of production was
present from the beginning of the Association or came about as a result of perusing
the reports of the Association. See Pabst, *op. cit.,* p. 47.
[73] *Summarized Data of Copper Production, op. cit.,* facing p. 32.

90   PERIODS OF UNUSUAL PRICE BEHAVIOR

In 1909, a prosperous year for the copper industry, there were
many rumors of important consolidations for the purpose of better
controlling output, and some of the plans did go through. But plans
for the larger consolidations were abandoned, apparently with a
dominant consideration being the court decisions in the Standard
Oil and American Tobacco cases. Had the plans gone through, the
new combination would have had control over about the same percentage of U. S. output as Amalgamated had in 1899.[74]

The remaining problem for the prewar period is 1912 to 1913.
According to Skelton, European demand was very strong, especially
from Germany, and "not only held the price at about 13 cents, but
permitted a modest essay in price manipulation up to 18 cents in
1912–1913.[75] The nature of this "modest essay in price manipulation" is somewhat obscured by the comments of Elizabeth May in
the same volume. She was of the view that maintenance of equilibrium in the prewar years was facilitated by the Copper Producers'
Association, but had nothing unusual to report about 1912–13.[76]

What seems to have happened was that the demand for copper
revived strongly in both the United States and Europe. So far as
quoted New York prices are concerned, there was a substantial
increase during the first half of 1912 from a level of 12–13 cents to
about 17.5 cents. One commentator characterizes the last half of
1912 as "the famous period of pegged prices."[77] During this period,
the larger companies, which were maintaining the pegged prices,
found their share of the sales diminishing while the smaller companies which were not co-operating did not restrict their sales. The
result was that in 1912 copper companies failed "by far" to attain

[74] See *Mineral Resources of the United States, 1909, Part I* (GPO, 1911), p. 153,
and *1919, Part I* (GPO, 1922), p. 158; and *The Mineral Industry, 1909*, statistical
supplement to *Engineering and Mining Journal* (New York: 1910), p. 152. The
last source was of the view that the power of the new combination, had it not
aborted, would have been nil in a very few years in view of prospective large
increases in output coming from new producers.

[75] *Op. cit.*, p. 399.

[76] *Ibid.*, p. 558.

[77] *The Mineral Industry, 1913*, annual statistical supplement to *Engineering
and Mining Journal* (New York: 1914), p. 135. See also p. 132 of the *1913* supplement and that of *1912* (New York: 1913), p. 169.

Price Manipulation—1870 to World War I 91

the quotational average and also differed as much as a cent in average realized price. In 1913, after the price break in December 1912 and January 1913, the quoted prices constituted a better description of what was happening.

On the basis of this account, Skelton's statement that there was a modest essay in price manipulation in 1912–13 seems justified, although the course of the quoted price exaggerates its importance. The action taken, a temporary restriction of output by the larger firms, is not a new pattern of behavior but is of the same general nature as a number of the earlier episodes.

NON-FERROUS METALS

ALUMINUM

Aluminum is a versatile metal which possesses the valuable properties of electrical conductivity, high ductility, high thermal conductivity, resistance to corrosion, and high reflectivity for light and heat. Raw aluminum, sold mainly in ingots, may be rolled, forged, or cast into common commercial forms as well as powdered for use

---

[1] League of Nations, *Circular*, E. 946, June 5, 1936, p. 27.
[2] *Kartell-Rundschau*, 1939, pp. 53, 361.
[3] *Circular*, E. 1067, March 15, 1939. See also *Kartell-Rundschau, 1938*, p. 640.

---

[1] Bone Committee, *Patent Hearings*, Part 5, pp. 2338, 2339; Ballande, *Ententes*, pp. 79 ff.; *Kartell-Rundschau*, 1936, p. 580.
[2] Eugene Staley, *Raw Materials in Peace and War* (New York, 1937), pp. 309 ff. (Hereafter cited Staley, *Raw Materials*.)
[3] Leith *et al.*, *World Minerals*, p. 28.

Non-Ferrous Metals   217

in paints. Combined with other metals it forms an extensive range of alloys and is indispensible in mass production of airplanes. Thus it is an important material in both peace and war.

Metallic aluminum is usually extracted from the mineral bauxite, which contains from 50 per cent to 60 per cent aluminum. The most important requirement in the production of aluminum is an abundance of electric power at reasonably low cost. To produce one short ton of aluminum 20,000 kilowatt hours of electricity, about four tons of crude ore, and about 5 tons of coal, in addition to other materials, are used. Though the basic patents for producing aluminum expired many years ago, certain processes are still covered by patents and a good deal of the technological know-how is still secret.[1] From the inception of the industry there have been close financial connections between various aluminum companies. These intimate intercorporate relationships have naturally tended toward concentration and integration. There is abundant literature covering both the cartels and the corporate combinations in this industry.[2]

French, British, Swiss, and Canadian producers of aluminum first formed a cartel in 1901. Canada was represented in the cartel by the Northern Aluminum Company, subsidiary of the Pittsburgh Reduction Company. The cartel disintegrated in 1908 and was revived in 1912. Some time later Italian and Norwegian firms also became members. The newly formed Aluminum Company of America (Alcoa) entered the first combination indirectly by an agreement concluded September 25, 1908, between the Northern Aluminum Company, Limited, and the leading company of the cartel, the *Société Anonyme pour l'Industrie d'Aluminium,* of Neuhausen (Switzerland). This agreement remained valid despite the disintegration of the European cartel in 1908. On June 7, 1912, the District Court for the Western district of Pennsylvania heard the petition of the United States Attorney-General to enjoin Alcoa from pursuing illegal activities including participation in this agreement. In the resultant consent decree, Alcoa was perpetually prohibited from entering into any agreement that would restrict exports from or imports to the United States.[8] The

---

[1] See Bone Committee, *Patent Hearings,* Part 5, pp. 2340 f.

[2] Donald H. Wallace, *Market Control in the Aluminum Industry,* Cambridge, Mass., 1937; *International Ententes,* pp. 31 ff.; TNEC, *Monograph 21,* p. 6911; in *Magarin der Deutschen Wirtschaft* (Berlin) [Aug. 1, 1929], pp. 1210 ff.; Alfred Gautschi, *Die Aluminiumindustrie,* Zürich, 1925; Dr. von Schoenebeck, *Das Aluminiumzollproblem,* Berlin, 1929.

[8] The consent decree signed by Alcoa is reprinted in D. H. Wallace, *op. cit.,* pp. 547 ff. On Oct. 25, 1922, the decree was modified to permit the Aluminum Co.

218   *International Cartels*

second cartel, established in 1912, automatically disintegrated with the
First World War. The third cartel, established in 1923, was based on
price fixing agreements among big European producers. The fourth
cartel, established November 15, 1926, was composed of French, Swiss,
German, British, and other European producers.[4] It chartered the
Aluminium Association, with headquarters in Switzerland, and a special bureau to explore and propagandize new uses for aluminum.
Experts in the League of Nations drew up a report analyzing these
aluminum agreements up to 1930. It is interesting to note that in
their opinion, this cartel reduced the number of middlemen and hence
lowered distribution costs. According to the same report, "the constitution of the cartel has done away with sales of metal between
producing countries, which necessitated the payment of customs duties
and transport charges that were quite unnecessary and sometimes
ridiculous—as, for example, when transports were proceeding simultaneously in exactly opposite directions." The same report emphasizes
that the cartel had practically put an end to dumping by fixing prices.[5]
The cartel agreement did not regulate capacity and total output although it fixed quotas for domestic and export sales, and covered
aluminum sold in the form of alloys. However, sales to North
American markets were not regulated. According to D. H. Wallace,
this agreement was ineffectual in preventing expansion.[6] Competition

to purchase a subsidiary in Norway. After this, another antitrust action was brought
against Alcoa in the courts of the United States. The brief to this action, filed Oct.
3, 1938, in the District Court, Southern District of New York, and the decision of the
District Court which dismissed the complaint contain interesting source material. The
law suit came to the Supreme Court of the United States by virtue of an appeal of the
Attorney General. This court was unable to make a decision because of lack of
quorum. The suit was therefore transferred for decision to the Circuit Court of Appeals
of New York. This tribunal reversed, March 12, 1945, in the main the decision of
the District Court and upheld the principal items of the complaint of the Government.
Although the decision relates mostly to the domestic situation, it contains many interesting details concerning the relationship between the American and Canadian companies and between the Canadians and the cartel.
    [4] Broadly speaking the cartel developed as follows: a) 1901-1908, b) 1912-1914,
c) 1923-1926, d) 1926-1930, e) 1931. . . .
    [5] League of Nations, *Review of the Economic Aspects of Several International
Industrial Agreements*, prepared by A. S. Benni and others (Geneva, 1930), p. 28.
(Hereafter cited Benni *et al., Industrial Agreements.*) Louis Marlio, one of the
authors, was also the president of the French aluminum cartel. The text of the agreement of the Aluminium Association contained the following guiding principles: 1)
To regulate and control the aluminum sales of each of its members by exchange of
market in formation, 2) to promote the use of aluminum, 3) to take care that consumers receive the needed quantities and qualities, and 4) to reduce overhead and
transportation expenses.
    [6] *Op. cit.,* p. 306.

Non-Ferrous Metals 219

from Canadian outsiders disturbed considerably the policies of the cartel on export markets. For this reason the Aluminium Association approached the Canadians with offers of common marketing organization. These negotiations culminated in a new cartel (the fifth) in 1931 with the Canadians included as prominent members. The other participants were British, German, French, Swiss, and Norwegian producers of aluminum as well as their subsidiaries in Austria, Spain, and Sweden. The agreement of July 3, 1931, was called the Foundation Agreement and was signed in Paris. A special joint stock company was established to administer the agreement. The shares of the cartel agency, Alliance Aluminium Company (Alliance) which was incorporated at Basle, Switzerland, were distributed in proportion to production rates at that time. The capital of the company was 35 million Swiss francs; one quarter of the shares was paid for in cash, the rest in aluminum.[7] The obligations of the members under the agreement extended to their present and future subsidiaries. Investments in outside plants were prohibited unless a dominant influence in outsiders' facilities was acquired, and thus their adherence to the cartel was ensured.

Under the previous cartel there had been no regulation of output, with the consequence that the gains derived from cartellization were somewhat dissipated by unlimited expansion and production. This "weakness" was therefore corrected by the institution of production quotas fixed by the executive board every three months. The first quotas were the following: 28 per cent for the Canadians, 21.36 per cent for the French, 19.64 per cent for the Germans, 15.42 per cent for the Swiss, and 15 per cent for the British. One rather unusual provision in the agreement authorized the cartel to confiscate production without compensation if the production quota was exceeded by more than 5 per cent per annum. In the course of time the severity of this provision was relaxed.[8] Sales territories were not allocated except that an agreement made in July, 1930, was reaffirmed according to which the exclusive sales agent for the Japanese market became the Canadian company with a share of 52 per cent in that territory.[9] Members were forbidden to co-operate with outside plants through capital investments or technological experience unless they were able to exert significant influence upon those outsiders.

There is little doubt that the cartel members made certain agreements concerning their domestic price policies, although no such ex-

[7] *International Ententes*, p. 33.   [8] *Ibid.*, p. 34.
[9] Borkin and Welsh, *Master Plan*, p. 212.

2 2 0   *International Cartels*

press provision in this regard was contained in the cartel agreement.[10] Surplus stocks of aluminum were pooled and disposed of by the Alliance at prices determined by cartel agencies. These prices automatically became the minimum standard prices for all export sales of aluminum. World prices of aluminum were not published, but it is known that they decreased between 1931 and 1939. The monthly average prices of aluminum are the following: 99 per cent virgin ingot in cents per pound were approximately: in 1895, 58.66; in 1913, 23.64; in 1914, 18.63; in January, 1931 to January, 1934, 23.30; from February, 1934, to February, 1937, between 21.65 and 20.50; from March, 1937, to the end of 1939, 20.00.

Although the cartel did not control more than three-fifths of the world production of aluminum, it regulated practically the whole volume of exports. The largest "outsider" was Alcoa, whose exports were insignificant. At the end of 1935, negotiations took place between the cartel and the Soviet Union, another outsider. It is highly probable that an understanding was reached in which Russia promised not to disturb the controlled world market with large exports.[11]

The German national group of the cartel announced in 1934 that it wanted to be freed from quota restrictions pertaining to domestic production.[12] The German Government intended to expand productive capacity for military reasons without regard to cartel policies. The other members strongly opposed the German suggestions. Ultimately, however, they agreed to a compromise by which Germany was allowed to increase her capacity on condition that for every ton exported she should buy from the cartel one ton for her domestic use. In addition, Germany agreed to increase her domestic prices of aluminum except for government supplies. This compromise did not work well and the cartel structure had to be reshaped effective January 1, 1936. The Alliance discontinued buying surplus stocks and setting minimum prices. Fines were introduced for those companies exceeding production quotas. Even this system did not operate successfully, and during 1936 the quota system was practically abandoned. The chief reason

[10] See T. W. Stadler, *Kartelle und Schutzzoll* (Berlin, 1933), pp. 49 ff.

[11] Borkin and Welsh, *Master Plan*, p. 216.

[12] The German national group was dominated by the *Vereinigte Aluminiumwerke A.G.*, a government-owned company. German exporters often objected that the price policies of this firm completely disregarded public interest, being directed only to make corporate profits. One writer, criticizing the domestic price policies of that company, stated that if a privately-owned company would charge such exorbitant prices, the government would certainly intervene. Cf. Anonymous, in *Magazin der Wirtschaft* (Berlin, August 1, 1929), p. 1214.

Non-Ferrous Metals   221

for the disintegration of quota restrictions was the sharp demand for aluminum in anticipation of the needs of war. According to Joseph Borkin and Charles H. Welsh, Alliance has been dormant since about 1938,[13] though the agreement was still nominally in force in 1939. Research and propaganda services of the cartel were centralized in a separate organization.

The relationship between Alcoa and the cartel has been the subject of much controversy. Alcoa transferred its European aluminum interests to its sister company Canadian Aluminum, Ltd., in 1928. The capital stock of the Canadian concern was distributed among the stockholders of Alcoa. The two companies continued to protect each other's markets. It is certainly no exaggeration to say that the two companies, while legally independent, always maintained close contacts. For that reason, many writers have felt that Canadian membership in the international cartel indirectly also bound Alcoa.[14] It is probable that the cartel did not feel anxiety in regard to the operation of the American company on the export market. In fact, Thurman Arnold, the Assistant Attorney-General in charge of the Antitrust Division, claimed that Alcoa pressed its Canadian affiliate to join the cartel so that the mounting foreign output would not invade the United States market.[15] It is noteworthy that, according to Joseph Borkin and Charles Welsh, the executive staff of Alliance consisted of two managers who for many years were in the employ of the Aluminum Company of America.[16] The exports from and imports to the United States in aluminum are given in Table 9.

TABLE 9

U. S. EXPORTS AND IMPORTS OF ALUMINUM IN SHORT TONS

Year	Exports	Imports	Year	Exports	Imports
1931	2,350	7,416	1936	803	12,781
1932	2,218	4,092	1937	2,692	22,589
1933	2,853	7,623	1938	6,309	8,870
1934	4,183	9,296	1939	37,085	14,336
1935	1,985	10,646			

Source: Bureau of Foreign and Domestic Commerce.

[13] *Master Plan*, p. 220.

[14] TNEC, *Monograph No. 21*, pp. 70, 71. It is important to note that the decision of the Circuit Court of Appeals of March 12, 1945 (*U. S. vs. Aluminum Co. of America et al.*), concludes that Alcoa was not a party to the "Alliance" and did not violate the Sherman Act as far as foreign trade is concerned.

[15] *Ottawa Gazette*, November 5, 1942.

[16] *Master Plan*, p. 214.

2 3 8   *International Cartels*

TIN

The most important deposits of tin ore appear in the form of a mineral called cassiterite or "tinstone." Although tin is fairly abundant throughout the world, it is unimportant commercially except in a few localities. Extensive deposits of good ores have been found in Malaya, the Dutch East Indies, Nigeria, Bolivia, Thailand, and the Belgian Congo.

Tin is divided into two main grades, A and B. While Class B may fall to 99 per cent metallic tin content, Class A is required to assay 99.75 per cent. Certain low-grade ores create difficulties in refining but they are nevertheless important.

Another class of tin is tin scrap or secondary tin which comes chiefly from scrap resulting from the manufacture of tin-bearing articles. Although new processes have been developed for its recovery, secondary tin does not influence the market as copper scrap does the copper market, or scrap steel the steel market. The amount of secondary tin recovered fluctuates widely because it is not used in large quantities except under unusual circumstances such as war or when tin buyers wish to exert pressure on the market due to shortages, high prices, etc.

The search for tin substitutes has been extensive, but for most uses no satisfactory material has been discovered. Tin bonderized steel and the electrolytic tin plate, carrying less than one-third the tin formerly used in the manufacture of tin cans, have been adopted. Both of these processes require extensive plant installations.

Tin is a raw material of political importance both because it is indispensable in armaments, where it has practically no substitute, and because tin production is concentrated chiefly in the Far East and dominated by only a few governments. Several governments, including that of the United States, have complained bitterly that the supply and price policies in the tin industry have hampered their efforts to

Non-Ferrous Metals 239

carry on war and have led to exorbitant exploitation in peacetime. Tin problems have been the subject of many a diplomatic note. Because of the great distances from sources of supply, governments have contemplated the accumulation of stockpiles of tin for use in case of war, but this was never accomplished satisfactorily.[1]

Great Britain occupies a focal position in the tin industries for several reasons. First, a large part of the world's supply of tin ore is produced within British territories. Second, an even larger quantity of tin ores is smelted in British factories, chiefly at Liverpool, Singapore, and Penang. Third, through financial and other intercorporate relations England exerts influence on many tin-producing and tin-refining plants outside Britain. Finally, the marketing control agencies of tin are located in London, and are partially administered by British Government officials.

The prices of tin ore wherever produced, and of metallic tin wherever smelted, were governed by the quotations on the London Metal Exchange, and metallic tin was primarily sold by the smelteries through agents or dealers directly, or indirectly, connected with the Exchange. Tin was also bought and sold on the Exchange by speculators who did not intend to supply or accept real tin but who wanted to make money from the price fluctuations. Because of these speculative transactions, the turnover on the London Exchange was increased in periods from two to ten times the actual consumption needs.[2] Some tin is bought and sold on the New York Commodity Exchange as well.[3]

A significant role in tin was played by the Netherlands Government. The Dutch East Indies produced a substantial part of the tin ores, most of which were smelted at Arnhem, Holland. Whereas the British Government acted in the interests of its banks, and its many hundreds of investors, in Holland the Government itself was a large shareholder in the tin mines.

---

[1] A Subcommittee of the House Committee on Foreign Affairs in 1935 vetoed the idea. Its reasons were expressed as follows: "The difficulty of purchasing such an amount of tin without drastically disturbing the present price would be so great as to be almost insurmountable. Regardless of assurance given by any legislation, the very existence of such a stock with the ever present possibility of liquidation would threaten the value of inventories as long as the stock was held. The fundamental disadvantage, however, lies in the fact that the plan offers protection only for an emergency." *Report of the Subcommittee of the House Committee on Foreign Affairs on H.R. 404*, 73rd Congress, 2nd Session, and H.R. 71, 74th Congress, 1st Session, 1935, p. 37. (Hereafter cited *Tin Investigation*.)

[2] ITC, *Tin Control*, pp. 15, 20.

[3] The tin by-laws of the New York Commodity Exchange are contained in *Tin Investigation*, pp. 492 ff.

The tin industry is the most important factor in the domestic and foreign economy of Bolivia. The export duties on tin, the import duties on mining materials, and other taxes paid by the tin companies amount to more than four-fifths of all the state's revenue. Many writers have remarked that the tin industry alone paid for the military expedition against Paraguay.[4] The romantic story of the rise of Señor Patiño from a poor workman to a captain of Bolivian industry and politics has been recounted frequently. Patiño's financial interests have expanded into stock ownership in British and Malayan smelters. Before the war the United States Congress was urged from time to time to prohibit the export of tin scrap to Japan in order to conserve the tin the U. S. possessed, but this was considered impracticable. Since then Bolivian tin ores have been of particular importance to our war economy. A new smelter has been built in the United States to accommodate the smelting of these low-grade Bolivian ores.[4a]

Trade associations played a significant part in the tin marketing controls. These associations were largely responsible for the regulation of markets at the start of international co-operation. Although they became less noticeable when international public agencies participated in the control schemes, even the superficial observer should have realized that government marketing controls could not have operated successfully without the support and guidance of the private entrepreneur associations. Tin producers first formed local associations which expanded into national groups. There were many producers' associations, especially in Malaya and Nigeria, some of which were connected with the chambers of commerce. The first comprehensive association of tin producers was established at a meeting in July of 1929 in London, with some three hundred delegates of the largest tin mining interests in the British Empire present. According to reports, this meeting resulted from a letter appearing in *The Times* of June 6, 1929, signed by representatives of tin mining interests from Malaya, Siam, Nigeria, and Burma. This formation of the Tin Producers' Association marked the first important attempt to establish an international marketing control on a voluntary basis. One motivating force leading to this organization was the fact that while the prices of other

---

[4] *International Ententes,* p. 20. See also K. E. Knorr, *Tin Under Control* (Stanford University, 1945), entire. See also additional material quoted in this volume.

[4a] According to recent reports, this smelter is expected to be kept in operation after the Second World War and to be supplied also by Dutch concentrates. American interests hope that the export duty on Malayan concentrates, discriminating against non-British smelters, will be repealed. Cf. the *New York Times,* April 30, 1945, p. 26.

Non-Ferrous Metals 241

non-ferrous metals increased in 1929 over those in 1928, tin prices dropped in that year and stocks rose. The Council of the Association consisted of 21 members who met for the first time on September 3, 1929. Originally it represented only a small part of the output and was regarded as an association of financial interests, until, in December, 1929, at the general assembly of the Association, it was announced that Bolivian and Dutch East Indies' producers had agreed to join. Thereupon many other British interests joined. Originally the Dutch producers had been reluctant to join the Association because, they argued, they had not expanded production tremendously during the early post-war boom as had the others and therefore should not be expected to curtail production.[5] All members were asked at this first general meeting to stop production for eight days from February 8 to February 16, 1930, and for another eight days from March 15 to March 23. In addition, members were requested to stop production every week-end for at least 30 hours during the whole of 1930 after the first of February.

The Council thought that these two measures would bring about a reduction of some 20,000 long tons by the end of 1930, but by the beginning of April they saw that there were complicating factors which would prevent such reduction. Then they decided to urge members to reduce output in 1930 to 80 per cent of the 1929 output, hoping it would reduce the total by 30,000 tons. By July they realized that 20 per cent was insufficient, and the members agreed in addition to this curtailment to suspend operations during two of the three succeeding months. The Dutch producers threatened to leave the Association because of the lack of discipline and enforcement of the restrictive measures. The Dutch suggested that these measures should be implemented by governmental compulsion. By the end of 1930, all the producers had concurred in this suggestion. The first agreement between governments on a tin restrictions scheme was concluded on February 27, 1931, to be effective on March 1.[6] Public opinion in producing countries received this new type of organization with rather favorable comments.

As a rule, international marketing controls in the non-ferrous metal industries found that attempts to stabilize prices only by influencing production were not adequate, and that other methods had to be adopted to supplement and enforce them. In the tin industry,

---

[5] Rowe, *Markets*, p. 160.
[6] This agreement is published in ILO, *Intergovernmental Commodity Control Agreements*, pp. 73 ff.

242 *International Cartels*

buffer stock schemes were employed to adjust market policies over short periods. These schemes attempted to maintain the price of tin between certain limits by buying or selling on the London market. Long term policies, however, continued to depend on the regulation of tin production.

One of the first instances of co-operation among tin producers was the formation of the so-called Bandoeng Pool. This scheme, like others in the non-ferrous metals, followed the close of the First World War in 1918-1919. It was organized under the auspices of the British and Dutch Governments and was designed to liquidate excess stocks. It succeeded in facilitating an orderly liquidation, and although it was not intended primarily as a measure of price regulation, it did help to restore tin prices to normal levels.[7]

The first international tin stock was formed in August, 1931, by British and Dutch tin producers within the Tin Producers' Association. This first stock scheme was established primarily to prevent a disastrous fall in the price of tin through co-operation by acquiring a large part of the excessive stocks then overhanging the market. It was reported that this tin pool had the financial backing of the Midland Bank, the Anglo-Oriental Corporation, the Patiño interests, and the Netherlands Government. The operation of the pool was shrouded in such secrecy that one participant was said to have remarked that most of the members of the pool were not even informed of the share of the other members.[8] Since the International Tin Control Scheme had already gone into effect the fact that the tin pool was a private operation occasioned some criticism.[9]

An agreement providing for the establishment of a buffer-stock scheme by the governments signatory to the international tin cartel was signed on July 10, 1934. Since the buffer stock could not begin operations until April, 1935, a producer's stock was formed by the Dutch and British interests to carry on during the interim. This was the first stock that had as its definite objective the maintenance of tin prices between certain limits. During this period the price fluctuations amounted to no more than 3.7 per cent; whereas, during the same period copper prices varied 21.3 per cent. The official governmental buffer-stock scheme went into effect on April 12, 1935, but was

---

[7] ITC, *Tin Control*, p. 30.

[8] Elliott *et al.*, *International Control*, p. 332. The executive of the pool was the late Sir John Campbell, Chairman of the International Tin Committee. See also Knorr, *op. cit.*, pp. 119 ff.

[9] W. F. Holland (ed.), *Commodity Control in the Pacific Area* (Stanford, 1935). p. 386. (Hereafter cited Holland, *Commodity Control*.)

Non-Ferrous Metals 243

terminated in June, 1935, when Bolivia decided not to co-operate in the venture. It was finally liquidated in September of 1935. On March 14, 1938, the Council of the Tin Producers' Association unanimously approved the draft of a new buffer-stock plan and urged the Secretary of State for the Colonies and the International Tin Committee to set up the necessary machinery as soon as possible. Since there was some opposition to the idea in Malaya, a referendum was held which resulted in a two to one decision there in favor of the scheme. This buffer-stock scheme, adopted on June 2, 1938, was administered as an adjunct to the international control. The stock consisted first of approximately 10,000 tons of tin and was later increased to 15,000 tons. The signatories were entitled to contribute in proportion to their standard tonnages. When the buffer-stock scheme came to an end finally on December 31, 1942, its stock was liquidated. During the operation of the scheme, a special executive was appointed to administer under strict secrecy the purchases and sales of tin on the London market. The general opinion of the producers and many others was that the buffer stock was influential in stabilizing tin prices to a considerable extent.[10]

The members of the basic agreement were the four governments of the Netherlands, Nigeria, the Malay states, and Bolivia. On September 1, 1931, Siam joined the agreement. The cartel then included 93 per cent of all tin production. Its administration was placed in the hands of the International Tin Committee with headquarters in London. The Committee was composed of governmental delegates although the governments were free to delegate entrepreneurs as their representatives. This committee was no automaton but a powerful executive. Each participant was allotted a standard tonnage based on his 1929 output. The production quotas determined periodically by the Committee were based on the standard quotas. Table 13 shows the changes in quotas from 1931 to 1940. Each group apportioned among its members the assigned output as it saw fit.

Quotas were considerably reduced until in June, 1932, they stood at 43.8 per cent of standard tonnages. The Tin Producers' Association, which remained a powerful group, interfered and told the Committee that this reduction was still not enough. It urged more drastic measures in the so-called Byrne Restriction Scheme which recommended that quotas be reduced to 33.3 per cent, and also advocated an export holiday. The plan was adopted by the Committee and

---

[10] The official publication, ITC *Tin Control,* discusses this problem thoroughly.

244 ## *International Cartels*

went into effect on July 1. These were the smallest quotes ever set during the whole period of restriction.[11]

The opinion of the London Monetary and Economic Conference on the tin restriction scheme and the Tin Pool was drafted in a separate sub-committee with the participation of representatives from the United States and the Chairman of the International Tin Committee. Though the representative of the United States emphasized the necessity of protecting the interests of consumers no substantive criticism of the scheme was made and no suggestions offered as to its amendment or as to any alternative methods of control. The report of the Sub-Committee adopted by the conference shows that the existing control was regarded as proceeding on sound lines. The conference went so far as to urge those tin-producing countries, not at the time members, to join the scheme.[12]

The first agreement expired at the end of February, 1933, but was prolonged without modification until the end of 1933. In October, 1933, a second agreement to be effective on January 1, 1934, for three years was announced. Beginning in July, 1934, French Indo-China, the Belgian Congo, Portugal, and Great Britain (Cornwall) adhered to the scheme. Portugal and Cornwall, however, dropped out in 1937 because their demands for increased quotas could not be met.

The third restriction scheme was based on an agreement signed at Brussels January 5, 1937, to expire at the close of 1941. This scheme contained a provision for consumer representation. Representatives from the two largest tin consuming countries were invited to attend ITC meetings and to tender advice to the Committee regarding world stocks and consumption. This was simply a recognition of the informal consumer representation that had already been practiced in the summer of 1934, after the rubber scheme had adopted a similar measure. In an agreement signed in London September 9, 1942, consumer representation, as formulated in the agreement of 1937, was altered by providing that two persons should represent the consumer interests of the United States (one to be appointed by the government of the United States and the other to be the direct representative of tin consumers), and a third person to represent tin consumers other than those in the United States. This mechanism has been frequently discussed in connection with cartels. It is very difficult to obtain reliable reports as to whether these representatives functioned effectively. Did

---

[11] Holland, *Commodity Control*, p. 387.

[12] *Journal of the London Monetary and Economic Conference*, July 19, 1933, pp. 201 f.; also July 21, 1933, pp. 204 f.; and July 27, 1933, pp. 239 f.

Non-Ferrous Metals 245

they really represent the interests of consumers and influence the decisions of the governing body? Eugene Staley is of the opinion that they were ineffective.[13] According to reliable private sources, the United States Government was represented in the Consumers' Panel by diplomatic officials of the American Embassy in London. American tin consumers appointed as their representative the American agent of the Steel Export Association of America in London. British and other tin consumers were represented by a delegate of the trade association of the tinplate producers of Great Britain. A private source expressed its opinion on the effectiveness of representation as follows: "It is my understanding that in general American consumers of tin found it helpful to have representation on the International Tin Committee. That representation proved effective in the matter of current official information about developments in tin production." Whether the British consumer representative consulted with other than the British (and American) consumers is not known to this writer.

The 1937 agreement incorporated the principle of majority vote on all important matters. Thus any proposal supported by eleven votes was carried. The small countries, if combined with one of the larger countries, could outvote the others. The votes were distributed as follows: Malaya, 5; Bolivia, 4; Dutch East Indies, 4; Siam, 2; Belgian Congo, 2; Nigeria, 2; and French Indo-China, 1.

The agreement, which expired at the end of 1941, was prolonged with a few changes in a new agreement concluded in London September 9, 1942, effective January, 1942, to remain in force until December 31, 1946. This new agreement was concluded by the governments of Belgium, Bolivia, the United Kingdom, and the Netherlands.

The first agreement authorized the Tin Committee to set up a special agency for research on the development and consumption of the uses of tin. The principles for the research bureaus were embodied in a special agreement on a Tin Research Scheme signed in London January 25, 1938, and amended in 1939. The research scheme was administered by a General Council of Control. This body appointed the directors of Research, Development and Statistics, and outlined their powers. The Statistical Office maintained headquarters at The Hague until the German occupation, when it was moved to London. The Research Bureau had offices in London and in New York, where it was connected with the American Tin Plate Trade

---

[13] *Raw Materials*, p. 135. According to *International Ententes*, p. 26, "The Advisory Panel of Consumers established in 1934 appears to have given its whole-hearted support to the management."

246   *International Cartels*

Association. It is ironical to think that today the Research Council is engaging in activities to conserve the uses of tin, whereas its chief concern formerly was to boost the sales of tin through propaganda and development of new uses of this commodity.

In the last few years one of the outsiders, the Chinese, exported little tin. Since Japan began its extensive Far Eastern campaign, French Indo-China, Siam, Malaya, Burma, and the Dutch East Indies have ceased to be tin suppliers for the world. There remain only Nigeria, Bolivia, and the Belgian Congo with about 90,000 long tons available for consumption by allied and neutral nations compared to a former peacetime export of some 200,000 tons. In 1943, the International Tin Committee increased the quotas for Nigeria, Belgian Congo, and Japanese-occupied regions much more than the Bolivian quota. It has been stated that: "The American tin trade suspects that the cartel increased the allowance for Far Eastern mines along with the increase for African production to keep the record for the two areas in balance pending the ousting of the Japs. They also observe that the Bolivian quota probably was not raised because the country is producing just about all the ore it can."[14]

The fairness of the cartel's price policies was often doubted. The question of to whom the prices were fair naturally arises. The answer to this is further complicated because production costs varied from mine to mine. The administration of a marketing scheme by governments of large, democratic countries implies that marketing policies are determined in accordance with public interests. When the first tin agreement was made by governments, public opinion took this point of view for granted. It should be emphasized, however, that it is especially hard to determine the public interest in the case of a scheme that relates to a world market.

There has been considerable publicity on the Tin Restriction Scheme. The agreements have been published as official documents by the British Government. The International Tin Research and Development Council has issued several reports on its research and statistical activities. But despite the large body of literature there is only one comprehensive work of an analytical and critical nature on the operation of the International Tin Restriction schemes.[15]

---

[14] *Business Week,* July 31, 1943, pp. 16, 17.

[15] Knorr, *op. cit., passim.* All the tin agreements are contained in ILO, *Intergovernmental Commodity Agreements.* The official papers of the International Tin Control Scheme are published in London as Cmd. 4825, Cmd. 5879, and Cmd. 6396. See also Rowe, *Markets,* Chapter VII; Staley, *Raw Materials,* pp. 306 ff.; Holland, *Commodity Control,* Chapter XII; International Chamber of Commerce, *International Ententes; Tin Investigation,* Parts 1-3.

Non-Ferrous Metals 247

TABLE 13

TIN PRICES

London— £ per long ton

Year	STANDARD CASH Highest	Lowest	Average Sterling currency	Gold £	Equivalent in Dutch currency (florins p. ton)	Backwardation (−) contango (+) for tin on 3 months	PREMIUM ALLOWED OVER STANDARD Straits	Banka	English (common)
1928..	266.0	205.8	227.2		2748	−1.45	2.2	4.0	0.6
1929..	229.8	174.1	203.9		2465	+2.50	3.4	7.8	0.4
1930..	180.6	104.6	142.0		1714	+1.93	2.6	5.5	1.5
1931..	141.9	100.3	118.5	108.9	1324	+2.00	2.8	6.6	2.2
1932..	157.8	102.4	135.9	97.6	1177	+1.80	4.5	10.6	2.4
1933..	227.4	141.1	194.6	132.1	1597	+0.16	8.0	8.0	1.6
1934..	244.0	222.3	230.4	142.3	1723	−0.96	2.0	3.4	1.1
1935..	245.5	208.3	225.7	135.0	1634	−7.85	4.4	5.3	0.5
1936..	244.6	175.3	204.6	123.9	1600	−4.22	2.6	1.7	−0.4
1937..	311.3	180.9	242.3	146.2	2177	−1.24	3.0	...	0.4
1938..	217.3	153.3	189.6	112.9	1684	+0.67	4.3	...	1.3
1939..	272.3	208.9	226.3	124.1	1878	−1.80			
1940..	290.3	231.8	256.6	129.6	....	+0.24			

New York—$ cents per lb.

Year	STRAITS CASH Highest	Lowest	Average Dollar currency	Gold £
1928........	57.75	45.75	50.46	
1929........	50.38	38.38	45.19	
1930........	39.75	23.75	31.70	
1931........	27.50	20.60	24.46	
1932........	25.63	18.35	22.01	
1933........	55.80	21.80	39.12	29.78
1934........	56.65	50.00	52.16	30.86
1935........	54.00	45.75	50.39	29.76
1936........	53.50	40.50	46.42	47.41
1937........	66.63	41.00	54.24	32.04
1938........	46.75	35.00	42.26	24.96
1939........	75.00	45.00	50.20	29.65
1940........	58.00	44.75	49.82	29.42

Source: *Statistical Bulletin* of the International Tin Research and Development Council, February, 1940.

248   *International Cartels*

TABLE 14

PRODUCTION OF TIN AND TIN IN ORE IN LONG TONS

The grand total represents almost the entire world output of tin, excepting only the quantities refined and consumed locally in China, in respect of which no information is available.

	1933	1934	1935	1936	1937	1938	1939	1940
Belgian Congo[1]	2,225	4,602	6,481	7,310	8,856	7,318	9,663	12,392
Bolivia[1]	14,725	20,634	27,168	24.074	25.024	25.371	27,215	37,940
French Indo China[1]	1,038	1,070	1,421	1,409	1,531	1,575	e 1,392	1,560
Malaya[1]	24,904	34,059	45,955	66,806	77,542	43,247	55.950	85,384
Netherlands East Indies[1]	14,406	18,678	24,719	31,684	39,825	21,024	31,281	44,563
Nigeria[1]	3,672	4,996	7,029	9,634	10,468	7,313	10,855	10,257
Thailand[1-6]	10,324	10,587	9,779	12,678	16,494	13,520	16,991	17,447
Total signatory Countries	71,384	94,626	122,552	153,595	179,740	119,368	153,347	209,500
Germany	—	25	30	50	76	300	e 300	
Italy	—	—	—	—	75	271	e 229	
Portugal	418	540	697	812	1,152	1,052		
Spain[4]	258	261	300	180	6	—		
United Kingdom	1,542	1,999	2,050	2,099	1,986	2,010	e 1,712	
Cameroons[5]	50	130	220	220	240	220		
Morocco	e 30	40	40	20	14	27		
Northern Rhodesia	—	—	5	4	5	3		
Southern Rhodesia	11	8	7	47	139	267		
Southwest Africa[2]	142	142	167	163	169	164	e 153	
Swaziland	71	114	127	128	108	174	e 180	
Tanganyika[2]	59	103	139	207	197	263	222	
Uganda[3]	278	306	386	408	374	358		
Union of So. Africa	539	570	622	634	537	558		
U.S.A.	3	8	45	101	168	109	e 120	
Argentina	50	230	630	890	1,335	1,719		
Mexico	123	16	621	368	373	249	273	
Peru	—	1	—	97	195	103		
Burma[r]	3,070	3,498	4,540	5,131	5,257	5,014	p 5,750	
China[3]	8,104	8,145	9,398	10,664	10,457	11,246		
Japan	1,522	1,803	2,197	2,382	e 2,175	e 2,186	e 1,700	
Australia	2,810	2,986	3,130	3,027	3,256	3,329	e 3,300	
Total non-sign. Countries	19,080	20,925	25,351	27,632	28,294	29,622	e 29,200	28,300
Sundries	1,170	697	726	627	1,077	724		
Grand Total	91,600	116,200	148,600	181,900	209,100	149,700	p183,700	237,800

[r] Revised.
[e] Estimated or partly estimated.
[p] Preliminary.
[1] Official exports as from the years in which these countries joined the International Tin Control Scheme.
[2] Up to and including 1936 reports, thereafter production.
[3] Exports.
[4] As from 1934 imports into smelting countries.
[5] As from 1939 exports.
[6] The true essay value of Thai ore is taken to be 72.5 per cent for the second half of 1939 and the first half of 1940.
Source: *Statistical Bulletin* of the International Tin Research and Development Council, February, 1940.

Non-Ferrous Metals 249

ZINC

The best known international zinc cartel was first established in May, 1928, and disintegrated in the latter part of 1929. It was revived in 1931 only to dissolve again in 1934. The cartel was extremely unstable and collapsed as a consequence of Germany's introduction of a premium on domestic zinc production and Great Britain's levying of a

GRAPH I

MONTHLY AVERAGES OF CASH PRICES IN LONDON PER LONG TON OF STANDARD TIN

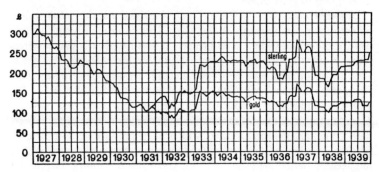

Source: Statistical Bulletin of the International Tin Research and Development Council, February, 1940.

TABLE 15

APPLIED PERCENTAGES OF STANDARD QUOTAS UNDER THE INTERNATIONAL
TIN CONTROL SCHEME

1st agreement	2nd agreement	3rd agreement	
1931 Mar.-May 77.7% June-Dec. 64.4%	1934 1st qtr 40%[4] 2nd qtr 50%[4] 3rd qtr 50%[4] 4th qtr 40%[4]	1937 1st qtr 100% 2nd qtr 110% 3rd qtr 110% 4th qtr 110%	1940 1st qtr 120% 2nd qtr 80% 3rd qtr 130% 4th qtr 130%
1932 Jan.-May 56.2% June 43.8% July-Dec. 33.3%	1935 1st qtr 40% 2nd qtr 45% 3rd qtr 70% 4th qtr 80%	1938 1st qtr 70% 2nd qtr 55% 3rd qtr 35%[3] 4th qtr 35%[3]	1941 130%
1933 Jan.-Dec. 33.3%	1936 1st qtr 90% 2nd qtr 85% 3rd qtr 90%[1] 4th qtr 105%[2]	1939 1st qtr 35%[3] 2nd qtr 40% 3rd qtr 120% 4th qtr 100%	

[1] Quota for Bolivia 75 per cent.
[2] Quota for Bolivia 90 per cent.
[3] Excluding the additional quota of 10 per cent for the buffer stock.
[4] Excluding the extra quota of 4 per cent for compensating over and under exports, and excluding the additional quota of 5 per cent for the buffer stock.
Source: *Statistical Bulletin* of the International Tin Research and Development Council.

10 per cent duty on non-Empire zinc.[1] The most recent meeting of French, Belgian, and British interests in Paris in June, 1939, failed to revive the old cartel. There are indications that British interests promised to press their government to reduce custom duties on zinc if foreign exporters would agree to form a cartel with them.[2] But Germany, Italy, and Japan were not interested in a cartel which would lower zinc production. Another difficulty was the close connection between lead and zinc production necessitating a reduction in lead if restriction of zinc were agreed upon.[3]

Another collective marketing control existed on the international market up to the outbreak of the war. This control, although incomplete, exercised considerable influence. It was based on a patent agreement concerning the most practical process for refining high-grade zinc. The process was developed in 1935 by the New Jersey Zinc Company in New York City. The license agreements directly and indirectly influenced producing, marketing, and exporting policies. The American company made direct agreements restricting exports with Canadian, British, German, and Belgian producers. The Belgian licensee, i.e., *Société Générale Des Minéraux,* was authorized to give sub-licenses to the Belgian Colonies, the French Empire, Czechoslovakia, Italy, Holland, Norway, Poland, Spain, and Luxembourg.[4] One curious feature employed to enforce exporting restrictions was the earmarking of zinc bars under the production licenses.[5] The shortage in high-grade zinc in the United States after war was declared was attributed to the restrictions mentioned above.

Arrangements among British Empire producers of metallic zinc (on the one side the Hudson Bay Company, Consolidated Mining Company, Electrolytic Zinc, and Rhodesian Broken Hill, and on the other side Imperial Smelting Company) existed by which the Imperial Smelting Company agreed to limit its output to 60,000 tons and the other companies agreed to pay 10 shillings cash to Imperial Smelting for each ton of zinc imported and sold in the United Kingdom.[6]

Another regional pact was arrived at on January 1, 1936, between Czechoslovak, German, and Polish producers for the export of zinc.

---

[1] Cf. Elliott *et al., International Control,* Chs. XII and XIII.

[2] Military Affairs Committee, *Monograph No. 1,* p. 46.

[3] *Kartell-Rundschau,* 1939, p. 54.

[4] The license agreements with all the countries mentioned are reprinted in Bone Committee, *Patent Hearings,* Part 3, pp. 1631 ff.

[5] *Ibid.,* p. 1524.

[6] *The Mineral Industry,* 1939, p. 619. See also the pamphlet by Ernest V. Gent, Secretary to the American Zinc Institute, Inc., *The Zinc Industry in 1939,* p. 27.

Non-Metallic Minerals 251

This was to remain in force for one year and was then to be renewed.[7]

In February, 1938, an International Zinc Sheet Cartel was formed with headquarters at the Belgian domestic cartel's offices in Liège. This cartel included members from the United Kingdom, Belgium, Holland, Germany, France, Spain, Hungary, Poland, Yugoslavia, and Czechoslovakia. Italy did not enter the cartel but Belgian control of the Italian rolling mills ensured Italian co-operation.[8] This cartel regulated prices and established export quotas.[9] Within this cartel, it seems likely that a previously (1934) established International Convention for the Export of Rolled Zinc Products operated with members from Poland, Germany, and Czechoslovakia.[10]

NON-METALLIC MINERALS

DIAMONDS

Diamonds, the most valuable of all the precious stones, have varied important industrial uses. The world production of diamonds is figured for 1941 at about 9,350,000 metric carats[1] (value approximately $26,000,000). In 1940 it reached 14,300,000 metric carats.

Any adequate discussion of the diamond trade must take up the separate processes of production, selling, and cutting. The economist realizes that the monopolistic features of the industry, while perhaps sensational, are not typical of industrial organization as a whole. The monopolistic position of the diamond industry has been strengthened by the fact that no substitute material or synthetic product discovered has been satisfactory.

Governments themselves have often fortified private monopolies in the diamond industry by licensing the monopolistic organizations, by participating in them as shareholders, or by reserving mining and selling rights. In South Africa, for example, through the passage of a statute all rights from the discoveries of mines made after July, 1926, were assigned to the Crown. This did not protect small, independent producers because ultimately the government entered into an agreement with the world diamond syndicate.[2] Several governments shared in the revenue from diamonds by levying export duties. Bel-

---

[7] *Czechoslovak Cartel Book*, p. 204. The *Polish Political and Economic Yearbook 1938*, p. 761, says it was established in 1933.
[8] *Minerals Yearbook*, 1938 (1939), p. 165.
[9] *Ibid.* See also International Chamber of Commerce, Document 6484, 1938; League of Nations, *Circular*, E, 1039, 1938, p. 13.
[10] *Polish Political and Economic Yearbook 1938*, p. 761.

---

[1] One metric carat is ⅕ gram weight.
[2] Staley, *Raw Materials*, pp. 271 f.

252   *International Cartels*

gian Congo, for instance, the largest producer of diamonds by weight, imposed an export duty of six francs per carat on gem stones and 0.40 francs per carat on industrial diamonds. In another case, an agreement was formulated between the Sierra Leone Trust, Ltd., and its government, and was commented upon in the following manner by a British official publication: "This company holds a monopoly for winning diamonds in Sierra Leone and in return the Government participates in the profits. The prospect is that the Government will receive a large annual income from this source."[3]

The Diamond Corporation of London (established in 1930) purchases 95 per cent (in value) of the world gem and industrial diamond production. The Diamond Trading Company, Ltd., in London, jointly owned by Diamond Corporation and De Beers Consolidated Mines, Ltd., sells the rough diamonds to carefully selected brokers and cutters. Diamond Trading Company is now the sole selling agency for 99 per cent of all diamonds produced in Africa and 95 per cent of all diamonds produced throughout the world. The Diamond Corporation embraced the producers' organization and regulated through its purchasing policy the amount of diamonds put up for sale on the market as well as the prices they would bear. That this policy was successful is shown by the following passage from an authoritative market analysis: "For the first time in the past six years, production exceeded sales of rough and the stocks of the Diamond Corporation and those of most producers increased. At certain times, however, during the year fine large rough and fine small round were difficult to obtain."[4] That restrictions on total output did not preclude expansion everywhere is demonstrated by the fact that the diamond production in the Belgian Congo increased, from 1933 to 1938, from 3.3 million carats to 7.2 million carats and in Sierra Leone from 69 thousand carats to 900 thousand carats.

The formal organization of the cartel, establishing production quotas, was set up in 1934 in the framework of a trade association, the Diamond Producers' Association in London. The members of this trade association included representatives from the governments of the Union of South Africa and the Administration of Southwest Africa. The most significant member of this association, however, was the De Beers Consolidated Mines, Ltd., which was the controlling

---

[3] British Colonial Office, *An Economic Survey of the Colonial Empire*, (1936), p. 150.

[4] Sidney H. Ball, "The Diamond Industry in 1938," *The Jewelers' Circular-Keystone* (New York, 1939), p. 5.

Non-Metallic Minerals   253

shareholder of the Diamond Corporation. De Beers was the most important producer of diamonds in value and was a more potent force in the diamond trade than was any other mine. During 1941, De Beers absorbed Cape Coast Exploration, Ltd., so that it now owns or controls all important diamond mines in the Union of South Africa and Southwest Africa except the state mines at Namaqualand. The President of De Beers, Sir Ernest Oppenheimer, exerted great personal influence in co-ordinating diamond production and trade. Although De Beers was mainly concerned with the production and selling of diamonds, it owned jointly with Imperial Chemical, Ltd., the African Explosives and Industries, manufacturers in South Africa of heavy chemicals, explosives, and fertilizers.

The former center of the diamond trade was London. Only after the outbreak of the Second World War did the diamond syndicate consider transferring part of its activities to New York. According to a publication of C. K. Leith, J. W. Furness, and Cleona Lewis the Department of Justice would not give the syndicate assurance that it would be exempt from prosecution under the American antitrust acts, so it continued to operate in London.[5] On January 29, 1945, the Department of Justice filed a civil suit charging nine British, Belgian, and Portuguese corporations (including De Beers, Diamond Corporation, and Diamond Trading Co.) with restraining and monopolizing the foreign trade of the United States in gem and industrial stones in violation of the Sherman Antitrust Act and the Wilson Tariff Act.[6] However, the Diamond Trading Company has since opened a branch office in Hamilton, Bermuda, to deal with cutters and brokers residing in the United States.

In 1942, the British Government in London assumed control over the Diamond Corporation.[7] A quota adjustment of the diamond cartel was made in June, 1939.[8]

The distribution of diamonds has been in the hands of a few brokers and privileged customers whom the Diamond Corporation regarded as worthy of that task.

Early in 1939 Belgian, German, Dutch, and French diamond cutters established a trade association called the International Commission of the Commerce of the Diamond Industry. The association was formed by the master cutters and unions of the principal cutting centers, namely, Amsterdam, Antwerp, and the lower Rhine cities,

---

[5] Leith *et al., World Minerals*, p. 129.
[6] Department of Justice, Press Release, Jan. 29, 1945.
[7] Leith *et al., World Minerals*, p. 129.   [8] *The Economist*, July 1, 1939, p. 27.

in an attempt to put certain of the shops on a part-time basis and to reduce wages. They held many meetings during 1938 and 1939 but their efforts to exercise market control were unsuccessful.

There is fairly satisfactory publicity about the diamond industry.[9]

---

[9] See *Fortune*, May, 1935, pp. 67-74; Sidney H. Ball, *op. cit.;* and Leith *et al.*, *World Minerals*, pp. 126 ff.; *Minerals Yearbook* for 1939 (1940), p. 1157; *The Economist*, Sept. 4, 1943; *Kartell-Rundschau*, 1937, p. 490; *New York Herald-Tribune*, Financial and Business Section, Oct. 3, 1943, pp. 8 and 11.

PETROLEUM

Crude petroleum is a mixture of a large number of hydrocarbons. Through the process of distillation these hydrocarbons may be divided into progressively higher cuts. The principal cuts are gasoline, kerosene, fuel oils, and lubricating distillates. The residue, after distillation of the lighter parts, may be sold as bunker fuel oil or it may be subjected to further distillation. Gasoline can be obtained also by physical separation from natural gas. In addition, petroleum products can be made synthetically. There are few commodities which occupy as important a position in value and volume of international trade as crude oil and petroleum products.

Technological progress in petroleum production is perhaps more rapid than in any other branch of industrial production. The invention and improvements in synthetic production of petroleum products from coal, oil shales, etc., has altered the military and political status of natural crude petroleum. However, oil policies are still in the forefront of international political discussions. Diplomacy exercises great influence on marketing in private international trade.

Marketing control problems have to be considered from the aspect of crude oil production, transportation of crude oil, refining of natural products, synthetic production, and marketing of finished products. Large petroleum companies of world-wide significance are highly integrated and have more or less completely controlled subsidiaries all over the world.

The international market in petroleum products before the Second World War was dominated by the Standard Oil Company of New Jersey (Jersey) and the British-Dutch controlled Shell group. There were many related companies attached to the Jersey group. According to reliable evidence, Jersey by its own initiative frequently safeguarded the foreign interests of all American oil companies.[1] This fact made Jersey's leadership in international relations more efficient. Shell also had many subsidiaries and related groups. In addition, it shared almost all of its internationally significant business transactions with its junior partner, the British government-owned Anglo-Iranian Oil Company. These two petroleum concerns (Jersey and

---

[1] See for an interesting example Bone Committee, *Patent Hearings*, Part 7, p. 3666.

Shell) exercised controlling influence, except in Germany, over newly invented processes for the production of synthetic oil and modern refining processes as well.

No doubt this leadership on international markets was not watertight. Other American[2] and various European groups also participated in exploitation of foreign oil fields, in exports, and in financial and commercial connections with refiners and marketers all over the world. Such companies frequently defied the two leading groups. But the competing groups were not very significant in international trade as compared with Jersey and Shell on the basis of ownership of patents, technological experience, oil fields, tankers, and pipelines. Nor did they possess the marketing mechanisms, political connections, and financial capacities to the extent of Jersey and Shell. The Standard Oil Company of California and the Texas Company formed the American Eastern Petroleum Company as a holding company for their jointly owned companies (with exception of their Arabian and Bolivian interests) principally devoted to the exploration of oil properties in Egypt, New Zealand, Australia, and the Dutch East Indies.[2a]

The tremendous amount of literature about technological and trade problems of petroleum contains relatively little material on co-operation and competitive relationships of big oil groups in the pre- and post-First-World-War periods.[3] In many countries cartels regulated domestic markets, and in Poland an export cartel operated among Polish producers. In the early twenties diplomatic discussions and disagreements overshadowed private efforts to compete, co-operate, and to secure important positions, especially in the Near and Middle East. It is depressing to read how misunderstandings poisoned American-British relations, especially after the First World War.[4] The romantic struggle between big oil groups after the First World War may be regarded as terminated by 1927. The last battles were fought over the market in India and over securing supplies from Russia.[5]

[2] E.g., The Gulf Exploration Company (subsidiary of the Gulf Oil Corporation) had an equal share with Anglo-Iranian in the oil fields of Kuwait. The huge oil concessions in Saudi Arabia and Bahrein were owned in equal shares by the Standard Oil Company of California and the Texas Company. Cf. Herbert Feis, *Petroleum and American Foreign Policy* (Stanford University, 1944), pp. 32-33. See also Plummer, *International Combines*, pp. 7-8.

[2a] See *New York Times*, August 22, 1944, p. 22.

[3] See Plummer, *International Combines*, pp. 7 and 71-72; and Leith *et al.*, *World Minerals*, pp. 110 ff. See also Frederick Hausmann, "World Oil Control," *Social Research*, 1942, pp. 334 ff.

[4] See Herbert Feis, *Petroleum, passim*.

[5] Cf. Leith *et al.*, *World Minerals*, pp. 111 ff.; Glyn Roberts, *The Most Powerful Man in the World: The Life of Sir Henri Deterding* (New York, 1938), *passim*.

258   *International Cartels*

There is sufficient evidence to show that in 1928 Standard Oil Company of New Jersey and the Shell group made a comprehensive agreement about the maintenance of their power positions with reference to consumption[6] in foreign markets and with reference to the acquisition of foreign oil interests.   This agreement was called the "as is" agreement, or "Achnacarry" agreement.[7] There is little doubt that this agreement maintained the status quo (as of 1928-29) of all American exporting companies.   In addition, European, Asiatic, and Latin-American exporting groups, including producers, refiners, and marketers, that were American or Shell subsidiaries, adhered more or less informally to that agreement and to Jersey-Shell leadership. Several smaller oil groups remained outside and were regarded as disturbing elements.[8]   In addition, several other agreements were made between Jersey and the Shell-Anglo-Persian group. Available evidence indicates that the two principal world concerns regarded their close co-operation as very important.[9]   Their alliance remained the backbone of co-operation in oil. In other fields Jersey wanted to have a free hand in dealing with Shell.[10] Considerable extension of the Jersey-Shell co-operation was contemplated in 1935 and later in 1939.[11] Though there was much quibbling as to whether Shell should be a full 50 per cent

---

[6] In 1933 a discussion took place on whether consumption quotas are "relative" or "total" consumption quotas. One of the participants in the discussion wrote the following: "It is my understanding that quotas in the principal European markets such as England, Germany, and possibly Italy are on a relative percentage basis, while South America are on a total consumption basis. The latter likewise applies to the Far East. The relative percentage basis has proven recently very detrimental to the Anglo." See Bone Committee, *Patent Hearings*, Part 7, p. 3678. See also p. 486.

[7] See Bone Committee, *Patent Hearings*, Part 7, pp. 3660, 3678, 3679.

[8] See *The Economist*, Dec. 21, 1929, pp. 1196-97.

[9] See Bone Committee, *Patent Hearings*, Part 7, p. 3676. The relationship between Jersey and Shell is excellently described by Jersey in the following words (quoted from *Ibid.*, p. 3683): "Anglo-Persian, Shell and Jersey not only enjoy the great bulk of the foreign marketing business but also control most of the low-cost foreign crude. Each of these companies has sufficient crude supplies to permit of its doing a still larger share of the total. No one of them, therefore, can expect to obtain an increased outlet for its own production at the expense of another. An attempt to do this, with each determined to hold his share, can only result in destructive prices and excessive duplication of facilities. On the other hand, if the three companies respect each other's position and co-operate with this primary fundamental in mind, it should be possible for them to maintain their aggregate share of the total business with satisfactory earnings and a minimum duplication of investment. It is believed that all of our people agree as to the essential need for the closest possible co-operation among those three companies in the foreign markets."

[10] When Shell approached Jersey in 1938 to make a common front against IG, Jersey, according to a reliable report, stated its position as being "together with Shell only in the oil field." Cf. Bone Committee, *Patent Hearings*, Part 7, p. 3736.

[11] See Bone Committee, *Patent Hearings*, Part 7, pp. 3683-84, and 4121-23.

Non-Metallic Minerals   259

partner of Jersey in the ownership of patents and technological processes related to hydrogenation and refining of oil, there was no doubt
that Shell should be a partner.[12]

In the United States in 1929 one serious attempt was made to
bring petroleum exporters under two (interlocking) common controls.
Two Webb-Pomerene associations were formed, the Export Petroleum
Association, Inc., with seventeen members, and the Standard Oil Export Corporation, with six members.[13]   During 1929 and 1930 these
export associations were in serious discussion with European groups
concerning marketing collaboration.[14]   Though the two export associations existed up to 1936, their operation and collaboration had practically collapsed in 1931.   This disintegration prompted Jersey to
consider a possible dissolution of its agreements with Shell,[15] although
no change was made in their relationships.

This co-operation between the dominant export groups, Jersey and
Shell, was never successful in building a comprehensive world-wide
marketing control in petroleum.   That they envisaged and desired such
control is shown in a recent study subtitled "Impediments in cartelisation,'" written by one of the leaders of the oil industry.[16]   The
building of a world-wide marketing control became more urgent with
the onset of the great depression when petroleum prices on national
and international markets dropped to a very low level.[17]   Rumanian
producers, controlled by capitalistic groups of various nations, chiefly
British, frustrated many attempts for collaboration by their exaggerated
demands.   After several conferences of prominent exporting groups,
a meeting in Paris in July, 1932, was successful in bringing Rumania
in line with a rather high export quota.[18]   The Soviets refused at that

---

[12] *Ibid.*, pp. 3658-59, 3662.   One statement of Jersey reads: ". . . whether we wish
to work out a general agreement for cross-licensing and pooling of exploitation profits
with Shell throughout the world . . . the importance of this question is far greater
than the total of all others put together."—*Ibid.*, p. 3658.

[13] TNEC, *Monograph No. 6*, pp. 187 and 218.

[14] See Bone Committee, *Patent Hearings*, Part 7, p. 3677.

[15] *Ibid.*, p. 3679.

[16] J.B.A. Kessler, "The Oil Industry in the World Crisis," *International Cartels*,
No. 1, 1939, pp. 2 ff.

[17] The percentage change in average gold export prices of petroleum of United States
from 1929 to 1938 is shown by the League of Nations (*Review of World Trade 1938*,
p. 13) as follows:

1929 to 1932	— 47	1935 to 1936	+ 8
1932 to 1933	— 24	1936 to 1937	+10
1933 to 1934	— 21	1937 to 1938	— 9
1934 to 1935	—0.7	1929 to 1938	—66

[18] *The Economist*, September 3, 1932, p. 425.   About Rumanian and Russian competition, cf. Bone Committee, *Patent Hearings*, Part 7, p. 3679.

time to restrict their exports.[19]   However, the Rumanians kept to their export restrictions only a few weeks because (according to Rumania) Americans did not live up to their obligations required by the Paris Agreement and were responsible that prices did not rise as expected.[20]

French, Italian, and German industrial and capitalistic groups were very ambitious to play a role on the world petroleum market.   However, they had only moderate success.[21]

The export policies of the Soviet State Oil Trust were considered by Jersey and Shell as a disturbing element on international markets. There is little doubt that several attempts were made to arrive at some understanding with it, and although the Soviet Trust did not oppose co-operation in principle, it remained an outsider as far as Jersey and Shell were concerned.[22]

According to Mr. R. W. Gallagher, President of the Standard Oil Company of New Jersey, Jersey was obliged to make restrictive agreements in France, Italy, Argentina, Uruguay, Chile, and other countries in order to be allowed to engage in the oil business there.   He stated that in France, for instance, in order to promote domestic oil refining, the government in 1928 set up a system of import licenses which limited the amount of petroleum shipped into the country.   It also issued licenses specifying the amount of crude petroleum a company could refine.   A syndicate of practically all oil companies operating in France was formed.   The government did not fix prices but controlled them to the extent that prices could not be lowered or increased without review by a government agency.[23]

One of the most interesting international combinations showing British-American co-operation in petroleum is the so-called Red Line

---

[19] Leith, *et al.*, *World Minerals*, p. 113.

[20] As a matter of fact, prices rose considerably after the conclusion of the Paris Agreement.   Another reason for the Rumanian behavior is attributed to the fact that the Soviets did not participate in the arrangement.   Cf. Leith, *et al.*, *World Minerals*, pp. 113-14, and Plummer, *Industrial Combines*, p. 72.   According to Plummer (p. 73) the simultaneous rise of prices of Soviet petroleum points to some sort of understanding between the Soviets and other oil groups.

[21] Cf. Louis Pineau and Others, *Le Pétrole et son Economie* (Paris, 1935), pp. 13 ff.

[22] In February, 1934, J.B.A. Kessler charged in *Mining Journal* (London) that the Soviets were unco-operative and were cutting prices on world markets. In February, 1935, these charges were answered by a Soviet source in *World Petroleum* (New York). According to that source the Soviets declared themselves willing to co-operate in a collective organization of world petroleum markets, although they evaluated such collaboration as a mere "palliative" measure. See Glyn Roberts, *op. cit.*, p. 291.

[23] *A Statement by Ralph W. Gallagher* before the O'Mahoney Subcommittee of the Senate Committee on the Judiciary, May 23, 1944 (Pamphlet), published by Standard Oil Company of New Jersey (New York, 1944), p. 7.

Agreement. It relates to the production, transportation, refining, and marketing of the petroleum of Iraq. The main purpose of the agreement was to forestall British, American, and French competition in the acquisition of oil rights in Iraq. Shell and Anglo-Iranian has a 47½ per cent, and Standard Oil of New Jersey and Socony Vacuum Oil Company a 23⅔ per cent participation. French capital was interested as well. According to the President of Standard Oil of New Jersey, Ralph W. Gallagher, "As a condition of particiaption, the Americans agreed as the other (British, French, and Dutch) interests had already agreed, not to engage in petroleum activities in an area considerably more extensive than the concession area, except through the corporate vehicle operating the joint enterprise. But if America was to get any of the oil of Iraq, American companies had to accept these conditions."[24]

During the Second World War new forms of co-operation among oil companies have been instituted. Technological progress has advanced rapidly in the last few years. The reader may obtain information about these technological developments, so far as they can be disclosed, in the documents of the Truman and Bone Committees of the United States Senate.

Desiring to eliminate friction on oil problems among governments in the postwar period, the American and British Governments started discussions in the spring of 1944. It was assumed that at a later date other governments would be invited. According to official statements not only broad principles but also specific problems relating to the production, distribution, and transportation of oil were discussed. Rumors that the conference had considered the outlawing of cartels between foreign oil companies were denied. In this respect, it is interesting to note the official statement to the press: "We were not dealing with the rationing of scarcity, and therefore with cartels. . . . The whole discussion was based on the belief that we will be dealing with expanding, not contracting markets."[25]

Conferences among experts were followed by official discussions between the American and British Governments in Washington, D. C., July 25, 1944. The result was the Anglo-American Oil Accord, published August 8, 1944.[26] The Petroleum Industry War Council

---

[24] *Statement* before the O'Mahoney Subcommittee, *ibid.*, p. 7.

[25] See *The New York Times*, May 4, 1944, p. 9.

[26] The introductory article of the Anglo-American Oil Accord reads as follows: "The Government of the United States of America and the Government of the United Kingdom of Great Britain and Northern Ireland, whose nationals hold, to a substantial

262 *International Cartels*

formulated its objections to the oil compact and asked the Senate to reject the treaty. There is no hope that it will be approved by the Senate.[27] The Anglo-American Oil Accord laid out a pattern for agreements covering important commodities in international trade.

extent jointly, rights to explore and develop petroleum resources in other countries, recognize:

1. That ample supplies of petroleum, available in international trade to meet increasing market demands, are essential for both the security and economic well-being of nations;

2. That for the foreseeable future the petroleum resources of the world are adequate to assure the availability of such supplies;

3. That such supplies should be derived from the various producing areas of the world with due consideration of such factors as available reserves, sound engineering practices, relevant economic factors, and the interests of producing and consuming countries, and with a view to the full satisfaction of expanding demand;

4. That such supplies should be available in accordance with the principles of the Atlantic Charter and in order to serve the needs of collective security;

5. That the general adoption of these principles can best be promoted by international agreement among all countries interested in the petroleum trade whether as producers or consumers.—*The New York Times*, Aug. 9, 1944, p. 8.

[27] The recommendations of the American oil companies may be found in Feis, *Petroleum*, pp. 54 ff. J. H. Pew, President of the Sun Oil Company, assailed the Petroleum Pact as a step to "Super-State Cartel."—The *New York Times*, Aug. 21, 1944, p. 18. The objections of the Petroleum Industry War Council may be found in the *New York Times*, Dec. 3, 1944, p. 25.

[12]

Excerpt from *International Control in the Non-ferrous Metals*, 663–83.

CHAPTER XI

THE LEAD INDUSTRY IN THE UNITED STATES

The history of lead mining in the United States antedates the formation of the Union : there is record of lead mining at Falling Creek, Virginia, as early as 1621 ; in what is now Missouri, as early as 1720 ; in what is now Wisconsin and Iowa, as early as 1788. Moreover the lead mining industry has had tariff protection since 1789, almost as long as the United States has had a Constitution.

Since the early mining was very primitive and the treatment as simple as could be imagined, it was not until the nineteenth century that the deposits were worked on an extensive scale. Between 1830 and 1850, particularly after 1840, the Missouri and Wisconsin areas were more fully developed and became the most important source of lead in the United States. These two areas caused the United States' production to reach almost 20 per cent of the world's output, so that the country became, in the decade of the 1840's, an exporting instead of an importing nation. In spite of the three-cents-a-pound tariff on imports, and a price in New York higher than in London, the exports continued to increase until 1847.

Although the expansion when it came was not the result of new prospecting, since the Missouri and Wisconsin areas had long been known, it may be that the tariff of one cent a pound enacted in 1789, two cents a pound after 1824, and three cents a pound after 1828, did encourage the extension of the mining enterprise ; it is possible that without the tariff the industry would never have reached the exporting stage. If so, consumers paid a high price for the domestic industry in the form of revenue on lead imports for fifty years. From the evidence, however, it seems much more reasonable to believe that at least until the tariff of 1897 the import duty was distinctly subordinate to other influences in stimulating new discoveries and causing the expansion of the industry. After exports began in the 1840's, on the other hand,

663

664   CONTROL OF NON–FERROUS METALS

tariff was probably instrumental in maintaining the differential between New York and London prices, which went into the pockets of the lead producers, and thus in making for a more speedy extraction of the mineral than would otherwise have occurred. Since in the interest of the conservation of natural resources a hastening of the rate of recovery is detrimental, there is considerable basis for the argument that the tariff should then have been removed.

It is true that in 1846 the tariff was lowered from three cents a pound to 20 per cent *ad valorem* (which amounted to about 0.75 to 0.8 cent per pound), but it was not removed, perhaps because the miners in the Wisconsin areas voiced strong objection to the proposed change, after they had suffered some set-back because it was lowered. But miners are seldom interested in conservation and seldom recognize that the tariff which increases their immediate profits also helps to shorten the life of their properties. They did not admit that, partly because of the tariff, the surface areas became exhausted; nor did they believe that even if the tariff had not been lowered the Wisconsin areas would have declined, as they did, and that exports would have fallen off. Yet it is probable that by 1846 the Wisconsin deposits had passed their peak of production. The decline in the output of the area was expedited after the California discoveries because of the emigration of workers. In addition, working at lower depths in Wisconsin was unduly expensive, and, with the mining methods then in use, was completely impossible after the water level had been reached.[1]

After 1847 there was no other period when lead was exported in any quantity until the cataclysm precipitated by the World War in 1914. In fact, production declined steadily until a new era of prospecting in the 1870's. As a percentage of the world's output, production in the United States fell from 19.21 per cent in the 1840's to 8.92 per cent in the 1850's and 5.87 per cent in

[1] The conclusion that the Wisconsin areas would have declined even if the tariff had not been lowered is reached by W. R. Ingalls, on page 137 of his volume, *Lead and Zinc in the United States*, New York, 1908. The entire discussion of the history of lead mining up to 1907 draws heavily on this study. Other material was secured from United States Department of Commerce, Bureau of Mines, Economic Paper No. 5, *Summarized Data of Lead Production*, 1929; T. A. Rickard, *History of American Mining*, New York, 1932; and a summary of the tariff history of lead ore and metal compiled by the United States Department of Commerce, Bureau of Foreign and Domestic Commerce, Tariff Division.

LEAD INDUSTRY IN THE UNITED STATES 665

the 1860's. Although the tariff, which was further reduced in 1857, was raised in 1861, again in 1862 (when for the first time a duty was imposed on the lead content of ore), and still again in 1864, the increase did not deter the steady decline of production from Wisconsin and Missouri nor cause new areas to be discovered. High prices during the Civil War days brought into operation some new deposits in the Eastern states, but they were not extensive enough to affect appreciably the nation's lead output. For practically every year between 1850 and 1870 the differential between the London and New York prices was more than the United States duty.

When an impetus did come to lead prospecting, and the prospecting brought new discoveries, the cause was the completion of the first transcontinental railway in 1869 rather than any tariff changes. In fact, during the decade of the discoveries, 1870–1879, the tariff was lowered by 10 per cent in 1872, though the reduction was repealed in 1875.

The most notable of the discoveries were made at Eureka, Nevada; Big and Little Cottonwood Canyon, Park City, and Bingham Canyon, Utah; Leadville, Colorado; Cerro Gordo, California; and Bonne Terre and Joplin, Missouri. From the present point of view, one of the most important of these locations was that at Bonne Terre, Missouri. The St. Joseph Lead Company discovered at a depth of 120 feet very large deposits of disseminated lead. Like the later "porphyry" coppers, these areas were of low grade, but of great extent. Although the first deposit of its kind to be discovered in the United States, the value was appreciated at once; and St. Joseph Lead became then, as it is now, an important producer. Of the 1870 discoveries only Southeast Missouri (including other deposits in the vicinity of Bonne Terre), Southwest Missouri (Joplin), and Park City and Bingham Canyon, Utah, are lead-producing regions worth mention today. The other regions reached the peak of production and have declined. Although it reached its maximum output in 1883, one of the most spectacular in its time was Leadville, which caused a furor in 1878, and which owed its fall, in part at least, to the decline in the price of silver.

After these discoveries, and apparently because of the increased production, the price was reduced; and for the first time the

666   CONTROL OF NON–FERROUS METALS

differential between the London and New York prices was, for a continuous period, less than the amount of the duty. The United States' percentage of world production increased from 5.87 between 1861 and 1870 to 16.58 between 1871 and 1880; but, though imports fell off, exports were not induced. Expanding industrial activity required as much and more than could be produced in the United States. The really great increase in demand came in 1879, and coincided with the Leadville boom, so that, in spite of greatly increased production, the price was forced very high. From a low level in 1878 when the New York price was actually below that in London, the price rose until in 1879 importation of lead over the tariff wall became profitable.

The tremendous expansion of the industry in the United States led to proposals of tariff reduction in the 1880's, at the instigation of Eastern manufacturers. Producers in Utah and Nevada were not politically expressive, because though they preferred tariff protection from European imports when the demand for lead was strong in the United States, the exportation of a surplus was at times very convenient. Missouri producers, however, were very vigorous in their opposition, and, in spite of the recommendation of the Tariff Commission that the rates be reduced, the opposition was successful. In fact the rates on sheet lead and lead in ore were raised slightly.

The increased production was sufficient to raise the percentage of United States' production from 16.58 between 1871 and 1880 to 27.80 between 1881 and 1890, and to lower the differential between London and New York prices to less than the tariff, but still exports did not occur. Consumers took all that Utah, Nevada, and Missouri could produce, and even absorbed the output from a new discovery, an area which is still important today, Coeur d'Alene, Idaho. Like the St. Joseph Lead Company's deposits, the ore bodies are very extensive.

Although the 1890's witnessed no new discoveries, the United States continued to mine about the same percentage of world production, and the differential between prices in New York and London remained less than the duty. About this time a controversy began that proved to be of continuing importance not only for the lead industry but for all those interested in tariff policy. In 1886 for the first time a noticeable quantity of lead-

LEAD INDUSTRY IN THE UNITED STATES   667

silver ore was imported into the United States from Mexico. This ore had the great advantage of being an excellent fluxing ore to help in reducing American silicious silver ores; it was of value not only for its metallic content but also for its power as a metallurgical agent.   As Mr. Ingalls has explained,[2] silver-lead smelting needs ore of various kinds, silicious ore, limestone, and iron ores in order to get a good fluxing mixture and avoid adding other fluxing agents;   and, since the American ores did not contain sufficient quantity of certain elements to be found in the Mexican ore, it was natural to depend on the Mexican supply. The needs of the United States smelting interests were met by the tariff ruling, in 1886, that since this Mexican ore contained a higher value of silver than of lead (though the quantity of lead was greater), it should be admitted as a silver ore, duty free, there being no rule in regard to composite ore.   This ruling was, however, reversed by the McKinley tariff of 1890, which, besides lowering slightly the rate on sheet lead, enacted that on the lead content of a composite ore there should be a duty equivalent to the duty on lead.   The smelters found they incurred the less substantial loss by continuing to import the Mexican ore, though they were forced to increase the smelting charges.   This is certainly a very nice example of a tariff that fails to protect the interests it serves, the failure here being the result of the insufficient refinement of the tariff schedule.   Though the act of 1894 lowered all the rates, it did not exempt the Mexican ores that were needed for fluxing.

By far the most important tendency initiated in the 1890's was the consolidation of the industry into larger and larger financial groups.   Although this was part of the general industrial movement in the country at large, it resulted in a degree of consolidation in the lead smelting and lead processing industries that is notable. The National Lead Trust, which had been organized previously, was succeeded by the National Lead Company in 1891, an organization which controlled the principal corroders of lead.   Another important branch of fabricating, the making of shot, was also considerably integrated by the end of the 1890's, under the auspices of the American Shot Company.   At the other end of the lead industry, the lead miners had begun to consolidate in

[2] Ingalls, *op. cit.*, p. 239.

668   CONTROL OF NON–FERROUS METALS

the Cœur d'Alene district of Idaho, but consolidations among miners never went very far.

The most important amalgamations, however, were among the smelters.   In 1878 the American Pig Lead Association had been formed with an agreement not to sell lead at less than four cents delivered in New York.   With a market price of 3.75 cents, and very divergent interests in the industry, enforcement of the agreement was never possible.   In 1883, low prices for lead had induced the formation of the Western Mining and Smelting Association to consider restricting production and reducing wage rates and freight rates, but no action had been taken.   In 1894, then, the outstanding smelters at Leadville formed an association to limit the price to be paid for ores.   Squeezed from two sides by the miners and the refiners, these smelting interests hoped that in agreement there might be protection.   But with a loose organization, they were unable to keep even a semblance of corporate form later than 1895.

If not at once successful, the smelting interests were at least persistent, so that in 1897 a general smelting association was organized, to act as an ore-buying agency.   The necessity for different kinds of ores in order to secure a good fluxing mixture often put the smelters at the mercy of the producers of ore of the requisite composition ; therefore the smelters decided that pooled-buying of ore might solve problems for all of them.   The arrangement was that there should be a clearing house to purchase on a fixed schedule and distribute to each smelter the proper proportion of the total purchases and the necessary proportion of each kind of ore.   Contrary to predictions of refiners and consumers, the existence of this smelting association did not cause unduly high prices.

With an example of a successful smelting association, it became easy to convince smelting interests that a stronger consolidation, an actual financial amalgamation, would achieve even greater efficiency.   Therefore in 1899 there began the organization of what was later the American Smelting and Refining Company. The promoters suggested that smelters as a whole would be better off if they agreed permanently to eliminate competition in the buying of ore, to close antiquated plants, to concentrate operations in the most favorable locations, to exchange technical

LEAD INDUSTRY IN THE UNITED STATES 669

information, and to negotiate for more favorable transportation rates.

Some of the old smelting units sold out to the new group; others simply exchanged stock of old units for stock in the new company, the owners of the old companies becoming directors in the new. In capitalizing the new corporation, the worth of the old plants was less than half the nominal amount of preferred stock created, and there was again as much common as preferred. As Mr. Ingalls has pointed out,[3] this was a very large allowance for intangibles. The new company bought up a great many units and actually scrapped many of them until in 1901 — when the Guggenheim interests, who had been the most powerful outsiders, bought into the consolidation — the only units excluded were the Balbach Smelting and Refining Company, the Selby Smelting and Lead Company, the Puget Sound Reduction Company, and the Tacoma Smelting Company. The Guggenheims secured shares in the American Smelting and Refining Company in exchange for their own smelter at Monterey and Aguascalientes, Mexico, the smelter at Pueblo, Colorado, the smelter in Chile, and the refinery at Perth Amboy, New Jersey, a transfer which was very advantageous to the consolidation and which initiated what has continued to be a very strong financial connection. The Guggenheims started with the mining of ore in Leadville, financed by a lace industry controlled by them. They depended in the first instances, as they have continued to depend, on outsiders for technical, metallurgical and engineering skill; but in their choice of technical advisers they have displayed as great discrimination as in their choice of financial opportunities. Though it was at first considered that they exacted too high a price for giving up independent direction of their own smelting and refining, it soon became apparent that their contribution was a very important condition of the success of the American Smelting and Refining Company.

In 1905 the Trust purchased the Selby works through a subsidiary, the American Smelters Securities Company, and later some of the other outside interests were drawn in. The only new competition was that provided by the United States Smelting, Refining, and Mining Company, organized in 1905, which in 1906

[3] Ingalls, *op. cit.*, p. 241.

670   CONTROL OF NON-FERROUS METALS

opened an electrolytic lead refinery near Chicago, the first electrolytic lead refinery in the United States.

The consolidation now controlled almost all of the United States' output of desilverized lead, and came to be known as the "Smelter Trust," though it was really not a trust in its corporate structure. Only after achieving success in lead smelting and refining did it undertake other kinds of smelting, particularly the processing of copper. In the general smelting and refining field it has, however, never achieved the degree of importance it secured, and still holds, in lead.

The smelting amalgamation secured its ore and concentrate from a great number of mining interests, but for its outlet it depended on but two important manufacturers, the National Lead Company, successor to the National Lead Trust, and the United Lead Company, successor to the American Shot Company. The National Lead Company produced white lead, oxides of lead, solder, babbitt metal, and sheet lead ; the United Lead Company, besides controlling the shot manufacture of the country, owned the most important lead-alloy works and some white lead works. With all competition a thing of the past, the American Smelting and Refining Company was in a position to control the price of lead. It is possible that at one time this control was even easier than would appear, because of some interest of the Guggenheim group in the National Lead Company.[4]

The dictation of prices by the American Smelting and Refining Company was justified by its managers as a means of stabilizing prices, which, it was said, was in the interests both of the ultimate consumers and of the manufacturers who needed to buy lead. The first test, and, as it turned out, the first vindication, of the power of the new organization came in 1901 when prices were low and stocks had accumulated unduly. The Trust arranged with the principal producers to reduce their output, and so caused the abnormal stocks to be gradually absorbed. Soon afterwards it inaugurated the practice of supplying manufacturers at minimum prices only if they bought on contract, a premium of 2.5 cents per

[4] Though this association was apparently short-lived, Mr. Ingalls asserted (*op. cit.*, pp. 251–252) that it had been initiated in 1906, but that according to the report of National Lead in 1907 no single outside interest was in control. Certainly the interests of the National Lead and the Guggenheims in Bolivian tin would seem to be rivals today, for the National Lead has its investments in the Patiño Mines and Enterprises, and the Guggenheims are independent owners.

LEAD INDUSTRY IN THE UNITED STATES 671

pound being charged for prompt delivery. This no doubt facilitated control of the market, and the rising prices for lead from 1901 to 1907 contributed to the ease with which prices could be dictated. In 1907, however, when prices were falling, and an open market grew up which undercut the charges made for the Trust's sales, the Trust recognized the weakness of its position and sold at the open market price for a time.

No doubt one condition for the formation of the American Smelting and Refining Company was the increased tariff of 1897, imposed, it was said, to exclude lead from British Columbia. From one cent a pound on pig lead, 1.25 cents on sheets, the rates were raised to $2\frac{1}{8}$ cents and 2.5 cents respectively. On lead ore the rate of $\frac{3}{4}$ cent was raised to 1.5 cents on the lead content; lead dross, however, on which the rate had been $\frac{3}{4}$ cent, was assessed the same rate as pig lead. After this time American production expanded absolutely and in relation to the rest of the world, the percentage of world production being increased from 26.85 in the decade of the 1890's to 31.51 in the decade of the 1900's. No doubt the ability to overcome the excessive stocks of 1901 depended on the tariff, for without the exclusion of foreign lead the curtailment of production would doubtless have been less effective, perhaps the agreement to curtail would never have been secured. But, more important, the increase in the differential between New York and London prices up to but not exceeding the amount of the duty was probably only possible because of the existence of the partial monopoly in smelting. As in other industries, the monopoly in lead was doubtless formed for the primary purpose of taking advantage of the duty in order to raise domestic prices.

Until 1913 the tariff on pig and bar lead remained at $2\frac{1}{8}$ cents per pound, the rate established in 1897. With the differential less than the duty, and neither imports nor exports important, the American Smelting and Refining Company regained by 1909 or 1910 the predominance over the market which it had lost for a time after 1907. In 1913, however, the rates were lowered to 25 per cent *ad valorem*, the average collected between October 4, 1913, and September 21, 1922, being 1.1 cents per pound. But before the new rates had time to exert their full effects the coming

672   CONTROL OF NON–FERROUS METALS

of the war in Europe changed the entire position of the American lead-producing industry.

In 1914 the New York price not only did not exceed the London price by the amount of the duty, but was actually lower. Therefore for the second time the United States became an exporter of lead. Although in 1914 the foreign demand was not much greater than it had been before the war, the internal political troubles in Mexico and labor difficulties in Spain and Australia made it necessary for the United States to supply an increasing proportion of the world's needs. By 1915 demand began to increase, and, since supply did not expand in proportion, the price was raised until it reached a maximum of 12.25 cents in June, 1917, though the average for 1917 was but 8.6 cents per pound.

The smelter output of the United States was increased considerably between 1914 and 1918, among the units that were expanded being such important plants as that of the Balbach Smelting and Refining Company in Newark, New Jersey; the Hercules Mining Company and Bunker Hill and Sullivan Company in the Coeur d'Alene district of Idaho; the American Smelting and Refining Company at El Paso, Texas, and East Helena, Montana; the then-consolidated Eagle White Lead and Picher Lead at Joplin, Missouri, Galena, Kansas, and elsewhere; and the St. Joseph Lead at Herculaneum, Missouri.[5] The increased construction enabled producers to increase their output by about 22 per cent and to increase their proportion of the world's output to 40.45 per cent in the decade 1911 to 1920, as compared with 31.51 per cent in the decade 1901 to 1910.[6] During all the war period exports expanded, in spite of the import duty, which, though lowered in 1913, was still continued.

For the first six months after the United States entered the war the increased needs of the government, which in July, 1917, amounted to as much as one-sixth of the national production, were supplied at the direction of a committee of producers. Although the price for government purchases was eight cents per

[5] See United States Department of Commerce, Bureau of Mines, *Mineral Resources of the United States* (hereafter *Mineral Resources*), 1914, 1915, 1916, 1917, and 1918, Parts I, sections on smelter changes in chapters on lead industry, where a full list and description of smelter changes is given. For the increase in smelter output during this period see Chart No. 2, Chapter X, p. 655.

[6] United States Department of Commerce, Bureau of Mines, *Summarized Data of Lead Production*, Economic Paper No. 5, 1929.

LEAD INDUSTRY IN THE UNITED STATES   673

pound, and the current market price in June and July was between
ten and twelve cents, output was inadequate.   Therefore after
October, 1917, when the Council of National Defense was established, more systematic rationing became necessary.   By August,
1918, shipments to China and Japan were refused; and shortly
after, when all exports were stopped, retailers were asked to cease
selling lead for non-essential uses.   Not until the Armistice was
rationing discontinued [7] and then, as in other industries, the
accumulated supply proved excessive.

In 1919 production was reduced as prices fell until, exactly
as in other industries, the revival in the early part of 1920 raised
prices and production.   (See Chart No. 1, page 654, and No. 10
following page 662.)   The recovery in lead was also short-lived,
however, so that in 1921 prices averaged only 4.545 cents per
pound as compared with 8.787 in 1917.   But since the demand for
lead increased more promptly than did the demand for other
metals, producers were able to put out in 1923 almost as much as
in 1918.   The foreign market was, it is true, almost completely
cut off once more because of the tariff, whose rates were increased
in 1922, and prices in New York maintained a premium over
London prices, though the premium did not equal the amount of
the duty.   Those imports that continued were base bullion and
ore, increasingly ore, sent to the United States for processing,
primarily from Mexico; exports were for the most part refined
pig lead derived from foreign ore and base bullion.   In spite of
the absence of a foreign market, however, the increase in domestic
demand would have been sufficient to insure real domestic recovery
except for one fact — the radical changes in methods of processing
which altered the relative advantages of mining in different
districts and changed the make-up of the American lead-producing
industry.

The chief advance in lead metallurgy was the more complete
separation of lead from the zinc with which lead ore is commonly
associated in nature.   Only the introduction of Wilfley tables in
the 1890's made possible even partial segregation of zinc.   Though
a relatively successful method for Mississippi Valley zinc, it was
inefficient for the ores of the Western states in which copper and

---

[7] See *Mineral Resources*, 1918, Part I, pp. 954-960, for a history of the lead industry during the war.

674   CONTROL OF NON–FERROUS METALS

iron sulphides were often found with the lead and zinc sulphides. For the more complex ores the zinc that was removed was lost, and what remained caused a lower price for the lead ore.   After 1918, however, selective flotation for lead-zinc ores [8] became available on a commercial scale, and caused profound changes in the American industry after 1924.   (See Chart No. 5, page 658.)   The change brought the greatest benefit to the producers of Western ores, for the zinc could be not only completely separated from the lead, but could itself be recovered as a marketable product.   In consequence the competitive position of the Western producers was increased at the expense of those in the Mississippi Valley, such as the St. Joseph Lead Company, who could secure no such radical advantage for treating their relatively simple ores, and who for the most part lacked the advantage enjoyed by the Western miners of securing some credits for small amounts of gold and silver.   Furthermore, the small Mississippi Valley zinc producers located in the so-called Tri-state district, who had previously put some lead on the market, found it no longer profitable to do so.   The Western producers took full advantage of the new method, so that by 1927 at least 56 per cent of their lead was recovered by selective flotation.[9]

The effect of these changes [10] on the Mississippi Valley producers was reflected in their output, which reached a peak in 1925 and then declined.   Though the output of the Western areas also

[8] See Chapter XII, pp. 686-688.
[9] For an account of the changes in the lead industry wrought by introduction of selective flotation, see *Mineral Resources*, 1927, Part I, p. 345.

[10] REGIONAL MINE PRODUCTION OF LEAD IN THE UNITED STATES

	1921	1925	1927
	Short Tons	Short Tons	Short Tons
Mississippi Valley			
Southeastern Missouri	178,735	208,915	196,251
Tri-state district	61,581	105,372	81,686
(*1921 = 100*)	240,316	314,287	277,937
	(*100*)	(*131*)	(*115*)
Western Areas			
Coeur d'Alene, Idaho	94,543	120,856	141,948
Bingham, Utah	12,288	54,982	55,508
Tintic, Utah	18,158	45,982	45,045
Park City, Utah	8,846	40,656	41,403
(*1921 = 100*)	133,835	262,383	283,904
	(*100*)	(*196*)	(*212*)

Calculated from a table entitled "Mine Production of Recoverable Lead in the Principal Lead-producing Districts of the United States," *Mineral Resources*, 1928, Part I, p. 618.

LEAD INDUSTRY IN THE UNITED STATES 675

declined after 1927, it had, between 1921 and 1925, expanded by a far greater degree than that of the Mississippi regions, 96 per cent as compared with 31 per cent, and had kept on increasing until in 1927 production was 112 per cent greater than in 1921.

During the period of metallurgical changes, between 1923 and 1927, when potential output was definitely expanding, the changes in the character of demand were no less notable, and therefore explain the profits in increased utilization of the technical advances that were made available. (See Chart No. 4, page 657.) The very great increase in the use of automobiles made necessary a far greater supply of storage batteries, and the later development of the radio expanded further the storage battery market until the introduction of radio sets which could be attached to lighting fixtures for their supply of power. Furthermore, the tendency to lay all power lines underground expanded the demand for lead cable sheathing. Between 1923 and 1928 the amount of lead used annually in storage batteries increased from 143,000 to 220,000 tons, while between 1923 and 1929 lead in cable sheathing increased from 131,000 to 220,000 tons. These changes were relative as well as absolute : the lead in storage batteries in 1928 requiring 23.64 per cent of all the lead used in that year as compared with 18.62 per cent in 1923, and the lead in cable coverings requiring 22.63 per cent in 1929 as compared with 17.06 per cent in 1923. The only more important uses for lead were for paint in the form of white lead, red lead, and litharge, but these uses declined absolutely and relatively between 1923 and 1929.[11] Undoubtedly this diminution in lead consumption will be increasingly noticeable, because white lead, which was during the nineteenth century the outstanding pigment base for paints, is being displaced by zinc oxide, by lithopone (a pigment in which the chief constituent is zinc oxide), and by nitrocellulose paint, lacquer, and enamel. Besides certain superior properties of the

[11] PRODUCTION OF WHITE LEAD, RED LEAD, AND LITHARGE

	1923		1929	
	Short Tons	Per Cent	Short Tons	Per Cent
White lead	130,000	16.92	119,700	13.21
Red lead and litharge	46,000	5.99	30,000	3.09
Other uses of lead in U. S.. . . .		77.09		84.60
		100.00		100.00

("Use of Lead in the United States," American Bureau of Metal Statistics, *Yearbook* (hereafter *A.B.M.S.*), 1932, p. 54.)

676   CONTROL OF NON–FERROUS METALS

newer pigments, they all lack the poisonous qualities of white lead.[12]

Though a very considerable amount of new equipment was built between 1925 and 1927,[13] consumption began definitely to fall off in 1927. There was, it is true, a minor industrial recession, but the decline in the consumption of lead was more marked than that of other non-ferrous metals. The reduction in demand resulted primarily from a lessened requirement for lead for storage batteries and cable coverings, two uses which, though they had been steadily increasing and did later increase again, reflected the decline in construction activity. The only exception to the general tendency was the demand for lead in paint, which, though it had previously been falling off, increased somewhat. In spite of the temporary set-back to the industry, however, the exploitation of new methods continued.[14]

By 1927, furthermore, the lead industry began to suffer from other dangers of disequilibrium. This was not so great as it might have been — or not so great as it was, in fact, in the copper industry — for the spectacular new and improved foreign sources of supply were quite effectively cut off by the tariff.[15] The degree to which lead could be reclaimed, however, particularly the lead in storage batteries, was very much underestimated when new plant was constructed, and this constituted an important reason for lack of balance between the productive capacity and the demand for new lead. (See Chart No. 9, page 662.) In 1928, for instance, the production of secondary lead represented 49 per cent of the production of refined lead.[16] That the importance of secondary lead had increased very greatly is evident, for in 1913 secondary lead represented but 18 per cent of the primary production; in 1918, 18 per cent; in 1921, 26 per cent; and in 1924, 36 per cent.

Partly because of more general recognition of the advantages

[12] *Mineral Resources*, 1928, Part I, pp. 350–352.
[13] For a statement of plant changes, see the *Mineral Industry, Its Statistics, Technology, and Trade*, New York, annual (hereafter the *Mineral Industry*), 1925, p. 427; 1926, pp. 210–213, 217–223.
[14] *Mineral Industry*, 1927, p. 340.
[15] By 1927 the Sullivan mine in Canada, Pennaroya in Spain, and Burma Corporation in Burma, had already demonstrated their producing ability, and at Mount Isa, Australia, extensive reserves were reported. See Chapter X.
[16] United States Department of Commerce, Bureau of Mines, *Minerals Yearbook* (hereafter *Minerals Yearbook*), 1932–1933, p. 59.

LEAD INDUSTRY IN THE UNITED STATES 677

of trade associations, but also, no doubt, because of the inherent weaknesses within the lead industry, the Lead Industries Association was formed in November, 1928. With a membership of both consumers and producers in Mexico, Canada, and South America, as well as within the United States, the organization was in a position to inform its members about the activities of competitors and the market for the various products.[17]

Mere dissemination of statistical information, however, did not deter the activity of forces that were adverse to prosperity for lead producers. Though by the end of 1928 the market had improved somewhat, the improvement was neither great enough to warrant lead producers in believing they had shared the general prosperity of the country nor financially important enough to enable them to lay aside any reserves for future declines in consumption.

Stocks of refined pig lead, which had been low in 1926, increased considerably in 1927, and slightly in 1928 and 1929, in spite of the fact that total production, which had fallen noticeably in 1927, was practically unchanged in 1928 and lower in 1929. These general changes, however, had little effect on the relative positions of the various producing districts; only the Coeur d'Alene district of Idaho produced appreciably more in subsequent years than in 1926. The decline in production was primarily in response to the fall in price which even at the end of 1928 had not reached the comparatively low level of 1927, nor did the higher prices in March and April of 1929 raise the 1929 level considerably above 1928 or 1927. Consumption was simply too sluggish to permit higher prices. The steadiest consumer of lead, the paint industry, was gradually shifting to other pigments; and the new arrivals among lead consumers, the consumers of lead for storage batteries and for cable sheaths, though more spectacular in the intensity with which their demand expanded, were also more fickle. The total demand for lead was distinctly affected by the decline in the process of electrification, the increased use of old lead for storage batteries, and the lessened requirement for storage batteries in radios. Therefore as in other industries here studied, copper and tin particularly, the lead industry showed distinct signs of excessive equipment and excessive stocks some time before the stock

[17] *Mineral Resources*, 1928, Part I, pp. 608–609.

678   CONTROL OF NON–FERROUS METALS

market crisis of 1929. Indeed, the lead industry never really revived after the minor relapse of 1927.[17a]

During the years 1929 to 1932, when plants were closing and profits were first eaten into and then completely devoured, the lead industry fared less badly in some respects than the copper industry. Whereas in 1932 copper prices dropped to about 30 per cent of what they had been in 1929, lead prices dropped to only 46 per cent of what they had been. Though the consumption of lead dropped relatively almost as much as that of copper, the production dropped far less. Without intimating that lead producers were not affected by the depression, these comparisons indicate that lead producers were perhaps in a better position to undertake renewed activity.

As in the copper industry, however, the various producers of lead were unequally fitted for revival. From the calculations of Mr. Furness, to which reference has already been made, it is possible to essay some estimate of the relative advantages enjoyed by the individual producers during the period 1922 to 1932.[18] Although the study is limited to producers of just over 51 per cent of the lead output, it includes the larger companies. Even though the results are complicated by the fact that most of the mines yield lead-zinc ore in varying proportions, significant conclusions are possible if the companies are classified into those that produce primarily lead, those that produce lead and zinc in about equal proportions, and those that produce primarily zinc.

Of the lead-zinc mining companies for which lead is most important,[19] the two high-cost units are St. Joseph Lead and

[17a] See Charts No. 1, 2, 3, and 10 in Chapter X, pp. 654, 655, 656, and following 662, respectively.
[18] H. D. Keiser, " Costs, Codes, and the Future," *Engineering and Mining Journal* (hereafter *E.M.J.*), April 1934, p. 176.

[19] LEAD-ZINC MINING COMPANIES PRODUCING PRIMARILY LEAD

Bingham Mines Co., Bingham, Utah, acquired, 1929, by the United States Smelting, Refining, and Mining Co. Lead 89.8%.
Bunker Hill and Sullivan Mining and Concentrating Co., Coeur d'Alene district, Idaho. Owns 50% interest in Treadwell Yukon Co., Tybo, Nevada; 69.25% in Northwest Lead Co. of Seattle, Washington; and 50% in Sullivan Mining Co., Coeur d'Alene district, Idaho. Lead 95.0%.
Chief Consolidated Mining Co., Tintic district, Utah, and elsewhere. Lead 84.7%.
Dayrock Mining Co., Coeur d'Alene district, Idaho. Lead 99.7%.
Hecla Mining Co., Coeur d'Alene district, Idaho. Part owner of Sullivan Mining Co., Coeur d'Alene district, Idaho. Lead 98.8%.

LEAD INDUSTRY IN THE UNITED STATES 679

Utah-Apex.   St. Joseph Lead, which was once a very efficient producer, is still a very important source of lead, indeed it is the largest producer in the United States.[20]   Its chief mining property, located in southeast Missouri, was the first large deposit of disseminated lead ore discovered.   Though the company's mine and plant investment per-pound-of-lead-produced is not unduly high as compared with other lead producing companies in this category, its working capital is low.   In spite of the fact that its net earnings and dividends per pound of lead are distinctly less than those of other producers, the company actually produced in 1932 a larger percentage of the lead output of the United States than in 1929, though of course its actual output declined considerably.

The Utah-Apex, on the other hand, is a relatively small producer, but like the St. Joseph Lead its net earnings and dividends per pound were low.   Unlike St. Joseph Lead, mining was suspended in May, 1931, though developments were continued until June, 1932.

Four other companies which are primarily lead producers, Bunker Hill and Sullivan, Hecla, Silver King Coalition, and

North Lily Mining Co., Tintic district, Utah, controlled by Anaconda through International Smelting Co.   Lead 98.6%.

Silver King Coalition Mines Co., Park City, Utah.   Lead 79.8%, zinc 16.9%.

St. Joseph Lead Co., Southeast Missouri, and Barker district, Montana.   Lead 79.8%, zinc 16.9%.

Tintic Standard Mining Co., Tintic district, Utah.   Lead 97.1%.

United States Smelting, Refining, and Mining Co., Bingham and Tintic districts, Utah.   Lead 65.8%, zinc 28.7%.

Utah-Apex Mining Co., Bingham Canyon, Carr, Fork, and West Mountain districts, Utah.   Lead 63.4%, zinc 26.7%.

[20] LEAD PRODUCTION OF INDIVIDUAL COMPANIES AS A PROPORTION OF UNITED STATES LEAD PRODUCTION

	1929	1932
Bingham Mines	0.52% [a]	— [b]
Bunker Hill and Sullivan	6.45%	14.7 %
Chief Consolidated	0.89%	0.058%
Dayrock	0.55%	—
Hecla	4.25%	6.55 %
North Lily	2.4 %	0.017%
Silver King Coalition	3.22%	4.45 %
St. Joseph Lead	25.8 %	38.6 %
Tintic Standard	2.8 %	3.28 %
United States Smelting, Refining, and Mining	8.75%	14.4 %
Utah-Apex	1.24%	—

[a] January to July only.
[b] Included in United States Smelting, Refining, and Mining Co.

680   CONTROL OF NON–FERROUS METALS

Tintic Standard, are all located in Utah or Idaho; all have costs that are relatively low and not very different. Silver King Coalition and Tintic Standard, the two Utah companies, each have average net earnings and dividends per pound that are relatively higher than those of either Bunker Hill and Sullivan, or Hecla.   Bunker Hill and Sullivan, however, has a low working capital and a heavy investment in plant and mining property as compared with the others, though the figure given is actually an underestimate, since the allowance for depreciation was not really comparable.   Of these four only the Silver King produces appreciable amounts of zinc.   Though neither of the others produces even a noticeable amount of gold, Silver King and Tintic Standard each have a higher gold content in their ore than any other copper, lead, or zinc producer studied by Mr. Furness.[21]

Three companies are about equally dependent on lead and zinc : Callahan Zinc-Lead, Federal Mining and Smelting, and Park Utah.[22]   The Callahan Zinc-Lead Company is scarcely comparable because its position is so unfavorable, the company having had a high deficit instead of net earnings during the eleven years studied.   Calculating per-pound costs on the basis of net earnings, the costs for this company average 10.699 cents per pound as compared with the average of 4.676 cents for the industry.   Its fixed investment is fantastically high, $4.96 per-pound-produced as compared with 23.6 cents for the group here considered; moreover its working capital is low, only 1.6 cents per pound as compared with the average for the industry of 2.6 cents per pound. It is not strange, therefore, that mining and milling were dis-

---

[21] The remaining companies that are primarily lead producers, Bingham Mines, Chief Consolidated, Dayrock, North Lily, and the United States Smelting, Refining, and Mining Co., are not discussed here individually because for one reason or another they are not comparable.   Bingham Mines was acquired by the United States Smelting, Refining, and Mining Co. in 1929.   Chief Consolidated reports are not given in full.   Dayrock and North Lily did not operate for the full eleven years, Dayrock being operative only from 1923 to 1930, North Lily from 1928 to 1932. The United States Smelting, Refining, and Mining Co. gives no separate report on its mining activities.

[22] LEAD–ZINC MINING COMPANIES EQUALLY DEPENDENT ON LEAD AND ZINC

Callahan Zinc-Lead Co., Coeur d'Alene district, Idaho.   Lead 46.9%, zinc 52%.
Federal Mining and Smelting Co., controlled by American Smelting and Refining Co., Idaho, and Tri-State (Oklahoma, Kansas, and Missouri).   Lead 53.2%, zinc 46.6%.
Park Utah Consolidated Mines Co., Park City, Utah.   Lead 52.1%, zinc 45.2%.

LEAD INDUSTRY IN THE UNITED STATES   681

continued in 1931.[23] It is only strange that the company should have continued as long as it did and that one manual should report in 1931 : "The management has been able and progressive and is endeavoring to perpetuate the organization by the acquisition of new properties." [24]

The only comparison, then, for companies that produce about equal amounts of lead and zinc is Federal Mining and Smelting, and Park Utah.[25] The Federal Mining and Smelting is the only producer of considerable importance and it is therefore unfortunate that the data are incomplete.[26] Though these two companies have per-pound investment in mine development, plant, and machinery and per-pound working capital which are exactly the same, the dividends and bonded indebtedness of Federal Mining and Smelting are less than the average. The dividends of Park Utah (which has no bonded indebtedness) are more than the average. In spite of its high dividends, Park Utah has a cost based on net earnings that is higher than the average for the companies that produce primarily lead.

From this detailed statement it is clear that the best lead companies are those in Utah and Idaho which depend largely on lead, and which have a considerable profit from gold as a by-product, though St. Joseph Lead is still by far the greatest producer.

Though the lead industry during 1933 by no means regained its balance, the code of fair competition expressed no demand for unreasonable power; rather, it was particularly cautious, being no more than a means of regulating wages and hours and of disseminating trade information.[27] Advanced by the Lead Indus-

[23] Moody's *Manual of Industrials*, New York, 1933.
[24] *Mines Handbook*, New York, 1931.

[25] LEAD PRODUCTION OF INDIVIDUAL COMPANIES AS A PROPORTION OF UNITED STATES LEAD PRODUCTION

	1929	1932
Callahan Zinc-Lead	0.116	—
Federal Mining and Smelting	6.55	4.35
Park Utah	2.9	—

[26] Mr. Furness has been unable to secure more data for this company than for the mining and smelting companies, though this company really does only mining, turning over its concentrate for smelting to its parent company, the American Smelting and Refining Company.

[27] National Recovery Administration, "Code of Fair Competition for the Lead Industry," as approved on May 24, 1934, Washington, 1934.

682   CONTROL OF NON-FERROUS METALS

tries Association, it had the support of virtually the entire industry.[28]

From the point of view of the code authorities, however, even if they had been well armed, there was little hope of conquest. Although domestic production in 1933 was less than in 1932,[29] stocks reached the highest point yet attained in March.[30] The price was somewhat improved [31] but the chance of improved consumption was slight. It was perhaps not strange, therefore, that lead producers hailed the increased prices for precious metals which began to affect lead prices in 1934. Interestingly enough, authorities pointed out that though increase in revenues from precious metals was confined to lead producers in Western states, the increased production of lead in 1934, a mere five per cent, was shared about equally by those who produced precious metals and those who did not. It is possible, however, that without the increase in the price of gold and silver even this small increment in the production of lead might have been impossible, and the price of lead might have been lower.[32]

Though the world industry revived very considerably, producers in the United States derived little benefit. Prices fell as compared with 1933 and stocks were augmented. Primary producers may have secured some comfort in the realization that the ratio of secondary to domestic refined primary lead declined, but with a ratio still at 70 per cent, comfort could not be unalloyed. As the National Resources Board said,[33] the price of lead was kept at a very low level by the potential competition of new low cost production from abroad.

"As with copper, the committee concludes that the formulation of specific plans should originate with the industry. We would suggest for immediate consideration, however, (1) development of better statistics of secondary lead to supplement the mar-

---

[28] O. W. Roskill, "Lead and Zinc in 1933," *Mining Journal*, London, January 17, 1934, p. 15; and *E.M.J.*, January, 1934, p. 40.

[29] Being 273,690 short tons in 1933, compared with 292,947 short tons in 1932.

[30] *E. M. J.*, April, 1934, p. 147; and *Metal and Mineral Markets*, March 22, 1934.

[31] An average of 3.900 cents per pound in the first three months of 1934 as compared with 3.735, the average for 1933.

[32] *Minerals Yearbook*, 1935, pp. 78, 79.

[33] United States National Resources Board, *A Report on National Planning and Public Works in Relation to Natural Resources and Including Land Use and Water Resources with Findings and Recommendations*, Washington, 1934, p. 412.

LEAD INDUSTRY IN THE UNITED STATES   683

ket information services already available for this industry;
(2) establishment of consumption forecasts, to be made by a
Government agency, such as the Bureau of Mines, in coöperation
with producers and organized consumers; and (3) joint action
by the industry under public supervision to control the accumulation of excess stocks."

Here is a suggestion that there is one more industry which is,
if not legally, at least economically, affected with the public
interest.

ELIZABETH S. MAY

[13]

Excerpt from *Journal of Economic History*, 1952, **XII**, 411–24.

The Standard Oil Company (New Jersey)

Ralph W. Hidy

USA
L7.1
N5 1
L12

THE aim of this discussion is to elucidate the evolution of the management concepts, organizational patterns, and policies of the
Standard Oil Company (New Jersey).[1] In point of fact, these topics
are discussed primarily with reference to the origin and development
of the Standard Oil combination under its various legal titles prior to
1911. The policies and practices, both sound and unsound, of the men
who administered the Jersey Company in its early years were largely
those of the men who created the combination.

I

Relative to the advisability of presenting the early development of
Standard Oil policies and procedures in general, it must be remembered that the Standard Oil Company (New Jersey) has played a
number of roles since its birth in 1882. Executives of the combination
organized it in accordance with a specific provision of the agreement
creating the Standard Oil Trust. During its first ten years Jersey Standard acted solely as an operating company engaged chiefly in manufacturing. At the end of that period the Ohio Supreme Court denied the
right of the Standard Oil Company (Ohio) to pay dividends or to be
subject to the policies of the trustees. Between 1892 and 1899 the administrators of Standard Oil affairs expanded their New Jersey unit
into one of their most important manufacturing and marketing
agencies and simultaneously made it one of several holding corporations among the leading twenty companies under their direction as a
community of interest. In 1899, while retaining operating functions,
Jersey Standard became the parent holding company of the combination. This dual role continued after the separation of thirty-three corporations from the parent company in 1911, but since 1927 Standard
Oil Company (New Jersey) has served, with the minor exception of
marine operations for a short time, only as a holding company.

Inasmuch as the Standard Oil combination was a pioneer in large-
scale enterprise in the United States, the policies and practices of John
D. Rockefeller and his colleagues well deserve detailed analysis. Those

---

[1] These generalizations are based upon the forthcoming publication by Ralph W. and
Muriel E. Hidy, "The History of the Standard Oil Company (New Jersey), 1882–1911."

Ralph W. Hidy

men engineered a radical new departure in the administration and operation of industrial activity in this country. The railroad and tele- graph industries had engaged in big business before the 1870's, but the oil combination constituted the first successful attempt to organize and operate, on a massive scale, the production and distribution of goods rather than services. Much criticism was directed at Standard Oil executives, sometimes with justification, sometimes without justi- fication. Rockefeller and his associates were open to criticism as man- agers of a private business which maintained an overwhelming domi- nance of its industry, but many reactions stemmed from the facts that it was new and that it ran counter both to the interests of some people and to many prevailing American ideals and fixed ideas. Inquiry reveals that Standard Oil men actually created an effective new behavior pat- tern by merging new concepts with several business practices of long standing.

In common with many other administrators before and since, Stand- ard Oil executives between 1882 and 1911 adhered reasonably closely to a number of managerial concepts, even if all were not clearly visu- alized or formally stated. Basic to all other ideas was the desire to make profits over a period of years—for the long pull, not the short run. Profits were definitely not without honor in the Standard Oil man- sion—26 Broadway. To achieve that goal, managers of the combina- tion early adopted and followed numerous principles of action. Many of these principles were not fully attained and were frequently quali- fied in practice over time. Even before the dismemberment of Jersey Standard in 1911, many of the basic concepts were modified as a result of changing personnel and of almost innumerable alterations in con- ditions of operation. Differing stimuli produced differing reactions.

During the early years of the combination, Standard Oil executives endeavored to stabilize the petroleum industry by eliminating as far as possible some, though not all, of the variables in the business. The instrument was a giant horizontal and vertical combination owned in common by a small group of investors. Through excluding some re- finers and at first all producing operations, John D. Rockefeller and his associates deliberately stopped short of monopoly, although they pos- sessed overwhelming dominance of the market in the United States and of the export trade in petroleum products. In this fashion Standard Oil managers sought security for themselves, the same elusive and ephemeral goal so earnestly pursued by farmers and others in the twentieth century. The oilmen differed from their later emulators by

Large-Scale Organization   413

relying exclusively upon private action to attain their objective. As subsequent discussion will indicate, changing circumstances induced the managers of the combination to alter the implementation of the basic concept as time passed.

Into the combination Rockefeller and his colleagues carried many of the concepts characteristic of the business mores of the time and previously utilized by them as small businessmen. Among these ideas were the convictions that the owners should manage their own business and that the affairs of the enterprise should be kept secret from competitors—age-old habits of thought. Closely associated with those two expressions of the concept "My business is my own" were the desires to be financially independent at all times and to observe consistently the letter of the law.

Strange as it may seem to believers of Henry Demarest Lloyd and Ida Minerva Tarbell, conformity to the letter of the law constituted a cardinal principle of Standard Oil leadership. To make certain, as far as possible, of that conformity, Rockefeller and his associates retained one of the best corporation lawyers in the United States—S. C. T. Dodd. Both he and his successor utilized a whole battery of assistants in connection with different companies on state and regional issues throughout the years from 1880 to 1911.

All the top executives of the combination believed in the virtues of competition, though they preferred to modify the unrestrained variety. They encouraged individuals and units within the organization to compete with each other as a means of keeping managers and their teams on their toes. For the same reason the members of the Executive Committee accepted willingly a measure of competition with outsiders. The latter were left roughly 15 per cent of the market in the United States in 1881, but many factors aided them in increasing their share of an expanding market about another 10 per cent of the total by 1911. It is noteworthy that not all field managers shared this faith in competition with those in the top echelon; some Standard Oil marketers preferred to annihilate competitors, if possible. All agreed, however, with efficient industrialists everywhere that continuous reduction of unit costs in manufacturing was a major competitive weapon and at least as important an item in the delivered price as getting the best possible transportation rates through bargaining with railroads.

Specialization within the organization and careful attention to the possibilities of new methods were other concepts applied by Standard Oil men. They thought that greater efficiency would ensue if each man

414   *Ralph W. Hidy*

applied all his energy and skill to the function for which he had greatest aptitude and knowledge. Standard Oil leaders insisted upon getting for each task the best possible ideas, skills, and techniques available at the time. The formation of the alliance in 1874–1875 brought together several of the most able and successful businessmen in the American petroleum industry. Some businesses were bought to acquire patents, inventors, and administrators. In some cases Standard Oil executives perfected new techniques by promoting experimentation within the organization, on lubricants for example. In others they borrowed, expanded, and systematized ideas tried out by competitors; Standard Oil men built a network of trunk pipe lines for crude oil after that method of transport was first proved commercially successful by the Columbia Conduit Company and subsequently dramatized by the Tidewater Pipe Company, Limited. When Standard Oil managers were unable to devise a satisfactory process for manufacturing marketable products from sulphur-laden Lima-Indiana crude oil, they hired the leading petroleum chemist of the 1880's—Herman Frasch—to attain their objective. All activities were characterized by as meticulous attention to detail as was ever boasted by Napoleon in the conduct of his campaigns.

To co-ordinate the labors of multitudinous specialists in two-score companies and to maintain a balanced relationship between the functions of producing, purchasing, transporting, storing, manufacturing, and marketing petroleum and its derivatives, Rockefeller and his associates had to adopt some creative managerial concepts. They recognized early that policy formulation for the combination as a whole should be centralized in a specific agency, even if in so large an organization suggestions and recommendations must necessarily come from below. Appreciation of that fact was instrumental in creating the trust. At the same time, many factors encouraged a large measure of individual and corporate autonomy. Among these were general legal requirements, existing contracts with the companies and individuals, performance of functions by different units, ownership of shares in various Standard Oil companies by investors outside the group in the alliance, respect for personal characteristics and abilities of associated executives, and conviction that a man gave his best only when delegated responsibility. In such a complex situation effective management involved a compromise between centralization and decentralization of authority and called for systematic administration based upon the maintenance of continuous checks and controls. In the course of evolving and operating their system, Standard Oil executives had the ideal of working as a team, par-

Large-Scale Organization   415

ticularly of reaching decisions through consultation and agreement.

As in all businesses, the last stage on the road to Standard Oil profits was the market. From the beginning of their united efforts, managers of the combination thought in terms of an expanding market, not a static one, and of a world-wide market, not one limited to the United States. Kerosene was going into practically every major seaport of the world before the alliance was formed. Some firms had specialized in manufacturing export oil prior to joining the alliance and several members of the combination had previously shared in export sales. Thus, the effective operation of all Standard Oil units depended, in the final analysis, upon sales in markets as varied as Siam and the United States, as China and Germany. American oilmen were subject to competition from many local petroleum industries and to regulations by scores of municipal, provincial, and national ruling bodies, not to mention fluctuations in economic conditions in all sections of the globe. A giant market had bred a giant combination in the world's leading national petroleum industry. Small wonder that Standard Oil executives, caught between the erratic flow of oil from the wells of the Appalachians and the equally formidable variations in the vast market for American petroleum products, elected to attempt to co-ordinate and control the functions performed between the two—a concept not unique to Rockefeller and his colleagues, but certainly unique in breadth and size at the time.

II

In the course of implementing their basic concepts, and in response to a variety of stimuli—internal and external—Standard Oil managers from time to time changed the organizational pattern of the combination.

From 1874 to the end of 1881 the combination was an alliance—a community of interest—of 41 owners, including one two-man partnership. The organization was a makeshift, a hodgepodge. Though all Standard Oil properties belonged to the 41 owners, their rights were expressly vested in a mixture of corporations, limited partnership associations, co-partnerships, individual trusteeships, and a special trusteeship of three men with no power of administration. Persons outside the Standard Oil group owned either a minority or majority interest in 27 of the 40 operating units in the alliance. Authority for managing the activities of the constituent elements in the combination was legally delegated to no man or group of men, though the few dominant owners actually administered many operations. Difficulties lurked in the possibility of death among both the leading executives and the various trustees. Transfers of property and shares were complicated. Order and system seemed imperative for the successful administration of the alliance, in itself a pooling of patents, trade-marks, brands, good will, properties, skills, techniques, brains, and personalities.

At the same time, a mélange of circumstances dictated the retention of separate and distinct companies. Among those factors were the heritage of many companies from the seventies, personal pride of many executives in the firms created by them, outside ownership of shares in many of the affiliated concerns, state and Federal regulatory legislation, tax laws and administration, functional differentiation among the associated companies, and regional and national objectives. Most of these have operated to the same end since 1882. However, ownership by a group of investors of all or part of a large number of companies indicated the desirability of forming and maintaining a holding mechanism.

Though other alternatives were considered, through the efforts of S. C. T. Dodd and H. M. Flagler the agreement for the creation of the Standard Oil Trust was drawn up and signed on January 2, 1882. Among many other items, the document provided for the organization of a Standard Oil Company in New Jersey. The contract also vested control and management in nine trustees, who together owned over half of the certificates in the trust. John D. Rockefeller became president, William Rockefeller vice-president, J. A. Bostwick treasurer, and H. M. Flagler secretary of the Board of Trustees.

In practice, neither the president alone nor all the four officers managed the Standard Oil combination. From the beginning, administration depended upon daily consultation and agreement by almost two-score executives. Members of the Board of Trustees did far more than merely ratify the decisions of the officers at occasional meetings. Everybody in the top echelon labored and was aided by daily advice from the second rank of executives. The instrument was a series of committees.

As provided in the bylaws of the trust, the trustees formed an executive committee. At first it included eight of their own number. Later, the committee often embraced men not within the select circle of trustees; for example, from 1888 to his death in 1898 James McGee, an expert on sales for export, was a member of the group. John D. Rockefeller's most arduous task was to preside over the daily meetings of the Executive Committee, while attending members listened to suggestions from their colleagues, and then argued and compromised on courses of action for the benefit of the stockholders in the Standard Oil combination—for "the general interest," to use their own phrase of 1882. This phrase is still in current use in Jersey Standard.

By 1886 a galaxy of committees, enjoying full advisory and a measure of administrative powers, had grown up on the level just below the Executive Committee. The names of the seven major advisory units at that time reveal their functions—transportation, manufacturing, lubricating oil, cooperage, case and can, export trade, and domestic trade. A production committee reported to John D. Archbold after the Executive Committee decided to embark on producing crude oil. As different problems arose and new functions assumed importance, new committees were created to make investigations and recommendations—on salary schedules, ship construction and operation, and labor disputes, to give three examples.

This system of management by consultation and of working top managers, who were the directors of Jersey Standard from 1899 onward, has continued to the present day, not only in the New Jersey corporation but also in other former members of the Standard Oil family. Between 1899 and 1911 some of the directors were inactive, but all the active ones worked diligently. In the history of the Jersey Company the committee system appears to have been less important between 1911 and 1927 than before or since. So much have committees proliferated within the parent company and affiliates during recent years that executives sometimes regard themselves as working members of a perpetual debating society. Co-ordination of committees and departments is an imperative recognized by management, as the recent articles in *Fortune* on Jersey Standard and its associated corporations point out.

The reasons for the emergence of management by consultation through the committee system were simple, indeed. No one man, nor any one family, ever owned a majority of the stock in the combination. Hence, no individual was able at any time to assert control arbitrarily. The owner of the largest block of stock, John D. Rockefeller, never believed in dictatorial methods of management. He consistently adhered to a policy of consultation, first with his brother William, then with H. M. Flagler, and by 1872 with J. A. Bostwick, O. H. Payne, and Benjamin Brewster in addition.

Within another three years necessity supplemented inclination in the adoption of consultation and team play in the administration of the

Ralph W. Hidy

Standard Oil alliance. All the leading figures among the top managers came into the combination on the basis of equality, like the states into the Federal union. Before entry into the alliance, such men as W. G. Warden, J. J. Vandergrift, Charles Lockhart, Charles Pratt, H. H. Rogers, and John D. Archbold were strong and vigorous men in their own right. These members in the top echelon of management, not to mention more than a score of former independent businessmen in the second rank of Standard Oil executives, were the epitome of rugged individualism. Nobody impinged upon their independence of judgment and, to be certain of maximum effectiveness in performance of duties, no manager dared ignore their personal feelings.

Recognition of these facts often led to extreme caution in consultation. "I have conferred with all the parties that are, as I think, likely to have opinions or feelings upon this subject," wrote one man to his colleagues on the Cooperage Committee, "and the recommendations that I make are satisfactory to them."[2] In a similar spirit, all letters from top managers to subordinates "suggested" or "recommended," never "ordered," a practice still followed by directors of Jersey Standard.

Assurance that the decisions of the committees would be implemented by operating companies was achieved at first in many instances by selecting directors and officers of corporations from the executive and advisory units. As chairman of the Executive Committee, John D. Rockefeller could feel reasonably sure that John D. Rockefeller, president of Ohio Standard, would carry out any recommendations of the policy-forming group. The same might be said for H. M. Flagler, the first president of the Jersey Company.

In practice there were limits to the control exercised under the system of identical top committeemen and officers of affiliated companies. At 26 Broadway the executive committeemen and their associates laid down general policy, leaving the vice-presidents and general managers of operating companies to carry out the ideas for "the general interest" as they saw fit. In describing the qualities of the man desired to take charge of Kentucky Standard's marketing activities south of the Ohio River in 1886, W. P. Thompson expressed to John D. Rockefeller both the ideal and the reason for it: "He should be big enough to run the entire business subject only to general advice on general policy. It is too big and complicated to be run at arms length."[3] A year earlier Rocke-

---

[2] Socony Paint Products Company Records, Memorandum of G. H. Hopper enclosed in letter of T. H. Wheeler to the Executive Committee, February 20, 1885.
[3] Rockefeller Records, W. P. Thompson to J. D. Rockefeller, October 19, 1886.

Large-Scale Organization   419

feller had stated broadly another reason for the granting of autonomy to Thompson regarding operations of Ohio Standard and simultaneously sounded a warning as to the extent of independent behavior: "You gentlemen on the ground can judge better than we about this matter, but let us not drift into arrangements where we cannot control the policy." [4]

In the early days of the Standard Oil Trust there were noteworthy examples that control did not ensue from identity of committeemen with directors of affiliates. Men from the top echelons of managers exercised no more than slight influence as directors of the Vacuum Oil Company and the Galena Oil Works, to give but two of several possible illustrations. Management of those two companies rested almost exclusively with C. M. Everest and Charles Miller, respectively, as long as they remained in the Standard Oil family. Such examples of divorcing operations of subsidiaries from policy making for "the general interest" may be regarded as "the wave of the future" finally recognized in the 1930's.

Over the nine years from 1924 to 1933 top-level policy formulation was gradually separated from operations. In the reorganization of 1927, in itself a product of three years' study, some directors of Jersey Standard were directors and officers of affiliates. Six years later top managers decided that the best plan was to separate more effectively operations and formulation of top policy. Hence, since that time, directors of the parent company have not held office in affiliates, although every member of the Big Board has the responsibility of maintaining continuous contact with certain corporations and functions. In this fashion Jersey Standard directors strive to effect a workable compromise between centralization and decentralization—between consideration of decisions for the entire family of affiliates and the autonomous operation of each associated unit.

III

Operating policies, the tactical measures of top strategists, had to be altered more often than basic concepts. Rockefeller and his associates adjusted their policies of producing crude oil, storing, transporting, manufacturing, and marketing to innumerable circumstances and pressures, including those from outside suppliers of crude petroleum, con-

[4] Rockefeller Records, J. D. Rockefeller to W. P. Thompson, November 5, 1885.

Ralph W. Hidy

sumers, competitors in the oil industry at home and abroad, and competition from coal producers, manufacturers of artificial gas, and the burgeoning electrical industry.

In order to assure a steady flow of crude oil to refineries, which necessitated having a price which would encourage producers to keep active and at the same time enable Standard Oil manufacturers to make a profit on finished goods, top managers worked out a complex of interrelated gathering, transporting, storing, and purchasing techniques in the early 1880's. They left the production of crude oil to outsiders. Standard Oil pipe-line units ran gathering lines to the storage tanks of almost every well, provided storage facilities for all oil run from field tanks, and gave a negotiable certificate for each 1,000 barrels received and stored. The Joseph Seep Purchasing Agency, an adjunct of Standard Oil's National Transit Company, did practically all the purchasing in the field for the combination. Seep's purchasing price, for any given day, was the closing price for oil certificates on the oil exchanges. Standard Oil men built a trunk pipe-line system between 1879 and 1885 to carry their purchased crude oil to all their refineries. Rebates on shipments of raw petroleum by railroads were a thing of the past to Standard Oil refiners in Pittsburgh by 1877, in Cleveland and Olean by 1880, in Bayonne and Brooklyn by 1881, in Buffalo by 1882, in Philadelphia and Baltimore by 1883, and in Parkersburg by 1885.

Within a few years changing conditions forced a radical modification of the foregoing pattern of operations. The Standard Oil combination went into large-scale production of crude petroleum in 1889, although it provided for only a portion of its needs in this way. In terms of its share in the amount of crude oil produced in the United States, Standard Oil reached its peak in 1898 with approximately 33 per cent, after which there was a marked decline. In 1895 Standard Oil purchasers officially adopted the policy of buying according to posted prices, a practice still in use today. The use of certificates practically ceased at that time. Centralized purchasing had been modified in the late eighties as the Lima-Indiana producing area developed. Pipe lines ultimately became the chief Standard Oil purchasing agents in that area and others. The oil was bought at posted prices as it entered the pipes, or shortly thereafter, in Illinois, Kansas, Oklahoma, Texas, and Louisiana, but Jersey Standard's affiliate in California made purchases from producers on one- to three-year contracts. In these newer producing regions Standard Oil units utilized their own storage tanks for

Large-Scale Organization   421

their own oil, thus ceasing to be bankers of oil owned by others, as they had earlier in the Appalachians.

The drive to reduce the unit costs of manufacturing—a basic urge of Standard Oil managers inherited from their days of relatively unrestricted competition—resulted in a policy of mass production. The process was gradual and embraced a number of simultaneously conducted operations. Rockefeller and his team eliminated submarginal units, expanded or erected large, strategically located refineries, and manufactured a complete range of finished products in accordance with changes in demand. They attempted to assure uniformity in quality by means of inspection both at each plant and in a centralized laboratory and to improve quality through ceaseless experimentation, particularly on lubricants. They engaged in at least ten auxiliary fabricating activities: they made their own acid, glue, cases, cans, both wooden and steel barrels, tank cars, tank wagons, wicks, paint, and pumps. They utilized the assembly-line technique in fabricating and filling cans and cases as early as the 1870's. Over the years prior to 1911 Standard Oil refiners devised or adopted scores of improvements in the technology of manufacturing operations, the outstanding changes in refining being the utilization of continuous distillation and of selective condensation by means of towers invented by J. W. Van Dyke of the Atlantic Refining Company.

Even more slowly than in the case of mass manufacturing, Standard Oil executives carried out a policy of mass distribution of petroleum products. At the time that Jersey Standard was born, the change was in process. Standard Oil refiners sold many types of lubricating oils and gasolines direct to industrial consumers, a practice continued for those items, for fuel oil to factories and railroads, and for gas oil to manufacturers of artificial gas. Prior to 1881, various components of the combination, including the Standard Oil Company (Ohio), had either erected or purchased some wholesaling facilities in the form of 130 bulk stations from which retailers were supplied kerosene in barrels. Over the years other units of the organization gradually assumed the wholesale and jobbing function in marketing kerosene, gasoline, and packaged lubricants. They also substituted delivery of kerosene and gasoline to retailers by tank wagon for distribution in barrels for over 70 per cent of the volume by 1911. The pattern of bulk stations and tank wagon delivery was continued but later improved by the motorization of the wagon.

Achieving mass marketing embraced a host of procedures beyond

the assumption and systematic organization of the wholesaling function. Among corollary activities were greater efforts to expand sales
of by-products (lubricants, gas oil, fuel oil, gasoline, and paraffin wax),
the use of inherited and new brand names and trade-marks, and buying
out rather than fighting out competitors. Other methods included
increased use of packaging and a gradual expansion of advertising.
Three techniques of Standard Oil marketers, though not unique to
their operations, elicited widespread criticism and legal action—making arrangements for the lowest possible railroad transport costs allowed by the letter of the law, watching the activities of competitors
and compiling statistics on sales, and utilizing hidden companies, a
practice which they discontinued in 1904 in the United States.

As to price policy, instead of always "cutting to kill" as Miss Tarbell
inferred, the combination usually, though not always, was "last down
and first up." This normal behavior of the leader was accompanied
by variations in price levels according to the remoteness of areas and
volume of sales. An observing competitor, T. B. Westgate, testified in
1899: "If I sell a limited amount of oil, very limited, say a tenth of the
consumption in Syracuse, there are nine chances in ten that the prices
will not be cut [by Standard Oil]. But it is different if I attempt to get
one-third or one-half of the trade, as I did have in Auburn." [5] Throughout the years to 1911 Standard Oil units actually maintained a price
umbrella, though a relatively low one, which, in conjunction with the
development of new producing areas, resulted in a slow, steady growth
of competition and a decline in the combination's share of the market,
a trend quite noticeable before 1911.

In export trade Standard Oil executives gradually adapted their
American techniques to foreign markets. When Jersey Standard was
created, the combination's products going abroad were sold to outside
exporters or to local representatives of foreign merchants. In order
to expand foreign sales and to hold markets against foreign competition led by the Nobels and the Rothschilds, Standard Oil men began
to organize their own marketing outlets in Europe in 1888 and to
establish their own bulk stations in the Far East five years later. As
Royal Dutch and the Shell Transport and Trading Company rose to
strong competitive positions during the late nineties, Standard Oil
sought producing properties abroad with a view to establishing integrated operations on a regional or national basis. Aided by govern-

---

[5] *Industrial Commission, Preliminary Report on Trusts and Industrial Combinations* (Washington, D. C., 1900), I, 367.

Large-Scale Organization 423

ments, competitors succeeded in barring Standard Oil from production in the Netherlands East Indies and Burma. The creation of an integrated enterprise in Japan (1900–1907) proved a financial failure. In Rumania and Canada integrated businesses succeeded on a small scale and stayed in the Jersey Standard fold after 1911. Henry Clay Pierce through Standard Oil's Missouri affiliate, the Waters-Pierce Oil Company, also developed producing, manufacturing, and marketing operations in Mexico, but that connection was lost to the Jersey Company through separation in 1911. National customs, mores, regulations, legislation, and administration caused the establishment of a remarkably varied pattern in Standard Oil operations abroad and the variety persists in a large measure even today.

Expansion of all Standard Oil operations after 1881 was financed within the combination. Rockefeller and his associates resorted to banks for a few short-term loans in the early 1880's, but by the latter half of that decade the organization had surplus funds to put into the call-loan market. Funds for expansion came out of earnings, in relation to which dividends were kept low. Since expenditures of $5,000 or more were referred to the Executive Committee for approval, the flow of funds and the early development of accounting and auditing made for a planned growth of the Standard Oil combination.

Probably the greatest error in the financial policy and public relations of Jersey Standard between 1899 and 1911 was the failure to change the capitalization as earnings were plowed back and net worth of the business rose. Both earnings and dividends thereby appeared to be excessively high in relation to outstanding capital stock, a point seized upon by counsel for the Federal Government in the dissolution suit and weighted heavily by the judges in rendering their decision to break up the combination.

This essay is consciously an extremely general analysis of the evolution of the managerial concepts, organizational patterns, and operating policies of the Standard Oil Company (New Jersey) and its parent, the Standard Oil Trust. Substantiation of all points and a portrayal of additional policies—on employee relations and public relations, to cite two examples—may be found in the forthcoming volume on the history of Jersey Standard from 1882 to 1911. Frictions in working out policies and mistakes in decisions also receive attention. Developments and modification of early practices may be followed in the second and third volumes of the series. It is hoped that enough data have been presented herein to suggest that, although many of the contributions of Standard

                          Ralph W. Hidy

Oil men to the almost innumerable techniques of large-scale petroleum enterprise in the United States were obviously not unique, the success with which they created and systematically managed an integrated business catering to a world market was revolutionary in scope and in long-term socioeconomic significance. Privately, the executives of the combination regarded themselves, to quote from one of their letters in 1889, as builders of "the greatest commercial organization of modern times." [6]

RALPH W. HIDY, *New York University*

[6] Rockefeller Records, W. P. Thompson to J. D. Rockefeller, June 14, 1889.

[14]

By William Graebner
ASSISTANT PROFESSOR OF HISTORY
STATE UNIVERSITY COLLEGE
FREDONIA, N.Y.

Great Expectations: The Search for Order in Bituminous Coal, 1890-1917*

❡ *Arguing that the American bituminous coal industry suffered from "excessive competition," this study traces the industry's repeated failures to control output or prices, whether by various kinds of trade associations, mergers, or by attempts to secure government sanctions for cooperation. Although an over-zealous Department of Justice must bear some responsibility for the industry's "sick" condition, Professor Graebner concludes, the fundamental problem lay in the basic economic conditions in the industry.*

Between 1890 and 1917 the American bituminous coal industry experienced rapid growth, largely in response to exceptional demands for industrial and domestic steam coals and coking coals to service the iron and steel industry. Stagnant in the early years of the 1890s, bituminous production doubled between 1894 and 1901 and doubled again by 1912. In 1918 some 579,000,000 short tons were produced, a figure not reached again until 1942.[1] But in the midst of this expansion, conditions in the coal trade were widely regarded — by operators, miners and their unions, engineers, scientists, and government officials — as wasteful, inefficient, excessively competitive, and insufficiently profitable.[2] Operator attorney D. W. Kuhn said: "Among the Falstaff army of industries of this country, too poor to fight, too cowardly or too virtuous to steal, the coal mining industry presents itself as one of the most bedraggled members of these ragged recruits."[3] The military analogy also seemed

Business History Review, Vol. XLVIII, No. 1 (Spring, 1973). Copyright © The President and Fellows of Harvard College.
* The author wishes to thank the Research Foundation of the State University of New York for financial support in conducting the research for this study.

[1] U.S. Bureau of the Census, *Historical Statistics of the United States, Colonial Times to 1957* (Washington, D.C., 1960), 356.

[2] *United Mine Workers Journal*, May 12, 1910, 4, and May 20, 1910, 4; American Mining Congress, *Proceedings of the Thirteenth Annual Session*, XIII (1910), 225; clipping from *Nation's Business*, April 15, 1913, 12, found in United States Bureau of Mines, Records, Record Group 70, National Record Center, Suitland, Maryland, box 55; and H. M. Chance, "A New Method for Working Deep-Coal Beds," *Transactions* of the American Institute of Mining Engineers, XXX (February–September, 1900), 287.

[3] D. W. Kuhn, "Sherman Anti-Trust Law with Special Reference to the Coal Mining Industry," *AMC Proceedings*, XIV (1911), 264.

appropriate to Pennsylvania's Chief Mine Inspector, James Roderick. "The rapid growth of the industry," he said, "has prevented systematic development and today the operators constitute a great army of antagonistic elements and unorganized forces . . . they continue to indulge in a cut-throat war-fare." [4] As one public official commented, "the old idea of a coal baron is a myth." [5]

These subjective evaluations were based on fact. In most major coal markets east of the Mississippi, coals from several states were in competition. Pennsylvania, West Virginia, and Ohio coals moved by rail and lake steamer to the distribution and consumption centers of Chicago, Milwaukee, and Duluth-Superior, where they were competitively priced with lower-grade coals produced in Illinois and Indiana. Kentucky coals shipped north became significant market influences in every midwestern state from Ohio to Minnesota. The nation's two largest producers after 1910, Pennsylvania and West Virginia, effectively dominated the coal trade in the eastern tidewater, in select western markets like Cincinnati, and in one particular product market, coke. Seldom did Illinois and Indiana coals enter these or other eastern markets.[6] This interstate competition reflected the wide availability of coal and the labor to mine it, the relatively low capital requirements for its development, and the ease with which one coal (or an alternative energy source) could be substituted for another. The result was a low-profit industry with chronic and growing excess capacity and an extremely low level of concentration. The bituminous coal industry had its large firms, but none had significant market power beyond the local marketing area.[7]

From 1890 to 1917 coal operators, like businessmen in cotton textiles, agriculture, steel, and other industries, attempted to deal individually and cooperatively with the problems posed by excessive

[4] Commonwealth of Pennsylvania, *Report of the Department of Mines of Pennsylvania, Part II — Bituminous, 1910* (Harrisburg, 1911), 4.
[5] Herbert M. Wilson, "Safety Measures in the Bituminous Coal Mines of Western Pennsylvania," National Safety Council *Proceedings*, I (1912), 116. Wilson was with the U.S. Bureau of Mines.
[6] U.S. Department of the Interior, Geological Survey, *Mineral Resources of the United States, 1915, Part II — Nonmetals* (Washington, D.C., 1917), 487–492; *ibid.*, 1910, 32–33; E. L. Moran, "The Coal Traffic of the Great Lakes," *Journal of Geography*, XV (January, 1917), 150–159; *Coal Trade*, 1896, 58, and *ibid.*, 1911, 102; West Virginia, *Annual Report of the Department of Mines for the Year Ending June 30, 1910* (Charleston, 1911), 81–87; International Commerce, *Coal Trade of the U.S.*, 1900, 2853–2865.
[7] Walton H. Hamilton and Helen R. Wright, *The Case of Bituminous Coal* (New York, 1925), 56–57; U.S. Department of Commerce, Bureau of the Census, *Thirteenth Census of the United States*, Volume XI, *Mines and Quarries* (1909), *General Report and Analysis* (Washington, D.C., 1913), 204–231; *Twenty-Ninth Annual Coal Report of the Illinois Bureau of Labor Statistics, 1910* (Springfield, Ill., 1911), 1–2; and *Black Diamond*, XLVIII (January 6, 1912), 24. The lack of uniform accounting practices would make an accounting determination of profits virtually impossible before 1917 or 1918. This essay accepts the contemporary view that profits were low, a logical consequence of the industry's industrial and market structure.

competition; they tried to bring order to the chaos of competition that was the coal industry. Few of the cures had much effect; some made the patient worse, and none went to the source of the illness. Real progress became possible only after 1912, when the industry turned in earnest to the national government. Five years later it was clear that although the search had taken some new forms under the aegis of politics, operator expectations had not been fulfilled. For all its efforts, the industry of 1917 looked much the same as it had some thirty years earlier; only the mechanism for change — politics — was well established. Coal's search for order had been frustrating and essentially futile.[8]

The coal industry's most common response to disorder, logical for the firm but self-defeating on an industry-wide basis, was to attempt to cut costs of production and distribution or to prevent them from increasing. Concern with labor costs in part explains the rapid mechanization of the industry after 1900 and the operators' efforts to prevent unionization in the 1890s. Enthusiasm for cost-cutting also led to waste of natural and human resources and resistance to cost-increasing innovations such as state safety legislation.[9]

Just as ineffective as cost-cutting was the trade's effort to find foreign markets to absorb surplus output. The export movement, led by the American Consular Service and occasionally promoted by the journals of the coal trade, interested few operators. A 1908 trade association report suggesting that coal operators viewed the export market as a "safety valve . . . at a time when the demand in the home market may be slow," was wishful thinking or propaganda.[10] Aside from export surges in 1899–1900 and 1911–1913, shipments abroad, largely to Canada, Mexico, and Cuba, grew very slowly. Nor was a major proportion of total production exported during this period. In 1898 only 1.8 per cent of total bituminous production found its way abroad; by 1915 that had increased to a still unimpressive 4.2 per cent. It was not uncommon for European and South American consuls to report available but unexploited markets, and in 1911 *Coal and Coke Operator* speculated that the

[8] The title is, of course, from Robert H. Wiebe, *The Search for Order, 1877–1920* (New York, 1967). Wiebe's use of the term is much broader than its use here, but it includes industrial organization. For another discussion of the problem of order and organization, see Louis Galambos, "The Emerging Organizational Synthesis in Modern American History," *Business History Review,* XLIV (Autumn, 1970), 279-290.

[9] The word "waste" is not intended here to have a timeless economic meaning; it is conceivable that the use operators made of productive factors was economically viable, even in the long run. For an interesting statement of the problem, see Warren C. Scoville, "Did Colonial Farmers 'Waste' Our Land?" *Southern Economic Journal,* XX (October, 1953), 178–181.

[10] *A Report to the Bituminous Coal Trade Association on the Present and Future of the Bituminous Coal Trade, 1908* (n.p., 1908), 11.

BITUMINOUS COAL, 1890–1917   51

foreign market could not serve as an outlet for surplus production because "we have no ships to carry it at a transportation rate that would enable us to meet the competition from European countries, Australia, and Japan."[11] While the coal industry could not help but participate in the national interest in foreign markets, there is no evidence that operators saw foreign markets as an industry panacea. They correctly perceived that the "Open Door" was largely irrelevant to an industry with chronic overcapacity and virtually unlimited productive potential.[12]

Cost-cutting and the search for markets placed coal operators within the traditional framework of competition. In these years, however, the operators began to move beyond this framework toward solutions which minimized competition. Of great appeal for many operators was the attempt to equalize costs of production and distribution over a competitive geographical area. When state legislation was a factor in increasing the cost of production, operators interested in cost equalization tried to insure that legislative increments to cost were roughly equivalent in competitive regions or states. The mechanism was uniform state legislation, pursued in matters of safety and accident compensation and a favorite project of Illinois operators who saw their marketing region invaded by eastern operators with lower production costs. Working with the National Civic Federation and other groups, the American Mining Congress achieved virtual uniformity in workmen's compensation legislation by about 1916; in that year, however, the movement for uniform state legislation was hopelessly stalled by the failure of Ohio and West Virginia representatives to participate in the Uniform Mining Laws Conference.[13]

A similar but more potent mechanism — national rather than uniform state legislation — was used to stabilize and equalize transportation costs. As Joseph Lambie has demonstrated, coal producers and the railroads serving them were both interested in

[11] XII (January 26, 1911), 62.

[12] Export statistics are computed from *Historical Statistics of the United States*, 356; *Coal Trade Bulletin*, XV (June 1, 1906), 35, and (August 1, 1906), 53; *Coal Trade Journal*, XXXV (September 16, 1896), 531, and XXXVIII (April 26, 1899), 217; *Black Diamond*, XXII (March 11, 1899), 267. On the Open Door idea, see William Appleman Williams, *The Tragedy of American Diplomacy* (New York, 1959); Martin J. Sklar, "Woodrow Wilson and the Political Economy of Modern United States Liberalism," *Studies on the Left*, I (Fall 1960), reprinted in James Weinstein and David W. Eakins, eds., *For a New America* (New York, 1970), 46–100; and Thomas J. McCormick, *China Market* (Chicago, 1967).

[13] *Report of the Uniform Mining Laws Conference*, Chicago, Illinois, November 13, 14, 15, 1916 (Springfield, Ill., n.d.); James Weinstein, "Big Business and the Origins of Workmen's Compensation," *Labor History*, VIII (Spring, 1967), 156–174; American Mining Congress, *Proceedings*, XIX (1916), 157–158. The U.S. Bureau of Mines was created in 1910 partly to provide a scientific underpinning for uniform legislation. See William Sievers Graebner, "Coal Mining Safety: National Solutions in the Progressive Period" (Ph.D. dissertation, University of Illinois at Urbana-Champaign, 1970), 67.

maintaining volume and prices. Price-cutting initiated through cutthroat rail competition was just as harmful to coal operators as self-initiated cutting, and before 1900 it was a regular feature of transportation into competitive markets like Cincinnati, Chicago, and the eastern tidewater.[14] The carriers' inability to maintain rates rendered futile attempts to fix prices and production such as that mounted in 1887 by the Seaboard Steam Coal Association for the tidewater trade. When the railroads moved beyond self-regulation to government regulation with the Elkins and Hepburn Acts, competition was not eliminated, only reduced through bureaucratization. Regional coal operators' associations continually sought redress from unfair competition at the offices of the Interstate Commerce Commission.[15] Most common were requests for rate adjustments from central Pennsylvania coal operators, who faced stiff Virginia and West Virginia competition in New England, and from Ohio producers who were fighting a losing battle to control the coal trade in their own state and to keep their share of the traffic on the Great Lakes. And, although the Interstate Commerce Commission denied having the authority or the intent to maintain inter-regional competition, that, rather than a diminution of the competition, appears to have been the overall impact of federal regulation.[16]

Cost equalization also played a minor though significant role in the epic struggle between operators and miners over unionization. Labor costs, some 75 per cent of production costs, were a critical element in a region's competitive ability; the disabilities of Illinois, Indiana, Ohio, and sections of Pennsylvania can in part be traced to the intimidating non-union competition of West Virginia, which survived the 1897 union drive untouched. Since one of its major goals was to raise wages and thus production costs, the union was, in one sense, the universal adversary. Non-union operators in West Virginia believed in the existence of a conspiracy of Illinois, Indiana, Pennsylvania, and Ohio operators to unionize the state; a 1912 governor-commissioned report found West Virginia operators "within their rights in declining to recognize a union which would place them in a helpless minority when joined to those of the four

---

[14] Joseph T. Lambie, *From Mine to Market: The History of Coal Transportation on the Norfolk and Western Railway* (New York, 1954), 59; U.S. House of Representatives, *Report on Discriminations and Monopolies in Coal and Oil*, Interstate Commerce Commission, H. Doc. 561, 50th Cong., 2d Sess., 1907.

[15] Lambie, 87ff., 180ff., 189–190; Gabriel Kolko, *Railroads and Regulation, 1877–1916* (New York, 1965), 94ff.

[16] *Coal Trade*, 1911, 22, 60, and *ibid.*, 1910, 33; *Mineral Resources, 1915, Part II*, 191–192 and 406; *Twenty-Fourth Annual Report of the Chief Inspector of Mines, To the Governor of the State of Ohio, for the Year 1898* (Columbus, Ohio, 1890), 9, 22–23, 303; *ibid.*, 1909, 5, and *ibid.*, 1912, 64.

competitive States." [17] In the regions participating in the Interstate
Joint Conference, there were frequent complaints that mining rates
were not uniformly drawn. Ohio operators threatened to walk out
of the Joint Conference in 1910, a threat Illinois operators had
carried out two years earlier. [18]

In another sense, however, the union was not an adversary but a
mechanism for internal adjustment in the industry. Herman Justi,
Commissioner of the Illinois Coal Operators' Association, said as
much in his testimony to the U.S. Industrial Commission in 1901: [19]

> Severe as we find competition to-day in the bituminous coal field it has
> its limitations which it did not have before. The reason for this is plain.
> Relatively speaking, every operator in the bituminous field pays the same
> scale of wages and is governed by the same mining conditions. As the
> miner pays no rebates, each operator knows substantially what it costs his
> rival to produce coal, and hence the selling price is more nearly uniform.

When wages were not the subject of formal collective bargaining
procedures, they were sometimes equalized locally through informal operator agreements. Wage fixing and price fixing were
intimately related. In Iowa, for example, operators agreed on a
wage scale at the same meeting at which they fixed prices. In
Illinois in 1898, the union settlement led to an operator organization
designed to fix selling prices. "This action," said the *Coal Trade
Journal*, "has been forced upon the operators by the drift of
circumstances. It is the natural sequence of the uniform mining
scale." [20] The unionization of much of the bituminous industry in
1897 should be seen not only as the consequence of a victory of
miners over operators, but as the result of a conscious decision on
the part of farsighted operators to use the union to equalize an
important cost of production. Even those operators who had
strongly opposed the union could see that once their mines were
unionized, they would remain at a disadvantage until competitive
mines were also brought under union control. Although the primary
union-operator relationship was and continued to be one of conflict, a secondary relationship found the two sides in rough agree-

[17] *Coal and Coke Operator*, XV (December 12, 1912), 369; *Coal and Coke Operator
and The Fuel Magazine*, XXI (September 25, 1913), 486.
[18] *Coal and Coke Operator*, X (February 17, 1910), 107; letter A. J. Moorshead, Madison Coal Corporation, to T. L. Lewis, President, United Mine Workers of America (April
9, 1908), in Edward A. Wieck Papers, Archives of Labor History and Urban Affairs, Wayne
State University, Detroit, Michigan, box 1, book 3. The Interstate Joint Conference was
the bargaining forum for miners and operators.
[19] U.S. House of Representatives, Industrial Commission, *Report on the Relations and
Conditions of Capital and Labor Employed in the Mining Industry*, XIII (Washington,
1901), 678.
[20] *Coal Trade Journal*, XXXVII (March 23, 1898), 157, and XXXV (September 2,
1896), 502.

ment on the economic problems of the coal industry. For a time this produced labor-management agreement on solutions as well, most notably a 1915 consensus that the Sherman Act was harmful insofar as it was interpreted to prevent trade agreements fixing the selling price of coal. In short, as early as 1897 labor was in a small way integrated into the coal industry's scheme of things and had adopted the major assumptions of the search for order.[21]

The culmination of this effort to bring order to the industry by stabilizing labor conditions came in 1912 with an abortive attempt to establish a national association of operators. No such organization would have been necessary had the joint conference functioned satisfactorily, but the efficiency of that body had been seriously impaired by the periodic absence of key groups of operators. Impetus for the new organization came from Illinois, the state which had earlier separated from the joint conference but which now found its competitive position eroding. Illinois, said Chicago's *Black Diamond*, "was pleading for some united action that would bring a harmonious result in the various states. She wanted to end the practice of the miners of dividing the operators into groups and whipping them piecemeal." [22]

Not long after negotiations began in 1909, it became clear that not all operators saw Illinois' suggestion of a national organization as benign. A. B. Fleming, former Governor of West Virginia and president of the mammoth Fairmont Coal Company, expressed the viewpoint of most West Virginia operators. "It seems to me," he said, "that it would be impossible for our West Virginia Association to become a member unless we intend to 'unionize' and recognize the United Mine Workers, as I suppose all will do who join the

---

[21] Letter John P. White, UMWA President, to Charles S. Keith, President, Central Coal and Coke Co., Kansas City, Mo. (September 20, 1915), in Federal Trade Commission, General Correspondence, 1914-1921, Record Group 122, National Archives, Washington, D.C., box 44, file 8149-13; letter T. L. Lewis to editor, *Pittsburgh Daily Headlight* (March 10, 1911), in Wieck Papers, box 16, book 3; Robert H. Harlan, "Is Uniform Mining Legislation Advisable?" *AMC Proceedings*, XIX (1916), 600-601; speech of William B. Wilson, in UMWA District 2 *Proceedings*, March 25, 1908 session (1908), 76-77; *United Mine Workers Journal*, October 28, 1915, 4, and November 4, 1915, 4; and U.S. House of Representatives, *Hearings Before the Committee on Mines and Mining, To Consider the Question of the Establishment of a Bureau of Mines*, 1908 (Washington, D.C., 1908), 32-33.

On the integration of labor into the corporate order, the place to begin is Ronald Radosh, "The Corporate Ideology of American Labor Leaders from Gompers to Hillman," *Studies on the Left*, VI (November–December, 1966), 66-88, and the comment on that piece by Philip S. Foner in the same issue, 89-96. David Brody briefly considers the problem in "Labor and the Great Depression: The Interpretative Prospects," *Labor History*, XIII (Spring, 1972), 231-244. Melvyn Dubofsky makes the argument in *When Workers Organize: New York City in the Progressive Era* (Amherst, Mass., 1968), 44. The above analysis is intended to supplement, not replace the more traditional views; it recognizes that the essence of labor-management relations (at least in this period) was conflict. Radosh goes considerably further, but then he was dealing with Samuel Gompers and the AF of L, not the United Mine Workers.

[22] *Black Diamond*, XLVIII (January 27, 1912), 35.

National Association."[23] Pittsburgh district operators, essential to the organization's success, also proved unwilling; they viewed the Illinois proposition as an attempt to impose costly western mining conditions on the eastern states. Like Ohio operators, they were incapable of assuming a leadership role or even of unified action. At a time when the coal trade needed a "Moses to lead it out of the wilderness of doubt and uncertainty to a land of steadiness and profit," Ohio operators required three associations to harbor their divisions, and Pittsburgh district producers could only "lag behind quarrel and fuss and fume, spit fire and hiss at each other like cats and dogs."[24] West Virginia, Ohio, and Pittsburgh remained out of the organizing meetings of the association, leaving Kentucky as the only participating state east of Indiana. These omissions were fatal. The American Federation of Coal Operators remained a regional, rather than a national association, and as such it was incapable of contributing much to the industry's search for stability.[25]

Cost equalization — whether through uniform state legislation, federal legislation, or unionization — was only one element in the coal industry's master plan for industrial reform. The heart of that plan was cooperation between coal operators, and its method (before 1899 at any rate) was the trade association. A great many of the associations serving the coal industry in the depression decade of the 1890s had no direct connection with trade conditions and were concerned with safety, education, or labor relations. The trade-oriented units were of two basic types. The more common type was the simple agreement to maintain prices among producers from a particular region or selling in a particular market. The price fixing agreement was generally considered inferior to the second type, the joint sales agency, under which producers agreed to sell their output through (or to) one sales agency at or above an established minimum price.

What was probably the first joint sales agency, the Coal Producers' Contract, was established in the Pocahontas region of West Virginia in 1886 to sell that area's output at tidewater. Oper-

[23] Letter Fleming to Neil Robinson (December 31, 1909), in Aretas Brooks Fleming Papers, West Virginia University Library, Morgantown, West Virginia, box August–December 1909; *Coal and Coke Operator,* XIII (December 14, 1911), 388.
[24] *Coal and Coke Operator,* XIII (August 10, 1911), 91; XIV (January 11, 1912), 24; XIV (January 18, 1912), 37; and XII (January 26, 1911), 60; *Coal and Coke Operator and Fuel,* XXI (May 15, 1913), 66; (May 8, 1913), 35.
[25] *Coal and Coke Operator,* XIII (December 14, 1911), 381; Arthur E. Suffern, *The Coal Miners' Struggle for Industrial Status* (New York, 1926), 168–170, and Suffern, *Conciliation and Arbitration in the Coal Industry of America* (Boston, 1915), 128–134. The stated objective of the association was to "promote the common interests of the coal operators of America by all lawful means; but the Federation shall not deal with matters relating to freight rates, prices or sale of coal."

ators received the average price of all the coal sold through the agency. After 1890 the sales agency was a common, though usually transient feature of other coal fields. By 1892 demoralized conditions had spawned talk of a huge company to buy and sell the entire ouput of the Hocking Valley, Ohio, coal mines. Like Ohio associations to follow, it fell apart when major operators, reluctant to submerge their identities and sensing benefits in railroad car distribution from remaining outside, refused to participate. When the object of the selling agreement was isolated to a particular market, the chances of success were better. Hocking operators apparently managed to coalesce for the purpose of marketing in the Chicago area. That city was also the target of the Northern Coal Association, selling out of Streator, Illinois, and the Brazil Coal Company, which sold most of the output of the Indiana Block district after 1896. Another highly competitive market, Cincinnati, was the focus of a West Virginia agency designed to eliminate price competition between producers in that state's Kanawha and New River regions. For varying periods, operators in the Indiana territory, the Jellico district of Tennessee, the Connellsville coke region of Pennsylvania, and the Mystic Block and Walnut Block areas of Iowa marketed all or much of their coal through one seller. Selling agencies appear to have been limited to producers in one state and usually to a region producing a single type of coal.[26]

Like the selling agencies, price fixing associations were widely used throughout the coal fields and were usually aimed at particular markets and distribution centers, notably Chicago, Cincinnati, the lake ports, and the eastern tidewater. Several were especially successful, including the American Coal Operators Association, which had some influence over coal prices in the Hocking Valley from 1892 to 1897. Perhaps because the commitment was a lesser one, interstate price agreements were more common than interstate selling agencies. One impressive interstate group was the Southern Coal Association, formed in 1895 of nearly all the leading operators in Tennessee, Alabama, and Kentucky and including nine coal producing districts and some eighty companies. Interstate arrangements were worked out among Virginia, West

[26] Lambie, 48; *Coal Trade Journal*, XXXI (December 7, 1892), 583; (December 14, 1892), 591; XXXII (January 4, 1893), 2; (January 11, 1893), 23; (February 15, 1893), 95; XXXIII (October 24, 1894), 780; XXXIV (September 25, 1895), 725; XXXVI (June 16, 1897), 309; *Black Diamond*, XXII (March 18, 1899), 300; *Coal and Coke Operator*, XI (November 24, 1910), 757; memorandum by U.S. Attorney on New River and Pocahontas Arrangement (January 31, 1917), in Department of Justice Central Files, Classified Subject Files, Correspondence, Record Group 60, National Archives, Washington, D.C., box 607, file 60–187–16 (these records are hereinafter referred to as DJ-CS); and letter C. P. McKenzie to James R. Garfield (January 25, 1907), in Bureau of Corporations Records, Record Group 122, National Archives, Washington, D.C., box 198, file 4439–9.

Virginia, and Pennsylvania operators serving Cincinnati in 1895 and in the Ohio-Pittsburgh district in 1896.[27]

Occasionally operators combined with dealers to fix prices in local markets. Usually, however, dealer associations were restricted to retailers, and when that was the case they did little to stabilize the trade on the production level. Indeed, these "local coal barons" sometimes engaged in buying-price agreements under which re-tailers and jobbers agreed to hold the selling price of coal at the mine as close as possible to the cost of production. As a result, said the *United Mine Workers Journal* in 1915, "many of our best friends among the operators are being forced to the wall."[28]

Price fixing associations and sales agencies multiplied rapidly during the 1893 depression and, in spite of ongoing declines in production and prices, there was some optimism among producers. Following the formation of several associations in the spring and summer of 1895, the *Coal Trade Journal* commented: "Observant men in the coal trade think they discern in these associations, proof of a drift toward conditions which might make it possible to bring soft coal under a control as concentrated as that dominating Anthracite."[29]

This sanguine view proved unfounded. From the beginning, coal trade associations were neither easy to form nor easy to keep together. The Southern Coal Association was troubled first by Tennessee operators who were in the association but insisted on competing with each other regardless of the fixed schedule of prices and grades, then by Alabama members who threatened to resign. The Indiana Block Coal Company, a sales agency, had to close its doors when important operators refused to join. Operators attempting to maintain association prices in the face of undercutting sustained heavy losses. Certain companies, the M. A. Hanna Coal Co. in the Pittsburgh district, for example, acquired reputations for price cutting, and a major operator in the central Pennsylvania region, Edward J. Berwind, reportedly "would never join any

---

[27] *Coal Trade Journal,* XXXII (February 15, 1893), 104; XXXIV (August 28, 1895), 627; (February 6, 1895), 101; (July 31, 1895), 564; (August 7, 1895), 573; (August 21, 1895), 615; XXXV (January 22, 1896), 46; (March 25, 1896), 178. For an account of the Seaboard Steam Coal Association, see Lambie, 87–110.

[28] October 7, 1915, 4; letter F. P. Carey, Clearfield, Iowa, to George B. Cortelyou (March 25, 1903), Bureau of Corporations Records, file 0–40–31; clipping from *San Francisco Chronicle* enclosed in letter F. A. Lacey to James R. Garfield (September 23, 1907), Bureau of Corporations Records, box 598, file 4439–14; *Coal Trade Journal,* XXXI (April 6, 1892), 185; *Coal and Coke Operator,* XIV (April 4, 1912), 224; *Coal and Coke,* IX (August 1, 1902), 18; and file 60–187–9 in DJ–CS, box 606. Retailers were also organized regionally and nationally, but beyond the local level their economic functions were increasingly restricted. KoKoal, the national retail organization, was largely a social institution.

[29] XXXIV (October 9, 1895), 758.

operators association, holding that they were all right for the ordinary operator but were beneath his dignity." [30] Such intra-regional differences produced situations such as that in the Pittsburgh district in 1898, when three different associations existed, "all having purposes in some instances radically different from the others." [31] If an association managed to survive internal strains, it might succumb to the interregional assaults of the Pittsburgh operators or non-union West Virginia.[32]

By 1900, moreover, the whole climate for price fixing and sales associations had noticeably soured. The return to normal trade conditions exacerbated centrifugal tendencies as operators found the associations less necessary. The near-lethal blow, however, was delivered by the national government with the prosecution and conviction in 1899 of the New River Consolidated Coal and Coke Company, organized to sell the output of the New River and Kanawha fields. The government case emphasized the destruction of competition through a minimum selling price, and the company was held to be a combination in restraint of trade under the Sherman Act. This decision was in line with the Supreme Court's new and profound hostility to any limitations on competition. Some associations continued to exist, but only because the Justice Department was remarkably inactive.[33]

By 1900 it was clear that price fixing and sales associations were no longer appropriate solutions to the problems of the coal industry. Legal liabilities aside, they had failed to bring significant structural change to the coal markets. Although operators continued to experiment with these organizational forms, the new century found the industry looking for a solution through a new mechanism, corporate consolidation. The first significant merger movement in the history of the bituminous coal industry began in 1898 or soon afterwards in most of the major coal producing regions and continued with some intensity until after 1910. Despite frequent claims that efficiency was the great motivator, consolidations were designed, like the associations before them, to achieve price stability and

[30] W. P. Tams, Jr., *The Smokeless Coal Fields of West Virginia* (Morgantown, 1963), 78; *Coal Trade Journal*, XXXV (January 22, 1896), 46; (June 10, 1896), 339; XXXVI (February 17, 1897), 87; (June 16, 1897), 309.
[31] *Coal Trade Journal*, XXXVII (February 16, 1898), 92; and U.S. Industrial Commission, *Report*, XIII, 119.
[32] *Coal Trade Journal*, XXXVIII (January 11, 1899), 19; *Coal and Coke Operator*, XIV (April 11, 1912), 233. The few attempts to limit output failed.
[33] DJ-CS, box 617, file 60–187–94; *Black Diamond*, XXII (May 13, 1899), 520; James D. Norris, "The Missouri and Kansas Zinc Miners' Association, 1899–1905," *Business History Review*, XL (Autumn, 1966), 334; Henry R. Seager and Charles A. Gulick, Jr., *Trust and Corporation Problems* (New York, 1929), 94–95 and 383–384; William Letwin, *Law and Economic Policy in America: The Evolution of the Sherman Antitrust Act* (New York, 1964), chapters 4 and 5.

restrict competition.[34] By 1901, operators in the Pittsburgh district
had merged into two great operating companies. The Pittsburgh
Coal Co. controlled, through purchase, more than 100 mines (including the M. A. Hanna property) which shipped their product
by rail. To the south and east, the Monongahela River Consolidated
Coal and Coke Co. acquired all those properties shipping down the
Monongahela River through the city of Pittsburgh. Coke making
was relatively concentrated as early as 1895, when the H. C. Frick
Co. owned two-thirds of the ovens in the world famous Connellsville
region. Although the Frick company continued to add to its oven
holdings, the percentage of ownership changed little. Merger of
merchant coke companies, producing for a market rather than captive producers for the steel industry like Frick, began in 1910.[35]
Consolidation in West Virginia began in 1901, when coal properties
in the state's northern counties were brought together under the
Fairmont Coal Co. Two years later controlling shares in the Fairmont company and the Clarksburg Fuel Co., itself a major combination, were purchased by Consolidation Coal Co., an operating
firm organized in 1860. By 1909, Consolidation mined coal in Maryland, West Virginia, and Pennsylvania and was producing almost
2 per cent of the total national production of bituminous coal. Major
consolidation also took place in the state's Pocahontas field in 1900,
in the New River district in 1905, and in the Cabin Creek district
in 1907.[36]

To the west, operators also participated in the merger movement,
but with less enthusiasm and fewer results. Consolidation in Illinois
began early in the 1890s and culminated in the formation of a number of medium-sized corporations in 1905. Bridging the interstate
barrier was the Dering Co., with interests in two Illinois and three
Indiana counties. Ohio's equivalent was the 1905 merger of the
Continental Coal Co. and the Sunday Creek Coal Co., with the
product an interstate company with interests in West Virginia as

[34] This conclusion discounts the role of economies of scale (minimal in bituminous coal
production) and is in general agreement with the findings of Alfred S. Eichner in *The
Emergence of Oligopoly: Sugar Refining as a Case Study* (Baltimore, 1969). Unlike sugar
refining, however, the problems of the coal industry were precipitated in part by the trans-
portation-stimulated emergence of a national market. See Eichner, *Emergence*, 94, and
Joe S. Bain, "Industrial Concentration and Anti-Trust Policy," in Harold F. Williamson,
ed., *The Growth of the American Economy* (New York, 1951), 616–630.
[35] *Coal and Coke Operator*, X (June 9, 1910), 369; XI (November 24, 1910), 757;
(December 22, 1910), 840; XVI (April 3, 1913), 252; U.S. Industrial Commission, *Final
Report* (1902), 229–230; and *ibid.*, XIII (1901), 100–102; *Coal Trade Journal*, XXXII
(June 28, 1893), 400; XXXVIII (May 17, 1899), 255; (August 23, 1899), 438; *Mineral
Resources, 1900*, 274; 1905, p. 746; and 1915, 549; *Coal Trade*, 1896, 8; *Coal and Coke
Operator*, X (June 9, 1910), 369.
[36] *Coal Trade*, 1901, 39; memorandum, October 11, 1911, in Fleming Papers, box
September 1911–February 1912; Phil Conley, *History of the West Virginia Coal Industry*
(Charleston, W. Va., 1960), 98, 168, 221, 235; *Moody's Manual of Railroads and Corpora-
tion Securities, 1910* (New York, 1910).

well as the Buckeye State. Between 1909 and 1911 there was talk in the Midwest of a scheme to consolidate the region's coal mining properties into a series of district companies, operated by a parent company. U. S. Steel and Standard Oil were conceived as models, and, according to *Coal and Coke Operator*, J. P. Morgan was asked to undertake the task of reorganization. Morgan's field agents, however, brought back reports of the excessive prices operators wanted for their properties. Although Morgan's 1911 European trip may have included a personal look at the German coal syndicates, the trade lost interest in this grand scheme after 1912. The Supreme Court's 1911 decision in the Standard Oil Case was no doubt the critical element in the change of opinion.[37]

Consolidation did not produce stability. Even in the coke markets, with a relatively homogeneous product and a natural price leader in the Connellsville product, price maintenance proved impossible. In the Pittsburgh district, where concentration was carried the furthest, independents continued to be a factor and the two giants, rather than cooperating, invaded each other's markets. Pessimism in midwestern trade circles was aptly expressed by *Black Diamond*: "It is apparently impossible for any consolidation of bituminous coal mines which falls short of a monopoly, to effect any radical increase in the price of fuel to the consumer." [38]

Behind this failure lay the same economic realities — widely available resources, easily developed — which had rendered powerless the price fixing and sales associations of the previous decade. Those realities were now abetted by an uncertain political atmosphere. Although no coal merger was prosecuted under Theodore Roosevelt or William Taft, neither President was receptive when operators presented their economic analyses of the industry. Whatever its role in other areas of the economy, the Bureau of Corporations functioned as a funnel for an undercurrent of public opposition to concentration in the coal industry, referring complainants to the dynamic center of federal opposition to consolidation, the Department of Justice. More than once coal operators found Justice officials uncooperative. In 1910, lawyer D. W. Kuhn of the Pittsburgh-

---

[37] *Coal Trade Journal*, XXXVII (March 23, 1898), 157; Harry Mitchell Dixon, "The Illinois Coal Mining Industry" (Ph.D. dissertation, University of Illinois, 1951), 74, 96; *Mineral Resources*, 1905, 505–506; *Coal Trade Bulletin*, September 1, 1906, 45, and October 1, 1906, 27; *Ohio Mine Inspectors' Report*, 1909, 5–6; *Coal and Coke Operator*, XII (February 23, 1911), 128–129; (March 2, 1911), 142–143; XIII (September 21, 1911), 186. A plan similar to the midwestern one was mentioned for the Appalachian region. See *Coal and Coke Operator*, XI (October 6, 1910), 642. For statistics on bituminous mergers, see Ralph L. Nelson, *Merger Movements in American Industry, 1895–1956* (Princeton, 1959), 46, 62, and Appendices B and C.

[38] *Black Diamond*, XL (February 22, 1908), 17; *Coal and Coke Operator*, XV (July 11, 1912), 27; *Coal and Coke*, IX (January 1, 1902), 12–13, and (April 1, 1902), 8–9.

Westmoreland Coal Co. thought the antitrust climate sufficiently
threatening to warrant a letter to the Department of Justice. Kuhn
explained and justified a proposed consolidation of seven or eight
coal companies and requested assurance that Justice would not
prosecute the combination. The Department refused. The same
process took place in 1912 when the Pittsburgh Coal Co. sought
a merger with the Monongahela River Consolidated Coal and Coke
Co. Justice officials again would offer no advice and, upon receipt
of newspaper notice of the merger, sent agents into the Pittsburgh
district to conduct an inquiry. Little wonder that numerous operators saw the Sherman Act as the enemy of consolidation.[39]

The second post-1900 institution designed to confine competition
within reasonable bounds was the statistical trade association. Also
called open price associations, these organizations were based on
the assumption that operators who were fully knowledgeable about
prices, contracts, inventories, shipments, selling and production
costs, and other terms of the trade would be less likely to sell below
cost and more likely to maintain prices individually or by informal
agreement.[40] The idea was introduced into the coal industry in
1897, but before 1911 there was only one statistical association of
any importance. Established in February 1903, the Bituminous
Coal Trade Association served operators shipping east from eight
regions in Pennsylvania, West Virginia, Virginia, and Maryland.
"The Association," explained its chairman, L. N. Lovell, "cannot
take up individual questions of competition. . . . nor can there be
any agreements on prices. The latter is a matter prohibited by law
and, quite apart from that, always made inoperative by the exigen-
cies of business. But the members can meet, confer on the various
matters of mutual interests, and there is no law, statute or moral,
to prevent [it]." [41]

[39] *Black Diamond*, XLVIII (April 13, 1912), 18; letter John Mitchell to Joseph A.
Holmes (November 27, 1909), in John Mitchell Papers, Mullen Library, Catholic Uni-
versity, Washington, D.C., box A3–15, file 63; *The Independent*, LX (April 26, 1906),
991–992; letter U.S. Attorney, Topeka, Kansas, to Attorney General (April 10, 1912), in
DJ–CS, box 607, file 60–187–21; letter D. W. Kuhn to W. S. Kenyon, Assistant Attorney
General (April 28, 1910), *ibid.*, box 606, file 60–187–3; letter Cyrus E. Woods to George
W. Wickersham (February 3, 1912), *ibid.*, and Wickersham to Woods (February 8, 1912),
ibid.; letter J. F. Shotts to James R. Garfield (October 25, 1906), in Bureau of Corporations Records, box 598, file 4439–8; letter W. P. Atkins to Theodore Roosevelt (September
11, 1907), *ibid.*, file 4439–11; letter A. L. Brandenburg (January 20, 1909), *ibid.*, file
4439–18; *Coal and Coke Operator*, XV (July 11, 1912), 27; X (March 3, 1910), 137;
Glenn W. Traer, "Conservation in the Coal Industry, Protection of Life and Prevention
of Waste," AMC *Proceedings*, XI (1908), part 2, 161–163; and Letwin, *Law and
Economic Policy*, 240-266.
[40] Milton Nels Nelson, "Open Price Associations," *University of Illinois Studies in the
Social Sciences*, X (June, 1922), 9-10, 14–15; Seager and Gulick, 305, 318–319; and
Louis Galambos, *Competition and Cooperation: The Emergence of a National Trade Association* (Baltimore, 1966), 78–83.
[41] From the Report of the Annual Meeting of February 11, 1904, 4–5, copy in Bureau
of Corporations Records, file 5091-6; *Coal Trade Journal*, XXXVI (January 20, 1897), 29.

The coal industry participated in the national infatuation with such associations which began in 1911 and reached a peak about 1916. In coal, as elsewhere, the major reasons are clear. Most important, the industry's previous solutions to the problem of competition — sales agencies, price fixing associations, mergers — were now suspect. The case against mergers was simple; they completely failed to stabilize the industry. Sales agencies and price fixing associations, used extensively before 1900, had been on shaky legal ground since 1897 and particularly after Taft assumed the presidency. In November 1909, a committee of coal operators met with the President and asked for his cooperation in modifying the Sherman Act so that producers could " 'get together' and arrange for a price on bituminous coal at the mine." Taft, according to their report, "could see no escape from a continuance of the present system of vigorous competition." [42] All doubt concerning the administration position was dispelled the next spring, when Attorney General George W. Wickersham threatened a suit against a combination of New River and Pocahontas operators for price maintenance. With the U. S. Steel indictment in 1911, the administration placed the open price system itself under suspicion, and the election year found Justice Department agents investigating Pennsylvania merchant coke producers for uniform pricing based on uniform accounting systems. These actions insured Taft's alienation from the coal operators. One in particular, a prominent producer from the new Winding Gulf region of West Virginia, termed the President "unquestionably a stiff, with the judicial mind, who would sit still and let the country go to the devil while prosecuting every man and every concern in the country that had made good." [43]

The decreasing usefulness of mergers and price fixing made little difference between 1899 and 1909, years of growth in the coal industry. But when stagnation began in 1910, the statistical association took on increasing appeal as a new device for securing stability. Cautious because of the steel indictment and the new President, coal operators waited until May 1915. Then, with the industry in the depths of depression and reasonably sure that statistical associations would not be prosecuted, midwestern opera-

---

[42] Letter Holmes to Mitchell (no date), in Mitchell Papers, box A3-15, file 63.
[43] Letter Justus Collins to Isaac T. Mann (February 29, 1912), in Justus Collins Papers, West Virginia University Library, Morgantown, W. Va., series I, box 10, folder 67; *Coal and Coke Operator*, X (May 19, 1910), 314; (April 14, 1910), 236-237; XIII (September 28, 1911), 201; XV (July 11, 1912), 27; Robert H. Wiebe, *Businessmen and Reform: A Study of the Progressive Movement* (Chicago, 1968), 82-84; James Weinstein, *The Corporate Ideal in the Liberal State, 1900-1918* (Boston, 1968), 83-84 and 149-150; and James C. German, Jr., "The Taft Administration and the Sherman Antitrust Act," *Mid-America*, LIV (July 1972), 172-186.

tors took action, forming district statistical associations that eastern-
ers "first met with scorn, then disbelief." [44] Within eighteen months,
nearly every major producing district had its own association,
"co-operating with the sanction of the Federal Trade Commission
in the exchange of information." [45] The associations emphasized
their informational functions and denied any intent to fix the price
of coal. Since the numbers collected and dispensed by the associations were meaningless unless they represented comparable units,
the open price movement implied and encouraged uniform sizing
of coal and uniform cost accounting.[46]

The tone and performance of the Taft administration did a good
deal more than motivate coal operators to consider the statistical
association. In conjunction with the industry's ubiquitous economic
problems, it convinced the operators of the need to redefine the
government-industry relationship and make it predictable. Restive
even under Theodore Roosevelt, in 1908 coal producers joined with
the National Civic Federation and past and present Commissioners
of the Bureau of Corporations in ill-fated support of amendments
to the Sherman Act, predictably conceived to be restrictive, repressive, and partly responsible for the maintenance of destructive
competition.[47] Their efforts centered on the Hepburn bill, which
provided for the registration of corporations and associations with
the Commissioner of Corporations and gave him, with the concurrence of the Secretary of Commerce and Labor, the power to judge
whether contracts or combinations filed with the Bureau of Corporations were "reasonable." [48]

Between 1911 and 1914 the operators again sought to make the
federal government a full partner in the search for order and appealed once more for a legislative solution to the problem of exces-

[44] *Coal Trade*, 1916, 70; *Fuel Magazine*, XX (February 5, 1913), 7–8.
[45] Edward W. Parker, "Cooperation, Conservation and Competition in Coal," AMC
Proceedings, XIX (1916), 242; *Black Diamond*, LVI (January 1, 1916), 1; (June 17,
1916), 498.
[46] *Black Diamond*, LIV (March 13, 1915), 210–211; LVII (December 30, 1916),
578; letter Bulkley, Hauxhurst, Inglis, and Saeger, Attorneys, to Department of Justice
(May 24, 1916), in DJ-CS, box 607, file 60–187–13; typescript of address by Robert E.
Belt, FTC, delivered March 23, 1916, in FTC General Records, 1914–21, box 42, file
8140–2–8; American Mining Congress, *Proceedings*, XIX (1916) 78–83 and 186–192.
[47] *Report of the Pennsylvania Department of Mines*, 1909, iii; D. W. Kuhn, "Sherman
Anti-Trust Law with Special Reference to the Coal Mining Industry," AMC *Proceedings*,
XIV (1911), 259; *Coal and Coke Operator and Fuel*, XXI (October 23, 1913), 562;
Black Diamond, LII (April 18, 1914), 312; *Coal Age*, I (November 11, 1911), 143; and
Outlook, December 11, 1909, 797–798.
[48] Letter James R. Garfield to Henry Knox Smith (May 7, 1908), in James R. Garfield
Papers, Manuscript Division, U.S. Library of Congress, Washington, D.C., Office Files,
box 128; *Black Diamond*, XL (May 2, 1908), 17; *Coal and Coke Operator*, XI (October
6, 1910), 642; Gabriel Kolko, *The Triumph of Conservatism: A Reinterpretation of
American History, 1900–1916* (Chicago, 1967), 133–138; Wiebe, *Businessmen and Re-
form*, 80–81; Weinstein, *The Corporate Ideal in the Liberal State*, 77–82; and George
Cullom Davis, Jr., "The Federal Trade Commission: Promise and Practice in Regulating
Business, 1900–1929" (Ph.D. dissertation, University of Illinois, 1969), 16–17.

sive competition. They were united on one specific proposition — the need to transfer regulatory functions from the Department of Justice, which had "caused so much uncertainty [and] disturbance to orderly pursuit of business," to a commission.[49] One suggestion, which appealed to the more radical operators, was for a National Mining Commission with "universal and complete jurisdiction over the mining business." [50] Advocates of such a commission viewed trade agreements as essential but inadequate solutions to destructive competition. Illinois operator A. J. Moorshead, for example, envisioned a commission which would restrict the opening of new mines and equalize supply and demand. Nonetheless, the vast majority of operators, represented in the American Mining Congress, again found common ground with the National Civic Federation in advocating a general commission which would investigate contracts, trade agreements, and combinations, and determine their legal status under the Sherman Act, amended if possible. The commission proposed by the AMC and the NCF would have the crucial power of prior approval — power to determine conclusively the legality of industrial arrangements submitted by corporations. If the commissioners found an agreement to be an unreasonable restraint of trade, they could request the participants to discontinue their illegal activities. Only if they failed to do so within a reasonable period would prosecution result.[51]

Operators were in general agreement not only on the means to be used in achieving industrial recovery, but on ends as well. Basic to their vision was the district confederation, a natural response to American conditions and one which reflected the widely admired German syndicate structure.[52] Under trade agreements sanctioned by a commission, operators within one production district (e.g., Indiana-Illinois, Pittsburgh, eastern Kentucky-western West Virginia) might limit production or restrict the opening of new mines; "group" output in order to eliminate seasonal overproduction; or employ a central sales agency to raise the price of coal or to achieve distributive economies. Differences between operators arose largely

[49] *Coal and Coke Operator,* XVI (February 27, 1913); and Weinstein, *Corporate Ideal,* 82.
[50] AMC *Proceedings,* XIV (1911), 39–41; *Coal Age,* I (January 6, 1912), 433; *Coal and Coke Operator,* XIV (April 11, 1912), 235; and *Black Diamond,* XLVIII (April 13, 1912), 18.
[51] A. J. Moorshead, "Condition of the Bituminous Coal Industry," AMC *Proceedings,* XIV (1911), 251; AMC *Proceedings,* XIV (1911), 42 and 279; *Black Diamond,* XLVIII (June 1, 1912), 20; LII (April 18, 1914), 312; *Coal and Coke Operator,* XIV (May 2, 1912), 278–279; and *Coal and Coke Operator and Fuel,* XXII (December 25, 1913), 137–138.
[52] *Coal and Coke Operator,* XIII (September 28, 1911), 196; (November 2, 1911), 281; and *Coal Age,* I (May 18, 1912), 1049–1050.

over the question of pricing. Speaking before the Senate Interstate
Commerce Committee for the operators of Indiana, Walter S. Bogle
emphasized production and selling agreements and admitted they
would be of little value unless the result was some control over
price. He was willing to see the federal government decide what
constituted a reasonable price. Illinois operator Glenn Traer spoke
in favor of restraint of trade but claimed to draw the line at output
limitations or "arbitrary" control of prices. Admitting to the committee that he was "considerably at variance" with Bogle, Traer
suggested that district operators agree to operate only enough mines
to supply the trade. S. A. Taylor, representing the Pittsburgh Coal
Operators' Association but also president of the American Mining
Congress, did his best to emphasize possible economies of scale in
sales and marketing; still, it was clear that his conception included
control of supply, fixing of minimum selling prices, and the possibility of government regulation of prices. Industry spokesmen
were aware of the need for a radical restructuring of the industry
into a highly concentrated trade agreement oligopoly.[53]

Of the vocal members of the Senate Committee on Interstate
Commerce, only West Virginia's Clarence Watson, a coal operator,
showed much sympathy with the operators' recommendations or an
understanding of industry economics. Chairman Moses Clapp of
Minnesota traced industry difficulties to "poor business policy [in]
opening these mines in excess of the real demand for their product." [54] Albert Cummins of Iowa and Frank Brandegee of Connec-
ticut apparently could discern no difference between the coal industry and any other industry. Failing to recognize the problem
(excessive competition), the Senators could hardly countenance the
solution (the trade agreement). Nor could the committee conceive
of an industrial structure between perfect competition and monopoly. American Mining Congress lobbyist James Callbreath told of
a revealing exchange with Clapp. Clapp said: "When you will show
me how it is possible to lock the stable door and still have it closed,
or, having it closed, may at the same time have it open, I will understand how what you want can be accomplished." Callbreath
replied: "Between the stable and the garden is a plot of grass going
to waste and needing to be cropped. In the stable is a horse suffering
for want of this grass. I am going to put a halter on that horse, give
you the end of the halter-strap and allow you to supervise the

---

[53] U.S. Senate, Committee on Interstate Commerce, *Hearings Pursuant to Senate Resolution 98*, Vol. II, 62nd Cong., 1912, 2320-2332, 2354-2368, 2371, 2381-2393, 2400;
Coal and Coke Operator, XV (August 29, 1912), 138; X (March 3, 1910), 137.
[54] Senate Committee on Interstate Commerce, *Hearings Pursuant to SR 98*, 2363.

grazing, and whenever the horse attempts to go into the garden you can pull him back, and, if he persists, you can put him back in the stable." [55]

It should come as no surprise that the Federal Trade Commission Act as signed into law on September 26, 1914, was not what the coal operators had requested. Prior approval was not mentioned. The hoped-for article on trade agreements was replaced with Section 5, declaring "unfair methods of competition" unlawful and empowering the commission to issue cease and desist orders in case such "unfair methods" were employed. Moreover, in spite of repeated requests, the coal industry did not succeed in placing the informed and politically adept Callbreath on the commission.[56] Nonetheless, the initial reaction to the trade commission was surprisingly favorable. *Coal Age* appreciated the commission's investigatory powers and predicted the body would make a careful study of the industry which "will lead to the tacit or open sanctioning of suitable working agreements." [57] A lengthy meeting between Indiana and Illinois operators and Interior Secretary Franklin K. Lane in December 1914 led to speculation that the commission would not only give advance advice on trade agreements but would declare most of them permissible. *Black Diamond* forecast "the co-operative era in American business" and looked forward to statistical associations and cooperative production, storage, and marketing.[58]

From the last days of 1914, however, the industry was profoundly ambivalent toward the FTC. Amid positive statements there was uncertainty and even hostility. Aware that the act itself offered little, *Black Diamond* wondered if Wilsonian cooperation might be limited to cost-reducing distribution schemes and sidestep the real need — cooperation to curtail production. A new and powerful spokesman for the industry, Charles S. Keith of Kansas City, Missouri, claimed the public was misinformed. The trade commission, he said, was not an administrative body to supervise restraint of trade, but an investigative body which reported to the Department of Justice: "It is consequently a repressive rather than a constructive measure. . . . under the new act, with the court ruling on facts as pre-determined by the Commission and by this same cause prejudiced against the defendant, we can expect more convictions,

[55] *Coal and Coke Operator*, XVI (February 20, 1913), 147; Senate Committee on Interstate Commerce, *Hearings Pursuant to SR 98*, 2324, 2331, 2334 2335, 2359, 2362, 2366, 2368, 2390, 2393, 2397, 2404; U.S. House of Representatives, Committee on Interstate and Foreign Commerce, *Hearings, Interstate Trade Commission, 1914*, 1914, 460–461.
[56] U.S. *Statutes at Large*, XXXVIII, 717ff.; *Black Diamond*, LIII (July 18, 1914), 50; (August 1, 1914), 90 91; (August 15, 1914), 131.
[57] *Coal Age*, VI (November 21, 1914), 844.
[58] LIII (December 19, 1914), 29, and (December 29, 1914), 525.

greater fears, less investment, and less initiative on the part of business." [59] By late 1915, it was clear to many operators, including Keith, that the FTC Act had failed to correct even the uncertainty which had prevailed under Taft and Roosevelt. They expressed their disappointment in a December 1915 appeal to the U. S. Chamber of Commerce for help in obtaining new legislation: "In the present state of the law business is prevented from indulging in co-operation due to the uncertain state of the law touching our Federal Trust statutes. . . . Doubt, itself, is equivalent to prohibition." [60]

These operators were responding to an FTC-Justice Department policy of cooperating with business that was extremely narrow in scope and hostile to all but the most primitive of trade agreements. Neither government agency exercised prior approval over any trade agreement, and their passive encouragement was limited to strictly statistical associations. Operators could take some solace in the views of FTC Vice-Chairman Edward Hurley, who publicly advocated cooperation through joint selling agencies. But Hurley's insistence that such cooperation "necessarily presupposes strict Federal regulation of the cooperating concerns" apparently involved too much federal interference for most operators.[61] Moreover, Hurley's legacy to the operators was not his broad vision but rather uniform accounting, a pet project which he promoted in coal, lumber, and other atomistic industries. Hurley's purpose, and the Commission's, was not to encourage price maintenance but to eliminate "unintelligent" competition based on faulty estimates of production cost. The end was notably conservative.[62]

The statistical associations, moreover, were carefully watched. An April 1915 memorandum prepared by an FTC agent asserted that a typical open price association in Franklin County, Illinois, "might be of considerable influence in preventing active price competition;" by early 1915, according to one report, "members of the Trade Commission [were] becoming increasingly suspicious of the operation of many of these trade asociations; they are not limiting

[59] *Black Diamond*, LIV (May 15, 1915), 414; and LIII (December 26, 1914), 525.
[60] December 2, 1915, in FTC General Correspondence, 1914–1921, box 44, file 8149–13. See also Davis, *The Federal Trade Commission*, 131; Nathan B. Williams, "The Federal Trade Commission Law," *Annals*, LXIII (January, 1916), 20–21; and AMC *Proceedings*, XIX (1916), 242.
[61] Edward N. Hurley, *Awakening of Business* (n.p., 1916), 202.
[62] Typescript of Belt Address, FTC Records; typescript of "Informal Conference with Illinois and Indiana Coal Operators," May 15, 1916, in FTC General Records, 1914–1921, box 201, file 8508–572–2–1, 7–8, 90; letter L. C. Boyle to Joseph Davies (March 30, 1916), FTC General Records, box 44, file 8149–13; FTC General Records, box 38, file 8116–2; and letter W. C. Saeger to Department of Justice (May 24, 1916), DJ-CS, box 607, file 60–187–13; Hurley, *Awakening of Business*, 197–200.

themselves to their legitimate functions, but are getting into the price-fixing, territory-dividing field." [63]

Justice Department officials remained largely uninvolved in the question of statistical associations until early 1917, when complaints of high coal prices led the attorney general to consider possible violations of the antitrust laws. Although the ensuing investigation emphasized dealer combinations, operator open price associations were examined to determine if they had been used "as a cover for price fixing purposes." [64] The Justice Department discovered that the Indiana Trade Bureau, ostensibly a straightforward statistical association, had been issuing circular selling instructions to its members in an effort to maintain prices. George Anderson, special assistant to the attorney general, wrote of "the desirability of wiping out of existence all these associations" because they engaged in illegal practices such as price fixing and division of territories. The FTC, he suggested, could do all the statistical work done by the associations. Nonetheless, as of 1918 Justice had entered no indictments against associations which limited their functions to collecting and disseminating statistics. Three West Virginia associations which transgressed department guidelines were indicted for price fixing through joint sales agencies; no convictions were obtained. [65]

The rest of the operator program for industry stabilization, including district confederations, sales agencies, and production restrictions, received no assistance from any branch of the federal government. A test case developed early in 1915 when a group of Indiana operators, led by Bogle and Callbreath, asked FTC approval for a sales corporation which would market some 80 per cent of the state's output and restrict production through a pooling of mine operating time. Their presentation emphasized anticipated economies in production and sales and the natural limits on price increases imposed by interstate competition. An FTC investigation revealed little empathy. It questioned whether the coal industry really suffered from excessive competition and low profits, criticized

[63] Letter George W. Anderson, Special Assistant to the Attorney General, to Attorney General (January 6, 1917), Department of Justice Central Files, Straight Numerical Files, box 1874, file 181092 (1–99) (these files are hereinafter referred to as DJ–SN); memorandum signed D. A. Morrow, "Preliminary Memoranda in Regard to Proposed Agreement of Indiana Coal Operators and Conditions in the Coal Mining Industry of Illinois," in FTC General Correspondence, box 196, file 8508–10–2–1; and *Declaration of Purposes, Articles of Association and By-Laws of the Franklin County, Illinois, Coal Operators' Association* (n.p., 1904), copy in FTC General Records, *ibid.*, file 8508–10–1–1.
[64] Letter Attorney General Thomas Gregory to William Howard, House of Representatives (July 25, 1917), DJ–SN, box 1874, file 181092 (310).
[65] Letter Anderson to Gregory (January 6, 1917), DJ–SN, box 1874, file 181092 (1–99); letter Anderson to Gregory (January 10, 1917), *ibid.* (100–179); Assistant to Attorney General to Charles F. Kingsley (June 15, 1917), *ibid.* (250–309); and DJ–CS, box 607, file 60–187–16.

the output and sales provisions of the agreement, and conjured the spectre of district sales agencies eventually combining to effect a monopoly.[66] Following meetings with trade commission and Justice officials in April 1915, there were reports of an agreement between the Justice Department and the Indiana operators. G. Carroll Todd, who handled these meetings for Justice, was upset by the suggestion of a deal and privately communicated his feeling that the coal operators were working "not quite fairly to create an atmosphere of having committed the Department to an approval of their plans." [67] It seems likely that the Federal Trade Commission and the Justice Department refrained from encouraging the Indiana operators in this critical test. Deprived of government aid, the Indiana association never became a major factor in the coal trade; prosecution was unnecessary.

The post-1914 "co-operative era" was punctuated with frustration and disappointment. While a few operators continued to see the FTC as the coal industry's benefactor, most were dissatisfied with an organization which tolerated only the most limited form of cooperation and was oblivious to the very real need — often articulated by industry spokesmen — for production restrictions.[68] Dissatisfied operators joined the United Mine Workers and the U. S. Chamber of Commerce in an attempt to secure amendments to the antitrust laws. "If the Commission as it is now construed," wrote one operator, "has not the power to advise with industries along broad and constructive lines, then, indeed, this power should be conferred upon it." [69] This group planned to secure amendments to Section 5 of the FTC Act, so as "to empower the Commission to permit reasonable cooperation in business and industry." [70] If the FTC was the captive of politically oriented big businessmen, coal operators were not among the captors.[71]

[66] Letter W. S. Bogle, *et al.*, to Joseph E. Davies (March 25, 1915), FTC General Records, box 196, file 8508-10-1-1; D. A. Morrow, "Preliminary Memoranda."
[67] Letter Anderson to Gregory (January 10, 1917), DJ-SN, box 1874, file 181092 (100–179). Anderson's recollections were based on personal notes taken at the April 21, 1915 meeting between Todd and the Indiana operators (letter L. L. Bracken [February 23, 1917], in FTC General Records, box 190, file 8502-297).
[68] This is particularly obvious in the May 15, 1916 FTC-Illinois-Indiana Conference, report in FTC General Records, 12, 14, 83; also *Black Diamond*, LVI (May 27, 1916), 444-445. In 1962, G. Cullom Davis made the point that until 1925, the commission tried "to execute a strict regulatory policy in accordance with the progressive ideals of economic reform." But Davis dismissed the years before 1918 and offered little proof for his thesis before that date. See "The Transformation of the Federal Trade Commission, 1914–1929," *Mississippi Valley Historical Review*, XLIX (December, 1962), 437–455.
[69] Letter Boyle to Davies (January 22, 1916), FTC General Records, box 44, file 8149-13; Wiebe, *Businessmen and Reform*, 84.
[70] Letter Charles S. Keith and W. R. Fairley to Samuel Gompers and John Fahey (January 19, 1916), FTC General Records, box 44, file 8149-13; *Black Diamond*, LV (October 23, 1915), 325; and *Coal and Coke Operator*, XXI (February 1917), 15.
[71] Recent critiques of Progressivism from the New Left have overemphasized harmony and underemphasized conflict in business-government relationships. See Sklar, 78-79,

Contrary to what operators hoped, the FTC had not replaced Justice as the arbiter of trade agreements. And the attorney general had responded to an increasing flow of anti-coal operator mail with his own industry-wide investigation of coal trade associations and ultimately with indictments. "In regulating the coal business," commented *Black Diamond* in April 1917, "the government and the Department of Justice have tampered with the roots. They began to bear down on coal before any organization at all was effected. Therefore they began to hack at it before anything which makes for efficiency had become a part of the coal routine." [72]

On the eve of American entry into World War I, the coal industry remained undisciplined, wasteful of natural and human resources. Three decades of remedies for a sick industry had produced minor victories (a slight increase in concentration, some statistical associations, and a degree of uniformity in wages and other costs) and major defeats (price fixing associations, joint selling agencies, the merger movement, and the limited nature of FTC cooperation). An over-zealous Department of Justice, particularly under Presidents McKinley and Taft, must bear some of the responsibility for the industry's continued predicament, but fundamentally the problem lay not in politics but in the basic economic conditions in a natural resource industry with regional and national markets. These conditions did not change after 1917. Wartime surges in demand and price fixing brought relief in the form of higher profits, but it was only temporary and was accompanied by considerable friction between coal operators and federal officials.[73] After 1920 an increasingly divided industry, troubled by an anti-union southern wing, resisted the associational approach of Herbert Hoover and the Com-

---

Weinstein, *Corporate Ideal*, 89, 91, and Kolko, *Triumph of Conservatism*, 268-270. "The business community," states Kolko, "knew what it wanted from the commission, and what it wanted was almost precisely what the commission sought to do." (*Ibid.*, 278.) Only further research will indicate conclusively whether the coal industry's relationship to the federal government was typical or uniquely frustrating, the exception that proves the rule. There are indications that other groups, presumably without the divisions and disabilities of the coal industry, were also unable to obtain precisely what they wanted. The National Civic Federation, for example, was no more successful than the coal industry in getting Congress to act on its trust program. See Senate Committee on Interstate Commerce, *Hearings Pursuant to SR 98*, 515-516, 519, 521, 527, 529. There is reason to doubt Weinstein's claim that "the ideas embodied in the Federal Trade Commission Act represented a triumph of the agitation and education done by the NCF over the previous seven years" (*Corporate Ideal*, 89).

[72] *Black Diamond*, LVIII (April 28, 1917), 355; and JD-SN, box 1874, file 181092 (100-179).

[73] Daniel R. Beaver, *Newton D. Baker and the American War Effort, 1917-1919* (Lincoln, Nebraska, 1966), 64-66; Letter Anderson to Gregory (June 30, 1917), JD-SN, box 1874, file 181092 (250-309); letter Judge Isaac R. Oeland to Gregory (July 13, 1917), DJ-CS, box 607, file 60-187-16; memorandum, undated and unsigned, on formation of the National Coal Association, JD-SN, box 1874, file 181092 (250-309); *Black Diamond*, LVIII (June 30, 1917), 552; (July 28, 1917), 61; (August 4, 1917), 87; and (September 29, 1917), 249.

merce Department. Even the regulatory legislation of the New
Deal reflected the industry's divisions and centrifugal tendencies,
and not until late 1940 did the minimum price provisions of the
Guffey-Vinson Act go into effect.[74] The great expectations of the
1890s were just beginning to be fulfilled.

[74] Ellis W. Hawley, "Secretary Hoover and the Bituminous Coal Problem, 1921–1928,"
Business History Review, XLII (Autumn, 1968), 247–270; James P. Johnson, "Drafting
the NRA Code of Fair Competition for the Bituminous Coal Industry," *Journal of American
History*, LIII (December, 1966), 521–541; and Ellis W. Hawley, *The New Deal and the
Problem of Monopoly: A Study in Economic Ambivalence* (Princeton, 1966), 205–212.

[15]

CHAPTER 8

COAL:

CONCERTED PRACTICES

The European coal industry has been organized since World War I with outside help, usually given by the government, for the sake of enabling the large number of producers to stabilize prices and income over the course of the business cycle. (The treaty provisions regarding concerted actions that interfere with the market have already been discussed in Chapter 7 while the lack of antitrust sentiment in Europe has been mentioned in Chapter 5.) Collective action and control is universal in the European coal industry, and is directly encouraged by governments and the High Authority, which has authorized concerted action subject to its inspection and control, according to rules which are designed to protect the public interest.

THE INTERWAR PERIOD

Each domestic market was organized with varying degrees of success, though the European coal industry failed to reach any comprehensive international agreements during the interwar period.

Background

The coal industry was more overexpanded even than the steel industry after the first world war. In the late 1920s—when business was still fairly good—25 per cent of German, 25 to 33 per cent of British and 50 per cent of Polish capacity was idle. Twenty-seven per cent of American capacity also was idle at that time.[1] The French mines were less overexpanded.[2] The Polish coal in-

---

[1] ILO, *The World Coal-Mining Industry*, Geneva, 1938, Vol. I, pp. 74, 111–112; Temporary National Economic Committee, *Competition and Monopoly in American Industry*, Monograph No. 21, Washington, 1940, p. 24.

[2] André Dubosq, *Le Conflit contemporain des houillères européennes (Perspectives d'entente)*, Librairie Technique et Economique, Paris, 1936, pp. 28–29.

251

252   *Europe's Coal and Steel Community*

dustry was in the greatest difficulty. Poland had acquired East Upper Silesia from Germany after the first world war. This region had produced 30 million tons of coal before the war and thereafter accounted for 80 per cent of Polish output, which had quadrupled as a result. So large an increase in an essentially agricultural country gave Poland a large export surplus.[3]

Coal producing capacity in the United Kingdom and on the Continent increased between 1913 and the 1920s though coal production in the interwar years never, except for 1929, exceeded that of 1913. Demand failed to keep pace because improvements in the use of coal yielded more energy per unit, because coal importing areas increased their own production, and because the use of water power and petroleum increased.[4]

The decline of overseas demand was particularly sharp. Coal exports from the United Kingdom in the late 1920s were about 75 per cent of the prewar volume and declined to 60 per cent in the 1930s.[5] German exports in the like periods declined to 85 and 80 per cent, respectively, of 1913.[6] The British coal industry was in greater trouble than the German because Poland's entry into the export market had created more difficulties for the former. The United Kingdom and Poland were each large exporters of coal for steam-raising uses to overseas areas, but Germany enjoyed the advantage of supplying metallurgical fuels over interior lines of transport. The United Kingdom and Poland eventually reached an agreement on exports in December 1934 that regulated distribution rather than export prices.[7]

Only six countries—the United Kingdom, Germany, Poland, France, Belgium and the Netherlands—would have had to agree in order to control 90 per cent of the European coal output and nearly all the exports. But their interests proved too contradictory. As a large importer and small exporter France had more to gain from British-German rivalry. The British industry wished to restore the prewar export patterns more favorable to it, though there had been a chronic deterioration in its competitive ability.[8] Resting on a property structure determined by the small leasehold, British coal production was dispersed over many firms. Internal organization in the United Kingdom was consequently weak and prevented it from dictating terms to the

---

[3] *Statistische Übersicht über die Kohlenwirtschaft im Jahre 1936*, in *Jahresbericht des Reichskohlenverbandes, 1936–37*, p. 22; hereafter cited as *Statistische Übersicht*. For the effect of surplus capacity on export prices, see *The World Coal-Mining Industry*, Vol. I, pp. 195–219.

[4] *The World Coal-Mining Industry*, Vol. I, pp. 104–110.

[5] *Statistische Übersicht*, p. 50.

[6] *Ibid.*, p. 36. Coke is excluded. The comparison would be more favorable to Germany if exports from East Upper Silesia were credited to Germany.

[7] The agreement is summarized in *The World Coal-Mining Industry*, Vol. I, pp. 249–250.

[8] *Coal Mining*, Report of the Technical Advisory Committee, Charles C. Reid, Chairman, HMSO, London, March 1945, p. 29; cited hereafter as Reid Report, one of the best on the problems of the British coal industry in the interwar period.

Coal: Concerted Practices 253

German coal exporters. Unreconciled to its loss of ground, the United Kingdom tried to recapture its former position by currency manipulation, dumping and bilateral agreements. The devaluation of the pound in 1931 gave the British industry a temporary advantage. The Anglo-German negotiations of 1934 for an agreement on coal, which coincided with the negotiations for the steel cartel and the naval agreement, failed because the United Kingdom thought an agreement on coal prices would be sufficient while the Germans wanted to fix export quotas also.[9]

Instead of adjusting capacity to demand, the European coal mines engaged in cutthroat competition and discrimination in order to maintain volume and cover fixed costs. Since labor costs accounted for 55 to 65 per cent of the selling price, competition meant manipulation of wages and working hours. A League of Nations report observed: "It would . . . appear that the competitive lowering of coal prices after 1929 was facilitated to a large degree by the flexibility of the wage-cost factor. And certainly part of this competitive lowering of sales prices was made possible by the breakdown of wage rates."[10] In an era of general unemployment, mining labor had few alternative opportunities for employment. To counteract the practice by which each country tried to export unemployment to the other countries, the International Miners Federation and the League of Nations favored an international agreement on coal in the belief that it would help maintain the labor standards gained during the first world war.[11]

The coke export trade proved to be the only field in which a private multilateral agreement could be reached. The coke producers of Germany, the United Kingdom, Belgium, the Netherlands and Poland founded the International Coke Cartel in April 1937 after several years of negotiation. Each country received an export quota and preference in certain markets. Minimum prices were agreed.[12]

Government Influence

As economic conditions declined in the 1930s, the coal problem became increasingly political, though the amalgamation of individual properties and improvement of the conditions of labor had received political attention long before the first world war.[13] The governments controlled production, prices, distribution, wages, working conditions and profits during that war. As living

---

[9] Dubosq, *op. cit.*, pp. 243–244.

[10] *The World Coal-Mining Industry*, Vol. I, p. 217.

[11] Dubosq, *op. cit.*, pp. 185–186, 194–195; *Raw Materials Problems and Policies*, League of Nations, Geneva, 1946, p. 51.

[12] *The World Coal-Mining Industry*, Vol. 1, pp. 248–251; Dubosq, *op. cit.*, pp. 207–208.

[13] *The World Coal-Mining Industry*, Vol. I, pp. 4–5.

254   *Europe's Coal and Steel Community*

standards for miners had improved during the war, the miners later resisted the efforts to reduce them.[14]

Economic nationalism took a turn for the worse in the interwar years as government influence increased. National protective measures in the European coal industry produced some of the outstanding examples of economic nationalism witnessed in the interwar period. The rivalry for export markets in coal was not an example of salutary competition but of dumping, subsidies, discriminatory prices, tie-in sales, currency manipulation, special tax relief, preferential freight rates and domestic market control.[15] The simultaneous pursuit of protection for home production and of dumping on export markets led to a crazy quilt of international countermeasures and discriminations, especially in the 1930s. As in an armaments race, every device stimulated a counterdevice, every alliance a counteralliance. "Private" and "public" measures became hopelessly entangled and the division between them meaningless.

The tariff, exceptional in the 1920s, became the rule in the following decade, but was not the main device for limiting imports. Besides the normal import duty, there were equalization taxes, import license fees, port and river charges. Germany, France, Italy, Belgium and the Netherlands had import quota limitations by 1936.[16] The importing countries extended preferential treatment to selected sources of supply within the framework of preferential bilateral trade agreements. These agreements helped the partners to exchange goods that were surplus to each of them. The United Kingdom made such arrangements with the Scandinavian and Baltic countries in 1933–1934. German coal enjoyed preference in Belgium, the Netherlands and France under agreements that regulated the importation of German coal.[17]

The 1938 League of Nations report saw these "complex systems" of economic supervision and control as "the beginnings of an international mechanism for regulating competition between coal exporting countries."[18] Whatever it was that this was the beginning of, it was certainly the end of the free market mechanism in the coal industry. As the report indicates: ". . . the European coal trade must be viewed as a case of commercial dealing which is far removed from 'perfect competition.'"[19]

In the 1930s the United States also abandoned the free market. The National Recovery Act of 1933 suspended the antitrust laws and provided for minimum prices and wages under government supervision. After the NRA

[14] See *ibid.*, pp. 6–8, 220.
[15] See *ibid.*, pp. 158, 194–200 for details.
[16] *Ibid.*, pp. 158 ff.
[17] *Ibid.*, pp. 188–190, 249–250; Dubosq, *op. cit.*, pp. 102–103, 173–174.
[18] *The World Coal-Mining Industry*, Vol. I, p. 220.
[19] *Ibid.*, p. 190.

Coal: Concerted Practices 255

had been declared unconstitutional, price control in bituminous coal was continued under the Bituminous Coal Conservation Act of 1935 and later under the Bituminous Coal Act of 1937, but the latter was soon emasculated by an unfavorable Federal Court decision on the minimum price provisions. The anthracite industry was regulated by the laws of the state of Pennsylvania.[20] Overseas exports were, however, of minor significance to the United States coal industry in the prewar period.

AFTER WORLD WAR II

As coal and labor were scarce, the great competitive struggles of the past disappeared after the second world war. Export prices were higher than internal ones—the reverse of the interwar relationship—but the additional revenue on export sales was small in any case, for a smaller proportion of production was exported.

Since the end of the second world war internal coal prices charged by privately as well as publicly owned enterprises have been controlled at low levels in relation to costs and the paucity of coal, first by the individual governments, then by the High Authority and, again, by the governments informally after price controls had been lifted by the High Authority.

Since the second world war all governments in Western Europe have in practice assumed the obligation of stabilizing production, employment and wages and of encouraging modernization and investments, whether the mines are publicly or privately owned. The common sales agency selling for a large number of, or for all, the firms in a given producing district is one of the major devices by which the objectives common to governments and producers are carried out in privately owned areas. In nationalized mining areas concerted action rests on the fact of nationalization itself. The privately owned as well as publicly owned mines are subject to government influence in Europe because the earnings of capital and labor cannot be stabilized unless prices, production and sales by the large number of firms whose costs vary considerably are coordinated. Many firms, furthermore, could not survive when prices are pegged without some form of aid that sometimes goes as far as interfirm compensation.

Several common sales agencies were operating in the non-nationalized portions of the coal industry on the eve of the ECSC. These were in the Ruhr, Aachen, Lower Saxony, Belgium and in the southern German coal market. In France the Association Technique de l'Importation Charbonnière (ATIC) controlled imports of solid fuels. The High Authority's disposition of the sales

[20] *Ibid.*, pp. 239–241.

256   *Europe's Coal and Steel Community*

agency for the Ruhr, which controlled half the production in the ECSC, set a
pattern for High Authority policy in the other areas. Three years of protracted
negotiations between the High Authority, the Ruhr coal industry and the
German government went by before the High Authority established a policy
for the sale of Ruhr solid fuels. The High Authority subsequently took action
with respect to ATIC and the sales agencies in Belgium and southern
Germany.

RUHR SOLID FUELS

The sale of Ruhr solid fuels has been centralized since 1893. The Rheinische
Westfälische Kohlen Syndikat (RWKS) was organized that year to stabilize
prices. The captive coal mines joined the cartel in 1903 after having obtained
important concessions. The RWKS encompassed about 90 per cent of Ruhr
solid fuels by 1913 and acquired 100 per cent membership in the first world
war, when the State-owned mines joined.[21]

INTERWAR PERIOD

The RWKS emerged stronger than ever from the first world war. In 1919,
the German socialists, then in power, passed a socialization bill (Kohlenwirtschaftsgesetz). Expressing the Weimar Republic's wish for economic democracy, the act provided for compulsory membership in the regional coal cartels
in order to facilitate public control. It also provided for nationalization but
that was not carried out.[22] The RWKS took over the sale of Aachen coal in
1934 and of Saar coal the following year when the latter rejoined Germany.
Each of the other coal producing districts—mainly German Silesia, and several
minor basins—also had its sales organization before the second world war.

The RWKS—many of the provisions of the Kohlenwirtschaftsgesetz were
modeled on it—was an incorporated limited liability company, the stock of
which was owned by the coal companies, which had voting rights proportionate to their sales quotas. The RWKS established prices, levies, penalties
and quotas for the individual firms. Arrangements between the RWKS and
individual firms were made by periodic contracts. Each member had a sales
quota and a separate quota for coke and briquettes, adjusted periodically in

[21] William N. Parker, *Fuel Supply and Industrial Strength,* unpublished Ph.D. thesis, Harvard
University, Cambridge, 1951, pp. 115–120, 126–128. Frederick Haussmann, *The Reorganization of
the German Coal Industry and Its International Aspects* (undated mimeographed study written after
the second world war), pp. 27–33, contains an excellent summary of the RWKS.

[22] *The World Coal-Mining Industry,* Vol. I, p. 6; Franz Neumann, *Behemoth,* Oxford, New
York, 1942, p. 266. Parker, *op. cit.,* pp. 115–124, describes the structure of public control.

Coal: Concerted Practices 257

relation to demand. Each member had a consumption quota, in addition to the sales quota, to cover the requirements of the mine, of auxiliary operations and of vertically integrated firms.

Markets in Germany were divided into "uncontested" and "contested" areas. The regional cartel had a sales monopoly in the uncontested area. Contested areas were served by more than one cartel or by imported coal. Among the contested areas were northern Germany, where United Kingdom coal was imported, and southern Germany, where coal was delivered from the Ruhr, Aachen, Bavaria, the Saar and Lorraine.

Prices in uncontested areas were higher than those in contested areas, which also encompassed exports. The RWKS taxed its members in order to cover the lower prices. This tax, called the *Umlage*, equalized unit returns among producers, regardless of the destination of the coal from individual firms. Unit revenue in each firm was therefore determined by the average unit revenue on all the coal distributed in uncontested, contested and export markets. Uncontested markets, contested markets and integrated consumption each absorbed roughly one third the Ruhr coal output.[23]

As the integrated coal mining firms obtained control of the RWKS, they improved their position by obtaining a lower *Umlage* on consumption quotas. High book prices on coking smalls, which represented the major part of the consumption quota, also helped improve their position.[24] The demand for high consumption quotas on the part of integrated firms was a source of sharp conflict between them and the independents.

Official prices in the uncontested areas, approved by the government, were monopoly prices, reflecting the costs of the less efficient producers.[25] Prices in the contested areas took account of the delivered price of coal from other producers. Although average receipts per ton of solid fuels exported by the RWKS declined by more than 50 per cent from 1930 to 1934, the official price in uncontested areas declined by less than 20 per cent. Official prices in uncontested areas must have been about 50 per cent higher than export prices in 1934; the differential at pithead must have been even larger because the export price included freight to the border.[26] The monopoly price in uncontested areas thus subsidized the price in contested markets.

The regional coal producing cartels marketed their coal in contested areas through a common sales agency, referred to as a Kohlenkontor, which also

[23] Robert Lafitte-Laplace, *L'Economie charbonnière de la France*, Marcel Giard, Paris, 1933, pp. 545–551.

[24] See Parker, *op. cit.*, pp. 129–157; Dubosq, *op. cit.*, pp. 132–138; Lafitte-Laplace, *op. cit.*, pp. 545–551; *The World Coal-Mining Industry*, Vol. I, pp. 235–239.

[25] Reid Report, pp. 30–31.

[26] These estimates are calculated from data in *Statistische Übersicht*, 1936, p. 46.

258 *Europe's Coal and Steel Community*

handled imported coal. The Kohlenkontor sold directly to large consumers and to authorized first-hand merchants. The contested areas were therefore not competitive either; they were simply controlled by different ground rules.[27]

One contested area, south Germany, deserves particular attention. The Kohlenkontor in this area handled coal coming from the RWKS, the Saar (incorporated with RWKS in 1935), Lorraine and the Bavarian mines. This Kohlenkontor also controlled inbound transport on the Rhine, an essential and profitable part of the system. The delivered base price in southern Germany for coal from all origins was determined by the RWKS price for that area plus the freight cost, which was based on published rates.[28]

EVE OF THE COMMON MARKET

The RWKS was abolished after the war by the British Military Government.[29] The centralized sale of Ruhr solid fuels was, however, continued by the Deutsche Kohlen Verkauf (DKV), established by the occupation authorities, to which it was responsible.[30] The occupation authorities established the DKV because the acute paucity of solid fuels and the ceiling on prices required centralized control of distribution and exports. The DKV coordinated all coal supplied to the German market by the Ruhr mines, by imports and by the common sales agencies for Aachen and Lower Saxony. It consequently controlled all sources and markets and enjoyed as much influence as the old RWKS, if not more.

The allied occupation officials, particularly those of the United States, considered the DKV temporary pending completion of the deconcentration program. They and the German government, represented by members of the mining industry and the labor unions, later agreed to dissolve the DKV and to establish six sales agencies for Ruhr solid fuels and a coordinating agency called Georg (Gemeinschaftsorganisation). These new organizations were established in February 1953. It was understood at the time that Georg would simply provide central statistical and technical service for the six agencies and would coordinate only when necessary without controlling prices or sales at any time. The sixty-odd mining firms in the Ruhr were to sell through the six sales agencies.

When the common market for coal began in February 1953, the High

---

[27] *The World Coal-Mining Industry*, Vol. I, pp. 235–239.

[28] Lafitte-Laplace, *op. cit.*, pp. 123–137, 141; Dubosq, *op. cit.*, pp. 132–138.

[29] It had abolished all cartels by Article 1 of Ordinance 78, February 12, 1947, and the coal cartel specifically by Order No. 5 of Public Law No. 52; B. Ruhm von Oppen, ed., *Documents on Germany Under Occupation*, Oxford, London, 1955, pp. 203 ff.

[30] By Public Law No. 75, November 10, 1948; von Oppen, *op. cit.*, p. 337.

Coal: Concerted Practices 259

Authority discovered that the package it had inherited was a completely centralized pricing and sales mechanism through the medium of Georg.[31]

SALE OF RUHR SOLID FUELS
IN THE COMMON MARKET

Article 65, relative to cartels, having become effective in July 1953,[32] the Ruhr coal sales agencies applied to the High Authority in August for permission to continue.

Sales Agencies for Aachen and Lower Saxony

While its negotiations with the Ruhr mining firms proceeded, the High Authority in June 1954 authorized the mining firms in Aachen and those in Lower Saxony to operate common sales agencies in accordance with Section 2 of Article 65, because they produced only 2.3 per cent and 1 per cent, respectively, of the coal in the ECSC and because two of the three firms in each basin were too small to sell "rationally."[33]

Why Common Sales Agencies in the Ruhr Were Continued

The High Authority decided the fate of the Ruhr coal sales agencies in February 1956.[34] It allowed the Ruhr to maintain a common sales agency for export to third countries, the Ruhrkohlenexportgesellschaft, on the ground that it did not restrain internal commerce.[35] The High Authority established three sales agencies, instead of six, to handle the sale of Ruhr solid fuels in the common market. It also established a coordinating agency, Bureau Commun, and a Commission des Normes to provide common rules of operation.

[31] H. Aszkenazy, "La Reorganisation des comptoirs de charbon de la Ruhr," in *Revue française de l'énergie*, June 1956, p. 337. The Allied High Commission protested to the German Minister for Economics in a letter dated March 18, 1953, a copy of which was sent to the High Authority. Sidney Willner, in W. Friedmann, ed., *Anti-Trust Laws, A Comparative Symposium*, Stevens and Sons, London, 1956, p. 186, has observed: "In actual operation the central body . . . assumed the direction over sales policies and continued its old market allocation and price fixing functions, thus violating the letter and the spirit of the agreed solution."

[32] HA, Decision 37–53, in *Journal officiel*, July 21, 1953, p. 153; see Chapter 6.

[33] These two sales agencies, called Comptoir Aachener Kohlen-Verkauf and Comptoir Niedersächsischer Kohlen-Verkauf, were authorized by HA, Decisions 32–54 and 34–54, respectively, in *Journal officiel*, July 6, 1954, pp. 434, 436. These two agencies had been established in 1950. A fourth mine in Aachen, Gewerkschaft Sophia Jacoba, which traditionally sold through the RWKS, was subsequently authorized to sell through one of the Ruhr sales agencies called Geitling; *Journal officiel*, March 13, 1956, p. 36. This mine withdrew from Geitling in April 1959; HA, Decision 7–59, in *Journal officiel*, February 11, 1959, p. 192.

[34] HA, Decisions 5–56, 6–56, 7–56 and 8–56, all dated February 15, 1956, are in *Journal officiel*, March 13, 1956. A minor amendment was made in Decisions 10–57, 11–57 and 12–57, in *Journal officiel*, April 16, 1957, pp. 159 ff. See also a decision of the Court with reference to the definition of the wholesaler in *Journal officiel*, April 16, 1957, pp. 166 ff. These decisions, as well as those for other coal producers and purchasers, were to expire March 31, 1959. They were later extended for one year; *Handelsblatt*, December 22, 1958, p. 2.

[35] *Journal officiel*, March 13, 1956, p. 31.

260   *Europe's Coal and Steel Community*

The High Authority accepted the centralization of Ruhr coal sales for three reasons:

(1) to enable the firms to provide the required volume and grades of solid fuels at the required time and place;

(2) to enable the firms to equalize production and employment when coal is surplus;

(3) to enable the firms to distribute supplies equitably when coal is scarce.

Thus the High Authority affirmed the proposition that sixty-odd mining firms cannot each sell solid fuels and still satisfy the collective interests of the coal mine operators, of the employees and of the consumers.

The allied authorities had already conceded as much when they created six sales agencies and Georg.[36] They pointed out that all the groups they had consulted—labor unions, the coal industry, the federation of German industry, the railroads, wholesalers and retailers—unanimously favored centralized sales.[37]

The High Authority was in no stronger political position than the allied authorities had been to propose any solution other than centralization. The interests on which it could rely in support of decentralization were few. The groups outside Germany which might have wished to weaken the Ruhr coal cartel favored concerted action in their own coal industries. The Ruhr mining firms made much of the fact that all French coal production was centralized.[38] That there is need of centralized regulation of production, prices and sales in order to mitigate the effects of the business cycle is a proposition that goes nearly unchallenged in Europe.

In spite of the acceptance of centralization by the allied authorities and, later, by the High Authority, both were eager to avoid monopoly and to protect the wholesalers' position. They thus tried to create several independent sales agencies; where the allies had established six, the High Authority created three. Under the High Authority's arrangement each mining firm in the Ruhr is in one of the agencies and each agency encompasses one third the output.

Are the Three Sales Agencies Independent?

While no mining firm is in more than one sales agency, some of the proprietary groups are represented in two, or even in all three, of them. The dis-

---

[36] Allied High Commission, "Report of the Committee on Coal Distribution Problems Relative to the Dissolution of the DKV," October 29, 1951, and Appendix, November 9, 1951.

[37] *Ibid.*, Appendix, p. 1; Aszkenazy, *op. cit.*, pp. 337–338, describes the achievements of the RWKS in stabilizing employment and production.

[38] Friedmann, *op. cit.*, p. 513.

Coal: Concerted Practices   261

tribution of proprietary interests in Geitling, Präsident, and Mausegatt, as the sales agencies are called, is shown in Table 46. Sixty-six per cent of the produc-

Table 46

DISTRIBUTION OF PROPRIETARY INTERESTS AMONG
RUHR COAL SALES AGENCIES, 1959[a]

(Amount in Thousands of Metric Tons)

Group	Geitling Amount	Geitling Per Cent	Präsident Amount	Präsident Per Cent	Mausegatt Amount	Mausegatt Per Cent
Private German steel groups:						
Thyssen	5,201	12.6	—	—	6,939	17.1
Krupp	4,813	11.7	408	1.0	2,165	5.3
Haniel	5,453	13.2	4,569	11.6	—	—
Hoesch	2,931	7.1	3,644	9.3	—	—
Rheinische	—	—	5,198	13.2	—	—
Mannesmann	—	—	6,563	16.7	—	—
Klöckner	—	—	5,238	13.3	—	—
Michel group	—	—	—	—	1,398	3.4
Dortmund–Hörder	—	—	—	—	4,640	11.5
Stumm	1,792	4.3	—	—	—	—
Ilseder[b]	1,558	3.8	—	—	—	—
German State	—	—	2,684	6.8	16,454	40.6
Gelsenkirchener[c]	3,401	8.2	2,628	6.7	2,519	6.2
Stinnes	3,445	8.3	—	—	2,088	5.2
Total	28,594	69.2	30,932	78.8	36,203	89.3
Foreign interests:						
Arbed	2,033	4.9	—	—	—	—
De Wendel	1,562	3.8	2,138	5.4	—	—
Sidechar	7,798	18.9	—	—	—	—
Total	11,393	27.6	2,138	5.4	—	—
Other groups[d]	—	—	4,277	10.9	2,339	5.8
Independents[e]	(1,300)	3.2	1,924	4.9	1,973	4.9
TOTAL[f]	41,287	100.0	39,271	100.0	40,515	100.0

Sources: HA, Decisions 5 to 7–56, inclusive, in *Journal officiel*, March 13, 1956, for the mining firms in each sales comptoir; *Jahrbuch,* for production; Table 5–6, Appendix E, for proprietary control of firms.

[a] Production data as of 1955 but proprietary relationships as of early 1959.

[b] The State has a 25 per cent interest.

[c] Includes only GBAG's 100 per cent owned mines; the mines in which Dortmund-Hörder and August Thyssen Hütte purchased a 51 per cent interest are excluded.

[d] German industrial groups not previously listed; each of them is represented in one agency only.

[e] Each independent is of course represented in one agency only.

[f] The grand total covers 100 per cent of the Ruhr.

tion organized in Geitling, 41 per cent of that organized in Präsident and 85 per cent of that in Mausegatt has proprietary ties to mining firms in one of the other two agencies. In view of the fact that the interests of the proprietary groups spill over into more than one sales organization, the prospects for independence among the three agencies are small.

The High Authority evidently placed the mining firms controlled by the foreign steel groups, and those controlled by the German State, where they might exercise some independence. Thus, foreign steel groups without ties to the other agencies control more than one fourth of the coal represented in Geitling. But there is no evidence to suggest that the foreign groups are taking advantage of the opportunity. Neither is the German State. The State-owned mines, accounting for 41 per cent of the production organized in Mausegatt, could wield a great influence in that sales agency, though they also have a small interest in Präsident. But the State-owned mines refused the opportunity to exercise independence when the Ruhr coal operators raised prices at the end of 1957, to the government's intense displeasure. Ludwig Erhard, the Minister for Economics, threatened to break the common price policy by pulling Hibernia, the State-owned firm, out of the common price list. Hibernia accounts for one fourth the coal organized in Mausegatt and 9 per cent of all the Ruhr output. The common price list for all mining firms in the Ruhr is the cornerstone of control. Erhard did not follow through; had he done so he would have dealt a serious blow to the whole structure of control. Instead he had the Preussag mines in Lower Saxony maintain the old price, but this was merely a gesture because Preussag produces only one fourth as much coal as Hibernia and, located in Lower Saxony rather than the Ruhr, does not compete with Ruhr coal.[39]

The High Authority tried to safeguard the independence of each sales agency by forbidding the officers of one agency to hold office in another and by controlling the transfer of funds and of solid fuels from one sales agency to another.[40]

Wholesalers and Dealers

The RWKS had selected and controlled the merchants and had given them exclusive sales rights. They had been organized in merchants' associations in which the RWKS was represented. The RWKS had granted exclusive rights in foreign markets to one or two large merchants.[41] These devices were important features of market control.

The High Authority has carefully tried to protect the merchant's status and his access to supply. Consumers who consume over 30,000 tons of solid fuels

---

[39] Details on the incident are from *Handelsblatt*, October 4-5, 1957, p. 2, and October 7, 1957, p. 2.

[40] See, e.g., Articles 2 and 3 of Decision 5–56, *Journal officiel*, March 13, 1956, pp. 36–37.

[41] Aszkenazy, *op. cit.*, p. 338.

Coal: Concerted Practices 263

annually may deal directly with the sales agencies; those who consume over 50,000 tons may deal with the Bureau Commun, described later. Mining firms may sell directly to local customers who consume less than 12,500 tons annually. A consumer large enough to qualify for direct purchases from the sales agencies may also purchase from a merchant for a limited period if he has been accustomed to using the latter. All other consumers must purchase from first- or second-degree merchants according to size; the first-degree merchant purchases from the Ruhr sales agency, but the second-degree merchant obtains his coal from the first-degree merchant. The first-degree merchant sells at the list prices established by the Ruhr sales agency and deducts a commission agreed between him and the agency; i.e., the latter earns a lower net return on the solid fuels distributed through merchant channels.[42]

To qualify as first-degree merchant, a dealer must have handled a minimum tonnage of Ruhr solid fuels in a historical reference period and must have sold a minimum tonnage in any one of seven sales zones. The zonal provision limits the number of first-degree merchants in any zone and attempts to spread them geographically throughout the common market. Non-German merchants may qualify.

The qualifications set for the merchants were too restrictive and fewer merchants qualified than had been hoped. The High Authority therefore successively reduced the size qualifications by amendment.[43] The number of qualified first-degree merchants in the several sales zones increased slightly or remained fairly stationary from 1956 to the first quarter of 1958.[44]

Freight Charges

The customer who purchases from the sales agency has the right to specify the point at which he takes delivery, i.e., f.o.b. mine, f.o.b. Rhine River port, or f.o.b. seaport. This provision is particularly important because the seller can engage in secret price discrimination by fixing the delivery point. The provision thus protects the consumer against phantom freight charges and allows him to use the most economical means of transport.[45]

Coordination Among the Three Sales Agencies

The Commission des Normes and the Bureau Commun are the coordinating

[42] HA, Decision 5-56, *Journal officiel*, Article 3 (8).

[43] HA, *Journal officiel*, March 13, 1956, pp. 279 ff. Articles 7, 8, 9, 10, 11 of HA, Decision 5-56, deal with the merchant trade. The amendments are contained in a series of decisions published in the *Journal officiel* beginning August 10, 1957.

[44] Assemblée Parlementaire Européenne, Commission du Marché Intérieur, Doc. No. 12, 1958, p. 37.

[45] HA, Decision 5-56, *Journal officiel*, March 13, 1956, Article 3 (5) (6) (7).

264   *Europe's Coal and Steel Community*

bodies for the sale of Ruhr solid fuels.[46] The Commission des Normes is a sort of legislative assembly in which the mining firms are represented. It may establish common standards for all the mines with respect to:

(1) The rules that determine the quantity of solid fuels used for Werksselbstverbrauch (mines' consumption, miners' coal, consumption by vertical affiliates) and the quantity sold by the sales agencies to local and other customers. Each sales agency sells about 15 million tons of coal plus 5 to 6 million tons of coke, exclusive of Werksselbstverbrauch and local sales; local sales— small in the aggregate—are made directly by the mines. All three sales agencies combined thus sell 45 million tons of coal—roughly one third the total output of the Ruhr and more than 60 per cent of the coal after coking requirements are deducted—and about 15 million tons of coke, about 40 per cent of the total Ruhr output. The remainder of each class of product goes to Werksselbstverbrauch and to local sales made directly by the mining firms. About one third the solid fuels produced in the Ruhr was used for Werksselbstverbrauch in the interwar period; the proportion increased to one half in the 1950s.

(2) The rules by which mining firms and their corporate affiliates buy solid fuels from one another in order to equalize employment and operating rates during a recession or to give up some of their solid fuels when coal is scarce. These provisions affect the Werksselbstverbrauch. The Commission des Normes established a rule requiring the steel firms that are vertically integrated with the mines to purchase a fixed quantity of coal; the steel firms tried to reduce their obligations as a result of the 1958 recession.

(3) The rules by which orders from other customers will be distributed among mining firms in order to stabilize employment.

(4) The minimum base production tonnage for each mining firm. When there is surplus coal producing capacity, the sales agencies and the Bureau Commun distribute orders in order to enable each firm to come up to the minimum rate of operation. The mining firms that operate above the minimum may be required to pay an indemnity of up to 5 DM per ton of coal to those firms that are below the minimum. This provision and the 5 DM indemnity were applied in the 1958 recession, when sales were running from 10 to 15 per cent below Ruhr mining capacity.[47]

The rules adopted by the Commission des Normes are subject to High Authority approval. The Commission must give the High Authority an annual forecast of the tonnage of coal retained for Werksselbstverbauch and a quarterly report on actual performance.

[46] See HA, Decision 8–56 in *Journal officiel*, March 13, 1956.
[47] *Handelsblatt*, July 30, 1958, p. 1.

Coal: Concerted Practices 265

Whereas the Commission des Normes provides the rules for coordination, the Bureau Commun is the executive body. It is headed by one representative from each sales agency; the three select a president by unanimous agreement.

The Bureau Commun deals with consumers who consume over 50,000 tons annually and who promise to use the Bureau exclusively for at least a year. But contracts are between the consumer and one of the three sales agencies. The Bureau Commun may manipulate deliveries in order to facilitate vessel loading and to help ship the right quantity of the specific grades and sizes of coal. The Bureau Commun is really a fourth sales agency acting as a balance wheel. The Bureau distributes orders to equalize employment when there is surplus coal producing capacity. When solid fuels are scarce it helps the sales agencies to provide all customers with a fair share.

The Bureau Commun also acts as a financial agency. It administers the subsidy for mines that operate below the minimum base tonnage when coal producing capacity is not fully utilized. It administers payments that equalize the cost of freight absorption among mining firms that sell at delivery points other than f.o.b. mine. When the customer accepts delivery f.o.b. seaport or f.o.b. Duisburg-Ruhrort, a uniform freight charge is applied. The uniform charge must be equal to the average weighted real cost. The mines are compensated or debited for the difference between the actual freight cost and the uniform charge. If the mines absorb freight in order to compete with imported coal, the Bureau may fix the quantities and the charge to be absorbed and may equalize the financial burden among all the mines. When solid fuels were scarce in 1956 and 1957, the High Authority gave the Bureau Commun a delegation of power to apportion supplies. The High Authority could authorize it to establish production quotas when there is a surplus of coal producing capacity.

Public Supervision

The allied authorities had subordinated Georg to a tripartite committee representing the mines, the unions and consumers. They also had envisaged a substantial degree of public supervision by the High Authority and the German government owing to the danger of "monopolistic tendencies" on the part of a "private control selling agency."[48]

The principle of public supervision was later adopted by the High Authority for the sales agencies it authorized. The High Authority has the right to ascertain whether or not the coal mining firms, the selling agencies, the Bureau Commun and the Commission des Normes conform to the terms of the authorization. The High Authority required the mining firms to establish a Consultative Committee of nine producers, nine labor representatives and

[48] Allied High Commission, *op. cit.*, Appendix, November 9, 1951, p. 7.

266   *Europe's Coal and Steel Community*

nine consumers and merchants, and to keep this committee informed of the activities of the Bureau Commun. The High Authority and the German government may also participate in the Consultative Committee.

Conclusion

Are the Ruhr solid fuels sales agencies independent and do they compete with each other?

The High Authority believed that none of the three sales agencies would control a substantial part of the market because it encompasses no more than 13 per cent of the coal output in the Ruhr or 6 per cent of the total output in the ECSC and because, further, it encompasses no more than 11 per cent of the coke output in the Ruhr and 5 per cent of that in the ECSC.[49] The importance of considering these matters from the regional point of view has already been pointed out in Chapter 5. The position of Ruhr coal in regional markets or even in the common market as a whole cannot be measured in percentages alone. Nor is it very realistic to measure the strength of the sales agencies by taking each one separately as though one were completely independent of the others. Though the centralized selling arrangements do not, furthermore, preclude the Ruhr mines as a group from invading the markets of other coal producing districts, the sales agencies refrained during the 1958 recession from challenging the mines in southern Belgium, the most vulnerable of all producing districts, and asked the High Authority to maintain its ban on price alignments between producing districts.[50]

Though the High Authority's authorization does not provide for concerted pricing, the mining firms use a common price list; the common sales agencies are the administrative core for concerted prices. Was the High Authority very realistic to assume that the Ruhr coal industry, in view of its history and wishes, would stop short of concerted pricing after having been authorized to concert on so many other aspects of sales and distribution? The overlapping of proprietary interests points to a reply in the negative. Since the provisions authorized by the High Authority call for an equalized distribution of orders and operating rates between mining firms, as well as for interfirm compensation, when there is surplus producing capacity, why should the mines compete if the results of competition are to be neutralized in a buyers' market? In October 1957 several members of the Common Assembly asked the High Authority whether simultaneous price changes "prove that the facade of Ruhr sales agencies hides a true homogeneous cartel, eluding public control." The

---

[49] These percentages differ somewhat from those given earlier in this chapter because they are calculated on a somewhat different basis.

[50] *Handelsblatt*, February 3, 1958, p. 9.

Coal: Concerted Practices 267

High Authority replied that simultaneous price changes do not provide con-clusive evidence but that it had started an inquiry.[51]

Fifteen months later, in March 1959, the High Authority ruled that the three sales agencies had concerted on sales and prices. Asserting that the firms should be free to sell independently, the High Authority ruled that the sales agencies would have to be modified or dissolved. But it prolonged their exist-ence, as well as that of the Bureau Commun, the Commission des Normes and the common financial measures, to March 1960 with the possibility of another year's extension for the three sales agencies only. The High Authority was to supervise the three agencies more closely in the meantime. It also ruled that it would meanwhile, together with the operators, labor and the German government, study the measures to be taken to *stabilize employment and earnings* in the Ruhr coal industry. The Ruhr coal operators challenged the decision before the Court.[52]

Does this decision presage the introduction of price competition between the mining firms in the Ruhr. It would be necessary to await the decisions of the High Authority before reaching any conclusions. In view of the High Authority's explicit desire to stabilize employment, the concentration of own-ership, the long history of cartelization, and the high degree of nationalization prevailing in other parts of the Community, the High Authority has set itself a hard task indeed if it expects to alter the basic ground rules. The High Au-thority in any case has thus far authorized a publicly sponsored monopoly in the Ruhr coal industry.[53]

THE FRENCH MARKET

Interwar Period

The French coal problem was simpler than the British, German or Polish.[54] Since France is essentially an importing country, the coal producers there did not depend on overseas outlets and consequently were less overexpanded. The industry was protected by import restrictions and by regional cartels.

At the suggestion of the government, the coal producers in 1931 and 1932 organized the three producing districts, Nord and Pas-de-Calais, Centre-Midi

[51] *Journal officiel*, December 7, 1957, pp. 571 ff.

[52] HA, Decision No. 17–59, *Journal officiel*, March 7, 1959; *Handelsblatt*, March 27-28, 1959, p. 3.

[53] Miriam Camps, *The European Common Market and American Policy*, Center of Interna-tional Studies, Princeton, November 1956, p. 27, refers to the authorization of the Ruhr sales agency by the High Authority as a "sobering" experience and calls attention to the opposition the High Authority would have encountered had it interpreted the treaty more strictly.

[54] The 1920s are omitted from discussion; that decade was largely dominated by problems con-nected with the receipt of solid fuels from the Ruhr on reparations and related accounts. Lafitte-Laplace, *op. cit.*, contains a good analysis of the period.

and Lorraine, into separate marketing cartels. Until 1935 the Saar mines were in the cartel for Lorraine. The country was divided into four sales zones and a functional zone of large consumers called the R zone. The northern mines obtained preference in Zone A, which covered the northern market, Paris and Rouen. The eastern mines enjoyed preference in Zone B in eastern France though the northern mines enjoyed preference in supplying coke to the steel plants in this zone; the Centre-Midi mines, in Zone C in southern and central France; all three mining regions had equal status in Zone D. But no zone was exclusively reserved to any producing region. Zone R encompassed the railroads, gas works, etc., which purchased directly from coal producers. Operating rates were equalized between the three mining regions. Each producer received a share of the regional quota. The four sales zones had a common statistical office and an office that adjusted orders so as to coordinate sales with production quotas. The R zone also proved useful in this connection.[55]

The Comptoir de Douai, as the northern coal producers' group was called, exercised leadership over the other French coal producers. It fixed minimum prices for its coal, and hence for all coal in all the French zones.

Since France imported from a quarter to a third of the solid fuels it consumed, import controls were an important means of protecting the French coal producers. To regulate imports into the coastal areas, where briquetting plants predominated, the northern mines in 1928 organized the Comptoir des Charbons Classés et Agglomérés, in which the other regional producers, the import merchants and the briquetting plants joined. This cartel purchased coal for import and sold coal to the briquetting plants.[56] From 1927 to 1939, the Convention des Gailleteries, an agreement among the mining firms in the Ruhr, Netherlands, Belgium and Nord and Pas-de-Calais, regulated the sale and prices of small-sized heating coal in the French market.[57] Beginning in 1933 the northern French coal producers "exchanged views" with the Belgian producers regarding the coal market in northern France for the other types of coal.[58]

With the onset of the Great Depression, the French government adjusted the rate of import regularly. Import license taxes, import duties and turnover taxes were applied selectively to the different sources of imported supplies in accordance with a preferential system. German solid fuels enjoyed preference. The import of coal from South Wales, another important source, varied with the British purchase of French pit props.[59]

[55] *Ibid.*, pp. 722–726.
[56] Dubosq, *op. cit.*, pp. 139–144.
[57] *Ibid.*, p. 171; *The World Coal-Mining Industry*, Vol. I, p. 244.
[58] Lafitte-Laplace, *op. cit.*, p. 720.
[59] Dubosq, *op. cit.*, pp. 170–171.

Coal: Concerted Practices 269

In 1936, when Léon Blum was Premier, Parliament passed the Coal Industry Act, which gave the government power to fix the price of domestic and imported coal, to subsidize high-cost mines and to conduct an inquiry for the preparation of regional and national marketing controls under closer government supervision.[60]

Since the Common Market

The French coal mines were nationalized after the second world war. The Charbonnages de France was established and given responsibility for the administration of coal production and sales. Commercial and policy-making activities are centralized although mining operations and sales are decentralized in nine regional divisions. According to an official of Charbonnages de France:[61]

The Charbonnages de France enjoys a monopoly, at the least a quasi-monopoly, of French coal production. If the decentralization arising from the existence of nine mining divisions prevents us from calling it a monopoly, Charbonnages de France from the commercial point of view is nevertheless a single sales unit in many respects.

A parallel organization, Association Technique de l'Importation Charbonnière (ATIC), operating by government decree since 1944, monopolizes the import of solid fuels into France—except that imported by the French steel industry for its own use—and thus acts as a shield for the protection of the nationalized mines. Petroleum imports and refining also are regulated by the government to prevent competition in the fuels industries, a policy that has been followed since the interwar period. ATIC has the right to veto any contract for the purchase of non-French solid fuels. French consumers and merchants cannot purchase from other producers or merchants in the common market without mediation by ATIC. Officials of the Ministry of Industry and of Charbonnages de France are on ATIC's Board of Directors. Centralization of imports also has helped the government to equalize the difference between the price of French and imported coal; since the common market this adjustment is made only for solid fuels imported from suppliers outside of the ECSC.[62]

ATIC's role in controlling imports may be appreciated from the fact that when the French government devalued the franc in August 1957, retaining the

[60] *The World Coal-Mining Industry*, Vol. I, pp. 243–246.

[61] Paul Gardent, "Les Houillères françaises et la concurrence sur le marché commun," *Colloque des Facultés de Droit*, Grenoble, June 1955, mimeographed, page 1.

[62] For the French point of view on ATIC's relation to the over-all coal policy in France, see Paul Gardent, "Les Importations de charbon américain et le problème des contrats à long terme," *Revue française de l'énergie*, December 1957, p. 109.

270   *Europe's Coal and Steel Community*

old rate on imports of raw materials, speculative imports of steel rose sharply but coal imports remained constant.[63]

Having disposed of the problem of the Ruhr sales agencies in February 1956, the High Authority then took on the problem of ATIC. ATIC really involved the French government, with whose sanction it operates. The French steel industry has a common purchasing agency for solid fuels called ORCIS, which is represented in ATIC. The government agreed to the High Authority's request that membership in ORCIS be voluntary rather than obligatory. The French government conceded several other points but none involving ATIC's basic operations.[64]

The High Authority brought matters to a head in December 1957 on the strength of Articles 86 and 88, since Article 65 is applicable only to private organizations. The High Authority ruled:

(1) That ATIC's role as sole purchaser in its own name be abolished within one year and that its role as purchaser in the name of other clients be abolished within two years.

(2) That French consumers be given direct access to non-French merchants within two years.

The French government appealed to the Court of Justice in February 1958. The outcome still rested with the Court as of early 1959. The High Authority's decision, if upheld, will not affect ATIC's powers over imports from third-party countries.

The French government has justified ATIC on the ground that France must coordinate its large volume of imports, that the individual buyer is no match for the powerful Ruhr sales agencies, that the Ruhr must be prevented from dumping coal in France during a recession, and that the Ruhr coal producers must be prevented from dominating the French coal importers as they did before the war.[65] The French government insisted that ATIC was simply the counterweight to the sales agencies for Ruhr solid fuels. The French government's defense of ATIC therefore shows little confidence in the High Authority's attempt to regulate the Ruhr sales agencies. The High Authority, on the other hand, felt morally obligated—and the Germans expected it—to reduce ATIC's power once the matter of Georg had been disposed of. Though the French government defended ATIC on the ground that it shielded the Charbonnages de France from the monopoly power exercised by the Ruhr coal industry, the German government had defended the centralized sales agencies

[63] *Handelsblatt*, October 25-26, 1957, p. 1.

[64] The High Authority's *Bulletin mensuel d'information*, July 1956, pp. 33 ff, and January–February 1958, pp. 23 ff, contains a good analysis of the subject, describing the High Authority's efforts to reach a mutual agreement with the French government's concurrence.

[65] *Le Monde*, June 29, 1956, p. 10.

Coal: Concerted Practices 271

for Ruhr solid fuels on the ground that the Charbonnages de France was a monopoly.

A NOTE ON CENTRALIZED IMPORTS BY LUXEMBOURG

The government of Luxembourg has its own ATIC-type organization, called the Office Commercial Luxembourgeois, which controls the importation of solid fuels for all consumers other than the steel mills, which handle their own imports. The Office Commercial Luxembourgeois imports a small quantity of solid fuels. It had once equalized the delivered price of imported fuels coming from diverse sources in order to sell them to the consumer on a common price list and generally below cost. This subsidy was, and is, financed by a tax on coal for industrial consumption—in practice a tax on steel production. The High Authority and the Court of Justice considered this subsidy to be an indirect tax for revenue equally applicable to all industry, and therefore legal. The High Authority, however, advised the Office Commercial Luxembourgeois that it was illegal to equalize prices—which interferes with competition among suppliers in the Luxembourgeois market—but not illegal to reduce the price of all imported solid fuels by the same percentage.

The High Authority later endeavored to loosen the monopolistic features of the Office Commercial Luxembourgeois by applying measures similar to those it recommended with respect to ATIC.[66] The outcome in both cases still rested with the Court of Justice as of early 1959.

SALE OF COAL PRODUCED IN THE SAAR AND LORRAINE

The Saar and Lorraine supply similar grades of coal to southern Germany and to eastern France.

SAAR MARKETS

The Saar having too small a local market to be able to survive without "exports," and too small an export surplus to dominate any other market, the distribution of Saar coal in France has been organized in relation to the coal supplied by the Lorraine mines. Its distribution in southern Germany has been organized in relation to the coal supplied to that area by the mines in Lorraine, Aachen and the Ruhr.

[66] HA, *Bulletin mensuel d'information*, April 1958, p. 15, May 1956, p. 14, November 1956, paragraph 49; HA, *Sixième rapport général*, Vol. II, pp. 99–100; Court of Justice, *Recueil de la jurisprudence*, Vol. II, cases 7–54 through 10–54, inclusive.

272   *Europe's Coal and Steel Community*

Interwar Period

These arrangements have survived successive territorial changes. When the RWKS assumed exclusive control of the distribution of Saar coal in 1935, the delivery of Saar coal to France was regulated by the Naples Agreement of February 1935 between France and Germany; it stipulated, among other things, that Germany would ship to designated consumers in France 2 million tons of Saar coal annually until 1940.

Saar coal was distributed in southern Germany by the Kohlenkontor for that region.[67]

Saar Coal in French Markets

In 1955 the Saar distributed 14.5 million tons of coal and coke as follows (exclusive of coal consumed locally by the mines and cokeries):[68]

Destination	Tons (Millions)	Per Cent
France	4.5	32
Saar	5.2	36
Southern Germany	3.7	24
Austria, Italy, Switzerland	1.1	8
Total	14.5	100

Seventy per cent of the Saar coal distributed in France that year was sold directly by the Saarbergwerke, then under French control, to nationalized industries, such as the French railways, Electricité de France, Gaz de France, and to ORCIS (the centralized purchase organization for the French steel industry). Saarbergwerke also sold directly to the Saar railways and the Saar steel industry. The remaining 30 per cent of the sales in France were handled by two French centralized sales agencies, AREPIC for eastern France and LORSAR for the rest of France.

Coordination of Saar and Lorraine Coal

The transfer of the Saar to Germany, beginning January 1957, would have threatened these arrangements, as well as the coordinated sale of Saar and Lorraine coal in southern Germany, had not the German and French governments regulated the matter in the treaty for the transfer of the Saar.[69] The treaty obliged the French gradually to abandon mining in the Warndt area, astride the Lorraine-Saar frontier. The French government had made large

[67] Dubosq, *op. cit.*, p. 33; Lafitte-Laplace, *op. cit.*, pp. 454–455.

[68] *Glückauf*, December 8, 1956, p. 1503.

[69] Published by the French government as "Sarre-Moselle-Rhin Conventions de janvier 1957," *Journal officiel de la République de France*, No. 57–4S, Paris, January 1957.

Coal: Concerted Practices 273

postwar investments in the Warndt mines despite protest from the Saar, which accused France of mining coal from the Saar's side of the frontier. The ECSC, unfortunately, did not help allay national rivalry over the possession of coal reserves.

The pertinent provisions of the Saar treaty of 1957 are listed below; the first two items are related to the Warndt question.

(1) The French will draw from the Warndt a total of 20 million tons of coal in 1957–1961 and a total of 46 million tons in 1962–1981.

(2) From 1962 to 1981 the German government will deliver an additional 1.2 million tons of Saar coal annually to Houillères de Lorraine, the regional coal division of Charbonnages de France, at prevailing prices for Saar coal.[70]

(3) The Saar mining organization will, in addition, offer one third of its salable coal annually, at prices prevailing for Saar coal, to an organization named by the French government for distribution in France. This provision, valid for twenty-five years, obligated France to purchase the tonnage offered. The provision adds that if "international authorities" (obviously the High Authority) disturb this commitment, the German government will inform them of the special nature of the case.[71] The French government subsequently requested ATIC to take charge of this tonnage and founded Covesar (Comptoir de Vente des Charbons Sarrois) to distribute the coal.[72]

(4) A private Franco-German enterprise, valid for twenty-five years, will be created to "coordinate" the sale of Saar and Lorraine coal in southern Germany; German and French capital will each have an equal share, and control, in this enterprise. The enterprise's rules for the coordination of sales are subject to approval by the two governments.[73] The two governments subsequently organized Saarlar (Saar-Lothringische Kohlenunion), which will coordinate sales at prices fixed by the mines. It may also buy and sell solid fuels in other parts of the ECSC. The mines in Lorraine and the Saar control 85 per cent of Saarlar's capital.[74]

These arrangements, except for the first item, provide for concerted practices under public authority. The High Authority, demurring, reserved its rights by notifying the two governments of the following points:[75]

(1) The French government may not require anyone to take any portion of the 1.2 million tons against his will (item 2 of the Saar treaty as given above).

(2) Articles 58 and 59 of the ECSC treaty take precedence over any of the

[70] *Ibid.*, p. 42.
[71] *Ibid.*, Article 83 of Convention, p. 43, and Annex 28, p. 201.
[72] ATIC, *Exercice 1957*, p. 6.
[73] "Sarre-Moselle-Rhin Conventions de janvier 1957," Article 84, pp. 43–44.
[74] HA, Decision No. 6–59, *Journal officiel*, February 11, 1959, p. 189.
[75] *Journal officiel*, November 23, 1956, pp. 325 ff.

274   **Europe's Coal and Steel Community**

envisaged deliveries. (These articles provide for limitations on production and sales, respectively, as the case may be.)

(3) The agency appointed by the French government to take delivery of one third of the Saar coal (item 3 of the Saar treaty as given above) has no authority to divide the tonnage among French consumers.

(4) With respect to the agency to coordinate the shipment of coal from the Saar and Lorraine to southern Germany (item 4 of the Saar treaty as given above), the High Authority observed:

(a) That the High Authority will examine its legality when it knows the scope of its action, the distribution of capital stock in it, and the proportion of capital stock, if any, to be owned by the coal producers.

(b) That the agency will, in any case, have to file a request for authorization under Article 65 of the ECSC treaty.

(c) That the two governments should not lose sight of the pertinent parts of the ECSC treaty, nor of the fact that the Saar treaty does not relieve them of any of their obligations to the former treaty.

It is too early to determine the full outcome of these reservations made by the High Authority, but it approved Saarlar with reservations early in 1959.[76]

Prior to the Saar treaty of 1957, coal and coke from the Saar and Lorraine were distributed everywhere—but in France and in the Saar—by a monopoly, Union Charbonnière Rhénane, called Unichar. The French owned 65 per cent and the Saarbergwerke 35 per cent of Unichar.[77] Its principal market was in southern Germany; but it also distributed solid fuels in Austria, Italy and Switzerland. Unichar handled about 32 per cent of the Saar's solid fuels available for sale in 1955 and less than 10 per cent of the coal produced in Lorraine.

Unichar was not a sales but a distributing agency; it distributed solid fuels to sales subsidiaries or affiliates and added a 5 per cent service charge to the list price of the mines. It owned capital stock in all its affiliates and granted them exclusive sales rights over the coal which it distributed. Oberrheinische Kohlenunion (OKU) had exclusive sales rights over the solid fuels distributed by Unichar in southern Germany. OKU also monopolized the distribution of solid fuels from the Ruhr and Aachen in southern Germany.

Saarlar replaced Unichar by the terms of the Saar treaty of 1957 (item 4 of the Saar treaty as given above), German and French interests each acquiring 50 per cent control. Saarlar will continue to sell solid fuels from the Saar and Lorraine everywhere but in France and the Saar. (It will not sell to the German railways either.) Sales coordination of solid fuels from the Saar and Lorraine

---

[76] HA, Decision No. 6–59, *Journal officiel*, February 11, 1959.

[77] *Handelsblatt*, April 18, 1956, lists the French interests in Unichar as follows: ATIC, 17 per cent; Houillères de Lorraine, 10 per cent; Charbonnages de France, 3 per cent; other French interests, 35 per cent.

Coal: Concerted Practices 275

in the French market will remain substantially unchanged.[78] The German interest in Saarlar's local affiliates will rise to correspond with its 50 per cent interest in Saarlar as compared with 35 per cent in Unichar.[79]

THE SOUTH GERMAN MARKET

Before August 1957

From 1945 to the end of 1952 Kohlenkontor Weyhenmeyer, Mannheim, controlled the distribution of coal in the United States Zone of Germany and the Oberrheinische Kohlenunion (OKU) performed the same function in the French Zone. Kohlenkontor Weyhenmeyer was a branch office of Deutsche Kohlen Verkauf (DKV), which under supervision of the allied authorities controlled all the solid fuels distributed in Germany. In 1945 the United States Military Government had ordered Kohlenkontor Weyhenmeyer to sell only to wholesalers, and hoped that the wholesalers would compete among themselves. But DKV partly circumvented this order by selling directly to the larger consumers in the south German market. In 1952, for example, DKV handled 15 per cent of the solid fuels in the south German market and the wholesalers handled the remainder. The wholesalers, on the rare occasion of a buyers' market, competed by absorbing part of the 3 per cent commission allowed them by Kohlenkontor Weyhenmeyer within the list price.

In the French Zone OKU sold directly to all customers who consumed over 2,400 tons of solid fuels annually; very little was left for the wholesalers. In the British Zone (northern Germany) all customers that consumed 12,500 tons or more of solid fuels annually were reserved to DKV.

All wholesalers in the United States Zone were forced to purchase from Kohlenkontor Weyhenmeyer. All those in the French Zone purchased only from OKU. Both these distribution agencies controlled transport on the upper Rhine to Mannheim and Ludwigshafen, the basing points for coal sold in southern Germany. The wholesalers thus were without means of transporting coal to that area had they wished to circumvent the distribution agencies on which they were dependent.

The prospective dissolution of DKV (which occurred in 1953) spelled the end of Kohlenkontor Weyhenmeyer. With the handwriting on the wall, Kohlenkontor Weyhenmeyer and OKU drew up a fusion agreement in 1950 to control the south German coal market. It was pocket-vetoed by the United

[78] See *Glückauf,* December 8, 1956, p. 1504; *Revue française de l'énergie,* September 1956, p. 424.

[79] *Handelsblatt,* April 18, 1956.

276   *Europe's Coal and Steel Community*

States Military Government but supported by the French Military Government, as well as by the German principals. The dormant agreement was executed by its sponsors in 1952 without the approval of the United States Military Government. The new organization, also called OKU, began operations in April 1953. It sold directly to all customers that consumed 30,000 tons or more of solid fuels annually. It sold directly to all wholesalers, who dealt with the smaller consumers. OKU thus handled all the solid fuels consumed in southern Germany and also controlled transport on the upper Rhine and the coal blending facilities at Mannheim.

Unichar owned 3.6 per cent of the capital stock of OKU, the mining firms in the Ruhr and Aachen owned 32 per cent of the stock and several large wholesalers in southern Germany owned about 50 per cent of OKU.[80] But since the mining firms in the Ruhr exercised proprietary control in several large wholesale firms in southern Germany, the coal mining firms as a whole that sold in that market—the Saar, Lorraine, Ruhr and Aachen mines—controlled OKU through direct and indirect ownership ties. These mining firms as a whole furnished two thirds of all the solid fuels consumed in southern Germany. That portion of the two thirds that was transported on the Rhine River—about 7 million tons annually—accounted for about one fifth of all upstream traffic.[81]

In July 1953 the High Authority issued a "recommendation" (which is binding as to objectives but leaves the principal free to select his means) to OKU. It indicated that OKU monopolizes the distribution of solid fuels in southern Germany and divides the clientele between itself and the wholesalers, the latter being able to sell only to customers that consume less than 30,000 tons annually. The High Authority therefore recommended that OKU should take "appropriate measures to eliminate the practices contrary to Article 4 of the Treaty."[82] But this recommendation was simply a holding action that deferred the real solution to the time when Georg should be dissolved—an event that occurred nearly three years later.

After Reorganization by the High Authority (August 1957)[83]

The High Authority as of August 1957 transformed OKU from a common sales agency for the producers into a common purchasing agency for wholesalers. The coal mining firms in the Ruhr and Aachen were required to withdraw from OKU as members and owners. The Saar and Lorraine producers,

[80] *Ibid.*

[81] HA, Decision No. 19–57, *Journal officiel*, August 10, 1957, pp. 352–353.

[82] HA, Recommendation of July 11, 1953, *Journal officiel*, July 21, 1953, p. 154.

[83] HA, Decision No. 19–57, *Journal officiel*, August 10, 1957, pp. 352 ff. The decision, effective August 1, 1957, is summarized in HA, *Bulletin mensuel d'information*, October 1957, p. 11.

Coal: Concerted Practices 277

as well as Unichar (later Saarlar), were also required to withdraw but were accorded a respite to March 1958. This respite gave them time to establish commercial relations with the wholesalers in the area—relations that the firms in the Ruhr and Aachen had already had for a long time.[84] Designated wholesalers in France were given the opportunity until March 1958 to extend their activities to southern Germany in order to qualify as first-hand wholesalers and purchasers of capital stock in OKU.

Each wholesaler was authorized to own capital shares in OKU in proportion to the volume of solid fuels it purchased through it. The High Authority decision stipulated that wholesalers that are controlled by the Ruhr mining firms or that have proprietary interests in those firms may not capture control of OKU.

The High Authority decision required OKU to become purely a service organization for its members. OKU may not sell solid fuels to consumers, or fix prices or make any agreements limiting the use and availability of Rhine transport. It must purchase for the account of the wholesaler on the latter's instructions as to source and price; at the wholesaler's request, it must try to purchase from any producing district in the ECSC. Where the mining firms in a producing region sell through common sales agencies, OKU must purchase from the latter, not from the former.

OKU was not authorized to monopolize purchases. Consumers that purchase over 30,000 tons of solid fuels annually and first-hand wholesalers may also purchase directly from mining firms or their agents. The wholesalers were not required to join OKU but OKU was obliged to admit any wholesaler who fulfilled the conditions. OKU was thus required to be only a voluntary common purchasing agency.

OKU was authorized to maintain blending facilities, to operate a shipping pool on the Rhine and to maintain stockpiles, in order to coordinate supplies and transports. It was obliged to furnish shipping facilities to nonmembers to the extent available.

The High Authority can review OKU's activities to see that it complies with the authorization. It may if necessary request OKU to help spread orders among the mining firms during a business recession or to help distribute coal fairly when it is scarce.

Southern Germany accounts for about 10 per cent of the solid fuels consumed by the ECSC as a whole. In reorganizing OKU, the High Authority tried to induce the suppliers in that market—the Ruhr, Aachen, the Saar and Lorraine—to compete. This matter is discussed further in Chapter 9.

[84] This respite was prolonged once by the High Authority; a request for a second prolongation was denied. *Journal officiel*, August 4, 1958, p. 286.

278   *Europe's Coal and Steel Community*

THE BELGIAN MARKET

Interwar Period

The efforts of the Belgian coal industry to control markets before the second world war were as turbulent as those of the steel industry. The large number of small independents in the southern coal fields and differences between government and industry created most of the difficulties.

A socialist minister of industry and labor in 1927 proposed that the mines establish a centralized sales agency. This proposal was abandoned under attack from the industry. In April 1929 Société Générale and the Banque de Bruxelles helped found the Comptoir Belge des Charbons Industriels; it lasted until 1934. This agency, in cooperation with another for the Liége mining district, centralized the sale of coal to industry and the exportation and importation of industrial coal; it handled in all about 8 million tons of coal annually on a total production of 26 million tons. Coke was controlled by another agreement. The Comptoir Belge des Charbons Industriels ran into difficulties in 1934 owing to differences between the coal industry and the government. The former was unhappy with the volume of coal imported under the Belgo-German Commercial Treaty and the latter was unhappy with a 5 per cent wage reduction made by the industry. The government introduced a bill early in 1934 calling for government control of production, sales, imports and exports until 1935. The coal industry attacked it as "dirigistic" but appointed a committee to negotiate with the government on the latter's invitation. The government in the meantime reimbursed the employees for the 5 per cent wage cut. Another bill was passed later in 1934; it authorized the government to control the industry by decree. Under this law the producers founded a cooperative called Office National des Charbons in December 1934. The Belgian government simultaneously denounced the commercial treaty with Germany. The Office National des Charbons consisted of eight sections, one for each type of coal. It controlled production, assigned production quotas, regulated prices and foreign trade. It had exclusive control over sales to major public and private consumers and to foreign customers. The cost of the control scheme, under which exports were subsidized also, was covered by a levy of 2 francs per ton of coal produced.[85] An Office Belge des Cokes with similar functions was created in 1937.

Under the Common Market

The High Authority's decision to authorize common sales agencies for the mining firms in the Ruhr set the pattern for the firms in Belgium, one of the few other places where private firms still control most or all of the production.

[85] Dubosq, *op. cit.*, pp. 151–155; *The World Coal-Mining Industry*, Vol. I, pp. 246–247.

Coal: Concerted Practices 279

In October 1956, several months after the establishment of the three sales agencies in the Ruhr, the High Authority authorized the Belgian coal mines to operate a central sales agency for similar reasons.[86] Comptoir Belge des Charbons (Cobechar), organized in 1934, was authorized to sell coal for the mining firms to certain customers. It was also authorized to fix prices and sales conditions for all sales, including those made by the mining firms themselves. Cobechar also was empowered to fix the rules for delivery terms, for basing points, for discounts and for long-term contracts. Unlike Ruhr firms, the mining firms in Belgium are authorized to concert on prices.

Practically all the mining firms are represented in Cobechar. Each firm has capital shares and voting rights in Cobechar in proportion to its production. Since the Société Générale and the Launoit groups control a large part of the coal industry, the presidency of Cobechar rotates between the two groups from one year to the next.[87]

Cobechar was not authorized to control production but it was authorized to equalize employment and the distribution of orders when there is idle capacity.[88] This stipulation is included as a "restriction" on the powers of Cobechar, and was evidently meant to protect the independent producers.

The large consumers, defined functionally rather than by annual consumption—the independent cokeries, steel plant cokeries, public utilities, public railroads, bunkers, cement, glass and patent fuel plants—are all reserved to Cobechar. Cobechar was to sell to Italian customers until July 1958 unless any of the latter preferred to employ a merchant instead. Cobechar was not authorized to insist on exclusive sales arrangements in the Luxembourg or French coal markets.

The mining firms may sell to all other customers, to firms that own 75 per cent of their capital and to any consumers that have bought from the mines on long-term contracts. The mines may sell directly or through merchants. The High Authority decision does not attempt to protect or define the status of merchant or to divide merchants into zones as it does for the sale of Ruhr coal, although it offers them the general protection of Articles 4(b) and 4(d) of the treaty.[89] If Cobechar fixes the rules for sale to merchants, it must first obtain the High Authority's approval. In Belgium as in the Ruhr, the High

---

[86] Decision No. 30-56, *Journal officiel*, October 18, 1956, and the amendment thereto, Decision No. 27-57, *Journal officiel*, December 27, 1957.

[87] H. Aszkenazy, "Le Fonctionnement du marché charbonnier en Belgique et en Hollande," *Annales des mines*, May 1957, p. 322.

[88] Article 9 of HA, Decision No. 30–56.

[89] The merchants' markup, fixed by government decree, is added to the list price of the mining firm so that consumers ordinarily prefer to purchase directly from the mine. On sales to the retailer the wholesale merchant may add 3.3 per cent to the mine price. The markup on imports is also fixed by the Belgian government. Aszkenazy, "Le Fonctionement du marché charbonnier en Belgique et en Hollande," p. 324.

280   *Europe's Coal and Steel Community*

Authority decision gives the customer the right to take delivery at mine, inland port or Antwerp and to arrange his own transportation.

The mining firms are authorized to establish uniform freight charges for delivery at Liége, Gand and Antwerp, provided the uniform charge does not exceed the actual average freight charge. The firms may operate a financial scheme to debit and credit the firms for the difference between the uniform charge and the actual freight cost.

Belgium produced an annual average of 29.5 million tons of coal in 1956–1957; 6.5 million tons were consumed by the mines and affiliated concerns, leaving 23 million tons for sale. Cobechar handles about 17 million tons, nearly 60 per cent of the total output or three fourths of the coal available for sale. The mining firms handle the rest. There are more than fifty mining firms. The High Authority decision theoretically provides for a large number of sellers. But sales are more coordinated in practice than appearance indicates, because Cobechar fixes prices and sales conditions for all coal whether sold by it or by the mining firms, because the Société Générale and the Launoit groups dominate Cobechar, and because nearly all the mining firms belong to Cobechar. The coal sold directly by the mining firms is therefore sold by firms that also belong to Cobechar.

OTHER ECSC MARKETS

The Netherlands

The State controls about two thirds of the coal output in the Netherlands. A foreign-owned mining firm controls another 20 per cent. The Dutch coal industry is thus effectively centralized as producer and seller. The Netherlands normally imports nearly two thirds as much as it produces. Germany, Belgium and the United States supply most of the coal imported. Though imports are not centralized, the government supervises the volume of coal imported by the merchants.

Italy

Nearly all the coal consumed by Italy is imported. Italy has no domestic coal industry to protect and therefore has every reason to import freely from the lowest-priced sources. Imports are arranged by the several large consumers and distributors.

CONCLUSIONS

The mining firms in all the mining districts where coal is produced by more than one firm, as in Aachen, Lower Saxony, the Ruhr and Belgium, have been authorized to sell in common. The High Authority and the individual governments stand behind this policy. The High Authority has also authorized common purchasing arrangements among wholesalers in southern Germany. This principle will no doubt apply to importers of solid fuels in France as well, provided the French government agrees to eliminate ATIC's exclusive power over imports and to convert ATIC into a voluntary purchasing agency for the importers and consumers that wish to employ its know-how.

There appears to be very little likelihood of rivalry between mining firms in the same producing district for local or distant markets. Will the sales agencies for different coal fields compete among themselves? Such rivalry is still potentially possible in those markets that are supplied by more than one regional source and especially in those markets that are accessible to imports from overseas sources, notably from the United States. The markets in southern and northern Germany, in Italy, and those served through the Low Country ports, meet these conditions. These prospects are discussed in Chapters 9 and 10, for which the present chapter serves as background.

Coal

The coal industry which was taken over by the NCB at the beginning of 1947 had had a dismal record under private ownership and had got worse during the Second World War, when output, manpower, productivity and stocks fell appreciably, while absenteeism and costs rose.[2] The take-over took place at a time of immediate fuel shortage, bad enough to disrupt electricity supplies and the operation of industry, and in conditions which suggested that insufficient energy supplies might be the greatest long-term threat to post-war

92 *The State in Business: 1945 to the mid-1980s*

recovery and growth.[3] For ten years after the war it was taken for granted that almost all energy must come from coal. So, although the government looked to the NCB to reverse all the adverse trends of the war years, the purpose which was emphasised above all others was the achievement of a continual increase in the supply of coal. Attempts were made to make mining a more attractive occupation by increasing wages and reducing the normal working week; capital was made readily available and a large number of small schemes which spread best practice more widely in the industry helped to increase efficiency in the early years, after which a Plan for Coal, adopted in 1950 with governmental approval, introduced a decade of comprehensive modernisation and expansion by major reconstructions of existing mines and new sinkings.[4] Opencast mining, which had been adopted as a desperate wartime expedient to get a little extra coal at high cost, was kept going, though it was such a lossmaker that the NCB initially refused to take it over and until 1952 it was directly undertaken by the Ministry of Fuel and Power. After 1952 the NCB not only made it profitable but, by continual exploration, identified sufficient reserves of shallow coal to continue this 'temporary' expedient into the 21st century. By 1952 total output of coal had been increased from its 1946 level of 193.0 million tonnes to 228.4 million tonnes (which proved to be its peak, though deep-mined output was slightly higher in 1954 than 1952) and Plan for Coal was aiming to raise the total to 240 million tons (that is, 243.8 million tonnes) by 1965. Yet in 1952 the Ridley Committee[5] reported to the government that this was not enough to keep pace with demand and the target for 1965 ought to be 20 million tons higher. So the pressure to keep expanding output was made even stronger and there was a temporary (and unnecessary) inclination to supplement supplies by importing, which showed in the figures for 1954–7.

For several reasons a policy giving overriding priority to the maximisation of supplies was bound to be financially difficult for the NCB. Higher output could not be attained without the continued use of a lot of high-cost capacity. The coal industry had long been accustomed to appreciable differences in costs of production between districts. Immediately before nationalisation they had been dealt with partly by a levy on low-cost producers to help high-cost producers and partly by Exchequer subsidy, which ceased when the industry passed into public ownership. Subsequently the cost differentials tended to widen. Mining was labour-intensive. The attempt to recruit many more miners at a time of generally high employment put them in a strong bargaining position. Wage increases were negotiated nationally, as they had not been before, and similar wage increases added a relatively greater cost burden where the productivity of labour was lowest. This feature was reinforced because it was the policy of the National Union of Mineworkers to narrow, and eventually remove, wage differentials between districts, although down to 1939 the miners in high-cost districts had generally agreed to lower wages than those elsewhere. The less efficient collieries thus diverged further from the average costs of the industry, and the trend was strengthened by the need to concentrate cost-reducing investment, which helped labour productivity, on the collieries with the best prospects. The policy of seeking ever higher output also required heavy investment in extra capacity. As this had to be financed by borrowing at a time of rising interest rates, a further growing financial burden resulted.

It would have been financially possible, though politically difficult, to accommodate these problems by substantial price increases because the British coal industry, in terms of average costs, remained competitive in international terms in the 1950s. This competitive achievement was a source of further difficulty because the government required the NCB not only to do all the importing of coal but to sell the imports, which cost much more than British production, at the same price as equivalent grades of British coal. In its earlier years losses on imports were the most adverse of the influences on the NCB's profit and loss account.[6] The government would never agree to price increases which would have removed such difficulties. Except for about four years from the end of 1947 coal prices rose in real terms until the late 1950s, but not sufficiently to prevent about half the collieries operating at a loss. Several members of the Ridley Committee proposed in 1952 that the NCB should move towards marginal cost pricing on lines which at that time would not have put British coal prices out of line internationally and

94   *The State in Business: 1945 to the mid-1980s*

could be expected to yield a surplus of £200 million a year. Such a figure would have enabled all investment to be financed out of revenue and the building of reserves, which would have proved an adequate cushion against all the difficulties encountered at least down to the early 1970s.[7] But nobody in authority seriously contemplated such a course of action.

The NCB was able to cope with its financial circumstances in a variety of ways until the early 1960s. It had generally profitable non-mining businesses, chiefly in coal products (coke, manufactured fuel, and the by-products of carbonisation) and brickmaking – inheriting the latter from the colliery companies made it one of the country's largest brickmaking undertakings until it sold nearly all its brickworks in the early 1970s. From the mid-1950s it had a steady and generally growing source of profits in opencast mining, which in the long run proved to be its greatest business success. From the mid-1950s also it was getting well launched on the application of the new techniques which, over a period of about fifteen years, transformed coalface operations and underground haulage, though the benefits to productivity showed mainly in the 1960s. And in deep mining there was the successful operation of the two principal central regions, Yorkshire and the East Midlands (Derbyshire, Nottinghamshire, and Leicestershire), whose profits had practically to carry the losses of the high cost coalfields.

But from 1957 external conditions changed permanently. The market for coal started to contract, mainly because of the growing abundance of cheap oil and technical changes in important coal-using industries such as the railways, gas, and (to a lesser extent) steel, and in domestic heating. At least from 1967 (and rather less blatantly from a little earlier) it was also the government's proclaimed policy for coal to have a declining share in a four-fuel economy, so there was a propagandist pressure pushing any wavering users to switch from coal to something else. All this began before most of the investment in Plan for Coal had come to fruition and while further expenditure was still needed on the completion of projects which had gone too far for their abandonment to be economic. Whatever was done, it was impossible to prevent some deterioration in the financial position: the accumulation of reserves which could be drawn on had not been permitted; and a financial reconstruction became unavoidable. Under the terms of the Coal Industry Act 1965 this applied from the end of the 1965–6 financial year and involved the writing-off of £415 million, much of it representing closed capacity which had remained on the books, and a change in the terms of the remaining loans. The immediate effect on the revenue account was to reduce interest payments by £21.5 million and depreciation charges by £14.1 million.[8]

Once the accounting basis of a public corporation has been changed in such a way, the appraisal of its financial performance over the long term becomes increasingly a matter of uncertainty and opinion, especially when further changes followed in later years, as they did for the NCB. Perhaps the most that can safely be attempted is to record what was done by way of relief to the capital structure. This is the purpose of Table 5.1. It should be borne in mind that, because of very high rates of inflation, roughly similar figures at different dates meant very different things in terms of practical effect. It should also be remembered that the table does not include revenue grants in direct aid to operations. These, of course, prevented some deficits emerging or slightly increased an annual surplus, either of which would have subsequently affected the capital position. Between 1972–3 and 1982–3 there were £240 million of such government grants.

Some aspects of the industry's performance can be presented more certainly, even if the appearance is less misleadingly precise. The response to a contracting market was in many ways economically impressive in the 1960s. It was to reduce capacity by closing large numbers of near-exhausted and high cost collieries, to market coal more attractively, and to keep a tight hold on costs and prices. In ten years output fell by more than a quarter, the number of collieries and the labour force by more than half, yet the mechanisation of coalface operations and haulage went on rapidly, and output per manshift rose by 60 per cent. From 1961 to 1969 coal prices were on average kept steady in real terms and for the most efficient coalfields they fell on that basis.

But it was a success achieved at the cost of great strain. Employment at collieries fell by an average of 30 000 a year

96

TABLE 5.1 *NCB financial reconstructions and comparable financial reliefs, 1947–1983 (£ million)*

	1965–6	1972	1973	1974	1980–3	TOTAL
Accumulated deficit extinguished	115.6		174.6			290.2
Other capital written off	299.4		275.0			574.4
Special government grant to keep deficit within statutory limit		100.0		130.7		230.7
Deficit grants					1110.6	1110.6
TOTAL	415.0	100.0	449.6	130.7	1110.6	2205.9

for a decade, which was a traumatic experience, and the wages of miners, though they were maintained in real terms, fell appreciably in relation to those in other industries. The pressure to use the most efficient coalfields to retain more customers for the whole industry led to such tight pricing that even Yorkshire was driven into loss and the profits of the East Midlands were seriously reduced. The NCB was left with no margin for facing any new shocks. And, though the modernisation of working methods in the retained collieries went on apace, there was after the mid-1960s hardly any investment in the creation of new capacity, and this left the industry in a poor position to take advantage of any new market opportunities that might emerge.[9]

These strains are part of the explanation of what happened in the 1970s. After 1969 it was impossible to maintain price stability any longer and there were rapid rises in the next few years. The frustrations of the miners began to boil over and led to their successful national strike in 1972, which ended the period in which miners' wages had made a significant contribution to coping with adverse market pressures. Inflation and incomes policies eroded the relative gains which underground workers had obtained in 1972, the government intervened without doing anything effective to satisfy any of the parties, and there was another national strike, again largely successful, in 1974. These two strikes caused greater financial losses to the NCB than any previous influence had done and their outcome helped to maintain the recent rise in the level of production costs.[10] The government's response included the second capital reconstruction, in 1973, and other special grants in 1972 and 1974, as recorded in Table 5.1. It also included provisions for grants towards costs of production, if required, that is, in effect, subsidies.[11] This was, of course, at a time when government preoccupations with attempts to limit price rises led to somewhat similar assistance to a number of nationalised industries.

The 1970s saw a curiously mixed record by the NCB. Market prospects appeared much better because of the huge rises (especially in 1973–4 and again in 1979) in the price of oil, which had been the main competitor. But the benefits of this change were very limited for several reasons. Most of the large

98   *The State in Business: 1945 to the mid-1980s*

consumers of the past were now committed to combustion equipment which did not directly use coal and they would not find it easy to change back. The NCB had become mainly a supplier of fuel to the electricity and steel industries, the second of which ran into severe problems of contraction. So increased sales depended mainly on an increased demand for electricity generated from British coal. In any case, the absence of capital for investment in new capacity since the early 1960s had created conditions in which any large increase of deep-mined output was not immediately attainable. In 1974 a new Plan for Coal was brought into operation to remedy this state of affairs, but its execution was still far from complete when oil prices again fell drastically in the mid-1980s; and as it had to be financed from loans at enormously high rates of interest it imposed heavy financial burdens. Apart from this, it proved so difficult to keep down costs that the competitive advantages were less than had been hoped. Many of these costs related to inputs over which the coal industry had no control. But it was a severe handicap that the productivity of labour, which had risen so impressively in the 1960s, changed little in the 1970s. This was partly due to physical and technological reasons, but partly also to some lack of co-operation by workers, who had lost some incentive as all had moved on to day-wages, and who would not agree to any system of incentive payments until 1978. There was also, because of union opposition which appeared to be approved by the Labour governments of 1974–9, great difficulty in closing old collieries of declining efficiency as improved capacity became available elsewhere, although such closures were an essential part of the 1974 Plan for Coal, which the National Union of Mineworkers had publicly endorsed. There remained a good deal of British coal output which was not competitive in cost with available foreign supplies.[12]

In financial terms the record after the 1974 strike was much better than had been feared, particularly because the state of the international energy market allowed coal prices to rise enough to compensate for the great rise in costs which had occurred. Until the early 1980s, when recession in the large energy-using industries brought mounting difficulties, dependence on grants to aid production was very small and the NCB normally made an operating profit, but the rapidly growing interest burden associated with the new investment programme turned this into an overall deficit in most years. The sources of the operating profits were, however, likely to cause some heartsearching. The combination of higher coal prices and continuing low costs turned opencast mining into a splendid profit-maker, and there were still profits from non-mining business, mainly from the production of North Sea gas until the government transferred this to the British National Oil Corporation in 1976, and from merchanting in coal and heating appliances, even though coke ovens had become a financial burden. But, because of the retention of so many high cost collieries, deep mining (which was the main *raison d' être* of the NCB) was, as a whole, not profitable.[13]

To carry consideration beyond the early 1980s would be more confusing for coal than for any other industry, unless it were done in great detail. This is because of the unique causes and effects of the year-long strike of 1984–5, which was very different from the strikes of 1972 and 1974 and had irrationalities and political significances which did not relate exclusively to the economics and technicalities of the coal industry.[14] In business terms, one may merely note that it took the industry into a new era in which users had learned to manage with a smaller amount of British coal and the obstacles to the closure of high-cost capacity and to the more intensive working of the most efficient collieries had been greatly reduced.

But it is worth giving particular attention to the performance of coal among the nationalised industries down to 1983. It was the most acclaimed symbol of the post-war nationalisation programme and was then regarded as the most basic of all the industries taken into public ownership; it had exceptional continuity in its statutory position; and it came to be a special target of hostile critics of public ownership. Some of the fundamental data for judgment can be fairly easily summarised, though it is necessary to note that in some respects there were breaks in continuity. The financial reconstructions break up the uniformity of the data, and the effect of the 1972 strike – not only on costs but on attitudes to costs, including acceptance of the view that government grants in aid of production could be a permanent element in finance – also indicates an important turning point. Table 5.2 presents some of the physical statistics,

100

TABLE 5.2 *NCB statistics 1947–1987/8*

	1947	1957	1967–8	1972–3	1977–8	1982–3	1987–8
Coal output* (m. tonnes)	200.0	227.2	173.6	140.5	120.9	120.9	99.6
Output per manshift (tonnes)	1.09	1.26	1.98	2.33	2.19	2.44	3.62
Output per man-year (tonnes)	267	300	421	480	441	504	789
Men on colliery books+ ('000)	703.9	703.8	391.9	268.0	240.5	207.6	104.4

* Includes licensed mines and opencast
+ Average for year

Table 5.3 summarises the operating results, and Table 5.4 analyses for the initial period, where there are uniform data, the elements in the situation which first caused a need for financial reconstruction.[15]

At first sight it does not look an impressive record, especially if attention is also given to the writing-off of deficits as shown in Table 5.1. It is relevant to note that in the eleven years from 1972–3, when Table 5.3 shows only £265 million of operating profits (after grants of £240 million to aid production), £1613 million was paid out in interest on capital, so that larger deficits than ever emerged. Clearly the record is worse from 1972 than before. Nevertheless, there are other points worth noting, not all of them adverse, about the period as a whole.

The supreme initial task set the nationalised coal industry was to remove the threat of energy shortage by producing more. This was, in fact, done and was done at much lower prices than would have been paid if reliance had been mainly on imported fuels. The NCB was neither required nor permitted to make an appreciable surplus. It was required to expand to an extent for which there was no permanent need and to finance its expansion by loans at gradually rising rates of interest. Despite all the pressure to retain the output of high cost collieries, it would not have run into deficit if it had been paying a low dividend on equity capital and had not had the losses on coal imports loaded on to its accounts. Even with these burdens, a Coal Board for England and Wales (and still more one for England alone) would have earned enough to have had

TABLE 5.3 *NCB operating profits (losses) 1947–1982/3 (£ million)*

	1947 to 1971–2	1972–3 to 1982–3*	1947 to 1982–3*
Non-mining	86	186	272
Opencast	138	1012	1150
Deep mining	226	(933)	(707)
TOTAL	450	265	715

*These results are after crediting £240 million of government grants in direct aid to operations. Of this sum £72 million was for non-mining activities and £168 million for mining, almost all for deep mining.

102 *The State in Business: 1945 to the mid-1980s*

TABLE 5.4 *Sources of NCB deficits before the financial reconstruction of 1965–1966 (£ million)*

(a) *Financial results 1946 to 1965–6 inclusive*

Profit on deep mining	400.5	
Profit on opencast	70.0	
Profit on non-mining	39.1	
Loss on imported coal	(74.1)	
Total operating profit		435.5
Interest paid		(509.6)
Other charges		(41.5)
OVERALL DEFICIT		(115.6)

(b) *Regional contributions to financial results to 1965–66* (excluding opencast)*

	Surpluses		Deficits
Yorkshire	113.6	Scotland	156.5
East Midlands	250.8	Northumberland	
		and Durham	128.8
		North Western +	80.2
		West Midlands	0.8
		South Western + +	126.2
		Kent	12.4

* Brickworks were excluded from 1962 and coal products from 1963–4 as a result of their removal from the regional organisation. The figures are after charging interest and apportionment of losses on imports.
+ Cumberland, Lancashire, and North Wales.
+ + South Wales, Forest of Dean, Bristol and Somerset.

no need of financial reconstruction in 1965–6, as appears from Table 5.4(b). A separate Coal Board for Scotland had been suggested in pre-nationalisation discussions. It would have had a hard life but the main NCB would have fared better. Indeed for most of its existence the NCB could probably have run a profitable business if it had been free to mine anywhere by opencasting and had restricted deep mining to an area of middle England with its corners in Bradford, York, Melton Mowbray, Coventry and Newcastle-under-Lyme. But there would have been a serious lack of quantity in the earlier years and some significant reduction in variety of coal types at all times and, rightly or wrongly, this was seen as contrary to national need.

The high cost of servicing loans which formed virtually the whole capital of the business, and the losses and continuing additions to costs which resulted when the national strikes took place, appear as the principal source of NCB deficits. Both features might be interpreted, at least in part, as managerial failures. Even the peculiar financial structure should not divert attention from the need to earn a reasonable return on capital. It looks particularly alarming that, over its existence as a whole, the NCB did not make even an operating profit on deep mining, its main activity. Yet the same organisation was able to run some of its smaller ancillary undertakings very successfully and had an impressive record of achievement in opencasting; and this was true of the otherwise difficult decade of the 1970s. It does not look like general managerial or organisational failure. In fact, when the performance in deep mining is put into a wider context some rather different questions come to mind. The British coal industry in private ownership down to 1946 and most West European coal industries since then have some very poor results to show, while within its longer record of difficulty the British industry achieved in the 1960s a remarkable adjustment to a contracting market. One is left suspecting that if, over the long period, financial expectations were repeatedly disappointed the reason was not that the activity was nationalised but that it was coalmining.[16]

[17]

365-77
[1989]

Global
L72
L32
N50
N40

The role of state owned enterprises in the international metal mining industry

Marian Radetzki

State ownership in the non-socialist world mineral industries grew from insignificance in the 1950s to account for about one-third of total production capacity in the early 1980s. The motivations for this growth are explored. It is concluded that the period of expansion has now come to an end. The characteristic features and behavioural patterns of state owned enterprises are described. The implications of a large and increasingly mature state owned universe for international mineral markets and for the privately owned industry are analysed. The analyses point to the painful disruptions to which many multinational firms were subjected by the successive waves of nationalization in the 1960s and 1970s. But they also indicate that there is little foundation for the frequent claims that state owned firms constitute a survival threat to the private industry.

The author is at the Institute for International Economic Studies, University of Stockholm, S-10691 Stockholm, Sweden. He is also Visiting Professor at the Mineral Economics Department, Colorado School of Mines, Golden, CO 80401, USA.

[1]The analysis draws heavily on the research underlying M. Radetzki, *State Mineral Enterprises: An Investigation into Their Impact on International Mineral Markets*, Resources for the Future, Washington, DC, 1985.

The purpose of this paper is to explore the implications for the international mineral markets of the fast growth of state ownership in the mineral industries over the past two decades. The present investigation focuses on the change in market structure and the shifts in relative competitive position of different suppliers, resulting from the proliferation of state owned enterprises.

The paper is concerned with state owned mineral enterprises in the market economy countries only.[1] State ownership in all industries is a matter of course in the socialist countries and has been so ever since socialism was established.

There is a heavy emphasis throughout the following account on the developing countries. This is because the rapid growth of state ownership in mineral industries worldwide has been predominantly due to the widespread nationalizations that occurred in these countries after the break up of the colonial empires.

The analysis proceeds as follows. The first section analyses the motivations and describes the modes for establishing state ownership positions in the mineral industries. The second section assesses the growth and current size of the state mineral universe, after first considering the methodological and definitional issues involved. The prospects for further growth of state ownership in the mineral industries are also considered. In the third section the features which distinguish state owned mineral enterprises from private ones are identified and the market impact from the introduction of the new agents on the supply side is analysed. The final section is concerned with the implications for the private mineral industry of the presence of large and increasingly mature state owned enterprises.

Why state ownership in the mineral industries?

The mineral sector throughout the world has been a favourite area for government intervention in a variety of forms, including the taking up of direct equity positions. The authorities' desire to be involved and to control has a variety of explanations. First, the widespread perception of mineral wealth as a national patrimony has often been used to sanction public involvement, for instance to prevent private interests from profiteering or to assure adequate mineral supplies for future generations. Second, the inability to move mineral deposits exploited by mining firms facilitates far reaching public intervention in such exploitation without a risk of the activity moving beyond the government's reach. Third, the frequent generation of high rents in mineral endeavours, coupled with the difficulty of appropriating such rents through fiscal measures, provides the temptation for a greater degree of public involvement. And fourth, the extraction and processing of minerals is often regarded as strategically important, either because of the very large size of many mineral ventures or because such activities assure a domestic supply of key inputs into manufacturing, including the defence industry.

Arguments such as these explain many of the public ownership positions in mineral industries in the industrialized market economies. The more important ones include all stages of aluminium production in France, aluminium smelting in FRGermany, Italy, Norway and Spain, copper mining through to refining in Finland, iron ore production in France and Sweden and steel manufacturing in several Western European countries. The modes for establishing these ownership positions varied. In a few cases they resulted from confiscation of enemy property at the end of the second world war. In some instances the state acquired its ownership stake by bailing out bankrupt private enterprise. In others, the government purchased the equity at a price agreed through negotiations (Swedish iron ore) or determined unilaterally through a government decree (French aluminium).

However, a major proportion of the state owned mineral enterprises outside the socialist economies is found in the developing countries. Although the arguments enumerated above are certainly valid in explaining the existence of state ownership in the developing country group, an additional perspective is required for a fuller understanding of the emergence and growth of the publicly owned mineral sector in the Third World.

The 1960s and 1970s involved a historically unique economic emancipation process for a majority of the developing countries, following the severance of formal or informal colonial bonds. With improving administrative, technical and managerial capabilities in the post-colonial period, the ambitions and abilities of the authorities to promote development through control and direction of national economies were expanded. The great importance of the mineral sector in many cases, its predominantly foreign ownership and secluded enclave character *vis-à-vis* the national economy made it a major target for public policy initiatives.

These initiatives took a variety of forms. The ultimate and most far reaching measure in the developing countries heavily dependent on mineral exports was to nationalize the industry, in part or completely. The motivation to nationalize was usually based on the view that other intervention measures, like taxation or specific regulation pertaining to eg investment, employment or exports, were inadequate and that only direct equity ownership could provide the means for effective control over this key industry. The practice of compensation payments to previous owners varied from none at all to sums which might appear as

State owned enterprises in the international metal mining industry

adequate to impartial observers. However, the former owners invariably complained about the compensation received.

For reasons to be explored below, the urge to nationalize appears to have lost its force in the present decade. This underlines the historical uniqueness of the very fast growth of state ownership during the preceding two decades.

State ownership in the mineral industries quantified

Quantification of the state mineral enterprise universe raises some intricate problems. What criteria should be used in defining state mineral enterprises? A high degree of government control and a high share of public equity ownership are two possible criteria for including mineral firms in this category. Qualitative discussions often assume a close relationship between degree of public ownership and public control. This is not always so. Very heavy public involvement can sometimes be based on quite small government shareholding while in other cases the government may be uninterested in exercising its power to control despite a majority equity holding.

The degree of government control is probably a more relevant criterion for defining state enterprise than the extent of public equity ownership, given this paper's concern about changes in market structure and competitive strength brought about by the growth of state enterprises. Any systematic differences between private and public mineral firms are more likely to depend on control than on formal ownership. As noted, ownership can be passive. Control, on the other hand, implies active involvement.

The use of government control to define and quantify state mineral enterprise raises formidable difficulties, however. To determine the extent of such control would require in depth studies of individual mineral enterprises, which is hardly practicable in the context of global quantification.

Defining state mineral enterprise by the equity ownership criterion, though not entirely relevant for the purpose at hand, is infinitely simpler. Even when this classification criterion is employed some tricky issues must be resolved. For instance, Table 1 below provides three alternative measures of the state mineral enterprise universe. The least restrictive includes in the state owned category all firms in which public bodies hold 5% or more of the total equity. The most restrictive measure, in contrast, classifies as state enterprises only the ones in which government has a majority equity holding. The one in between takes state owned capacity to be proportional to the government's equity holding in each firm.

The division of enterprises into state and private portions according to the respective equity holdings will be employed in the following assessments of the size of the state owned universe. Though it is convenient for quantification purposes, the measure has the disadvantage of impeding clear cut identification of individual enterprises as either state or private.

Table 1, based on detailed analyses by company, presents an overview of state ownership at different stages of aluminium and copper production and in iron ore. In addition to providing Western world[2] totals, the table also details the prevalence of state enterprise in the developing countries.

[2] Western world is defined to include the entire world with the exception of the socialist countries of Eastern Europe, Asia and Cuba.

State owned enterprises in the international metal mining industry

Table 1. Government ownership positions in three major mineral industries, 1981.

	Aluminium (actual weight)[a] Mining	Refining	Smelting	Copper (metal content) Mining	Smelting	Refining	Iron ore (actual weight)[b]
Western World							
Total capacity (tons × 10³)	92 500	30 790	14 040	7 820	8 780	9 120	543 000
Percentage of capacity with significant government ownership[c]	45.3	24.2	22.8	40.5	30.6	25.9	55.6
Percentage of equity held by government	27.8	15.1	18.5	32.4	26.1	21.6	40.0
Percentage of capacity with majority government ownership	23.2	13.2	19.4	34.7	29.7	24.3	na
Developing countries							
Total capacity (tons × 10³)	54 000	6 530	2 190	4 120	3 340	2 580	216 900
Percentage of capacity with significant government ownership[c]	71.1	54.9	60.3	73.0	75.5	82.6	94.7
Percentage of equity held by government	41.1	21.1	44.7	57.8	64.0	67.6	61.8
Percentage of capacity with majority government ownership	33.3	12.3	45.6	62.0	72.9	77.0	na

Source: M. Radetzki, *State Mineral Enterprises*, Resources for the Future, Washington, DC, 1985.

[a]Figures for aluminium are for 1980; [b]figures for iron ore are based on production and not on capacity; [c]defined as 5% and upwards of total equity.

In the early 1980s, Western world state enterprise, measured as capacity proportional to government equity holding, represented 45% of total capacity in bauxite and 41% in copper mining. The figures were substantially lower at the further processing stages of bauxite and copper ores. In iron ore, the state owned proportion was more than 55%. Less detailed analyses for some other metal minerals suggest Western world state owned shares of about 70% in cobalt, more than 30% in tin, 20–25% in lead and zinc, roughly 17% in chromium and 15% in nickel and molybdenum.[3]

In all cases the state owned shares are substantially higher when only the developing countries are considered. In fact, the variation in the Western world state owned share is strongly correlated with the LDCs share of each metal in total Western world output.

Despite their limitations, the above data indicate that public ownership involvement in Western world mineral industries is very substantial. They also point to a very considerable concentration of state enterprises in the developing countries. An attempt to aggregate by assigning weights to the respective minerals according to output value suggests that in the early 1980s roughly one-third of Western world mineral industry, and about one-half of the mineral production capacity located in the developing countries, was state owned.

Attempts to track the growth of state enterprise over time present tricky problems but whatever data are available suggest that the expansion was explosive in the 1960s and 1970s. Public ownership was relatively insignificant in the early 1950s. The present importance of public engagement in the mineral sector has been attained primarily through a combination of nationalizations of existing privately owned firms, growth in capacity of existing state owned companies and substantial government participation in joint ventures with mining multinationals in the development of new capacity.

Several factors suggest that the fast growth phase has now come to an end. The post-colonial push for economic emancipation, a major force behind many nationalizations, was completed in the majority of developing countries by the early 1980s. The most conspicuous foreign

[3]*Op cit*, Ref 1.

State owned enterprises in the international metal mining industry

ownership positions have already been taken over by the national authorities. Relations between governments in developing countries and multinational mining firms have improved and amicable joint venture arrangements for the development of new projects have become common. During the 1980s a worldwide resentment against excessive public involvement in industry has led to many privatizations of state enterprises. Though few, if any, state owned mineral firms have been sold off, the likelihood of a further significant expansion of the state owned share in the mineral industries in industrialized economies or developing countries appears to be small. Prospects for the coming years are for a substantial but relatively static proportion of Western world mineral production to be supplied by an increasingly mature group of state owned enterprises.

State mineral enterprises: distinguishing features and market impact

From an analyst's point of view the ideal situation would be one where a clear cut distinction could be drawn between the profit maximizing mineral firms on the one hand and the state owned mineral enterprises, characterized by their pursuit of a different set of goals, on the other. In the real world, the distinction between the two is blurred. Private firms seldom conform to the pure microeconomic paradigm. Private mineral enterprises in many countries have been increasingly conditioned, by law or convention and especially during the most recent decades, to assume many functions other than profit maximization. The characteristics of state owned mineral enterprises appear to range widely between forms quite akin to private corporations at one extreme and ones where social considerations predominate over concerns with return on capital at the other.

However, although the line is blurred, there does appear to be a significant difference in goals, characteristics and behavioural patterns between the average private and state owned mineral firm. The following paragraphs try to describe this difference. The statements are based on widespread empirical observation as reflected in the literature and are supported by common sense and economic logic.

The emphasis is on the state owned mineral firms in developing countries, since this group has experienced the fastest growth and currently accounts for a dominant share of the total state owned universe in the mineral industry.

Inefficiency of new state owned firms

A transient but very important feature that has characterized a significant proportion of the state mineral enterprise universe during the past 20 years has been a high degree of inefficiency. As noted, the fast growth of the state mineral enterprise universe came about most notably through nationalizations of private foreign investments in developing countries. Nationalizations frequently involved extended and heavy set up costs. The national firms set up to manage the operations that were taken over from foreigners usually had a difficult start. The old owners, dissatisfied with the compensation offered, were often unwilling to provide assistance. The new managers regularly lacked the appropriate experience; yet they had to take on wide ranging responsibilities long before they had a chance to acquire the necessary expertise.

The result was almost invariably a disruption in operations that reached a maximum soon after takeover and then gradually subsided over a long period of time. Initially, inexperienced management was often unable to maintain production at full capacity levels and the cost of output tended to rise. The ability to undertake investment in new capacity, probably the most complex task faced by managements of mineral firms, usually took the longest time to master.

Empirical evidence suggests a wide variation in the time needed to overcome the disruptions and inefficiencies due to managerial inexperience after nationalization. The speed of results appears to be related to the level of economic development of the country, the extent of earlier exposure of the national managers to the problems of the industry and the ability to strike a constructive arrangement with outside specialists for managerial support and training. Overcoming the loss of efficiency due to inexperience at the time of nationalization took no more than five years in the case of Venezuela's iron ore operations. In Indonesia's tin industry more than 20 years were needed to develop a national management cadre of international quality standards after the industry was taken over from the Dutch in the early 1950s. In Zambia, where the government took a majority holding of the copper industry in 1969, the process has not yet been completed.[4]

As a consequence of the successive nationalizations, a considerable proportion of the state owned mineral enterprises has been operated by inexperienced managements throughout the past two decades. The result has been a lower rate of capacity utilization, a higher level of costs and a lesser extent of capacity expansion than would have occurred in the absence of state takeovers.

The impact just described is transient. Since the process of nationalization appears to have come to an end we can expect that the state mineral enterprises still suffering from managerial inexperience and related inefficiencies will gradually overcome these predicaments.

Characteristics of mature state owned mineral firms

Other characteristics of state mineral enterprises are more permanent. Such enterprises regularly have a much more diversified goal structure than privately owned firms. In addition to the requirements that a return on capital should be earned, state enterprises often pursue employment, regional development or skill creation and technological progress objectives at the national level.

The addition of non-profit objectives to the goals of the state owned firm is bound to involve a cost and so to result in permanently higher costs of mineral production. Furthermore, the subordination of the profit motive is likely to lessen the pressure on management to minimize costs,[5] especially since a high cost to produce the mineral can always be justified by the pursuit of some social objective. The ensuing inefficiency will tend to increase costs even further.

For the reasons just spelled out, the costs of producing minerals in state owned mineral enterprises will be higher, on average, than in private firms exploiting mineral deposits of a corresponding quality. It should be stressed, however, that the importance of this difference will vary. In those state owned firms where return on capital is the overriding objective, the cost efficiency will not be very different from that in private operations.

The suppression of the profit goal and the influence exerted by the

[4] *Ibid.*
[5] H. Leiberstein, 'X-efficiency and the analysis of state enterprise', Paper presented at the Second BAPEG Conference on Public Enterprises in Mixed Economy LDCs, Boston, April 1980.

government can be assumed to make the state owned enterprises more amenable to considering social benefit, including externalities that they will not reap, as a guiding criterion for their actions. In mineral exporting developing countries, unemployment is a common problem and so the shadow wage would be lower than the actual wage. At least during periods of mineral price depression the current account of such countries would often show a deficit and so the shadow rate of exchange for their currency would be lower than the official one.[6] An application of these shadow rates will lower the supply curve and raise the demand curve in relation to the ones that would prevail if the market rates were used. This will provide economic justification for higher capacity utilization at each level of mineral prices in dollars and so a lesser degree of output adjustment to varying price levels.

A reciprocal of the costly concerns of the state mineral firms is an implicit guarantee of financial survival, regularly provided by their owners. State enterprises are rarely allowed to go bankrupt. Undercapitalization resulting from unprofitable operation is regularly remedied through new financial infusions. The implications of such a guarantee should not be overemphasized. Excepting periods of severe mineral price depression, a majority of the large state mineral firms reap significant Ricardian rents which assure financial comfort even after their social obligations have been covered.

What systematic differences in investment behaviour can be identified between state owned firms and private multinational corporations in the mineral industry? State enterprises, like private ones, would ordinarily develop new production units only when it was commercially justifiable to do so. The capital invested has to yield sufficient return to service the loans and to provide a return on equity after costs have been covered. Through their owners, state owned firms may have a somewhat easier access to sources of credit on concessional terms eg from the World Bank or the Regional Development Banks. But such creditors have typically required careful feasibility studies proving commercial viability of the projects to be financed.

In some cases, governments have used their control to make state enterprises invest in uncommercial ventures eg to promote regional development or to satisfy the national strategic needs of output. Ownership is not a unique means of achieving such public ends. Support of private firms through subsidies or tariffs has accomplished identical objectives in countries where the government has abstained from owning the mineral industry.

There will be a large difference in the rate of return on investments required by state owned and private mineral firms in countries where private foreign investors feel exposed to political risk. The expected return on private mineral projects has to be increased sufficiently to provide an adequate risk premium. State owned enterprises, by definition, are not exposed to the risk of expropriation or milder forms of nationalization. For this reason, in the circumstances just described, their rate of return requirements will be lower.

Turning to the geographical spread of investments, a distinguishing characteristic of state mineral enterprises is their strong preference for investing at home. Exceptions, like the investments of Chilean Codelco and Zambian ZCCM in European downstream processing of copper, only underline the rule. The nationalizations of the 1960s and 1970s frequently involved a rupture of the international vertical integration

[6]Shadow wage rates and rates of exchange are defined as those rates at which full employment and a balanced current account would be attained.

chains maintained by the private mining companies. (The downstream processing facilities located in the mineral importing countries were out of reach of nationalization efforts.) The lower extent of vertical integration that resulted from state takeovers has ever since remained because of the unwillingness of state enterprises to invest in processing facilities abroad. The markets for unprocessed and semiprocessed metal minerals have become more competitive as a result of the increasing importance of the arm's length transactions that have ensued.

Available evidence does not permit a conclusion that state owned mineral enterprises are more or less aggressive than private ones in expanding their market share. Some, like ZCCM in Zambia and Ferrominera in Venezuela, have not invested very aggressively and have been losing market shares ever since nationalization. Others, like Brazil's CVRD (in iron ore) have been expanding their relative market positions at very fast rates, but then, so have some private multinationals eg RTZ (in copper). Yet other state owned mineral firms eg PT Timah in Indonesia and Codelco in Chile have experienced extended periods of market contraction after they became state owned, followed by periods of very fast growth that permitted them to restore their former market shares.

Market impact: a summary

The market impact resulting from the above observations can now be summarized.

- The inexperience of the state appointed managers who became responsible for running the many mineral companies that were nationalized in the 1960s and 1970s led to an extended but temporary increase in the cost of production, and a retardation of investments in the state owned universe.
- Because of the multiple goals that they are required to pursue, state owned mineral firms will tend to have permanently higher costs of production than equally endowed private companies.
- State owned firms have a virtual assurance about financial survival from their owners. Compared to the private mining corporations, their investments have sometimes benefited from an easier access to credit on concessional terms from international agencies.
- The tendency to focus on social benefit instead of corporate profit will often lower the marginal cost schedule and raise the demand schedule of state mineral firms, and hence reduce their preparedness to adjust output to variations in mineral price.
- The rupture of the international vertical integration chains at the time of nationalization, and the unwillingness of the state owned firms to invest abroad, has permanently reduced the extent of vertical integration in the mineral industry. This has increased competition in the markets for semiprocessed mineral products.

While these conclusions emerge clearly from casual empiricism and are supported by economic logic, it is extremely difficult to provide a formal and definitive empirical vindication for any of them. The major problem is that of detailed and reliable data; but it may also be that the tendencies are not strong enough to be borne out unambiguously in formal tests. For instance, a detailed econometric analysis of the copper industry[7] failed to confirm a lesser price sensitivity of supply in state owned than in privately owned industries, though it suggested that such

[7]A. Markowski and M. Radetzki, 'State ownership and the price sensitivity of supply: the case of the copper mining industry', *Resources Policy*, Vol 13, No 1, March 1987, pp 19–34.

sensitivity was lower in poor countries and especially in countries heavily dependent on copper exports.

Implications for the private mineral industry

What have been the consequences of the emergence, fast growth and increasing maturity of state owned enterprises on the competitiveness and viability of the private mineral industry? Several distinctly different impacts can be identified.

Nationalizations

The waves of nationalization, through which a large proportion of the present state mineral enterprises were established, without question had a very detrimental impact on the privately owned mineral industry. This impact was felt both at the microlevel of the individual firm and at the industry-wide level.

Decisions about state takeover were usually preceded by periods of very tense relations between the foreign mineral investor and the host government. Impressed by the impending risk of drastic government intervention, the foreign enterprises often resorted to actions that hurt their own long-run interest. When it was implemented, nationalization often involved the amputation of very low cost sources of corporate raw material supply. Even where compensation was paid the sums were invariably considered to be grossly inadequate by the former foreign owners. In this way the preludes to nationalization, as well as nationalization itself, disturbed and disrupted the operations of the affected mineral firms.

At the industry-wide level, the nationalization implied, *ceteris paribus*, a corresponding relative shrinkage of the market share of the privately owned sector. Over two decades, the Western world state owned capacity grew from insignificance to one-third of the total. At least one-half of this was probably established through nationalizations. It is therefore reasonable to claim that the state takeovers of existing operations resulted in a shrinkage of the market share held by private enterprise by almost 1 percentage point per year as compared to what it would otherwise have been. With the virtual cessation of nationalizations since about 1980, this detrimental impact is no longer in force.

Ruptured vertical integration

As should be apparent from Table 1, the setting up of state enterprises has been much more common at the mining stage than at the latter stages of production. Nationalization often ruptured existing international vertical integration links and increased the importance of raw materials trade between independent units. Establishment of new state owned mines has further reinforced this tendency. Given the economics of locating mineral processing plants close to the final consumption markets in many cases and the unwillingness of the state owned firms to invest abroad, the degree of vertical integration in international mineral markets in the 1980s is much less than it was 20 years earlier.

As a result of these developments many of the multinational firms in the mineral sector have become increasingly dependent on arm's length transactions for their raw material needs. This change has made them potentially more vulnerable to the vagaries of the market. The vertical integration links built up by these firms in earlier decades provided a

State owned enterprises in the international metal mining industry

Table 2. Tin production in Indonesia and Malaysia.

	1950		1970		1980	
	Tons ×10³	% share of world production	Tons ×10³	% share of world production	Tons ×10³	% share of world production
Indonesia	32.6	19.8	19.1	10.2	32.5	16.1
Malaysia	58.7	35.7	73.8	39.6	61.4	30.5

Source: Metallgesellschaft, *Metal Statistics*, annual, several issues.

considerable degree of control over raw material costs and perceived assurance of supply. Conditions are less predictable, though not necessarily less advantageous, now that a large number of the vertical links have disintegrated. The price of raw materials purchased from independent producers varies much more than did the cost of output in wholly owned mines and the procurement of concentrates and ores necessitates a much more active effort than was needed when in house supplies satisified the entire requirement.

We may speculate, however, that the greater degree of competition implied in expanding arm's length trade has reduced the cost of mineral raw materials. At the same time it is hard to find evidence that ruptured vertical integration has reduced the reliability of supply. After all, the supply disruptions from far away mines that have occurred were usually caused by strikes and political upheavals that would have disturbed the operations of foreign owned subsidiaries in equal measure.

The implications of the setting up cost of state enterprise

The conclusions that nationalization involves a heavy and extended setting up cost and that managerial inexperience has reduced the average efficiency of the state enterprise universe through the past two decades lead logically to very important implications for the private mineral industry.

The increase in costs, reduction in capacity utilization and inability to expand capacity that typically follow nationalization must have given a temporary competitive edge to the private sector in markets where governments had recently taken over a significant share of total capacity. This advantage should have lasted as long as nationalization continued on a significant scale because that assured continued inefficiency in a large part of the state owned sector. Now that nationalization has virtually ceased and even the most recently established state owned firms have become increasingly mature, the competitive advantage enjoyed by the private industry must be gradually disappearing.

Developments in the international supply of tin provide qualitative support for the above argument. As already noted, the Indonesian government's takeover of the country's tin industry involved a very painful and politically inflamed process. The industry remained highly disorganized over a long period of time and lost substantial market share. Only in the mid- to late 1970s did the state owned tin corporation succeed in developing national managerial and technical talent at an adequate quality level and in recovering the earlier losses in production. Table 2 compares the developments in Indonesia with those in Malaysia, its main competitor, where the industry remained privately owned until the mid-1970s. The rise and subsequent decline of Malaysia's tin production was certainly related to the emergence and gradual resolution of the problems of state ownership in Indonesian tin.

Pursuit of social objectives and public subsidies

Through the 1980s, continuous and very vocal concern has been expressed by the representatives of North America's mineral industry about the unfair competition this industry has faced from state owned enterprises in developing countries. The latter, it was held, continued to produce at high rates of capacity utilization, despite the low level of demand, and so contributed to a further depression of the already low metal prices. The resultant losses that they incurred were compensated by their owner governments by fresh capital infusions. Private industry in North America did not have access to corresponding public support. In consequence its viability was being threatened by the aggressive and economically unmotivated production policies of the state enterprises.[8] No convincing empirical support has been provided for these claims and the following paragraphs will clarify their meaning and substance.

From a historical perspective, metal prices were quite low in the 1980s, measured in real terms. The World Bank index of constant metal and mineral prices indicates a 1981–85 level 19% below that which prevailed in 1975–79 and 37% lower than in 1965–74.[9] A number of factors have contributed to the price weakness, but the depressed level of demand has been an important one.

On many earlier occasions metal industries have reacted to depressed prices by coordinated measures to cut supply and so to force prices to rise to more remunerative levels. Such action has commonly presupposed proportional supply cuts by all producers participating in the scheme. One interpretation of the above views could be that state enterprises and their owners, governments, are less willing than private multinational firms in the mineral industry to enter into collusive market arrangements. This view could hardly be sustained at a more general level, given the experiences of the petroleum and bauxite markets of the 1970s, where governments took a leading role in the efforts to restrict supply and raise prices.

Where there is no supplier collusion the expected impact of low prices is that producers will cut their capacity utilization whenever their marginal costs exceed price. Application of this rule will imply that producers with high operating costs will implement substantial cuts, while those with more advantageous cost structures continue to operate close to full capacity. Another interpretation of the North American industry's claims is that state enterprises have not abided by the above rule and have continued to operate even when their marginal costs exceeded price.

There may be some truth in the contention that state enterprises maintain output at price levels that would induce private firms in identical circumstances to cut production. By implicitly or explicitly considering shadow rates of exchange and shadow wage rates, publicly owned firms in many developing countries will perceive a higher demand curve and a lower supply curve than if actual market rates had been applied. They will hence produce more at each price level. Even if such behaviour could be verified, it need not involve a net disadvantage to the private industry if we compare it with an undistorted purely competitive situation. The differences between the market rates of exchange and wages on the one hand, and the shadow ones on the other, signify distortions in the national economy commonly resulting from the government's economic policies. Application of shadow rates, in this sense, implies a rectification of these distortions insofar as the

[8] For a summary of these views, see for instance *Mining Journal*, 9 December 1983; or Metallgesellschaft, 'Pressmeldungen über die Metallmärkte', January 1984.
[9] World Bank, Commodities Division, 'Primary commodity price forecasts', 18 August 1986.

state owned firm is concerned and a reinstatement of the conditions that would have prevailed in a competitive equilibrium.

Formidable difficulties are encountered in attempts to verify a behavioural difference between state owned and private mineral enterprises concerning rates of capacity utilization. The observation that the North American, almost exclusively privately owned mineral industry, undertook large-scale reductions in capacity utilization during the 1980s, while industries in developing countries where state ownership predominates did not, is not a proof of behavioural deviation in state owned enterprises since such a difference could be due simply to differences in operating cost levels. But then, such cost levels are immensely difficult to establish and verify.[10] Scattered evidence for various metals suggests that production costs in North America around 1980 were significantly above the world average.[11] In the ensuing years the relative cost levels in the USA and Canada have increased substantially as a result of the strong appreciation of the US dollar. Between 1980 and 1984 the real appreciation of the dollar ie the combination of differences in rates of inflation and exchange rate changes, amounted to 61% versus Zambia, 52% versus South Africa, 23% versus Australia, 37% versus Indonesia and the Philippines, 35% versus Mexico, 55% versus Chile, 76% versus Sweden but no more than 3% versus Canada.[12]

The figures suggest a very strong reduction in the relative competitiveness of the USA and Canada as metal producers in relation to the countries enumerated. This, along with the relatively weak competitive position at the beginning of the period, may be sufficient to explain why virtually all capacity reductions in response to weak prices took place in North America. US and Canadian metal producers became increasingly marginal suppliers in consequence of the rising dollar. Their output cuts – as well as the maintenance of production elsewhere – can be explained by standard microeconomic theory. In this light state ownership becomes irrelevant. Output of copper from Chile would not have been cut, even if the great mines in that country had remained in private US ownership, simply because the cost of producing that output was lower than the cost of production in most US installations.

There is some truth in the statement that mineral firms under public ownership enjoy a degree of assurance from their owners against financial distress. Such firms have also at times received subsidized financial support from their governments. In some cases governments have simply forwarded to their companies loans on advantageous terms, obtained from international agencies like the World Bank group. Where financial assurances and financial subsidies have been provided they have obviously strengthened the competitive position of the state owned firms *vis-à-vis* private industry. But to get a complete picture, these advantages must be juxtaposed against the costs of pursuing various social goals imposed on such firms. It is reasonable to regard the financial benefits as compensation for the cost of the social obligations that the state enterprises are asked to fulfil. When these obligations are taken into account it is by no means certain that the state enterprises reap a net gain in competitive strength from the financial support they receive from their owners. It should be added that, excepting the oil exporting countries during the OPEC decade, the mineral exporting developing countries' governments have seldom had the resources to support their state owned mineral firms financially on a sustained basis.

[10]*Op cit*, Ref 7.
[11]This is apparent, for instance, from several reports issued in the early 1980s by the Commodities Research Unit. For evidence from a specific industry, see A.F. Barsotti and R.D. Rosencranz, 'Estimated costs for the recovery of copper from demonstrated resources in market economy countries', *Natural Resources Forum*, No 2, 1983.
[12]K. Takeuchi, J.E. Strongman, S. Maeda and C.S. Tan, *The World Copper Industry: Its Changing Structure and Future Prospects*, World Bank, Washington, DC, 1987.

On the contrary, in a somewhat longer run, these firms have been invariably required to make positive contributions to their owners.

Does state ownership impose a survival threat to the private mineral industry?

To summarize the arguments of this section, the widespread nationalizations through which a large part of the state owned mineral enterprise universe was established during the 1960s and 1970s, constituted a very serious threat to the private mineral industry. Its proportion of total mineral production capacity was heavily curtailed, it suffered from inadequate compensation for the assets taken over and many individual multinational firms were severely mutilated in the process. This threat is no longer in force, since the nationalization process appears to have come to an end.

Nationalization brought about an important and apparently permanent change to the market structure in many mineral markets by rupturing existing international vertical integration chains. As a result, the private multinational mineral firms have to rely to a much greater extent than before on arm's length trade for their raw materials supply.

The establishment of state enterprises through nationalization regularly involved a heavy and extended setting up cost. Over the past two decades, the average efficiency of the state owned enterprise universe has been depressed by the inexperience of the newly set up firms. This provided a distinct competitive advantage to the private industry. Nationalization has by and large ceased since the early 1980s and so the inefficiencies due to inexperience have gradually been overcome as state owned enterprises have become increasingly mature. The competitive advantage enjoyed by the privately owned sector on this count is consequently being eroded.

It is possible, but very hard to prove, that the output of state owned enterprises is less responsive to price than that of private firms. To the extent that this is because of the use of shadow exchange and wage rates rather than the rates that prevail in the market, the behaviour of the state enterprises can be seen to rectify policy induced distortions in the countries where they operate. A more likely explanation for the lesser responsiveness to price change is that many state firms have lower costs than their private competitors.

The findings emerging from the above analyses do not support the claim that state owned mineral enterprises constitute a survival threat to the private mineral industry. The claim has come, in the main, from North American industry representatives and has been voiced especially loudly during the 1980s. The North American mineral industry has indeed gone through a very difficult time. Contributing to its difficulties has been the relative depletion of its mineral wealth, depressed metal demand, low metal prices but above all the severe deterioration in the industry's international competitiveness caused by the exchange rate changes that occurred between 1980 and 1985. These factors, and not the behaviour of state owned mineral enterprises, constitute, for a time, a survival threat to the North American mining and mineral processing industry.

[18]

Excerpt from Thomas R. Navin, *Copper Mining and Management*, 97–109, 371.

CHAPTER 8

Pollution, Politics,
and Proven Reserves

The anonymity of the executives in the American copper industry quickly disappeared after the passage of the "Clean Air Act of 1970," which established the Environmental Protection Agency (EPA). Until that time few of the industry's executives had had occasion to address public meetings, conduct press interviews, testify at public hearings, or meet with legislators, either state or national. And few of them had had the experience, to them unpleasant, of seeing their names in the newspapers. After 1970 all that changed. For many copper officials, the glare of the limelight was discomfiting. Trained in engineering, as most of them were, they had few personal resources on which to draw for support in their new ordeal.

National concern for environmental deterioration had arisen, far from the mining industry, in the nation's major cities, particularly in New York, Chicago, Philadelphia, Los Angeles, and Pittsburgh. At first most of that concern focused on city smog — and on the contribution to that problem made by automobile emissions. In 1963 the *New York Times* was averaging about an article a week on smog-related subjects. By 1969 the frequency of articles in the *New York Times* had increased to an average of one a day. By then attention was being directed to other sources of pollution, especially to the smoke (particulate) emissions from coal-burning utility power plants. Included in the power plant smoke emissions was some sulfur dioxide (SO_2). Consequently, when the EPA issued its first set of air standards (1971), it included on the list a standard for SO_2 emissions. Since the standards applied across the nation, not just to the major cities, and since copper smelters emitted substantial quantities of SO_2 (although in total only about a fifth as much as the amount emitted by all the power plants in the nation — and near no major cities), the copper industry suddenly became involved in the antipollution movement.

Smelter emissions of SO_2 were, to be sure, not a new issue in the copper industry. Almost from the very beginning of the treatment of sulfide ores in

[97]

98   MANAGEMENT OF TECHNOLOGY

the American West (from the early 1890s), the copper smelters had been a source of public controversy. Some of the earliest smelters had been forced to close when irate farmers took the issue of crop damage to court. The smeltermen had responded to public condemnation principally by constructing very tall gas stacks to disperse the smelter fumes high into the atmosphere.[1] Even with high stacks, weather conditions sometimes drove the SO_2 close to the ground and created damage to crops near the smelter; in such instances, the smelter companies settled with the farmers out of court simply by buying their crops. Sometimes, when the problems were persistent, they would even buy their farms.

In the 1950s more active measures were taken to reduce pollution. Electrostatic precipitators (see Chapter 21 for more on the Cottrell precipitators) were installed for dust control. Efforts were made to dilute the SO_2 escaping into the atmosphere. Experiments were conducted on the company-owned farms to determine the relationship between weather conditions and crop damage.[2]

It may seem odd that the copper industry should have allowed air pollution, so damaging to their public image, to prevail into the mid-twentieth century. It seems less odd when one reflects on the true nature of copper mining and smelting. Looked at from a physical point of view, the copper companies are, in a sense, in the waste-disposal business, a business in which copper is merely a by-product of the major physical effort: the digging and moving and smelting of earth and rock. From this viewpoint the copper companies are, in fact, about 600 times as much involved in waste disposal as in copper production. Their output in physical terms is in the following approximate ratios — 1/600th of which has to carry the cost of all the rest:

Unwanted earthen materials	400
Tailings	195
Slag	3
Sulfur	1
Copper	1
Total	600

Since the waste-disposal business is not only massively dominant but also nonrevenue producing, it must be conducted with the utmost efficiency. Since pyrometallurgy (smelting) is an extremely effective way of processing a lot of those materials and since no other method has anything like smelting's low-cost efficiency, the old way has endured.

---

1. To the general public these tall structures, which can be seen for great distances, are smokestacks; to smeltermen they are merely stacks, and what they emit is not smoke but gas.

2. These farms were also used to accumulate evidence in the instances in which companies regarded lawsuits as unjustified. Some companies hired photographers to take aerial pictures of the surrounding countryside to monitor crop damage and to gather protective evidence.

Sulfur, as it exists in the earth in the form of copper sulfides and iron sulfides, is inert and harmless. It becomes potentially harmful only when it is separated from its natural compounds. In removing the sulfur from the copper sulfides, the smelting process, unfortunately, also removes the sulfur from the iron sulfides; consequently, the copper companies produce at least as much sulfur as copper — and sometimes up to four times as much.

On the basis of a study conducted by the engineering consulting firm of Arthur G. McKee & Company, the EPA concluded that the attack on SO_2 pollution should be conducted in two phases. The primary phase was intended to reduce emissions below the level at which they were deemed harmful to humans. This level (called the "ambient air" standard) was defined as an average, over a year's time, of 80 micrograms of SO_2 concentration per cubic centimeter of the atmosphere at ground level near the point of emission. The secondary phase was intended to reduce emissions to a level that would not be harmful to materials (corrosion) or to plant life.

Insofar as smelter emissions were concerned, the key state was Arizona. Of the nation's sixteen copper smelters in 1970, Arizona had eight; no other state had more than one. Based on the experience of London (which had had smog control since 1956), the Arizona state environment agency decided that the state's smelters should be allowed to emit into the air only 10 percent of their sulfur input, and this standard was soon adopted by other western states as well. Expressed another way, 90 percent of the sulfur was to be removed and disposed of in a harmless way. The ruling, with a deadline of 1975, created a storm of controversy. The smeltermen maintained that the technology used in London (wet-limestone scrubbing) might be suitable for coal-burning power plants but not for copper smelters — and they formed an industry association to investigate alternative technologies.

Arizona's smelters found that meeting the primary standard was costly (more than $300 million) but technologically feasible, and by 1974 all of them were in the process of conforming by one means or another. To effect this achievement they had to resort to one or both of two procedures. Previously a central concern of all smeltermen had been to emit into the atmosphere as *dilute* a stream of SO_2 as possible; after the EPA Act, however, they had to make the stream coming off the furnaces as *rich* as possible (higher than 4 percent) to be able to collect the SO_2 and convert it into sulfuric acid (H_2SO_4) in a specially designed acid plant. In addition, they sometimes had to establish, within a 15-mile radius, monitoring stations which permitted the reduction of smelter throughput whenever weather conditions (such as temperature inversions and lack of wind) caused SO_2 concentrations to approach the ambient air limits. The acid-plant system was capable of preventing between 55 and 70 percent of the processed sulfur from escaping into the ambient air, and the closed-loop system guarded against those periods when weather conditions made the 55-70 percent removal insufficient. The closed-loop system had the unfortunate effect,

100   MANAGEMENT OF TECHNOLOGY

however, of reducing the annual throughput (operating capacity) of the smelters to which they were linked.

In 1972 the national EPA ruled that the secondary standard (90 percent removal, later increased to 95 percent) would apply only to new construction. This ruling raised two questions: How were the existing smelters to be expanded in such a way as to meet the secondary standard? And, what technology was to be used in the construction of new smelters?

Smelter expansion posed the most immediate dilemmas. By any conceivable technology it would cost perhaps four times as much to remove 90 percent of the sulfur as it had cost to remove 55-70 percent. A number of possible solutions were advanced, but all of them shared two or more of the following drawbacks: they were very expensive both in terms of initial capital expenditures and subsequent operating costs; there was no assurance that they were technologically feasible; and there was no assurance that, once operative, they were capable of meeting the 90 percent requirement. It seemed probable that no single solution could be applied widely, so different were the smelting conditions from one region to another, and that the nation would be facing a long period of constrained smelter capacity until these uncertainties had been resolved.

What was particularly disconcerting to the copper executives was the fact that there was no established proof that the 90-percent removal was required to meet the *qualitative* goal of eliminating hazards to materials and to plant life. In metropolitan areas the 90-percent removal might be desirable, but in the vast open spaces of the mountainous West, where most of the smelters were located, the ambient air standards were thought to be sufficient — and Phelps Dodge set up a research center to gather information relative to the contribution of various pollution sources, both man-made and natural, to Arizona's air quality in order to develop a better understanding of how to combat pollution-caused problems.

The main stumbling block to the improvement of emission control was the reverberatory furnace, the second of the three basic steps in smelting (see Chapter 4). If "reverb" emissions could be better controlled, the new standards might be reached by a modification of existing technology. Capital expenditures and operating costs would not be prohibitive, and a proven technology would be preserved. If, on the other hand, the reverbs had to be replaced, both capital and operating costs would be extremely high and the risk of technological failure would be great. No techniques yet known could match the reverb's capability of handling a wide variety of concentrates, including the dirty ones that contain arsenic, mercury, and antimony. The trouble with the reverbs is that they emit a great deal of dilute SO_2, well below the 4 percent recapturable level for sulfuric acid. The reverb furnace is where most of the heat is applied in smelting, and the combustion process creates quantities of flue gasses so great that they dilute the sulfur dioxide.[3]

Among the several conceivable ways of "saving" the reverbs, one merits special attention. The nation's smelters could return to roasting, the first stage in the pyrometallurgical process. As stated in Chapter 4, the trend in recent times has been toward bypassing the roasting stage and "green-feeding" the concentrates directly from flotation into the reverbs. More than half the nation's smelters have either abandoned roasting or have been built without roasters. The advantage of reviving the roasting process derives from the fact that a rich stream of sulfur can be driven off at that stage, leaving less to escape from the reverbs. The disadvantage is that those smelters which gave up roasting did so in part to recapture valuable plant site space which they are now using for other purposes, while the newer smelters never had roasters. Kennecott, by adding roasting to its smelter at Hayden, Arizona, was able, most of the time, to meet the 90 percent sulfur-removal standard. It is important to note, however, that Kennecott enjoyed a three-way advantage in opting for this solution. First, it had the space. Second, its mine at Ray was rich in (formerly one would have said plagued with) sulfur-bearing pyrites, permitting an increase at will of the sulfur content of its materials to a point where a rich stream of gasses from the roaster could be assured. Third, a large quantity of leachable ores, which would benefit from the application of cheap sulfuric acid, were present at Ray. No other smelter was so advantaged.

Even if the reverbs are made obsolete, there are those who advocate at least sticking with pyrometallurgy because of its proven worth. Of several new pyrometallurgical processes, two merit attention. The first is the electric furnace, a Swedish development, which, by eliminating combustion, eliminates the combustion fumes. It may seem contralogical to burn coal to make electricity to heat the electric furnace, instead of using coal to heat the furnace in the first place, but at least such a process meets the pollution standards. The Inspiration company has replaced its reverb with an electric furnace and has become the second Arizona smelter to meet the 90 percent standard — further "proof" that it can be met.[4] The electric furnace requires the prior use of a roaster, but, even with roasting, there are some dirty ores that the electric furnace cannot handle. In the immediate future this limitation may be of little consequence. In the long run, however, this nation may discover that many of its untapped orebodies will require greater

----

3. Until the rationing of natural gas, most reverbs used natural gas as their energy source. By 1974 most of them had converted to fuel oil or coal.

4. Inspiration deserves credit for having moved early to effect pollution abatement. However, its decision was made at a time when power rates were much lower than they subsequently became. As a result, the operational costs of the decision proved to be much higher than anticipated.

102 MANAGEMENT OF TECHNOLOGY

versatility than the electric furnace is capable of providing, and the copper from such orebodies will therefore not be available for use.

A second pyrometallurgical substitute for the reverb is the flash furnace. The Outokumpu company of Finland has developed such a furnace and has made several installations throughout the world. The Outokumpu process can easily meet the primary standards but probably cannot be made to meet the secondary ones; consequently, it has been rejected by several American copper companies. There is no way to use this process at an existing smelter. A new smelter has to be built. Since the economics of scale require that a new smelter be capable of handling 200 million pounds of copper a year, a huge capital investment is required. Only Phelps Dodge has elected to make use of the Outokumpu process — to supplement its aged (1910) smelter at Douglas — the decision having been made before the secondary standards were applied to all new construction. The cost of the new smelter at Hidalgo, New Mexico, will approximate $200 million, of which $82 million is due to antipollution devices. The Hidalgo smelter was originally designed to produce elemental sulfur, using natural gas, but the scarcity and rapidly rising cost of natural gas has forced the abandonment of this technology in favor of the production of sulfuric acid.

There are some advantages and many disadvantages to producing a lot of sulfuric acid. Acid can be used advantageously by copper companies to leach their oxide ores. In the past, when sulfur sold in the range of $20 to $40 a ton, it was not economical to leach with other than fairly dilute acid. With acid in oversupply, especially in the Southwest, the price may drop to a quarter of what it used to be, permitting intensified leaching. In addition, availability of cheaper acid opens the possibility of leaching waste dumps (below 0.2 percent copper) and even tailings (which contain only about 0.05 percent copper). Much will depend on future price levels of refined copper, since the use of concentrated acid will require safeguards (in themselves expensive) to keep the more concentrated acid from seeping down to the water table.

Sulfuric acid is, however, highly corrosive, a fact that creates severe potential problems. Any breakdown in the acid plant will force a shutdown of the smelter and perhaps of the supporting mine as well. Once the acid is produced, it must be almost immediately shipped, no matter what the condition of the marketplace. The amounts of acid produced per hour are very large, and storage of more than a few days' production is prohibitively expensive. Since acid is costly to ship, the market for smelter acid is limited to the western half of the United States. Smelters will be tempted to sell their acid at prices that cover at least part of the shipping costs (in effect giving away the acid to anyone who will share in the shipping costs), a predictable result of which will be the elimination of the region's independent acid merchants. If the price falls low enough, some smelters will find it cheaper to neutralize the acid with limestone and dump it on wastelands nearby. Since it takes about three tons of limestone to neutralize a ton of acid, this alternative will be open only to smelters with a large limestone quarry within economical shipping distance. Dumping neutralized acid creates still further potential environmental problems.

If we are to avoid all the problems of excessive acid production, we shall have to abandon pyrometallurgy in favor of some form of hydro-metallurgy (a collective term covering a wide variety of electrochemical methods of extracting copper). Hydrometallurgy has the theoretical capability of taking copper directly from concentrates to semirefined form, thus bypassing the smelting process. Its sulfur by-product can come out in a solid form — including gypsum or ammonium sulfate. A number of new hydrometallurgical processes are under consideration. Three merit discussion, although none has yet proven a success.

Anaconda's process is designed to produce sulfur in a form suitable for use as a fertilizer. Duval's process will also produce sulfur in a fertilizer form, a particular advantage to Duval since, through its potash division, it is already in the fertilizer business. Cyprus is experimenting with a process that will produce elemental sulfur. It is worth noting that the last two processes are being developed by the nation's two largest nonintegrated mining ventures. Both Duval and Cyprus, because they have no investment in smelters, have nothing to lose but their research and development expenditures, while they have much to gain by developing their own ability to bypass the smelting operation for which they are presently paying toll charges.

Hydrometallurgy is inferior to pyrometallurgy in two respects. It is not as effective in screening out some of the unwanted minerals, and it often screens out too many of the valuable precious metals that are found in copper deposits.

All hydrometallurgical extraction processes require a substantial degree of technological sophistication. They can be made to work under research conditions with the use of highly educated personnel; the question of whether they can be made to work under mass-production circumstances using mass-production workers remains to be answered. In addition, hydrometallurgical methods have become very costly because they are energy-intensive. Conventional smelters conserve energy through the combustion of the sulfur to SO_2. Conversion to hydrometallurgical methods reduces air pollution at one place, the smelter, while increasing it at another, the power plant.

Probably the greatest drawback to the development of hydrometallurgy is its cost. Hydrometallurgy will probably never cost less than pyrometallurgy; in all likelihood, it will cost more. Any mine that has its output

104   MANAGEMENT OF TECHNOLOGY

processed by the new technology will therefore be at a competitive disadvantage to mines using the old technology, unless special taxes are levied on the old technology, as has been proposed.

The strategy of the major copper companies has been to gain time in the form of exemptions (called variances), while striving to meet the primary standards through the construction of acid plants, closed-loop systems, or both. They have fought hard to preserve the reverberatory process (for expansion and/or for future new construction), but on this issue they are likely to lose, in which case existing smelters will probably not be expanded. Future smelting needs may have to come from new plants which, in order to meet the secondary standards, will have to use a completely new technology. Since none of the new technologies has been tested, the future is highly problematical. Among those most directly affected by this great uncertainty are the oil companies that have recently discovered new copper deposits in the Southwest (see Chapter 2). With existing smelters operating at reduced capacities and with no assurance that they will be able to expand, some or all of the oil companies may have to rely on processing units not yet built, to be constructed by themselves or others, using a technology not yet identified, at the risk that these new units may not work or may not prove economically competitive with the old but obsolete smelters with their reverberatory furnaces.

There are several other pollution problems facing the copper industry, but they are minor compared with the problems created by SO_2 emissions. The copper industry is a heavy user of water; hence, water pollution must be guarded against. The heaviest use of water is at the concentrator (for flotation), at the smelter (for cooling of the outside furnace bricks), and at the refinery (for use in sulfuric acid). It takes about 200 pounds of water to produce a single pound of copper, but, since the water is constantly recycled, the *net* consumption is only about 15 pounds of water per pound of copper, most of the loss occurring through evaporation. In the arid Southwest where most of the water comes from the water table, the major issue is not pollution but competition for a scarce (and diminishing) resource, the principal competitor being farming, a much heavier net consumer of water than mining. Neutralization and disposal of refinery acids is a fairly simple and inexpensive procedure.

Tailings ponds, because of the fineness of their ground earthen materials, are capable of producing unpleasant dust storms, but the sides of active ponds and the tops of abandoned ponds can be planted to reduce the wind erosion. Waste dumps can be unsightly, but mining companies have learned to bulldoze them into level plateaus and to plant their side slopes. The day will come when some of them, because of their elevation, their commanding vistas, their established access roads, and their level terrain (permitting low-cost development), will make admirable homesites.

Other environmental considerations closely related to pollution are land utilization, energy consumption, and the size of future mineral reserves. Land-use environmentalists have focused much of their attention on strip mining, a technique widely used in coal mining but not at all in copper. They have also lobbied vigorously for changes in the nation's basic mining law, the Act of 1872. The mining industry would also like to see the act changed. The law is antiquated, but an agreement on how it should be changed is difficult. Because so much of the West and all of Alaska were obtained through treaties with other governments, most of the undeveloped land in the United States remains in federal hands. Conservationists within the government, frustrated in their efforts to obtain changes in the 1872 act, have launched a vigorous campaign to have vast tracts of federal land declared wilderness areas, a source of grave concern to all the mining industries. Executives of the mining industries have argued that, while wilderness areas may be valuable as vacation lands, they benefit principally the affluent and they should not be "withdrawn" to such an extent as to prohibit exploration for mineral resources that would benefit the entire population.

Copper production is a heavy consumer of energy. Even in the days of cheap energy, the cost of energy accounted for about 8 percent of the total direct operating costs of producing copper; by 1974 this proportion had probably increased to 10 percent and was still rising. Different forms of energy are required at the different stages of processing copper, but the predominant form (more than half the total energy costs) is electricity, great quantities of which are needed, especially for crushing and grinding, as shown below:

	Share of total energy costs
Open-pit mining requires fuel for trucks and electricity for power shovels	18%
Crushing and grinding requires electricity	37
Smelting requires heat from natural gas, fuel oil, coal, or electricity	31
Refining requires electricity	14
Total energy costs	100%

Not only is the unit cost of energy increasing, but the amount of energy required to produce a pound of copper is also rising. As the grade of copper continues to decline, the power required to crush and grind enough earthen materials to get a pound of copper increases. Furthermore, the energy costs of producing copper are rising much faster than the energy costs of producing aluminum. At one time it took eight times as much energy to produce a pound of aluminum as it took to produce a pound of copper. By 1974 aluminum was consuming only three times as much energy — and the gap was

106   MANAGEMENT OF TECHNOLOGY

continuing to close. Aluminum uses energy at the reduction (refining) stage, where the energy technology is fairly stable. Copper uses energy principally at the mining and milling stages, where the technology is continuing to require more and more energy.

The increasing rate at which America has been consuming its mineral reserves has been a subject of national concern since the publication of the Paley Commission report of 1952 (see Chapter 14). So little has been done to implement the national policy recommendations of that report that a mounting public concern has been justified. However, relative to the future availability of energy, concern over the future availability of minerals (and especially of copper) has been somewhat misplaced. A basic assumption of conservationists is that the world contains a finite amount of minerals which, once gone, is gone forever. In the case of copper this assumption is, of course, not true since copper is so readily recyclable. But there are other special aspects of our copper reserves that are apparently too complex to be understood by the public, or at least by those who write for the public media. As was stated in Chapter 1, the earth's surface contains about 0.007 percent copper. Even if we assume that human beings will never be able to find adequate means of commercially mining copper with any grade lower than 0.1 percent, the world still has vast untapped reserves. Using the 0.1 percent grade as the ultimate cutoff point, it is predicted that, by the year 2000 the United States will have used up only about 16 percent of its total endowment of potentially minable copper. What worries the conservationists is the fact that by 2000 we may have used up our entire supply based on a cutoff point of 0.5 percent, the grade level that is currently commercially feasible without additional income from by-product minerals. There are a lot of reasons why this eventuality is extremely unlikely. Two of them are worth discussing.

The first relates to consumption. All forecasts are based on the assumption that the present upward trend in consumption will continue for the next twenty-five years. In the near future, at least, these forecasts are probably going to be inaccurate because of the smelter constraints existing in this country. As pointed out earlier, smelter capacity in this country is not expanding but contracting. The argument may be advanced that a stagnant smelter capacity will simply result in more imports, in which case it will be the foreign reserves and not ours that will be depleted at the projected rate. A second reason why our consumption of copper may not continue at extrapolated rates has to do with the costs of production. If production costs continue to rise more rapidly than the general price level, the users of copper may find alternative ways of meeting their needs. One reason why costs may outpace the general price level is the disappearance of cheap energy. As has been pointed out, copper production is a heavy consumer of energy and energy costs are almost certain to rise.[5] The expected rise in copper

5. There was a time when ocean-bed nodules were considered a potential source of additional copper (see Chapter 22), but, with present technology, five times as much

consumption will not take place if substitution becomes widespread. The segment of the copper industry most vulnerable to substitution is the brass mill segment; if brass becomes obsolescent, the present forecasts of consumption in the next quarter-century will prove to be too high.

If, however, projected consumption proves to be accurate, it will be because of some or all of the following eventualities. The anti-inflation forces in this country may become politically strong enough to counter the antipollution forces. In that case, copper prices may not rise more rapidly than other industrial prices. If labor relations in the copper industry do not deteriorate (as they have in the coal industry) so that it is possible to continue the present trend toward increased output per man-hour, then cost increases may be contained within reasonable levels. If mass production technologies continue to improve (even though the rate of increased improvement may decline), then, too, cost increases may be kept within competitive limits. None of these eventualities seems improbable. Therefore, the extrapolation of present consumption trends may, in fact, prove accurate. It is on the supply side that the doomsayers are more likely to be wrong.

All predictions relative to the supply of copper in the next quarter-century are based, at least in some degree, on the "proven reserves" reported by operating copper companies. Since it is normal procedure for a copper company to establish up to twenty-five years of proven reserves before opening a *new* mine (partly for the purpose of planning the infrastructure but also for the purpose of attracting loan capital), these figures are quite reliable and are on the conservative side. Since it is also normal practice for all mines, once in operation, to keep updating their planning horizon each year for a period of the next ten years, the proven reserves reported even by the *older* mines are also quite reliable — and are also on the conservative side. There are two reasons why mines keep their estimates conservative, both based on economics, one internal and the other external. Internally, there is no reason to spend money on drilling and mine planning for more than ten years in advance, given the fact that the "present value" of profits earned beyond that period of time is negligible. (Indeed, most detailed planning is done only five years in advance.) The external reason for not pushing any harder to explore developmentally for future reserves is the fear of taxation. It may be argued that the mines are doing the nation's economic planners a disservice by not providing better long-range data about the nation's critical resources, but the fact is that mining companies run grave risk of being severely penalized for doing so. They have the example of British Columbia to remind them of the risks involved.

In the 1960s British Columbia was one of the world's "hottest" regions for copper exploration. Led by Newmont, which invested in three of the province's copper mines, a number of American companies developed

---

energy would be required to process these nodules as is required by conventional copper technology.

108   MANAGEMENT OF TECHNOLOGY

medium-size (Class 3) orebodies.[6] In the early 1970s several new copper mines began operations. Most of them exported their copper, in the form of concentrates, to Japan on long-term contracts. In 1972 a fateful election took place. For the preceding twenty years the premier of British Columbia had been William A. C. Bennett, then 72, who, though a moderate socialist, had nevertheless been supportive of the efforts to find and develop the minerals resources of the province. His opponent was David (Dave) Barrett, a 42-year-old social worker recently turned politician. Barrett was an ardent conservationist who deplored the exportation of the people's copper to Japan and believed that minerals resources of the province were severely limited; he believed that, if steps were not taken to ration their exploitation, posterity would be left destitute and the present generation would be convicted as criminal exploiters before the tribunal of history. His platform was supported overwhelmingly at the polls. Once in office Barrett instituted a number of "reforms," among which was an increase in the tax on ore reserves. Any such increase was bound to discourage further exploration of the development type beyond what was absolutely necessary. Whereas British Columbia had been earlier regarded as one of the most promising areas for copper-mine development, it became an area where American capital sought to retrench and perhaps even withdraw.

The point is that the projections of copper availability based on proven reserves is, for political reasons, unrealistically conservative. The amount of copper already known to exist in commercially workable deposits is probably more than enough to accommodate even the most optimistic consumption needs of this country through the year 2000. Furthermore, the probability is high that the cutoff point of commercially workable deposits will, by then, have fallen well below the current 0.5 percent level (as it already has in some places; see Duval).

The assurance of adequate reserves for the next generation is, however, no reason for complacency. The American copper industry in the early 1970s was facing a hostile environment both abroad and at home. Most of the mineralized Third World nations, embittered by their resentment of colonialism, were making it difficult, if not impossible, for American companies to continue their exploration programs in black Africa and Latin America. Even nations long considered friendly were becoming inhospitable. At the same time as British Columbia was discouraging further mineral development by American companies, the Australians, under a Labour government, were causing Americans to abandon their exploration projects on the subcontinent. The only important mineralized nation with a policy of actively encouraging Americans to search for ore reserves was the Republic of South Africa, and

6. Only one Class 2 orebody was discovered (by a subsidiary of the Canadian Pacific Railway). A Class 1 orebody is the size of a Bingham or Morenci.

that nation's prosperity was built on a quicksand of social unrest. With the American government moving rapidly to exclude federal lands from mineral development, the major copper companies were impelled to focus attention on the arid regions of the American Southwest, and there they were encountering stiff competition from the exploration teams of the major oil companies. The strategic options left open were becoming increasingly few.

To summarize, it can be said that the American copper industry has done a commendable job of meeting the tasks prescribed for it by the Paley Commission report of 1952. It is the national government that has almost completely ignored the recommendations of that commission. There is no reason, for instance, why the major burden of finding alternatives to smelter pollution should fall so heavily on those few companies that stand to benefit from the research. Pollution is of concern to the body politic, and the cost of its solution should be borne, in major part at least, by the general public.

The highest near-term probability is that the consumption of copper in this country will be constrained by inadequate smelter capacity. The highest long-term probability is that costs of production will rise faster than the general price level and will cut down on expected consumption increases because of resultant substitution. The probability is slight that we shall become heavily dependent on imports for the foreseeable future. American copper production is still in the hands of extremely cost-conscious engineer-executives, while the competition abroad is now owned principally by government monopolies where cost-cutting runs counter to social needs and aspirations. This does not preclude the possibility that, for brief periods, the foreign producers may succeed in penetrating the American market by cutting their prices below production costs. In the long run, however, American copper should remain price-competitive with other copper producers unless there is a serious deterioration in labor-management relations or technological expertise. What is not at all likely is that this nation will run out of copper in the next two or three or even four generations. There are much more pressing problems to be solved before then. The worst that might happen from the point of view of the copper industry is that, because of substitution, we may decide not to use all the copper we have — and that should please the conservationists.

CHAPTER 8

Not surprisingly, most publications dealing with resources and the environment are government-sponsored. The Environmental Protection Agency commissioned a report, in three parts, by Arthur D. Little, Inc., called "Economic Impact of Anticipated Pollution Abatement Costs" (1972). In 1973 the U. S. Department of Interior published "An Economic Appraisal of the Supply of Copper from Primary Domestic Sources," Bureau of Mines Information Circular No. 8598. In 1975 the National Academy of Sciences published "Mineral Resources and the Environment."

In its February 1974 issue, *Metals and Materials* published P. F. Chapman's comparative study, "The Energy Costs of Producing Copper and Aluminum from Primary Sources."

Part IV
The Multinational Quest for Minerals and Relations with Hosts

[19]

Excerpt from *Business History*, 1990, **XXXII**, 98–119.

THE CITY AND INTERNATIONAL MINING, 1870–1914

By CHARLES HARVEY and JON PRESS

One of the enduring fascinations of British economic history in the years between 1870 and 1914 is the pre-eminence of London as a centre of international finance. In recent years, several scholars have produced books and articles which point to the complexity and variety of functions undertaken by City enterprises, and the rich diversity of institutional arrangements which existed throughout the Square Mile. Of particular interest is the work of Stanley Chapman and Ranald Michie. Chapman's work on investment groups identifies 29 networks of merchants, financiers and entrepreneurs through which capital was channelled into productive uses overseas. These investment groups were entrepreneurial or family concerns 'whose name and reputation was used to float a variety of subsidiary trading, mining or financial enterprises, invariably overseas and often widely dispersed'. He cites as an example, the Matheson group, which, through Matheson & Co. in London and Jardine-Matheson & Co. in Hong Kong, promoted large scale ventures in mining, financial services, textiles, shipping and railways, as far distant as Spain, China, the United States, South Africa and Russia. Not all of Chapman's investment groups were entirely British, but they 'all had a base (office) in Britain and conducted a large part of their trade or financial operations (or both) through London'. The City, according to Chapman, was not merely a mechanism for the transfer of funds from a multitude of savers to governments and firms at home and abroad; it was also a place where entrepreneurship flourished, and opportunity seeking was the natural concern of merchant banks, company promoters, speculators, exploration companies, investment trusts, merchant houses, and investment groups.[1] To this list might be added the solicitors, accountants, consulting engineers, stock brokers, and commodity brokers who frequently engaged in company promotion. Michie takes up this theme in his work on venture capital and the London Stock Exchange, emphatically rejecting the idea, lately revived by Kennedy, that City conservatism and prejudice lay at the heart of British economic difficulties in the late nineteenth century.[2]

This representation of the City as a large, vital, multi-functional cluster of organisations finds confirmation in the recent work of Mira Wilkins. In two important articles, she draws attention to the many thousands of 'free-standing' firms set up between 1870 and 1914 to manage investments abroad in transport, public utilities, banking, financial services, manufacturing, agriculture and mining. These did

THE CITY AND INTERNATIONAL MINING   99

not grow out of domestic operations, but were formed to manage a single investment. Promoters were to be found in all parts of Britain, but most were based in the City. International company promotion was a widespread and lucrative activity. The majority of free-standing companies had very sparse management, amounting to little more than a small head office staff and a board of directors. They offered a means of supervising overseas investments, and had the attraction that a ready market existed for their stocks and shares. However, because adequate management was lacking in most cases, all but a tiny minority of free-standing international companies can be seen to have failed. They simply did not have the technological, administrative and marketing know-how needed to survive in competitive markets. The only exceptions were firms which either somehow developed fitting management and organisational structures or had their assets managed for them by experienced intermediaries such as mining consultancies or agency houses.[3]

Wilkins' conclusion that the supply of capital and promotional talent in Britain outran the nation's ability to manage its assets overseas cannot be accepted without reservation. Certainly, many thousands of limited companies were registered to operate overseas, and most of them did sink without trace. Most of the 8,400 companies formed between 1880 and 1913 for mining and mine exploration abroad, for instance, are known to have generated very little serious activity. And, of those that did enter production, only a small proportion became profitable.[4] Yet facts such as these are not sufficient to demonstrate that, on the whole, the capital invested in British free-standing international companies was unremunerative. There have been few attempts to measure the rate of return on investments in overseas mining, and of these only the studies of Frankel and of Harvey and Taylor were conducted in a rigorous fashion. Both studies confirm that most international mining ventures failed financially, but that occasional successes were sufficiently lucrative to raise the industry rate of return on capital employed, as measured by internal rates of return, to positive levels. The main result of Frankel's study of gold mining in South Africa is that 'the average internal rates of return on capital investment in the gold mining industry have tended to equality with those calculated on the same basis in other comparable directions of international investment'. Having measured the average rate of return for all mines between 1887 and 1965 at 5.2 per cent, Frankel firmly rejects the 'widely held belief that, on the whole, the return to capital invested in the industry has been negative'.[5] Likewise, Harvey and Taylor compute a healthy rate of return of more than 10 per cent on British capital invested in Spanish mining between 1851 and 1913.[6]

The findings of Frankel and of Harvey and Taylor, though not sufficient to dispel the notion that free-standing companies were a poor vehicle for international investment, do point to the need for caution when generalising about British direct investment overseas before

100   MINING AND METALLURGY

1914. Many eminent scholars have been drawn to the problem of measuring international capital movements, but there remain substantial points of disagreement over the scale, timing, nature, direction and profitability of investment flows. The estimates-dispute-revision cycle, associated with the names of Simon, Edelstein and Platt amongst others, is hardly likely to be terminated with the publication of Davis and Huttenback's monumental study of the political economy of British imperialism in the 1860–1912 period, *Mammon and the Pursuit of Empire*. In this work, new estimates of the scale, distribution and profitability of British overseas financial movements are presented. The London capital market is confirmed as the 'conduit for the greatest international movement of capital in the history of the world'. Of the £5 billion which flowed through the Stock Exchange, 30 per cent was retained at home, 45 per cent went to Europe, the United States and other countries over which Britain had no direct political influence, 16 per cent went to Empire countries with a large measure of self-government, and just 9 per cent went to the dependent Empire. This movement of funds represented 'the largest absolute voluntary capital transfer in the history of the world'. The average rate of return on Empire investments was greater than on home investments before about 1880, but thereafter the gap between the two narrowed to the point of insignificance.[7]

Davis and Huttenback go further than earlier writers in disaggregating their results, analysing the distribution of financial flows and rates of return geographically, temporally, and by industrial group. Yet the degree of disaggregation is not sufficient to enable the information presented to serve as a basis for more detailed industrial or national studies. Mining is a case in point. On the basis of the minimum estimates presented in *Mammon*, it appears that 12.5 per cent of the capital directed to private (non-governmental) institutions overseas between 1865 and 1914 went into the natural resource industries. The flow was most substantial in the second half of the 1890s and between 1910 and 1914, when it amounted to 29.5 per cent and 14.1 per cent of total private investment respectively. Natural resource investment was widespread geographically, but as a proportion of private funding it was most concentrated in the Empire; accounting for 18.8 per cent of non-governmental capital movements between 1865 and 1914, with peaks in 1880–84 (23.2 per cent), 1895–99 (33.7 per cent) and 1910–14 (19.4 per cent).[8] These figures, and the patterns of natural resource investment revealed by Davis and Huttenback, are of considerable interest in highlighting the importance of the agricultural and extractive industries to economic development in particular places and at particular times. Unfortunately, the grouping of agricultural and mining activities in a single category means that the authors' data cannot be used as the platform for a detailed investigation of British foreign direct investment in the mineral industries. 'Agriculture and extractive', with activities as diverse as Chilean nitrates, Indian tea,

Malaysian rubber and South African gold, is not a very helpful classification for anyone interested in the international expansion of a single
industry.

There are problems also with the quantitative work that has been
done specifically on the history of British overseas investment in
the mineral industries. An early survey was conducted by Edward
Ashmead in 1908–9, under the title 'Twenty-Five Years of Mining: A
Retrospective Review, 1880–1904, of Mining Companies Registered
in Great Britain, with Notes and Comments, and the Names and
Capitals of the Principal Registrations'. It appeared in the *Mining
Journal* in several instalments and covered each of the main mining
regions of the world. Ashmead's figures have since been revised and
extended, first by McCarty and more recently by van Helten.[9] The
grave weakness of these estimates, however, as van Helten readily
acknowledges, is that the original data relate to the nominal capitalisation of newly formed companies, and these bear little resemblance to
sums actually sunk in mining ventures. It was common for mining
companies to register a very large capital, but more often than not the
capital actually issued amounted to no more than a small fraction of that
authorised. Van Helten nonetheless holds that the figures do give some
idea of the geographic and temporal distribution of British direct
investment in the mineral industries.[10] But this seems most unlikely, as
there is precious little evidence to suggest that the ratio between capital
employed and nominal capital was fixed over time and across mining
fields. The nominal capitalisation figures for Western Australia
between 1895 and 1900, for instance, are clearly far more inflated than
the corresponding figures for South Africa.

A better idea of the scale, timing and direction of British direct
investment in overseas mining might be gained from the analysis of the
data for individual companies published in *The Stock Exchange Year-
Book* (SEYB). These volumes are not comprehensive, excluding many
small and private ventures, but they do contain data on most of the
firms that made serious investments abroad. Individual company
entries contain information on the location and nature of company
activities and various financial and management details. An elaborate
database might be constructed as a tool for research into such matters as
capital flows and free-standing company formation. However, this
would be costly and time-consuming, and for present purposes a much
simpler and more limited exercise was decided upon. This involved
creating data files for the years 1875, 1894 and 1913 in which each
record corresponds to an entry in the SEYB. A record was created
for each non-ferrous metal mining company registered in Britain or
the British Empire. Each record contains fields for company name,
location of mine, principal metal(s), and long-term capital employed
(issued share capital plus debentures).

The main purpose of the exercise was to provide a reasonably
accurate description of the scale and direction of overseas activity, at

102   MINING AND METALLURGY

three significant points, as a starting point for an examination of the
processes and mechanisms of foreign direct investment in the mineral
industries. The year 1875 was selected because it saw the end of the
overseas mining boom of the early 1870s. Companies had been formed
to work properties abroad well before this time, but it was during the
early 1870s that London emerged as the recognised centre for international mining finance. The year 1913 was chosen simply because it lay
at the end of a period of vigorous expansion. The year 1894 stands
midway between 1875 and 1913, and has the advantage of coming after
the development of new mining fields in South Africa and elsewhere in
the 1880s, but before the dramatic South African and Australian gold
mining booms of the 1895–99 period. Thus the figures for 1875 capture
the results of a first wave of expansion associated largely with the early
1870s boom; the 1894 figures capture the results of a second wave of
developments in the 1880s; the 1913 figures describe the industry at its
prewar peak.

TABLE 1

BRITISH FOREIGN DIRECT INVESTMENT IN NON-FERROUS METAL MINING
(1875, 1894, 1913)

Year	No. of Companies	Total Invested * £	Mean Capital Employed * £
1875	39	11,391,271	292,084
1894	415	85,076,351	205,033
1913	957	240,018,465	250,803

Notes: *Investment and capital employed are defined as the sum of paid up share
capital, outstanding debentures and mortgage bonds.

Source: Stock Exchange Year-Book.

The summary statistics presented in Table 1 confirm the rapid
growth of British investment in international mining ventures in the
1870–1914 period. Long-term capital employed grew at an average
annual rate of more than 8 per cent, and the number of mining
companies listed climbed from 39 in 1875 to 957 in 1913. The general
impression is one of a vigorous response on the part of British capitalists
to investment opportunities around the world. The favoured vehicle
for the management of these investments, as Mira Wilkins suggests,
was the free-standing international company employing a relatively
modest capital.

The creation of an international metal mining industry centred on the City of London was inspired by two powerful economic forces. The first of these was the rising demand for base metals such as copper, tin and lead in consequence of the rising tempo of industrialisation in Europe, North America and Japan. Traditional users of non-ferrous metals, like shipbuilders, were experiencing buoyant growth at a time when the newer industries of the so-called 'second industrial revolution' were beginning to make their mark. The demand for tin, for example, was given a tremendous boost by the success of the food canning industry, which required large quantities of tinplate, and the motor vehicle industry, which needed tin for solder and for the alloys used in bearings. Copper, aluminium and zinc production, likewise, were each encouraged by the rise of the electricity and chemical industries. World mine production of copper and tin increased by factors of nine and four respectively between 1870–74 and 1910–14.[1] Britain, meanwhile, as a leading industrial power, faced an ever-increasing dependence upon imported ores and metals. Until about 1870 the country was virtually self-sufficient in copper, lead and tin. The domestic copper industry, however, had already begun to fade, and, although production of the other ores held up rather better, here too consumers were fated to import dependence. The expansion of British mining interests overseas before 1914 was stimulated to some degree by shortages of ores mined at home and their relatively high costs of extraction.

A second factor stimulating British mining entrepreneurs to look abroad was the international acceptance of gold as a medium of exchange. The widespread adoption of the gold standard among the major economic powers created a demand for gold which before the second half of the 1880s proved difficult to satisfy.[12] Rising levels of economic activity and international trade induced a search for gold across the globe, and between the 1880s and 1914 new sources of supply were brought into production in many countries. Of particular importance were developments in South Africa which, following the discovery of the Rand outcrops in 1886, forged ahead to become the world's largest producer of gold by the early twentieth century. Impressive increases in production were also recorded in the United States and Australia. In the former, the rush was to the frozen wastes of Alaska; in the latter, the discoveries at Kalgoorlie in Western Australia in 1893 were rich enough to sustain a doubling of national production in the second half of the 1890s. Elsewhere in the world new mines were entering production on a substantial scale. Siberia, Canada, India, Mexico, New Zealand and the Gold Coast all made significant contributions to the expansion of world production which is recorded in Table 2.

British companies were to be found wherever and whenever there was an intensification of mining activities. No part of the world was considered out of bounds, though some were viewed with more interest

104   MINING AND METALLURGY

TABLE 2

WORLD MINE PRODUCTION OF GOLD, 1870–1914

Period	World Production (Tonnes)	Index of World Production (1870-74=100)	Percentage Shares of World Production				
			USA	Australia	Russia	S. Africa	Others
1870-74	752	100.0	39.8	34.3	23.8	0.0	2.1
1875-79	827	110.0	38.2	24.5	23.2	0.0	14.1
1880-84	749	99.6	32.9	24.1	24.2	0.0	18.8
1885-89	812	107.9	30.7	21.9	20.4	1.7	25.3
1890-94	1,082	143.8	24.2	20.4	17.4	16.2	21.8
1895-99	1,859	247.1	23.7	20.3	10.5	24.0	21.5
1900-04	2,234	297.0	26.4	24.4	8.1	12.5	28.6
1905-09	3,142	417.7	22.2	16.2	6.4	31.2	24.0
1910-14	3,434	456.5	20.3	10.7	6.3	38.1	24.6

Source: C.J. Schmitz, *World Non-ferrous Metal Production and Prices, 1700–1976* (1979), pp.80–5.

than others. It was the United States and Spanish mining booms of the early 1870s which really established London at the hub of the world industry. Between 1870 and 1873, at least 65 companies were registered in Britain to carry on mining and milling operations in Colorado, Nevada and Utah.[13] In the same period 13 companies were formed to exploit Spanish concessions, and the successful launch in 1873 of the Rio Tinto Co., with an issued share capital of £2 million, signalled that very large sums could be raised for overseas ventures if they were skilfully promoted.[14] Copper, sulphur, lead and iron ore were the main attractions of Spain. In the United States, silver and gold mines were the main interest of British investors. Of the £11.3 million invested in overseas mining shares and debentures in 1875, a third was invested in Europe (mainly in Spain) and a third in the North America (mainly in the United States). Copper accounted for nearly two-fifths of the total and silver one-fifth.

The pattern of investment changed quite dramatically after 1875, as can be seen from Table 3. Particularly evident is the very substantial relative decline of European copper mining as a target for investment. In the 1870s and 1880s, exports from the British-owned Rio Tinto and Tharsis mines raised Spain to a leading position in the world copper market, almost on a par with Chile and the United States. Thereafter, however, as United States copper output continued to double every 10 years, leadership of the industry passed into American hands. Substantial new investments were made by British companies in copper mining in Australia and South Africa, but by the later 1880s gold had become the main preoccupation of British mining entrepreneurs and investors.

The discovery in 1886 of the Witwatersrand gold fields in the South African Republic stands as one of the most important landmarks in the history of international mining. In its wake came the formation of numerous gold mining companies and a rush of capital from Britain sufficient to establish southern Africa at the forefront of the world industry. The early outcrop mines were very easy to work and the ores simple to treat, and problems only began to occur following the discovery that the gold-bearing reef plunged steeply downward and that the ores became pyritic at depth. Deep level mines began to displace the earlier outcrop mines during the 1890s, encouraged by the commercial development of the cyanide process for the treatment of the complex pyritic ores. A second investment boom, beginning in 1895, greatly increased the capacity of the Rand mines, and, despite the setbacks of the Boer War, by 1913 South Africa was supplying two-fifths of the world market. In that year, 221 British gold mining companies were active in southern Africa employing a capital of £94.5 million. Most held concessions on the Rand, but a minority had mines in Southern Rhodesia where the industry grew quite rapidly between 1899 and 1913.[15]

Southern Africa accounted for about half the long-term capital employed by British overseas mining companies in 1913. The second most favoured region for investment was Australia, with 16 per cent of the total. Gold mining in Australia began in 1851 and was largely concentrated in Victoria. When output in that state began to fall in the early 1880s, it was at first counteracted by increases in Queensland and later, after 1895, by the rapid development of the riches of Western Australia. Besides the extension of gold mining, the mineral industries were boosted after the mid-1880s by the exploitation of the rich deposits of silver-lead-zinc ores at Broken Hill.[16] In addition, there was a marked acceleration in the production of coal and copper. As a result, minerals and metals actually displaced wool as the leading Australian export for a few years at the opening of the twentieth century. Before the 1880s, most of the capital required to exploit the mineral riches of Australia came from local sources, and it was only in the 1890s, when the Western Australian gold fields were opened up, that a large part of the necessary resources came from Britain. The West Australian boom coincided with the second wave of investment to southern Africa, and contributed to the spectacular rise in the volume of British capital directed into mining operations in the 1895–99 period.[17]

It was not only in southern Africa and Australia that gold proved a

TABLE 3

TOP TWENTY TARGETS FOR BRITISH DIRECT INVESTMENT IN OVERSEAS
METAL MINING, 1875–1913*

Field	Year	Rank	Number of Companies	Investment (£000)	Investment as a % of Total **
Southern	1875	14	1	110	1.0
African	1894	1	116	23,555	27.7
Gold	1913	1	221	94,558	39.4
Australasian	1875	7	2	248	2.2
Gold	1894	3	52	7,865	9.2
	1913	2	114	22,350	9.3
Southern	1875	-	-	-	-
Africa	1894	13	8	1,858	2.2
Other	1913	3	29	11,060	4.6
European	1875	1	3	3,672	32.2
Copper	1894	2	7	9,562	11.2
	1913	4	23	10,578	4.4
North American	1875	3	4	677	5.9
Gold	1894	4	21	3,353	3.9
	1913	5	24	6,971	2.9
Southern	1875	-	-	-	-
African	1894	5	29	3,110	3.7
Exploration	1913	6	43	6,837	2.8
Australasian	1875	13	1	140	1.2
Other	1894	44	2	86	0.1
	1913	7	24	6,441	2.7
North and	1875	-	-	-	-
Central	1894	-	-	-	-
African	1913	8	9	4,996	2.1
Other					
Australasian	1875	6	2	253	2.2
Copper	1894	27	2	326	0.4
	1913	9	22	4,224	1.8
Central	1875	-	-	-	-
American	1894	15	6	1,317	1.6
Silver-Gold	1913	10	13	4,072	1.7
North and	1875	-	-	-	-
Central African	1894	-	-	-	-
Tin	1913	11	53	3,938	1.6
Southern	1875	11	1	175	1.5
African	1894	16	2	879	1.0
Copper	1913	12	10	3,267	1.4
Indian	1875	-	-	-	-
Gold	1894	10	15	2,411	2.8
	1913	13	14	3,134	1.3

Continued overleaf

THE CITY AND INTERNATIONAL MINING   107

TABLE 3 (cont.)

Field	Year	Rank	Number of Companies	Investment (£000)	Investment as a % of Total **
Far Eastern	1875	-	-	-	-
Tin	1894	18	4	770	0.9
	1913	14	26	3,096	1.3
South	1875	9	1	200	1.8
American	1894	28	2	250	0.3
Copper	1913	15	11	2,987	1.2
South	1875	4	3	425	3.7
American	1894	8	20	2,696	3.2
Gold	1913	16	22	2,986	1.2
North	1875	15	1	105	0.9
American	1894	14	3	1,528	1.8
Copper	1913	17	7	2,949	1.2
European	1875	-	-	-	-
Gold	1894	24	3	403	0.5
	1913	18	7	2,756	1.2
Australasian	1875	-	-	-	-
Lead	1894	6	4	2,299	2.7
	1913	19	10	2,503	1.0
Central	1875	-	-	-	-
American	1894	22	6	549	0.7
Gold	1913	20	11	2,170	0.9

Notes: *The fields are ranked from 1 to 20 in accordance with capital employed in 1913. As a result, coverage for earlier years is less complete than for 1913. In fact, just 53 per cent of all capital was employed in these fields in 1875, compared with 75 per cent in 1894 and 84 per cent in 1913. The major omission in 1875 is North American silver, which accounted for 17.7 per cent of total capital employed in that year, but only 2.6 per cent in 1894 and 0.1 per cent in 1913.

**The relevant figures for total investment are £11,391,271 for 1875; £85,076,351 for 1894; £240,018,465 for 1913.

Source: Stock Exchange Year-Book.

powerful lure for British mining entrepreneurs and investors. Of the long-term capital employed by active British overseas metal mining companies in 1913, fully 60 per cent was tied up in gold mining ventures. The gold fields of North America, Central America, India, South America and Europe, and the silver-gold fields of Central America, all feature in the list of important targets for British metal mining investment presented in Table 3. As many as 477 gold and 20 silver-gold companies were active in 1913, and in certain locations, as in the Mysore district in India, British companies controlled virtually the entire industry. Furthermore, many of the firms classified in the exploration and other categories had some connection with gold mining. Exploration companies were very active in winning concessions over mineral-bearing land, and in the promotion of operating companies to exploit concessions. They were particularly conspicuous in the 1890s, when a large proportion (40 per cent in 1895) of all new international mining companies were created for purposes of exploration and company promotion. A large number of other companies, though involved in actual mining operations, had interests in more than one metal. This might arise because they were exploiting complex deposits which yielded several metals or because they owned and operated several concessions. Gold production was frequently one of the activities of these firms, and this largely accounts for their prevalence by 1913 in southern Africa and Australia.

The intensity of British interest in gold mining between 1880 and 1914 should not be allowed to obscure the fact that sizeable investments continued to be made in base metal mining. British firms operating in southern Spain, for example, progressively expanded their mining operations and integrated forwards into copper and lead smelting. The copper companies alone employed more than 25,000 men on the eve of the First World War.[18] Other copper companies – in Australia, South Africa and Russia – built large mining and smelting complexes and employed capitals in excess of £1 million. Impressive achievements were also recorded in tin mining. Before the turn of the century, British firms found it hard to compete in Malaya with Chinese entrepreneurs who controlled the supply of labour and who owned the best mineral bearing alluvial deposits. The adoption of more capital intensive recovery techniques, originally used to work alluvial gold, altered the competitive balance. Armed with the new technologies of gravel pumping and dredging, British companies were able dramatically to reduce their labour requirements and treat lower grade deposits. In 1900, European firms accounted for just 10 per cent of Malayan tin production; the corresponding figure for 1915 was 28 per cent. After 1920, British firms pressed home their advantage to gain effective control of the industry.[19] Experience gained in Malaya was readily transported elsewhere. High tin prices and improved communications promoted a boom in Nigerian tin mining after 1911, and by 1913 as many as 53 companies were active with a combined long-term capital of £3.9 million.

The surge in British direct investment in metal mining overseas after 1870 was not without foundation. Britain had led the world in the production of copper, tin and lead for much of the eighteenth and nineteenth centuries, and over this long period a large pool of expertise had been accumulated – technological, managerial and financial. This expertise resided partly in the regions, in the mining districts of Cornwall, Devon and Derbyshire and elsewhere, but it resided equally in London. From the 1820s onwards, ties were created between London and the provinces, as mine promoters looked increasingly to the metropolis for the funds needed to work mines at ever greater depths. A market for provincial mining stocks gradually developed in the City; the number of mining ventures quoted in the share lists of the *Mining Journal* rising from 30 in the mid-1830s to about 500 in the 1850s. The volume of mining share transactions was sufficient to encourage various attempts to set up a specialist mining stock exchange, although eventually the London Stock Exchange itself provided a satisfactory market for the higher class of mining stocks and shares.[20] London was emerging by the 1850s as the centre of the national mining industry. Leading mining engineers and promoters, like John Taylor & Sons, naturally gravitated towards the City and made it their base. Mining overseas was for them but a further extension of their field of vision. In the 1850s, Taylor did not hesitate to take on the promotion and management of a group of lead mines in southern Spain. This step marked the beginning of his firm's long and distinguished career as one of London's most important international mining houses.[21]

After 1870, British mining entrepreneurs, already accustomed to promoting and managing companies in many different fields, had every incentive to seek and respond to investment opportunities abroad. It was apparent by the beginning of the period that domestic production of copper, tin and lead would increasingly fall short of domestic consumption, and that Britain could never become a major supplier of precious metals. The continued prosperity of many consulting engineers, equipment suppliers, promoters, brokers, commodity dealers and financiers depended on keeping up the supply of metals and metal mining companies, and the development of prospects overseas must have appealed to each of them as the obvious way of protecting and extending their interests. Whenever circumstances were propitious, as when the price of a particular metal shot up in consequence of temporary shortages, a fresh crop of mining ventures would be launched and placed before the public. What is stunning to the casual observer is the immediacy of the City's response to opportunity and the sheer number and variety of mining prospects available to company promoters.

The fact that a large number of mining concessions were always available to London-based company promoters reflects the special position of the City at the centre of a global information network. British merchants were present in all parts of the world; they had ready access to local information; and they corresponded on a regular basis with traders and financiers in the City of London. Most correspondence dealt with detailed matters relating to commodity prices, credit and orders, but when promising investment opportunities arose, these would be related back home as a matter of course. The situation in mining was little different to that in shipping, railways, tramways, water, manufacturing and financial services. A merchant house with British connections would become aware of a potentially lucrative investment, often through influential local contacts; details would be sent back to London and a syndicate formed; a concession would be secured by the syndicate in the host country; a company would be floated in London to exploit the syndicate. The main promotional gains accrued at the point of transfer of a concession from a syndicate to a newly-formed operating company. Usually a substantial price was paid for the concession in cash, debentures or shares, and besides this contracts for construction, management services and supplies might well be granted to syndicate members.

There were, of course, many variations on the basic pattern. The Rio Tinto Co. flotation of 1873 was exceptional because of the large size of the capital needed to purchase the mines, but the way the company was brought into being was typical of the period. The availability of the mines was brought to the attention of Matheson & Co. in London through Heinrich Doetsch of Sundheim & Doetsch, general merchants based in Huelva in southern Spain. Doetsch had the foresight to see that, if the Rio Tinto mines were developed to their full potential, then his business eventually stood to gain from a large increase in trade. A syndicate to purchase the Rio Tinto concession was organised by Hugh Matheson in London. The mines were purchased by the syndicate and immediately sold to the Rio Tinto Co. The new company was floated on the London Stock Exchange. The syndicate divided up £600,000 in eight per cent debentures and £150,000 in cash. Matheson & Co. was appointed as commercial agent for the new company, and the civil engineers Clark, Punchard & Co. won the contract to build the Rio Tinto railway and shipping pier. Hugh Matheson was appointed as first chairman of the Rio Tinto Co. with Heinrich Doetsch as his deputy.[22]

Merchant interests were no less important in the development of mining in southern Africa. It was the discovery of diamonds in the early 1870s in the region known as Griqualand West that first attracted the attention of London capitalists. The diamond-bearing deposits found on the Dutoitspan and Bultfontein farms were at first worked by large numbers of individual diggers working a myriad of claims. The system was supported by Governor Southey, who, fearing the consequences of large-scale company exploitation, resisted all attempts to consolidate claims. Following his removal in 1875, official policy was reversed and a process of consolidation ensued. Southey had been supported by the Kimberley merchants who, backed by the coastal merchants of Port Elizabeth, had prospered as suppliers of goods and credit to the diggers. Once he had gone, however, the more progressive merchants led the way in buying up claims and promoting companies. Some of these were general merchants like James Ferguson, and E.W. Tarry & Co., the largest importers of machinery on the field. Many more were diamond merchants with partners or correspondents in London or Paris. Some of the most successful of these were Jules Porges & Co., A. Mosenthal & Sons, the Barnato Brothers, Alfred Beit, and Martin Lilienfeld & Co. British and continental capital flowed in after July 1876, and by the beginning of 1880 the majority of claims were in the hands of just 12 operating companies with an aggregate capital of

THE CITY AND INTERNATIONAL MINING   111

£2.5 million. Companies like the Cape Diamond Co., the Kimberley Mining Co. and the Griqualand Diamond Mining Co. were directly controlled by London diamond merchant élite and their financial allies.[23]

In large measure, it was the diamond magnates of Kimberley who took the lead in the development of the Witwatersrand gold mining industry following the first surge in the registration of claims in 1886. Hundreds of mining companies were formed between 1886 and 1889 as the scramble to secure title to gold-bearing sections of land continued, but the first flush of enthusiasm was abruptly curtailed once the discovery was made that mining and recovery costs were set to rise sharply as deep mining and capital-intensive recovery techniques became the norm. At this stage, the more powerful and well connected mining capitalists were able to step in and secure large numbers of concessions across the whole length of the Rand. The most powerful group to emerge was that organised by the diamond merchants Julius Wernher and Alfred Beit, who had made their fortunes with Jules Porges & Co. The firm was reorganised in 1890 following the retirement of Jules Porges to Paris, and renamed Wernher, Beit & Co. Its operations on the Rand were conducted through Eckstein & Co. which had the services of Hermann Eckstein, a shrewd negotiator and strategic thinker, and James Taylor, one of the few men capable of assessing the true worth of a prospective mine. Eckstein and Taylor acquired and developed some of the best properties on the central Rand. Wernher, Beit & Co. took a keen interest in mining finance, technology and economics. Strong links were formed between mining capitalists in London, Paris and South Africa. When Rand Mines Ltd., a powerful holding company with a controlling interest in a clutch of deep level ventures, was founded in 1893, its initial funding came from a range of prestigious sources, including the London-based merchant banker, Ernest Cassel, various members of the Diamond Syndicate, a group of leading consulting mining engineers, and the Rothschilds.[24]

Each of the 15 or so mining groups which rose to prominence on the Rand after 1889 owed its position to some degree to the ready availability of European capital and expertise. Cecil Rhodes may have enjoyed disparaging the efforts of London bankers, but without them Consolidated Gold Fields of South Africa, which he founded with Charles Rudd in 1887, would never have got off the ground.[25] The relationships formed between enterprising men in the field, like Rhodes and Rudd, and their metropolitan backers, were evidently mutually rewarding and borne of necessity. Fortune seekers like Wernher, Beit, Rhodes, Barney Barnato, Joseph Robinson and George Farrar had the wit, foresight and energy needed to gain control of tracts of gold-bearing land and to create organisations that might retain control of any operating companies formed to exploit them. Their associates in Europe were skilled in company promotion, and could offer, directly or indirectly, a range of services of vital importance to fledgling mining enterprises. Both parties stood to gain large fortunes through their involvement in mining company promotion and management. Large amounts of money were made through the issue of vendors' shares to concession owners. The buying and selling of shares in volatile markets and with insider information was another rich source of profit. Management fees and fees for financial and technical services were a more regular source of income. Equipment, shipping and other contracts were a further much cherished source of gain.

The same pattern can be observed in tin mining in Malaya and Nigeria. In both cases, the extension and formalisation of British territorial control was followed by attempts by European merchants to secure title to mineral bearing lands. In the Selangor and Perak provinces of Malaya in the early 1880s, for instance, the lead was taken by agency houses whose partners were closely associated with the British administration. At least three of the concessionaires were members or ex-members of the Straits Legislative Council, and four out of six concessions came under the control of two Singapore managing houses, Paterson, Simons & Co. and Syme & Co. Meanwhile, in 1883, Jardine, Matheson & Co. formed the Rawang Tin Mining Co. whose management was handed over to Scott & Co. of Singapore. Most of these early efforts to exploit the mineral riches of Selangor and Perak failed, but the colonial capitalist élite persisted and eventually succeeded in attracting British capital and expertise to Malaya on a large scale.[26] In Nigeria, the lead was taken by the Niger Co., which in 1899 handed over to the British government its territorial administrative responsibilities and privileges in exchange for cash and a share in the royalties resulting from subsequent mineral exploitation. Over the next few years, the Niger Co. succeeded in monopolising mineral rights in the most promising regions of the interior. The intention was not that the company should abandon its traditional role as a trading enterprise in favour of tin mining, but that it should be in a position to profit from any escalation of mining activity. Between 1910 and 1914, prospecting licenses were granted to large numbers of firms, and two promotional booms ensued, punctuated by a crash in 1912. The Niger Co. sought profit in the short term through the licensing system and company promotion, and in the longer term through its control of transport in the mining regions, trading activities and royalty payments.[27]

The activities of entrepreneurs based overseas but with connections in the City of London were clearly very important in stimulating British capitalists to invest in international mining ventures. Metropolitan businessmen were ever responsive to investment opportunities brought to their attention, and with time many of them became opportunity seekers. The relative advance of companies in the 'exploration' and 'other' categories recorded in Table 3 reflects in part an increasing need for London-based company promoters to keep up the supply of new mining prospects, and systematise the development process. They were, as van Helten and others have noted, troubled by the number of barren prospects brought to the market in the 1880s and 1890s, and they had a vested interest in improving procedures for finding and evaluating prospective mines.[28] Yet, even so, as the situation in Nigeria demonstrates, the model which best characterises the 1870–1914 period as whole, is one of peripheral initiation and metropolitan response. And the pull from the periphery was at its strongest in territories of increasing British influence, with an entrepreneurially-minded merchant community, and countries lacking in capital and mining know-how. British involvement in mining in southern Africa, India, Malaya and Nigeria stemmed ultimately from colonial political and economic developments, whereas the British presence in metal mining in Spain and Russia was purely a consequence of the technological and financial impoverishment of those countries. British mining capitalists did not enjoy the same degree of success in countries with ample local supplies of capital and know-how or in countries that naturally looked elsewhere to remedy local deficiencies. British involvement in mining in the United States diminished as that country grew richer, and in Australia, although the British presence was substantial, a large part of the mining effort was sustained by domestic resources – human and financial. In Mexico, a resource-deficient nation which looked to the United States not Britain for support, the pre-1914 boom in precious metal mining was sponsored mainly by American companies, which invested 5.7 times more than their British counterparts.[29] A similar situation existed in other countries in Central and South America.

Neither the sharp advance of American interests in international mining after 1900, nor the eventual displacement of London by New York at the centre of the world industry, should be allowed to detract from the achievements of British mining capitalists before 1914. As domestic investment opportunities dwindled, full advantage was taken of promising developments abroad. The City of London offered a number of services which proved very attractive to mining concession holders, brokers and developers in the colonies and elsewhere. The first of these services involved the formation and promotion of companies, and the raising of funds for mine development through the issue of shares and debentures. Hall and others have described the promotional techniques used to launch new mining companies, and the profits that flowed to vendors and promoters.[30] The emphasis in the literature has been on corruption and attempts to stamp out fraud. One unfortunate consequence of this bias is that the essential efficiency of the London market has been neglected. The costs of raising capital, including those resulting from fraud, have not been estimated with any degree of precision; just as systematic studies of mining profitability remain a rarity. The openness of the London market, and the large amount of freely available information in publications like the *Mining Journal*, suggest that the extent of financial corruption may well have been exaggerated, and that part of the appeal of London lay in the possibility of raising cash for inherently speculative ventures on terms that gave a prospective mine at least a fighting chance of success.

A second attraction of London was that the metropolitan business community could offer clients a bundle of competitively priced services. Merchant bankers like the Rothschilds did a large amount of business with all the mining companies in which they took a major interest. For the gold mining companies of the South African Rand, the Rothschilds could act as gold refiners, metal brokers, insurance agents, shipping brokers, financial advisers and bankers. Short term credit was readily available to customers against the security of sales on the London bullion and base metal markets. These forms of support, and the position of London at the heart of the international trade and payments systems, made London the natural home for large numbers of international mining companies.[31] Many of these, though precisely how many it is impossible to say, were actually owned and operated by foreigners. The attractions of London for these firms lay mainly in the range of financial services on offer. The London share market was very open and it was possible to generate trade in a company's shares and fixed interest securities more easily than elsewhere. Market specialists, like 'kaffir' jobbers, or brokers who dealt exclusively in Australian gold shares, could be employed to good effect at times of crisis. The position in London contrasted sharply with that in Germany and Paris where a much more cautious approach was taken towards dealings in international mining securities.[32]

In addition to financial and marketing services, City firms had the skills needed to develop and manage mining properties. Mining and civil engineers, together with the merchants, bankers and stock brokers, were numbered among the more active promoters of international mining companies. A prospectus for a new company or a reconstruction of an old company would almost invariably contain a report from a mining expert, and newly-formed companies would generally employ a consulting engineer.[33] This practice had developed in Devon and Cornwall and was straightway adopted by international companies. By the end of the 1870s, most of the top British mining engineers were based in London. The practices of many remained small, employing a few apprentices and one or two senior engineers; others grew to quite a size. The largest of them took on mine management in addition to surveying, estimating and planning. John Taylor & Sons controlled a clutch of lead mines in southern Spain and reigned supreme in the goldfields of India. Equally, Bewick, Moreing & Co., which employed engineers of the calibre of Herbert Hoover, was responsible for the management of many of the gold mines of Western Australia and elsewhere. The London-based mining engineers who worked for these and other consulting firms saw themselves as internationally mobile professionals with valuable technological and managerial skills. They took the lead in forming their own professional association in 1892 – the Institution of Mining and Metallurgy – which by 1914 had 2,310 members employed in all parts of the world.[34]

Any explanation of the pattern and intensity of British involvement in international mining before 1914 must take account of both the economic and political realities in investment receiving countries and the capacity of the City of London to respond flexibly to a wide range of opportunities and problems. Businessmen operating abroad regularly approached City promoters with new mining propositions; the geographic distribution of which depended ultimately on the strength of political and commercial ties between London and the host country, and levels of demand in the latter for foreign capital and expertise. The propositions brought forward were evaluated from various angles by a metal mining community which included financiers, stock brokers, merchants, metal dealers, equipment suppliers, contractors and consultant mining engineers. Members of the community as a matter of course involved others in any proposition in which they took an interest. They did so because they often required complementary forms of expertise, and as a means of spreading risks. The inherently uncertain nature of overseas mining recommended joint ventures over concentrated ownership. It was also wise for promoters to take a long-term view of mining propositions, as a successful venture might boost incomes in many ways over a long period. For mining companies to be successful, they needed the services of well trained and financially astute mining engineers.

This view of the City and international mining between 1870 and 1914 differs from that of earlier accounts in highlighting the importance of information flows and business networks rather than speculation and share manias. Of the many thousands of companies registered for the purpose of taking up mining concessions, a large majority never entered production. The City had a propensity to create companies. It was an easy matter, and a useful way of investigating a prospect without risking too much capital. Companies were formed and liquidated by collaborating groups of firms and individuals in the normal course of business. It was understood by all concerned that only a minority of mines would ever be worth developing. Through involvement in numerous exploratory projects, promoters might expect to gain participation in at least some successful ventures. Shares in unlikely properties could be unloaded whenever the market boomed. The aim of the most ambitious mining entrepreneurs was to acquire a controlling interest in a number of first-class companies; and, indeed, large numbers of nominally free-standing companies were under the dominion of powerful capitalists, acting individually or in concert. Nowhere was this more true than in the goldfields of South Africa. By 1913, for instance, following a series of amalgamations in 1908–9, the Corner House group led by Wernher, Beit & Co. controlled 15 Rand mines with an issued share capital of more than £14 million.[35] The free-standing company may have been an important vehicle for British foreign direct investment, as Mira Wilkins asserts, but sight should not be lost of the fact that many legally separate enterprises were controlled and operated by more powerful groups which themselves represented a complex of interests.

The British were by no means exceptional in this. Several German firms, most notably Metallgesellschaft, Aron Hirsch and Beer Sondheimer, controlled international networks of mining and metal-trading businesses before 1914. The most vigorous of these, Metallgesellschaft, worked through powerful subsidiaries like the American Metal Co. and the Australian Metal Co. which had interests in a long succession of new ventures.[36] And when operating away from home, American groups operated in a manner very similar to that of their British and continental European counterparts. The Guggenheims operated in Mexico as an investment group looking for multiple sources of profit, not as a classic United States multinational. They were politically well connected, and dominated the Mexican mining industry through an elaborate web of companies. Not all Guggenheim properties were controlled through their main vehicle, the American Smelting and Refining Co. (ASARCO). Active subsidiaries like the Mexican Ore Co., the Aguascalientes Metal Co., the American Smelters' Securities Co. and the Guggenheim Exploration Co. were involved in making deals and floating companies in all parts of Mexico. The Guggenheims were not alone. Mexico was a land of opportunity for American mining companies, and New York was to that country as London was to southern Africa. Large numbers of concessions were bought up and mining companies launched. Most of them failed, but a mighty industry was built by powerful groups consisting of financiers, stock and metal brokers, equipment suppliers and mining engineers.[37]

It is not fully evident, in the light of what we know of international mining between 1870 and 1914, that the British were unique in the way they organised and managed their international business activities. Much more comparative research, of the kind undertaken by Michie, will be needed before we can make definitive statements about the nature and organisation of international business enterprise in different countries. Equally, there is a need for further research of the kind undertaken by Chapman on relationships between major centres of international trade and finance and the peripheral economies of the developing world. For the moment, however, it seems reasonable to conclude that, in the case of the British Empire, developments on the periphery must be weighed more heavily in the analytical balance than Cain and Hopkins are inclined to allow for in their challenging thesis on gentlemanly capitalism and the new imperialism of the later nineteenth century.[38]

Royal Holloway and Bedford New College, London
Bath College of Higher Education

NOTES

1. S. Chapman, 'British-based Investment Groups before 1914', *Economic History Review*, second series, Vol. XXXVIII (1985), pp.230–47; idem, 'Venture Capital and Financial Organisation: London and South Africa in the Nineteenth Century', in S. Jones (ed.), *Banking and Business in South Africa* (1988), pp.27–45.
2. R. Michie, *The New York and London Stock Exchanges, 1850–1914* (1987), pp.249–84; idem, 'Options, Concessions, Syndicates, and the Provision of Venture Capital, 1880–1913', *Business History*, Vol. XXIII (1981), pp.159–60.
3. M. Wilkins, 'The Free-Standing Company, 1870–1914: An Important Type of British Foreign Direct Investment', *Economic History Review*, second series, Vol. XLI (1988), pp.259–82; idem, 'European and American Multinationals, 1870–1914: Comparisons and Contrasts', *Business History*, Vol. XXX (1988), pp.8–45.
4. J.-J. van Helten, 'Mining, Share Manias and Speculation; British Investment in Overseas Mining, 1880–1913', *Business History Review*, forthcoming.
5. S.H. Frankel, *Investment and the Return to Equity Capital in the South African Gold Mining Industry, 1887–1965: An International Comparison* (Cambridge, MA, 1967), p.7.
6. C. Harvey and P. Taylor, 'Mineral Wealth and Economic Development: Foreign Direct Investment in Spain, 1851–1913', *Economic History Review*, second series, Vol. XL (1987), p.199.
7. L. Davis and R. Huttenback, *Mammon and the Pursuit of Empire: A Political Economy of British Imperialism, 1860–1912* (Cambridge, 1986), pp.30–72.
8. Computed from ibid., pp.54–5, Table 2.6.
9. Ashmead's articles were subsequently published in book form in 1909, under the same title. J.W. McCarty, 'British Investment in Overseas Mining, 1880–1914' (unpublished D.Phil. thesis, University of Cambridge, 1960); idem, 'British Investment in Western Australian Gold Mining, 1894–1914', *University Studies in History*, Vol. 4 (1961/62), pp.7–23; Van Helten, 'Share Manias'.
10. Van Helten, 'Share Manias'.
11. C.J. Schmitz, *World Non-ferrous Metal Production and Prices, 1700–1976* (1979), pp.69, 164, 168; W.Y. Elliott *et al.*, *International Control in the Non-ferrous Metals* (New York, 1937), pp.392–4.
12. L.D. Stanforth, *Gold Production and Prices before and after the First World War* (New York, 1983); M. De Cecco, *The International Gold Standard: Money and Empire* (2nd ed., 1984); J.-J. van Helten, 'Empire and High Finance: South Africa and the International Gold Standard, 1980–1914', *Journal of African History*, Vol. 23 (1982), pp.532–3.
13. C.C. Spence, *British Investments and the American Mining Frontier, 1860–1901* (New York, 1958), pp.241–60.
14. C. Harvey, 'Public Relations and the Creation of a Victorian Mining Company: Rio Tinto, 1873–1875', *Business Archives*, Vol. 41 (1976), pp.44–58; idem, *The Rio Tinto Company: An Economic History of a Leading International Mining Concern, 1873–1954* (Penzance, 1981), pp.28–35.
15. Table 3. See also D. Innes, *Anglo American and the Rise of Modern South Africa* (1984), especially pp.45–74; J.H. Hammond, *Autobiography of John Hays Hammond*, 2 vols. (New York, 1935); R.V. Kubicek, *Economic Imperialism in Theory and Practice: The Case of South African Gold Mining Finance, 1886–1914* (Durham, NC, 1979); P. Richardson and J.-J. van Helten, 'The Development of the South African Gold Mining Industry, 1895–1918', *Economic History Review*, second series, Vol. XXXVII (1984), pp.319–40. On Rhodesia, see for example I.R. Phimister, 'The Reconstruction of the Southern Rhodesian Gold Mining Industry, 1903–10', *Economic History Review*, second series, Vol. XXIX (1986), pp.465–81.
16. G. Blainey, *The Rush that Never Ended: A History of Australian Mining* (Melbourne, 3rd ed., 1978), pp.142–58.
17. A.R. Hall, *The London Capital Market and Australia, 1870–1914* (Canberra,

118   MINING AND METALLURGY

1963), pp.9–20, 132–3, 176–8; Blainey, *Rush that Never Ended*, pp.248–56.
18. Harvey, *Rio Tinto*, pp.124–8.
19. Wong Lin Ken, *The Malayan Tin Industry to 1914* (Tucson, 1965), pp.153–4, 216–7; idem, 'Western Enterprise and the Development of the Malaysian Tin Industry to 1914', in C.D. Cowan (ed.), *The Economic Development of South-East Asia* (1964), pp.127–53; Hoong Yip, *The Development of the Tin Mining Industry of Malaya* (Singapore, 1969), pp.95–109, 127–152; J.-F. Hennart, 'Internalisation in Practice: Early Foreign Direct Investments in Malaysian Tin Mining', *Journal of International Business Studies*, Vol. 17 (1986), pp.131–43.
20. R. Burt, 'The London Mining Exchange, 1850–1900', *Business History*, Vol. XIV (1972), pp.124–43.
21. C. Harvey and J. Press, 'Overseas Investment and the Professional Advance of British Metal Mining Engineers, 1851–1914', *Economic History Review*, second series, Vol. XLII (1989), pp.66, 69. On Taylor's career generally, see R. Burt, *John Taylor: Mining Engineer and Entrepreneur, 1779–1863* (Buxton, 1977).
22. Harvey, *Rio Tinto*, pp.5–11, 25–36.
23. R.V. Turrell, *Capital and Labour on the Kimberley Diamond Fields, 1871–1890* (Cambridge, 1987), pp.59–65, 73–82; C. Newbury, 'Technology, Capital and Consolidation: The Performance of De Beers Mining Company Limited, 1880–1889', *Business History Review*, Vol. 61 (1987), pp.1–42; T. Gregory, *Ernest Oppenheimer and the Economic Development of South Africa* (1962), p.47.
24. Kubicek, *Economic Imperialism*, pp.53–71; R.V. Turrell with J.-J. van Helten, 'The Rothschilds, the Exploration Company and Mining Finance', *Business History*, Vol. XXVIII (1986), pp.181–205; D.J. Jeremy (ed.), *Dictionary of Business Biography*, entries on Sir Julius Wernher and Sir Alfred Beit, Vol. I (1984), pp.253–5, and Vol. V (1985), pp.736–40.
25. Kubicek, *Economic Imperialism*, pp.87–90. See also Consolidated Gold Fields of South Africa Ltd., *The Gold Fields, 1887–1937* (1937), pp.8–10; A.P. Cartwright, *Gold Paved the Way: The Story of the Gold Fields Group of Companies* (1967), p.26.
26. Wong Lin Ken, *Malayan Tin Industry*, pp.119–67, 211–39.
27. W. Freund, *Capital and Labour in the Nigerian Tin Mines* (1981), pp.32–41.
28. See van Helten, 'Share Manias'; Harvey and Press, 'Mining Engineers', pp.76–8; H. Hoover, *Principles of Mining: Valuation, Organisation and Administration* (New York, 1909), passim; idem, 'Mining Valuation and Mining Finance', *Mining Magazine*, Vol. VII (1912), pp.275–7; G. Nash, *The Life of Herbert Hoover: The Engineer, 1874–1914* (New York, 1983), pp.277–86; A.G. Charleton, *General Principles of Successful Mine Management* (1800).
29. M.D. Bernstein, *The Mexican Mining Industry, 1890–1950: A Study of the Interaction of Politics, Economics and Technology* (New York, 1965), p.75. On American mining enterprise and investment, also see C.J. Schmitz, 'The Rise of Big Business in the World Copper Industry, 1870–1930', *Economic History Review*, second series, Vol. XXXIX (1986), pp.392–410; H. Barger and S.H. Schurr, *The Mining Industries, 1899–1939: A Study of Output, Employment and Productivity* (New York, 1944).
30. Hall, *London Capital Market and Australia*, pp.61–77, 111 et seq. Also see van Helten, 'Share Manias'; Spence, *British Investments*, passim.
31. Van Helten, 'Empire and High Finance', pp.539–43.
32. Van Helten, 'Share Manias'.
33. Harvey and Press, 'Mining Engineers', pp.69, 73; Spence, *British Investments*, pp.70–1, 101–4; J. Rowe, *The Hard Rock Men: Cornish Immigrants and the North American Mining Frontier* (Liverpool, 1974), pp.255–7.
34. C. Harvey and J. Press, 'The Origins and Early History of the Institution of Mining and Metallurgy, 1892–1914', *Transactions of the Institution of Mining and Metallurgy*, Vol. 95 (1986), pp.171–5.
35. Kubicek, *Economic Imperialism*, p.54.
36. Schmitz, 'Rise of Big Business', p.395.

THE CITY AND INTERNATIONAL MINING   119

37. Bernstein, *Mexican Mining Industry*, pp.49–77.
38. P.J. Cain and A.G. Hopkins, 'Gentlemanly Capitalism and British Imperialism,
    II: New Imperialism, 1850–1945', *Economic History Review*, second series, Vol.
    XL (1987), pp.1–26.

[20]

3 The British in Foreign Oilfields

I THE BRITISH OIL INDUSTRY

The half century before the First World War saw a massive export of British capital overseas, arguably to the detriment of the domestic economy. Between 1905 and 1914 some 5 to 7 per cent of the British National Income was sent abroad, almost double the rate of domestic capital formation. By 1914 the United Kingdom had about £4000 million invested overseas, over 40 per cent of this sum being in railways.

It is difficult to give an exact figure for the amount of British capital invested in the world oil industry. Foreign investment statistics for the period before 1914 are notoriously unreliable. Sir George Paish, an eminent statistician, produced some useful foreign investment statistics before the First World War, although he only covered foreign portfolio investment and not direct investment abroad. He estimated that the amount of British capital 'publicly invested' in the oil industry abroad was £14.3 million at the end of 1907, and £40 million at the end of 1913. Another indicator of the size of British investment in the oil industry is Skinner's *Oil and Petroleum Manual*. The 1912 edition of this reference work on the British oil industry listed some 592 companies, with a total nominal capital of £137 million. This included transport and distribution companies, the Scottish shale oil firms, and a host of small speculative ventures. About half of the £137 million nominal capital was represented by companies which appear to have had producing interests in foreign oilfields, and a proportion of this £68.5 million represented capital authorised but not paid up.[1]

If the exact dimension of British oil investment abroad remains elusive, it is clear that this investment represented a considerable divergence from the norm of British overseas investment. While

47

48   THE EMERGENCE OF THE BRITISH OIL INDUSTRY

most British foreign investment was portfolio, involving no managerial control, oil investment was often associated with entrepreneurship. While British investors had a strong preference for high-grade foreign bonds and other reliable securities, oil investments were frequently risky, although Paish's figure of 4.5 per cent for the rate of return for British capital invested in the foreign oil industry at the end of 1907 was only a little below his average of 5.2 per cent for total British overseas investment. There was also a marked difference in the geographical destination of the investment. Almost half of British overseas investment was in the Empire, and another 40 per cent in the Americas. British oilmen and investors, however, spread their interests far more widely. Both Paish and Skinner's statistics indicate that Russia attracted a very substantial share of British oil investment, although under 3 per cent of total British prewar investment was placed in that country. Some £8.1 million, or 60 per cent, of Paish's £14.3 million of British capital invested in the oil industry overseas at the end of 1907, was in Russia. The Empire came next in importance with £6 million, followed by the United States, with £3.6 million. The list of companies given by Skinner confirms this geographical pattern. The *Oil and Petroleum Manual* for 1912 listed companies with a total nominal capital of £21.7 million operating in Russia; £10.2 million in North America; £8.6 million in South America; £7.2 million in Asia; £6.3 million in Austria–Hungary; £4 million in Rumania; £3.8 million in North Africa and the Middle East, and various small amounts spread around the rest of the world.

The age of Middle Eastern oil had obviously not arrived by 1914. Eastern Europe and the Americas were the main focus of attention of British oil investors. This chapter is concerned with the spread of British enterprise and capital into two of the countries of those regions, Russia and Mexico, while subsequent chapters will examine the growth of British oil investment in the Middle East and the Empire. It is often overlooked, however, that by 1900 Britain had possessed an indigenous oil industry in Scotland for over fifty years, and this experience proved of some assistance when British entrepreneurs began to take an interest in foreign oilfields.

The origins of the Scottish shale industry can be dated from the early 1850s when James Young developed a process for distilling oil from shale. Within a few years Young's kerosene was being widely sold on the Continent. The industry subsequently suffered greatly from imports of cheap American and later Russian petroleum, but it survived into the twentieth century, albeit with a greatly reduced number of firms. The 90 shale oil companies in 1870 had been reduced to 13 by 1894 and to half a dozen by the turn of the century. Yet the remaining companies were able to pay steady and reliable dividends in the 1900s. The most successful company, Pumpherston, paid on average dividends of 33 per cent per annum on its ordinary shares between 1900 and 1910, and annual shale oil production increased from over 2 million to over 3 million tons in the two decades prior to the First World War.[2]

The very respectable dividend record of the leading firms in the industry greatly impressed contemporaries, and they were frequently taken as models for other British oil companies by the trade press. 'What a pity the majority of our petroleum companies', lamented the *Petroleum Review* in January 1910, 'cannot show such a good record for Stock Exchange quotations.'[3] However, these dividends were built on a vulnerable long-term position. By the late nineteenth century the profitability of the industry had become dependent on the sales of by-products such as sulphate of ammonia and paraffin wax, and a fall in the prices of these products rapidly embarrassed the companies. After 1910 a combination of low prices for both kerosene and paraffin wax forced the industry into financial difficulties. In 1911 three of the companies, Youngs, Broxburn and Oakbank, paid no dividends. The offer which the Scottish shale oil industry made before the Royal Commission in 1913 to switch its entire production to fuel oil, provided the Admiralty were prepared to guarantee to take it, made considerable economic sense. It would have meant a switch from a high-risk, volatile market situation to a low-risk stable one. The Admiralty market was especially valuable because it was uniquely immune from foreign competition, for it was the very nationality of Scottish shale which the Admiralty was likely to find most attractive.

Scotland was also the home of two of the more successful British oil companies operating overseas, whose activities will be examined in subsequent chapters. The Burmah Oil Company was established in Glasgow in 1886, with its shares being quoted on the Glasgow Stock Exchange. The company's dividend record attracted much favourable comment, it only once paying out a dividend of less than 15 per cent on its ordinary shares between

50   THE EMERGENCE OF THE BRITISH OIL INDUSTRY

1902 and 1913. In 1905 Burmah Oil became involved in the search for oil in Persia, and after a great oilfield had been located there it floated the Anglo-Persian Oil Company on the Glasgow Exchange in 1909.

II THE OILFIELDS OF RUSSIA

The Glasgow-based companies represented, however, only a small percentage of British capital invested in the oil industry. Considerable amounts of British capital flowed into the oil industries of eastern Europe. The British were involved in the Rumanian oil industry over a period of nearly fifty years before 1914. Their record was undistinguished. One pioneer company, Jackson and Company, invested heavily in buying leases and constructing facilities. Unfortunately, it subsequently experienced a series of disasters, beginning with gas explosions in the oil pits, followed by the loss through disease of the oxen on which its distribution relied, and finally the gutting by fire of its refinery. In the 1890s the Anglo-Rumanian Oil Company of London brought American machinery and drillers to the Rumanian oilfields for the first time, but they found no oil. By the outbreak of the First World War the British stake in Rumanian oil by value of investments was 20 per cent of all foreign capital, but it was spread among numbers of enterprises. Only one major concern was British-managed and that was a recent consolidation in 1912.[4]

The oil industry of Russia attracted large amounts of British capital. According to the estimates of the Russian statistician P. V. Ol', published in the early 1920s, the petroleum industry attracted a third, the largest single amount, of the £53.7 million of British capital invested in Russian industry before the Revolution.[5]

The British arrived, however, relatively late in the history of the Russian oil industry. By the time British oil companies appeared in Russia, foreigners had already made a notable contribution to the oil industry, the main centres of which are shown in Map 3.1 Before 1872 a primitive oil industry had existed around Baku, operated alternately by the State and by a farming-out system to private enterprise. Between 1850 and 1872 a monopoly was held by a Russian merchant. In 1872 the Government began to auction off oil-bearing lands on a long-term basis in return for a

THE BRITISH IN FOREIGN OILFIELDS   51

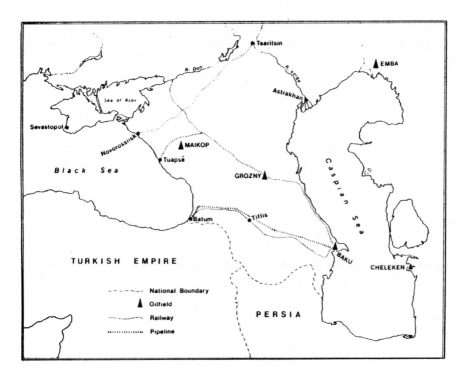

MAP 3.1   The oilfields of the Caucasus before 1914

lump sum payment and a low annual rental. This legislative change provided the pre-conditions for the birth of a modern oil industry. In March 1873 one of the Swedish Nobel brothers, Robert, visited Baku in search of walnut trees for use as riflestocks in the Nobel family business at St Petersburg. Robert Nobel, a chemist by training, purchased some oil properties instead of walnut trees, and constructed a refinery which was soon producing the highest quality kerosene ever made in Russia. In 1876 his brother, Ludwig, arrived in Baku, and there followed a veritable revolution in the Russian oil industry. The Swedes closely scrutinised the American industry, and, on the basis of this, introduced reforms in every branch of the Russian oil industry. In 1878 six Pennsylvanian drillers were brought to Baku, and the American 'rope' system of drilling was introduced, though this was later modified to meet Russian geological

52   THE EMERGENCE OF THE BRITISH OIL INDUSTRY

conditions. The industry in Russia had been greatly hampered by transport bottlenecks. Oil was transported from the wells to Baku in wooden barrels on carts known as *arbas*. This traffic stopped every time it rained as the rain made the roads impassable. The oil was refined when it reached Baku, and then transported in sailing vessels to the Volga and from there to the interior of Russia. Unfortunately, the Volga was only navigable during the summer months of the year, while the demand for kerosene naturally peaked during the winter. The Nobels responded to the inefficiency of this system, and the rising cost of the wood used for the barrels, by introducing pipeline technology into Russia from America. The first successful pipeline for the carriage of crude petroleum had been built in the United States in 1865. The Nobels began the construction of a pipeline from the oilfields to their refinery in 1877. Shortly afterwards, the Swedes pioneered techniques for the bulk transportation of oil. In 1879 they had the world's first ship for carrying oil in bulk, the *Zoroaster*, built in a Swedish shipyard. The use of railways for the transportation of oil was also pioneered. By 1881 a Nobel train was delivering oil by rail to St Petersburg. Further advances were made in refining. By 1880 Ludwig Nobel had built one of the world's first 'continuous distillation' refineries, a technique not used in the United States for another twenty-five years. This refinery greatly increased the amount of kerosene obtained from the 'heavy' Baku crude. Nobel crude yielded 35 per cent kerosene, while some of the other Russian refineries only gave yields of 20 per cent.

The second major foreign group to become involved in the Russian oil industry were the Paris Rothschilds. The Rothschilds had had some connection with the petroleum industry for several years before they became interested in Russia. During the 1870s they had been involved in the importing of American oil into France. Later they initiated a refining industry in Spain, and constructed a refinery at Fiume on the Adriatic for the supply of oil to the Austro-Hungarian Empire. From about 1880 Rothschild officials began to consider Russia as a possible source of supply for their Fiume factory. In 1883 a group of Russian producers, unable to raise sufficient capital to complete their project of constructing a rail line from Baku to Batum on the Black Sea, approached the Rothschilds. The Paris house lent money, in exchange for mortgages on refineries, wells and transportation facilities. By this means the Rothschilds soon became owners of various oilfields and storage depots. In 1886 they formed the Société Commerciale de Naphte Caspienne et de la Mer Noire, usually known as Bnito, the initials of its Russian name. The Rothschilds were always interested in exporting Russian oil rather than in supplying the interior markets of that country, and as part of this process they developed Batum into the major exporting port for Russian oil. A marketing organisation was developed abroad, with Fred Lane playing a key role. In 1898 the Rothschild oil empire was consolidated by the formation, with the International Commercial Bank of St Petersburg, of the Société Commerciale et Industrielle de Naphte, or Mazout.[6]

The dynamism of the Nobels and the Rothschilds made possible a great expansion of the Russian oil industry. The production of crude oil grew from 1.7 million poods in 1870 to 229 million in 1890 and over 630 million in 1900.[7] (There were 62 poods in 1 long ton.) At the turn of the century Russia was briefly the largest petroleum producer in the world, and Russian oil held a very strong position in world markets. Russian oil was well placed to compete with that from America. Russian production costs were between 30 per cent and 50 per cent lower than those of the United States, partly because of the concentration of the industry around the extremely prolific oilfields of Baku and partly because continuous distillation reduced refining costs. A high excise tax imposed in 1888 encouraged Russian producers to export, and the marketing methods of the Russian producers were more effective than those of Standard Oil. By 1884 American oil had disappeared from Russian markets, and its pre-eminent position in the rest of Europe had come under attack. After 1891 Russian oil also began to penetrate the markets of the Far East.[8]

The Nobels and the Rothschilds dominated the industry. By 1904 they controlled between them 40 per cent of the total sales of fuel oil and 50 per cent of the sales of kerosene in Russia.[9] The policy of both enterprises was always in the direction of co-operation rather than competition. The first attempts to form an alliance came as early as 1884. Ten years later a market-sharing agreement for foreign countries was signed between the Nobels, the Rothschilds and the third largest Russian refiner, Mantashev. At the turn of the century Nobels and Mazout joined together in a cartel, known as Nobmazout, which had 50 per cent of all Russian oil exports under its control.[10] The Rothschilds and the Nobels also sought an alliance with Standard Oil, something

54 THE EMERGENCE OF THE BRITISH OIL INDUSTRY

which the Americans, with their tradition of destroying rather than co-operating with rivals, at first eschewed. The first contacts between Nobels and Standard Oil were in 1886, and in 1894 the Swedes suggested that the American company should purchase 49 per cent of the Nobel interests. From 1887 Rothschild officials were also seeking to arrange an alliance with Standard Oil. The closest the Americans and the Russians came to co-operation was a grandiose agreement signed in March in 1895 between the Nobels and the Rothschilds, 'on behalf of the petroleum industry of Russia', and Standard Oil, 'on behalf of the petroleum industry of the United States'. The Americans were to be allocated 75 per cent of the world's oil export trade and the Russians the remaining 25 per cent. The agreement was scheduled to last for ten years, but the negotiations broke down even before all the details were finalised.[11]

The large-scale entry of British capital into the Russian oil industry came at the very end of the nineteenth century, at a time when Russia was almost the largest oil-producing country in the world. However, the British connection with Russian oil pre-dated this capital inflow. A number of British writers and journalists had been fascinated by the Baku oil industry.[12] Admiral Selwyn had watched with great interest the early experiments with the burning of fuel oil on Russian ships. A Scottish engineer, Thomas Urquhart, who was employed with the Grozny and Tsaritsyn Railway in south-east Russia, pioneered the development of fuel oil burning in Russian trains in the early 1880s.

Two British entrepreneurs played a particularly distinguished role in the early Russian oil industry. One was Fred Lane, whose involvement with the marketing of Russian oil was discussed in Chapter 1. The other was an equally neglected figure, Alfred Suart. Suart was an entrepreneurial risk-taker *par excellence*, but unfortunately a man with more foresight and initiative than commercial judgement. His extraordinary career, therefore, was marked by a series of bold pioneering initiatives, which turned into financial disasters. Suart's involvement in Russian oil stemmed, as did Fred Lane's, from his shipping interests. In this connection he rapidly followed the Nobels initiative in building specially-designed ships to carry oil, and he was responsible for the first British-owned tanker built in a British shipyard, the *Bakuin*, launched in 1884. He brought the first British ships to

THE BRITISH IN FOREIGN OILFIELDS 55

Batum. He persuaded Armstrongs to build a tanker in sections, so it could be conveyed from the Baltic to the Caspian Sea. Between 1885 and 1889 he converted several steamers into tankers for carrying Russian oil from Batum across the Mediterranean, and in 1887 across the Atlantic to Philadelphia. His *Chigwall* was the first British tanker to dock in the United States. By 1892 Suart had some sixteen tankers of various kinds under his control. He dealt with Fred Lane in Bnito oil, and it was in this connection that he met Marcus Samuel when he visited Baku in 1890.

In 1893 Suart launched a completely new initiative, buying a property in Grozny, which was eventually to become Russia's second major oilfield. Characteristically Suart's investment was both extremely successful and financially ruinous. His borings hit a 'spouter', the Russian equivalent of American 'gushers'. This 'spouter' produced some 20,000 poods of oil on the first day and drenched the neighbouring countryside. Suart was faced by huge claims for compensation from neighbouring landowners, and as a consequence was forced to dispose of his Grozny property 'for a song'.[13] Suart remained undaunted. In 1896, in order to maintain his independence from the Nobels and Rothschilds, he purchased the Zatourov property in Baku. The deal also included properties in Galacia and Rumania, and a fleet of oil tankers. Using this purchase as the basis, he founded the first British oil company in Baku, the European Petroleum Company, with a capital of £1 million. Suart achieved yet another first in the following year, when his *Baku Standard* became the first oil-fired tanker to cross the Atlantic. Once again this proved a technical triumph and a financial flop. In the last years of the century Suart embarked on an ambitious, but eventually unsuccessful, scheme to shatter the position of the Rothschild – Shell Transport alliance by uniting the British oil companies in Baku with the Royal Dutch.[14]

Despite Suart's personal fortunes, his initiatives were taken up by other British entrepreneurs. The formation of the European Petroleum Company in 1896 was followed by the floating of several other British oil companies to operate in Russia. In 1897 the Russian Petroleum and Liquid Fuel Company was formed by the purchase of property worth £530,000 in Baku. In the following year the Baku Russian Petroleum Company and the Schibaieff Company bought Russian property for £370, 400 and £740,750 respectively.[15] British capital rapidly established an important place in the Russian oil industry. By 1901 foreigners

56   THE EMERGENCE OF THE BRITISH OIL INDUSTRY

contributed 30 per cent of the total capital invested in the Baku oil industry, and £4 million of the £5.9 million of this foreign capital was British.[16] The British, moreover, did not restrict themselves solely to Baku. Despite Suart's unfortunate experience, they resumed the development of Grozny oilfields. By 1903 the 7 British firms established at Grozny had a capital of £1.2 million.[17] British companies were responsible for about one sixth of the oil produced at Grozny between 1896 and 1906.[18]

The infusion of British capital was warmly welcomed by the Russian Minister of Finance, Count Witte, and like-minded officials in the government.[19] The agent of the Ministry of Finance in London wrote to St Petersburg in January 1898 that English capital would help Russia keep her 'proper place' in the world oil market next to Standard Oil.[20] Russian officials appreciated the enterprise of men like Fred Lane, and regarded British investment as an important means of keeping Standard Oil out of Russia, and indeed preventing monopolisation of the Russian oil industry by the large oil groups.[21] British investment in Russian oil, however, also served a useful function in providing many Britishers with a sound training in the oil industry. Beeby Thompson, who went out to work with the European Petroleum Company in 1898, regarded Baku as the 'nursery of British oilmen.'[22]

By 1905, however, it was clear that all was not well in the 'nursery'. The dividends of the Anglo-Russian oil companies fell sharply after the turn of the century. Russian Petroleum paid 50 per cent on its ordinary shares in 1899–1900, but by 1904–5 this had been reduced to 2½ per cent. The Spies Company, the largest British oil company at Grozny, paid out one dividend of 5 per cent in 1900–1, and then nothing until 1905.

A number of things had gone wrong with British oil investment in Russia. The profitability of all foreign enterprises in Russia slumped during the 1900–5 depression. Whereas foreign capital in joint-stock companies was receiving returns of 8.9 per cent in 1895, the return had fallen to a low of 3.8 per cent by 1905.[23] The rapid expansion of the oil industry following the influx of foreign capital led to overproduction, and to a sharp fall in prices in 1901.[24] Moreover, yields from the old Baku oilfields were beginning to fall, and 'spouters' becoming rarer.

The British oil companies were ill-prepared to adjust to these more difficult circumstances. The typical company had started life by the purchase of a plot from a Russian owner, often for a very high price. The Armenian or Tartar owners invariably sold the property because, in the words of Beeby Thompson, they believed they 'had extracted the cream'.[25] The second of the British oil companies to arrive in Baku, Russian Petroleum, was fortunate in this respect. The property it purchased turned out to be very far from exhausted, producing about 3 million barrels (105 million imperial gallons) of oil during the first month of operation. This success, however, was entirely fortuitous. The company had paid remarkably little attention to either the legal or the economic position of the property it purchased. Soon after completing the deal, Russian Petroleum discovered that under a Russian law dating from June 1892 property could not be owned by a foreign company, a well-known fact of commercial life which the company promoters had overlooked. The property had to be made over to a trustee, and the company chose the British Vice-Consul at St Petersburg, a Russian subject. This was hardly a satisfactory arrangement. Had the Vice-Consul died, the company would have been liable to pay about £40,000 in death duties. Moreover, the Vice-Consul was known to be involved in various dubious businesses, and if any of these had gone bankrupt, Russian Petroleum's property would have been confiscated. The secretary of the company rightly described his firm's position in January 1898 as a 'very precarious one'.[26] Russian Petroleum's rights of ownership were not recognised until the summer of that year, thanks to the intervention of the Minister of Finance, Count Witte.[27] The company also seems not to have taken the precaution of surveying its property before the purchase, and was consequently greatly distressed to discover its condition. The former owner's policy, reported the General Manager, 'appears to have been to get as much out of the land as possible, by sinking the smallest amount of capital'.[28] In other words, the property had been sold just when heavy capital expenditure began to be required.

The organisation of the Anglo-Russian oil companies was extremely defective. There was the constant problem that companies were undercapitalised in relation to risks. The trade press was full of complaints about this, and about the 'watering' of capital. Britain's lack of a significant domestic oil industry meant that there was no reservoir of skilled personnel to manage her investments in foreign oilfields. Many of the expatriate managers

58   THE EMERGENCE OF THE BRITISH OIL INDUSTRY

in Russia were ill-qualified for their posts. In 1911 the *Petroleum World* attacked the 'professional gentlemen imported from London' who ran British oil companies overseas. 'The "swell" Manager', continued the journal, 'is a by-word among the Russians, some of whom take advantage of his ignorance, sell him second-rate goods, and watch with equanimity the money of the shareholders gradually disappearing under his hands.'[29] The companies had a very primitive level of technical sophistication. 'Personally I am not at all in favour of a Geological expert', the General Manager of Russian Petroleum informed his London office in January 1899. 'I have always found that such men have too many theories and fads and not sufficient practical experience.'[30] This was fourteen years after the Nobels had hired their first geologist to work at Baku.

These management defects were not confined to the British oil companies operating in Russia. Shell Transport had been brought to the verge of disaster by inadequate management before its merger with Royal Dutch. The Burmah Oil and Anglo-Persian companies were also to experience considerable problems with management deficiencies. British oil companies seemed generally prone to amateurism in management, and to the retention of obsolete methods of organisation. The companies which prospered were those which either located large supplies of crude oil or, as in the case of Shell, merged with a better managed foreign company.

The weak British oil companies were in no position to withstand the revolutionary disturbances of 1904/5, particularly since the Baku region was badly affected. The average age of the workmen on the Baku oilfield in 1900 was 25–30 years, and fewer than 50 per cent of them stayed at their jobs for one year or more. This youthful and transient labour force became increasingly involved in the strike movement. The first really serious strikes began in 1903, just when the oil producers were recovering from the depression at the turn of the century. In December 1904 there was the first general strike of oil workers, and this was followed by an outbreak of exceptionally savage racial warfare between Tartars and Armenians.[31] Serious racial and labour disturbances lasted until 1906, and the amount of physical damage done to the oil industry was substantial. Russian oil production in 1905 was 30 per cent lower than in 1904, and the 1904 level of production was not reached again until 1928. Beeby Thompson estimated in

THE BRITISH IN FOREIGN OILFIELDS 59

1908 that at least £2 million worth of property on the oilfields had been destroyed during this period.[32] 'The Russian petroleum industry for the present time has ceased to exist', the *Petroleum Review* gloomily observed in September 1905, 'the producing fields around Baku have all been fired, and some hundreds of derricks, together with the necessary plant destroyed.'[33] The British oil companies were spared the full fury that damaged the Rothschild properties, but their already enfeebled condition meant that even minor losses were sufficient to cause irreparable damage to a number of them. By the end of 1905 Russian Petroleum was claiming to have had between £80,000 and £90,000 worth of property destroyed.[34] A receiver was appointed for the company in 1908. The other British oil companies in Baku were in an equally miserable state after 1905. The Schibaieff Company paid no dividends after 1901, and in 1909 its position was described by the *Petroleum Review* as 'deplorable'.[35]

Yet British investors were far from totally disillusioned with the oilfields of Russia. The *entente* between Britain and Russia in 1907, and the return of general industrial prosperity to Russia in 1909, led to renewed interest in the country by English investors. In 1910 this attention became concentrated once more on the petroleum industry. During that year there was a sudden boom in oil shares and a flood of new oil companies appeared. 'Today oil shares upon the London Stock Exchange', observed the *Petroleum Review*, 'are the most sought after of any industrial securities on the market. We are, without doubt, in the midst of the greatest oil boom which this country has ever known.'[36] The boom in oil was triggered off by the annual Admiralty fuel oil contracts, which were taken by the London stock market as presaging a great expansion in the Royal Navy's use of fuel oil.[37]

The main object of the Stock Exchange's attention was a new and apparently prolific Russian oilfield at Maikop. The Maikop oilfield was located in the Kuban district of the Caucasus, in a very favourable geographical situation for the development of an export trade. It was only 50 miles from the port of Tuapsé on the Black Sea, and less than a hundred miles from the well-established oil export port of Novorossiisk. In 1909 a strong 'spouter' set off an oil boom in the area. In July the first British oil company, the Black Sea Oilfields Ltd, was formed to exploit the field, and in the following February this enterprise struck a great oil fountain on

60   THE EMERGENCE OF THE BRITISH OIL INDUSTRY

one of its plots. The apparently prolific nature of the oilfield, and its desirable geographical position, seemed to augur well for Maikop, and a large quantity of British capital was attracted into the area. Between 1909 and April 1911 some 53 Maikop companies were formed in Britain. By the eve of the Revolution there remained 25 British companies, with a capital of £4 million, concerned with the exploitation of Maikop oil.[38]

The Maikop companies were a disaster. Very little oil was found. 'With regard to Maikop', a witness told the Royal Commission on Fuel and Engines, 'perhaps the less said the better. Of the numerous companies operating there only two have paid dividends.'[39] In October 1911 the *Petroleum Review* observed that the failure at Maikop had left a 'distasteful flavour in the eyes of thousands of English investors'.[40] There was oil to be found at Maikop, and indeed under the Soviets Maikop was to become a major oil-producing region. The British companies, however, were not properly equipped to exploit the field. The geological conditions were different from the Baku and Grozny fields, but the only available skilled labour came from those established fields. Inappropriate drilling methods were therefore initially used.[41] Communications were poor, with a total absence of metalled roads in the region.[42] The port of Tuapsé did possess eighteen feet of water, but there was also a large submerged rock in the harbour which greatly hindered access. The construction of the infrastructure required for the successful commercial exploitation of a virgin oilfield was beyond the capacity of the dozens of small British oil companies.

Despite the depressing Maikop experience the British retained their interest in Russian oil. In the immediate prewar years British capital maintained the tradition, begun by Alfred Suart at Grozny, of pioneering new oil regions. The continued decline in production on the old Baku oilfields caused oil prices to rise sharply—the price of kerosene per pood at Baku tripled between 1910 and 1913—and this acted as a major stimulus for further exploration. The new areas of attention were Emba and Cheleken, in the Caspian region, and Sakhalin Island, off the coast of Siberia. British capital participated in the development of these regions in a variety of ways. Some British oil companies operated directly; others operated through the medium of companies, registered in Russia, but wholly British-owned; sometimes British investors held a part of the share capital of

THE BRITISH IN FOREIGN OILFIELDS 61

Russian enterprises. The British contribution, made in this variety of ways, to the growth of these new oil regions was substantial. By 1914 companies which were wholly or partly British owned were responsible for 50 per cent of the production of the Grozny oilfields, 75 per cent of Cheleken production, 90 per cent of Maikop production, and the whole of the oil production from the Emba region.[43]

British oil capital and enterprise in Russia in the prewar years was increasingly consolidated into a number of large and interrelated groups. The five British oil companies at Cheleken, for example, were all linked. The two dominant groups which emerged in Russia in the prewar years, however, were Shell and the Russian General Oil Corporation.

During 1911 the Shell Group began to acquire a number of Anglo-Russian oil companies. These included several enterprises operating in the new oil regions, such as the North Caucasian Oilfields and Spies Company at Grozny, and the Ural Caspian Company in the Emba region. The Shell Group's greatest *coup* came in 1912 when it purchased the Rothschild's 80 per cent holding in Bnito and Mazout. The management of these companies was reorganised, and the various firms placed under the control of a central management committee in St Petersburg, whose chairman was an ex-Nobel official, Ernest Grube. By 1914 the eleven Shell enterprises in Russia controlled 104.9 million poods of oil production, equivalent to just under a fifth of total Russian production.[44]

The second group was the Russian General Oil Corporation. 'Oil', as this group was commonly referred to, was a holding company formed by a group of Russian bankers and oil producers. The company was floated on the London Stock Exchange, and it attracted large amounts of British capital. The aim of the venture was to unite a large portion of the Baku oil industry, and within a short period of time it managed to bring the major independent ventures, such as Mantashev, Lianozov and Mirzoiev, under its banner. By the eve of the War a quarter of 'Oil's' capital, about £600,000, was held by British investors, and two British representatives sat on the board.[45]

It is difficult to give precise statistics for the amount of British capital which had been invested in the Russian oil industry since the late nineteenth century. Beeby Thompson estimated that the sum had reached £6½ million by 1904.[46] The next decade saw this

62   THE EMERGENCE OF THE BRITISH OIL INDUSTRY

amount expand considerably. By 1916 P. V. Ol' estimated that
British investment in the Russian oil industry was £18.1 million.
This compared with France's £5.4 million and Germany's £1.4
million. The British investment was distributed by region as
follows: Baku £5.2 million; Emba-Urals £3.3 million; Grozny
£2.7 million; Maikop £2.5 million; Cheleken £2.5 million;
Sakhalin £1.1 million; and other fields £800,000. A further £1.2
million of British capital was invested in various oil refining and
transporting businesses in Russia.[47]

The large British investment in Russian oil had clearly met with
mixed fortunes. While much money had been wasted in speculative ventures and the Anglo-Russian oil companies had not
earned the high dividends their founders had anticipated, British
enterprise and capital had pioneered new oil regions in Russia.
Moreover, British interests played an important role in the
consolidation of the Russian oil industry before 1914, a process
which raised hopes of renewal for the industry. The British
economy did not benefit greatly from the investment in Russian
oil. British capital did not develop new sources of oil for the
economy; indeed, Russian oil exports dwindled soon after the
arrival of the British. The dividends earned by British oil
companies in Russia after 1900 were very low, and most of the
investors' money in the Maikop and other speculative ventures
was lost even before the Bolshevik Revolution.

The Russian experience contributed greatly to the view of the
British capital markets that oil companies were a high-risk
investment. 'To the general public', wrote the *Economist* in 1910,
'perhaps the best known example of oil companies is the Russian
Petroleum.'[48] It was an unfortunate example. The experience of
Maikop was even less appealing, and, after the 1910 boom, oil
shares were an unattractive proposition for the remaining prewar
period. 'Everyone in London financial circles knows', the
Petroleum World observed in 1913, 'that at the present moment it
is a very difficult thing, in fact almost impossible, to induce the
public to take an interest in even a good oil proposition.'[49]

The reluctance of the money markets to supply funds for
speculative oil enterprises in these years gave certain of the
smaller oil companies a further reason for seeking an association
of some kind with the British Government. A number of oil
companies, aware of the strategic significance of the commodity
they produced, had made requests for financial assistance from

the State since the turn of the century. In 1903 the West Indian Petroleum Company, a small British oil company prospecting in Barbados, asked for a Government loan of £10,000, and in return offered the Admiralty the right of pre-emption over its production. In 1908 the Nigerian Bitumen Corporation proposed that the Government should join with it to explore for oil in Nigeria, the colonial government subsequently awarded the company £25,000. Requests for State finance increased in number after 1911. Nigerian Bitumen asked in 1912 for a further Government grant of £12,000 a year. The Cairo Syndicate, a small British oil company operating in Egypt, asked for a State loan of £100,000 for two years. The Newfoundland Oil Company put in a bid for a State loan of not more than £20,000. It was also in 1912 that the Anglo-Persian Oil Company began a campaign to secure a very large sum of money from the Government, and a year later the Mexican Eagle Petroleum Company offered to make a long-term fuel oil contract with the Royal Navy in return for a State loan of £5 million.[50]

III WEETMAN PEARSON AND MEXICAN OIL

The Americas were the second largest recipient, after eastern Europe, of British oil investment before 1914, and in general British oil companies proved rather more successful in the New World than in the Old. There were a number of relatively small but successful British oil companies in the United States. The California Oilfields Ltd was one of these. This company had been organised in 1902, with British capital and largely American management. Ten years later it had an annual production of 4.4 million barrels of crude oil, or 4.5 percent of total Californian production.[51]

This section, however, focuses on the most remarkable success of British oil enterprise in the Americas before the First World War. The man primarily responsible for this success was Weetman Pearson, later First Baron Cowdray. Pearson was born in 1856, and at the age of 16 he joined the family contracting business which had been founded by his grandfather. He became a partner in 1875, and by the turn of the century S. Pearson and Son had earned a worldwide reputation as contracting engineers. The firm constructed the Blackwall Tunnel under the Thames, built the four tunnels for the Pennsylvania Railway Company under the

64   THE EMERGENCE OF THE BRITISH OIL INDUSTRY

East River, which connected New York with Long Island, and became a major specialist in dock work. In 1889 S. Pearson and Son entered Mexico with a contract to drain the capital city. The construction of the Grand Canal to drain Mexico City's valley was completed in 1896, and over the next four years the firm built a modern harbour at Vera Cruz and a 200 mile railway across the Tehuantepec Isthmus (see map 3.2).

Pearson's interest in oil originated in 1901. One of the partners in S. Pearson and Son, J. B. Body, discovered petroleum deposits near San Cristobal while looking for rock for the firm's harbour works at Coatzacoulcos, soon to be renamed Puerto Mexico. No action was taken over this discovery until April 1901, when

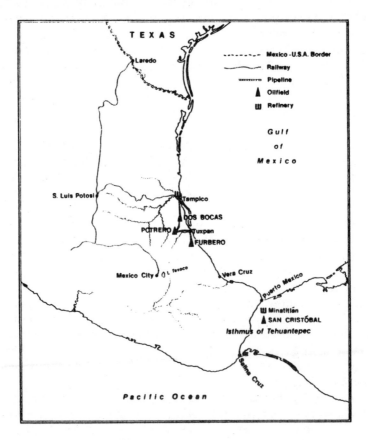

MAP 3.2   Mexico in 1914

Pearson, because of a missed train connection, was obliged to spend a night at Laredo on the Mexican-American border. The Spindletop gusher had just been struck about 300 miles away, and Laredo was in the grip of oil fever. It occurred to Pearson that if oil could be found on the Isthmus, it would provide an ideal fuel for the new Tehuantepec railway, especially since supplies of wood were inadequate. Pearson wrote immediately to Body, suggesting the acquisition of land around the San Cristobal oil seepages.[52]

Pearson was to become the most brilliantly successful, as well as the most personally attractive, of British oil entrepreneurs before the First World War. Yet in 1901 he was completely ignorant of the oil industry. This ignorance resulted in several costly mistakes. 'Now I know that it would have been wiser to surround myself with proven oilmen', he ruefully wrote to his son in 1908, 'and not relied upon commercial knowledge and hard work coupled with a superficial knowledge of the trade.'[53] Yet his great entrepreneurial skills eventually won him more success in oil than in any other branch of industry with which he was concerned. Pearson combined in an unusual way a number of qualities. He had both a complete grasp of details and a vision of the whole design, seeing both the wood and the trees at the same time. 'The Chief', as he was universally known to employees of S. Pearson and Son, was personally active in all of his business ventures and never asked anyone to undertake a risk he was not prepared to take himself. Yet he also knew how to delegate responsibility, something which became increasingly essential as the Pearson empire expanded. Pearson, motivated less by the desire for personal financial gain than by the sheer excitement of business, was always restless, always in search of the new challenge. On several occasions this was to bring him to the brink of disaster, and it was therefore fortunate that his greatest entrepreneurial gift was the proverbial 'Pearson luck'.

In 1902 Pearson acquired his first oil concessions. Further concessions were steadily acquired, largely because of the contractor's friendly relations with the Mexican dictator, Porfirio Diaz. Diaz was extremely impressed with Pearson's construction works in Mexico, especially the Tehuantepec Railway which S. Pearson and Son owned and operated in partnership with the Mexican government. The Englishman in turn respected the order and stability which Diaz had imposed on Mexico. The

66   THE EMERGENCE OF THE BRITISH OIL INDUSTRY

mutual respect between the two men developed into a personal
friendship which was to be of enormous consequence to the
eventual success of Pearson's enterprise. In November 1905 Diaz
promised J. B. Body that as soon as the company had sufficient
crude production in Mexico, he would increase the duty on
imported oils.[54] The major *coup*, however, came in 1906, when
Pearson's firm was granted huge new concessions on Federal and
State lands to the north of the San Cristobal oil fields in the
provinces of Veracruz, Tabasco, San Luis Potosi and Chiapas.
The concessions were for fifty years and were exempt from
taxation. By July 1907 the firm owned 600,000 acres and had
secured subsoil leases over 1 million acres of land.

Pearson made arrangements to market the large supplies of oil
he expected soon to possess. In 1905 plans were laid for a refinery
at Minatitlán, twenty miles from Puerto Mexico, the terminal
point of the Tehuantepec Railway on the Atlantic. After the vast
new concessions had been secured in 1906, Pearson ordered the
doubling of the original planned capacity of the refinery and it
eventually began operations early in 1908. A fleet of three small
tankers of sufficiently shallow draught to navigate the
Coatzacoulcos River was ordered. In 1907 the first 3000 ton
capacity tanker was ready for service. Pearson opened an oil
retailing department in London, and in 1907 a contract was
signed with the oldest firm of petroleum importers and distributors in the United Kingdom, C. T. Bowring and Company.[55]
August 1908 saw the first shipment to Britain of refined oil
produced at the Minatitlán refinery.

The one major obstacle to success was the lack of oil to sell
through this expanding distribution network. 'There is only left',
Pearson wrote to his wife in March 1909, 'the oil.'[56] The
production of the San Cristobal field was small and a ring of new
wells drilled around the original well were dry. In 1908 the San
Cristobal field was given just two years life.[57] Pearson was forced
to purchase crude from other producers to meet his supply
contracts. In late 1907 he made a contract with another English
company operating in Mexico, owned by Percy Furber. Pearson
agreed to buy a minimum of 2000 barrels of crude oil a day and a
maximum of 6000 for the next twelve years. The Furbero oilfield,
however, was also unproductive, and Pearson had to purchase oil
in the open market in Texas to maintain his supplies to Bowring.
The process of buying crude oil in Texas, refining it at Minatitlán

and re-exporting the refined products to Europe was financially disastrous. Overall, the first six years of the enterprise had proved extremely capital-intensive, and there had been no returns on the investment. In 1902 Pearson had resolved to put £1½ million into the oil venture. By 1908 he had spent £5 million, and his personal fortune was wholly pledged.

In 1908 the enterprise was hit by two major disasters, and it seemed that 'Pearson luck' had finally evaporated. Pearson drillers had switched their attention from the oilfields around San Cristobal to the new concession areas secured by the company in the north. In August 1908 they brought in a huge well at Dos Bocas in northern Veracruz. Unfortunately the well caught fire and burned for the next eight weeks, during which a million tons of oil were destroyed. Pearson was forced to pay heavy compensation to local landowners. A further disaster occurred within a few months when a serious fire destroyed the greater part of the Minatitlán refinery and immobilized it for months.

The same year saw the outbreak of a vicious trade war between Pearson and his major competitor in Mexico, the Walters, Pierce Oil Company. Two-thirds of the capital of Walters, Pierce was owned by Standard Oil, and the remainder by an American oilman, Henry Clay Pierce. The firm imported oil from the United States, and refined it at two refineries at Tampico at Vera Cruz. Walters, Pierce had held a monopoly over kerosene and lubricating oil sales in Mexico for over a decade before the arrival of Pearson. In 1903 Pearson met Pierce in New York, and expressed the hope that the two companies could work in harmony.[58] Clay Pierce was prepared to accept this proposal, provided that Pearson did not intend to enter the distribution trade within Mexico. Pearson, however, was not a man to suffer this kind of restriction for long, and relations with Clay Pierce steadily deteriorated. In June 1908 negotiations broke down between the two sides, and Pearson launched his company into the retail oil trade in Mexico. A bitter price war followed. Clay Pierce used every possible means to destroy his rival. Inspired press attacks on Pearson appeared in Mexican, American and European newspapers, charging him with having corrupted the Mexican government.[59] Detectives were employed to shadow Pearson and his associates, and attempts made to lure away Pearson employees. 'American methods', Pearson observed to his wife, 'are peculiar.'[60] They were not, however, very successful. Pearson, by

68   THE EMERGENCE OF THE BRITISH OIL INDUSTRY

virtue of a superior selling organisation, had secured 40 per cent
of the internal oil trade of Mexico within fifteen months of the
outbreak of the trade war.

The success against Clay Pierce, however, was only a partial
compensation for the continuing failure to locate a large supply of
crude oil. At times Pearson became deeply pessimistic. 'Until our
oil venture is a proved success', he wrote to his wife in February
1909, 'I continue nervous and sometimes despondent.'[61] In that
year Pearson decided to reorganise his geological service. During
the first years of the Mexican enterprise, he had made use of the
English petroleum consulting firm run by Boverton Redwood,
whose activities will be examined in greater detail in subsequent
chapters. W. H. Dalton, one of Redwood's senior geologists,
made a reconnaissance survey for Pearson in 1901, and it was his
findings that led to the commencement of the San Cristobal
drilling programme in 1902. A number of other geologists from
this firm were employed by Pearson, but without conspicuous
success. In April 1909 the Chief Geologist of the United States
Geological Survey, C. W. Hayes, visited the Pearson oil concessions, and expressed optimism about their prospects.[62]
Pearson persuaded Hayes to work for him on a part-time basis,
and to recruit some North American geological staff. The
contract with Redwood's firm was ended, and the British
geologists were replaced by promising young men from the
United States Geological Survey. In 1911 Hayes resigned from
public service, and went to Mexico as general manager in charge
of exploration and production of the Pearson enterprises.

In 1910 Pearson's persistence, and his new geologists, finally
brought success. In January 1910 a small well was struck at
Potrero de Llano. In the following month came the far larger
Potrero No. 1 well, which guaranteed Pearson a supply of crude
oil. In December the biggest gusher ever struck in Mexico was hit
at Potrero No. 4. The well, the largest in the world at that time,
ran wild for three months, flowing at a rate of 100,000 barrels (3.5
million imperial gallons) per day. Pearson was in Mexico City at
the time of the strike, and he left immediately for the field, where
he remained until the well had been successfully capped. The well
ceased to flow in December 1918, having given over 100 million
barrels of crude oil.[63] Other discoveries followed. By 1914
Mexico had emerged as the third largest oil producing country in
the world, with an annual production of 4 million metric tons.

Pearson controlled about 60 per cent of this output. 'Pearson luck' had been vindicated, and the success of the venture secured.

Pearson, who had been raised to the peerage as Baron Cowdray of Midhurst in July 1910, now saw his investment in downstream capacity pay handsome dividends, as his integrated oil business rapidly emerged as a major force in the world oil industry. A major reorganisation of the Pearson oil interests was undertaken. As early as 1908 Pearson had planned to establish a Mexican company to take over the production of oil in the country, partly because a 'Mexican company would be assured of Government support much more than a foreign company'.[64] On 31 August 1908 the Compañía Mexicana de Petróleo El Aguila—Mexican Eagle—was formed. In March 1909 Mexican Eagle acquired from S. Pearson and Son all the latter's oil interests except for the refinery and the tankers and in the following year the company made its first public issue of shares. The board included several prominent Mexicans, including Diaz's son, but Cowdray retained a majority holding.

The tanker side of the business was rapidly developed. Pearson's gamble of building tankers before he had oil meant that a tanker fleet was already available when large supplies of oil were located. Cowdray soon ordered a great expansion of his fleet. The Eagle Oil Transport Company was formed in February 1912, with the whole of the share capital taken up by Mexican Eagle except for some £500,000 ordinary shares owned by S. Pearson and Son. Eagle Oil immediately ordered twenty tankers. The fleet included ten 15,000 ton ships, which cost about £160,000 each and were the largest oil tankers in the world at that time.[65]

In 1912 a new distribution company was also founded. In January 1912 the Anglo-Mexican Petroleum Products Co. Ltd was formed to sell Mexican Eagle's oil outside Mexico and Central America. Cowdray's son, Clive Pearson, was made chairman of the company at the age of 25. It began trading in the United Kingdom in 1912, and within two years had absorbed the distribution facilities of Bowrings. The company won a major Admiralty contract in July 1913, when it arranged to supply the Royal Navy with 200,000 tons of fuel oil. Further branches were opened in Argentina, Brazil, Chile, Uruguay, Paraguay and Cuba, and an extensive trade established in fuel oil for ships' bunkers and bitumen for road-making. By 1913 Cowdray was even selling Mexican fuel oil to Russian railways.[66]

70   THE EMERGENCE OF THE BRITISH OIL INDUSTRY

The organisation of Anglo-Mexican was a model of a well-run oil company, and was markedly different in this respect from many of its British contemporaries. Its fine headquarters building at Finsbury Circus House, London, contained a staff of eight hundred. This staff was divided into five departments. The European Sales Department handled trade in Britain and Europe, through Bowrings in the case of kerosene, petrol and lubricating oils, and directly for crude and fuel oil, asphalt, road oils and paraffin wax. The Foreign Sales Department controlled sales to Central and South America, Canada, Australia, Asia and Africa. The Bunkering Department was concerned with the establishment of bunkering stations between New York and Buenos Aires and sales of bunker fuel. The two remaining sections were the Transportation Department and the Buying Department, which acted as a centralised purchasing agency for all the petroleum companies of the Pearson Group. The activities of the different departments were co-ordinated through daily conferences of directors and weekly board meetings.[67]

The distribution of Pearson products in Mexico and Central America was undertaken by Mexican Eagle. As the production of crude oil rose, this company expanded its refining capacity. During 1912 a site was secured on the Panuco River for a refinery at Tampico, the old refinery at Minatitlán being both geographically inconvenient for the new fields and equipped to refine only the lighter crudes found in the south. The profitability of the Mexican trade was seriously reduced while the war with Clay Pierce continued. Pierce persisted in his attacks on Cowdray, trying in 1911 to use his influence in Washington to block Mexican Eagle's employment of C. W. Hayes. This position, however, became steadily more untenable as Standard Oil began to withdraw their support from their erstwhile subsidiary. Standard Oil, in the middle of a trade war with the Shell Group, was eager to secure at least some of Cowdray's crude oil. In 1911 the President of Standard Oil formally apologised to Cowdray for the methods Pierce had used during his campaign, and in March 1912 Cowdray signed a contract with Standard Oil under which he agreed to supply the American company with ten million barrels of crude oil over the next seven years. In the following month the directors of Standard Oil gave Cowdray a fine dinner in New York to celebrate their new relationship. This reconciliation left Pierce in an exposed position. Following the dissolution of the Standard Oil trust, Pierce purchased their interest in his company. In 1912 the Mexican managements of the two companies agreed on a basis of co-operation for the sale of certain products, but Pierce again broke faith. 'No one whom I have ever met who has done business with Clay Pierce', Cowdray reflected in August 1912, 'will either believe his word or rely upon his bond.'[68] Continued pressure from Mexican Eagle, however, eventually forced him to come to terms. In 1913 Cowdray, with some magnanimity, agreed to give Clay Pierce a fifty-fifty share in the Mexican trade.

It was Cowdray's misfortune that his great achievements in the Mexican oil industry were almost immediately threatened by political upheaval. Cowdray's great ally, President Diaz, was eighty when Potrero No. 4 was struck. As his grip slackened revolts broke out in several parts of the country. In May 1911 Diaz fled from Mexico City to Vera Cruz, where he spent four days with J. B. Body before taking ship for Europe and exile. The new President was the mild-mannered and philosophic Francisco Madero. Cowdray met Madero in Mexico City shortly afterwards, and the validity of Mexican Eagle's oil leases was recognised by the new government.[69] Madero, however, was dependent for his success on wild guerrilla leaders such as Emiliano Zapata and Pancho Villa, and his term of office was marked by constant disturbances. In February 1913 Madero was overthrown, by a half-Indian General, Victoriano Huerta, and subsequently murdered. Chaos spread in Mexico as Villa and Zapata revolted against the new regime. After 1911 the northern part of Mexican Eagle's territory, from Tuxpan to Tampico, was repeatedly fought over or raided by insurgents.

Cowdray's difficulties were increased by the policy of the United States. Cowdray had been under personal attack in the United States for many years. Clay Pierce had spread rumours of his corruption of the Mexican government. It was a newspaper owned by Pierce which first coined the phrase 'Cowdray has taken more out of Mexico than any man since Cortez'.[70] The main problems came, however, with the advent of the new Democratic Administration of Woodrow Wilson in February 1913. Wilson hated Huerta, whom he regarded as the murderer of the 'democrat' Madero. The President was determined to bring American democracy to Latin America, and to end the series of violent revolutions which brought dictators such as Huerta to

72   THE EMERGENCE OF THE BRITISH OIL INDUSTRY

power. The crusade against Huerta soon developed into a crusade against Cowdray. When the British Government extended diplomatic recognition to the hated Huerta, Wilson became convinced that Cowdray was the main inspirer of this policy. The American Ambassador in London, W. H. Page, reported home that Cowdray was moving the Foreign Office in Huerta's favour.[71] Anglo-American tension was further increased in July 1913 when Sir Lionel Carden, a British diplomat notorious for his anti-Americanism, was appointed British Ambassador to Mexico. Cowdray was once more blamed for his appointment. The United States Administration had soon deluded itself that there was a massive conspiracy between the British Government and Cowdray to thwart the interests of the United States in Mexico and defy the Monroe Doctrine. The fuel oil contract which Anglo-Mexican signed with the British Admiralty in July 1913 provided the Americans with an obvious motive for the British Government's susceptibility to Lord Cowdray's wishes.[72]

The policy of the United States at this time differed greatly from that of the post-1918 world in that it was not strictly nationalistic. The attempt was made to exclude European capital from Mexico not only because it was European but because it was capital.[73] Wilson had fought the Presidential election as the champion of small business against the trusts and Wall Street. Standard Oil was hated as much as Cowdray by the Administration, and Cowdray's good relations with that company only further increased their hostility towards him.

The attitude of the United States government to Cowdray soon began to have effects beyond Mexico. In 1912 Cowdray had recruited the former Liberal Chief Whip, Lord Murray of Elibank, to work for S. Pearson and Son. Cowdray had been the Liberal Member of Parliament for Colchester between 1895 and 1910, and he was consequently well-connected in Liberal political circles. Murray's speciality was backroom political negotiations, and it was with this skill in mind that he was despatched to South America in January 1913 to negotiate at the highest level for oil contracts. It was unfortunate that just as Murray reached his destination his name was linked with the Marconi scandal then raging in Britain. This only provided further evidence to the Americans of the corrupt nature of the Pearson oil enterprises, and American diplomatic pressure was used to thwart Murray's attempts to secure oil concessions in Costa Rica, Ecuador and

Columbia. The bill granting Pearson a concession in Columbia had been given its first reading by the country's Congress when the United States forced its cancellation in July 1913.[74]

The American government's onslaught against Cowdray transformed a business venture into a matter of international politics. There was a similar tendency in several parts of the world at this time for oil to become a matter of inter-governmental tension and rivalry. This development provided the third area of interaction between British oil companies and the British Government, for the companies sought not only naval fuel oil contracts and State finance, but the protection of diplomatic support.

The relations between oil companies and their home governments in foreign countries have always been one of the more controversial aspects of the petroleum industry. The alleged collusion between oil companies and their home governments in the cause of exploiting the natural resources of less developed countries is a familiar theme. The whole subject is plagued by tantalising, but unanswered and perhaps unanswerable questions. Have Western governments regularly used oil companies to further their politico-economic aims? Or have those governments been used to benefit the shareholders of the oil companies? Or has there been, and perhaps still is, a conspiracy between companies and governments to exploit third parties? 'It was never clear', Anthony Sampson concluded from his study of the relations between the 'seven sisters' and their respective governments, 'who was using whom.'[75]

There were several requests from oil companies for British diplomatic assistance before the First World War. Perhaps the most direct, and characteristically untactful, request came from Marcus Samuel who, in his evidence before the Royal Commission on Fuel and Engines in November 1912, offered the Admiralty a fuel oil contract in return for, in the words of the horrified Director of Naval Contracts, 'on unconditional terms, Foreign Office and diplomatic support for [Shell] oil interests in various parts of the world'.[76] Usually, however, requests for diplomatic support were rather more specific. Shell Transport in 1907, for instance, requested the assistance of the Foreign Office in removing what were regarded as obnoxious regulations over the kerosene trade made by the Chinese authorities.[77] British diplomatic assistance was even valued by oil companies in Russia. During the revolutionary disturbances of 1904–6 several pleas for

74   THE EMERGENCE OF THE BRITISH OIL INDUSTRY

diplomatic assistance were made by British oil companies. In 1911 Waley Cohen argued that the Shell Group should operate in Russia through a British-registered company, since they 'should then enjoy the support of British diplomacy in Russia'.[78]

Diplomatic support became essential in several countries where there was Great Power rivalry. The German government, for example, gave extensive support to the Deutsche Bank in Turkey, and British oil companies of necessity needed the support of their government. In such a situation even Henri Deterding, the strongest of theoretical opponents of State intervention in the petroleum industry, recognised the commercial disadvantages of *not* having diplomatic support. Government might be rather unreliable 'old aunts', who best served everyone's interests by staying aloof from the petroleum industry, but their wrecking potential was high and could not be ignored.[79]

By 1913 Cowdray was at least in as much need of diplomatic support as any British oil interests in the Middle East. He was not to receive it. The Wilson Administration's view that the British government was the puppet of Lord Cowdray was pure fantasy. Cowdray was the most honest and incorruptible of all the British oilmen of this period. Moreover, Sir Edward Grey, the Foreign Secretary, though not in sympathy with Wilson's moral crusade against Huerta, had no intention of engaging in a major diplomatic dispute with the United States over Mexican oil. The Foreign Office placed wider considerations of Anglo–American relations above any disagreement over oil. The Foreign Office was particularly concerned to secure the repeal of the Panama Canal Act of 1912, which had exempted American shipping from Canal dues, and it would take no strong diplomatic action against the United States until Congress had repealed this legislation. In the autumn of 1913 Grey, concerned about the damage caused to Anglo–American relations by Mexican oil, sent Sir William Tyrrell, a career diplomat, to the American President to explain British policy. Tyrrell told Wilson that Britain would not recognise any special privileges granted by Huerta to Cowdray. The breach with the Americans was healed, at the price of ordering the British Ambassador in Mexico not to interfere with United States policy even in defence of British oil interests.[80] 'I find there is a complete understanding between the British and United States Governments', Cowdray wrote to J. B. Body. 'This of course, means that the British Government recognises that the United States is free to act as it is doing.'[81]

Eventually Cowdray was given the minimum of British diplomatic protection. After November 1913 Mexican Eagle's property was under constant attack by rival armies. In December the refinery at Tampico was taken by rebels, and then recaptured by Huerta's troops. Early in the New Year the United States Congress repealed the Panama Canal Toll Act, and this freed the Foreign Office to take a stronger line in defence of British property. Cowdray persuaded Lord Morley, the Lord President of the Council, to see the Prime Minister on his behalf, and plead for greater protection for his company in Mexico. As a result the British Ambassador in Washington was instructed to see the American President. At their meeting on 8 April, the Ambassador went beyond his strict instructions and made very strong representations to Wilson about the subject. On the following day, after a mistaken arrest by federal police of a party of American sailors, the U.S. Consul in Tampico was told to warn Government officials and rebels alike to respect the oilfields. The oilfields were effectively placed under joint Anglo–American protection.[82]

The uncertainty which faced Mexican Eagle after 1910 prompted Cowdray to give serious consideration to selling his interest in Mexican oil, or at least diversifying away from total dependence on it. In 1911 he was approached by two American companies, the Texas and Gulf Refining companies, about a possible amalgamation with Mexican Eagle, but the negotiations fell through owing to problems created by the anti-trust laws of Texas. In March 1913 a Standard Oil (New Jersey) director, A. C. Bedford, called upon Cowdray in London and discussed with him the purchase of Mexican Eagle. In September the President of that company, Archibold, wrote to Cowdray to say that he hoped soon to start negotiations about purchase. In the following October, however, Standard decided for both political and legal reasons, not to pursue the matter.[83] Another suitor had appeared a year earlier. In 1912 a M. Benard, a partner in a leading Paris firm of stockbrokers, saw Cowdray and suggested a working arrangement between the Royal Dutch and Mexican Eagle. Royal Dutch proposed a holding company for the two enterprises, but Cowdray insisted on a cash sale and the

76   THE EMERGENCE OF THE BRITISH OIL INDUSTRY

discussions ceased. Calouste Gulbenkian initiated further talks between Cowdray and the Shell Group in February and March 1913, but nothing came of them.[84]

In December 1913 Cowdray extended his policy of attempting to involve others in his company by offering to make a major supply contract with the Royal Navy, provided that the British Government invested £5 million in Mexican Eagle. A day or so after the meeting with Lloyd George, the Chancellor, during which this offer was made, Cowdray addressed a letter to the Government offering to 'specifically dedicate . . . the Mexican Eagle Oil Company to the primary purpose of supplying the Admiralty with fuel oil . . . . If it were desired that the control of the Company should remain in British hands for say seven years, this can be arranged. But it would mean that we have to look to the Government for financial assistance instead of selling the Company's securities to the public.'[85] Cowdray's motive was obvious. Nothing would have safeguarded Mexican Eagle's properties so well as to have the British Government committed as a majority shareholder. Cowdray's proposals, however, found little support within the Government. The Admiralty was close to reaching an agreement with the Anglo-Persian Oil Company, while the Foreign Office was not willing to support a measure which could only be interpreted by the Wilson Administration as an explicit attack on the Monroe Doctrine.

Meanwhile Cowdray, ever anxious for a new adventure, had begun to search for oil concessions elsewhere in the world. In September 1912 a separate department of S. Pearson and Son under Lord Murray was established for this purpose, and after Latin America had been blocked by the Americans, Murray began to seek concessions in Europe, Asia and Africa.

In 1912, as a result of a preliminary geological investigation, a controlling interest was secured in the Oran Oil Company Ltd, which held a concession in Algeria. In the same year S. Pearson and Son took an interest in a syndicate which had filed a number of claims for prospecting for oil in Morocco. In 1913 a geologist was sent out to China, but he discovered he had been pre-empted by Standard Oil. In March 1914 two Pearson geologists went to Hungary, and in the following June Lord Murray visited Vienna in order to negotiate a concession with the Austrian government. In May 1914 Pearson geologists were sent to Tunis, and in July to a region in the south west of France where the firm had been offered a concession. In the spring of 1914 Pearson came to an agreement with Vickers to explore for oil on the island of Sakhalin, and an expedition was despatched in the winter of 1914.[86] In January 1914 negotiations were also started aimed at securing an oil concession in the Indian Empire. S. Pearson and Son offered to join the Government of India in a partnership for the exploration and development of the oil resources of Baluchistan.[87]

IV THE GROWTH OF THE SHELL GROUP 1907–14

Apart from the extraordinary entry of Weetman Pearson into oil, the outstanding development in the British oil industry in the immediate prewar period was the growth of the Shell Group. The total assets of the two holding companies, Royal Dutch and Shell Transport and Trading, grew by over two and a half times between 1907 and 1914. By the outbreak of war Shell Transport's issued capital of over £6 million placed it amongst the largest British enterprises in terms of market valuation. After 1910 the Shell Group began to absorb a series of smaller oil companies, both British and foreign. In 1911 the Group's only remaining competitor in the Dutch East Indies, the Dordtsche Petroleum Industrie, was absorbed, and the Red Sea Oilfields in Egypt taken into Shell's orbit. In 1912 Deterding decided to invade Standard Oil's homeland, and the Group organised the Roxana Petroleum Company to operate in the Mid-Continent region of the United States. California Oilfields was added to Shell's American interests in 1913, and by 1915 the Group had a production of 5.7 million barrels of crude in the United States.[88] In 1913 Shell purchased controlling interests in the Carribbean Petroleum Company and the Colon Development Company of Venezuela, and thereby acquired a very substantial stake in the infant Venezuelan industry.[89]

The Shell Group's major growth area, as seen earlier in this chapter, was Russia. Shell not only became a large producer itself, but inherited the Rothschild policy of co-operation with the Nobels and the other large oil groups. The Russian General Oil Corporation ('Oil'), after its formation in 1912, briefly offered strong competition to Shell and the Nobels. The company, however, was over-ambitious, and in 1914 its independence was considerably reduced when it failed in a bid to purchase a large

78   THE EMERGENCE OF THE BRITISH OIL INDUSTRY

block of Nobel shares, and instead Nobels secured a large holding in 'Oil'. The two groups were from then on fairly closely allied. A. E. Putilov, the Chairman of 'Oil', joined the board of Nobels, while Emanuel Nobel joined the board of one of 'Oil's' subsidiaries.[90] The only change in this situation prior to the Revolution came early in 1917, when Neft', one of the member companies of 'Oil', left the group and emerged as the centre of a new oil alliance centred on French capital. Ambitious plans were being made for the growth of Neft' when the February Revolution broke out.

The cartelisation of the Russian oil industry had its equivalent in the petroleum markets of western Europe. The Shell Group was allied in various markets with the European Petroleum Union, representing the Deutsche Bank, the Nobels and the Rothschilds, and after 1906 many Standard Oil affiliates also concluded local marketing agreements with their European competitors. It was paradoxical that the trend in the United States was in the other direction, with the emergence of new companies and producing areas resulting in a growth of competition in the industry. By 1911 Standard Oil's competitors supplied 70 per cent of the nation's fuel oil and 45 per cent of its lubricants.[91] In 1911 the great Trust itself was broken up by the Supreme Court.

The process of concentration in the European petroleum industry provided the small British oil companies with a useful bargaining counter in their attempts to extract special favours from the British Government. The Royal Navy's dependence on foreign oil, and the consequent desirability of supporting British oil enterprise, was frequently referred to by companies seeking State assistance in the form of diplomatic support, finance or naval fuel oil contracts. Companies buttressed their cases by claiming that if special assistance was not forthcoming they would be absorbed by their carnivorous 'monopolistic' and foreign rivals. The small companies naturally made the most of the alleged dangers posed to consumers and the Government by Standard Oil and the Shell Group. This was a significant contribution to the growth of a hostile attitude towards these companies in government circles. This was far from being an exclusively British phenonomen. In Russia the Nobels and other companies made repeated pleas for assistance from the Tsarist government because of the alleged prosecution of Russian oil exporters by agressive foreign trusts.[92] Indeed, the large oil companies themselves were not averse to blackening each other's reputations. Deterding described Standard Oil to the German Government in 1910 as a company which worked 'more on the lines of a Secret Society than a bona fide Public Company'.[93] In more senses than one, the oil companies have only themselves to blame for the fact that their industry was, and still is, regarded as having one of the more 'unacceptable' faces of capitalism.

*   *   *   *   *

The two decades before the First World War had seen the appearance of British entrepreneurs in many of the oilfields of the world. Over £18 million of British capital had been invested in Russia, though with indifferent results. Certain individuals and companies made significant contributions to the Russian oil industry, but the British companies tended to suffer by inadequate management. They were badly weakened by the strikes and revolutionary disturbances in Russia in the early 1900s, and the unsuccessful outcome of the 'Maikop boom' further diminished their reputations. The whole investment was to be lost when the Bolsheviks seized power in October 1917. There were, however, success stories to be found in other parts of the world. Weetman Pearson pioneered the Mexican oil industry. Although Pearson's initial ignorance of the oil industry caused difficulties in the early days of the venture, Pearson's entrepreneurial skill, organisational ability and luck eventually led to brilliant success. The decade before 1914 also witnessed the dramatic growth of the Anglo-Dutch Shell Group into a fully-integrated international oil company.

The British Government was a peripheral element in this story. Yet certain oil companies had attempted to involve the State in one way or another. A number of small, risky, companies had tried to get finance from the Government, especially in the immediate prewar period when the collapse of the 'Maikop boom' made it difficult for such firms to attract public funding. Oil companies in certain areas of the world, such as Mexico, had also looked to the British Government for diplomatic support to protect their interests.

The State was attractive to oil companies in the early twentieth century as a market for fuel oil, a source of finance and a provider of diplomatic support against foreign governments. As a result,

80   THE EMERGENCE OF THE BRITISH OIL INDUSTRY

certain companies were interested in establishing close links with it. These companies, in order to strengthen their cases for State assistance, emphasised the dangers posed to Britain and the Royal Navy by the domination of the world petroleum industry by foreign 'trusts'. These requests for a 'special relationship', however, found little response within British governments until the eve of the First World War.

Notes

1. George Paish, 'Great Britain's Capital Investment in Industrial Colonial and Foreign Countries', *Journal of the Royal Statistical Society*, LXXIV (1911); Sir George Paish, 'The Export of Capital and the Cost of Living', *Transactions of the Manchester Statistical Society* (1913–14). H. Feis, *Europe: The World's Banker 1870–1914* (Yale, 1930) p. 27 gives a figure of £40.6 million for British overseas investment in the prewar oil industry. W. R. Skinner, *The Oil and Petroleum Manual* (London, 1912). For an overall assessment of British foreign investment within this period, see W. P. Kennedy, 'Foreign Investment, Trade and Growth in the United Kingdom, 1870–1913', *Explorations in Economic History*, II, 4 (1974).

2. Statistics for Scottish shale oil production are given in B. Redwood, *A Treatise on Petroleum*, vol. III, (London, 1922), p. 1127. There is an account of the early growth of the Scottish shale oil industry by J. Butt, 'Technical Change and the Growth of the British Shale Oil Industry 1680–1870', *Econ. Hist. Rev.*, 2nd series, XVII (1964–5).

3. *Petroleum Review* (1 January 1910).

4. See M. Pearton, *Oil and the Romanian State* (Oxford, 1971) *passim*.

5. P. V. Ol', *Inostrannye Kapitaly v Rossii* (Moscow, 1922) p. 43. Ol's data is still the main source for estimates of foreign corporate investment in Russia before 1917. A number of criticisms have been levelled at Ol's statistics, however, and it is now generally accepted that his figures may overestimate British and French investment, though there is evidence that he underestimates German investment in Russia.

6. For an account of the Nobel oil enterprises in Russia, see Robert W. Tolf, *The Russian Rockefellers: The Saga of the Nobel Family and the Russian Oil Industry* (Stanford, 1976). For the early years of the Rothschild's investment in Russian oil, see B. Gille, 'Capitaux Français et Pétroles Russes 1884–94', *Histoire des Enterprises*, 12 (1963). There is also useful data in R. Girault, *Emprunts Russes et Investissements Français en Russie 1887–1914* (Paris, 1973). For a Soviet view, see A. Fursenko, 'Parizhskie Rotshildy i Russkaia Neft', *Voprosy Istorii* 8 (1962) and ch. 4 of his book *Neftianye tresty i mirovaia politika* (Moscow/Leningrad, 1965).

7. The most recent statistics for Russian oil production are in W. J. Kelly and T. Kano, 'Crude Oil Production in the Russian Empire: 1818–1919', 6, 2, *Journal of European Economic History* (1977).

8. The best accounts of the oil marketing battles in the late nineteenth century are on the American side, e.g. R. W. and M. E. Hidy, *Pioneering in Big Business* (New York, 1955).

THE BRITISH IN FOREIGN OILFIELDS 81

9. P. V. Volobuev, 'Iz istorii monopolizatsii neftianoi promyshlennosti dore-voluzionnoi Rossii', *Istoricheskie Zapiski* (1955) 82–3.
10. A. Fursenko, *Voprosy Istorii*, 8 (1962), 42. For the growing co-operation between the Rothschilds and the Nobels, see R. W. Tolf, op. cit., *passim*.
11. For Nobel's contacts with Standard Oil, see R. W. Tolf, op. cit. The early Rothschild negotiations with Standard Oil are surveyed in B. Gille, op. cit. There is a copy of the March 1895 agreement in *Monopolisticheskii Kapital v neftianoi promyshlennosti Rossii 1883–1914* (Moscow, 1961) pp. 169–171.
12. See, for example, Charles Marvin, *Baku: the Petrolia of Europe* (London, 1884), and *The Region of the Eternal Fire* (London, 1884).
13. A. Beeby Thompson, *Oil Pioneer* (London, 1961) p. 70.
14. Information about Suart's activities is scattered in a wide range of sources. Among the most informative are: R. W. Tolf, op. cit.; A. Beeby Thompson, op. cit.; R. Henriques, *Marcus Samuel* (London, 1960). Soviet sources are also useful, especially about Suart's involvement in the later 1890s with the Eastern Oil Association. See A. Fursenko, *Neftianye tresty*, op. cit., *passim*.
15. B. U. Akhundov, *Monopolisticheskii Kapital v dorevoluzionnoi Bakinskoi neftianoi promyschlennosti* (Moscow, 1959) p. 45. The exchange rate has been taken as £1 = 9.45 rubles.
16. P. V. Volobuev, op. cit., 81.
17. A. Fursenko, *Neftiannye tresty*, op. cit., p. 134.
18. A. Beeby Thompson, *The Oilfields of Russia*, 2nd ed. (London, 1908) p. 131.
19. A. Fursenko, op. cit., pp. 110–11.
20. Letter from Mr G. P. Kamenskii, Agent of Ministry of Finance in London, to Mr V. E. Kovalevskii, Director of the Department of Trade and Manufacture, 28 January 1898, *Monopolisticheskii Kapital* (Moscow, 1961) pp. 214–16.
21. Ibid., pp. 224–5.
22. A. Beeby Thompson, *Oil Pioneer* (London, 1961) p. 295.
23. J. P. Mckay, 'Foreign Enterprise in Russian and Soviet Industry: A Long-Term Perspective', *Business History Review*, 48 (1974) 348.
24. A. Beeby Thompson, *The Oilfields of Russia* (London, 1904) pp. 33–6.
25. Ibid., p. 7. A. Beeby Thompson, *Oil Pioneer* (London, 1961) p. 55.
26. Secretary of Russian Petroleum and Liquid Fuel Company to J. B. Aug. Kessler, 31 January 1898, SHELL.
27. Ibid. Telegram from St Petersburg, 13 July 1898. The correspondence between Count Witte and the company on this matter has been published in M. Y. Gefter, A. M. Solov'ëva and L. E. Shepelev, 'O proniknovenii ang-liiskogo kapitala v neftianuiu promyshlennost' Rossii (1898–1902),' *Istoricheskii Arkhiv*, 6 (1960), pp. 82–6.
28. Ibid. Report by Mr Schumacher, 19/31 March 1898.
29. *Petroleum World* (Aug. 1911) 390.
30. Mr Schumacher to London, 16/26 January 1899, SHELL.
31. An account of these racial and labour disputes is given in R. W. Tolf, op. cit., esp. pp. 157–62. There is a contemporary version in J. D. Henry, *Baku: An Eventual History* (London, 1905) Part 2.
32. A. Beeby Thompson, *The Oilfields of Russia* (London, 1904) p. 38.
33. *Petroleum Review* (9 September 1905).
34. Ibid. (9 December 1905).

82   THE EMERGENCE OF THE BRITISH OIL INDUSTRY

35. Ibid. (3 July 1909).
36. Ibid. (26 February 1910).
37. *Economist* (26 February 1910).
38. P. V. Ol', op. cit., pp. 51–2.
39. Evidence of A. W. Eastlake to Fisher Commission, First Report, ADM 116 1208, p. 148.
40. *Petroleum Review* (21 October 1911).
41. W. Calder, 'The Maikop Oilfield, South Russia', *Transactions of the Institute of Mining Engineers*, XlVIII (1915) Part 2.
42. A. Beeby Thompson, *Oil Pioneer* (London, 1961) p. 306.
43. P. V. Ol', op. cit., pp. 47–54. Crude oil production in 1914 at Grozny was 98 million poods; Emba 16 million poods; Maikop 3 million poods; and Cheleken 17 million poods. Ol' gives total Russian oil production in 1914 as 540 million poods. There is room for discussion about the validity of Ol's definition of British owned or 'influenced' companies, but his general view of a very strong British role in the new oil regions of Russia seems to be correct.
44. P. V. Volobuev, op. cit., p. 95. There is a very useful analysis of the Rothschilds' decision to sell their oil properties in Russia to the Shell Group by V. I. Bovykin, 'Rossiiskaia Neft' i Rotshil'dy', *Voprosy Istorii*, 4, (1978). Bovykin has made full use of the archives of the French Rothschilds, which were recently deposited in the National Archives, Paris.
45. P. V. Ol', op. cit., pp. 44–6.
46. A. Beeby Thompson, *The Oilfields of Russia* (London, 1904). A. Fursenko, *Neftianye tresty*, op. cit., p. 134.
47. P. V. Ol', op. cit., p. 43. For some reservations about Ol's statistics, which have been used as the main source for quantitative statements about oil investment in Russia, see M. Falkus, 'Aspects of Foreign Investment in Tsarist Russia', *Journal of European Economic History*, 8, 1 (1979) 30–5.
48. *Economist* (26 February 1910).
49. *Petroleum World* (April, 1913). Nevertheless Paish (1913–14), op. cit., estimated that £5.7 million was subscribed to oil enterprises in 1913. This is compared with £6.4 million in 1912, £3.8 million in 1911, and £10.5 million in 1910.
50. For the first application of the Nigerian Bitumen Corporation, see *Petroleum World* (January, 1908), 12. For the 1912 applications of Nigerian Bitumen, the Cairo Syndicate and Newfoundland Oil, see the evidence given by the representatives of these companies to the Royal Commission on Fuel and Engines, ADM 116/1208 and 1209. For the West Indian Petroleum Company, Mexican Eagle and Anglo-Persian, see below.
51. K. Beaton, *Enterprise in Oil: A History of Shell in the United States* (New York, 1957) pp. 72–75.
52. W. D. Pearson to J. B. Body, 19 April 1901; 'How we went into Oil', by J. B. Body, 21 November 1928; S. Pearson and Son Archives, Box C43, File LCO 23/3. D. Young, *Member for Mexico* (London, 1966) pp. 119–22.
53. K. Middlemas, *The Master Builders* (London, 1963) p. 215.
54. J. B. Body to Weetman Pearson, 4 November 1905, Pearson Papers Box A4, File: Personal Correspondence, Cowdray–Body 1900–11.
55. D. Keir, *The Bowring Story* (London, 1962) pp. 230–1.

THE BRITISH IN FOREIGN OILFIELDS 83

56. Weetman Pearson to Lady Cowdray, 13 March 1909. Pearson Papers, Box A9, File: Letters to Lady Cowdray.
57. K. Middlemas, op. cit., p. 215.
58. Historical memo, Pearson papers, Box C44, File: Relations with Henry Clay Pierce.
59. D. Young, op. cit., p. 128.
60. Weetman Pearson to Lady Cowdray, 20 April 1909, Pearson Papers, Box A9, File: Letters to Lady Cowdray.
61. Ibid., Weetman Pearson to Lady Cowdray, 24 February, 1909.
62. Ibid., Weetman Pearson to Lady Cowdray, 20 April 1909.
63. J. A. Spencer, *Weetman Pearson, First Viscount Cowdray 1856-1927* (London, 1930) pp. 159-161.
64. Weetman Pearson to Lady Cowdray, 17 February 1908, Pearson Papers, Box A9, File: Letters to Lady Cowdray.
65. Eagle Oil Transport: Finance, Pearson Papers, Box C47.
66. Anglo-Mexican to President of the Vladicaucase Railway, 10 September 1913, SHELL.
67. Anglo-Mexican Petroleum Products, 7 September 1912, Pearson Papers, Box C50.
68. Private memo for Sir Edward Holden, 13 August 1912, Pearson Papers, Box C44, File: Relations with Henry Clay Pierce.
69. P. Calvert, *The Mexican Revolution 1910-1914* (Cambridge, 1968) p. 101.
70. K. Middlemas, op. cit., p. 223.
71. Ibid., p. 224.
72. P. Calvert, op. cit., p. 173.
73. Ibid., pp. 295-6.
74. P. Calvert, 'The Murray Contract: An Episode in International Finance and Diplomacy', *Pacific Historical Review* (1966).
75. A. Sampson, *The Seven Sisters* (London, 1976) p. 323.
76. Evidence of Marcus Samuel to Fisher Commission, First Report, ADM 116 1208, p. 368.
77. Marcus Samuel to Foreign Office, 24 June 1907, F(oreign) O(ffice), P.R.O., F.O. 371 230, no. 21015/21015.
78. F. C. Gerreston, *History of the Royal Dutch*, vol. IV (Leiden, 1958) 133.
79. The phrase was used by Deterding in relation to the government of the Dutch East Indies, but it expresses well his opinion of all governments. H. Deterding to H. Colijn, 9 April 1914, SHELL.
80. K. Middlemas, op. cit., p. 226.
81. D. Young, op. cit., p. 170.
82. K. Middlemas, op. cit., p. 228.
83. J. D. Archbold to Lord Cowdray, 17 October 1913, Pearson Papers, Box C44, File: Negotiations with Standard Oil.
84. History of S. Pearson and Son, Amalgamation Negotiations, Pearson Papers, Box C43, File: LCO 23/3.
85. Ibid.
86. Whitehall Petroleum Corporation: Oil History 1927, Pearson Papers, Box C52, File: LCO 6/89.
87. S. Pearson and Son to India Office, 16 January 1914, India Office Library, L/PS/10/358, no. P4554/1913. See also Pearson Papers, Box C17.

84   THE EMERGENCE OF THE BRITISH OIL INDUSTRY

88. K. Beaton, op. cit., p. 784.
89. F. C. Gerretson, loc. sit., pp. 274–81.
90. R. W. Tolf, op. cit., p. 190. P. V. Ol', op. cit., pp. 46–7.
91. O. D. Nash, *United States Oil Policy 1890–1964* (Pittsburg, 1968) p. 8.
92. A. Fursenko, 'The Beginnings of International Competition in Oil', *Seventh International Economic History Congress*, 1978: Four 'A' Themes, p. 50.
93. H. Deterding to German Ministry of Foreign Affairs, 29 December 1910, SHELL.

[21]

By Noel H. Pugach

ASSISTANT PROFESSOR OF HISTORY
UNIVERSITY OF NEW MEXICO

Standard Oil and Petroleum Development in Early Republican China*

❡ Despite the efforts of American government officials, attempts to establish a joint Chinese-American company to develop China's petroleum potential met with failure during the initial years of the Wilson administration. Duplicity and misunderstanding on the part of Standard Oil and of the Chinese government added another chapter to the dismal history of American business in China.

In the early years of the twentieth century, Standard Oil was undoubtedly the most successful American company operating in China. For the anxious rivals of the United States, Standard Oil and the Y.M.C.A. epitomized American influence in China. Although it was less successful than its British, Dutch, and Russian competitors in acquiring crude reserves and refining facilities throughout the Far East, it managed to hold its own in petroleum sales in the China market. Unlike most American firms which relied on European commercial houses in the treaty ports, Standard Oil built up its own modern, efficient distribution complex. By dispatching its specially trained men into the heart of China and introducing an improved and cheaper kerosene lamp, Standard Oil increased its sales and enhanced its reputation. In the process, it invested more than $20,000,000 in China, formed close ties with native merchants, and became a household word to many Chinese. Meanwhile, its products, primarily kerosene, formed a large and vital part of America's annual exports to China. While the American public was touched by the romantic image of providing oil for the lamps of China, businessmen and policymakers viewed Standard Oil as an important element in capturing the China market and expanding America's economic influence in the Far East.[1]

Business History Review, Vol. XLV, No. 1 (Winter, 1971). Copyright © The President and Fellows of Harvard College.
* The author wishes to thank the Research Allocations Committee of the University of New Mexico for a travel grant which enabled him to complete the research for this paper.
[1] F. C. Gerretson, History of the Royal Dutch, 4 vols., (Leiden, 1953–1957), passim; Ralph W. and Muriel Hidy, Pioneering in Big Business, 1882–1911, (New York, 1955), 137, 528, 750 n.46; Harold Williamson et. al., The American Petroleum Industry: The Age

In February 1914, William Edward Bemis announced to the Peking press corps that Standard Oil had just managed a significant feat. The Vice President of Standard Oil Company of New York (SOCONY) [2] confirmed the recurrent rumors that his company, which had heretofore limited itself to the profitable marketing of petroleum products, had signed an agreement with the Chinese government to explore for oil in north China. Not only did Standard Oil defeat its jealous and surprised rivals by obtaining a promising concession, but it also agreed to employ a novel device — a partnership between a private foreign firm and the Chinese government.

Set against the history of repeated American failures and embarrassments in China (from the early fiasco of the American China Development Company to President Wilson's recent withdrawal of the United States from the Six Power Financial Consortium), this coup seemed to augur well for Standard Oil, American economic interests, and the position of the United States in the Far East. It also appeared that the new Chinese Republic was taking a bold step to develop its resources and modernize its economy, thereby breaking away from the legacy of isolation, suspicion of foreigners, and resistance to change. It remained to be seen if Standard Oil and the Chinese government possessed the wisdom, leadership, and flexibility to make the project succeed; if a modern profit-seeking American corporation could really cooperate with a shaky government and aid a backward non-Western nation, perhaps setting the pattern for non-exploitative foreign investment; if a weak, unstable, and bankrupt Chinese government could control internal and foreign intrigue and wisely direct a growing national consciousness toward modernization and development.

In less than two years, however, it became evident that the joint project was a failure. Standard Oil virtually abandoned the effort and American economic expansion seemed to have suffered another major defeat in the Far East. An examination of this interesting

of Energy, 1899–1959 (Evanston, Ill., 1963), 258; New York *Times*, February 14 and 15, 1914; Paul S. Reinsch, *An American Diplomat in China* (Garden City, N.Y., 1922), 62. *An American Diplomat* is the condensed version of Reinsch's memoir originally entitled, "Six Years of American Action in China," which is in the Paul S. Reinsch Papers, Wisconsin State Historical Society (Madison, Wisconsin), Box 15. The published version will be referred to except where it differs significantly from the original manuscript.

[2] As the Standard Oil Company of New York (commonly called by its trademarked nickname, SOCONY) handled all Chinese marketing prior to 1911, it merely continued its established business after the dissolution of Standard Oil.

William Edward Bemis joined Standard Oil in 1882, developed its Statistical Department and later served on its Export Trade Committee, specializing in China. He directed a part of the oil selling program begun in 1903, which brought Standard Oil into the interior of China, and claimed credit for designing the improved *mei foo* lamp. Hidy and Hidy, *Pioneering in Big Business*, 331, 495; New York *Times*, February 15, 1914.

episode in Sino-American relations underscores the problems and complexities involved in doing business in China. It also raises important questions concerning the methods of American companies and their readiness to operate abroad as well as the consequent impact on the foreign policy goals of the United States.[3]

STANDARD'S EARLY EXPERIENCES IN CHINA

Standard Oil entered the field of petroleum development in China only after careful consideration of its need for crude oil and the general situation in the Far East.[4] Before the 1880's Standard Oil enjoyed a virtual monopoly in China, as it did throughout the world, which reinforced its tendency to regard exports as a convenient and often temporary "spillway" for the excess production in the United States, its primary market. As long as this situation prevailed, the early oil trade in the Orient was loosely and primitively organized; Standard Oil was content to sell American illuminating oil on consignment to local Chinese merchants, who took the speculative risks in dealing with unreliable and irregular demand. But in the 1880's Standard Oil was challenged by Russian oil and soon afterwards by the development of oil fields and refineries in the Netherlands Indies. By 1902, Standard's sales in China declined absolutely, and a larger share of the market was seized by the Nobels, Rothschilds, Shell Transport, and the rising international organization of Royal Dutch.

Standard Oil fought fiercely to regain supremacy in its most important Far Eastern market. It employed price cutting, but since that was often self-defeating it reached temporary agreements (1905–1910) dividing Far Eastern markets with the Asiatic Petroleum Company, a Royal Dutch-Shell-Rothschild combination. In addition, Standard Oil upgraded the quality of its products, marketed cheaper brands to meet Russian competition, introduced and sometimes gave away its inexpensive *mei foo* lamps designed to burn Standard's products, and greatly expanded and improved its sales organization. Although its position improved after 1902, the

[3] Because they focus on Jersey Standard after 1911, none of the major histories of Standard Oil discuss this incident. Writing from the perspective of Royal Dutch, Gerretson mentions it briefly. See Gerretson, *History of the Royal Dutch*, IV, 119–129. Roy W. Curry, *Woodrow Wilson and Far Eastern Policy, 1913–1921* (New York, 1957) does not mention the project. Tien-yi Li, *Woodrow Wilson's China Policy, 1913–1917* (New York, 1952) makes a passing reference to the contract of February 1914.

[4] The following analysis of Standard Oil's decision to engage in petroleum development in China is based on the following sources: Gerretson, *History of the Royal Dutch*; Williamson *et. al.*, *American Petroleum Industry*, 635, 644, 647–657, 665–676; Hidy and Hidy, *Pioneering in Big Business*, 136–154, 512–521, 528, 547–553.

long range picture looked dim because Standard's rivals enjoyed lower costs of production and closer sources of crude. Periodic shortages of American oil, the Russo-Japanese Treaty of 1910 (which gave the Nobels and Royal Dutch enormous advantages in Manchuria), and the outbreak of the commercial oil war with Royal Dutch in 1910 convinced Standard Oil that it would have to establish an integrated oil industry in the Far East based on local crude, just as it had been forced to do in Austria-Hungary and Rumania in order to maintain its position in Europe. And because the British Viceroy vetoed a concession in Burma, and Netherlands Indies producers (especially Royal Dutch and the Moeara Enim Petroleum Company) refused Standard's offers to take them over or buy their properties, the American oil giant was forced to focus on China.

DIFFICULTIES OF DEVELOPMENT

Oil development in China, however, posed many problems. Petroleum deposits were known to exist in several provinces; small Chinese companies operated a few wells in Shensi and a Peking syndicate partially controlled by the influential Shansi bankers held rights to fields in Shansi. A concession in Szechuan Province had been granted to the British adventurer J. Pritchard Morgan, but was abandoned because of insufficient financing, transportation problems, and difficulties caused by the Revolution of 1911. Indeed, many parts of China remained relatively inaccessible, in spite of the substantial increase in railroad building since the Boxer Rebellion. Chinese mining and company laws had been modernized on a western pattern, but were still subject to frequent changes and now required special grants by the central government. The latter introduced political considerations and, after the Chinese Revolution of 1911, loans were expected for all favors granted by Peking. The instability and weakness of the new Chinese Republic was especially discouraging in view of the need for government collaboration and assistance in new economic ventures.

Moreover, American businessmen and concessionaires had a history of failure in China. In view of the close connection between international politics and the the granting of concessions, President Wilson's decision to withdraw from the Six Power Financial Consortium was generally regarded as a fatal blow to American enterprise in China. The situation in China, the suspension of exploration in the Morgan concession, and Standard's difficult experiences in

Austria-Hungary and Rumania constantly troubled Standard Oil officials, who nevertheless concluded that the need for Asian crude made a closer look at oil development in China worthwhile.

From the Chinese point of view, the prospect of having the American oil giant extract China's natural wealth from the interior of the nation created many difficulties and raised serious doubts. Provincially organized economic groups resented and challenged the movement begun by the Imperial government at the end of the nineteenth century to nationalize natural resources and centralize economic development, especially in rail transportation. The uprising against the Manchus in 1911 was in fact partly set off by the opposition of Szechuan investors, united in the Szechuan Railway Protection League, to the foreign financed Hukuang Railway system. This provincialism combined with the ever present anti-foreign and anti-western outlook could have created an explosive situation.

A certain xenophobia had always characterized Chinese relations with the West, but it was vastly intensified by the imposition of the unequal treaties, western administration of the customs, and the scramble for concessions and spheres of influence by the western powers after 1897. It burst forth in the Boxer Rebellion and lingered on in boycotts of foreign goods and repeated opposition to new concessions and loans, especially for railways and mineral rights, which always meant foreign profiteering, the extension of political influence, and the influx of more western personnel, experts, and advisers. The formation of the First Chinese Consortium and the completion of the Reorganization Loan not only touched off an insurrection during the summer of 1913, but also inflamed the bourgeois supporters of Yuan Shih-k'ai. In an apparent move to satisfy emerging Chinese nationalism and maintain equal opportunities for Chinese investors, the Chinese Government issued revised mining regulations on March 11, 1914, a month after the agreement with Standard Oil. The new regulations limited foreign participation in mining enterprises to half the total shares and forced the foreign partners to submit all disputes for arbitration by the Director of Mining Supervision.[5]

Compared to other westerners, Americans enjoyed a more favor-

[5] George M. Beckmann, *The Modernization of China and Japan* (New York, 1962), 177, 221–22; Paul Varg, *The Making of a Myth: The United States and China, 1897–1912* (East Lansing, Mich., 1968); John Fincher, "Political Provincialism and the National Revolution," in Mary C. Wright, ed., *China in Revolution: The First Phase, 1900–1913* (New Haven, Conn., 1968), 185–226; Marie-Claire Bergère, "The Role of the Bourgeoisie," *ibid.*, 230–295; Reinsch to Bryan, March 21, 1914, Lansing to Reinsch, May 1, 1914, Reinsch to Bryan, June 1, 1914, Department of State, *Papers Relating to the Foreign Relations of the United States, 1914*, 133–35.

able image in China and benefited from the withdrawal of the United States from the consortium. But they did not escape Chinese suspicions and were haunted by the conduct of the American China Development Company. That company built only a few miles of an important railway line from Canton to Hankow and then turned over its rights to a Belgian syndicate; these were eventually repurchased by J. P. Morgan & Co. and sold back to the Chinese government at a considerable profit. Standard Oil was also under a cloud because of false rumors that it had engineered the overthrow of President Diaz in Mexico and had secretly agreed to support Sun Yat Sen for President in return for oil monopoly rights in China. Nevertheless, the overriding need for money forced the government of Yuan Shih-k'ai to enter into secret negotiations with Standard Oil.[6]

Talks between Standard Oil and the Chinese Government had begun during the final months of the Manchu regime and were picked up briefly in the spring of 1913 by the new republican government. They were then suspended for several months because of uncertainties created by the American withdrawal from the consortium and the Kuomintang-led uprising against Yuan in the summer of 1913.[7] By October 1913, the government of Yuan Shih-k'ai was desperate for funds and greatly desired to avoid total financial dependence on the Five Power Consortium, which had just completed the First Reorganization Loan. Hoping to be rescued by the United States, Chinese officials descended upon the American Legation in Peking with appeals for financial assistance and offers of lucrative concessions. On October 18, 1913, Premier Hsiung Hsi-ling suggested to E. T. Williams, the American chargé d'affaires, that Standard Oil could receive oil monopoly rights in Shansi Providence in exchange for a $15,000,000 loan to strengthen the Bank of China and institute currency reform. Though devoted to American economic expansion, Williams questioned the advisability

[6] In the course of the negotiations, the Chinese constantly reminded Standard Oil officials of the American China Development Company fiasco and alluded to Standard Oil's involvement in Mexican politics. See Bemis to Hsiung Hsi-ling and Chou Tzu-ch'i, June 19, 1915, in MacMurray to Lansing, August 17, 1915, 893.6363/20, RG 59, Department of State, National Archives (hereafter cited DSNA, with reference to RG 59 unless otherwise indicated). Also, Cyril Pearl, *Morrison of Peking*, (Sydney, 1967), 234.

[7] The available evidence is scanty and is limited to a few newspaper references and later State Department correspondence. See New York *Times*, March 29, 1913; Reinsch to Bryan, February 24, 1914, 893.6363/3 and enclosures in Reinsch to Bryan, March 16, 1914, 893.6363/4, DSNA. Both Standard Oil of New Jersey and Mobil Oil, the successor to SOCONY, have informed the author that they have no documents on the episode; they claim that files were either misplaced or destroyed because of the dissolution of Standard Oil and lack of space. Gerretson sees a direct connection between the Consortium and Standard Oil's negotiations, in view of the close ties between Standard Oil and National City Bank, one of the members in the American Group. Gerretson, *History of the Royal Dutch*, IV, 121.

of any American loan to China in view of her financial difficulties and the threat of foreign interference. Nevertheless, he passed on China's requests to Washington and agreed to ascertain Standard Oil's interest in the proposal.[8]

Standard Oil wanted to exploit China's oil resources as a strictly business proposition, but was unwilling to get involved in the hazardous though common practice of buying concessions or making political loans. In early December 1913, formal negotiations were started by Henry J. Everall and Dr. Robert Coltman, Jr., representatives of SOCONY in north China, and the Ministries of Communications and Finance. They soon reached an impasse as the Chinese tried to force Standard Oil to bid against Japanese offers and the company refused to play the game.[9]

At this point, Paul S. Reinsch, the new United States Minister to China, stepped in. Reinsch believed that it was essential to translate American professions of friendship into concerte assistance for China while upholding the Open Door against the other powers who sought to strengthen their spheres of influence. He relied upon private business interests, with certain assistance from the United States government, to achieve the task and hoped in the end to establish a real Sino-American partnership.[10] "With respect to all such matters," he later recalled, "I had made up my mind that if any reputable American interest on the ground should desire to engage in some constructive work in industry or commerce, I should extend all the assistance I could properly give. The Standard Oil Company had achieved a position to be proud of." [11]

Reinsch injected himself into every phase of the negotiations. He tried to prevent misunderstandings and delays, meet the objections of outsiders, and find a basis for agreement. With his guidance, a tentative agreement was reached in January 1914, under which the Chinese government would receive one-third of the stock in a Sino-American development company and a loan. But then Standard Oil refused to make the loan, its representatives withdrawing from Peking in disgust, and the Chinese were left with a bad impression of the company. Worried about Japanese ambitions and the loss of a great business opportunity, Reinsch

[8] Interview between Williams and Hsiung Hsi-ling, October 18, 1913, Reinsch Papers, Box 2; Williams to Bryan, October 21, 1913, 893.51/1477, DSNA.
[9] Reinsch to Bryan, February 16, 1914, 893.6363/1, DSNA; New York *Times*, December 5, 1913, February 14, 1914.
[10] Noel H. Pugach, "Making the Open Door Work: Paul S. Reinsch in China, 1913–1919," *Pacific Historical Review*, XXXVIII (May, 1969), 157–175.
[11] Reinsch, "Six Years of American Action in China," Reinsch Papers, Box 15; Reinsch to Bryan, December 2, 1913, RG 84, Peking Post File, 1913, vol. 18, file 800, National Archives.

worked on the Chinese. He convinced them that they were better off dealing with a reliable and experienced American firm that had no political aims. When the Chinese seemed to respond to his arguments, he called back SOCONY's officials and persuaded them to be more generous.[12]

Consequently, an agreement was signed on February 10, 1914. Standard Oil was given one year to search for oil in certain districts in Shensi and Chihli, during which time the Chinese government pledged not to grant oil concessions to any competitors. If commercial deposits were discovered, a Sino-American development company would be chartered in the United States and have an exclusive right to exploit, refine, and market all petroleum produced in those provinces. SOCONY would own 55 per cent of the stock in the company; the Chinese government would take 37½ per cent as payment for the franchise and have a two year option to buy the remaining shares. The Chinese government granted the joint company all pipelines and railways needed to transport oil and equipment and promised to support the company in every possible way. Standard Oil pledged to send its experts immediately and help China obtain a loan in the United States.[13]

Bemis was elated with the contract, for without having to make a loan, Standard Oil would obtain a sixty-year monopoly to exploit the oil of several north China provinces, should major deposits be found. He also exuded optimism about the American future in China and called upon American bankers to supply needed capital to China. "We are looking forward to the entrance of American companies and capital into the Chinese Republic close after us on a scale that will place the United States in the lead in the commerce of the Far East," he told reporters.[14] Spokesmen for the business community responded favorably, but with greater restraint; some saw it as a positive step in extending the China trade and speeding China's development. The *New York Journal of Commerce*, for example, considered it as a sign both of enlightened progress in China and of the broadening maturity of American relations with China since the debacle of the American China Development Company.[15]

[12] Reinsch, "Six Years of American Action in China," Reinsch Papers, Box 15; Reinsch to Bryan, February 16, 1914, 893.6363/1, DSNA.

[13] Reinsch to Bryan, February 16, 1914, 893.6363/1, DSNA; New York *Times*, February 14, 1914. The text of the agreement may be found in John V. A. MacMurray, *Treaties and Agreements with and Concerning China, 1894–1919* (New York, 1921), II, 1109–1113.

[14] New York *Times*, February 14 and 15, 1914.

[15] New York *Times*, February 14, 1914; *Journal of the American Asiatic Association*, XIV (March, 1914), 34, 40.

STANDARD OIL IN CHINA   459

Chinese officials were plainly disappointed with the way Standard Oil did business, but they hoped to improve the terms in time. Meanwhile, due in part to their handling of the matter, they encountered stiff opposition to the contract. The negotiations had been carried on with great secrecy to prevent foreign interference and political intrigue. The agreement thus aroused popular suspicions that the government had given away valuable national wealth to a foreign company which had no immediate plan to develop the resources for China's benefit. In addition, the government had nationalized oil deposits in the two provinces involved and had quietly taken over the interests of two small companies in Shensi. This infuriated the Shensi notables, who resented the fact that they were not informed of the negotiations and feared the growing centralization of power in the hands of Peking. To avoid further misrepresentations and quiet the opposition, Reinsch advised the Chinese government to publish the contract and urged Standard Oil to demonstrate good faith by inaugurating the work as quickly as possible.[16] Foreign powers, especially Japan and Britain, also made things uncomfortable for China by protesting the concession and demanding similar rights elsewhere.[17]

Reinsch was generally pleased with the American, as well as his personal, achievement. It accorded well with his plans for the peaceful development of China and the helpful and profitable American penetration of the Far East. He thought that the arrangement was equitable. Without investing much of her own money, China received a share in the enterprise and the promised development of her resources. Standard Oil obtained special benefits and an important role in China's economic life, but these were warranted by the expense and risks involved in searching for unproved oil deposits. But aware of past American experiences in China, the dangers of complacency, and the anger and activities of Standard's competitors, Reinsch was determined to ensure the success of the enterprise. He therefore stressed that the contract only constituted an opportunity and a legal right which must be cultivated rapidly and expanded into "actual control of promising oil fields." [18]

[16] Reinsch to Bryan, February 16, 1914, 893.6363/1, February 24, 1914, 893.6363/3, March 16, 1914, 893.6363/4, DSNA; New York *Times*, February 20, 1914.
[17] Reinsch to Bryan, February 16, 1914, 893.6363/1, March 16, 1914, 893.6363/4, including enclosure of interview between Japanese Minister Yamaza and Hsiung Hsi-ling; interview between Sir John Jordan and Hsiung Hsi-ling, May 29, 1914, enclosed in MacMurray to Lansing, August 17, 1915, 893.6363/20, DSNA; New York *Times*, February 13, 1914; Willard Straight to Reinsch, February 25, 1914, Reinsch Papers, Box 2; Straight to James A. Thomas, March 24, 1914, Willard Straight Papers (Olin Library, Cornell University).
[18] Reinsch to Bryan, February 16, 1914, 893.6363/1, March 16, 1914, 893.6363/4, DSNA.

With information and advice supplied by Roy S. Anderson, an employee of Standard Oil who knew China intimately, Reinsch prepared a program for action. In the provinces already granted, Standard Oil should hasten to conciliate local officials and develop the most promising districts with the help of local merchants. If Shensi turned out well, SOCONY should seek similar rights in Shensi and Szechuan and from the start form provincial companies with local men. By providing the necessary capital, SOCONY would retain control while it enlisted local support and neutralized charges of monopoly and foreign domination. As China was awakening to the value of her oil properties, SOCONY should send out more geologists to make comprehensive mineral surveys in order to select future properties. In addition, SOCONY must work closely with the newly created National Oil Administration and its Director, Hsiung Hsi-ling. This could be done by attaching an expert to the bureau, sending in frequent reports and maintaining an official in China (Reinsch suggested Bemis) with complete authority to make decisions. Above all, Standard Oil had to give the impression that it was working in the interest of China. "Your position and that of your Company in the development of China," Reinsch advised Charles H. Blake, "will not depend solely on the letter of your contracts, but upon the personal relation of confidence and cooperation which you will establish with the Chinese." [19] Unfortunately, Standard Oil officials generally ignored Reinsch's counsel and blueprint for establishing a predominant position in China.

The following months severely tested the sincerity of the Chinese and Standard Oil as well as their ability to organize a real partnership. The Chinese were the first to show bad faith. After its geologists cast doubt on the oil potential of Chihli, SOCONY moved its men and equipment into Shensi.[20] But its operations were obstructed by the notorious local bandit, "White Wolf," and that prompted Hsiung to suggest a postponement of the expedition. The Chinese government also commandeered the company's carts on the pretext that the army needed them to suppress the bandit. While the Minister of Finance was urging SOCONY to obtain a loan for China, Hsiung secretly negotiated with Belgian interests for a concession that would have prevented the American company

[19] Roy S. Anderson to Reinsch, March 17, 1914, Reinsch Papers, Box 2; Reinsch to W. E. Bemis, April 20, 1914, RG 84, Peking Post File, 1914, vol. 29, file 863, National Archives; Reinsch to Charles H. Blake, May 28, 1914, *ibid.*
[20] Standard Oil made an earnest effort to dispatch men and equipment to China. Eventually, the company employed five geologists in China and spent close to $2,000,000. See 893.6363C44/6, DSNA; Reinsch, *An American Diplomat*, 98.

from acquiring additional lands adjacent to the Shensi oil fields. It became clear to Reinsch, Anderson, and John V. A. MacMurray, the new First Secretary of the Legation, that some Chinese officials wanted more than the development of China's resources. They saw a plot, managed by Liang Shih-yi through Hsiung, to prevent Standard Oil from fulfilling its agreement in time, thereby returning the enterprise to the international trading block.[21] The Chinese ploy failed because of British objections and the outbreak of World War I. But the Chinese showed their displeasure by refusing to substitute another province for Chihli and by extending Standard Oil's option for only two months.[22]

Meanwhile, the negotiations on the creation of a development company produced little progress and much bitterness. There existed a great disparity between the Chinese and Standard Oil positions, which reflected very different aspirations and interpretations of the original agreement. Envisaging the creation of a national oil industry that would produce and market crude oil and refined products, the Chinese wanted the development company to be a large enterprise, capitalized at perhaps $100,000,000. Standard Oil rejected the Chinese plan, for it naturally had no desire to destroy its profitable distribution system and valuable reputation, for which it had invested so much money and time. Instead, it regarded the joint enterprise as a producing and pipeline company, supplying crude to SOCONY which would then refine and market it through its own system. Consequently, the Sino-American Development Company would be small, capitalized at perhaps $1,000,000 to start with; and as additional capital was needed, the company would borrow it from Standard Oil at interest. Conceived in this manner, Standard Oil would enjoy a privileged position in China, have ready access to crude oil in the Far East, dominate a highly lucrative operation, and at the same time minimize its capital investment. The Chinese, however, considered SOCONY's plan a preposterous and insulting violation of the spirit, if not the letter, of the original agreement. The government could not allow Standard Oil to retain the most profitable parts of the oil operation nor permit the development company, by virtue of SOCONY's majority control of the stock and creditor position, to become a mere subsidiary of the oil giant. The Chinese agreed to postpone a decision on capitalization until geological reports

[21] MacMurray to Reinsch, June 23, 1914, Reinsch Papers, Box 2; Reinsch to Bryan, July 2, 1914, 893.6363/9.
[22] Coltman to Reinsch, November 27, 1914, RG 84, Peking Post File, 1914, vol. 29, file 863, National Archives; Reinsch to Bryan, April 5, 1915, 893.6363/12, DSNA.

indicated the size of the operation. But they demanded a share in all the profits and a chance to develop Chinese industry and technology.[23]

The negotiations were complicated by other factors. Standard Oil's organization in north China was torn by an internal dispute that forced Anderson to resign. In addition, Standard Oil was disturbed by the endless pressure for a loan, the constant reminders of past American failures in China, and Peking's secret nationalization of all oil deposits while the contract of 1914 was being negotiated. The Chinese, especially Chou Tzu-ch'i, the Minister of Commerce and Agriculture, found it difficult to deal with Coltman and Everall, SOCONY's manager and attorney in north China. Irritated by the recurrent delays caused by the need to refer every question to New York, the Chinese insisted that SOCONY send an official who had the power to make decisions. Reinsch, who constantly pleaded with American companies to send their "big men" to conduct business in China, thought that the Chinese were basically right. He warned that foreign rivals were active and bluntly informed Secretary of State William J. Bryan on April 5, 1915 that he would not help the company obtain a further extension of its option unless it changed its methods, sent an authorized representative, and negotiated in the spirit of the 1914 agreement.[24]

In the early stages of the negotiations, Standard Oil never seemed anxious to act on the advice of Reinsch or the State Department. But Reinsch's telegram jarred SOCONY sufficiently to bring Bemis back to China.[25] Bemis arrived in Peking on June 7, 1915, shortly before Reinsch left for the United States to campaign for major American investments in China. Bemis conferred with Reinsch and agreed to discuss the larger project desired by the Chinese, including a national refinery, provided Standard Oil would be designated the sales agent, on a cost basis, for the Sino-American development company. Reinsch considered Bemis's plan reasonable, for Standard Oil would protect its organization and would share in the marketing profits only through its interest in the joint company. And he thought that it might be accepted if modifications insured China a fair share of the profits and the right to control future national development. He therefore proposed the

[23] Memoranda of the National Oil Administration to SOCONY, March 12, 1915 and April 5, 1915, Memorandum of SOCONY to the National Oil Administration, March 29, 1915, in MacMurray to Lansing, August 17, 1915, 893.6363/20; Reinsch to Bryan, April 5, 1915, 893.6363/12, DSNA.
[24] Reinsch to Bryan, April 5, 1915, 893.6363/12; Bemis to Hsiung and Chou, June 19, 1915, in 893.6363/20, DSNA.
[25] William H. Libby to Bryan, March 4, 1914, 893.6363/6; Bryan to Standard Oil, April 6, 1915, 893.6363/12; Bemis to Bryan, April 8, 1915, 893.6363/13, DSNA.

creation of an auditing system and a renegotiation of the marketing agreement when domestic oil constituted 50 per cent of SOCONY's sales in China.[26]

Before leaving China, Reinsch again warned Bemis that success depended on reassuring the Chinese of the company's good intentions and on conducting the negotiations "in the right way." He also explained the complicated political situation in China and the bitter feud that existed between Hsiung Hsi-ling and Chou Tzu-ch'i. Hsiung had never liked Bemis, had conspired with foreign interests against SOCONY, and was now more interested in demonstrating his protection of Chinese resources than in having the project succeed. His appointment as director-general of the National Oil Administration was partly designed to get him out of the Cabinet, and he had only limited political influence. Chou, on the other hand, was a pro-American progressive who believed wholeheartedly in Sino-American economic cooperation. He was Minister of Commerce and Agriculture and technically represented the Minister of Finance and President Yuan in the negotiations. Reinsch therefore instructed Bemis to rely on Chou, even if it meant antagonizing Hsiung.[27]

On June 19, and without consulting MacMurray, the chargé d'affaires, Bemis submitted his plan for the larger enterprise, including Reinsch's modifications of the marketing agreement. The Chinese Development Company would have a total authorized capital of 100,000,000 Mexican dollars, but would begin business with 7,000,000 Mexican dollars and borrow additional funds from SOCONY at 6 per cent interest. Standard Oil would retain 55 per cent of the stock and the Chinese government could own as much as 45 per cent. The joint company would have a right, though not a monopoly, to explore for oil in all provinces, but those districts surveyed and selected would be worked exclusively by the development company.[28]

The Chinese turned down Bemis's proposal. They were determined to establish a national refinery processing all of China's

[26] Reinsch memo, "Suggestions on the Standard Oil Company's Contract," June 14, 1915, MacMurray memos, July 21, 1915, July 22, 1915, enclosed in 893.6363/20; MacMurray to Lansing, August 17, 1915, 893.6363/20, DSNA.

[27] Reinsch memo, "Suggestion on the Standard Oil Company's Contract," June 14, 1915, MacMurray memos, July 21 and August 4, 1915, enclosed in 893.6363/20, DSNA.

[28] Bemis to Hsiung and Chou, June 19, 1915, MacMurray memo, June 29, 1915, enclosed in 893.6363/20, DSNA. Mexican dollars (or more correctly Mexican pesos) circulated on a large scale in China beginning with the late eighteenth century, mainly because they were silver coins of determined value and China used silver rather than gold. They were probably the most common coin in the treaty ports and were used extensively in foreign trade. These coins became the yardstick or standard against which other foreign coins or currencies were valued. Consequently, many contracts between foreign firms or governments and China stipulated amounts in terms of Mexican silver pesos.

crude, with no foreign involvement except as lenders enjoying the customary financial and security rights. They wanted a marketing system that would be free to replace imported oils as rapidly as domestic production would permit. Sensitive to foreign and internal complaints, the Chinese felt they could not grant monopoly rights for either exploration or distribution. The Chinese vigorously objected to the small initial capitalization and dependence on loans, contemptuously dismissing the proposal "as a childish trick to make the proposed company a debtor to the Standard Oil Company even before it had gotten started as a going concern." Finally the Chinese expected terms at least as favorable as those they claimed were being offered by British and Dutch oil interests.[29]

During most of July little progress was made; conferences were infrequent and the Chinese position seemed to harden. Then Bemis indicated a willingness to concede points to the Chinese if they would substitute Hunan Province for Chihli, grant the joint company a monopoly for piping crude from individual oil bearing districts and, most important, allow SOCONY to market oil products refined from the crude produced by the Sino-American company.[30] Towards the end of the month both sides seemed to accept an arrangement whereby separate agreements would be made for production, refining, and marketing.

However, a crisis was reached between July 29–31 when the Chinese raised their price for substituting Hunan for Chihli. The Chinese now demanded the right to fix uniform prices on oil produced in China, insisted on dividing the profits of the marketing company on a 50–50 basis, and claimed they were free to set up joint companies with other foreigners outside of the provinces granted to the Sino-American concern. Bemis was furious. He pointed out that the Chinese were introducing new terms that conflicted with the original agreement and, without consulting the Legation, he called off negotiations on the larger proposition. Then, on July 31, in a burst of temper, Bemis told the Chinese that, unless they gave him a "square deal," he would "queer" the Chinese government in the American money market.[31]

Personal enmity and political intrigue were partly responsible for the crisis. The Chinese also made last minute changes after

[29] MacMurray memo, July 21, 1915, enclosed in 893.6363/20; MacMurray to Lansing, August 17, 1915, 893.6363/20, DSNA.
[30] MacMurray memos, July 7, 21, 22, 23, 1915, enclosed in 893.6363/20, DSNA.
[31] Bemis to Hsiung and Chou, July 29, 1915, Chinese memo, July 29, 1915, Hsiung and Chou to Bemis, July 30, 1915, MacMurray memo, August 4, 1915, enclosed in 893.6363/20, DSNA; MacMurray to E. T. Williams, August 5, 1915, Box 49 of the John V. A. MacMurray Papers (Manuscripts Collection, Princeton University).

agreeing to proposals and took extreme positions. But Bemis did much to provoke the Chinese response. From the beginning of the negotiations he had been overbearing and suspicious; he rarely gave the Chinese a chance to clear up misunderstandings and failed to appreciate the Chinese manner of bargaining. For the Chinese, the formation of close personal relations was an essential part of doing business and because of the political infighting it was especially important for preliminary conferences to be informal, without committing understandings to paper. Bemis's aloofness and formality only accentuated the ill-feeling that already existed.

Bemis committed other major errors. Disregarding Reinsch's clear warning, he befriended Hsiung and ignored Chou. Chou, understandably, was very bitter. He had fathered the project and had often been the only Cabinet member who maintained faith in the helpfulness of American interests. Now he was being ridiculed by his colleagues and even twitted by the President. Having lost "face," he took a hard stand in the negotiations to prove that he was not selling out China to the American rogues and exploiters. Bemis further aggravated the situation by not informing the Legation of his plans and actions nor confiding in MacMurray, who was anxious to have the enterprise succeed. Not only was he frustrated in his efforts to straighten out difficulties, but the embarrassed chargé was also forced to learn about Bemis's proposals through Chinese officials who came to consult with him.[82]

Ironically, the conflicts of July 31 cleared the air and led to a resumption of the negotiations. MacMurray sought an interview with Chou who spoke candidly of the conflict of personalities which was wrecking the talks. If Bemis would only trust him and come to an understanding of what each side considered essential, he told MacMurray, a solution might yet be found. Although Bemis expressed skepticism, MacMurray convinced him of the minister's commitment to the project and that only Chou could cut through the maze of Chinese political intrigue.[83]

Bemis therefore went to see Chou and their meeting was so successful that it paved the way for a formal conference on the smaller joint production project. An understanding was apparently reached on August 5, which Bemis then put on paper. Two days

[82] MacMurray to Williams, August 5, 1915, MacMurray Papers, Box 49; MacMurray to Reinsch, June 22, 1915, Reinsch Papers, Box 3; MacMurray memos, June 29, 1915, July 21, 1915, August 4, 1915, enclosed in 893.6363/20; MacMurray to Lansing, August 17, 1915, 893.6363/20, DSNA.

[83] MacMurray to Williams, August 5, 1915, MacMurray Papers, Box 49; MacMurray memos, August 4 and 10, 1915, enclosed in 893.6363/20, DSNA.

later, however, the Chinese repudiated the agreement, probably because political intrigue forced the negotiators to obtain better terms, and they submitted a highly objectionable counterproposal. The Chinese terms called for the Chinese government to fix prices, subjected the joint company to Chinese law, and vested control of the Sino-American company in a local committee divided equally between Americans and Chinese.[34] With MacMurray's cognizance, Bemis postponed further negotiations but reserved the company's rights under the agreement of February, 1914. In his letter of August 9, Bemis reminded Hsiung and Chou that he came to China with the knowledge that preliminary investigations did not reveal "any production upon which we can, with commercial intelligence, base the organization of a company." And because of the Chinese attitude on both the larger and smaller projects, Standard Oil "will await definite developments in Shensi before considering the question of forming a company." [35]

The Chinese now realized that they had gone too far. On August 10, the Ministry for Foreign Affairs intervened and asked Mac-Murray to exercise his "personal and unofficial good offices" to reopen the negotiations. MacMurray suggested, if the Chinese were sincere, an agreement on the larger project might be reached if the Chinese would divide the profits of the marketing company according to the shares owned (55–45) and name Standard Oil as the sales agent until Chinese Oil supplied half of the nation's requirements. But MacMurray had reservations about his own involvement. Unlike Reinsch, MacMurray was uncomfortable carrying on backdoor and unofficial negotiations and feared he was exceeding his authority. Nor did he relish further dealings with Bemis, who had on the previous evening rejected his suggestion of another meeting with Chou. On the other hand, MacMurray felt that he had to avoid another American fiasco in China and prevent the enterprise from falling into the hands of America's jealous rivals. Haste was also required to take advantage of a change in Chinese internal affairs. Yuan and the Ministry for Foreign Affairs were now taking a direct interest in the matter; Hsiung's influence was in decline and he was ordered not to obstruct the talks; and Chou was planning to retire to a provincial post and his successor might be less friendly to American interests. Finally, on August 10, Hsiung and Chou notified MacMurray of

[34] Hsiung and Chou to Bemis, August 7, 1915, MacMurray memo, August 10, 1915, enclosed in 893.6363/20; MacMurray to Lansing, August 12, 1915, 893.6363/15, DSNA.
[35] MacMurray to Lansing, August 12, 1915, 893.6363/15; Bemis to Hsiung and Chou, August 9, 1915, MacMurray memo, August 10, 1915, enclosed in 893.6363/20, DSNA.

their acceptance of his proposal, which was almost identical to the one Bemis had urged in July.[36]

Consequently, MacMurray intervened in the negotiations more actively than ever before. On August 10, MacMurray informed Bemis of the Foreign Minister's démarche. Bemis displayed or feigned interest, but the next day he adopted and thereafter maintained an uncompromising attitude. He claimed that, as far as he was concerned, the negotiations had come to an end with the Chinese proposal of August 7 and that the new Chinese move was only a face saving device to conceal Chinese incompetence and place the onus of breaking off the talks on Standard Oil. "They are 'stringing' you," he insisted, "they are trying to make you, as representing the American Government believe that it is Mr. Bemis who is responsible for the failure." MacMurray retorted that if Bemis shut the door on their advances, he could only conclude that it was the American company "which had failed to make good on a showdown . . . and which had laid itself open to the imputation of not really having meant business." [37]

Both sides found excuses to hold the matter in abeyance and, on August 14, Bemis departed for Shanghai. But MacMurray realized that it would be far more difficult to resume the negotiations once Bemis left China. Hoping to persuade Bemis to return to Peking, MacMurray carefully persisted in his mediation efforts. After some additional haggling, Chou agreed to discuss the larger project again, in accordance with the terms suggested by MacMurray on August 10. Neither MacMurray nor T. R. Jernigan, SOCONY's legal adviser in China, however, could force Bemis to change his mind.[38]

Meanwhile, MacMurray had urged the State Department to impress upon Standard Oil the significance of Bemis's decision and suggested that Reinsch visit the company's headquarters and explain the situation. The State Department shared his concern and, while trying to locate Reinsch, asked SOCONY to keep Bemis in Peking. Reinsch called on Standard Oil's officials and was told that the negotiations were merely suspended pending further explorations in Shensi. In fact, they later informed the State Depart-

[36] MacMurray to Lansing, August 12, 1915, 893.6363/15; MacMurray to Lansing, August 13, 1915, 893.6363/17; MacMurray memo, August 10, 1915, enclosed in 893.6363/20; MacMurray to Lansing, 893.6363/20, DSNA.
[37] MacMurray memos, August 10, 11, 12, 1915, enclosed in 893.6363/20; MacMurray to Lansing, August 17, 1915, 893.6363/20, DSNA.
[38] MacMurray to Lansing, August 17, 1915, 893.6363/20; MacMurray to Lansing, August 18, 1915, 893.6363/18; MacMurray to Lansing, August 23, 1915, 893.6363/19; MacMurray to Lansing, September 23, 1915, with enclosures, 893.6363/23, DSNA.

ment that they were fully satisfied with the way Bemis handled the matter.[39]

Upon his return to Peking, Reinsch found the Chinese filled with bitter disappointment. Despite his preference for working with Americans, Chou had told MacMurray that he felt free to negotiate with the British (Pearson & Co.) and Dutch (Royal Dutch-Shell) companies that had been badgering the government for months. MacMurray managed to persuade Chou to wait for Reinsch's report on his talks in New York. Since Reinsch and MacMurray could not offer the Chinese any encouragement, they requested the State Department to approach other American oil companies. The State Department contacted Penn Refining Co., Standard Oil, Waters-Pierce Oil Co., the Texas Co., and Guffey Petroleum Co. But none of the independents showed any interest, and Standard Oil was content to leave the matter in abeyance.[40]

Yuan's scheme to ascend the Imperial Throne in the autumn of 1915 diverted Chinese attention from the oil business. In the meantime, SOCONY continued its explorations of Shensi and Chihli. By April 1917, it became convinced that those provinces lacked sufficient oil to embark on a major enterprise and by mutual agreement with the Chinese government the contract of February 1914 was cancelled. However, since the war prevented other foreign companies from developing the concession, Hsiung offered to grant exploratory rights to any American company.[41]

CONCLUSION

Once again, an American company returned home empty handed, leaving behind a tarnished reputation. In this instance, however, the United States government can hardly be faulted. The Departments of State and Commerce fully appreciated the importance of the venture and feared a disastrous effect on Chinese-American trade if another power gained control of China's oil fields. Commerce officials pointed out that kerosene had accounted for half

[39] MacMurray to Lansing, August 13, 1915, 893.6363/17; Lansing to SOCONY, August 14, 1915, 893.6363/17; Lansing to MacMurray, August 21, 1915, 893.6363/17; H. L. Pratt to Polk, September 24, 1915, 893.6363/22; Lansing to MacMurray, September 25, 1915, 893.6363/22, DSNA.
[40] See 893.6363/25 and Williams to Trade Advisers, November 13, 1915, 893.6363/24; MacMurray to Lansing, September 23, 1915, 893.6363/21 and /23; Reinsch to Lansing, November 12, 1915, 893.6363/24, DSNA.
[41] Reinsch to Lansing, June 19, 1916, 893.6363/25; April 5, 1917, 893.6363/26, April 26, 1917, 893.6363/27. In the early 1920's Jersey Standard as well as other American, British, Japanese, and Soviet concerns expressed interest in oil development in China, especially in Szechuan, but nothing substantial materialized. See, for example, William Warfield to Hughes, September 7, 1921, 893.6363/37, DSNA.

of American exports to China in 1914 and was the only major item that had not met Japanese competition. The Wilson administration tried to hasten the conclusion of an agreement and gave its full diplomatic support to the extent that it countenanced a temporary exclusive sales agency for SOCONY.[42]

The American Legation in Peking went much further. Reinsch and MacMurray tendered advice, mediated disputes, coaxed the Americans and pressured the Chinese. Reinsch practically wrote the agreement of 1914 and MacMurray, overcoming his qualms, had a hand in the final proposals of August 1915. The chargé finally recognized that he could no longer rely on Bemis to spare the United States "the discredit and humiliation of a complete failure in a matter which is not only important to the American interests directly concerned, but also to all American hopes in China." [43] And the Legation did its part in spite of the lack of cooperation from Standard Oil and the obstruction of its irascible and suspicious Vice President. MacMurray, who bore the brunt of Bemis's behavior in 1915, unburdened himself to his mother: "I am being called upon to exercise personal good offices to untangle the snarl into which they have got themselves by ignoring the Minister's advice and disregarding the Legation. The call on me is the more imperative, but the duty is none the easier, for the knowledge that it is our people who have failed to play the game and laid themselves open to the charge of making a bluff that was too easily called." [44]

Instead, China and Standard Oil must share the responsibility. The Chinese were perfectly justified in seeking the best possible arrangement, desiring to create a national oil industry and to reap the expected financial and technological benefits. Indeed, the Chinese often proved to be tough bargainers who awoke to the value of their natural resources and tried to exploit them without being saddled with western imperialism. To be sure, the Chinese played off Standard Oil against foreign rivals, but this was one of the few weapons available to the weak giant of the Orient. The Chinese also labored under certain difficulties: they were subjected to continuous foreign pressures and, in view of their experience with the First Consortium Loan, were sensitive to the internal opposition against foreign monopolies. On the other hand, Chinese officials

---

[42] Lansing to MacMurray, July 26, 1915, 893.6363/14, DSNA. New York *Journal of Commerce*, August 16, 1915; New York *Times*, August 15, San Francisco *Chronicle*, August 15, 1915.

[43] MacMurray to Williams, August 5, 1915, MacMurray Papers, Box 49.

[44] MacMurray to his mother, August 16, 1915, *ibid.*

practiced outright deception, as when they attempted to prevent
SOCONY from perfecting its rights in Shensi and Chihli, and often
made outrageous demands that violated the 1914 agreement. Chinese political intrigue interfered with the negotiations and sometimes forced Chou, who probably wanted the project to succeed,
to take an extreme position. The intervention of the President and
the Ministry for Foreign Affairs in August 1915 suggests that some
of the intrigue could have been stopped earlier.

Standard Oil originally approached the project with the intention
of getting access to Asian crude, controlling the enterprise and
carrying off all of the profits. It later indicated a willingness to
make major concessions as long as it could maintain its sales organization and its predominant position in China. But it resented
the intrusion of the State Department and the Legation and generally ignored their advice. Its chief representative was clearly
ill-suited to negotiate with the Chinese; Bemis was demanding,
defensive, tactless, and unable or unwilling to see the Chinese point
of view. This is all the more surprising considering Standard Oil's
long involvement in the Far East and Bemis's previous experience
in China.

The personality conflicts, emphasized by MacMurray in his dis-
patches to Washington, certainly interefered with the negotiations
and obscured the middle ground of mutual interest which the Legation claimed existed. MacMurray reported another trivial incident
which Bemis intimated was the "final factor" determining his decision to go home. Bemis had carefully arranged a farewell dinner
on August 12 for the Chinese negotiators, at which occasion he
planned to present them with souvenirs of the first deep-drilled oil
wells in China. First Hsiung asked to be excused because of his
mother's illness and then it was incorrectly reported that Chou had
telephoned his regrets. In another burst of anger, Bemis cancelled
the dinner. "It seemed that Mr. Chou would not eat Mr. Bemis's
dinner because Mr. Bemis would not do business, and Mr. Bemis
would not do business because Mr. Chou would not eat his dinner," MacMurray explained to the State Department. "And so the
project fell into abeyance, as solemnly as though this incident of
Mr. Bemis's business in China were an adventure of Alice in
Wonderland." [45]

Mr. Bemis's testimony to the contrary, a more basic factor
prompted SOCONY to terminate the negotiations. During the
summer of 1915, Standard Oil decided that it was unwise at that

[45] MacMurray to Lansing, August 17, 1915, 893.6363/20, DSNA.

point to invest millions of dollars in an uncertain and difficult enterprise. In his letter of August 9, Bemis told Hsiung and Chou that SOCONY was suspending the talks pending an evaluation of the Shensi fields; and before leaving Peking he admitted to Mac-Murray that the preliminary findings had been disappointing. Although the company never admitted it, Reinsch concluded from his conversations in New York that Standard Oil had already decided to limit operations to the profitable marketing business.[46]

Skeptics might argue that Standard Oil never intended to go through with the project; that Bemis was sent to China only to find a pretext to disengage and at the same time straighten out the company's confused affairs in north China. However, the available evidence suggests that Standard Oil wanted to expand its operations if its Vice President's first hand report found it warranted and if he could sign an advantageous agreement. In the course of his stay in Peking, Bemis became disenchanted with doing business with the Chinese and decided, on the basis of preliminary investigations, that it was not worthwhile. New York obviously concurred. Thus, in the final stages of the negotiations, Bemis was bluffing and was attempting to cast the blame on the Chinese in order to escape public ridicule and Washington's condemnation (as the American China Development Company had received from Theodore Roosevelt and the Wall Street bankers from Woodrow Wilson). MacMurray suspected as much when Bemis accidentally blurted out, "I won't let them [the Chinese] say they called Mr. Bemis's bluff."[47] In the end, therefore, Standard Oil may have indeed been more culpable than the Chinese, and in the process seriously compromised the American position in China.

However, it is unlikely that the discovery of large oil deposits would have led to a successful joint enterprise. Reinsch's conception of Sino-American cooperation — the marrying of profitable American investment with rapid Chinese development, the extension of American influence without the trappings of imperialism — was too advanced and demanded too much of both Standard Oil and China. A subsequent joint enterprise sponsored by Reinsch, the Chinese-American Bank of Commerce, did get started, but it experienced repeated conflict between the American managers and the Chinese directors.

[46] Bemis to Hsiung and Chou, August 9, 1915, Bemis to MacMurray, August 13, 1915, enclosed in 893.6363/20; Reinsch, *An American Diplomat*, 223; New York *Times*, October 31, 1915; San Francisco *Chronicle*, August 18, 1915.
[47] MacMurray to Lansing, August 17, 1915, 893.6363/20; DSNA.

Finally, the misadventures of Standard Oil adds another dimension to the attempt to understand the failure of the United States to make the Open Door work in China. The effort to win a place for American trade and investment in China encountered many obstacles. Foreign rivals, now led by Japan, challenged almost every American enterprise. Conditions in China played a large role: American investors were frightened by recurrent instability, political intrigue and deception, conflict between Peking and the provinces, and the general backwardness of China. The image of China welcoming any American offer or of Americans jumping at every opportunity must be modified. Washington was sometimes reluctant to give the strong support which American interests required and, though the Wilson administration was remedying the situation, the United States lacked the modern machinery for overseas operations. But American business must shoulder much of the blame. It was inefficient, tactless, deceptive, and generally unprepared for foreign operations; it was unwilling to take risks and afraid of repeating past American failures in China. Even where sound business considerations warranted abstention from an enterprise, it often lacked the courage and candor to admit it.[48] Because they depended upon American capital to make the Open Door work, Reinsch, MacMurray and other observers often muted their criticism of American business or cast the blame on Japan, China, or some other factor. Thus, there were similar episodes involving American enterprise in China.[49] But the prominence of Standard Oil in China at the time lends a certain significance to the story of its concession.

[48] With regard to these remarks, I would like to thank Professors Paul Varg and Lloyd Gardner for their insightful and critical comments on a paper I read to the Western Conference of the Association for Asian Studies (Bozeman, Montana, October 16, 1970), entitled "Chinese Impediments to American Economic Expansion, 1913–1920." Professor Varg has critically examined the myth of the China market for the period 1897–1912. See Paul A. Varg, *The Making of a Myth: The United States and China, 1897–1912.*

[49] The Huai River Conservancy Project is another prime example, and it had even wider ramifications.

[22]

Excerpt from *Economic History Review*, 1984, **XXXVII**, 54–67.

Finance and Foreign Control in Canadian Base Metal Mining, 1918-55

By ALEXANDER DOW

Two contrary interpretations seek to explain the history of Canada's extractive resources.[1] What may be termed the orthodox position considers the exploitation of Canada's non-renewable natural resources in the first half of the twentieth-century as a success story, in which foreign capital was married to Canadian materials to the benefit of all. Certainly this view prevails among those within the Canadian mining industry, as the following quotation illustrates:

> It is obvious that the proper development of the mining industry, and all the resource industries, requires capital. Like it or not, the internal sources of money are just not sufficient. Some foreign investment is absolutely necessary. In our reaction to the extent of American investment in our country, we tend to lose sight of the fact that this foreign capital is essential to us.[2]

Academic analysis stresses also the role of entrepreneurial talent and the latest U.S. technology which accompanied direct foreign investment in the development of Canadian resources. Hugh Aitkin's writing shows this approach:

> American capital, entrepreneurship and technology have not merely exploited opportunities—they have also created them. Their function has been not merely to facilitate the doing of things that would have been done anyway, but also to get things done that might not have been done at all.[3]

Thus the orthodox position, presented both in popular and academic form, acknowledges the positive contribution of substantial foreign participation in the development of Canada's extractive industries. Seen as a corollary to a necessary drawing on the pool of foreign savings, particularly from the United States, foreign ownership also brought human capital, providing an entrepreneurial thrust otherwise lacking within the Canadian mining industry. In addition to the need for capital the orthodoxy indicates that U.S. ownership was promoted by the development of the technology of mining and mineral processing in the United States, and was stimulated by demand originating

---

[1] A version of this paper was presented to the Annual Meeting of the Canadian Historical Association in Montreal (June, 1980). I would like to thank Dr P. Phillips (University of Manitoba), I. Spry (University of Ottawa), Dr I. M. Drummond (University of Toronto), and members of the University of Toronto Economic History Workshop for helpful comments. All references to $ are to Canadian dollars, unless otherwise indicated.
[2] R. M. Longo, *Historical Highlights of Canadian Mining* (Toronto, 1973), p. 164.
[3] H. Aitken, *American Capital and Canadian Resources* (Cambridge, Mass. 1961), p. 104.

south of the 49th parallel which formed the greater part of the market for Canadian minerals.[4]

An alternative, more sceptical, view of the benefits to the Canadian economy of foreign investment has been adopted by some revisionist staples theorists. Writers in the Canadian "staple" tradition insist that Canada's economic development has been distinctive and not simply an illustration of classical economic principles at work. They stress that natural resource exploitation, given an external demand, shapes the maturing of an economy dependent on relatively unprocessed "staple exports" and seems to explain this entire process.[5] Fish, fur, timber, and wheat were successive staples in Canada's historical experience, but in the early twentieth century, somewhat awkwardly, mining development has been interpreted by some as evidence that mining should also be regarded as a staple, and suitable for analysis in terms of the staples approach. In one version this approach has been seen as an export-led growth model, in which a particular staple influences economic development uniquely on account of the distinctive linkages it creates.[6] In another, the staples approach is recast in the framework of dependency theory, whereby emphasis is extended from linkage or multiplier effects to the distribution of the economic rents from staple production.[7] Foreign ownership and the leakage of economic rents from the domestic economy define a form of exploitation. With respect to extractive resources, including minerals and mineral fuels, these modern staples writers (sometimes called "Canadian Left Nationalists") argue that foreign ownership reflects the expansion of America's economic power.[8] One corollary of Britain's decline as imperial lodestar is the growing stock of U.S. investment in Canada, including the Canadian mining industry.

Echoing the dependency notion of a "comprador" bourgeoisie, this Left Nationalist or revisionist amalgam of staples and dependency thinking promoted the suggestion that Canada's indigenous capitalist class has been based to an unusual degree on commercial functions, rather than on manufacturing or any industrial activity requiring a long-term investment in fixed capital. As a result, investment in industries was neglected in contrast to involvement in, and financial support of, trades, transportation, and financial institutions;[9] Canadian savings were diverted from Canadian heavy industries. Though

[4] Only a few writers note, as does Hugh Aitken, the importance of re-invested earnings to the growth of foreign ownership. See Aitken, *American Capital*.

[5] The 'staples approach' identifies the work of a group of scholars in Canada in the 1920s and 1930s. W. A. Mackintosh of Queen's University and Harold Innis of the University of Toronto led this group. See D. G. Creighton, *Harold Adams Innis: Portrait of a Scholar* (Toronto 1957), p. 105.

[6] M. H. Watkins, 'A Staple Theory of Economic Growth', *Canadian Journal of Economics and Political Science*, XXIX (1962), pp. 14-58. For linkages see A. O. Hirschman, *The Strategy of Economic Development* (1958).

[7] M. H. Watkins, 'The Staple Theory Revisited', *Journal of Canadian Studies*, 12 (1977), pp. 83-95.

[8] This approach is found in the work of economists, political scientists, sociologists, and historians. A recent review of this literature was presented by D. McNally, 'Staple Theory as Commodity Fetishism: Marx, Innis and Canadian Political Economy', *Studies in Political Economy*, 6 (1981), pp. 35-63. See also D. Drache, 'Rediscovering Canadian Political Economy', *Journal of Canadian Studies*, 11 (1976), pp. 3-18.

[9] R. T. Naylor, 'The Rise and Fall of the Third Commercial Empire of the St. Lawrence' in G. Teeple, ed. *Capitalism and the National Question in Canada* (Toronto, 1973), pp. 1-41. R. T. Naylor, *The History of Canadian Business* (Toronto, 1975), I, pp. 2-18.

56   A. DOW

foreshadowed in the original staples approach of the 1930s, this assertion has proved contentious[10], leaving the issue which this article seeks to illustrate as yet unresolved.

I

A corollary of both orthodox and revisionist positions appears to be that Canadian industries in the twentieth century were starved of Canadian capital. The orthodox view perceives an absolute shortage, whereas the revisionists identify and deplore a direction of capital away from industries towards other forms of economic activity. Moreover, an influential work in the Left Nationalist stream explained foreign ownership of Canadian industry as partly due to an absence of entrepreneurial initiatives among Canadians.[11] Surprisingly, this view is shared by both orthodox and at least some revisionist economic historians. There is a degree of consensus that Canada's development has been hindered by the inability of industries to obtain access to adequate investment funds from the pool of Canadian savings, and by the failure by Canadians to acquire the entrepreneurial skills and to undertake the risks upon which success under industrial capitalism depends.

The mining sector is a particularly interesting test of the staples-oriented approach for by the mid-1950s many mining enterprises were under foreign ownership. The orthodox interpretation regards foreign involvement as the inevitable outcome of the industry's need to seek foreign finance. The Left Nationalists, however, argue that foreign ownership was a result of the Canadian inheritance of an institutional structure ill-suited to industrial development.[12] The base metal mining industry in Canada was heavily dominated by the output of nickel, copper, lead and zinc in the period 1918-55. Military demands, along with the "new industrialism" based on electricity and the internal combustion engine, saw production of these four metals in Canada rise from $74 million in 1918 to $632 million in 1955. The maintenance of the momentum of expansion required exploration and development on an ever increasing scale. Consequently, the industry employed large amounts of fixed capital, and used a standard technology with high capital/labour ratios. The characteristic industrial structure was that of oligopoly. By 1954 the mining, smelting and refining of nickel-copper was conducted by only six firms of which the most dominant, the International Nickel Co. (INCO), was controlled from the United States. Other major producers were Falconbridge Nickel Mines and Sherritt Gordon Mines, which while initially developed as Canadian firms were subsequently sold into U.S. ownership.

For lead-zinc mining, smelting, and refining, the concentration was such

---

[10] L. R. McDonald, 'Merchants against Industry: An Idea and its Origins', *Canadian Historical Review*, 56 (1975), pp. 263-81; C. Pentland, 'Marx and the Canadian Question', *Canadian Forum* (Jan. 1974), pp. 26-8.

[11] K. Levitt, *Silent Surrender: The Multinational Corporation in Canada* (Toronto, 1970), p. 40.

[12] Successful historical interpretations must explain adequately, or survive 'testing' by confrontation with events. The evolving Canadian base metal mining industry offers such a possibility of assessing the orthodox and revisionist schools of mining history described above. Information sources include company annual reports, the *Financial Post Survey of Mines* (various years), the *Financial Post Corporation (Yellow Card) Service*, and contemporary newspaper reports.

CANADIAN METAL MINING   57

that by 1954 the six largest firms contributed 86 per cent of the net value
added. In this case a Canadian firm, a subsidiary of the Canadian Pacific
Railway Co., was dominant, the Consolidated Mining and Smelting Co. of
Canada (COMINCO), at the heart of which was the Sullivan lead-zinc mine
in south-eastern British Columbia. For copper-gold mining, both smelting
and refining and concentration were similarly pronounced. About 88 per cent
of the net value added was created by the six biggest firms, of which the two
largest were owned by respectively U.S. and Canadian investors. The Hudson
Bay Mining and Smelting Co. in Manitoba was developed under U.S. patron-
age, but Noranda Mines in Quebec, initially a U.S. enterprise, became an
entirely Canadian company from the late 1920s. By tracing the financial
evolution of these large firms an assessment is possible of the validity of the
orthodox and Left Nationalist views, though our analysis of a single sector is
presented as no more than suggestive for the entire extractive industry. Similar
work is needed on precious metals and the mineral fuels, especially oil, to
complete a comprehensive evaluation of the contrasting interpretations.[13]

II

Nickel-copper deposits of a sulphide type are spotted throughout the
Canadian Shield, but the area which has been unique in the richness and
extent of its nickel-copper ores is the Sudbury basin in Northern Ontario.[14]
A valley 37 miles long and 17 miles wide, the rim of the basin contained the
various mines. When cutting in preparation for the transcontinental Canadian
Pacific Railway revealed an ore body in 1883, the copper content had excited
interest. Typically, the Ontario Government concession, bought by local
speculators for a nominal sum, was later sold to a larger business firm, H. H.
Vivian and Co. of Swansea.[15] The Murray Mine, as it was called, was worked
unprofitably from 1889-94, the ore being smelted locally and shipped to Wales
for refining. Later, during World War I, anxious to receive a reliable source
of nickel for war purposes the British Government bought the property, and
formed the British American Nickel Co., which mined it temporarily.[16] Only
one British firm survived in active production till 1928. The Mond Co. owned
a nickel-refining method invented by Dr Lindsay Mond, which was used as
the basis for designing a Welsh refinery supplied by ore from Sudbury.[17]
However, it was American entrepreneurship which triumphed when the
International Nickel Co. (INCO) was formed by the fusion of the American-
led Canadian Copper Co. (owning properties in Sudbury) with the Orford Co.,

[13] Comparatively little has been written on the extractive industry of Canada by economic historians,
though anecdotal publications are plentiful. Still unchallenged in scope is H. A. Innis, *Settlement and the
Mining Frontier* (Toronto, 1936). More recently, for Ontario, there appeared H. V. Nelles, *The Politics
of Development: Forests, Mines and Hydro-Power in Ontario, 1849-1951* (Toronto, 1974). A specialized
bibliography is W. G. Richardson, *A Survey of Canadian Mining History* (The Canadian Institute of Mining
and Metallurgy, Special Volume 14, 1974).
[14] See D. M. LeBourdais, *The Sudbury Basin* (Toronto, 1953).
[15] The British North America Act (1867) of the Westminster Parliament established the Canadian
constitution, by which property rights over natural resources were vested in the provinces.
[16] See T. W. Gibson, *Mining in Ontario* (Toronto, 1937), p. 78.
[17] Royal Ontario Nickel Commission, *Report* (Toronto, 1917), p. 59.

which had refining works in the U.S.A. The new company was incorporated in
New Jersey in 1902.[18]

Although the initial experience of nickel-copper mining in Canada was of
British and American impetus, with the formation and growth of INCO the
American interests came to dominate. Almost all INCO's shares were held
by U.S. residents in 1915, suggesting an influx of U.S. capital into Canada
which was the consequence of the Sudbury activities of the American firm.[19]
The merger and formation of INCO cost no more than $10 million, and by
1916 no less than $30 million had been distributed in dividends,[20] an indication
of the very substantial return to American investors, which was achieved, in
part, from economic rent from Sudbury ores. Such an exodus of Canadian
mineral wealth has to be offset against the undoubted financial inflows required
to establish the mining and smelting operation in Sudbury. Of course, new
capital was required to finance the expansion of output during the First World
War. Furthermore, the International Nickel Co. of Canada, a wholly-owned
subsidiary, was established in 1916 with a Dominion charter. This move
represented the culmination of a long political struggle to have nickel refined
in Canada, instead of shipping smelter matte overseas.[21] INCO had resisted
such a suggestion for many years, but the pressure of the Royal Ontario Nickel
Commission, a scandal over Sudbury nickel which had reached Germany by
submarine, and the attraction of cheap Ontario hydro-power, had broken the
Company's resistance. Investment in the new subsidiary took the form of
building the refinery at Port Colborne, Ontario, for which, it was reported,
the finance came from the American company.[22]

After a few lean years, the peacetime demand for nickel in automobiles and
in speciality steels began to grow in the 1920s, and INCO's growth was
described by contemporaries as follows: "In 1926 the company undertook a
program of expansion, largely in Canada, which cost $52 million before its
completion in 1933. Seventy-one per cent of the capital was provided by the
sale of securities and the rest out of earnings and reserves".[23] This conclusion
of Marshall and Southard was somewhat misleading, however, for the major
part of a 1924 stock issue related to the takeover of the Mond Co., and thus
involved a transfer of assets, with concomitant financial flow, between foreign
principals. Once again, a capital inflow of impressive scale turns out to have
been more modest on closer examination. By 1934, when the dust from
complicated stock transactions had settled, Canadians owned 21 per cent of
the shares, British residents owned 33 per cent, and U.S. residents owned 42
per cent. Assets in Canada and abroad were valued at $200 million. The main

[18] For details on INCO see O. W. Main, *The Canadian Nickel Industry* (Toronto, 1955), pp. 76-123.
J. F. Thomson and N. Beasley, *For the Years to Come* (Toronto, 1960), pp. 139-90. D. M. LeBourdais,
Metals and Men (Toronto, 1957), pp. 119-26.
[19] RONC, *Report*, p. 73.
[20] A. C. Dow, 'The Canadian Base Metal Mining Industry (Non-ferrous) and its Impact on Economic
Development in Canada, 1918-55' (unpublished PhD thesis, University of Manitoba, 1980), pp. 138-43.
[21] The ore removed from a mine would contain less than 4 per cent of recoverable metals. By milling
and smelting the mineral, for example, nickel matte was made 95 per cent pure. Refining improved the
purity to over 99 per cent. See J. R. Boldt and P. Quesneau, *The Winning of Nickel* (Toronto, 1967),
pp. 350-5.
[22] H. Marshall and F. Southard, *Canadian-American Industry* (Toronto, 1976), p. 98.
[23] Ibid.

CANADIAN METAL MINING 59

source of capital propelling expansion came from ploughed back profits and economic rents. In every year from 1920 to 1934 profits were ploughed back into fixed capital formation, some $64 million in total over the years by one estimate.[24] In short, INCO represents a model of internally generated growth, supported by some occasional and modest infusions of U.S. capital. From 1930 to 1955 there were no further equity issues in INCO of Canada.

Mond having been absorbed, INCO's monopoly position in nickel was at its strongest in 1929. Though Le Nickel continued to mine New Caledonian ore, only one small competitor remained in Sudbury. Falconbridge Nickel Mines was a small and speculative concern when it was established with an Ontario charter in 1928 by Thayer Lindsley, an American engineer and mining promoter. Perhaps from fear of the anti-combine legislation in the U.S.A., or influenced by a report that the young company had obtained an independent nickel refinery in Norway, INCO seemingly allowed Falconbridge to develop the European market unchallenged. The small firm may have created a helpful illusion of serious competition. More than a simple producer, Falconbridge Nickel Mines became the flagship for a corporate empire dedicated to financing and developing new mines in Canada and abroad.[25] The Sudbury property, the surpluses from which were to fund so many new mines, was bought from Minneapolis owners for $2·5 million. Never before had so much been paid for a Sudbury property, and presumably the sum reflects a considerable element of economic rent. It seems likely that the realization of resource rent in this instance caused an outflow across the capital account of the Canadian balance of payments. The purchase was financed not by Thayer's own money, for he was not initially wealthy, but from a sale of shares (some through the Toronto Standard Stock and Mining Exchange) in two holding companies, Ventures Ltd. and Sudbury Basin Mines. Of course, to the extent that U.S. residents bought the shares, the capital outflow was mitigated. Falconbridge needed fresh capital in 1936 as the sales of nickel recovered from the depression. In the mid 1930s an extensive construction programme was initiated involving improvements to the Falconbridge mine and smelter and to the upgrading of the Norwegian refinery. Total expenditures for the construction were $2·1 million. Cash balances had been invested from 1932 in several Canadian gold-mining stocks, which reflected the buoyant gold market of the depression years. When the reserves were liquidated, a capital gain of about a half million dollars was realized[26] and applied to the expansion programme. Thus, through the mobilization of capital gains, equity shares in other mining companies contributed to finance nickel development.

Prior to World War II, Falconbridge was a comparatively small producer of nickel and copper. Only after the war, when it was still a Canadian company in the Lindsley empire, did Falconbridge start to challenge INCO. Anxious to increase nickel production and to build sources of supply separate from

---

[24] A. Skelton, 'Nickel' in W. Y. Elliot et al. *International Control in the Non Ferrous Metals* (New York, 1937), p. 191.
[25] For details on Falconbridge see D. M. LeBourdais, *The Sudbury Basin* (Toronto, 1953), p. 138; J. Deverall, *Falconbridge* (Toronto, 1975), pp. 39-51. F. S. Moore, *American Influence in Canadian Mining* (Toronto, 1941), p. 35. R. M. Longo, ed. *Historical Highlights of Canadian Mining* (Toronto, 1973), pp. 63-5.
[26] Falconbridge Nickel Mines, *Annual Report* (1936).

60   A. DOW

INCO, the U.S. government sponsored, among others, two Lindsley firms, Falconbridge and Sherritt Gordon Mines. In each case the chain of events leading to changed ownership can be traced to the strain placed on the financial capabilities of the firms as a result of attempts to increase sales dramatically to the U.S. government in the late 1940s and early 1950s.[27] A study of Falconbridge shows that ploughed back profits and economic rents were of major importance in financing growth. Shareholders even complained, at times, about the small proportion of profits distributed as dividends. There was, indeed, an injection of American funds, less in the initial stages than one might suppose from a casual assessment, but more in the hidden form of bonuses on contracts in the 1950s,[28] and some in the growth of Falconbridge to multinational status. The Canadian equity and bond markets provided the funds at various stages, but throughout the company's history American entrepreneurial flair was instrumental to success.[29]

Incorporated under Ontario charter in 1927 as part of the Lindsley group of companies, the initial focus of Sherritt-Gordon Mines was on the Sherridon deposits of copper, zinc, gold, and silver in Northern Manitoba. Production started in 1931, but the mine closed because of low metal prices from 1932 to 1936. Exhaustion of the Sherridon ore was complete by the late 1940s, when the Company's focus switched to nickel mined from a new site at Lynn Lake, some 150 miles north of Sherridon. Most of the finance for Sherritt-Gordon Mines before 1946 came from equity shares issued in the booming stock market conditions of the late 1920s. Unusual for such a remote mine-site, the proximity to the smelter and hydro-power supply of Hudson Bay Mining and Smelting, with which company appropriate contracts were signed, meant that neither power facilities nor smelter facilities had to be financed. A railway feeder line, 42 miles in length to the main Hudson Bay Railway, was supplied by Canadian National Railways (CNR) in 1929, with financial assistance from the Dominion.[30]

Sherridon's exhaustion was intimately tied to the eventual American take-over of Sherritt-Gordon. Lynn Lake was established as an alternative mine site in the years 1945-53, when the company became primarily a nickel, rather than a copper, producer. Such a transition required the building of new

[27] In fact, McIntyre Porcupine Mines, a Canadian gold producer, bought Falconbridge in 1957 when cash-flow problems emerged. Not until 1967 did a U.S. company, Superior Oil, take over.

[28] Falconbridge signed the first five year contract for nickel with the U.S. government in 1948. During the Korean conflict in 1951 the U.S. Defence Materials Procurement Agency agreed to a ten-year contract at market prices for each year along with $6 million advance. Then the U.S. government, in the biggest order of the three, contracted to buy large quantities of refined nickel over nine years at market prices plus a premium of 40 cents a pound. At that time (1953) the market price for nickel was 60 cents a pound. With an expected sale of 100 million pounds of refined nickel, the bonus amounted to an anticipated $40 million. These bonuses, which allowed a substantial expansion to be undertaken, represent capital inflow of an unusual sort.

[29] However, another Falconbridge career is noteworthy. Born in Saskatchewan, Horace Fraser graduated from the University of Manitoba in 1924 with a B.Sc. in chemistry. After a Harvard Ph.D. in geology, he worked briefly for INCO before accepting a university teaching position in California. During World War II he worked in Washington, D.C. in the area of minerals procurement. Sought out by Lindsley, Fraser joined Falconbridge after the war rising to become president and managing director in 1957. His success is a reminder of the part played by Canadians in the entrepreneurial function within firms such as Falconbridge.

[30] Canada, *Debates of the House of Commons*, 82nd Session, 17th parliament, 21 May, 1931, pp. 1858-60.

CANADIAN METAL MINING 61

capacity to smelt and refine the nickel, and for technical reasons severing the hitherto convenient arrangement with Hudson Bay Mining and Smelting. A new reduction plant in Alberta was built, based on the experimental leaching technology (which proved considerably more expensive than envisaged in the initial budget), and a power site had to be developed on the Churchill River in Saskatchewan. In combination, these developments led the investment needs of the Sherritt-Gordon Mines to outrun the capacity (or willingness) of the existing shareholders to supply capital. Takeover by the Newmont Mining Corporation of the U.S.A. was the result. Even a five-year contract with the U.S. government beginning in 1950, and other contracts with American steel producers, proved inadequate to ensure sufficient financing within Canada.

How can the American takeover be explained? The immediate cause was the financial strain imposed by the development of Lynn Lake and the Alberta leaching plant. However, an explanation is also required for the inadequacy of Sherritt-Gordon's internal resources, as is an answer to the question why was Canadian capital not forthcoming when required? Bearing on both these issues is the operation of wartime price controls in Canada. Following the practice of all Lindsley companies, Sherritt-Gordon ploughed back a high proportion of gross profits into exploration. Lynn Lake represents one of the fruits of this policy. However, as shown in the Annual Report for 1951, the bulk of the firm's Sherridon ore was mined under conditions when its full value could not be realized. Together with other copper producers in the British Empire, in 1939 the company agreed to supply the British government "at a fair price".[31] About three-quarters of the output of Sherritt-Gordon was earmarked in this way, the balance being sold in Canada, but domestic prices were also controlled from between 1942 and 1947. Thus, after a period of closure during the depression, followed by price restrictions during the war, Sherritt-Gordon lacked reserves to provide for the postwar removal and expansion.[32] The lack of Canadian risk capital to finance Sherritt-Gordon's development is suggestive at a more general level. A plausible general conclusion might be that after Canadian business emerged from the depression, price controls and heavier taxation associated with World War II forced Canadian business into a disadvantageous position in comparison with its counterpart in the U.S. Is it plausible, therefore, to regard Canada's contribution to the war effort as explaining the relative absence of risk capital in Canada in the late 1940s and early 1950s?

III

Lead and zinc mining, smelting and refining comprised the main business of COMINCO. The Canadian Pacific Railway Company (CPR) built the southerly Crows Nest Pass route through the Rockies to Kootenay Lake, whence from 1898, by steamer and rail, shipments could be transferred north to the CPR main line. Engaged in a battle with American promoters of railroads and steamship lines for the traffic of south-eastern British Columbia,

[31] Sherritt-Gordon Mines, *Annual Report* (1939).
[32] Considering that exhaustion loomed, it is remarkable that over two-thirds of the company's profits from exploiting the Sherridon deposits came in the period from 1947 to 1951.

62   A. DOW

in 1898 the CPR purchased the recently completed smelter at Trail, the owner of which had had grand ambitions for railway development of his own. To ensure a steady supply of ore to the smelter the CPR was drawn gradually into the business of mining. COMINCO was incorporated under Dominion Charter in 1906, by which time in addition to the original copper-gold smelter the Trail metallurgical works included a blast furnace to produce smelter lead and a small electrolytic lead-refining plant. Beyond the Trail complex COMINCO's operations extended to mines in nearby Rossland and along the tracks to Moyie in East Kootenay. In 1910 the company acquired the Sullivan Mine in East Kootenay, which contained a rich lead-zinc ore so complex that nobody could then economically separate it. A Canadian research effort located in Trail solved that metallurgical problem, first by subsidized electrolytic methods in 1916, then with increasing commercial success by a process of selective flotation started in 1920 and improved thereafter. The richness of the Sullivan Mine enabled the company to grow within three decades into a multinational corporation whose activities included mining and metallurgical operations and, via by-products of the Sullivan ore, fertilizer and chemical manufacture.[33]

The capital structure of the firm was straightforward. Bonds issued in 1918 to the amount of $3 million (later increased to $4 million) were retired in 1925, returning to a simple capital structure based on equity shares. Mine development and the expansion of reduction plants were financed to some extent by fresh stock issues, but relied most heavily on the re-investment of profits and economic rents.[34] Unusual for a mining company, COMINCO had a large bank overdraft with the Bank of Montreal. The security for this facility was inventory built up in expectation of sales to the Imperial Munitions Board, and credit amounted to just over $2 million in 1917 when the issued capital stood at almost $10·5 million. Over the next three years the amount of this bank lending increased and included a bridging loan in anticipation of funding, which reached a peak in excess of $5 million in 1920. Not until 1925 was this element of COMINCO's financing eliminated. Bank borrowing again occurred in 1930 which increased to a total of almost $3·9 million in 1932, the purpose of which was to finance increased inventories and to establish fertilizer production. It seems likely that COMINCO's favourable financial position resulted from the prestige of the CPR and its close links with the Montreal financial community, and that such connections were probably influential in securing substantial sums of capital at critical periods in the company's development in a form most unusual for a mining company. The major source of finance was ploughed back profits and economic rents, and in this respect the basis for COMINCO's growth resembled that of INCO. Financing was available from Canadian sources when needed. Of course, since the CPR was a stock widely owned in Britain (though control of the company rested in Canada), an appreciable percentage of the COMINCO stock and bond financing may have involved an inflow of British portfolio capital. No bonds were issued between 1936-55, nor was any new finance raised by stock issues during these years.

[33] See 'The Story of COMINCO', *Canadian Mining Journal*, 75 (1954), pp. 151-393.
[34] T. W. Bingay, 'A Brief History of The Consolidated M and S Co.', *Miner*, 9 (1936), pp. 49-51.

CANADIAN METAL MINING 63

A legal quirk caused Noranda Mines Ltd. to become incorporated in Ontario.[35] An American syndicate, headed by Samuel Thomson and Humphrey Chadborne, had been formed in New York in 1922 with a view to buying and developing promising mineral properties. Soon after its formation the syndicate took an option on the Tremoy Lake property in Quebec staked by Ed Horne and owned by the Tremoy syndicate in which he held an interest. A Canadian lawyer, James Murdoch, who represented the Thomson and Chadborne syndicate noticed that under Ontario law the members of the syndicate were personally liable for the mining interest they held in Ontario. To remove this potential embarrassment, for small mining ventures were prone to fail, Noranda Mines Ltd. was incorporated in Ontario in 1922, and the shrewd Canadian lawyer became interim president of what was still a small concern. He remained, however, after the Noranda smelter was built at Rouyn and even when the locus of control shifted to Canada in 1927 continued as president. He retired in 1952, having been intimately involved in the pace and direction of the company's expansion and its emergence as a multinational company.

The general manager in charge of mine development, including the erection of the Rouyn smelter, was Ernest Hibbert, a British immigrant. For assistance Hibbert employed two men who had worked with him in the defunct British American Nickel venture at Sudbury. These men, H. L. Roscoe and R. V. Porritt, were responsible for the underground development of the new mine. Porritt was a McGill University graduate in mining engineering who rose within the company to become president in 1964; Roscoe, an American, became senior vice-president in 1956. Also involved in the Noranda mine site and smelter construction was J. R. Bradfield, another McGill University graduate, who, having worked in the U.S., joined the New York designers in 1926 with a view to becoming on-site civil engineer at Rouyn. He became company president in 1956 and chairman of the board in 1964. The managerial personnel of Noranda, therefore, provides no support for those who argue that a lack of entrepreneurial or technical skill explains the U.S. presence in Canadian mining. But was this case exceptional?

Three features of the case explain the success of Noranda as a Canadian mining corporation. First, Murdoch was something of a nationalist. Second, and more important, fortuitous and unique circumstances affected Noranda, for the Lower H ore body found in 1929 which proved to be the lode, rich in copper and gold on which Noranda's prosperity in the 1930s depended, occurred two years after advance in Canadian ownership in the Company had taken place. The original development had occurred on the basis of a supply of ore assured for only three years. Yet in the late 1920s the price of Noranda Mines stock soared. The New York interests decided to unload Noranda at a substantial premium on the original investment. The Annual Report for 1927 recorded a change in share ownership since 1926, the result of which was that a majority of the issued shares were registered in the names of shareholders resident in Canada, and a new Toronto office soon replaced that in New York, which closed. Two years were to pass before the discovery of the Lower H

---

[35] L. Roberts, *Noranda* (Toronto, 1956), p. 52.

64   A. DOW

ore body transformed a small and speculative enterprise into a rich and burgeoning corporation based on Canadian enterprise, technical skills, and capital. For the final circumstances that explains Noranda's Canadianization was the ready availability of Canadian capital. A factor here was the coincident occurrence of gold as well as copper in the Noranda ore deposits. Successful gold mining in Ontario had built up reserves of capital in Porcupine and Kirkland Lake since before World War I, and investment tended to be attracted into similar activity. Consequently, some of these funds were deployed through the equity market to finance Noranda. Further strength derived from the flexibility of the Company's output mix resulting from the existence within the Noranda property both of gold- and copper-rich ores.

One of the major figures in the Canadianization of Noranda was Noah Timmins, owner of the Hollinger Mines, whose wealth, accumulated from gold mining, enabled him to invest in Noranda and to join the board in 1925. A $3 million issue in 1927 of 7 per cent first mortgage sinking-fund gold bonds was taken up exclusively by Hollinger, which received as part of the deal a bonus of 30,000 Noranda shares. Two years later the entire Noranda 1927 bond issue was repaid from an equity issue. However, the bonus shares, added to shares obtained earlier by Noah Timmins in exchange for claims held beside the Horne property, perpetuated his influence as a major stockholder in Noranda. From 1930 Noranda's growth was financed by internally generated profits and economic rents which accrued to the enterprise. The refinery built for Noranda in Montreal in 1931 was owned by Canadian Copper Refiners, a joint venture. Nichols Copper (an American concern linked with Phelps Dodge) and British Metals, a marketing organization, joined with Noranda as senior participant in the share subscription of the new company which combined within a single organization refinery, technology, and market outlets. Over and above equity funding for the refinery's construction, Noranda guaranteed a $2·5 million bond issue of Canadian Copper Refiners to ensure adequate finance. The origins of Noranda's capital, therefore, are clearly identified. In the long run it came mainly from Noranda's successful exploitation of its Quebec deposits. The crucial early financing came from the United States. Thereafter, a combination of the booming market in Noranda shares, the backing of funds accumulated from gold mining profits at the Hollinger Mines, and the fortuitous timing of the discovery of the richer ore lodes, enabled Canadian entrepreneurs to assume control of the corporation.

The Dominion Charter of the Hudson Bay Mining and Smelting Company was granted in 1927. A technology having been found to separate the Flin Flon (Manitoba) copper-zinc ores by research in Denver and by field experimentation, the Whitney group of New York exercised an option on the property and launched what was then a massive investment in the north of Manitoba. Not surprisingly, American entrepreneurship, capital, and technology played prominent parts in this development. Perhaps most striking is the willingness of an American entrepreneurial group to experiment with a flotation method, which in the 1920s was coming into widespread commercial use.[36] It was the successful application of this method which transformed the

[36] Selective flotation is a method of separating metal-bearing ore from crude rock based on the principle that a substance will tend to stick to an air bubble, if the surface is not wetted by water. In flotation tanks the desired minerals are made hydrophobic by the addition of suitable chemicals to a liquid ore pulp. See J. R. Boldt and P. Quesneau, *The Winning of Nickel* (Toronto, 1967), pp. 199-204.

CANADIAN METAL MINING   65

ore deposits, known since 1915, into a commerical success involving mining and smelting operations. Refining was carried out by Canadian Copper Refiners in Montreal, in whose refinery Noranda possessed an interest. Funding for Hudson Bay Mining and Smelting came from the sale of shares which Canadian investors appeared eager to acquire when the company was first formed. The purpose of initial financing was to raise $15 million to $20 million in cash to bring the enterprise into commercial operation. In January 1928, however, the *Northern Miner* reported that few shares of Hudson Bay Mining and Smelting were available to the Canadian public, since the New York interests were keeping nearly all their stock;[37] moreover, share listing on the Toronto Standard Exchange was not yet achieved. The New York share distribution was private, but reportedly widespread;[38] nonetheless, at his death in 1930 Harry Payne Whitney owned 30 per cent of the company's $5 million bonds issue in addition to 30 per cent of the common stock.

While most of the capital to launch this enterprise was obtained in New York, this seems to have been the result of rationing, at least in part. Canadians were eager to purchase equity but the conditions under which the company was launched initially frustrated their intentions. We conclude, therefore, that even in this case, which might seem at first glance to be unambiguous, shortage of risk capital does not explain the American ownership of a major new deposit; the explanation is to be found in the mode of operation of American financiers when the company was floated. Thereafter, apart from the bond issue of 1930, the financing of Hudson Bay Mining and Smelting depended entirely on ploughed back profits and economic rents. The $5 million bond issue took the form of convertible debentures, all of which were retired before July 1935 by purchase or conversion into capital stock. Control remained in U.S. hands until 1955.[39]

IV

A comparison of the total assets of those companies whose histories we have examined provide a wider perspective (Table 1). First, the relative importance of INCO is apparent in both 1935 and 1955; the rich Sudbury deposits

Table 1. *Total Assets of Leading Companies in Canadian Base Metal Mining, 1935 and 1955*

	($ million)	
	1935	*1955*
Inco	210·6	519·6
Cominco	49·9	200·8
Noranda	34·0	113·6
Hudson Bay M and S	34·6	74·1
Falconbridge	9·6	68·8
Sherritt-Gordon	8·6	58·2

Source: Survey of Mines (Financial Post, 1936, 1957).

[37] *Northern Miner*, 19 January, 1928.
[38] 'Flin Flon Deal Outlines', *Northern Miner*, 26 January, 1928.
[39] Subsequently in the 1960s the company was sold to South African interests.

66   A. DOW

and the world monopoly achieved by the 1920s rendered INCO a unique phenomenon in Canadian mining history. We have remarked already that a limited infusion of U.S. capital seems to have been necessary for INCO's success. COMINCO and Noranda both grew faster than INCO from 1935 to 1955, in each case using primarily Canadian capital. At the same time, Falconbridge and Sherritt-Gordon grew to become multi-nationals in their own right. The former relied throughout mainly on Canadian capital, while not until the early 1950s was Sherritt-Gordon acquired by American funds. Hudson Bay Mining and Smelting did employ American capital to become established in the late 1920s, but not, apparently, because of a lack of Canadian investment interest. The histories of leading firms suggest than any notion that there was heavy involvement of foreign firms in the Canadian base metal mining industry due to a shortage of Canadian capital in their development stages is quite false.

The main source of development finance for base metal mining between the wars was the reinvested surplus generated within each of the major concerns. From the original gold mines of Ontario, too, a certain surplus which had accumulated was attracted to the related copper-gold mining industry in Quebec. For the mass of speculative small concerns, which accounted for but a small part of output, the Toronto Standard Stock and Mining Exchange provided a channel into mining, for Canadian risk capital until its absorption in 1934 by the Toronto Stock Exchange, which continued the tradition. Montreal also served as a market for some small mining stocks. That there was American investment in Canadian mining is not surprising, given the opportunities; but it would be incorrect to conclude that this investment by its size was the critical factor which propelled the Canadian mining industry. Canadian economic rents, rather than the American capital, are to be seen as the motive force of the industry from 1918-39. Only in the 1950s did bonus contracts and capital injections create a situation where there may be some truth in Hugh Aitken's aphorism that American capital got things done that might not have been done at all. However, it seems likely that American policies supporting high base-metal prices may have been more significant than were direct capital injections, even in the 1950s. After World War II the dynamic seems to have resulted from market manipulation rather than from vigorous inflows of U.S. capital. Furthermore, the view that Canada could not develop necessary technologies but required American "packages", including technical expertise, entrepreneurship, and capital, seems to be invalidated by the historical experience of base metal mining. Sometimes, indeed, this was the reality, for example at Flin Flon where the Whitney group of financial interests possessed the expertise to devise in Denver, Colorado, a commercial production technique on which Hudson Bay Mining and Smelting flourished. At Trail, by contrast, a Canadian research effort supported by Canadian financial backing solved the problem of separating the Sullivan ore by a commercially successful process. The Noranda Mines in Quebec employed Canadians who proved to be extremely effective entre-preneurs. Market access and technical needs were solved in that case by establishing bilateral links with American and British concerns in the joint financing of the Montreal refinery. In short, the reality was much more

CANADIAN METAL MINING   67

diverse, and is more difficult to explain than the easy generalization of the orthodox school would have us believe.

The Left Nationalist view should be seen in the light of the history of COMINCO. Twice at crucial points in the company's development injections of capital were received from the sphere of commerce. As it was owned by Canadian Pacific, COMINCO's connections with Canadian commercial capital were of the best. Yet bank lending was available in these instances for essentially long term purposes: for the launching of the selective flotation technique of separation in 1920, and for the establishment of fertilizer operations from waste sulphur in 1930. In certain circumstances it seems as if Canadian commercial and financial capital could penetrate the production sphere, which raises the possibility that examples might be found in other sectors of the Canadian economy. The Noranda and the Lindsley companies were able to tap a variety of sources of Canadian capital to finance their growth, which also suggests that while no direct assistance was provided the dominance of commercial capital in Canada was not such as to inhibit the flow of indiginous finance for productive industry. Furthermore, Canadian entrepreneurship was in evidence throughout the industry during the entire period. There is little support, therefore, for either orthodox or revisionist interpretations from the experience of base metal mining from 1918 to 1955. The history is one of considerable Canadian achievement combined with U.S. involvement, and suggests that foreign domination of the industry must be explained in terms other than a shortage of Canadian capital or a lack of Canadian entrepreneurship.

University of Stirling

[23]

Excerpt from Theodore H. Moran, *Multinational Corporations and the Politics of Dependence: Copper in Chile*, 119–52.

CHAPTER 5

From Chileanization to Nationalization: Success and Revenge in the Movement away from *Dependencia*

The growth of economic nationalism in Chile began with frustration at the feelings of *dependencia* after the Second World War and reached an initial peak with the sales monopoly of 1952—as a first unsuccessful attempt to end that *dependencia*.

A second phase in the growth of economic nationalism began with the failure of the sales monopoly and ended with the rejection of the *Nuevo Trato* and its philosophy of foreign investment. Disappointment with the results of the *Nuevo Trato* revived the sense of frustration at having large, vitally important foreign corporations in the midst of the affairs of the country, foreign corporations whose internal decisions were crucial to the course of domestic development but whose behavior seemed both mystifying and exploitative.

The third phase in the growth of economic nationalism began with the Christian Democratic program of Chileanization and ended with the nationalization of the large US copper companies. The take-over of Kennecott and Anaconda was initiated—firmly but cautiously—by the Frei regime. The final nationalization of Anaconda and Kennecott and Cerro was finished—audaciously and inefficiently, but irreversibly—under Allende. Domestic control of the copper industry is in all likelihood one of the few achievements of this period whose legitimacy will effectively survive the bloody struggle over Chile's new constitutional order. This chapter will trace the movement from Chileanization to nationalization. Chapter 8 will outline some of the difficulties as well as the achievements of the post-nationalization period.

119

From Chileanization to Nationalization

Eduardo Frei began in 1964 as the candidate of moderation, with a strategy of "progress through negotiation"—
indeed, in a political slogan that would fall leadenly on
North American ears, the Christian Democrats summed up
their approach as *progreso contratado*. Their policy would
be pragmatic rather than dogmatic, cooperative rather than
—in a phrase that would fall leadenly on Chilean ears—
zero-sum.

The Frei Chileanization program achieved substantial
benefits for Chile. Huge new investment funds were
brought to the domestic industry to increase mining, smelting, and refining capacity. Chilean-dictated pricing policy
during the Vietnam War resulted in unprecedented levels
of foreign exchange flowing into the national treasury. The
terms of trade were reversed. The capacity to import was
expanded. In contrast to the *Nuevo Trato*'s failure, this attempt at "progress through negotiation" was, by any but the
most stingy standards, clearly a success.

Yet Frei's own administration ended with the nationalization of Anaconda. And it ended with all three candidates
for the next administration pledging to uphold, if not extend, the policy of nationalization.[1]

Following the election of Dr. Salvador Allende in 1970,
the new marxist President moved swiftly with broad public
support on copper policy. A Chilean Congress dominated
by the non-marxist opposition passed without a single dis-
senting vote a constitutional amendment directing the nationalization of all the large foreign copper companies.
With solemn Chilean declarations about the international
right of exercising national sovereignty and with exuberant
Chilean feelings of expropriating the expropriators, Anaconda, Kennecott, and Cerro were taken over.

[1] Salvador Allende and Radomiro Tomic (the Christian Democratic
candidate) both wanted to expand the policy of nationalization. Alessandri was the only candidate whose position was equivocal. For one
of the clearer statements of his program, see *El Mercurio*, February
7, 1970.

From Chileanization to Nationalization

There were two basic factors underlying the movement from Chileanization to nationalization: (1) increased Chilean confidence in the domestic ability to run the copper industry at the production stage and (evidently) to set copper policy on the international level as well; and (2) a continuing—indeed, accelerated—loss of political support for the US copper companies among domestic groups of the center and right in Chile. Their net effect was a projection of only small costs to set against huge benefits for nationalization of the *Gran Minería*—a projection that was persuasive to a broad spectrum of Chilean opinion.

As a result, in a moment of Chilean confidence and corporate vulnerability, the country moved once and for all to end the condition of *dependencia*.

I

In formulating and carrying through the Chileanization program in the mid-1960's, Eduardo Frei could draw on the expertise of a widening pool of Chilean *técnicos*—lawyers, administrators, and economists—who had experience in running large enterprises and, in some cases, competence in monitoring the behavior of the copper industry itself.

This was in marked contrast to the situation at the time of the first Chilean sales monopoly during the Korean War, or at the time of the writing of the *Nuevo Trato*.

In 1952, as the commercial monopoly directed by the Central Bank began to falter, the Chilean Congress had called on the Comptroller General of the Republic, as an independent auditor, to present a report on the condition of the domestic copper industry.[2] The Comptroller General responded with a sworn statement that except for the foreign management of the companies nobody, including himself, had any idea of what was going on in the industry or had ever had the basis for making a judgment! There was

[2] See the commentary on this report in *Historia de la ley 11.828*, Vól. 1, September 15, 1954, pp. 3734 *et seq.* For earlier comments, see *Panorama Económico*, January 16, 1953.

From Chileanization to Nationalization

no audit of how much the foreign companies were actually producing, shipping, storing, paying in taxes, earning as profits, or receiving as prices.[3] The Ministry of Mines, he asserted, published exactly what figures the companies gave it to publish, and had no others. The Internal Revenue Service, the Office of Ports and Customs, the Commission on Foreign Trade all published figures. All the figures were different. And, he claimed, they could not be reconciled.

The Comptroller General had to admit that his office too would have to go to Anaconda and Kennecott to get the figures to do the study to check the figures of the companies!

If Chile in the early 1950's did not have the facilities set up to monitor, accurately and authoritatively, even what was happening in the domestic industry, it is not surprising that the capacity to analyze international oligopoly strategy was even less finely developed. In the debates surrounding the *Nuevo Trato*, decisions involving hundreds of millions of dollars were made or rejected at the highest levels of the Chilean administration on the basis of information copied from a stockbroker's opinion received by chance in the mail from New York. When Senator Ignacio Palma, for example, tried to persuade his colleagues from the floor of the Senate as to how to reconstruct the nation's mining legislation, he waved in his hand a stock analysis by Loeb, Rhoades & Co. as definitive evidence about the global strategy of Anaconda and Kennecott.[4]

[3] One of the first attempts to improve this situation was the study of mineral taxation commissioned by Felipe Herrera, then Minister of the Treasury, and carried out by Félix Ruiz, *Tributación directa e indirecta a las grandes empresas de cobre* (Santiago: Sección Estadística del Banco Central, August 1953).

[4] *Historia de la ley 11.828*, Vol. 1, September 16, 1954, p. 3970. Ironically, the brokers in question argued that Anaconda and Kennecott felt a priority to use available funds to diversify out of Chile. If the Senate had drawn the proper conclusions from this (as argued in Chapter 4)—and had not relied on the rhetoric of the "automatic incentive" of the "profit motive" that would supposedly pull the

From Chileanization to Nationalization

Certainly even then there were some prominent members of the Chilean Congress—such as Senators Videla Lira, von Mühlenbrock, Duran, Palma, Tomic—who had experience in domestic business and in international negotiations. But their knowledge tended to be impressionistic, and their experience haphazard. As late as 1955 it was clear that able and sophisticated Chileans were trying to make decisions affecting the growth and welfare of their nation on the basis of almost no independent information, with little expertise, and with no institution devoted to the accumulation and verification of what few data were available.

The *Nuevo Trato* law of 1955 took a major step forward in providing an institution to develop Chilean competence in monitoring the copper industry. As a rearguard action in 1954, the more critical opponents of the *Nuevo Trato* succeeded in attaching a provision to the legislation for a Chilean "Copper Department" to watch over the actions of the foreign companies.[5] Once established, the Departamento del Cobre began by collecting statistics on production, prices, taxation, profits, dividends—statistics supplied primarily by the companies or gathered from international trade journals. Gradually, new efforts were made to check and verify, to compare year by year, the figures that were collected. A bureaucracy (of lawyers, engineers, accountants, businessmen, and economists) with some expertise was built up, and it became familiar with analyzing and making sense of the companies' balance sheets and income statements. It had a responsibility to supply information to

---

companies' capital into Chile—Chile would have been saved millions of dollars.

[5] This position was argued most strongly by the Falangistas and Radicals in the debates of 1954–1955, *Historia de la ley 11.828, passim.* See also the well-reasoned statements by Jorge Fontaine in favor of a strong Copper Department, in *Panorama Económico,* May 27, 1955, and August 5, 1955. The editorial position of *Panorama Económico* in favor of extended powers for a Copper Department can be found in the issues of September 24, 1954, and March 4, 1955.

From Chileanization to Nationalization

the Congress and the Executive, and since the Department's "experts" could be used to challenge the figures or the arguments of the companies, Anaconda and Kennecott had an (unenthusiastically greeted) vested interest in keeping the institution informed about what was happening in the industry.[6]

The Copper Department was important in putting pressure on the foreign companies to expand local procurement; it lobbied for more Chilean personnel in responsible positions in the US companies; and it took a capricious interest in sales policy.[7] While Jorge Alessandri was President (1958–1964), the government sided with the companies (against its own Copper Department) in almost all important disputes.[8] The initiatives of the Department tended to be muzzled rather than encouraged, since President Ales-

[6] Unfortunately there is no study of the historical development of the Departamento del Cobre or its successor, the Corporación del Cobre. The material here has been compiled from interviews with members and former members of these two institutions, from the *Annual Reports* of the Kennecott and Anaconda subsidiaries in Chile, from the *Boletín Minero*, and from *Panorama Económico*, as well as from congressional discussions in *Historia de la ley 16.425*, Vols. 1–3, 1964–1966.

There were parallel improvements in data-gathering and in the accumulation of expertise in the Ministry of Mining itself, and in the National Mining Society (Sociedad Nacional de Minería) under Hernán Videla Lira and Francisco Cuevas Mackenna.

[7] Although Braden, for example, fought pressures from the Copper Department to make local purchases in many specific instances, the company adopted a policy of local procurement after the *Nuevo Trato* was passed. Braden reported that local purchases grew from $4 million in 1955 to $20 million in 1969, from 57% of operating expenses in 1959 to 70% in 1968. *Expropriation of the El Teniente Copper Mine by the Chilean Government*, Kennecott Copper Corporation, 1971, p. 6, and *Annual Reports*, Braden Copper Company, 1955–1966.

On sales policy, one on-going dispute arose from the hostility of the Copper Department to long-term sales commitments (for delivery at a price determined by market conditions at the time of delivery). Such corporate practice represented an "entanglement" to the Chileans, similar to being "captive production".

[8] *Annual Reports*, Braden Copper Company, 1958–1964.

From Chileanization to Nationalization

sandri did not believe in government "interference" in private enterprise. But by the time President Eduardo Frei reconstituted the Copper Department as the Corporación del Cobre, he could pull together from within and without the old Department a number of talented and, more importantly, experienced Chilean personnel who felt at home using most of the standard data in the copper industry, analyzing many of the important problems, explaining and interpreting most of the behavior of the mining companies.

Alejandro Hales, who as Minister of Mines directed the nationalization of Anaconda under Frei in 1969, had also been Minister of Mines under President Ibáñez and had helped draw up the legislation creating the Copper Department in 1955. Javier Lagarrigue, who was one of Frei's most skillful negotiators with the companies, had been chief of the commercial section and later a vice-president in the Copper Department.

Clearly, not all of the *técnicos* who contributed to the formation of Frei's copper policy had backgrounds within the Department.[9] Others came from state-run industries or positions in private business. Raúl Sáez, an economist who had been head of the National Electricity Company (ENDENSA) and a member of the Alliance for Progress Committee of Nine, led the negotiations in 1964 with the US companies.[10] One of his principal co-workers, Flavian Levine, had been president of the National Steel Company (CAP).

To be sure, not all of the bright young *técnicos* with skill and experience in analyzing the behavior of the copper industry worked for the Frei government or supported the

[9] According to *Panorama Económico* (March 1969), the campaigns of 1958 and 1964 put large strains on the *técnico puro o objetivo* aspect of many academicians who wanted to give active support to the political positions of various candidates. As a result of the drain of *técnicos* into the Frei administration, *Panorama Económico* was not published from 1964 to 1969.

[10] For Sáez's defense of Chileanization, see Raúl Sáez, *Chile y el cobre* (Santiago: Departamento del Cobre, January 1965).

125

From Chileanization to Nationalization

Chileanization program. Mario Vera Valenzuela, an economist from the Instituto de Economía of the University of
Chile, who had written the most detailed and sophisticated
Chilean critique of the results of the *Nuevo Trato* legislation, was highly critical of Frei's Chileanization legislation.[11] As advisor to the National Copper Workers' Confederation and to leftwing political parties, Vera argued
strongly for nationalization.

The pool of domestic talent and expertise could provide
a basis for sharpening the country's bargaining position
with the companies, and Frei used his advisors to this end.
But more was changing than mere bargaining position. Increased Chilean competence meant that the perception of
the foreign "contribution" was reduced at the same time
that a group interested in taking more control was created.
At a minimum the companies would be expected to put
more and more of their own talents, resources, and expertise at the service of the host country just in order to maintain a position in Chile. To a growing number of talented
Chileans, increased Chilean competence reduced the perception of loss and heightened the perception of gain if the
foreigners were "replaced". The companies could be more
than "pushed against"—they could be pushed out. Nationalization became more than a credible threat. It became a
credible, and appealing, alternative.

At a moment when the companies had just finished a
large lump investment and would not be willing to make
any further commitment for some time, they would be particularly vulnerable. If this coincided with a moment when

[11] Vera's analysis of the *Nuevo Trato* is contained in his *La política
económica del cobre en Chile* (Santiago: Universidad de Chile, 1961).
His critique of Frei's program can be found in frequent articles for
Cobre, the magazine of the National Copperworkers' Union. His proposals for nationalization are most thoroughly stated in *Una política
definitiva para nuestras riquezas básicas* (Santiago: Prensa Latino-
americana, 1964).

Both Socialists and Communists used Vera's work in the debates on
Chileanization, *Historia de la ley 16.425, passim.*

From Chileanization to Nationalization

most domestic groups identified their own interests with the expulsion rather than the preservation of the foreign presence in the industry, the result for the companies would be sharper than a serpent's tooth.

These two moments began to coincide at the end of Frei's administration.

II

Eduardo Frei insisted that the Chileanization program for copper was the main plank (*viga maestra*) of his plan for the nation. Upon achievements in copper policy would depend success in financing agrarian reform, urban welfare, and economic development. During the campaign, Frei revealed that he intended to seek a definite commitment for substantial increases in Chilean production through stiff negotiations with the North American companies—he would fulfill through legal contract what the *Nuevo Trato* had unsuccessfully promised nearly ten years before. He also affirmed that he would seek some sort of Chilean participation in the ownership of the mines, although exactly what form this participation would take was left deliberately vague.[12]

Frei hoped for a supportive response from the companies, rather than confrontation. He was claiming to be the best alternative to the threat of communism and marxism. He had the wholehearted approval of the United States government and the funds of the Alliance for Progress behind him. And he expected that the copper companies would indeed want to contribute to the success of his program and his administration.

Doubtless, the narrow defeat of the marxist Allende in 1964 was an occasion of joy and relief for the North American copper companies. But the bargaining position of the new Christian Democratic administration was not necessarily as strong as the initial enthusiasm for the Frei vic-

[12] For a good comparison of Frei's and Allende's programs, see *Cobre*, July 6, 1964.

From Chileanization to Nationalization

tory seemed to indicate. Chile's twin aspirations for increased copper production and for equity participation
could be played off against each other by the companies in
any tight bargaining situation. It was by no means clear that
the corporate boards of directors for Anaconda and Kennecott (and now Cerro) would easily decide to begin long-
term capital commitments during the regime of a six-year
President who could not succeed himself.

Thus, it was a stroke of good fortune for the newly
elected regime when, even before Frei took office, Kennecott met with his representatives and, to their surprise, told
them Kennecott wanted to sell a majority share of the Chilean subsidiary.[13] In conjunction with the sale of 51% of the
equity, Kennecott proposed a program to expand production at El Teniente by over 50%—from a capacity of about
180,000 tons per year to about 280,000 tons—and to reconstruct the living arrangements for most of the mineworkers.
Kennecott would arrange for the bulk of the financing of
this program itself, and would stay and manage the new
joint venture through the difficult period of expansion and
on for at least ten years.

The details of the Kennecott offer startled (and irritated!) Anaconda.[14] Anaconda itself had been prepared to
put together some kind of conventional expansion program.
But the idea of sharing The Anaconda Company's sov-

[13] The Chileanization of El Teniente was the most spectacular part
of the Frei program when he announced it to the nation on December
21, 1964. Frei's negotiators had actually met first with Cerro and arranged minority participation (25%) for the Chilean government in
the new medium-sized Andina mine. Then the negotiators met with
Anaconda, where they found stiff resistance to any proposals of joint-
ownership. The negotiations with Kennecott came last. Cf. Raymond
F. Mikesell, ed., *Foreign Investment in the Petroleum and Mineral
Industries* (Baltimore: Johns Hopkins Press, 1971), ch. 15.

[14] This account is based on interviews with the most senior Anaconda officials in New York (July 1970). Anaconda was finally persuaded to accept minority ownership by the Chilean government (25%)
in the small, new Exotica mine.

128

From Chileanization to Nationalization

ereignty over internal operations with a government—any government—offended the company's basic philosophy of the separation of business and government. Consequently, the top management resisted from the start any suggestion of offering equity participation in their major operations, especially majority participation, to Chile.

Thus, the Kennecott offer took everybody by surprise. In Washington it was greeted as an act of statesmanship in accord with the spirit of the Alliance for Progress. The Kennecott decision to sell 51% of El Teniente, the world's largest underground mine, set the tone of the Chileanization program and gave the new Chilean administration an immediate image of success.

Why had Kennecott decided to sell?

III

The Braden Copper Company, Kennecott's subsidiary operating El Teniente, had never been an aggressive copper miner in Chile.[15] The company had lived since the 1920's as a *rentier*. The mountain of rich copper ore at El Teniente had seemed inexhaustible, and the company invested just enough out of depreciation each year to keep production running relatively smoothly. Between 1930 and 1965, for example, Kennecott had a net capital disinvestment of −$5 million in Chile, while Anaconda had a net capital investment of +$93 million. Anaconda had undertaken two major expansion programs during that period, including the opening of the new El Salvador mine, while Kennecott had done no more than hold its own. The production capacity

[15] This interpretation is based on interviews with the leading Kennecott officials in New York and Santiago. It is confirmed in two analyses of Kennecott's corporate strategy: John McDonald, "The World of Kennecott", *Fortune*, November 1951; and Rush Loving, Jr., "How Kennecott Got Hooked with Catch-22", *Fortune*, September 1971. It is considerably different from the tone of the company's defense of its behavior in Chile: *Expropriation of the El Teniente Copper Mine by the Chilean Government* (New York: Kennecott Public Relations Department, 1971–1973), 6 sections.

From Chileanization to Nationalization

of El Teniente in 1964 was approximately the same as it had been in 1937.[16] There was little active exploration for new ore-bodies and no indication of a desire by the Kennecott parent that Chilean operations be significantly increased.

Kennecott's attitudes began to change in 1959–1960. In 1955 the company had had no concrete plans for the development of new productive capacity in Chile, nor was it required to develop such plans under the *Nuevo Trato* mining laws. By the late 1950's, however, it was increasingly difficult for El Teniente even to maintain production at existing levels. Water and electricity were in short supply, transportation and haulage were difficult, and workers' housing was getting older and more dilapidated. The company could not keep production up enough to avoid the variable surtax that could push the total rate as high as 75%.

To Kennecott's economic difficulties were added political difficulties generated by the lack of response to the *Nuevo Trato*. The company's management accepted the fact that left-wing political groups had always been ideologically hostile to foreign capitalist domination of the copper industry. Increasingly, Kennecott officials felt, their company was receiving what they called "bad publicity" from right-wing political groups and the business sector in Chile.[17]

Then, in 1959–1960, exploratory drilling indicated that the basic El Teniente ore-body was much larger than previously realized.[18] Kennecott management began to con-

[16] The company defense states that Braden's annual copper productive capacity was 16,000 tons in 1916 and increased to 180,000 tons by 1967 for a 4.9% annual growth rate. This defense ignores the fact that productive capacity was not far below 180,000 by the middle 1930's— a capacity it barely maintained for the following thirty years.

[17] This account is based on interviews with the top Kennecott mining officials in New York and Santiago. Executives in corresponding positions in Anaconda had been privately distressed with the behavior of Kennecott and its failure to respond to the *Nuevo Trato*. They blamed Kennecott for the "bad name" the companies were getting in Chile in the late 1950's.

[18] *Annual Report*, Braden, 1959 and 1960.

From Chileanization to Nationalization

sider the possibility that all of their problems could be solved with one large expansion program—production could be increased substantially, the tax rate could be reduced, and "bad publicity" about the failure of the *Nuevo Trato* could be stilled. This program was called the Codegua Project.

Yet within two years all plans for the Codegua Project were dropped. Why?

Kennecott was unwilling to undertake the large financial commitment necessary for the expansion project without what it considered effective twenty-year guarantees of inviolability. But, with the disintegration of domestic support for the foreign copper companies, the company could not get such guarantees, even during President Alessandri's conservative administration. Kennecott finally concluded that even if guarantees were passed by Congress, they would mean little.

The new element that was responsible for the deterioration in support for the US copper companies was the Alliance for Progress and the resentment it caused among conservative political and business groups.

The Alliance spoke in strong terms about the need for social change in Latin America, and demanded a meaningful land reform before US funds would be dispensed. The next chapter will analyze in detail the behavior of the Chilean right as it reacted to the Alliance for Progress and the threat of land reform. In brief, the response of conservative political and economic groups was to use the companies' failure under the *Nuevo Trato* as a scapegoat for the development problems of Chile—while denying the allegations about domestic maldistribution of income, about local monopolies, about the need for social reform. In fact, as the threat of land reform became more menacing, the strategy of the conservative parties became more Machiavellian. They proposed the nationalization of Anaconda and Kennecott in an effort to hold them as hostages to gain concessions on land reform.

131

From Chileanization to Nationalization

President Alessandri in 1961 was able to patch over the splits in his cabinet, where the Minister of Mines, Enrique Serrano, a Conservative Party member, was leading the attack on the companies. With Alessandri's help, the first right-wing plan to hold the companies as hostage was finally blocked before it got to the Congress; but so was the legislation for Kennecott's large Codegua expansion program.[19] And, in the uproar over the Alliance and the companies, bills were passed that increased taxes on Anaconda and Kennecott by 10%–12%.

If it was previously possible to overlook the relatively mild attack on the US copper companies from the right wing over the "failure" of the *Nuevo Trato*, by now the pattern was clear. Long-term guarantees for operations in Chile—risky even in the best of times—were losing their meaning. Kennecott realized this. Anaconda did not. Shortly after the first outburst against the Alliance and the US copper companies (the Bulnes-Serrano crisis) Kennecott dropped its plans for the Codegua Project and began to entertain the idea of selling 51% of its Chilean operations to the government.[20]

IV

This was the basis for the paradox in the Kennecott decision to enter into partnership with the Chilean government: the joint-venture and expansion program were an effort to build domestic support and to improve the corporation's public image in Chile; they were also an effort to pull back from Chile and defend a deteriorating position through international rather than domestic ties.

[19] *Annual Report*, Braden, 1961.

[20] *Ibid.* This analysis is also based on interviews with leading Kennecott executives in Santiago and New York. They explained the difference in corporate approaches as a function of Anaconda's belief that it could keep manipulating the politics of Chile behind the scenes as it had always done in Montana (and as they supposedly did not).

132

From Chileanization to Nationalization

The Kennecott program was not simple to analyze:[21] the company would sell 51% of its Chilean operations to the Chilean government; it would arrange the financing for about $203 million or 85% of the huge increase in capacity; it would manage the new joint company for ten years or more, and supervise the completion of the expansion project as well as the arrangements for selling the increase in output.

Kennecott asked, in return for this, payment of more than twice book value for 51% of its property and a reassessment of the "worth" of the remaining assets at a multiple substantially higher than that; it wanted an immediate reduction in the tax rate on its share of the returns; it wanted a Chilean commitment for more than half of the capital needed for the expansion, and more for related social overhead expenses; and it wanted a formal twenty-year government guarantee for the entire project.

Yet Kennecott was not in fact bringing one new corporate dollar into Chile or raising a single *escudo* locally in the company name. The parent was counting on the Export-Import Bank of Washington, under some pressure from enthusiastic Alliance officials in the US State Department, to provide $110 million of the $230 million required for the expansion. The rest of its share of the financing would consist of the Chilean payment ($80 million, plus interest) for 51% equity in the new joint venture, which Kennecott would loan back to the new company. The Chilean government would then contribute an additional $27.5 million.

[21] Cf. *Historia de la ley 16.425*, Vols. 1–3, *passim*; Sáez, *Chile y el Cobre*; Kennecott *Annual Reports* and *Letters to Stockholders*; and interviews with Kennecott executives in New York and Santiago.

This is an analysis of the initial proposal for El Teniente. Later, as this chapter points out, an additional $45 million was raised by selling contracts for future output to Japanese and European customers.

Both Chile and Kennecott claimed credit for "contributing" the $80 million that Chile paid for a 51% interest and Kennecott loaned back to the new joint venture.

133

From Chileanization to Nationalization

The value of Kennecott's operations in Chile would increase substantially. From a balance sheet perspective, Kennecott would still be a 49% owner of a company worth about four times as much ($286 million) as it had been ($69 million) before. From a cash-flow perspective, Kennecott would be receiving 49% of the proceeds from an operation exporting almost 64% more output at a tax rate reduced from over 80% to 44%. The Chilean government would guarantee the $110 million loan from the Export-Import Bank of Washington, and the $80 million loan from Kennecott. These arrangements were calculated, negotiated, and approved as being profitable for Kennecott at a copper price of 29¢ per pound (with 1964 mining costs) before copper prices in the 80¢–90¢ per pound range during the Vietnam War turned mining operations into an old-fashioned bonanza.

Kennecott hoped that the sale of majority interest in El Teniente would create public support for the company's continued presence in Chile—or at least reduce public antagonism. But Kennecott was taking no chances with what seemed like clearly deteriorating domestic alliances. The company wanted to protect its position in Chile as far as possible through international alliances of both a governmental and a non-governmental nature.

Kennecott management had never placed enough trust in the ability of the US State Department or the US Congress to provide a rapid and effective response in case of expropriation to have confidence in the Hickenlooper Amendment.[22] Therefore, the company decided it would have to protect its Chilean holdings through means other than merely hoping for direct diplomatic pressure. Kennecott was not sure how secure its position could be made, but the company was determined not to pass away in silence.

To line up supporters who would come to the company's

[22] Based on interviews with Kennecott officials in New York and Santiago.

134

From Chileanization to Nationalization

aid in case of expropriation, Kennecott began by insuring the amount of the sale of equity ($80 million) supplied by Chile but committed to the joint project by Kennecott under a US AID Contract of Guarantee against expropriation (later assumed by the Overseas Private Investment Corporation). Thus, upon entering into the joint venture with Chile, the Kennecott parent had bypassed Congress and the State Department and arranged an immediate US government guarantee to pay an amount in case of expropriation larger than the net worth of its total Chilean operations had been prior to the reassessment of book value. At the same time Kennecott demanded that the sale amount and the Ex-Im Bank loan be unconditionally guaranteed by the Chilean state and made subject to the laws of the State of New York. These arrangements meant that Kennecott would have a general claim against the Chilean state should the Chilean operations be expropriated, and that the Ex-Im Bank, the State Department (AID), and the Congress would feel the effects of any nationalization simultaneously with Kennecott. The Ex-Im Bank would want its loan repaid by Chile as soon as the Kennecott management contract was broken; State (AID) would object to paying off a huge insurance claim; and these agencies plus Kennecott could join in mobilizing support for the Hickenlooper Amendment in Congress. Washington would not be able to ignore harm done to Kennecott's Chilean operations. The goal of Kennecott was to make any threat of nationalization result unavoidably in a face-to-face confrontation between the US and the Chilean governments.

Finally, to assure itself of an international reaction to any threat of nationalization, Kennecott raised the capital to cover a cost-overrun of $45 million for the joint project by writing long-term contracts for the new output with European and Asian customers, and then by selling collection rights on these contracts to a consortium of European banks headed by the Banca Comerciale Italiana ($30 million) and

135

From Chileanization to Nationalization

to a consortium of Japanese institutions headed by Mitsui & Co. ($15 million). This operation—similar to "factoring" in business finance or the selling of accounts receivable at a discount to a financial intermediary—was designed to bring international pressure on any nationalistic administration in Chile not to void the Kennecott management contract and not to repudiate the debt obligations of the El Teniente joint venture. Since repayment of the $45 million to the foreign banks depended upon faithful fulfillment of the long-term sales contracts to the customers, a crisis of confidence in the future of production (brought about by any threat to the Kennecott management contract, if Chile could not take over production dependably itself) would provoke outbursts from financial institutions as well as from customers in Europe and Asia.

"The aim of these arrangements," explained Robert Haldeman, executive vice-president of Kennecott's Chilean operations, "is to insure that nobody expropriates Kennecott without upsetting relations to customers, creditors, and governments on three continents."[23]

V

Anaconda, in contrast, was determined to maintain its corporate sovereignty intact and was prepared to undertake a major new commitment in Chile in its own name.[24] Chilean operations were to be increased by over 200,000 tons per year in new production. To finance this expansion, Anaconda would provide $72.55 million and the Export-Import Bank of Washington would provide $58.7 million. Since Anaconda refused to enter into any major joint association with the Chilean government, the only Chilean capital contribution was $3.75 million in payment for 25% of the equity in a small new mine near Chuquicamata named

[23] Interview, Santiago, May 27, 1970.
[24] Cf. *Historia de la ley 14.625*, Vols. 1–3, *passim*; Sáez, *Chile y el Cobre*; Anaconda *Annual Reports*; and interviews with Anaconda executives in New York and Santiago.

From Chileanization to Nationalization

Exotica. And payment on the Ex-Im Bank loan was guaranteed by Anaconda, not Chile.

In return for these commitments, Anaconda was promised a tax reduction from an effective rate near 62% to about 52% on the returns from this substantially expanded output. Even this concession was not as straightforward as it seemed, however, since some prior benefits in the form of provisions for accelerated depreciation and rebates on refined copper were taken away. The result was that, in marked contrast to Kennecott, most of the advantages would accrue to Anaconda later in the 1970's, and not immediately.

A third company was included in the Chileanization negotiations—the Cerro Corporation—which wanted to open its first Chilean mine high in the mountains at Rio Blanco.[25] Cerro's approach was more similar to Kennecott's than to Anaconda's, and its financing was even more complex. The new Andina subsidiary of Cerro was expected to produce about 230,000 tons of 30% copper concentrate per year beginning in 1971. The original capital cost of the project was estimated at $89 million but later raised to $157 million. Cerro would provide $49.9 million, the Export-Import Bank $56.4 million, a group of Japanese customers (headed by Sumitomo Metal Mining Company) would provide $32.1 million, and Chile would provide $18.6 million. In all, 70% of the company's equity would be owned by Cerro, 30% by Chile. The Chilean government also committed itself to invest in a major electrical power station and supply electricity to the new company at favorable rates. The Chilean government guaranteed $35.4 million of the Ex-Im loan and $10.1 million of the Japanese loan. The tax rates on the profits of the new joint venture would be 15%, plus an additional 30% withholding tax on Cerro's dividends. About 67.5% of the initial output of concentrates would be covered by a 15-year contract to the Japanese smelters.

[25] Cf. *Historia de la ley 14.625*, Vols. 1–3, *passim*; Sáez, *Chile y el Cobre*; and Cerro *Annual Reports*.

137

From Chileanization to Nationalization

Thus, there were clear differences between the approaches of Kennecott and Anaconda, with Cerro standing somewhere in the middle. Kennecott and Cerro were sharing equity ownership with Chile. They seemed to be participating more directly in the program of the Frei administration than Anaconda. They had the image of "Chileanization". Their deals were new and spectacular. They were "partners" with Chile. Yet they were doing everything they could to minimize the actual financial commitment that they were making in Chile, and to protect themselves against the risk of expropriation.

Anaconda, on the other hand, stuck to its traditional methods. The company was in fact providing more of its own resources for the new copper program than either of the other two companies. It was bearing the burden of the new expansion itself, in terms of both cost and risk, especially in the short run. In the longer run, of course, Anaconda would not have to split the benefits of the expansion program in the same measure as those companies that shared equity ownership with the host government.

Most importantly for the Anaconda management, there would be no outside Chilean directors sitting in on the board meetings of Anaconda's subsidiaries, except for the relatively insignificant Exotica. The necessary capital would be raised, as it always had been, through Anaconda's name in New York and guaranteed by the parent company directly. Anaconda would maintain its own sovereignty over internal decision-making intact.

This would be one of the central reasons why Anaconda would come under new Chilean attack even before the Frei administration had left office. The principal fault with the Anaconda strategy—straight equity investment, corporate sovereignty, foreign control—was not that it was more unjust or exploitative than other forms of foreign participation in natural resource development, but rather that it belonged to a system of rights and expectations that was (and is) rapidly disappearing.

138

From Chileanization to Nationalization

VI

In total, President Frei's Chileanization program was calculated to increase aggregate copper production from about 630,000 metric tons per year to nearly 1,090,000 metric tons per year in the course of a six-year period. Compared with the results of previous administrations, this would represent a spectacular achievement. During the twenty years from 1945 to 1964, Chilean production rose only 160,000 metric tons, Frei reminded the nation, while his plan contemplated an increase of 460,000 metric tons in six years.[26]

Chilean experience, Chilean competence, and Chilean confidence were notably increasing at the production level. By the middle of Frei's administration (1966), exports from the small and medium mines (about 124,000 tons) made the country the fifth largest copper exporter in the world—greater than the total of all exports from Peru or the Soviet Union. At the large foreign mines, Chileans were taking over more and more of the mining and smelting and refining operations, including managerial responsibilities. The joint venture with Kennecott at El Teniente, employing 10,000 persons (including construction workers), was the most advanced in this respect. By 1968–1969 there were fewer than ten non-Chileans with responsibility for any

[26] In a fascinating cost-benefit analysis of the Chileanization program, Keith Griffin, *Underdevelopment in Spanish America: An Interpretation* (Cambridge, Mass.: MIT Press, 1969), ch. 4, concludes that nationalization in 1964 would have had more beneficial results for Chile than Frei's program, even if Chile had financed the expansion of the *Gran Minería* out of domestic savings. Because an increasing number of state enterprises were run entirely by Chileans, Griffin assigns a dubious value of zero to the "contribution" of the foreign mining companies in managing the massive construction projects or in introducing Chilean *técnicos* to industry practices. Griffin's analysis does not include the dynamic possibility, stressed here, that the optimal strategy for a nationalist may be to induce foreign companies to put operations successfully on-line and then tighten the terms—with the ultimate aim, perhaps, of taking them over.

139

From Chileanization to Nationalization

activities having to do with mining, smelting, or refining—
all the rest, including supervisory and executive personnel,
were Chilean.[27] The Anaconda mines employed a larger
number of foreigners, but there too the trend was toward
Chilean supervision at all levels of operation.

The country was also building up its own competence in
refining. To the older state works at Paipote, the National
Mining Enterprise (ENAMI) in 1964 added a large new
electrolytic refining plant at Las Ventanas with a capacity
of 84,000 metric tons.[28] Frei began the process of expanding
Las Ventanas to 120,000 metric tons per year of electrolytic
copper, which would make ENAMI one of the largest state-
owned smelting complexes in the world. The quality of
ENAMI output was dependable and its reputation excellent, and both Kennecott and Cerro wrote contracts with
the state enterprise to have portions of their own output
refined there.

Members of Frei's government and technical administrators from the Chilean state bureaucracies participated in
the affairs of the companies to an extent never before permitted. Detailed audits of Kennecott's Chilean operations
were carried out by North American and Chilean companies, the results reviewed by representatives of the Copper Department, and a new appraisal value for El Teniente
set. Chilean representatives went over the details of the
engineering plans for the Kennecott, Cerro, and Anaconda
projects, and Chilean as well as North American companies
were contracted to carry out the construction. Chilean financial representatives were taken into the negotiations to
obtain capital for Kennecott and Cerro from the United

[27] Based on interviews with the top Kennecott executives in Santiago in 1969–1970. Kennecott states that, of 10,000 employees in
1971, only two were American citizens (*Expropriation of the El Teniente Copper Mine by the Chilean Government*, p. 5).
[28] The original government smelter and refinery at Paipote had been
planned by the Corporación de Fomento in the late 1930's but not
completed until after the Second World War. The newer works at Las
Ventanas had been constructed during the Alessandri regime.

From Chileanization to Nationalization

States, Japan, and Western Europe, since the Chilean government was being asked to guarantee the international loans. Representatives from the commercial section of the Corporación del Cobre traveled with executives of the Kennecott Sales Corporation and the Anaconda Sales Corporation to Europe, Japan, and the United States to begin the process of selling contracts for future output.

Chilean participation in the inner workings of negotiations about construction, sales, and finance was a great advance for Chilean experience and Chilean confidence. A great deal of pride was certainly justified. Nevertheless, the huge expansion programs at the Anaconda, Kennecott, and Cerro mines were directed by the North American parent companies, financed through their reputations, and carried out under the supervision of US building and mining contractors. Host country "participation" largely meant watching at first hand the dealings of others more used to taking risks and probably less exposed to the consequences of miscalculation.[29]

[29] For example, in the expansion projects themselves, the feasibility of the engineering designs had already been passed on by the North American parent corporations, and North American construction companies had been charged with developing the detailed specifications before Chilean authorities were invited to review the plans or Chilean companies were given subcontracts for some of the construction. Even so, there was at least one major miscalculation. The Cerro Corporation with its contractors Parsons-Jurden and Morrison-Knudsen (Constructora Emkay, S.A.) made an initial calculation for the Rio Blanco venture at $89 million and in the course of construction had to raise the estimate to $157 million—for a cost over-run of nearly 100%. Cerro was able to persuade the Japanese customers and the North American financiers to go along with the new calculation. There was not even a ripple in Chilean politics. Surely it would be more difficult for a Chilean agency, acting as manager in developing a risky new enterprise, to persuade creditors to go along with or to survive domestic criticism of a 100% cost over-run.

The analysis of the Cerro cost over-runs is based on the *Annual Reports* of the parent. I have also had the opportunity to discuss the over-runs with various North American and Chilean mining engineers in Santiago.

141

From Chileanization to Nationalization

There was nevertheless one important area in which Chile took direct control under Frei—in dictating international price policy. As the Vietnam War escalated from 1964 to 1966, the disparity between the US producers' price and the London Metals Exchange open-market price increased. The Johnson administration had opted not to impose formal price controls on the US economy, but the President jawboned the companies to keep their prices for primary copper from climbing too rapidly. This indirect pressure was backed by sales from the US stockpile, by mandatory set-asides of production for the Defense Department, and finally by export restrictions to prevent domestic copper from flowing to the higher-priced markets in Europe and Japan. Thus, the North American price for copper remained at the beginning of the war near the 35¢–38¢ per pound level, while the LME price soared to the 65¢–90¢ range.

Anaconda and Kennecott kept their price for Chilean copper at the level of the US producers' price, and, at first, the Frei administration was persuaded to go along.[30] But since most Chilean copper was in fact being sold in Europe and Japan to consumers willing to pay a higher price, the Frei administration decided in 1966 to break the pattern of price moderation during periods of peak demand. The Chilean government took over direct control of price policy and by August was pricing Chilean copper directly at the high LME quotation. In June 1967 representatives of the Frei government met at Lusaka with their counterparts from Zambia, Peru, and the Congo, to form the In-

[30] President Lyndon Johnson sent Ambassador Averell Harriman to Santiago in 1966 to negotiate a sale of 100,000 tons to US fabricators at the US producers' price of 36¢ per lb. In return for this, the US government agreed to give Chile a $10 million loan, repayable over 40 years at less than 1% interest, and Anaconda was required to make an additional tax payment on this copper of $3.5 million to the Chilean government. Cf. *Historia de la ley 16.425*, and Thomas O'Hanlon, "The Perilous Prosperity of Anaconda", *Fortune*, May 1966, p. 119.

From Chileanization to Nationalization

tergovernmental Council of Copper Exporting Countries (CIPEC). The LME quotation was adopted as the basis for all of the sales of this group, and plans were advanced for cutbacks in production, when necessary, to keep prices high.

The new Chilean price policy, combined with wartime demand and a long copperworkers' strike in the United States, resulted in enormous increases in copper revenues. From 1966 to 1970, Chilean tax revenues from the large foreign companies averaged $195 million per year in comparison to revenues during the Alessandri administration averaging only $80 million per year. Such spectacular results seemed to prove the wisdom of carrying out what the country had wanted to do all along—ditch the corporate producers' price system and go for all the market could bear.

By 1969 Chile had already increased copper production to 687,000 tons, and copper revenues to $216 million. The expansion programs of all three foreign companies, Kennecott, Anaconda, and Cerro, were well ahead of schedule, and due for completion in 1970 or 1971. Chileans were supervising more and more of their own mining, smelting, and refining. They were "participating" in the arrangement of international finance and marketing. And they were dictating pricing policy, with phenomenal success.

At El Teniente, the Kennecott hierarchy counted on the joint participation to be more a process of education for the Chileans into the management practices of Kennecott than a process of allowing Chilean control to spread over Kennecott. But education into the ways of Kennecott was in fact a means of breaking into those areas of expertise and experience that hitherto had been the monopoly of the foreigner. The potential to imitate Kennecott management could also be viewed as the potential to replace Kennecott management.

Many of those Chileans who watched from the inside the efficiency of North American management, the necessity of maintaining labor productivity, the risk of engineering an

143

From Chileanization to Nationalization

expansion program and bringing new production on-line, the complexities of assuring long-term foreign sales, or the trust and dependability needed to arrange international finance doubtless felt that the foreigners' presence was a valuable asset, at least in the short run. But those Chileans who had a modest view of their own growing competence and those who had an enthusiastic view of the obvious national successes were not always the same people. Members of the Congress and the press who could observe only the phenomenal results of the new Chilean-dictated pricing policy, or the rapid completion of the expansion program, or the maintaining of efficiency as Chileans took over more and more supervisory roles argued that the foreign presence was contributing less and less while the benefits from replacing the foreigner in the copper industry were growing more and more.[31]

This might be the rare historical moment, many argued, when, through an act of national will, the country could end its condition of *dependencia* forever.

VII

The 1969 attack on Anaconda began from within the Christian Democratic Party. In April, Congressional Dep-

---

[31] A representative popular view on Chilean capabilities can be found in *Clarín*, March 25, 1970, in an editorial by "Castor" entitled "Tenemos que nacionalizar el cobre".

Panorama Económico, however, was more cautious in appraising likely Chilean administrative behavior after the foreign copper companies were nationalized. The editors were afraid that the industry would be run "politically" rather than "purely commercially" (No. 246, July 1969).

Contributing to the general mood of domestic optimism, however, Chileans could point at the same time to the competence of other state-run enterprises outside of the mining area. Senator Rafael Tarud, for example, cited the State Development Agency (CORFO), the State Electricity Administration (ENDENSA), the State Steel Enterprise (CAP), the State Telephone and Telegraph Agency (ENTEL), the State Petroleum Company (ENAP), and the State Airlines (LANCHILE) as examples of excellent national administration, run by Chilean workers and managed by Chilean *técnicos*.

144

From Chileanization to Nationalization

uty Narciso Irureta denounced mining claims that Anaconda had filed for 80,000 hectares (or an area significantly larger than the state of Delaware) in the northern Chilean desert.

This incident sparked a general "re-evaluation" of the country's relations with the companies. The demands and the scope of such a re-evaluation quickly spread. Other members of the Christian Democratic Party, besides Irureta, delighted by the success of the Chilean-imposed pricing policy, wanted to use this uproar to impose a surtax on copper profits in order to capture more of the benefits for Chile. The switch to the LME price peg, combined with the tax cuts provided in the Chileanization agreements, meant that a large stream of the earnings generated by the Chilean maneuver were flowing as profits to Anaconda and Kennecott. In 1968 alone, for example, Kennecott had received after-tax profits from its 49% interest in El Teniente equal to almost 40% of the (old) book value of all the company's investments in Chile.

What about the twenty-year guarantees of "inviolability" that the Chilean Congress had given to the companies? *Rebus* were no longer *stantibus*, argued the Chilean lawyers—conditions (at least of bargaining power) had changed. Since the original agreements had been calculated on the basis of 29¢ (per pound) copper and since Chilean policy was responsible for the shift to a price near 90¢, Frei argued that his administration was not "violating" the twenty-year guarantees by imposing a surtax. What choice did the companies have? They had sunk their investment. Output was expanding even more rapidly than expected. The program was a success for everybody, but Chilean public opinion insisted that the fruits should be enjoyed more fully by the host country.

Neither Anaconda nor Kennecott protested too strenuously, as a matter of fact, against the reasoning of the Frei administration on the surtax.[32] For years prior to the invest-

---

[32] Against Congressman Narciso Irureta, Anaconda defended its new claim on between two and three thousand square miles in northern

145

From Chileanization to Nationalization

ment Kennecott had attached transcendent importance to the twenty-year government guarantee. But now that the investment was largely sunk and the operations were a roaring success, Kennecott and Anaconda rapidly consented to pay the surtax.

But in this round of "readjustment" the foreign copper companies were once again dominating the headlines. Conservative and Liberal Party leaders, in the midst of a bitterly contested Agrarian Reform, were under heavy constituent pressure not to support the US investors. Some groups within the Christian Democratic Party were joining the Communists and the Socialists and the Radicals in declaring that now was the time for nationalization. Chilean production was up, the Chilean share of the world market was up, copper prices were high, and Chileans could run the mines on their own!

When Frei demanded that negotiations be reopened with Anaconda, he actually pressed only for Chileanization, or 51% Chilean control with compensation, similar to the arrangement with Kennecott. But Anaconda did not want to make a new bargain after it had just completed a large corporate commitment. It refused to submit to Chileanization. It was afraid that this process of pushing and giving would just go on until it was expropriated. So it asked to be nationalized with compensation. The agreements were announced on June 26, 1969.

Frei called the nationalization of Anaconda Chile's Second Independence. Alejandro Hales, the Minister of Mines who had worked out the arrangements for nationalization, wept in public, saying that he had fulfilled a lifelong dream.

Chile with equanimity in public, but admitted in private that the move had been a "mistake in public relations".

Anaconda argued that the company had laid claim to the vast salt flats in the north to try to organize a joint chemical venture with Dow Chemical. Chileans suspected, however, that the claims were staked out to prevent other miners from moving into the area.

From Chileanization to Nationalization

Workers were found who gave up their salaries and peasants their produce to help pay the compensation for Anaconda.[33]

But it was clear that the Final Battle was yet to be won.

VIII

Shortly after taking office in 1970, the new marxist President, Dr. Salvador Allende, introduced the long-awaited bill for complete nationalization as a final solution to the problem of *dependencia*. It provided for an immediate take-over of all the Chilean subsidiaries of Anaconda, Kennecott, and Cerro with compensation to be paid over a thirty-year period—compensation that was more than off-set for the first two companies by a deduction for the "excessive profits" that had been earned since the beginning of the *Nuevo Trato* in 1955.

The nationalization legislation was passed unanimously as a Constitutional Amendment by the Congress on July 16, 1971.

As for Kennecott's strategy of self-protection, pressures on the Allende government to assume the international obligations of the El Teniente joint venture did come from all the directions that the company had mapped out in advance.[34] The customers who had bought long-term con-

[33] Cf. *Tercera de la Hora*, July 1, 1969. The self-conscious attempt to show grass-roots sacrifice for the nationalization of Anaconda, reminiscent of the nationalization of US petroleum companies by Cárdenas in Mexico, was not very successful.

[34] Cf. "Chile's Threatened US Property Seizure May Drain Federal Insurance Unit's Funds," *New York Times*, February 2, 1971; "Chile's Move Spurs US to 'Get Tough' ", *ibid.*, September 30, 1971; "Chile Assailed by Rogers for Compensation Stand," *ibid.*, October 14, 1971; "Six Concerns Embroiled in Seizures Are Called in by Rogers," *Wall Street Journal*, October 25, 1971; "US Tells Chile Seizures Could Endanger Aid to Needy Nations," *New York Times*, October 16, 1971; "Chile to Nationalize Foreign-Owned Firms Legally, Allende Says", *Wall Street Journal*, October 30, 1971; "Chile, Reserves Low,

From Chileanization to Nationalization

tracts for Chilean copper in Europe and Japan and the
international financial institutions that had lent money to El
Teniente on the basis of those contracts were putting pressure, through their governments, on the Group of Ten in
Paris to make assumption of the old obligations a condition
for refunding the Chilean debt. The US government, under
pressure from Anaconda and Kennecott and from Congressional supporters of the Ex-Im Bank and the Overseas Private Investment Corporation (which had taken over the
AID foreign investment insurance program), was pushing
to make immediate compensation a requirement for rolling
over the Chilean debt. Kennecott, on its own, was using the
unconditional guarantees that the Chilean government had
given for the original sale amount to obtain writs of attachment in the US Federal Courts against all Chilean property
in the State of New York, including the jets of LANCHILE
when they landed.

In response to this accumulation of pressures, President
Allende announced in October 1971 that his government
would directly assume the international obligations of the
nationalized El Teniente company. It would honor the long-
term sales contracts with customers in Europe and Japan.
And it would take over the debts that the nationalized company had contracted with the Ex-Im Bank of Washington,
with the Banca Comerciale Italiana, and with Mitsui &
Co. Payment to the latter two creditors would clearly depend upon faithful fulfillment of the original long-term production contracts with customers in Europe and Asia. But
the Allende government simply ignored the Kennecott management provision contained in the contracts, and pledged
to supply the output itself.

Finally, four months later, in February 1972, Dr. Allende

Will Seek Renegotiation of Payments on Her $3-Billion Foreign
Debt," *New York Times*, November 10, 1971.

    I have also benefitted from interviews with representatives of the
US copper companies and of the Chilean government.

From Chileanization to Nationalization

went all the way and announced that his government would pay compensation to Kennecott equal to the sale amount that had been unconditionally guaranteed by the Chilean state. Despite the pledge of the Socialists of "Ni un centavo!" in compensation, Kennecott was to receive $80 million plus interest from the Allende administration.[35]

Thus, the Allende government successfully unraveled most of the transnational web spun by Kennecott.[36]

With payment pledged to cover the Chilean state guarantee to Kennecott, the company was obliged to drop the writs of attachment levied against Chilean property in New York. This pledge of payment to Kennecott also removed the threat of bankrupting the new Overseas Private Investment Corporation with a huge claim. With OPIC safe and

[35] "Chile Says She Will Pay $84 Million to Kennecott," *New York Times*, February 26, 1972. After several payments, the Allende government before its overthrow in 1973 again suspended payments.

For a commentary on the legal position of the Allende administration, see Eduardo Novoa Monreal, *La batalla por el cobre* (Santiago: Quimantu, 1972).

[36] Kennecott claimed that, in addition to the $80 million in debt, it had an uncompensated equity holding in El Teniente valued at approximately $178 million. ("Memorandum Governing International Law Principles" by Covington & Burling, *Expropriation of El Teniente*, New York: Kennecott Public Relations Department, 1971.) On this basis it sued in various European countries to block payments for Chilean copper from final customers. The Chilean tribunal had ruled that Kennecott was entitled to compensation for the book value of its equity interest, but that reductions for excess profits and deficiencies more than offset any compensation.

To side with Kennecott's suit for the commercial value of its equity in a nationalized mine, courts in France or Germany or Italy would have had to overrule the Chilean determination of excess profits, overrule the claim of deficiencies in installations, and (perhaps) overrule the claim in Spanish law that private corporations do not gain possession of unmined reserves through a concession agreement that grants only rights of exploitation.

A more important impact of the threat of legal action against customers is the pressure it puts on consumers to choose that country only as supplier of last resort. For more on this matter, see Chapter 7.

149

From Chileanization to Nationalization

the Ex-Im Bank being repaid by Chile, Congressional interest dissipated.

Kennecott's strategy had, however, enabled the company to expand very profitably in the late 1960's with no new risk to itself and leave, after the nationalization in 1971, with compensation greater than the net worth of its holdings had been in 1964—despite the occurrence of the worst eventuality the company had envisioned.[37] From 1964 to 1970 Kennecott had received approximately $115 million in profits from Chile on an investment with an initial net worth of $69 million, and had left with what appeared to be at least $93 million in compensation ($80 million plus interest).

Anaconda, in contrast, which had not spread its risk or protected itself through a strategy of building transnational alliances, lost its old holdings, lost the new capital it had committed during the Frei regime, and was nationalized in 1971 without any hope of compensation. The company had applied for partial coverage on its new investments during the Frei period through a stand-by arrangement with AID. But after Anaconda was finally pressured into selling 51% of its Chilean operations to the Frei government in 1969, this insurance was apparently allowed to lapse.[38] The notes in payment for the sale of the majority interest in 1969 were not made unconditional obligations of the Chilean state but guaranteed only by the Corporación de Fomento (Corfo) and the Corporación del Cobre (Codelco), two subagencies of the Chilean government.

Despite Anaconda's huge losses, the Hickenlooper Amendment was not applied. That unhappy company, with writs of attachment that could only harass the activities of

[37] On the spread of transnational strategies similar to Kennecott's through the natural resource field, see my article, "Transnational Strategies of Protection and Defense by Multinational Corporations: Spreading the Risk and Raising the Cost for Nationalization in Natural Resources," *International Organization*, Vol. 27, No. 2 (Spring 1973).

[38] Overseas Private Investment Corporation, *Annual Report*, 1971, p. 34; and "U.S. Foreign-Investment Insurer Seeks Profit Rise, Takes Tough Line on Anaconda", *New York Times*, December 6, 1971.

From Chileanization to Nationalization

Corfo and Codelco, with a disputed claim to any US government insurance, and with long-term contracts and debts made in its own name, had few options for mobilizing either national or international support. Payments for the nationalized properties of Anaconda were cut off under Allende and the company received no promise of compensation. The only reasonable course for Anaconda's board of directors—which it took—was to fire the entire top management and hire a new set of executive officers who could do their best to forget about Chile.

With regard to Cerro, Chile negotiated an amicable arrangement to buy the Andina subsidiary at approximately book value and Cerro helped the state finish bringing the mine successfully on-line.

Once Chile had assumed the contracts and debts owned in Europe and Asia, the private and public creditors in those regions faced a choice similar to that of accepting the shaky promise of an on-going concern or of trying to preside over a bankruptcy. The European and Asian customers whose long-term contracts for Chilean copper had been sold to raise capital for Chile were given a pledge of preferential delivery. The financial institutions in Italy and Japan that had bought those contracts and supplied the Chilean joint venture with investment capital were pledged payment. The Allende offer of settlement made the hope of stable production in a stable Chile the least risky alternative for the Europeans and Asians. The Nixon administration did continue to fight in Paris for the principle of full payment for expropriations as a condition of refunding the Chilean debt, but the Group of Ten refused to go along.[39] Chile's

[39] Cf. "Debt-ridden Chile Is Reported to Get Soviet Offer of $50-million in Credits", *New York Times*, January 16, 1972; "Nixon Announces a Tough US Stand on Expropriation", *ibid.*, January 20, 1972; "Chile, $3-Billion in Debt, Asks Creditors to Accept a Moratorium on Payments", *ibid.*, January 20, 1972; "Plea by Chile to Delay Debt Payment Is Slated for Discussion in Paris", *Wall Street Journal* January 26, 1972; "Allende Confers with Foreign Officials on Debts",

From Chileanization to Nationalization

major public creditors were not anxious to see that country's dwindling foreign exchange reserves flow with priority to Anaconda and Kennecott. The United States had to acquiesce in a credit agreement that did not mention the principle of full compensation for expropriated properties.

The country had at last, irreversibly, taken complete control of its domestic copper industry.

There would be no more "inherent conflict" between the powerful foreign corporations acting according to their own "narrow" corporate strategies and the Chilean government wanting to act according to the "broader" dictates of national development.

Within the horizon of its perception of foreign investor–host country conflict, Chile had at last pulled itself out of a condition that had plagued the nation for more than a century.

Dependencia would be replaced by *independencia*.

New York Times, April 15, 1972; "US Joins in Credit Accord with Chile", *ibid.*, April 21, 1972.

The Nixon Administration, however, continued to oppose loans for Chile from the World Bank, the Inter-American Development Bank, and the Export-Import Bank. See James Petras and Robert LaPorte, "Can We Do Business with Radical Nationalists?—Chile: No", *Foreign Policy*, No. 7 (Summer 1972); and *idem*, "An Exchange on Chile," *Foreign Policy*, No. 8 (Fall 1972).

Chile successfully negotiated a rescheduling of 1971–1972 maturities with the Group of Ten in Paris, but went into default again in 1973. Immediately after the coup, the Group allowed the junta a moratorium until 1974. "Chilean Debt Talks Put Off by Creditors," *Washington Post*, October 3, 1973.

[24]

CHAPTER VI

Towards Joint Venture 1949–54

By early 1949, one year after the establishment of the Union of Burma, its government was beginning to come to terms with the reality of administering an independent country. During the honeymoon period in the first half of 1948 it had introduced a plethora of nationalisation and social measures; one measure involved taking the Irrawaddy Flotilla Company into state ownership. Since Burma was rich in agricultural, mineral and other products, the new rulers were convinced that once the country received the full financial returns from that wealth, instead of seeing them 'drained away' to Britain, India or elsewhere, Burma could be prosperous as never before.

On the other hand, the relatively conciliatory attitude of the new regime towards the oil industry was mentioned in Chapter V. The Burmah Oil directors in London had spoken candidly to the Burmese authorities about the special needs and difficulties of oil operations there. As a consequence, U Nu had agreed to think about taking the less radical path of a joint venture. However, when the company asked him what share the government of Burma would wish to acquire, he was unable to give a precise reply. His country's Treasury was desperately short of funds, and a stake in oil was only one of the many contemplated projects that would inevitably require heavy outlays.

Harper in London knew very well, both from his own people in Rangoon and from the Foreign Office, of the dilemma facing U Nu. The Union of Burma's constitution laid down that no

171

official licences could be granted to any organisation in which the state did not have an interest of at least 60 per cent, while the Burmah Oil directors saw no benefit for anyone in the government's joint-venture share being smaller than one-third. They had calculated the value of the oil properties in Burma as follows:

Value of undestroyed physical assets	£7.0 million
Expenditure on reconstruction, 1945 to end 1948	£6.5 million
Estimated cost of reconstruction still to be undertaken	£10.5 million
	£24.0 million

One third came to £8 million, to which would be added a £1 million share of extra working capital. That totalled £9 million, which the directors would expect the government of Burma to take up. Yet Burma had a budget deficit equivalent to £6 million in 1948/49 and the total central government revenue forecast for 1949/50 was only about £32.5 million.

The government's plan was to borrow the funds from Britain, and at the turn of the year it therefore sent a request to London for a substantial loan, partly for the joint venture and partly to help with balancing the budget. As soon as the loan was granted, it intended to make a payment of £1 million to Burmah Oil as an earnest of its serious intentions, and then pay off to the company the remainder in monthly instalments of £250,000 to £300,000. Harper, during his first trip to the East as chairman, was in Rangoon during January 1949; after some tough bargaining, the government of Burma accepted, subject to certain modifications, some draft heads of agreement on the joint venture. It would in the first instance buy a one-third share.

Later that month, the British cabinet's Economic Policy Committee, headed by Attlee as prime minister, considered the loan application from Rangoon. However, the committee decided that Burma still came well down the priority list of those countries in need of help, and that it could make no firm decision about a loan for the time being. Astonishingly enough, the Burmese government was not told officially until the following December that the loan application would, at best, be seriously delayed. Also in January 1949, Weva passed on some

Towards Joint Venture 1949–54 173

startling news to officials in the Ministry of Fuel and Power.

The company had perforce concluded that Burma's economic future looked too uncertain to justify further capital investment at that stage. Yet the consequences of halting oil rehabilitation could clearly be grave for both the company and the Burmese economy. Burmah Oil would, for instance, incur a £1 million penalty if it did not accept delivery by August of some refining plant on which it held an option. Moreover, the company would have to discharge up to 6,000 employees; that could only lead to serious unrest among the increasingly assertive labour unions, as well as the work-force generally, and sour Burmah Oil's relations with the government in Rangoon.

The directors therefore laid down a deadline of 9 March 1949 for a suspension of investment and the shedding of labour. Officials in Whitehall reacted with speed, inducing them to postpone their programme of sackings for a further month after the date, and hinting that ministers would use the time to consider what could be done in the longer term. On 9 February, the British government agreed to guarantee the company financially against future losses in Burma: that is, to meet the additional expense that could be shown to be directly attributable to its request for postponement. The reason for the guarantee, given confidentially by the Foreign Office, was that Britain's official policy towards South-East Asia was to arrest the spread of communism in the region. The linch-pin in that strategy was a prosperous and truly independent Burma.

To be sure, the world had moved on inexorably since the halcyon pre-1942 era when R. I. Watson had foretold to Roper that a self-governing Burma would be compelled, but at the same time would welcome the opportunity, to maintain very close defence and diplomatic links with Britain, within the cosy protection of the Commonwealth. Now Burma ran its own affairs independently: U Nu often used the simile of his country being 'hemmed in like a tender gourd among the cactus',[2] surrounded as it was by more powerful nations than itself, notably China with its new communist regime. Britain therefore felt an obligation to play a part, however reduced in the austere post-war circumstances, in assisting Burma. An additional factor was Burma's strategic proximity to several Commonwealth countries, one of which – namely Malaya –

was engaged in a long drawn-out battle with its own communist guerrillas. Moreover, Burma was of economic importance in the area, as a significant rice producer and exporter, while the close historical ties and on the whole amicable independence negotiations had ensured a valuable residue of goodwill towards Britain.

Hence the case for assisting Burmah Oil by loans and subsidies was a largely political one, as the Foreign Office admitted in a further briefing to other Whitehall departments. Any move to terminate the guarantee to the company, it declared, would gravely diminish the chances of restoring Burma to the peace and stability that were clearly essential if the loan, requested by the Rangoon government, were to be granted. That declaration did not deter the civil servants in the British Ministry of Fuel and Power from keeping up a barrage of criticism within Whitehall that the guarantee to Burmah Oil was 'totally unjustified' on economic grounds.

This subsidy can nowadays be recognised as an imaginative step to head off a particularly dangerous crisis, and as providing some tangible help at a time when disorder in Burma was spreading across much of the country. Most alarmingly of all, a number of regular battalions had mutinied, to be followed by the Karen regiments which had traditionally been the backbone of the Burmese army. The mutinous Karens were soon besieging Rangoon itself, and the government there survived only by the loyalty of the Chin and Kachin troops, hill warriors from northern Burma, who stood firm until the government could raise and train fresh troops.

Life among the British in Rangoon called forth the usual national phlegm. At Syriam, the strong Scottish influence among the engineers and chemists kept the atmosphere relaxed. Even though the insurgents were only a few miles away, the golfers among them insisted on rushing out on finishing work at 5 p.m., and taking advantage of the brief period of remaining daylight to play as many holes as possible. In Rangoon itself, initial apprehensions were eased when it became clear that the advance of the insurgents was being held, near as the lines of defence were to the capital, and that the sporadic outbreaks of shooting produced few casualties. Perhaps the nearest shave was when a concentrated burst of

Towards Joint Venture 1949–54   175

firing – apparently started by someone accidentally letting off a revolver – led to a spent bullet being fished out of a saucepan of soup in a kitchen at the managers' residences of Britannic Court. The Indian cook was shaken but not stirred. 'Hand not very steady, Sahib', he declared, 'but heart very strong.'

The British tried to keep their lives as normal as possible, some helping to cope with British, American and Indian refugees from Upper Burma who swarmed into Rangoon and for whom camps or individual accommodation had to be arranged. For those going out at night, road-blocks were a common inconvenience, and visits to the club or to friends had to be curtailed so as to be home before the nightly curfew. Some enterprising Burmese even cashed in on the siege by organising bus tours to the defence line. There the tourists could pay two annas to shoot off a rifle at the besiegers; a short burst of automatic fire was rather more expensive.

The government of Burma's financial troubles mounted as the disorder spread. In April Harper pleaded with Treasury officials in London to give the government of Burma a clear 'yes' or 'no' to its request for the loan it so sorely needed, but Whitehall had as yet no answer to make. In fact, it was very energetically seeking to persuade neighbouring Commonwealth countries to join in a programme of financial aid to Burma; by December India, Pakistan and Malaya had promised help and Australia came in during January 1950. The joint aid would comprise a loan to assist with both the budget deficit and expansion of the rice crop. A proposal to lend £6 million was put to and accepted by Rangoon in the early months of 1950. Yet all that Whitehall could do in May 1949 was to hold the line by agreeing to extend indefinitely the guarantee given to Burmah Oil.

Almost incredibly, Attlee's government kept that guarantee a close secret. The Burmah Oil directors were in the circumstances bound to silence, only letting the general manager in Rangoon know personally in the strictest confidence; the Foreign Office likewise notified the British ambassador in Rangoon in conditions of secrecy. Not until August 1949 was the government of Burma, which after all was supposed to be the ultimate beneficiary, informed unofficially; even then no details of the precise arrangements were given. Instead of appearing justifiably indignant, Burmese ministers took the news very well. At Westminster, the House of Commons was not told until almost the end of the financial year in March 1950, when a supplementary budget estimate for the cost had to be put forward: so well could secrets be kept in days when investigative journalists were virtually unknown and state papers were leaked for crates of whisky rather than to score political or ideological points. The far from convincing official reasons given for the secrecy were that premature disclosure would have encouraged unhealthy rumours in both London and Rangoon about Whitehall's future policy towards the Burmese oil industry, and might have helped to scupper Burma's own efforts to reimpose law and order.

The company's British employees at the main oilfields of Chauk and Yenangyaung were about to find themselves at the centre of perhaps the second most traumatic period in the company's entire history to date, eclipsed only by the denial episode of 1942.[3] This second period was to be one of high drama, as well as of constant anxiety, for the diminishing band of expatriate Burmah Oil men, who felt it their duty to remain at almost any cost. They realised only too well that if the last vestige of the British presence had for any reason to be withdrawn from the oilfields as a whole, very serious consequences could well follow for the company. For them physical conditions in the fields were uncomfortable, and at times they even went in fear of their lives.

Late in February 1949 instructions arrived from Rangoon to evacuate wives and children; although for some it was a repetition of what had happened in 1942, the families accepted the inevitable and were taken to Rangoon by RAF flying boat. A few hours later there arrived units of the People's Volunteer Organisation, a guerrilla band pledged to the overthrow of the regime. The first real sign of danger for the company men came when the rebels demanded for themselves the equivalent of £14,000, which was the sum paid monthly to the government in Rangoon for oil royalties and excise duty. The company's aircraft and radio station were surrounded, and only one radio message was permitted to Rangoon; not surprisingly, that was a request to pay out that sum. The general manager, after consulting Burmese ministers, agreed: needless to say, the

Towards Joint Venture *1949–54* 177

money had later to be paid all over again to the government of Burma.

The way in which Burmah Oil's managerial staff coped with the insurgents' general behaviour says much about the British character. Ill-trained in the use of arms, these rebels were fairly harmless as long as safety-catches were kept on rifles, and pins in grenades; but fear or anger might well have driven them to some foolhardy actions. The oilfields manager at Chauk, Cecil Maxwell-Lefroy, decided that one way of building up some rapport with them was to instruct them in arms drill, learnt many years before in the Officers' Training Corps at his public school. This drill both helped to gratify the Burmese love of display and to keep the troops occupied.

Thus the British knack of submitting with good nature and even with a degree of humour to the tiresome consequences of *force majeure* clearly warded off much potential trouble. Burmah Oil's general managers in the Indian subcontinent sometimes found relaxed responses similarly useful in times of crisis. The general manager at Karachi at about this time had to refuse some request or other by the local trade union, and in consequence had his effigy burnt. To make sure that he did not miss the fun, the secretary of the union burst into his office and exclaimed, 'Sir, sir, we are burning you on the maidan [the open space in front of the office].' 'So what?' the general manager enquired, without displaying interest. 'But it is so very much like you,' came the excited response. 'You should come and see.' Taking a discreet peep from the side of the window, the general manager agreed it was a good likeness, although privately convinced that any resemblance with the scarecrow-figure being consumed by fire could only be in the eye of the beholder. As he wrote later, 'There was no violence in the occasion – it was a kind of catharsis for frustration, in the main healthy.' At least two other among the company's general managers in the East are known to have been 'victims' of effigy burning about this time.

Negotiations between the Rangoon government and the company over joint venture proceeded intermittently. For the company, Lingeman was the negotiator on the spot until he retired in June 1949; Rupert Carey, son of a former eminent

Burma civil servant, then took over as general manager. Law and order, so far from improving as the year wore on, markedly worsened; however, the company strove to keep up, as best it could, work in the oilfields and the refinery. A programme of clearing wells was undertaken, and the refinery site was prepared for eventual reconstruction.

Yet this was merely a continuation of the unreal world that had existed since 1942. With the oilfields cut off by land from Rangoon, only limited quantities of products could be turned out, to feed the very local market still open to the company. As long as the pipeline was out of action and much of the territory through which it ran remained in insurgents' hands, a new refinery at Syriam was inconceivable. Instead Burmah Oil had to import most of its product requirements. Of the 500,000 barrels of petrol and 250,000 barrels of kerosene consumed in Burma during 1948, the bulk had come by sea from Abadan.

The Burmese operatives themselves knew that much of what they did was no better than invented work. The company was no longer allowed to use the pre-war sanctions of sacking malefactors or of banning them from the vicinity of refinery or fields; hence indiscipline, gambling and theft were widespread. Oil was regularly stolen, and the Burmese found angle-irons and braces of the old electric pylons that ran from Yenangyaung to Chauk very useful for constructing bedsteads, frames for bullock cart-wheels and the long knives called *dahs*. Even where the rehabilitation equipment itself could be protected from pilfering, it was becoming short in supply. By May 1949 stocks of fields and refinery equipment were very low. About the only bright spot in this darkening scene was that the problem of unwanted plant ordered for the refinery, with its £1 million penalty clause, was overcome when it was offered, with the government of Burma's consent, to Anglo-Iranian. That company was only too happy to purchase such equipment, which was still scarce all over the world.

Since the joint-venture negotiations were turning out to be so protracted, Harper was anxious that Burmese ministers should detect no sign of weakness on the part of Burmah Oil's directors. After months of parleying, in July he wrote to Carey, 'We are proceeding only by faith – and because it is at others' expense – that one day Burma will once again come to its

Towards Joint Venture 1949–54 179

senses, but it would be as well [if ministers were] not to try our faith too highly.' Should the government of Burma be unwilling to accept reasonable financial terms, he continued, the company must not be expected to reduce its offer below what it had already decided as the irreducible minimum. In such a case, he would reluctantly conclude that ministers in Rangoon were not suitable partners to take into the oil business.

In mid-1949, the company decided to withdraw its six British employees from Yenangyaung. Although that town had fallen into rebel hands the previous February, about the same time as Chauk, the employees had stayed put and had succeeded in persuading the rebels not to harm the fields in any way. In return, however, company managers were forced, with Burmese government approval, to sell their production to the rebels, who also demanded and received protection money in the form of royalty payments. The local trade union leaders took advantage of the rebel occupation to make the workers down tools and then get some discharged men reinstated, with their lost pay made up. It was the third time in eight months that they had wrung concessions out of the company, and the lucrative gains that could be won from direct action were not lost on them.

Although government troops recaptured Yenangyaung in June, the rebels twice unsuccessfully launched a counter-attack. The second time, on 6 July, no fewer than 150 were killed and their bodies laid out on the company's sports ground; the local inhabitants were reported to have flocked out eagerly to gape at and count the corpses. The fighting had been so close to the company office that some shots had actually hit the building, but had fortunately not injured the staff inside. As the rebels still occupied the surrounding countryside, however, they could well renew their attacks on the oilfields at any time.

Carey, alarmed for the safety of the British employees there, at this time sought U Nu's advice on whether or not they should be pulled out. U Nu, realising the serious implications of any British citizens becoming casualties, echoed his concern and advised him to contact the Burmese War Office in Rangoon. It happened that Weva had just dropped in, on one of his regular visits as the company's managing director. He at once flew up to the fields with Carey, under military protection. As fighting seemed very likely to flare up again at or near the Yenangyaung office, he gave instructions for the British staff there to be evacuated, and for 2,000 non-European employees to be discharged, leaving just under 200 to maintain essential services.

On returning to Rangoon, Weva found that U Nu was not available and therefore could not be told of this decision; instead he saw the Foreign Minister, who seems to have failed to grasp the implications of the withdrawal, notably that production at Yenangyaung would be completely halted. Weva also asked the government of Burma not to use the shut-down as a pretext to cancel Burmah Oil's concession there. Although that government later pressed hard for a resumption of the Yenangyaung operations, the company refused as long as the threat from the rebels persisted.

This evacuation episode, which was later the subject of a thorough investigation by an *Ad Hoc* Oilfields Enquiry Committee which the Burmese authorities set up in the autumn,[4] provides a classic case-study of the conflicts between a multinational enterprise and its host government. Each party had its separate objectives and preoccupations. Burmah Oil was concerned about the expense of keeping labour idle, perhaps for years ahead, and about risking the safety of its British employees. The restoration of order was entirely a political matter and therefore outside its competence altogether. The Burmese government, on the other hand, was after the maximum production of oil, since imports were costing very scarce foreign exchange, and it also wanted maximum employment levels, which it regarded as the key to the restoration of order. The more people were actually in real work, the fewer would be roaming about in a volatile state of discontent. By the dismissals it had made, however necessary in the circumstance, the company was undoubtedly building up potential trouble for itself with its hosts in Burma.

While on the same Burmese trip in July 1949, Weva seems to have broached to the Rangoon government the possibility of modifying the joint venture proposal. The company, he suggested, would value its assets in Burma at £15 million,

Towards Joint Venture 1949–54 181

considerably below the £24 million, but only the amount spent to date, then standing at £8 million, would be included in the aggregate sum. This revised figure had almost certainly not been agreed in advance with the board in London. Weva later claimed that it had come into his head during a conversation with U Nu; it had the advantage of being easily divisible into three. The government's one-third share would thus be around £5 million.

Yet it was a fairly realistic figure, assuming that the government of Burma would be prepared to put in its extra share every time new expenditure was incurred: in the first nine months of 1949 the company spent no less than £3 million there. The Burmah Oil board and Whitehall both gave their blessing to this new basis of negotiation, recognizing the advantage of greater flexibility than under the old system. By the beginning of September the overall figure of £15 million was officially accepted in Rangoon; however, a major condition was still the provision of a loan by the British government. That condition remained a worrying one. Should Whitehall refuse the loan and cause the joint venture to founder, the Burmah Oil directors could expect no co-operation from the government of Burma when they began to carry out the further staff reductions that they felt were becoming urgent.

With no progress made over the loan or the joint venture by late September, the company issued notices discharging 1,400 employees at Chauk and about 2,200 at Syriam. Carey had already discussed these possible reductions with Burma's Minister of Foreign Affairs, and in October he and the British ambassador, James Bowker, met U Nu. Neither meeting was particularly fruitful: ministers would go no further than a non-committal recognition of what was being done. Harper remained hawkish about the dismissals, declaring that he would not surrender to the Burmese unions and was prepared to face a show-down, since the company could not be expected to go on carrying surplus labour on its payroll, whether at its own or the British government's expense.

At a further meeting with the foreign minister, Bowker hinted that Whitehall, even if unable to grant a loan, might be ready to make available some short-term funds to cushion the effects of the redundancies. However, any aid would depend on rebel activities ceasing in the oilfields and law and order being restored. He declared bluntly that, if the labour leaders persisted in behaving irresponsibly, they would almost certainly bring about the total collapse of Burma's oil industry.

Hectoring of that kind by the British was all very well, but by then practically all existing industrial installations in the country, including the railways and river traffic, were at a standstill. At the end of October Harper felt that Burma's troubles were building up to some kind of climax. Yet while refusing to invest any more of the company's own capital there, he and his board were prepared to accept U Nu's offer of substantive negotiations on joint venture. When Carey met U Nu at the end of October, he portrayed the latter's charm memorably as follows: 'Both panels of his radiator of geniality were switched on.' However, Carey continued, 'both comforting panels will be switched off the moment the will of the Burmese Trade Union Congress is in any way disregarded by us.' Harper could not help wondering if the authorities in Rangoon were deliberately spinning talks out for their own purposes. 'The longer the Burmese government can keep the ball rolling, the more reconstruction [of oil assets] there would be to take over. And His Majesty's Government's dilatoriness is playing that game for them nicely.'

In November 1949 U Nu set up the *Ad Hoc* Oilfields Enquiry Committee. Before it could get under way, Bowker had to tell U Nu late in December that the British government would be unable to provide a loan for the joint venture. U Nu received that deeply disappointing news without a muscle moving in his impassive face; yet he knew that here was a further blow to his country's grave situation. Indeed, the early months of 1950 were later authoritatively described as the lowest point in Burma's post-war financial fortunes. Even Harry S. Truman's administration in the United States, sympathetic as it was to the new regime, had become convinced that the country was finished as a viable political and economic entity. The Oilfields Enquiry Committee reported in mid-March 1950. Its report sharply criticised Burmah Oil's policies in general and conduct over the Yenangyaung withdrawal in particular. Why, it asked, had oil production in British Borneo and Indonesia recovered so much more dramatically than in Burma, and why had Burmah Oil been so reluctant to pour rehabilitation funds into the country? Burmah Oil's reply was that the post-independence disturbances in the country had greatly exacerbated the problem and that in any case, the oilfields were a good distance from the coast, in contrast with Borneo and Indonesia. To put the case bluntly, the company argued, Burma's problems made it uneconomic to invest money in oil production there when an equivalent sum invested elsewhere would produce more oil at lower cost, not to mention lower risk.

In analysing recent events at Yenangyaung, the report implied that the company had seized the opportunity of a temporary reoccupation of the oilfields by the rebels to escape from an onerous and unprofitable commitment there. Moreover, it continued, Weva and Carey had acted with quite unnecessary haste and had misled the Burmese ministers concerned into thinking that any withdrawal of British staff would be temporary and not lead to a total stoppage of all work there. Weva strongly disagreed with this interpretation of events and made a sworn statement to the effect that he had at the time clearly and fully explained to ministers the consequences for Burmese labour of the withdrawal.

In a private comment on the report, the British embassy staff dryly observed that it was 'too much to expect that a Burmese government committee would admit' that ministers had not had the courage to face the disagreeable implications of the company's decision and to inform their colleagues accordingly. What the embassy did believe to contain a germ of truth was the report's criticisms about the paternalistic attitude of the company, a lack of imagination and of 'human contact' in dealings with non-European staff: criticisms originally made in an official Burmese report on the disturbances of 1938, less valid in post-war conditions but still – according to the embassy – central to the whole problem of the company's relationships with government and employees in Burma.[5] The more perceptive Drysdale, by then a manager in the London office, would have pointed not so much to personal contacts with local staff, which were good, but to the anomalous system whereby a foreign management was striving to cope with economic and political problems which directedly affected the livelihoods of thousands in the country.

On 23 December 1949 the British government informed the company that it would be withdrawing its financial guarantee as from the end of January 1950. The directors had already made it clear that, in the event of such a decision, further large-scale reductions of staff would have to take place: specifically, 2,500 at Chauk and 3,500 at the Syriam refinery. A press report, released in London and Rangoon, expressed the view of Whitehall that the widespread unrest in Burma no longer justified large amounts of expenditure on rehabilitation. At the same time the British government was examining, in consultation with other friendly governments, possible means of providing alternative forms of financial assistance. Carey sent a carefully drafted letter to U Nu. In the fields, he pointed out, the only work that could at the moment be usefully done was the production and refining of the limited quantity of oil which could be marketed locally. Elsewhere in Burma, labour was needed only for receiving and distributing imported oil from the ocean installations at Syriam.

The total expenditure incurred by the oil companies, arising from the extra labour kept on, during the guarantee period from March 1949 to January 1950 amounted to no less than £1.1 million. Just over a half had been spent in the oilfields, a third in the refineries and a small amount on servicing the still non-operative pipelines. British Burmah and Indo-Burma between them were responsible for only 7 per cent of the expenses. Since part of these could not be justified as having been essential, Burmah Oil agreed to accept £700,000 as its share. Bowker, the British ambassador, strove to persuade the government of Burma to assume responsibility for paying the redundant labour for an extra month or two, over and above the month's pay that the company was offering in lieu of notice. The labour forces affected had at once gone on strike, and the matter was referred to the Industrial Court in Burma. The company appealed to the Supreme Court to have the reference quashed, but the Supreme Court ruled that any such application was premature and that it was up to the Industrial Court to decide whether it had the legal powers to adjudicate in this

Towards Joint Venture 1949–54   185

case: this ruling not unexpectedly caused the company much dissatisfaction.

The Burmese authorities brought further pressure in March 1950, when Cecil Maxwell-Lefroy, the oilfields manager, was personally sued in the local court at Chauk for contravening the Trade Disputes Act. On his behalf, the company again pleaded that the dismissals arose from inescapable economic and political factors which prevented the maintenance of normal operations at the fields. It had not been responsible for any victimisation, nor for any illegal actions. There was a slight fear that Maxwell-Lefroy might become the victim of a show trial, but in the event he was released on bail and later quietly sentenced to a nominal fine, which the company paid. The Burmah Oil board later granted him £1,000 for the inconvenience and anxiety which he had undergone.

The directors in London were convinced that all these legal moves were part of an elaborate battle of wits against the company. One of the most acute minds on the Burmese side, the Indian-born M. A. Raschid, who was on the *Ad Hoc* committee and much involved in every aspect of the country's labour affairs, admitted publicly in April that Burma as a virtually bankrupt country had no choice but to seek capital from overseas until such time as it could stand on its own feet. That interim period, he believed, might last as long as 25–30 years, during which his government would have to decide how far existing foreign capital in the country could be constrained and imposed upon without being frightened away altogether.

That a joint venture plan for oil remained very much in Rangoon's mind was demonstrated when U Nu revived the notion in May at an informal meeting with Weva. The prime minister proposed that under the joint venture, topping plant facilities should be increased at Chauk, while a small refinery or topping plant would be erected at Syriam, to be fed by crude oil sent down on barges from the oilfields. Weva declined to discuss any proposals of that kind until the Industrial Court had reported; in any case he viewed such plans as unrealistic since communications by land between the fields and Rangoon were still interrupted by rebel action, and seemed unlikely to be restored for a long time to come. Privately, Weva felt that giving publicity to joint venture proposals at that stage would

be counter-productive by raising redundant workers' expectations of more jobs being created, which were quite unrealistic in
the existing circumstances.

At the end of May 1950 the Industrial Court announced its
findings.[6] The redundancies at Chauk were held to be reasonable, but at the same time illegal on technical grounds, because
actual discharge had taken place after the dispute had been
referred to the court. Wages should therefore be paid to the end
of May, and two months' redundancy payment in addition:
that represented an extra expense to the company of about
£40,000 a month gross. In London, Foreign Office officials
called a meeting a week later to discuss these findings; Harper,
Weva, Michie of the Burma Chamber of Commerce and
representatives of British Burmah and Indo-Burma were
present.

Michie declared that the Industrial Court's finding went
against the spirit of the letters exchanged between Attlee and U
Nu at the time of the 1947 Anglo-Burmese treaty, which had
agreed about safeguarding the interests of British companies in
Burma. Harper, too, was so dissatisfied with the court's ruling
that, on his board's authority, he arranged for Carey to lodge
an appeal with the Supreme Court in Rangoon. Should what he
termed a 'reasonable' decision be passed down there, the
company would be prepared to increase the output of oil
products from Chauk, always provided that communications
and transport facilities were suitable. It would also spend some
£250,000 on capital expenditure in transferring some recently
delivered refinery plant from Syriam to Chauk.

The Supreme Court's decision, announced in October,
turned out to be as 'reasonable' as the company could perhaps
have hoped for. The Industrial Court was judged to have had
no authority to tell Burmah Oil how it should carry on its
business. Hence the company's right to discharge surplus
labour at Syriam was upheld. At the same time, the discharges
at Chauk and the two months' redundancy payments there
and at Syriam were declared illegal, but the award of a
discharge allowance at Yenangyaung was quashed. The
company thereupon paid off the labour, at a total cost of
£150,000.

Towards Joint Venture 1949–54   187

Burmah Oil derived comfort from the fact that it had at least been able to reduce costs to a point at which production and sale of Burmese-raised oil would be showing a profit. Moreover, it was earning a good return on the imported oil products; in the three years since 1946 it had made a direct and indirect profit there of nearly £1.2 million. As the total net trading profit for Burma in 1949 came to £540,000 and in 1950 to £430,000, the company could not have been making much from its indigenous production and marketing there. In an interview with U Nu in November, Carey did not disguise his feeling about the 'colossal tragedy' of so many thousands of men losing their jobs. That tragedy was sadly intensified by the fact, vouched for by the Roman Catholic padre at the fields, that the ex-employees had squandered 60–70 per cent of the redundancy payments within ten days in gambling dens and drinking saloons, energetically assisted by what were described as 'evil exploiters, largely Chinese'.

Now that the various legal tangles were resolved, the government of Burma seemed likely to renew its proposal for a joint venture. That possibility made Harper more than ever determined to play hard to get. As the board minutes put it, he sought 'to remain in the position of the party being pressed to agree to such a joint venture rather than the party asking for it'. This was not merely a tactical move, since the company would then be able to seek, as part of a package deal, a 'constructive programme' of increased output and investment, and it could also insist on the government of Burma contributing its own quota of cash for its one-third share. Soon after the Supreme Court judgement, Carey saw U Nu, and in a conciliatory atmosphere explained the limited programme of fresh investment the company planned to undertake, such as extending the Chauk topping plant for the benefit of the growing domestic market. The renewal of cordiality gave hope that the two parties could move to a swift and mutually advantageous agreement on joint venture.

Towards the end of 1950, a gruelling year by any standards, Carey was clearly feeling the strain. He admitted in a letter to the directors at home – sent by safe hand – that, while he would do his level best to put across to the Burmese authorities the principles laid down by the board during the future joint

188					*A History of the Burmah Oil Company*

venture negotiations, he was not looking forward to the task. He went on,

> Frankly, I have great disrespect for some of the people I still have to deal with in this regard, and if it was not my duty to the company to have dealings with them, I should absolutely refuse to have any converse with them.

For the government of Burma, the new year of 1951 brought with it a modest revival of financial and economic prosperity. Underlying that revival was the painfully slow process of attrition against the rebels so that the government's writ still did not run in many parts of the country. Central Burma was largely rebel-held, which inhibited free internal movement of oil products. The outbreak of the Korean war in mid-1950 had led to a sharp commodity boom, in which Burma's rice shared. Hence there was to be in the next few years an unprecedented buoyancy in government revenues and a satisfactory building up of foreign currency reserves. Understandably, the people of Burma pressed for higher social welfare and other public expenditure; yet perhaps negotiations for a joint venture could now at last be opened on a more constructive basis than hitherto. When Weva visited Rangoon early in 1951, he discerned a notable improvement in Burma's political and military conditions, although he was by no means certain that that improvement would continue.[7]

In February 1951 the government of Burma revived the joint venture idea by announcing that it wished to take up a one-third interest, but only if the British government agreed to loan the £5 million that would be required. A formal application for a loan duly went to Whitehall, but a swift reply could not be expected: the Attlee government was yet again facing severe financial problems, this time over defence and increased raw material prices caused by the Korean commodity boom. The ailing Cripps had been succeeded as Chancellor of the Exchequer by Hugh Gaitskell towards the end of 1950.

It happened that Gaitskell knew a good deal about Burma, as his father had been in the civil service there, and his sister Bunty had married Hubert Ashton. Gaitskell was at one with his Treasury officials in believing that Rangoon was 'black-

Towards Joint Venture 1949–54 189

mailing' Britain into making a loan, at a time when Burma had plenty of sterling; in any case – to deploy an all too familiar Treasury argument – surrender in this case would create a bad precedent that other countries would seek to exploit.

However, Gaitskell found himself up against not only Attlee but also certain cabinet ministers such as Philip Noel-Baker and Patrick Gordon-Walker, each of whom had previously served as Commonwealth Secretary and who opposed the cheese-paring Treasury line. Gaitskell, in his diary, described Attlee and Noel-Baker as 'feeling positively passionate about Burma and insisting on giving them anything they wanted. I have voted against this unsuccessfully,' he continued. When the matter was thrashed out at ministerial level, Attlee for once lost his temper, went 'quite red in the face', and angrily exclaimed, 'If you go on like this, you will lose the whole of the Middle East.'[8]

The basis of Attlee's anger was the Abadan crisis, involving the government of Iran and the Anglo-Iranian Oil Company, which had recently erupted when in May 1951 Dr Mossadeq had nationalised that company's assets. Sir William Fraser had given the Burmah Oil board what was minuted as an 'interesting' account of events, and Harper had formally conveyed the board's 'good wishes for a satisfactory solution to difficult problems'. One of the Burmah Oil non-executive directors privately felt that 'one of the causes of our friends' trouble has been insufficient contact with the fields', by which he meant the host country of Iran. At the meeting with Gaitskell, the prime minister clearly feared that Burma too might turn sour and become a centre of discord in South-East Asia as Iran had become in the Middle East.

The Iranian moves against British interests, as U Nu informed Weva in July 1951, had indeed made a deep impression on the Burmese people and also raised their own expectations. U Nu hinted that nothing less than a 50:50 partnership would now do, although Weva after some persuasive argument brought him back to the one-third basis. 'It was also as clear as daylight', Weva reported home, 'that he did not intend to pay a penny of Burmese money for the participation.' U Nu did, perhaps to test out the company, drop hints about getting the 50:50 share by expropriation, but he was not really serious about such a drastic step.

In fact, relations between the government and the largest company in Burma could not have been more different from those in Iran. Remarkably, two very knowledgeable men, the minister of state at the Foreign Office, Kenneth Younger, and the labour adviser of Anglo-Iranian, in memoranda they wrote independently that year, blamed Anglo-Iranian for what had happened. According to the latter, that company was 'confused, hidebound, small-minded and blind'. The former criticised the chairman, Sir William Fraser, for a wanton neglect of the political dimension which Fraser explicitly stated did not concern him at all.[9] Politics of one kind or another were, on the other hand, a constant preoccupation of Burmah Oil's executive and of its general manager in the East.

Nor could Harper or Weva be accused of such insensitiveness towards the country that provided their oil. They understood the Burmese mind from the experience of many years' residence and thereafter the maintenance of regular personal contacts. Relations between the Burmah Oil directors and the authorities in Rangoon may from time to time have become strained, but both sides had a good deal of common ground. At his encounter with Attlee over the loan, Gaitskell retorted, 'It is your policy which will lose us the Middle East. By giving way to blackmail here, you will have it imposed on you everywhere else.' Gaitskell was outvoted, and the British cabinet approved the loan.

With the Iranian crisis rumbling on, and with virtually no prospect of a swift solution, Whitehall very much hoped that Burma at least would deliver an amicable accord. In mid-September Attlee sent a personal message to U Nu. A loan of £5 million would be excessive, he stated, but if the government of Burma and the company could agree on a joint venture scheme, Britain would offer £2.5 million. Since U Nu was persisting in his resolve not to put in any Burmese money, and Weva would not consent to Rangoon's share being less than one-third, an impasse was reached. U Nu merely responded to Attlee by expressing pleasure that Britain had offered a loan, without making public his disappointment that the full £5 million was not forthcoming. Weva privately admitted that he had spent a month or more in fending off a suggestion by Whitehall that the offer of £2.5 million should be linked with a statement that

Towards Joint Venture 1949–54   191

Burmah Oil would be prepared to make suitable arrangements to underwrite the remainder.

In November 1951 Weva arrived in Rangoon with definite proposals for the government of Burma. A general election had just been held in Britain, and Winston Churchill was once again prime minister. The Burmese were very apprehensive that, as Churchill had been so opposed to what he had called 'scuttle' from empire, Britain's official attitude towards them might sharply deteriorate. In fact, the Foreign Office told Weva before his departure that the new government was anxious to build up cordial relations with Burma, and in particular wished to see a joint oil venture settled. After much discussion, on 30 November an agreement was initialled whereby a new rupee company would be set up in Rangoon, the government of Burma holding a third share. Burmah Oil would appoint three directors, of whom one would act as chairman, and the government of Burma would appoint two directors. That government would in future be allowed to increase its own stake, after giving due notice. Once it had more than 51 per cent of shares, it would be entitled to have three directors and Burmah Oil only two. Marketing would not be affected, since that would remain in the hands of Burmah Oil's trading subsidiary.

The long-term objectives sought by Burmah Oil were written into the agreement, notably that production and refining at Chauk would be increased to about 1.6 million barrels annually and that, when security conditions permitted, the pipeline and Syriam refinery would be reconstructed to permit an eventual output of 3.7 million barrels a year and the restoration of Burma's export trade in oil. The government of Burma had the right to check the valuation of the assets; subject to that, the sale price was set at £15 million and the capital at the equivalent figure of 200 million *kyats*. The *kyat*, of 100 *pyas*, officially replaced the Burmese rupee on 1 July 1952.

Late in December 1951 R. A. Butler, recently appointed Chancellor of the Exchequer, wrote to Anthony Eden, the Foreign Secretary, deploying some 'powerful practical economic arguments' against lending the £2.5 million to the Burmese for the acquisition of what were British-owned assets. Burma, he pointed out, had left the Commonwealth by its own choice, and neighbouring Commonwealth countries could well be jealous if Burma were now singled out for special treatment. Moreover, Britain was short of foreign currency; and so on. The Treasury hostility to this loan had very evidently survived the change in government.

Eden replied with some political and 'politico-economic' counter-arguments. The Burmese government was in a very 'precarious' state; were it to fall, the Marxist element in the country was so strong that Burma might be lost to the West. Moreover, that event could upset the international balance throughout South-East Asia. On the politico-economic side, all peoples in that part of the world were watching carefully the progress of the Abadan crisis in Iran. For Burma, a joint oil venture launched with a loan from Britain could fend off pressure to nationalise outright not merely the oil interests there but also other important British enterprises. An interest-free loan repaid over twelve and a half years would, according to Eden, cost the Exchequer only £2 million in interest foregone: 'as an insurance premium, it does not seem unduly high, particularly if one considers that the Burmah Oil Company last year contributed something like £6½ million to the Exchequer by way of income tax.'

Butler riposted with the further point that the Burmese had not been repaying the money they still owed under the financial agreement of 1947, and that the loan should be withheld until some repayment was made. Eden did not care for the idea of linking the two issues, but as Burma did not appear to be pressing for the loan, the two ministers left the matter in abeyance.[10]

From the political and military viewpoints, conditions in Burma seemed to be somewhat more stable by the end of 1951. A general election had been successfully held there that year. Supervision of the polls may have been lax in places, and bizarre happenings occurred, including local detachments of the armed forces being taken in bodies to vote – naturally for the official candidates. The perhaps over-anxious Burmah Oil board saw the outcome of the election as indicating a 'worsening to the left', with U Nu apparently less securely in control than before. However, world opinion accepted that the

Towards Joint Venture 1949–54 193

renewed mandate for him broadly represented the will of the Burmese people.[11] On the military side, martial law had been brought to an end in mid-1951; although the government still failed to control large areas of the country, the rebels were no longer generally regarded as credible alternatives to the existing regime. As far as the joint venture proposals went, both parties had accepted the principles, and the task was now to settle the financial details.

A valuation commission set up by the Rangoon government duly visited the oilfields and Syriam, and in April 1952 came up with an asset value of £13.5 million. At a time when Whitehall had not yet decided on the precise terms of its loan, the government of Burma sought to place a lien on the sum of £700,000 which Burmah Oil had received from Whitehall for the guarantee period of 1949–50. After a good deal of parleying, the company offered to include the £700,000 in the new company's assets, whereupon Rangoon accepted the valuation in the agreement of £15 million. The government of Burma then tried to have the denial claims – still going through the country's courts at a snail's pace – included as well in the assets. It did not press the matter when the Burmah Oil board refused. 'Somewhat belatedly', as the board minutes described it, Rangoon then sought a ruling from its Supreme Court on whether a joint venture with a minority government stake was permissible under the constitution, which had laid down that the exploration of mineral rights should be entirely or largely in Burmese hands.

Not until February 1953 did the Supreme Court reach its decision on this matter. It held the joint venture to be constitutional, but declined to rule on the validity of Burmah Oil's existing leases after the company's counsel pleaded that it was inappropriate for the court to consider such an 'indefinite question'. However, instead of this decision spurring it into signing the agreement, in April the government of Burma sought to reopen the whole question of joint venture by exploring possible alternative arrangements for operating the country's oil industry.

After the Rangoon government had asked Carey for a detailed breakdown of the company's sources of profit in Burma – which Carey refused to give – U Nu dropped the hint that Weva might care to come out on a visit. Weva, unwilling to appear to be pushing matters, did not oblige, and in the absence of any serious negotiations U Nu blew hot and cold. In June he spoke encouragingly about the proposals, but by September was discussing the possibility of arranging a joint venture instead with certain Japanese and American interests. The latter possibility was not taken very seriously, and a recently arrived World Bank delegation gained the impression that Burmese opinion expected the arrangement with Burmah Oil to go ahead. What did irritate the government of Burma was the chaotic and unsatisfactory situation that had persisted in Yenangyaung, ever since the evacuation of the British staff; that was investigated by the company's board in London, which saw no reason to send its staff back there. Then in October the government of Burma informed British ministers that after all it had no need of the £2.5 million loan, since it would be able to pay the sum required from its own resources: at the end of 1952 the country's foreign exchange reserves had reached the equivalent of £75 million.

Despite all the problems of insurgency, equipment shortages and disrupted communications, oil production in Burma had steadily increased since 1947, as Table 4 shows. There had been a decline in both output and demand during the crisis year of 1949. However, in accordance with the agreement of November 1951, by 1953 the topping plants in Chauk had been replaced by a small integrated refinery, complete with wax processing equipment. This refinery had an initial throughput of 2,500 barrels a day; in January 1954 it was inaugurated by U Nu, who opened a valve, and molten wax flowed out. By the end of that year annual output in Burma, including that of the independent operators there, was just four times that of 1948. The difference between the amount of crude oil production and that of refined products from Burma illustrates the relatively low product yield – compared with pre-1942 – obtained from the topping plants.

Despite the increase in output, and the still high level of oil imports undertaken by the company, the amount of net trading profit contributed by Burma was falling: just over £290,000 in 1951 or almost half that of 1949, although it increased to an

TABLE 4

Oil production and consumption – Burma 1947–54

	Crude oil production (000 barrels)			Refined products (000 barrels)			Percentage of oil product needs from Burma (%)
	'Merger' co's*	Independent operators†	Total Burma	Indigenous	Imported	Total	
1947	72	11	83	n.a.	n.a.	n.a.	n.a.
1948	289	28	317	89	1098	1187	8
1949	219	28	247	86	772	858	10
1950	417	122	539	226	784	1010	22
1951	626	144	770	389	747	1136	34
1952	620	209	829	400	812	1212	33
1953	788	209	997	502	883	1385	36
1954	945	348	1293	707	798	1505	47

* Burmah Oil, British Burmah and Indo-Burma (For 1954, Burma Oil Co (1954) Ltd)

† Estimated

average of £410,000 annually between 1952 and 1954. That represented about 12 per cent of total profit, while investment income was contributing 45 per cent. Unless joint venture were able to increase profits from that source, the country where operations had originally started would soon become a negligible earner for the company.

At the end of 1953 Weva was in Rangoon, and he soon reached a definitive agreement with the government of Burma. Signed on 12 January 1954, it turned out to be substantially the same as the one initialled as long before as 1951. The new corporate body, to take over all functions apart from marketing, was to be called the Burma Oil Company (1954) Ltd. The government of Burma would hold one-third of the £15 million capital, paying £2.5 million in cash and the rest in instalments. The board in London was by then so anxious to resolve the joint venture question one way or another that, before Weva's departure, it had approved in advance a fall-back position of 50:50 shareholding if the earlier terms were rejected. However, this did not prove to be necessary.

Although Weva had done well in the negotiations, the board was not entirely happy with the final outcome. In particular, while the directors had authorised the payment of the £700,000 guarantee money to the new company, Weva had without board permission raised the sum payable to £750,000, just equal to a crore (or 10 million) of *kyats*, as the Burmese rupee was now called.

He had made this extra offer as a *coup de théâtre* on the actual day of signing. A number of cabinet ministers had been unhappy that U Nu had rushed through the accord without insisting on Britain binding itself to provide guarantees over the future capital needed to make Burma self-sufficient in oil. Nor, it appeared, had U Nu tried to gain for the government of Burma even titular control over what they regarded as some of the country's most valuable resources. Therefore ministers might well have vetoed the signing at the very last moment. The directors at home became further irritated when it emerged that the government of Burma was dragging its feet over the initial deposit, agreed at £2.5 million, and offering only £1.5 million in the first instance, with the balance to be paid in

March or April. This infuriated the board in London as constituting a breach of the agreement and it laid down that the 1954 company could not be registered until the full £2.5 million had been actually received in London. It seems probable, in retrospect, that these hiccups led to differences between Weva and his Burmah Oil colleagues which were never wholly resolved.

One administrative consequence of a joint venture being established in Rangoon was that the company's top man there was no longer designated as general manager in the East. Perhaps the division of territorial functions, making the general managers in India and Pakistan responsible directly to London, might have been arranged even as early as August 1947 when both countries received independence. However, it was only the far more specific new role for the Rangoon general manager, who was to be made chairman of the 1954 company, that made the change really necessary. Not until the end of April was the government of Burma's £2.5 million paid to London, but the company still had to be formally registered in Rangoon: as was noted in the Burmah Oil board minutes, 'largely it would appear because of the absence on tour of those concerned' in Burma.

Subsidiary agreements remained to be signed, but the board of the new company had been formed and had held its first meeting. Relations with the Burmese government-appointed directors were said to be good. On the other hand, the Burmah Oil board instructed the general manager that, until the subsidiary agreements had been signed, the new company would possess no assets and therefore had no right to engage in trading of any kind. That did not deter ministers in Rangoon from submitting a list of forty proposed changes to the agreements, only four of which Burmah Oil after consideration regarded as substantive. Not until 5 October were all the agreements signed; shares were then allotted on the 8th. The Burma Oil Company (1954) Ltd was in business.

The new board lost no time in bringing forward plans for a new refinery at Syriam, which it hoped to have completed in two years' time. The former Irrawaddy Flotilla Company, nationalised in 1948, had been renamed the Inland Water Transport Board (IWTB): not exactly a name to have set

198   *A History of the Burmah Oil Company*

Kipling's pulses racing. The 1954 company now asked the IWTB to give a firm date when new craft would be available to transport crude oil to Syriam; there seemed no chance of rehabilitating the pipeline within the two years that were contemplated as it ran through dacoit country, so that repairs and maintenance would pose a constant problem. It was irksome that the IWTB charged such high freights; the company pointed out that it cost five times as much to send petrol from Chauk to Rangoon as it did to ship it from the Gulf.

On the Burmese side, an undercurrent of annoyance persisted that Burmah Oil refused to consider making a similar partnership arrangement for its fully-owned Burma trading subsidiary. The latter was earning good profits, still running at £400,000 to £500,000 both on the marketing of indigenous products and on the considerable volume of imports that were being made. This issue flared up in the early 1960s. Meanwhile, however, what mattered was that a new and highly promising era in the oil industry of Burma appeared to have been inaugurated, with goodwill shown by all the parties concerned. Men on both sides of the world must have fervently hoped that the new joint venture would fully live up to its promises.

Notes

1 PRO POWE 33 1565–8, 'Burmah Oil Company's Claim under HMG's Guarantee', 1950–2, and 1569, 'Proposed Participation of Burmese Government in Joint Venture', 1950–1.
2 Tinker, *Union of Burma*, p. 337.
3 I am very grateful to C. A. Maxwell-Lefroy for letting me quote from his unpublished memoirs, especially Chapter 7, 'Burma Oilfields under Siege, 1949–50'.
4 PRO POWE 33/1566, *Report of the Ad Hoc Oilfields Enquiry Committee*, 16 March 1950, pp. 1–65.
5 Ibid. Rangoon Embassy, 'Comments on the Report of the Ad Hoc Oilfields Enquiry Committee', undated (c. March 1950).
6 PRO POWE 33/1565, copy of Industrial Court award, 31 May 1950, and subsequent meetings and correspondence with company. The Supreme Court judgment was reported by a greatly relieved Bevin to Attlee on 26 October 1950. FO 800/441, Bevin Papers.
7 PRO POWE 33/1569, letter of Petroleum Department to Foreign Office, 31 January 1951.

Towards Joint Venture 1949–54   199

8 P. M. Williams (ed.), *The Diary of Hugh Gaitskell 1945–1956*, 1983, p. 271.

9 Kenneth Younger's memo is in A. Sampson, *The Seven Sisters*, 1975, p. 120. That of AIOC's labour adviser, Sir Frederick Leggett, is in Morgan, *Labour in Power*, pp. 466–7.

10 PRO FO 800/753, Private Papers of Sir A. Eden, Burma 1952 and 1954, correspondence between Eden and Butler 29 Dec 1951–19 Apr 1952.

11 For the 1951 election, see Tinker, *Union of Burma*, pp. 71–2.

[25]

Excerpt from *Foreign Investment in the Petroleum and Mineral Industries*, 365–8.

CHAPTER 14

BETHLEHEM'S JOINT VENTURE IN

BRAZILIAN MANGANESE

Raymond F. Mikesell

In 1949 the Bethlehem Steel Corporation was invited to invest in Brazil as a minority stockholder in a mining company, Indústria e Comércio de Minérios, S.A. (ICOMI), organized and controlled by a private Brazilian mining engineer, Augusto Tranjano de Azevedo Antunes. The joint venture developed rich deposits of minerals, and there were no insuperable technical problems in producing and transporting the ores. In contrast with Hanna's experience, Bethlehem has experienced a minimum of legal, organizational, financial, political, and transportation problems in achieving its production and export goals. Bethlehem's principal interest in the manganese venture has been that of providing a source of high-grade manganese for its own steel plants in the United States. In fact, the output of Bethlehem's joint venture with the Antunes group has been somewhat higher than Bethlehem has regarded as optimum.

THE DISCOVERY OF MANGANESE IN AMAPÁ

In 1946 the discovery came to light of a body of high-grade manganese ore in the territory of Amapá in northeastern Brazil.[1] An initial survey made by federal government officials determined that the area was worthy of further exploration and it was therefore declared a "National Reserve" in 1946 by presidential decree upon recommendation of the National Council of Mines and Metallurgy. In 1947 the federal government called for bids for the exploration and study of the minerals in the area. Meanwhile, several companies, including the Hanna Mining Company; the U.S. Steel Corporation; and a private Brazilian company, ICOMI, under the direction of its founder, Dr. Augusto Antunes, were surveying the area containing the manganese. Under a decree signed by President Dutra on 4 December 1947, the governor of the territory of Amapá was authorized to contract with ICOMI for the further exploration and eventual development of the manganese mines in the region of the Amapari

[1] This discovery was made quite accidentally by a migrant merchant while trading in the gold mining region of the Amapari River in 1941. The merchant, who thought he had found a piece of iron ore (which he used as ballast for his canoe), delivered the ore five years later to the territorial governor of Amapá, who in turn took the ore to Rio for analysis where it was determined to be high-grade manganese ore. *Brazilian Business*, May 1963.

River.[2] The manganese ore deposits were discovered in an isolated jungle area far from any means of land transportation or navigable water.

THE CREATION OF
THE JOINT VENTURE

After a year of study, Dr. Antunes became convinced that he needed both a large amount of capital and considerable technical knowledge and experience to mine the ore and transport it over some 200 kilometers of jungle to the Amazon River where port facilities would have to be built to convey the ore to open sea. After contacting firms both in Europe and the United States, Antunes eventually associated his company with the Bethlehem Steel Corporation. The legal form of Antunes' company, ICOMI, was changed to that of a stock company (Sociedade Anónima, S.A.); and while the name of the original company, ICOMI, was retained, certain properties of the old ICOMI were stripped off and another company, ICOMINAS, was created to accommodate the mining properties of the old company in the state of Minas Gerais. The stock of ICOMI is held 51 percent by Cía. Auxiliar de Empresás de Mineracão (CAEMI), which in turn is controlled by Antunes and 49 percent by Bethlehem.

A fifty-year concession contract was negotiated between ICOMI and the territory of Amapá on 31 May 1950.[3] The agreement covered the production and transportation of manganese ore, including the building of a railroad, the royalties to be paid, the distribution of profits, and other conditions. The agreement provided, among other things, that ICOMI would pay the government of the territory of Amapá an amount of 4 percent of the sale value per metric ton of the exported manganese ore; that the corporation would export at least 50 thousand tons of ore a year (with certain provisions for exceptions); that the corporation would invest in new enterprise in the territory 20 percent of the net profits derived from the exploitation of the leased mines; that the corporation must reserve to Brazilians at least 51 percent of its share capital and might admit foreign shareholders whose participation in the equity capital would not exceed 49 percent; that the lease would last for about fifty years; that the corporation would be free to export a minimum of 500,000 tons of manganese ore and agreed to supply all the needs of the national industry for manganese ore at market prices; that the railroad to be constructed from the mines to the port of Macapá by the corporation would provide capacity for public and private shipping of freight other than manganese ore, according to fares stipulated by Brazilian law; and that the corporation undertook to supply electric power for residences, schools, industrial buildings, etc. in the communities in which it operated at rates to be established by public authorities. It seems clear that the provisions of the lease contract were not only in accordance with Brazilian law, but took into account the public interest in developing the largely undeveloped region of the Amapá territory in which ICOMI was operating.

Geological surveys and exploration work continued for several years before ICOMI was in a position to begin exporting ore. Intensive drilling covering some 65 percent of the area of known ore zones led to an estimate that the whole deposit contained at least 30 million tons of mineable ore. It became quite evident that the 200 million cruzeiros of paid-in capital (about $20 million), of which 49 percent was contributed by Bethlehem Steel, constituted only a small portion of the total capital required. The company first approached the World Bank and secured an agreement for a loan of $3.5 million.[4] It also

---

[2] *Brazilian Business,* May 1963; and *Diario Oficial,* 1 June 1950, for a history of ICOMI and of the various decrees relating to the contract of 2 December 1947, and the concession agreement of 31 May 1950.

[3] The agreement between ICOMI and the territory of Amapá was approved by the federal government by decree 28,162, dated 3 May 1951, and published in the *Diario Oficial,* 1 June 1951.

[4] The World Bank loan was guaranteed by the Brazilian government, by congressional law 1,235, 14 November 1950.

borrowed $1.9 million from Bethlehem. The
World Bank loan was never consummated
since the amount of capital required proved
to be much larger than had been estimated
earlier, so that in September 1952 a loan of
$67.5 million was secured from the Export-
Import Bank of Washington, $15.0 million of
which was covered by a market guarantee
from the U.S. government Defense Materials
Procurement Agency, which committed itself
to buy 5.5 million tons of ore. Not all of the
Export-Import Bank loan was required and
the loan was fully repaid five and one-half
years after ICOMI began production, whereas
the terms of the loan were for seven years,
with payments to start from the beginning of
operations.[5]

MINING OPERATIONS

With the industrial installations and the
railroad and port facilities completed in January 1957, 658,000 tons of ore were exported
in 1957. In recent years ICOMI has been exporting between seven and eight hundred
thousand tons of manganese ore. Virtually all
of ICOMI's output is exported, and about
one-third of its exports in 1964 (249,000
tons) went to Bethlehem Steel. The vast bulk
of the rest went to the U.S. Steel Corporation,
Republic Steel Corporation, and to firms in
Germany, the United Kingdom, France,
Japan, and Argentina. Only a few hundred
tons in 1964 went to the Brazilian steel plants
in the south of Brazil since it is much cheaper
to supply Brazilian plants from other sources,
including U.S. Steel subsidiary operations in
the south. Manganese output of ICOMI is
substantially less than its potential and, according to a company official, it could increase its output from the 1965 level of about
800 thousand tons per year to a million tons
per year with very little increase in investment. Over the 1957–65 period, total exports

amounted to about 6.7 million tons valued
at $257 million and total royalties paid to
Amapá were 2.4 billion cruzeiros (or $14.7
million equivalent). Total employment of
ICOMI in mines, railroads, and other operations was 4,000 in 1965.[6]

According to the American member of the
board of directors of ICOMI, Robert D.
Butler, relations between the Brazilian owners
headed by Antunes and Bethlehem are cordial
and no serious policy issues have arisen.
Three of the four members of the board of
directors are Brazilians, and both the president
and the vice-president (Paulo César de
Azeuedo Antunes) are Brazilians. I was informed that, while output could readily be
expanded, Bethlehem has little interest in
larger output. In fact, the ideal output as far
as Bethlehem is concerned would be about
600 thousand tons per year, or some 25 percent less than the 1965 level. Two reasons
were given for this. First, Bethlehem is interested in having an assured supply of high-
grade manganese. (There are thirty years'
proved reserves at the present rate of output
and perhaps an additional ten to fifteen years
of unproved reserves.) Second, profit remittance limitations by the Brazilian government
have only served to increase the supply of
cruzeiros which must be reinvested in Brazil.
Recently, Brazil's profit remittance law has
been changed, but the amount of profits re-
mitted to Bethlehem was not known at the
time of writing.

All export contracts must be cleared with
the Ministry of Mines. Taxation is similar to
that outlined in the previous chapter. ICOMI
officials state that they have had no problems
with government officials as regards prices
and do not anticipate any so long as they
follow world market trends in their export
pricing. In addition to investing 20 percent
of its profits in the territory of Amapá, some
of which have gone into a plywood plant and
other local industries, ICOMI is engaged in
a joint venture with an international company
Svenska Kullagerfabriken (SKF), for the pro-

[5] Jose Garrido Torres and Denio Nogueira, *Joint International Business Ventures in Brazil* (New York: Columbia University, September 1959), pp. 78–84; and "Breath-
ing Life into Amapá: The Story of ICOMI," *Brazilian
Business*, May-June 1963.

[6] Bill Williamson, "O Manganese do Amapá," mimeographed, February 1966.

duction of ball bearings in a plant in São Paulo. The royalties paid by ICOMI to the government have constituted the territorial government's largest source of revenue and have gone mainly to Cía de Eletricidade do Amapá (CEA), a mixed company engaged in the production and distribution of electric power in the territory. There are plans for the future construction by ICOMI of a ferro-manganese electric furnace plant when sufficient energy becomes available.

In addition to providing half of the equity capital and a $1.9 million loan, Bethlehem Steel has provided mining engineers and experts in various fields relating to mining and construction operations and the use of certain of its patents for which it is understood that royalties are not paid to Bethlehem. During the construction phase, 120 foreign technicians were working with ICOMI, but by early 1963 only six foreign technicians remained, all working under Brazilian managers.[7] Much of Bethlehem's assistance to ICOMI has reportedly been rendered on a gratis basis, and once ICOMI's operations in Amapá were well launched, Bethlehem personnel tended to fade out of the picture. A conscious effort appears to have been made to play down Bethlehem's role in ICOMI in its public statements.

I have been unable to find in the responsible Brazilian press any recent criticism of ICOMI and of its association with Bethlehem Steel, although there was some criticism of the concession contract at the time it was made because of the association of foreign interests.[8] Dr. Antunes pointed out that all attempts to interest Brazilian capital had failed and that in addition foreign technical assistance and experience were greatly needed. The contribution to the Amazon area of Amapá has been considerable; over 12 percent of the Amapá territory population has

directly or indirectly benefited from the operations of ICOMI in achieving a level of living thus far unknown in the Amazon region. Wages and fringe benefits are on a par with those found in the industrial centers in the south of Brazil and health and educational facilities, together with good housing, have been brought by the company to an equatorial region previously devoid of the comforts and advantages of modern life. The ICOMI contract with the government of Amapá has generally been regarded as quite favorable to Brazil. Dr. Antunes is very popular in Brazil and is apparently admired by all but the extreme leftists. He has established with his large fortune the first major philanthropic foundation in Brazil.

CONCLUSION

This short case history provides an example of a successful foreign investment in mineral resources which has taken the form of a joint venture from the beginning. Moreover, the mining rights were obtained by ICOMI according to procedures fully in accord with both the letter and the spirit of the 1934 Constitution. I believe that these facts are not unrelated to the minimum of legal and political difficulties which Bethlehem encountered in Brazil during a period in which certain other foreign investors were faced with substantial problems of a political origin. Bethlehem was, of course, especially fortunate in teaming up with such a congenial and competent partner. It is of interest that Hanna, whose experience is discussed in the previous chapter, is also expected to become associated with the Antunes mining group. However, as was pointed out in the previous chapter, the actual operations of Hanna and Bethlehem in their particular joint ventures with the Antunes group are expected to remain separate even though their interests may become a part of the same Brazilian corporate holding company structure.

[7] Paul V. Shaw, "Know-How Conquers Jungle," *Brazil Herald*, 19 March 1963.
[8] Governor Carlos Lacerda, who has attacked Hanna's operations in Brazil, told me that he is a great admirer of Dr. Antunes and of his contribution to Brazilian mineral development.

[26]

Excerpt from Duncan Innes, *Anglo American and the Rise of Modern South Africa*, 229–42.

CONCLUSION

Anglo American and South African Imperialism

This study has concentrated almost exclusively on Anglo American's position in the political economy of South Africa. In so doing it has focused not only on Anglo's rise to power within the industrial economy but also on the social and political conditions which surrounded and influenced that process. Such an approach has enabled us both to locate Anglo American in relation to the fundamental forces which motivate capitalist society in South Africa and to chart the evolution of that society over time. Inevitably, there must be omissions and short-comings in a work which attempts such an all-embracing study over a time-span of more than a hundred years. None the less, we would argue that such weaknesses do not detract from the validity of attempting this task, since the particular perspective or overview which it affords is one which no micro-study could hope to provide. However, there *are* omissions in this study and before closing this investigation some of these omissions need to be briefly dealt with. In this conclusion we will summarize those aspects of Anglo's activities which, though largely ignored so far, we feel it necessary to comment on before putting forward a final definition of the Group. These relate to the question of corporate control within the Group and to the international scope of its activities.

Throughout this study we have tended to view the interests of the Anglo American Group and those of its successive chairmen, Ernest and Harry Oppenheimer, as more or less synonymous with one another. The reason for this is obvious: since its inception the Anglo Group has been closely identified with subsequent generations of the Oppenheimer family. Anton Dunkelsbuhler, the Group's founder, was the uncle of both Ernest and Louis Oppenheimer, the two brothers who played such a crucial role in the Group's formative years. Ernest's son Harry followed his father as chairman and today Harry's son Nicholas is an important figure in the Group as is Harry's former son-in-law, Gordon Waddell. Furthermore, within the Group's structure—and yet never in the forefront of Group activity—are to be found private companies, such as Brenthurst Investment Trust (named

230   *Anglo American*

after Harry Oppenheimer's private home) and E. Oppenheimer and Son, which tend to be dominated by members of the Oppenheimer family. This latter company, whose origins date back to the 1860s, has had a particularly close association with the Group throughout its history. The question which immediately presents itself, of course, is that of the precise nature of the association between the Oppenheimer family and the Anglo American Group. Posed in general terms, the question of the relationship between families or individuals with large holdings in giant corporations and the operations of these corporations is one which is of particular interest to social scientists at a number of levels. One of these concerns the potential for manipulation that such a relationship might open up, while another concerns the issue of the way in which control is exercised within such a corporation. As far as the Oppenheimer family and Anglo American are concerned, we do not intend to explore the former question, but we are interested in the latter: i.e., in the nature of the relationship between the family and the Group to the extent that it raises theoretical questions about corporate control. There is a broad body of literature which argues that the diffusion of ownership which has accompanied the historical rise of large public corporations has been accompanied by an inevitable dilution of corporate control. Furthermore, some versions of this thesis claim that under monopoly capitalism 'ownership' and 'control' have been separated from one another, leading to a situation in which a 'managerial class' emerges in control of company operations (see, for instance, Berle, 1954; Burnham, 1960). At first sight it seems as if there is a good deal of truth in these propositions and that there is no reason why they should not be applicable to Anglo American. The Group does indeed consist largely of public corporations in which 'the public' is free to participate. Furthermore, the ownership structure within the Group is highly decentralized, thus suggesting a dilution of owners' control. However, against this, we have the undisputed fact of the Oppenheimer family's domination of the Group over many years. The question is: how does this domination occur and what are its implications for the application of the above theories to Anglo American?

The first point to note is that the internal control structure within the Anglo American Group is highly decentralized. Four holding companies form the inner core of the Group's control structure: the Anglo American Corporation, De Beers Consolidated, the Rand Selection Corporation and Charter Consolidated. Between them there is a complex network of cross-holdings through which each company holds only a minority share in each of its partners (see Figure 6 in Appendix 2). However, *together* these minority holdings add up to a substantial majority share in each company so that, as the *Financial Mail* put it: 'Any international giant attempting [a take-over] on a share swop basis

Conclusion   Anglo American and South African Imperialism   231

would probably end up in the uncomfortable position of having Oppenheimer as its biggest single shareholder.'[1] The importance of this from our present point of view is that it means that it is possible for the Oppenheimer family to dominate the Group as a whole through holding only a minority of the shares in each of the four leading companies. An examination of the Anglo American Corporation's share register at three-yearly intervals reveals that, in 1973, 1976 and 1979, Harry Oppenheimer and his son, Nicholas, between them owned respectively 20.4 per cent, 20.25 per cent and 16.4 per cent of the corporation's total share capital.[2] Though extremely large in absolute terms, these holdings on their own were not sufficient to exert direct control. In 1977, for instance, De Beers alone owned 33 per cent of the Anglo American Corporation. However, if the Oppenheimers' holdings in the Anglo American Corporation are combined with the family's minority shares in other Group companies (especially its stake in De Beers through Consolidated Diamond Mines of South West Africa), these holdings would seem to give the Oppenheimers an almost unassailable position in the Group.

Yet, of course, the family's position can never be totally secure. It is always possible that some outsider or some new coalition from within may appear and buy up sufficient shares to oust the Oppenheimers from their dominant position. At this point the role of a private company like E. Oppenheimer and Son seems to be important within the Group since it helps to promote a sense of *esprit de corps* among senior management and personnel. Not only does this help to discourage a possible internal coup but, in the face of a take-over threat from outside, the danger of disunity within the ranks is subverted. The way this works in practice is quite difficult to discern precisely, since E. Oppenheimer and Son is no longer a public corporation (it converted to a private concern on 1 February 1966) and therefore does not publicly divulge the kind of information which would facilitate an inquiry of this kind. However, prior to going private the company was controlled through a majority shareholding by the Oppenheimer family. In addition, the family encouraged minority participation by non-family members who were often senior Group management and personnel. In terms of the Articles of Association of the company, the terms on which this latter participation occurred were at the sole discretion of the directors who were, for instance, able to determine the price at which shares could be bought and sold.[3] In the light of this it is interesting to observe that in 1966 all the directors of the Anglo American Corporation were also shareholders in and nominees of E. Oppenheimer and Son.[4] Since most of these directors also held key positions on the boards of other Anglo Group companies, it seems reasonable to assume that the Oppenheimer family's control over E. Oppenheimer and Son gave it an effective influence over Group affairs which exceeded that

232 Anglo American

which was immediately apparent from a perusal of the share registers of the companies concerned. If this is so, then it plays havoc with theoretical notions that public ownership *necessarily* leads to a dilution of corporate control. On the contrary, it suggests that public ownership might do no more than obscure the existence of a highly centralized control structure.

Arising out of the analysis we have developed here, we would argue that under monopoly capitalism ownership and control in fact remain tightly interwoven. Certainly, we would not wish to dispute the notion that the emergence of large public corporations has brought with it a diffusion of ownership; nor even would we deny that monopolies have indeed spawned a professional, bureaucratic élite which administers the day-to-day affairs of these large and cumbersome institutions. But, following our investigation of Anglo American, we would argue that power may often be expressed through more subtle forms than simply control over 51 per cent of a company's shares and that the existence of a bureaucracy still leaves open the question of who controls the bureaucrats. Consequently, we have discovered nothing in our analysis of Anglo which leads us to believe that the era of monopoly capitalism brings with it a dilution of corporate control—or, more fundamentally, an end to the control of massive resources by a few. On the contrary, the monopoly era only throws up new organizational forms, such as multinational combines, through which ever greater financial and productive resources are brought within the reach of the few, thereby increasing their power in society a thousandfold.

This leads us to the second question we wished to address: that of the international scope of Anglo American's activities. So far we have addressed the Group largely as a South African-oriented concern and have examined the extent to which its power has increased in South African society. But Anglo American's activities are not confined to South Africa: the Group is, in every sense, an international combine whose various interests reach across five continents. In concluding this analysis of the Group we need to adopt an international perspective and look, briefly, at its position within world capitalism. This will help both to locate the Group in its international context and to illuminate an often neglected aspect of South African capitalist development: its impact on international affairs. As we shall see, the world-wide network of economic relations which Anglo American is constantly forging is no freak phenomenon: it expresses the growing strength of monopoly capitalism in South Africa. And in southern Africa, where it is most heavily concentrated, this strength emerges in the political and economic form of imperialism.

An inspection of the main holdings of the four financial companies which in 1976 formed the inner core of Anglo's Group structure reflects its character as predominantly a South African-based mining-

Conclusion   Anglo American and South African Imperialism   233

finance conglomerate (Appendix 2). But, as we saw in Chapter 6, one of these inner-core companies, Charter Consolidated, is based in London, from where it undertakes investment on a world scale. If we widen our scope to include the ten remaining companies which hold the majority of Group interests this same pattern of South African and non-South African companies emerges. Alongside companies like AMGOLD, AMCOAL, AMIC and AMAPROP (whose primary holdings, respectively, are in South African gold, coal, industry and property), we find a spread of holding companies located outside South Africa: Mineral and Resources Corporation (MINORCO), Anglo American Corporation of Rhodesia (RHOAM), Zambian Copper Investments, Anglo American Corporation of Canada (AMCAN) and Australian Anglo American (AUSTRAM). And if we go wider still and examine the 109 financial companies which hold many of the Group's more important interests we find an even wider spread of non-South African-based companies that includes: Anglo American Corporation of Botswana, Zambian Anglo American Industrial Corporation, Anglo De Beers Forest Services (Lesotho), Angloswazi Investments, Anglo American Corporation of Central Africa, Charter France, Charter Overseas NV (Curaçao), Euranglo Ltd, Societa Nazionale Svilieppo Impresse Industriale (Italy), Anglo American Corporation of South Africa (Portugal), De Beers European Holdings, Bahamas International Trust Company, Cayman International Trust Company, Anglo American International, Anglo American Corporation do Brazil Limitada, Debhold Canada, Engelhard Hanovia Inc., and Anglo American Corporation of the United States.

It is thus clear that (in addition to its South African-based companies) over the years Anglo American has established a number of companies whose specific purpose is to build up Group interests outside South Africa. However, one should not assume that these are the only channels for the Group's non-South African investments. Most of its South African-based companies also include within their portfolios a wide range of investments in companies operating outside South Africa. For instance, of the 139 subsidiaries which AMIC held in 1976, 69 were located outside South Africa: 7 in Zimbabwe; 8 in Zambia; 2 each in Swaziland and Mozambique; 1 each in Botswana and Liberia; 8 in Britain; 4 in Federal Germany; 3 in the Netherlands; 1 each in Switzerland, Norway, Portugal, Luxembourg, Ireland, Sweden, France and Italy; 5 each in the United States of America and Canada; 2 in Mexico; 1 each in Brazil, Costa Rica, Bahamas and Chile; 7 in Australia; and 1 each in New Zealand and the Philippines.[5] The spread of international investments is thus extremely large and involves companies in a range of different economic activities. In 1976 at least 11 of Anglo's 27 leading financial companies (like banks and insurance companies) were located outside South Africa, as were 45 of its 193 major industrial and agricul-

234   Anglo American

tural companies.⁶ But it is principally through mining that the Group spreads itself internationally.

In 1976 Anglo was involved in over 250 different companies which were active in mining in at least 22 different countries of the world. These interests, which included mine holding, exploration, production and marketing concerns, were spread throughout an astonishing range of minerals and included 48 gold mines (some of which were uranium producers as well), 31 prospecting companies, 29 diamond companies, 28 coal mines, 22 copper and nickel mines, 10 oil ventures (including North Sea oil), 7 platinum mines, 5 tin mines, 5 iron mines, 2 chrome mines, 2 lead mines, 2 vanadium mines and one mine each in uranium, asbestos, potash, soda, lime, scheelite, manganese and silver. The 22 countries through which these interests were spread were: South Africa, Namibia, Zimbabwe, Zambia, Botswana, Lesotho, Swaziland, Angola, Tanzania, Mauretania, Madagascar, Britain, Ireland, Sweden, France, Portugal, Canada, Australia, Brazil, Mexico, Chile and Malaysia). This vast array of companies and international operations provides the basis for Anglo to link up with some of the world's most important international mining companies, such as ALCAN, American Metal Climax, Bethlehem Steel (US), International Nickel of Canada, Rio Tinto Zinc, Kennecott Copper (US) and Newmont Mining. But Anglo's links with the world's leading multinationals go far wider than just these *mining* companies, taking in an assortment of at least 73 international *banking* and *industrial* concerns.⁷ Thus the Anglo American Group forms an important link in a vast and complex chain through which a relatively few massive international combines control the bulk of the productive resources in the capitalist world.

We will not go into any detail here on the way in which Anglo American rose to such international prominence, since that is itself a major task which goes well beyond our present scope. Yet a few comments on this theme do need to be made in order to assess correctly the relationship between Anglo's international operations and its base in South Africa. Perhaps most important is to identify the precise point in time at which this international expansion commenced.

Although (like all the major South African mining groups) Anglo had originally been based in London, the decision to transfer the Group's head office to South Africa and the subsequent collapse of the London-based Consolidated Mines Selection Co. resulted in Anglo's foreign interests being largely neglected. Although during the 1920s, 1930s and 1940s these were built up again the new investments tended to be concentrated in southern Africa, especially in Namibian and Angolan diamonds and in Northern and Southern Rhodesian copper and other minerals. The 1950s were spent mainly developing the new gold fields in South Africa, but in 1958 an event occurred which was to prove crucial to Anglo's subsequent international expansion: the take-over of

Conclusion   Anglo American and South African Imperialism   235

the Central Mining–Rand Mines Group. Carried through in conjunction with the American-based Engelhard Group, this coup gave Anglo an important foot-hold on the American continent. With a stream of revenue now pouring out of its South African gold mines, Anglo began to reorganize its scattered non-South African interests. Consolidated Mines Selection was resurrected in London to combine these interests under a centralized control at the same time as Anglo, again in conjunction with Engelhard, took control of a major Canadian mining conglomerate, the Hudson Bay Mining and Smelting Co. No sooner was this take-over completed than in 1964 Anglo merged Consolidated Mines Selection with the recently acquired Central Mining Company and with another old imperialist war-horse, the Chartered (or British South Africa) Co., to form Charter Consolidated. From that moment onwards Anglo American's international interests grew in both scope and size.

The important point here is that Anglo's growing international presence corresponds exactly with the early phase of its diversified expansion inside South Africa. At precisely the time Anglo was creating a local money market in South Africa and taking its first major steps into South African industry (such as through the Highveld Steel project) it was also making its first significant moves to carve out an international presence for itself through Charter. These very different phenomena in fact do have a common origin in the gold mines of the Orange Free State. It was the revenue being generated here which provided the stimulus and the financial means for both aspects of Group expansion, helping to establish Anglo American not only as a diversified industrial and financial conglomerate in South Africa, but also as a multinational combine.

There is, however, a further aspect of Anglo's international expansion which is of special interest—and that is the unlikely origins of MINORCO, which is Charter's most important partner in the international field. MINORCO began life as the Zambian Anglo American Corporation (ZAMANGLO), which held Anglo's interests in Zambia, consisting mainly of a half share in the country's large copper industry. Following political independence the Zambian government nationalized the copper mines, which involved *inter alia* buying up 51 per cent of ZAMANGLO. Full compensation was paid to the company's shareholders in American dollars and without any restriction being placed on their repatriation abroad. Shortly afterwards Anglo American established MINORCO in the Atlantic tax-haven of Bermuda. Fed with revenue from the Zambian copper mines (handily converted into dollars), MINORCO became a major international force during the 1970s. With Charter concentrating its investment programme on Africa, Europe and Australasia, MINORCO largely assumed responsibility for the American side, investing in Latin

236 Anglo American

America, Canada and the United States. Nor are these latter investments small-scale undertakings: by the start of the 1980s MINORCO had become the largest single foreign investor in the United States of America (with a total revenue of $26 570m). This position was held ahead of established oil giants like the Royal Dutch Shell Group (ranked second with a revenue of $19 830m) and BP (ranked third with a revenue of $11 023m).[8] It is one of the ironies of history that a struggling underdeveloped country such as Zambia should have created the original wealth which enabled a South African multinational to become subsequently the largest foreign investor in the world's most developed capitalist state.

These international developments establish beyond doubt that Anglo American can be understood in no other way than as a multinational—and one of the world's more important multinationals at that. The fact that its highly decentralized control structure prevents the Anglo Group from appearing on the list of the world's top 100 companies should not deceive anyone into believing that it does not belong in such exalted company. Individual Group companies, such as De Beers and the Anglo American Corporation itself, have on occasion reached the lower rungs of this list and, undoubtedly, were the Group's interests to be combined for these purposes it would be a permanent fixture. However, not only is the Group large by international standards, but the very way in which it conducts its international operations is an expression of its international strength. No longer does the Group simply spread itself across the world on an unco-ordinated basis: instead, it neatly divides the world up, creating Charter to take responsibility for Group expansion in one half and MINORCO to handle the other. Nor when we speak of the world in this context do we mean only the capitalist world. Recent evidence suggests that in certain spheres at least (such as diamonds, gold and platinum) collaboration takes place between Anglo American and the Soviet Union over international pricing policy.[9]

But perhaps it is through its American involvement that the Group's current international strength is most aptly expressed. The fact that Anglo should appear well ahead of such international giants as Shell, BP, ICI, Unilever and Volkswagen (to mention only a few) in the list of foreign investors in the United States suggests a major new direction in Anglo's international investment strategy. But even more startling is the fact that the Group commands sufficient financial resources to attain such a position. Such a development, of course, may have dire implications for classical theories of imperialism which assume a one-way flow of investment (export of capital) from the capitalist centre to the periphery (see, for instance, Lenin, 1973b, and Frank, 1970b). When corporations like Anglo emerge—based in the capitalist periphery and exporting capital to the centre—it seems as if these theories

Conclusion   Anglo American and South African Imperialism   237

are turned upside down. The question that underlies this debate is that of the relationship between Anglo American and South African capitalism. If one assumes that there is no integral relationship between the two—that Anglo is simply a free-floating international institution without a 'home base' in South Africa or anywhere else—then Anglo's growing investments in the capitalist centres tell us absolutely nothing about centre–periphery relations under capitalism. If, on the other hand, we argue that Anglo's massive presence in South Africa locates it as a specifically *South African* institution, then its growing involvement in the capitalist centres *does* have implications for centre–periphery theories of imperialism. In particular, it poses serious problems for those theories which assume that imperialism promotes growth in the centre at the inevitable expense of the chronic underdevelopment of the periphery.

In this work we have adopted the perspective that Anglo American can only be understood as a South African-based multinational combine. It is the monopoly control which the Group came to exert primarily in South African gold and diamond mining which has been the key to its subsequent success both in South Africa and abroad. Furthermore, we have argued that, primarily because of its position as a major producer of strategic minerals, South African capitalism has undergone important economic transformations, breaking free of chronic patterns of under-development and establishing a relatively strong industrial base (though still retaining a dependency relation with the capitalist centres). Similarly, we have argued that these changes in the nature of South African capitalism were accompanied by changes in its form, as monopoly relations permeated first mining and then the industrial and financial sectors of the economy, ultimately giving rise to monopoly capitalism. At every stage of this process we have seen that Anglo American played a decisive role. Of crucial significance here is the way in which these various processes coalesced in the late 1950s and 1960s. It was during this period that Anglo American, benefiting especially from its postwar investments in gold, began to diversify into local industry, finance and property, and to take its first major steps on the road to international expansion. Equally, it was during this period that South Africa's economy developed along monopoly lines. Thus Anglo's international 'take-off' occurs at precisely the time South African capitalism begins to transform itself into monopoly capitalism. The question is whether these changes are coincidental or whether they express another transition: that of the evolution of South African imperialism.

To answer this question one has to go far wider than simply recording South Africa's growing economic links internationally. In addition, one has to look at the nature of these links, their effect on the host economies, the political relations which accompany them and, most

238 Anglo American

important, the impact on the social classes in the host country. These questions clearly take us well beyond our present scope and, in any event, we would be foolish to try and argue that Anglo's involvement in the United States of America or Britain implies that these states are being colonized by South African capitalism. But what of smaller and weaker states which would be more susceptible to South Africa's economic and political influence? Does the transition to monopoly capitalism in South Africa have implications for these states and, if so, what are they?

There is in fact considerable evidence that South Africa's relations with African states, and in particular those in southern Africa, have undergone a profound change in the post-Second World War period in which monopoly capitalism established itself in South Africa. Namibia provides probably the most clear-cut example of this. Although administered by South Africa since 1919, the relationship between South Africa and Namibia changed dramatically after the Second World War. Between 1920 and 1942 Namibia's GDP did not grow at all and by 1945 was only 52 per cent higher than it had been in 1920. Between 1946 and 1962, however, the GDP grew by a massive 573 per cent and, between 1962 and 1973, by a further 320 per cent.[10] This high rate of postwar expansion is exceptional by international standards and reflects a new direction in South African economic policy in Namibia. Prior to the war South Africa had done virtually nothing to develop Namibia's economic resources: state aid had been largely confined to resettling a relatively small number of white farmers and Anglo American had actually reduced the productive capacity of its diamond mines in order to protect its other diamond interests. After the war, however, the South African state and individual capitalists were instrumental in initiating Namibia's economic recovery. Anglo rejuvenated the diamond industry and, together with other South African and international monopolies, participated in a range of other mining ventures. In 1964 the South African-appointed Odendaal Commission recommended 'a broad programme of capital expenditure' in Namibia and, following this, the South African state began pumping money into the Namibian economy (at least R150m was injected between 1964 and 1969).[11] The question is: what was it that produced this *volte face* in South Africa's economic policy?

Undoubtedly, social and political factors, like the growth of a Namibian resistance movement committed to securing political independence from South Africa and the United Nation's decision to put an end to South Africa's administration, were important influences in this respect. But it is revealing that this policy change begins at the same time as the South African economy begins to transform itself along monopoly lines—that is, during the 1950s—and that the restructuring of Namibia's political economy, which the Odendaal Commission in-

Conclusion   Anglo American and South African Imperialism   239

itiates, is carried through at precisely the time that the process of
monopoly transformation in South Africa reaches new heights—that is,
during the 1960s and 1970s. It is thus possible that the transition to
monopoly capitalism in South Africa also produced the phenomenon of
South African imperialism. This view is in fact confirmed by an inspection of the nature of the links forged over this period between South
Africa and Namibia and of their effects on Namibia's political and economic independence. In general, these links have tended to tie
Namibia into a position of increasingly strong dependence on South
African capitalism which denies its political independence, distorts its
economy and undermines its society as a whole.[12]

What seems to have happened is that in the pre-Second World War
period, despite the fact that South Africa was in political control of
Namibia, South African capitalism was too weak to gain any major
economic advantage from this relationship. As we saw, during that
period South African capitalism was itself restrained by its relationship
to the European imperialist powers. However, the gradual shift in the
form of that relationship during the 1930s and after, coupled with the
important developments in South African mining and industry after
the war, greatly strengthened South African capitalism, giving it the
capacity from then on to exploit Namibia's economic potential. As the
process of monopolization intensified in South Africa, so that country's
political, economic and military stranglehold over Namibia has tightened. Whatever the formal legal relation between the two countries,
Smuts's words spoken immediately after the war—that Namibia's
relationship to South Africa 'more nearly approximated to that of a
colonial possession than anything else'—have undoubtedly been
proved correct by history (cited in Wellington, 1967, p. 329).

But it is not just in South Africa's relationship with Namibia that the
former's imperialistic tendencies have manifested themselves since the
war. The extremely close economic ties which South Africa has forged
with the former High Commission Territories over the last few decades
have inevitably undermined the political independence of these states
as well. In 1965 South Africa's Prime Minister, Dr Verwoerd, stated: 'I
believe that the one thing which really counts in international relationships is common economic interests. So far as these Governments [of
Botswana, Lesotho and Swaziland] are concerned, their political interests will be dominated by their economic interests' (cited in Maryse-
Cockram, 1970). Nor was this just bombastic rhetoric. Botswana's first
President, Seretse Khama, openly acknowledged the strength of Verwoerd's position when he said:

> We fully appreciate that it is wholly in our interests to preserve as
> friendly and neighbourly relations with the Republic of South Africa as
> possible. Our economic links with the Republic are virtually indissolu-
> ble. Economically we are directly tied to the Republic for communica-

240   Anglo American

tions, for markets, for our beef exports, for labour on the mines, and in many other respects.[13]

The economic and political strength which South African capitalism acquired through its monopoly transformation enabled the state to spread its influence throughout the whole southern African region during the 1960s and 1970s, extending into Mozambique, Angola, Malawi, Zambia and (as it then was) Rhodesia. Nor has this influence been confined to southern Africa. The South African state's 'outward' policy of the 1960s, its 'dialogue' policy of the early 1970s and its 'detente' policy of the late 1970s were all intended to promote South Africa's influence throughout the African continent. And even today, though revolutions in Angola, Mozambique and Zimbabwe have forced the South African state to change tack and adopt a more militaristic policy, the fundamental drive towards outward expansion—towards imperialist domination—is stronger than ever.

It is not our purpose here to analyse whether or not this expansionist policy will be successful, nor even to analyse the social and political forces which are building up in opposition. All we are concerned to do is to establish that South Africa's transition to monopoly capitalism has been accompanied by a corresponding drive towards imperialism. If this is in fact the case then it means that, even though its influence is as yet largely confined only to southern Africa, South Africa has become an active participant in forging the international network of economic and political relations which constitutes the modern system of imperialism. As such South Africa can no longer be classified as simply an underdeveloped Third World country, but rather must be ranked as an imperialist power located on the periphery of world capitalism. Certainly, because of its historical location, South Africa is considerably weaker than those 'more traditional' imperialist powers which are located in the capitalist centres. Yet it would be quite wrong to assume that this means that therefore these powers will willingly exert pressure to force South Africa to abandon policies of which they might disapprove. Though the South African economy remains technologically dependent on the major imperialist powers, the links between South Africa and these powers, especially through monopoly investments, trade and finance, are so firmly integrated that it would be almost unthinkable that these imperialist powers would be willing to use this technological dependence as a weapon against South Africa.

The position which South African capitalism has achieved for itself is therefore one which makes a nonsense of any imperialist theory which argues that perpetual underdevelopment and economic backwardness are inevitable consequences for countries on the capitalist periphery. Clearly, the case of South Africa (as well as of others like Brazil) poses serious problems for theories which base themselves either on the historical experiences of the early twentieth century or on the current

Conclusion   Anglo American and South African Imperialism   241

experiences of countries which do not possess commodities for which
there is a large export demand. Without abandoning an historical approach, we need to evolve a theory of imperialism which draws on the
current experiences of countries like South Africa as much as those of
Tanzania, Upper Volta and Paraguay. Such a theory should not only be
sharply critical of traditional notions of 'development' and 'underdevelopment', but should also question whether historical notions of
'centre' and 'periphery' still have the same meaning today as before.
Does it in fact make sense to argue, as we have done in the preceding
paragraph, that South Africa is still located on the periphery of world
capitalism or is such an approach not too 'geographically' determined?
Should we not rather speak of South Africa as being today a part of a
wider capitalist centre, but if so, how then do we distinguish it from
the position of the older imperialist powers? And what, too, of the
changing relations among these latter powers and, especially, of the
implications of Britain's current industrial decline? Today the processes of economic and political change are developing more rapidly
than ever before and theories of imperialism which remain locked in
the events and conditions of the early years of this century are hopelessly inadequate as explanations of these modern developments.
There is an urgent necessity to produce a theory of imperialism which
can satisfactorily answer the kinds of questions which this study of
South Africa has raised.

Thus to conclude we would briefly sum up our findings on the nature
of Anglo American and its relationship to South African capitalism
today as follows. The Anglo American Group has evolved into a multinational combine which is engaged on a world scale in a wide range of
economic activities of which mining is the most important. These interests—and therefore the Group's influence—reach out from a power
base which is firmly rooted in South African society. That society itself
is far from static. Over the past one hundred years it has transformed
itself from an underdeveloped chattel of imperialism into an aggressive
imperialist power which exhibits many of the characteristics of a monopoly capitalist society. Foremost among these is the decisive power
which monopoly groups like Anglo American wield within that society.
Yet if over the past century Anglo American and South African capitalism have achieved an awesome degree of power it is as well to remember that in the process they have also created a countervailing force
which may well have the potential to wrest that power from them. The
capitalist class which developed the world's largest gold fields has also
produced the largest proletariat in Africa.

242   Anglo American

NOTES

1. *Financial Mail*, Special Survey, 'Inside the Anglo Power House', p. 17.
2. These holdings, which were split equally between the two, involved 13.25 million shares apiece in 1973; 13.34 million apiece in 1976; and 18.33 million apiece in 1979. (Anglo American Corp. of SA, *Annual Report, 1973, 1976* and *1979*.)
3. Para. 166(c)(i) of the company's Articles of Association stated: 'The shares shall be under the control of the Directors, who may allot issue or otherwise dispose of the same to such person or persons at such times and with such rights and privileges and generally on such terms and conditions and either at a premium or otherwise as the Directors may think fit.' See also para. 166(c)(ii).
4. Letter to Mr. H. Oppenheimer from H. B. Samuel, dated 2 September 1966.
5. AMIC, *Annual Report, 1976*, pp. 28–30.
6. Among Anglo's more important financial interests outside South Africa were: British and Rhodesian Discount House, Southampton Assurance Co. of Rhodesia, Rhodesian Acceptances, Merchant Bank (Zambia) Ltd, Standard Bank of Angola, Standard Bank of Mozambique, Standard Charter Bank Group, Compagnie Financière de Paris et des Pays-Bas, and International Pacific Corp. (Australia) Ltd.

    Among Anglo's more important industrial interests outside South Africa were: Chilanga Cement, Durham Industries of Canada, Dunlop (Zambia), Duncan Gilbey and Matheson (Zambia), Explosives (Zambia), Engelhard Industries, Industriade Caju Mocita (Mozambique), Kenya Fertilizers, Mozambique Fisheries, Metal Fabricators of Zambia, National Milling Company (Zambia), Zambia Breweries, Rhodesian Diamond and Carbide, Rhodesian Iron and Steel Corp., Rhodesian Alloys, South Wales Group, Scandiamant Aktiebolag, Terra Chemicals International, Rhodesian Milling Co., Unitor (Zambia), Werff Brothers, White Pass and Yukon, Wendt GMBH, Zinc Oxides of Canada, Zambia Clay Industries, Ultra High Pressure Units (Ireland), De Beers Industrial Diamond Division (Ireland), Industrias de Caju, Antenes SARL, Gerencia Industrial Limitada, and Christensen and Boart Oilfield Products. (See Appendix 2.)
7. These include: Banca Commerciale Italiane, Banque de Paris et des Pays-Bas, Crédit Foncier Franco-Canadien, Barclays Bank, Bowater Paper, Cayzer Group, British Steel Corp., Rheem International, Computer Sciences Corp., Cory Mann George, Deutsche Bank, Dunlop, Eastern Stainless Steel, First National City Bank of New York, ICI, IMI Japan, Johnson Matthey, Kleinwort Benson, Klöchner and Co., KZO, Volvo, Mazda, Lazard Brothers, Manbré and Gartons, Mitsubishi, Mitsui, Morgan Grenfell, Morgan Guaranty Trust, Nalco Chemicals, P. & O. Shipping Group, Petrofina, Rothschilds, Royal Dutch Shell, Selection Trust, Société Generale Belge, Société Nationale des Pétroles d'Aquitaine, Somic, Standard Chartered Bank, Standard Oil of Indiana, Titan Products, Union Bank of Switzerland, US Natural Oil, United Transport, Metropolitan Vickers, and Weyerhauser. In addition the Group is linked in one way or another in productive ventures with at least eight different governments: those of South Africa, Chile, Iran, Swaziland, Botswana, Tanzania, the United Kingdom and Zambia. (See Appendix 3.)
8. *Forbes*, Special Report: Spotlight on International Business, 6 July 1981, pp. 83–91.
9. 'Gold and Diamonds: The Kremlin Connection', BBC1 *Panorama* programme, 6 April 1981.
10. The figures for the GDP were as follows: 1920—R13.0m; 1942—R12.2m; 1945—R19.8m; 1946—R21.8m; 1962—R146.7m; and 1973—R615.6m. (Report of the Commission of Inquiry into South West African Affairs, 1962–3, RP no. 12/1964, p. 319; and SA Department of Statistics, *South West Africa Survey 1974*, p. 33.)
11. For details of these various economic changes and for an assessment of South African state policy see Innes (1981b, also 1978).
12. For details see the articles cited above.
13. Cited in South African Institute of Race Relations, *A Survey of Race Relations in South Africa 1966* (1967).

4. MINERAL DEVELOPMENT AND GOVERNMENT POLICY IN
MANCHUKUO

The latest estimates for mineral production in Manchuria for the years 1929 and 1933 to 1937 inclusive are compared with the goals of the original and the revised Five Year Plans in Table 103. Two facts are at once obvious. Though there was a considerable increase for a number of items, the actual volume of production was still very small in 1937 and was only a fraction of the result hoped for under the Five Year Plan. The production of gold, coke, magnesite, fire clay, cement and ammonium sulphate rose by more than 100 per cent between 1933 and 1937; the figures for iron ore and electricity generated by nearly 100 per cent, pig iron by approximately 65 per cent and coal by more than 35 per cent. The possibility of further increases during 1938 and 1939 will be discussed later in this chapter when the position of each of the important minerals will be reviewed for the Yen Bloc as a whole.

388 THE INDUSTRIALIZATION OF JAPAN AND MANCHUKUO

TABLE 103

MANCHURIA — MINERAL PRODUCTION, 1929–1937*
COMPARED WITH THE FIVE-YEAR PLAN

(Quantities in thousands of metric tons)

	1929	1933	1934	1935	1936	1937	OUTPUT GOAL FIVE-YEAR PLAN Original	Revised
Iron Ore	986	1,177	1,133	1,478	1,795	2,257	6,600	12,000
Pig Iron	294	434	476	608	647	739	2,400	4,860
Steel Ingots	...	...	...	...	...	...	2,500	3,500
Steel Rolled	...	...	...	...	...	...	...	2,000
Lead Ores	...	...	...	...	...	...	124	...
Manganese Ore	0.72	0.75	0.70	0.60	0.28	...	...	...
Gold Ore	14	18	...	...	...	...	{¥200** million	{¥300** million
Gold (in kilograms)	...	...	464	1,887	3,959	...		
Coal	10,024	9,063	10,619	11,187	12,082	12,540	27,000	38,000
Coke	388	476	521	667	712	1,114	...	...
Oil Shale	...	2,683	2,106	3,228	3,648	...	...	...
Crude Oil	...	87	58	120	123	...	...	...
Liquid Fuel	...	...	...	...	...	...	1,356	2,500
Coal Liquefaction	...	...	...	...	...	...	500	1,700
Shale Oil	...	...	...	...	...	...	800	650
Alcohol	...	...	...	...	...	...	56	150
Magnesite	32	71	100	225	192	350	...	...
Fire Clay	69	112	79	138	148	266	...	...
Dolomite	...	...	166	170	179	...	...	...
Limestone	630	693	419	651	1,002	939	...	...
Aluminum	...	...	...	...	...	...	20	...
Asbestos	...	...	0.12	0.07	0.07	...	15	...
Cement	...	...	331	371	650	797	...	...
Sulphate of Ammonia	...	...	26	156	181	182	...	...
Salt { Kwantung	242	291	243	505	413	429	...	...
Salt { Manchukuo	278	316	162	396	478	405	875	1,000
Soda Ash	...	...	...	...	...	...	72	...
Pulp	...	...	...	...	...	...	300	400
Electricity Generated (in million KWH)	...	...	782	949	1,248	1,481	...	...
Electric Power (in thousand KW)	...	...	...	...	...	420	1,445	2,600
Hydraulic	...	...	...	...	...	...	575	1,260
Coal	...	...	...	...	...	...	870	1,340

Sources: *Fifth Report on Progress in Manchuria to 1936*, p. 166; *Sixth Report on Progress in Manchuria to 1939*, p. 157; *Contemporary Manchuria*, July 1937, pp. 148–49; *Manshu Keizai Nempo* for 1938 (Manchuria Economic Year Book), South Manchuria Railway Company (Tokyo, 1939), pp. 92–4 and Appendix, p. 1.
* The production figures are estimates compiled by the South Manchuria Railway Company and by the Manchukuo government. The 1937 figures are preliminary estimates. For other versions, see *Contemporary Manchuria*, January, 1938, p. 148 and *Japan-Manchukuo Year Book*, 1939, p. 798.
** Over five years.

The reader may encounter different figures for production or for the aims of the various plans to increase industrial capacity. The statistics are constantly being revised in a most confusing manner so that as many as four or five different sets of figures may be published within a few months. Fortunately the differences are not very large in the case of important commodities such as iron ore, pig iron, coal, and gold. The most reliable reports for Manchukuo seem to be those issued by the South Manchuria Railway Company. The *Reports on Progress* appear at infrequent intervals, but *Contemporary Manchuria* appears several times a year.[19] It is not surprising that there should be difficulties and uncertainties when we realize that the boundaries of the country have changed from time to time since 1932; that statistics for the Japanese administered South Manchuria Railway Zone and Kwantung Leased territory were sometimes included and sometimes excluded, and that only a relatively small part of the huge territory has been settled and properly administered. The period covered may be the calendar year, the fiscal year, or the year ending June 30. It is not always clear whether coal production figures include coal produced and consumed by the railways or whether iron ore figures lump together concentrated ores and ores in their natural state. The railway zone ceased to be a separate administrative area on December 1, 1937, when Japan formally relinquished her extraterritorial rights, but Kwantung Leased Territory is still under Japanese jurisdiction.

It is possible that the statistics have improved but that figures of this kind are no longer being published for the usual strategic reasons. On the whole, however, information on Manchurian industry has been published much more freely in the recent period than

---

[19] One explanation of the statistical difficulties is offered in the foreword to the *Sixth Report on Progress in Manchuria to 1939*. "The statistical materials used in the present Report were derived principally from the Statistics Bureau and other branches of the Manchoukuo Government so far as they relate to Manchoukuo affairs and from the Kwantung Bureau and the South Manchuria Railway Company so far as they relate to Japanese jurisdictional matters and railway activities. An extensive revision of statistics heretofore accepted as authentic is still progressing under the able direction of the Statistics Bureau of the Manchoukuo Government as much of the Manchuria statistical materials in the past were estimates. This continues to explain occasional differences inevitably arising between the figures given in the previous Reports and the revised figures used in the present Report. Unless they are obviously clear, therefore, the sources of information are generally indicated. As a matter of general principle, the latest figures instead of the previously published ones should be used."

390 THE INDUSTRIALIZATION OF JAPAN AND MANCHUKUO

similar information on Japanese industry. There is yet another source of difficulty for anyone attempting to follow current developments in Korea and Manchukuo. There seem to be no good maps which make it possible to locate towns, mines or electric power sites which have become important recently. There have also been a number of changes of names and there seem to be several variations in the spelling of some names. To add to the confusion, the government has recently changed the method of romanization of Japanese names from the old *Hepburn* system to a new system called *Kokutci*. In government literature, for example, Chosen is now Tyosen and Fuji is now Huzi. Many scholars in the field hope that this attempt to change long familiar usage will be abandoned. There is considerable opposition to this innovation both at home and abroad. Because of these many difficulties, it was necessary to abandon the idea of including maps in this volume.

Though there were increases in the output of minerals from 1933 on, the results were disappointing to both Japan and Manchukuo. The magnitude of the task of developing Manchukuo had not been adequately appreciated. There was a feeling that the Japanese investment in men and materials was not likely to yield the returns anticipated and there was a growing reluctance on the part of Japanese capitalists to make further investments to develop the new state under the conditions imposed by the Manchukuo government. This feeling was shared by the Japanese government in 1935 when Finance Minister Takahashi warned the nation against a continuation of large military expenditures and capital exports to Manchukuo. The army groups were anxious to develop Manchuria for strategic reasons and resented this opposition.

The Kwantung Army which was generally anti-capitalist and opposed to the powerful position held by the big financial and industrial groups in Japan, influenced strongly the attitude of the Manchukuo government in the direction of a controlled economy and a "rational" development of resources. The fundamental policy was officially announced on March 1, 1933, in the General Outline of the Economic Construction Program of Manchukuo. This policy was designed "to avoid the baneful effects of unbridled capitalism through the application of a certain measure of national control so that a sound development in all branches of the people's economy

MINERAL RESOURCES OF JAPAN AND MANCHUKUO 391

may be realized." [20] It hoped, nevertheless, to enlist private capital from all parts of the world and placed special emphasis on the interdependence and the necessity for close co-operation in the economic sphere between Japan and Manchukuo.

There were various degrees of control. The mining and manufacturing industries most closely identified with the public interest and the national defense were to be placed under the management of official or semi-official corporations (usually referred to as special or semi-special companies). These included the production of gold in the state owned mines, essential minerals, light metals, iron and steel, shale oil, munitions, electric power, opium and weights and measures. These essential industries were to be carried on under strict government control; a second group could be operated under government permit; and a third group was left to free enterprise. The second group included cotton, wool, gas, automobile, ammonium sulphate, alcohol, soda and tobacco manufacturing and gold mining outside the state owned mines.

The Manchukuo government was determined to avoid the wastefulness and confusion attendant on private ownership and operation of natural resources in other parts of the world and wished to be in a position to mobilize strategic raw materials for industrial development and national defense. In 1934 and 1935 four special companies were established by the government in co-operation with the South Manchuria Railway Company to insure a rational exploitation of mineral resources with the railway company and the government each putting up half the capital in most cases. The Manchuria Petroleum Company, the Manchuria Gold Mining Company, the Manchuria Coal Mining Company and the Manchuria Mining Development Company were founded in this way. Late in 1937 three of these special companies and a number of semi-special companies were placed under the control of the newly organized Manchuria Industrial Development Company.

The government was especially interested in the unified development and management of sources of heat and power including petroleum production and refining, coal mining and electric power generation. It was in line with this general policy that the Manchuria Petroleum Company was formed in February, 1934, as a

[20] *Fifth Report on Progress in Manchuria to 1936*, p. 98.

392 THE INDUSTRIALIZATION OF JAPAN AND MANCHUKUO

special company to monopolize the exploitation and refining of crude petroleum, and the Oil Monopoly Law was promulgated in November, 1934, to apply to refined petroleum products such as gasoline, kerosene, light and heavy oil, benzine, and fuel oil substitutes. It made these petroleum products a government monopoly and permitted their manufacture, exportation, and importation only to authorized dealers. The government intended to manage these monopolies in such a way as to develop Manchurian resources and refining capacity at the expense of the importers of refined products. The foreign companies, including Standard Vacuum-Oil and Texas Oil, maintained that they were being forced out because the business left to them would no longer be profitable. The American, British, and Dutch governments protested to Tokyo that the Open Door Principle was being violated but their protests were not effective since Japan denied any responsibility, and the foreign governments could not negotiate directly with the government of Manchukuo which they had refused to recognize. The Manchuria Petroleum Company established a large plant at Kanseishi across the bay from Dairen where it refines imported crude oil and sells the refined products to the government, which has a monopoly on the sale of gasoline, kerosene, gas oil, heavy oil, benzol and fuel oil substitutes.

The emphasis on gold mining in the Japanese Empire and in Manchukuo is the consequence of an irrational turn in international economic relations. The United States and many other countries are reluctant to receive commodities in payment for other commodities in the course of international trade but will cheerfully take any amount of gold in payment for raw materials and manufactures. Increasing trade and exchange restrictions and prevailing uncertainties of all kinds have contributed to making gold mining more than ever a strategic industry in spite of the abandonment of the gold standard by many countries. The Manchuria Gold Mining Company was established in May, 1934, to develop all the state owned gold mines and alluvial gold beds in the country. It was empowered not only to mine and refine gold itself but also to entrust these enterprises to others. The Manchuria Coal Mining Company was established at the same time to acquire control over and to exploit the coal mines of Manchukuo with the exception of the mines belonging to the South Manchuria Railway Company and the Okura Company. Among the coal mines which it now controls are the Fuhsin and Peipiao mines in Chinchow Province, Hsian in Fengtien Province, Holikang in Sankiang Province, Mishan and Muleng in Mutankiang Province and Chalainor in North Hsingan Province.

The Mining Law of August, 1935, designated 40 legal minerals; provided that all minerals not yet mined should belong to the state; restricted mining rights to Manchurian subjects and corporations unless special permission was obtained from the Minister of Industry; permitted sub-leasing; and carefully defined mining rights in general. At the same time, the Manchuria Mining Development Company was established by an Imperial Ordinance. It was given the exclusive right to mine 23 important minerals including platinum, lead, zinc, tin, iron, antimony, aluminum, nickel, manganese, petroleum, oil shale, magnesite and asbestos. Anyone who discovers deposits of any of these minerals and wishes to mine them must obtain a lease from and pay a royalty to the company. It is part of the business of the Manchuria Mining Development Company to acquire leases and mining privileges, to refine ores and to invest in or otherwise finance refining enterprises. For the most part, the regulations outlined above which gave monopolistic privileges to the special companies did not affect mining rights in existence prior to the formation of the new state. The Showa Steel Works, a subsidiary of the South Manchuria Railway Company, continued to operate coal mines at Fushun and Yentai and iron mines at Anshan and Kungchungling. The Pensihu Iron Works, controlled by the Okura Company of Japan, retained their coal mines at Pensihu and the Miaoerhkou iron deposits. There was also the Manchuria Lead Mining Company, established by the railway company to exploit some promising lead mines. Later the Manchuria Industrial Development Company obtained a controlling interest in these three enterprises.

In addition to the special companies described above there were a number of other special and semi-special organizations promoted primarily by the Manchukuo Government and the South Manchuria Railway Company and also several joint Japanese-Manchurian corporations. The latter were financed by the Oriental Development Company, the Bank of Korea and such Japanese

394 THE INDUSTRIALIZATION OF JAPAN AND MANCHUKUO

financial cliques as Mitsui, Mitsubishi, Sumitomo and Okura. It was claimed that some of these investments were made under a certain amount of pressure as a proof of patriotism. There were 27 of these special companies in existence at the end of 1936; they covered banking, colonization, insurance and agriculture as well as mining and manufacturing.

The expansion of mineral and industrial production from 1933 to 1936 was disappointing. There was a great need of capital which was not forthcoming in sufficient amounts. Even the Japanese industrialists were reluctant to take risks under circumstances of government control which made profits very doubtful. It was rumored that the South Manchuria Railway Company lacked enthusiasm and that it was experiencing difficulty in raising funds for the new companies at the same time that it was expanding transportation facilities on such a large scale. Conditions began to improve in the second half of 1936 although the real reversal of policy came more than a year later under the stimulus of a wartime economy. The original German-Manchukuo Trade Agreement ran for one year from July 1, 1936, and was subsequently extended. In October, 1936, the Hsinking Government published its original Five Year Industrial Development Plan of which a summarized version is presented in Table 103. The plan was to be carried out in the years 1937 to 1941 inclusive. The Important Industries Control Act, which was put into operation in May, 1937, set legal limits to the economic control of the government, gave first consideration to the expansion of strategic industries, and provided for a co-ordinated Manchurian-Japanese industrial development. Soon the outbreak of the war with China in July, 1937, made it more important than ever that Manchurian materials should be available in large amounts for Japanese war industries. The final phase in the transition from a system of rigid state control, anti-capitalist in its outlook, to one which welcomed private capital and gave it unusual opportunities for profit was the formation of the Manchuria Industrial Development Company in December, 1937.

This gigantic holding company, capitalized at 450 million yuan, was authorized to invest in and manage the iron and steel, light metals, coal, automobile, and airplane industries or any part of them. It was also permitted to invest in the mining of gold, zinc,

## MINERAL RESOURCES OF JAPAN AND MANCHUKUO	395

lead, copper and other metals and in other enterprises, but had to obtain government permission for businesses other than mining. One half of the capital was to be subscribed by the Manchukuo government and the other half by the Japan Industry Company, better known as the Nissan interests. Nissan was itself a powerful Japanese holding company, founded in 1928 by Mr. Yoshisuke Aikawa, with extensive investments in the heavy industries. In less than ten years it was the second largest holding company in Japan (Mitsui Gomei was first) with 18 direct subsidiaries engaged in mining, machine, automobile and chemical manufacturing, electricity, and fishing. A list of the principal Japanese subsidiaries will be found in the concluding chapter. It represented a new form of capitalist organization in Japan in that it was an "open concern" with some 50,000 stockholders whereas the stock in the holding companies of the older financial cliques was closely held by small family groups.

The Japan Industry Company moved its head office to Hsinking and became a Manchurian corporation, with Mr. Aikawa as its president. The Manchukuo government purchased from the South Manchuria Railway Company a controlling interest in many of its industrial subsidiaries and turned them over to the new company as part of its subscription. At the time of organization the Manchuria Industrial Development Company controlled 9 principal subsidiaries in Manchukuo and 13 in Japan. Among the Manchurian companies were those listed in the table on page 396.

The steel and iron works were established by Japanese interests many years before the Manchurian Incident and were subsequently reorganized. The Coal, Gold and Mining Development Companies were special companies, the launching of which has already been described. Manchuria Light Metals (Aluminum Manufacturing) was established in November, 1936, for the purpose of producing aluminum from the aluminum shale found in abundance over some of the principal coal mines in Manchukuo. The South Manchuria Railway Company had long conducted experiments at its Fushun coal mines in an effort to perfect methods for obtaining oil and aluminum from shale on a commercial basis. The Dowa Automobile Company was formed in 1934 for the purpose of assembling and distributing in Manchukuo automobiles manufactured in

396 THE INDUSTRIALIZATION OF JAPAN AND MANCHUKUO

MANCHURIAN-INDUSTRIAL DEVELOPMENT CO. COMPANIES DECEMBER, 1937	CAPITAL IN MILLIONS OF YEN [21]			
	December, 1937		September, 1939	
	Authorized	Paid-up	Authorized	Paid-up
Showa Steel Works......................	100	90	200	175
Pensihu Colliery and Iron Works..........	10	10	100	100
Manchuria Coal Mining..................	80	32	200	140
Manchuria Mining Development...........	50	12.5	50	50
Manchuria Gold Mining.................	12	12	...	...
Manchuria Light Metals (Aluminum).......	25	6.25	50	50
Dowa Automobile......................	6.2	3.2	30	18.1
Manchuria Lead Mining.................	4	4	4	4
Manchuria Soya Bean Industry...........	5	2.5	...	...
COMPANIES ADDED LATER				
Manchuria Aircraft Manufacturing.........	...	...	20	20
Tungpientao Development................	...	...	75	41.25
Manchuria Automobile Manufacturing......	...	...	100	25.
Kyowa Iron Mining.....................	...	...	10	10.

Japan. The automobile industry of Japan has been relatively backward and it was part of the Four Year Plan to remedy this situation. The Nissan interests evidently felt that Manchukuo offered certain advantages as the center of an automobile industry. They decided, therefore, after consultation with the Manchukuo government to establish the Manchuria Automobile Manufacturing Company, capitalized at ¥100 million to manufacture automobiles and trucks at Mukden. The Tungpientao Development Company was formed for the purpose of mining iron and coal and producing steel in the southeastern frontier region where large deposits of coal and of high grade iron ores have been opened up in recent years. These were all special or semi-special companies with the exception of Manchuria Lead Mining and Soya Bean Industry.

As there has been no possibility of foreign borrowing by either Japan or Manchukuo since 1931, these developments have been financed almost entirely by Japanese capital [22] and the terms had to be made rather attractive at a time when war industries were booming at home. It was necessary also to change the conviction that the new state was anti-capitalist in its outlook and policies. The government guaranteed a return of 6 per cent for a period of ten

[21] *Sixth Report on Progress in Manchuria to 1939*, pp. 201, 202; "The Heavy Industry of Manchukuo," *East Asia Economic Intelligence Series*, No. 3, January, 1940, p. 28.

[22] Japan's investments in Manchuria will be discussed in the concluding chapter.

years. It also agreed that whenever the private shareholders received a dividend of less than 10 per cent, the government dividend should be half as much. Any excess above 10 per cent for private shares and 5 per cent for public shares was to be divided equally. It was expressly stipulated that there should be no restriction on the dividend rate (as there is now in Japan), no taxation of profits from undertakings outside Manchukuo and no taxation of dividends paid to shareholders outside Manchukuo. Moreover, in the event of a general change in the tax system of Manchukuo the government gave assurances that the functioning of the holding company by means of integrated management would not be impaired. These and other unusual privileges made the development of heavy industries in Manchukuo an attractive if somewhat dangerous venture for the younger financial groups in Japan. This type of enterprise was now less regulated than in Japan and there were guarantees that it would continue to be so.

The original Five Year Plan called for an investment of ¥2,800 million but this was subsequently raised to ¥4,800 million in the revised plan and then to ¥6,000 million in September, 1938. Shortly after the establishment of the Manchuria Industrial Development Company, Mr. Aikawa hoped to raise ¥3,000 million in new capital for his heavy industries alone. He planned to obtain ¥1,000 million in Manchukuo (mostly in kind), ¥1,000 million in Japan and a final ¥1,000 million abroad, mainly in the United States, in the form of commercial credits for machinery and technical services. His efforts to enlist foreign capital have not met with success as yet. So far there have been no long term loans or investments and only Germany has extended short term credits for the purchase of machinery on a limited scale. The outbreak of the China Incident which diverted labor and materials to war purposes and the failure to obtain foreign capital to finance the purchase of equipment from abroad have both contributed to the impossibility of realizing the aims of the Five Year Plan on schedule, though it is doubtful that so ambitious a plan could have been realized in so short a time even in the absence of complications. More recently it has become difficult to obtain machinery from Japan because of the shortage there of skilled labor and materials and from foreign countries because of the war in Europe and strong anti-Japanese sentiment in the United States.

398 THE INDUSTRIALIZATION OF JAPAN AND MANCHUKUO

The re-armament program in the United States will also make it even more difficult to obtain machine tools and other equipment from that country.

Total Japanese investments in Manchukuo were estimated at ¥3,441 million at the end of 1938, according to investigations made by the South Manchuria Railway Company and the Manchurian Affairs Bureau in Tokyo [23] and were undoubtedly in excess of ¥4,500 million at the end of 1939. Investments prior to the Manchurian Incident amounted to ¥1,617 million, of which ¥742 million, or 48 per cent, represented outlays by the South Manchuria Railway Company. Additional investments in the four year period, 1932–35, were estimated at ¥899 million and in the four year period, 1936–39, at ¥2,154 million. Shares in Manchurian corporations and the bonds of the South Manchuria Railway Company and of the Manchukuo government and its agencies were acquired by industrial or semi-official companies and by individuals in Japan. Manchukuo was expending large sums for labor, materials and equipment in the process of expanding her transportation facilities and in developing mines and industries. The Japanese investment was received in the form of imports of materials and machinery for mines and factories and of textile materials, flour and sugar for the labor employed. The export from Japan of both capital goods and consumption goods was stimulated by the Japanese investment in Manchukuo and these investments were further stimulated by high prices in Manchukuo.

From 1920 to 1932, Manchuria had a favorable balance of trade with exports consistently and considerably in excess of imports. The excess of exports may be taken as a rough measure of the returns to Japanese, Russian and Chinese investments in railways and other enterprises. In 1933, Manchukuo became a capital importing country and the balance of trade became increasingly unfavorable; the excess of exports was replaced by an excess of imports. The capital and the excess of commodity imports were supplied by Japan. The interdependence of foreign trade, industrial expansion, and Japanese investments is illustrated in the following table: [24]

[23] *Sixth Report on Progress in Manchuria to 1939*, pp. 80, 81. The figures for 1932–35 differ slightly from the latest estimates presented below in the text and in the table.

[24] *Fifth Report on Progress to 1936*, pp. 110, 111; *Sixth Report on Progress to 1939*, pp. 80, 81, 95, 96 and 99; *Contemporary Manchuria*, July, 1939, pp. 12 and 13; *Oriental Economist*, March, 1940, p. 153; April, 1940, p. 218.

MINERAL RESOURCES OF JAPAN AND MANCHUKUO 399

YEAR	FOREIGN TRADE OF MANCHUKUO (M¥1,000,000)				JAPANESE INVESTMENTS IN MANCHUKUO (¥1,000,000)	JAPANESE EMPIRE EXPORT SURPLUS WITH MANCHUKUO AND KWANTUNG (¥1,000,000)
	Imports	Exports	Balance	Imports of Construction Materials		
1932	337.7	618.2	+280.5	. . .	97.2	. . .
1933	515.8	448.5	− 67.4	. . .	151.2	. . .
1934	593.6	448.4	−145.1	154.3	271.7	. . .
1935	604.1	421.1	−183.1	157.8	378.6	. . .
1936	691.8	602.8	− 89.1	151.9	263.0	225
1937	887.4	645.3	−242.1	224.3	348.3	322
1938	1,274.7	725.5	−549.3	410.6	439.5	519
1939	1,783.4	826.2	−957.2	555	1,103.7	959

For the most part, however, the rising Manchurian exports paid for the consumption goods imported. A large part of the import excess is to be accounted for by construction materials which included iron and steel, machinery and tools, vehicles and vessels, electrical equipment, cement and timber. Japan supplied about 80 per cent of the imports in this group in recent years, with the United States, Germany and Great Britain supplying much smaller amounts of machinery and materials not available in Japan. Between 1934 and 1936 imports of iron, steel and cement decreased because of the rise in domestic production, but after 1936 there was a striking increase for all construction materials except cement as a result of the speeding up required by the Five Year Plan. Manchukuo had a favorable balance of trade with countries other than Japan and China until 1938 when the excess of imports from third countries was valued at ¥24 million. In 1939 the unfavorable balance with third countries rose to ¥70,000,000 as the result of large imports of industrial equipment. It would be in the nature of an oversimplification to expect the estimated Japanese investments to balance exactly the unfavorable balance of trade with Japan. There are other factors which influence the balance such as payments due Japan in the nature of dividends, interest and freight charges and on the other side short term credits extended by Japanese producers and exporters to Manchurian merchants. In reply to an interpellation at a meeting of the Diet in February, 1940, the Japanese Government stated that during 1939 about ¥200 million came back to Japan from Manchukuo in the form of dividends and interest and another ¥100 million as remittances and returns on private enter-

400 THE INDUSTRIALIZATION OF JAPAN AND MANCHUKUO

prise. The higher price level in Manchukuo stimulated exports from Japan to such an extent in 1938 and 1939 that the Japanese authorities took measures to restrict exports of textiles, based on imported raw materials and machinery not needed for wartime industries.

It must not be supposed that there are no small partnerships and corporations in Manchukuo and that all business is managed by huge holding companies closely allied to the government. It is primarily transportation, electricity, banking, colonization, the chemical and heavy industries, airplanes and automobiles which are being developed by special or semi-special companies. In other parts of the world, many of these enterprises are owned by the government or subjected to a high degree of government control, either because they function most efficiently under unified management, or sufficient private capital is not available, or they are essential for national defense purposes. What is unusual in the Manchurian situation is that this has all been planned from the founding of the new state. At the end of 1938 there had been established in Manchukuo 41 special or semi-special corporations with an authorized capital of ¥1,600 million and a paid-up capital of ¥1,150 million.[25] The Manchukuo government held about one-third of this capital (both authorized and paid-up). At the same date, December 31, 1938, there were 3,888 joint stock companies and partnerships with an authorized capital of ¥3,363 million and a paid-up capital of ¥2,479 million. Some of the more important groups were as follows:

CLASSIFICATION	NUMBER OF COMPANIES	AUTHORIZED CAPITAL	PAID-UP CAPITAL
		(¥1,000,000)	
Transportation and Express	164	903	762
Ceramics and Mining	186	734	603
Metals and Machinery	115	259	213
Electricity and Gas	28	191	144
Chemical Industry	119	263	128
Commercial	1,809	151	114

The South Manchuria Railway Company had financed or helped to finance almost every industrial undertaking in Manchukuo and

[25] For a list of these companies and for details about their capitalization, see *Progress to 1936*, p. 166; *Progress to 1939*, pp. 76, 77, 158; Kazue Kikuchi—Outline of Special Companies in Manchukuo and Investors—*Contemporary Opinions*, September 21, 1939.

MINERAL RESOURCES OF JAPAN AND MANCHUKUO   401

continued to have substantial interests in over 50 subsidiary and affiliated enterprises after it relinquished control over the heavy industries to the Manchuria Industrial Development Company at the end of 1937. Among its larger holdings were those in two joint Japanese-Manchurian corporations, the Manchuria Chemical Industry Company (May, 1933), which produced ammonium sulphate and sulphuric acid at Kanseishi, and the Manchuria Electric Industry Company, which was established in November, 1934, to amalgamate existing electric companies under unified control and to finance new undertakings. In the summer of 1939, the railway company announced that it was withdrawing from the industrial field and that it planned to devote itself exclusively to transportation in the future except that it would retain the Fushun coal mines and shale oil plants. Its holdings in diversified industries were to be disposed of gradually either by direct sale of subsidiary companies or by sale of stock holdings to the public. The company will retain subsidiaries directly related to transportation such as bus, tramway, steamship, dock and warehouse companies. The withdrawal from the industrial field is not a symptom of declining power and influence but rather the result of tremendously increased responsibilities in the transportation field. In the future, the company will operate not only the North Korea and the Manchukuo Railway systems but it will also have a substantial interest in the railways of North China through its participation in a subsidiary of the North China Development Company. The North China Traffic Company was formed in April, 1939, to operate the 3,000 miles of railway north of the Yellow River as well as to control the bus lines and inland navigation. It was capitalized at ¥300 million with the North China Development Company subscribing ¥150 million, the South Manchuria Railway Company ¥120 million and the Provisional Government at Pekin the remaining ¥30 million. It is believed that the South Manchuria Railway will be the dominant factor in the management of the railway system in North China while the Japanese occupation continues. The company will require more than a billion yen in new capital over the three years, 1940–42, to build new lines in Manchukuo, to carry out its part in the development of the Northern Frontier Provinces and to participate in the North China developments. With these programs in mind, the capitalization of the company was

402   THE INDUSTRIALIZATION OF JAPAN AND MANCHUKUO

increased from ¥800 million to ¥1,400 million at the end of 1939 with the Japanese government subscribing one-half of the increase.

It is difficult to see how capital can be raised in Japan for all the projects planned at home, in Manchukuo and in North China within the next few years. The yen value of these capital increases may have little significance if the pace of inflation continues at the rate which prevailed in the second half of 1939, but it is clear that every one of these plans demands labor, materials and equipment in larger and larger amounts. If one or two could be pushed at a time, there would be a real possibility of success, but the attempt to promote them all simultaneously while a major war is being waged, subjects the whole economy to increasing strain, which may paralyze it completely unless the war is brought to an end and plans for industrial expansion are considerably modified.

This strain became increasingly apparent in the second half of 1939 and in the first quarter of 1940. Many of the plans for industrial expansion called for comparatively small advances in 1937 and 1938 but much larger ones thereafter. The Manchurian Five Year Industrial Development Plan which was started in 1937, completed the first two years with satisfactory results but encountered great difficulties in 1939. As a consequence of the prolonged war in China and the decision to develop the Northern Frontier Provinces, the plan was revised for a third time in August, 1939. The production schedules for iron and steel, coal, liquid fuel and various non-ferrous metals were raised and the period of the plan was extended by another two years to 1943. The necessary machinery which could not be produced in Japan or Manchukuo was to be obtained from Germany and paid for in soya beans and other Manchurian produce, but the outbreak of the European War in September unsettled this arrangement and resulted in the adoption of the *concentration* policy. Under this policy, efforts were to be concentrated on projects which could be completed with materials and equipment obtainable at home and in Japan, but iron and steel, coal, liquid fuel and the non-ferrous metals were to be given preferential treatment.

The progress made in the three years 1937–39 has probably been greatest in the field of iron and steel production though plants have been built and equipped for the production of aluminum and synthetic oil and the first stations of the large scale hydro-electric power projects are nearing completion. The fact that coal production has increased only moderately is a serious problem because the development of the heavy industries in Manchukuo and Japan has resulted in a greatly increased consumption of coal. This failure has been due not so much to inadequate coal resources as to a shortage of labor and mining equipment. The Manchurian Government has recently encouraged the immigration of Chinese coolies and Korean laborers in large numbers to work in the mines, and great efforts are being made to increase the output of mining machinery in Japan. Early in 1940, the Japan Mining Machinery and Tools Association informed the government that mining machinery formerly imported from abroad could henceforth be produced in Japan from domestic materials without any infringement of patent rights.[26] While this may be possible it will doubtless take some time before self-sufficiency is achieved.

It has already been pointed out that before the establishment of Manchukuo in 1932 there was little mining activity outside the railway zones, where the Russians and the Japanese had special privileges granted in connection with the railway concessions. The Chinese refused to grant further mining privileges to foreigners and were themselves unable to explore and develop the mineral wealth of the country. This came to be one of the causes of friction in the years preceding the Manchurian Incident. The South Manchuria Railway Company, for example, had the right to mine coal at the Fushun mines. Over the coal, there was a thick layer of shale containing oil which had to be removed in the process of coal mining. When the company erected a plant to extract the oil from the shale, the Chinese Government protested that the mining rights applied to the coal only and not to the shale.

This policy was immediately reversed by the new government. Mining engineers and geologists were sent out to explore promising sites in many distant parts of the country. The American geologist, H. Foster Bain, toured the principal mining districts of Manchukuo in the spring of 1938. This work has not been completed by any means, but it is already clear that the mineral wealth of the country is much greater than had been supposed. The government is not

[26] *Japan Weekly Chronicle Commercial Supplement*, February 1, 1940.

404   THE INDUSTRIALIZATION OF JAPAN AND MANCHUKUO

publishing very much definite information at this time but the estimates of deposits of iron, coal, gold, copper, lead, zinc, magnesite,
aluminum and many other mineral resources have been revised
upwards very sharply in recent years. In 1934 the coal deposits of
South Manchuria were roughly estimated at 4.8 billion tons and the
iron deposits at 800 million tons (mostly low grade ore). By 1939
the coal deposits were estimated at 15 billion tons and the iron ore
deposits at about 2,500 million tons with a much larger proportion
of high grade ore.[27] Large deposits of high grade iron ore and coking
coal have been discovered close together in the Tungpientao or
Eastern Frontier District, a region in the southeast near the Korean
border. Thus far the exploration and development of new mineral
resources has been confined largely to South Manchuria and there
is still much to be done there. It may take several years before the
possibilities of North Manchuria can be appraised with any degree
of confidence.

Before 1932 pig iron was made from local ores in modest quantities at Anshan and Penhsihu along the Mukden-Dairen and
Mukden-Antung sections of the South Manchuria Railway, but the
available deposits of iron ore were mostly of low grade and expensive to work. The Anshan Iron Works was the leading producer;
it was built by the South Manchuria Railway Company, first produced pig iron in 1919, and was reorganized as the Showa Steel
Works in 1933. The Penhsihu Colliery and Iron Works was established as a joint Japanese-Chinese enterprise in 1914 on the initiative of the Okura interests. Both companies suffered severely in
the post-War depression, but began to expand output after 1926.
Steel was first produced in Manchukuo at the Showa Steel Works
in 1935. The Manchuria Industrial Development Company acquired
a controlling interest in Showa Steel and Penhsihu Iron at the end
of 1937, and the recent history has been one of rapid expansion of
capacity.

The great difficulty in the early years was that the available ores
were of low grade with an iron content of from 30 to 40 per cent
and that the hematite ores at Anshan could not be reduced by the
usual concentration or beneficiation methods employed on low grade

[27] *Fourth Report on Progress to 1934*, p. 210; *Sixth Report on Progress to 1939*,
p. 59; *Milestones of Progress*, April, 1939, p. 9.

ores in Germany. Low grade magnetite ores are crushed, separated magnetically into concentrates and tailings, and then concentrated or massed by briquetting or sintering. The ores at Anshan were mainly hematite, however, and did not respond to this treatment; they were hard and difficult to pulverize, they could not be separated magnetically, and the iron oxide was in very fine particles. Samples of the Anshan ores were sent to Germany and Sweden for experiment in 1920 and mining experts from the University of Minnesota came to Anshan without success. It was only in 1926 after years of patient research and experimentation that the South Manchuria Railway Company was able to solve this problem and produce pig iron at a profit by means of a process perfected by its own research department. The ores are roasted in a special reducing furnace which makes them brittle and easy to crush and magnetizes them artificially. Thereafter they are pulverized, separated magnetically and the particles containing 60 per cent or more of iron are sintered.[28] This special method seems to be employed only at Anshan; elsewhere in Manchukuo and in Korea where the "lean" ores are predominantly magnetite, the Krupp concentration process is employed.

It would be difficult to overestimate the value of the work done by the research organizations of the South Manchuria Railway Company with a view to the profitable exploitation of agricultural and mineral resources in Manchuria. We have made brief mention of some of the agricultural experiment stations in Chapter IX; the work with the Anshan ores has been described above. Among other noteworthy achievements were the experiments carried out at the Fushun coal mines which resulted in new methods for obtaining oil from shale and from coal in commercial quantities. In both these last examples the preliminary work took many years, but the experimental stage is over and production on a commercial scale has begun.

The output of pig iron increased rapidly after 1926 and was exported for the most part to Japan (Table 77). Estimates of the output of iron ore, pig iron and steel for the years 1925 to 1937 are presented below.

[28] For an account of this concentration process at the Showa Steel Works, see *Contemporary Manchuria*, January, 1938, pp. 60–70.

406 THE INDUSTRIALIZATION OF JAPAN AND MANCHUKUO

MANCHUKUO — PRODUCTION OF IRON ORE, PIG IRON AND STEEL [29]

(in thousand metric tons)

YEAR	IRON ORE			PIG IRON			STEEL INGOTS	STEEL MATE- RIALS[31]
	LEAN	RICH	TOTAL	SHOWA WORKS	PENHSIHU WORKS	TOTAL		
1925	1	140	140[30]	86	51	137	. . .	. . .
1927	457	173	631	193	51	244	. . .	. . .
1929	529	252	781	218	78	295	. . .	. . .
1931	673	251	924	277	66	342	. . .	. . .
1933	770	328	1,098	318	116	434	. . .	. . .
1934	740	394	1,133	322	153	476	. . .	. . .
1935	985	492	1,477	457	151	608	137	25
1936	1,325	579	1,905	473	160	633	344	135
1937	. . .	. . .	. . .	762		762	427	370

The great increase after 1925 was the result of using lean ores (iron content of 25 to 40 per cent) because the deposits of rich iron ores (iron content 52 to 65 per cent) then known and exploited were very small. This situation has now changed significantly with the discovery and exploitation of large deposits of rich ore in the Tungpientao region. The output of pig iron doubled between 1932 and 1937 and the production of steel ingots and rolled steel (sheets, rods, rails and plates) made rapid progress after 1935. In the year ending March 31, 1938, the Showa Steel Works produced 677,399 tons of pig iron, 515,347 tons of steel ingots and 455,809 tons of rolled steel.[32] It seems reasonable to suppose that the Penhsihu Iron Works produced about 200,000 tons of pig iron in that year and that total pig iron production approached 900,000 tons. Thereafter output figures were not published but the authorities in reporting on 1938, the second year of the Five Year Plan, stated that pig iron rose 17 per cent, steel ingots 18 per cent and rolled steel 50 per cent.[33] The revised Five Year Plan called for the production of 4,800,000 tons of pig iron, 3,500,000 tons of steel ingots and 2,000,000 tons of rolled steel by 1941 (Table 103). The pig iron not made into steel ingots and the steel ingots not made into rolled

[29] *Japan-Manchukuo Year Book*, 1939, pp. 802–03. Based on estimates of the South Manchuria Railway Company.

[30] Figures for iron ore are for 1922.

[31] Manufactured from the steel ingots.

[32] *Japan-Manchukuo Year Book*, 1939, p. 804.

[33] It is not clear whether these percentages refer to the calendar year, 1938, or to the fiscal year ending March 31, 1938, but it is assumed that they refer to the former.

MINERAL RESOURCES OF JAPAN AND MANCHUKUO   407

-steel were to be exported to Japan. The schedules have since been increased and the plan extended by two years.

This plan envisaged a considerable expansion of capacity at the Showa Steel Works and the Penhsihu Iron Works and also the development of new resources in the Tungpientao region. The proposed schedules have been revised many times and nothing which follows should be regarded as either definite or final. The Showa Steel Works in 1937 had an annual capacity of 700,000 tons of pig iron and 580,000 tons of steel. Pig iron capacity was increased by 1,000,000 tons to 1,700,000 tons during 1938 and early 1939 when four 700 ton blast furnaces were blown in. It is worthy of note that all parts of these blast furnaces with the exception of the winches for hoisting ores and accessory parts, which were imported from Germany, were manufactured in Manchukuo. As part of this program steel production was to be expanded by 125,000 tons in 1939 and by 375,000 tons in 1940. The pig iron capacity of the Penhsihu Iron Works was to be increased to 500,000 tons. In the spring of 1939, the directors of the Showa Steel Works announced new plans for increasing pig iron capacity to 3,060,000 tons and steel ingot capacity to 2,830,000 tons by the end of 1942 at an estimated expenditure of more than ¥600 million. It is not likely that pig iron production in 1939 approached anything like the capacity figure of 1,700,000 tons because of the impossibility of obtaining sufficient supplies of coke and concentrated ore, but there was probably a surplus for export to Japan. In 1938 Manchukuo had promised to ship 100,000 tons of pig iron and 210,000 tons of steel materials to Japan but because of increased consumption at home was not able to ship more than half of that amount. During 1939, with pig iron capacity greatly increased, it promised to export 600,000 tons of pig iron and 100,000 tons of steel materials to Japan.[34] It is becoming increasingly difficult to check or verify these press reports which are, however, usually released by Domei, the official press agency.

The opening up of the Tungpientao or Eastern Frontier District makes available for the first time to the Manchurian iron and steel industry large deposits of high grade iron ore found in close proximity to mines from which coking coal can be obtained. Estimates

[34] *Monthly Trade Report, Japan.* U. S. Department of Commerce, February, 1939, p. 18.

408 THE INDUSTRIALIZATION OF JAPAN AND MANCHUKUO

of all mineral resources in Manchukuo are as yet tentative and are being constantly revised upwards. According to a recent publication of the South Manchuria Railway Company *other* iron deposits (mostly of low grade ores with an iron content of from 25 to 40 per cent) were estimated at 1,200 million tons. The Tungpientao deposits were estimated at an additional 1,200 million tons with a fair proportion of high grade ore with an iron content of 52 to 63 per cent. These include "78 million tons at Talitzukou, 5 million tons at Chitaokou, 100 million tons at Laoling and no less than 1 billion tons in a vein covering 40 kilometers from Pataochiang to Ertaochiang." [35] A railroad has been completed which links this region with the main lines in South Manchuria and also with the railways of North Korea by means of a bridge across the Yalu. Mining operations began in 1938 and ore has been shipped to Japan. The Tungpientao Development Company hopes to produce 1,500,-000 tons of iron ore and 1,300,000 tons of coal, and to construct an iron and steel works with a capacity of 500,000 tons of pig iron and 100,000 tons of steel by the end of 1941.

Before 1932 the principal coal mines in Manchuria were the Fushun and Yentai mines of the South Manchuria Railway Company and the Penhsihu mine of the Okura Company. The output of the famous open-cut Fushun mine increased from 490,000 tons in 1908 when it was taken over by the railway company, to 9,590,000 tons in 1936. The relative importance of this single mine may be inferred from the fact that it often produced as much as 75 per cent of all the coal mined in Manchuria. Total production in 1936 was estimated at from 12 to 13.6 million tons. The smaller figure is that given in Table 103 and probably does not include the coal used in coke production which is also given in the same table. Of the larger total of 13,606,000 tons in 1936, the South Manchuria Railway Company produced 10,252,000 tons, the Manchuria Coal Mining Company 2,195,000 tons, and other mines 1,159,000 tons.[36] The Manchuria Coal Mining Company is a special company formed in 1934 to take over and develop all coal mines except those belong-

[35] *Sixth Report on Progress in Manchuria to 1939*, p. 59. These figures differ substantially from other estimates, but the editor of the publication quoted assured me that these are the latest and most authentic of the *published* estimates.
[36] The Coal Mining Industry in Manchuria, *Contemporary Manchuria*, November 1937, pp. 69–70.

MINERAL RESOURCES OF JAPAN AND MANCHUKUO   409

ing to the railway company and the Penhsihu Iron Works. Between 1927 and 1936, although domestic consumption was rising, Manchukuo exported from 3 to 4 million tons of coal a year to Japan,[37] Korea and China. The exports from Manchukuo to Japan would probably have been even larger had not the Japanese producers opposed this competition from outside.

COAL — MANCHUKUO, 1927–1936

ESTIMATES OF PRODUCTION, CONSUMPTION AND EXPORTS [38]

(in thousand metric tons)

YEAR	PRODUCTION FUSHUN	TOTAL PRODUCTION	CONSUMPTION	EXPORTS
1927	7,190	9,510	4,440	3,240
1929	7,690	10,530	5,250	4,010
1933	7,950	10,150	6,120	3,770
1934	8,660	11,420	7,250	3,900
1935	8,380	11,820	8,690	3,360
1936	9,590	13,600	9,580	2,990

The first Five Year Plan called for an annual production of 27 million tons by 1941 and the revised plan raised this figure to 38 million tons or nearly three times the 1937 output. Even this last figure was increased in the summer of 1939 and the period extended to 1943. Most of the increase is to be produced by mines under the control of the Manchuria Coal Mining Company which include Fuhsin and Peipiao in Chinchow Province, Hsian in Fengtein Province, Holikang in Sankiang Province, Mishan in Mutankiang Province and Chalainoerh in North Hsingan Province. It was reported originally that this company would produce from 10 to 15 million tons of coal a year; the figure was later raised to 20 million tons and toward the end of 1939 to 28 million tons. The authorized capital of the company was raised from ¥16 million in 1934 to ¥80 million in 1937 and to ¥200 million in 1939.

Adequate supplies of coal are of the utmost importance to the expansion of the heavy industries in Japan and Manchukuo, to the synthetic oil industry and to the extension of railways and electric power on a wide scale. One estimate indicates that of the total

[37] For Japanese imports of coal, see Table 90.
[38] *Contemporary Manchuria*, November, 1937, pp. 66–76. These figures are, of course, only estimates and somewhat different estimates may be found in other places.

410 THE INDUSTRIALIZATION OF JAPAN AND MANCHUKUO

domestic demand of 9.6 million tons in Manchuria in 1936, 1.6 million tons was consumed by the steel industry, 1.3 million tons by the electric and gas industry and 2 million tons by the railways. With the rapid industrialization of the country this demand has risen in a striking manner and will rise even more. No definite estimates of output and consumption under the latest plan have been published. Under the original Five Year Plan when an output of 27 million tons in 1941 was the aim, it was expected that 8,335,000 tons would be consumed by Manchuria's heavy industries, 3,000,000 tons by the railway, 8,810,000 tons by other industries, 1,150,000 tons by shipping and that 5,650,000 tons would be available for export.[39] It is probable that a number of these estimates have risen from 50 to 100 per cent for the year 1943.

Production has increased since 1936 but not nearly as rapidly as had been anticipated because of the shortage of labor, materials and equipment already mentioned. Much preliminary work had to be done in getting new mines ready for operation and the results have been disappointing as far as actual production is concerned. The authorities admit that coal output fell short of expectations in both 1937 and 1938; the latter year showed a gain of 5 per cent over 1937 but attained only 91 per cent of the goal set for the second year of the revised plan. A further modest gain was reported for 1939. Domestic requirements have risen rapidly with the result that exports of coal to Japan fell from 2,241,000 tons in 1937 to 752,000 tons in 1939.[40] According to one authority [41] the Manchuria Coal Mining Company has been operating 15 collieries, the output of which rose from 1,504,000 tons in 1934 to 2,156,000 tons in 1936, and to 4,388,000 tons in 1938. The most encouraging sign is the rapid increase in the output of the newly opened Fuhsin mine in Chinchow Province from 115,000 tons in 1936 to 607,000 tons in 1937 and to 1,488,000 tons in 1938. This is another great open-cut mine with estimated reserves of 4 billion tons which is expected to rival the already famous Fushun mine. Both mines are in South Manchuria and are connected by rail with important ports. The Fushun mine is about 30 miles east of Mukden on a line which joins the Mukden-Dairen main line; the Fuhsin mine is west of Mukden

[39] *Japan-Manchukuo Year Book*, 1939, p. 802.
[40] Japanese import statistics.
[41] John R. Stewart, *Far Eastern Survey*, March 13, 1940, p. 74.

MINERAL RESOURCES OF JAPAN AND MANCHUKUO   411

on a railway line which runs from Hsinlitun to the newly developed port of Hulutao. These locations should facilitate shipments to Japan when Manchurian production exceeds domestic requirements and harbor expansion plans have been completed.

Since Manchukuo has coal and oil shale in abundance but no petroleum, there have been many plans for producing liquid fuel from shale and coal with the object of reducing the great dependence on countries outside the Yen Bloc. There was much experimental work even before the Manchurian Incident but Chinese opposition and high costs of production retarded development on a commercial scale although crude oil has been extracted from shale since 1930. The original Five Year Plan called for the production of 800,000 tons of shale oil and 500,000 tons of oil from coal liquefaction; the revised plan for 650,000 tons of oil from shale and 1,700,000 tons from coal (Table 103). There was provision also for increases in the output of alcohol to be mixed with gasoline and used as a motor fuel. Somewhat different versions of these plans have been published and the revised plan seems to have been changed in some particulars since 1938.

It has been estimated that the reserves of oil shale immediately above the coal beds at Fushun exceed five billion tons with an average oil content of six per cent, ranging from 10 to 12 per cent in the upper part of the seam to 1 to 3 per cent at the lower level. The deposit of shale which is 450 feet deep in the thickest part must be removed in the process of open-cut mining. The South Manchuria Railway experimented with many methods for extracting the oil and by 1925 had evolved a process for the extraction of oil from the shale by means of dry distillation. It erected a plant at Fushun which began to produce crude oil and various by-products in 1930. The output in 1935 consisted of 65,000 tons of crude oil, 20,000 tons of crude paraffin, 5,000 tons of coke, 22,000 tons of ammonium sulphate and 16,000 tons of benzine.[42]

Production capacity was increased in 1935 from 70,000 tons a year to double that figure and plans were made to raise the capacity to 360,000 tons by 1938. In March, 1939, the directors of the South Manchuria Railway voted to raise production to 500,000 tons in 1941 and to 1,000,000 tons in 1943 at an estimated expenditure of

[42] *Fifth Report on Progress in Manchuria to 1936*, p. 102.

412 THE INDUSTRIALIZATION OF JAPAN AND MANCHUKUO

¥150 million. It was pointed out by President Matsuoka that there were great advantages in producing oil from shale rather than coal in that the method had been thoroughly tested, a worthless by-product was used and coal was conserved, and that the cost of production was appreciably lower. Because of the excellent record of the railway company in so many different fields one cannot dismiss this as just another plan.

This decision may mean that the South Manchuria Railway Company was not as optimistic about its coal liquefaction plant as about the shale enterprise. Since 1928 the Naval Fuel Depot and the Central Research Bureau of the railway have been working on a hydrogenation process which differs from the Bergius process perfected in Germany. The German process is adapted to lignite and the Japanese process to bituminous coal. An experimental plant with a capacity of 20,000 tons of oil a year was constructed at Fushun in 1936. The results of the experimental operations appear to have been satisfactory since orders for machinery of Japanese design adapted to this method were placed in both Germany and the United States during 1938 and 1939. At the end of 1939 three additional synthetic oil plants—all with larger capacities—were either completed or being constructed at Ssupingkai, Fuhsin and Kirin. The Manchuria Coal Liquefaction Company announced that it would produce 50,000 tons of crude oil and 10,000 tons of gasoline annually at Ssupinkai by means of direct liquefaction and also the low temperature carbonization of coal tar. It was reported that both this company and the Fushun plant of the South Manchuria Railway began production in 1938. The Manchuria Synthetic Fuel Company planned to produce 100,000 tons of fuel oil at Fuhsin by the use of the Fischer synthetic process with operations scheduled to begin at the end of 1939. The Kirin Artificial Oil Company was formed in 1939 to produce 300,000 tons of oil from 1,500,000 tons of coal to be brought to Kirin from the Shulan coal mine. This company plans to commence operations in 1941 when the great hydro-electric power generating plant on the Second Sungari will also be ready. The capital for these enterprises is being provided by the Manchukuo Government, the Imperial Japanese Fuel Company and private interests in Japan. The Mitsui interests provide part of the capital and will manage the Manchuria Synthetic Fuel

MINERAL RESOURCES OF JAPAN AND MANCHUKUO   413

Company and Jun Noguchi is performing the same service for the Kirin Artificial Oil Company.

When we turn to the non-ferrous metals in Manchukuo, the prospects for aluminum, magnesium, lead and zinc appear to be more promising at this stage than do those for gold and copper. Raw materials for the light metals, aluminum and magnesium, exist in abundance and there is also the prospect of plenty of cheap hydro-electric power to be used in the refining process. Aluminum is produced from fire-clay or aluminum shale of which there are enormous reserves between the coal strata at Yentai, Penhsihu, Fuchow and Chinchow. This shale contains a much lower percentage of alumina than does bauxite so that the problem is one of comparative cost of production. The South Manchuria Railway carried on experiments for many years at Fushun and participated in the organization in 1933 of the Japan-Manchuria Aluminum Company which was established to commercialize the product. This company was reported to have a capacity of 7,000 tons a year in 1939.[48] The Manchuria Light Metals (Aluminum) Manufacturing Company was organized in 1936 and has constructed a plant at Fushun which began operations in 1938 with an initial capacity of 4,000 tons. The deposit of high grade magnesite ore at Tashihchiao in Chinchow Province, South Manchuria, is estimated at more than a billion tons. Formerly used mostly for fire-proof linings in steel furnaces, it is now also used as a source of metallic magnesium, the metal which is even lighter than aluminum. The Japan-Manchuria Magnesium Company, organized in 1933, has two plants in Japan where metallic magnesium is produced from Manchurian magnesite. The Manchuria Magnesium Industry Company, a subsidiary of the Manchuria Industrial Development Company, was established in 1938 and built a plant at Yinkow near Tashihchiao. Manchukuo is now one of the world's leading producers of this light metal which is very important in airplane construction.

In contrast to the scarcity of lead and zinc in Japan, Manchukuo is supposed to have fairly large deposits of these minerals. The Manchuria Lead Mining Company which was formed to work the lead deposits at Yangchiachangtzu was taken over by the Manchuria Industrial Development Company in 1937. A recent press

[48] *Contemporary Opinions*, March 23, 1939.

414 THE INDUSTRIALIZATION OF JAPAN AND MANCHUKUO

report [44] states that this company was producing 13,500 tons of lead (ore) a month and expected to build a new zinc smelting plant; it was also planning to increase its capital from ¥4 million to ¥30 million in order that it might increase its output.

There are a number of low grade copper deposits in Manchukuo which can be worked only at very high cost. There are reports every now and then of the discovery of rich copper veins, but these reports cannot be verified.

The Manchuria Gold Mining Company was established in 1934 to develop all the state owned gold mines and alluvial gold beds in the country. The original Five Year Plan called for gold production of the value of MY200 million over the whole five years, rising from MY 15 million in 1937 to MY82 million in 1941. The revised plan increased the amount to MY300 million for the five year period. The official price of gold was raised to MY3.85 per gram on April 30, 1938. It was hoped that this move would encourage production and discourage smuggling as this was the approximate equivalent of the world price. Gold has been found in many parts of Manchuria, but some of the deposits are in remote spots along the Amur River or in Jehol and the mining methods have been very crude. Estimates of gold production rose from MY357,000 in 1934 to MY3,670,000 in 1935 and to MY10,025,000 in 1936. The Central Bank of Manchou bought gold to the value of MY13,000,000 in 1936 and to the value of MY14,000,000 in 1937. The reports of the Department of Industry indicate that gold production has not progressed as planned since 1937. There have been the usual explanations of labor shortage and lack of proper mining machinery. Toward the end of 1938 a number of gold dredgers were ordered in Japan to make possible a large scale exploitation of the alluvial or placer gold deposits of North Manchuria, and it was anticipated that some of them would be completed during 1939.

The development of coal liquefaction, of the chemical industry, and the refining of the non-ferrous metals, especially aluminum and magnesium, will require a large supply of cheap electric power. Before 1932 there was very little industrial demand for electric power in Manchukuo; power for lighting and for tramways was generated by a small number of steam power plants, the largest

[44] A dispatch from Domei to the *Japan Weekly Chronicle*, February 8, 1940.

MINERAL RESOURCES OF JAPAN AND MANCHUKUO   415

of which was at Fushun. The amount of electricity generated increased rapidly after 1932 but remained far from adequate for the industrial expansion program (Table 103). The revised Five Year Plan aimed at a capacity of 2,600,000 kilowatts, about equally divided between steam power and water power but recent reports have placed greater emphasis on the water power developments. The electric capacity of the country in 1939 was estimated at 500,000 kilowatts of steam power.[45] The work of expansion is being carried on by the Manchuria Electric Industry Company and the Yalu River Hydro-Electric Power Company. The Manchuria Electric Industry Company was established in 1934 as a joint Manchurian-Japanese corporation with a capital of ¥90 million to supply light and power, conduct affiliated undertakings and invest in allied undertakings. It was to amalgamate all electric companies operating in Manchuria and to effect a complete control and unification of the system.

Two outstanding hydro-electric power projects were started in 1937, one on the Second Sungari River above Kirin which is to produce 600,000 kilowatts an hour and the other on the Yalu River with an eventual capacity of 1,600,000 kilowatts. The first is being built by the Manchukuo Government; the second by the Yalu Hydro-Electric Power Company, a joint Manchurian-Japanese venture, the capital for which has been supplied by the two governments and by the Noguchi interests. The Yalu River forms the boundary between Manchukuo and Korea and the power generated will help develop the Tungpientao region in Manchukuo and the industrial and mining region of North Korea. The Manchuria Electric Industry Company has expanded the steam plant at Fuhsin and adopted a policy of concentrating steam power generation at a few large plants. It has also been engaged in developing all over Manchukuo a vast transmission system which will distribute the steam and hydro-electric power generated by the new stations as soon as it is available.

The dams and power stations under construction on the Second Sungari and Yalu Rivers rank among the greatest engineering undertakings in the world. Both are frequently compared in the Japanese press to Boulder Dam on the Colorado River in the United

[45] *Oriental Economist*, July, 1939, p. 465.

416   THE INDUSTRIALIZATION OF JAPAN AND MANCHUKUO

States.[46] The Second Sugari River has its source in the hills of the Changpai Range on the Korean boundary and runs through twenty counties in Fengtien and Kirin Provinces before joining the main Sungari River; its basin covers an area of 72,800 square kilometers. The dam and power plant are being constructed about 24 kilometers above Kirin; the estimated capacity of the plant is 600,000 kilowatts, of which 480,000 kilowatts are to be available by the end of 1941 and the remaining 120,000 by the end of 1944. Eventually other power plants may be built farther upstream. Of the eight 70,000 kilowatt generators required for this power station, three were ordered in the United States, three in Germany and two in Japan.[47] One of the American generators left San Francisco in January, 1940, and it was expected that the two remaining would be shipped by the end of June. It was also anticipated that the German machinery would be delivered in spite of the war. The dam above Kirin will aid agriculture by facilitating flood control and irrigation as well as building up an important industrial area where the Manchuria Electro-Chemical Company will manufacture carbide, synthetic rubber, acetic acid, calcium cyanide and other allied products, and the Kirin Artificial Oil Company will engage in coal liquefaction. The coal will come from the Shulan mine which is north of Kirin.

Work was started on the Yalu River dam and power station at Shuifengtung (or Suihodo) in December, 1937, with the plan of generating 300,000 kilowatts at the end of 1941 and 640,000 kilowatts at the end of 1942. Later with other power stations on the upper reaches of the Yalu River, the total generating capacity will be 1,600,000 kilowatts. So far as can be ascertained, progress on the electric power projects has been according to plan except for the fact that there may be some delay in obtaining equipment ordered in Germany. The Shuifengtung power plant, for example, planned to install seven gigantic hydraulic-turbine generators with a capacity of 92,000 (or 100,000) [48] kilowatts each, four of which were ordered from Germany and three from Japan. Early in 1940 it was reported

[46] *Contemporary Manchuria*, January, 1938, p. 145; *Milestones of Progress*, May, 1938, p. 164; *Oriental Economist*, November, 1939, p. 734.

[47] *Japan Weekly Chronicle*, February 15, 1940.

[48] The lower figure is given in *Contemporary Manchuria*, January, 1938, p. 145 and the higher one in the *Japan Weekly Chronicle*, February 15, 1940. At this time, it is not possible to verify from official sources.

MINERAL RESOURCES OF JAPAN AND MANCHUKUO   417

that five of these generators would be obtained from the Shibaura Engineering Works in Tokyo and the two others from the United States. The three generators originally ordered in Japan are expected to be ready in September, 1940, and the American machinery is to be installed by the end of 1941. If these deliveries are made on schedule, Manchukuo will have a much larger supply of cheap electric power within a short time.[49]

The Manchurian Five Year Industrial Development Plan was adopted at the end of 1936 before the outbreak of the China Incident and revised in April, 1938. The war in China resulted in a system of rigid exchange control and accentuated the emphasis on strategic industries. These influences are reflected in the developments of 1937 and 1938, the first and second years of the plan. At the end of the first year, 1937, the vice-minister of the Department of Industry reported as follows: "Better results than expected were obtained in the steel, electric, aluminum and soda industries; coal, zinc, salt, pulp, and the manufacture of rolling stock produced the expected results; liquid fuel and gold were slightly retarded in output, while the manufacture of automobiles, aeroplanes and munitions did not exceed the planning stage." [50] A report by the Department of Industry on 1938, the second year of the Five Year Plan, indicated that the best results were achieved by the iron and steel, shale oil and electric power industries which attained or exceeded their goals. Pig iron, steel ingots and steel materials increased 17, 18, and 50 per cent over the previous year. Work on the hydroelectric power plants advanced according to schedule, but there was a considerable delay in the construction of coal liquefaction plants as a consequence of difficulties in obtaining imported materials and equipment. Coal production increased only 5 per cent over the previous year and attained only 91 per cent of the goal set for 1938. Soda and ammonium sulphate made satisfactory progress, but the production of pulp did not measure up to the second year goal due to delays in utilizing the forest resources of the Hsingan Ranges.

---

[49] The power rates quoted are so low that one wonders if there is some mistake. In *Milestones of Progress*, September, 1939, it was stated that the Manchuria Electric Industry Company supplied 1.3 billion kilowatt hours in 1938 through special contracts at an average rate of M¥0.0186 and that it is planning to supply 3 billion kilowatt hours in 1940 at an average rate of M¥0.013 with the Yuan equal to $0.234 in early 1940.

[50] *Sixth Report on Progress in Manchuria to 1939*, p. 65.

418 THE INDUSTRIALIZATION OF JAPAN AND MANCHUKUO

The non-ferrous metals did not come up to expectations and the output of salt declined considerably because of excessive rainfall. No official report has been issued up to the present (March, 1940) on the year 1939, but it is clear that many of the plans were retarded by the shortage of labor, imported materials, and machinery. It became obvious in the summer of 1939, in the face of the long struggle in China with the added complication of the war in Europe, that it would be impossible to carry out all parts of the Five Year Plan as scheduled and it was decided to concentrate efforts on iron and steel, coal, liquid fuel and the non-ferrous metals. Even without the war in China and even with the aid of foreign capital it is difficult to see how all these plans for industrial expansion could have been carried out in so short a time. It is truly remarkable that so much has been accomplished under the conditions which have prevailed since 1937.

5. COAL AND OIL IN THE YEN BLOC

The various plans for industrial expansion in the Japanese Empire and Manchukuo involve great increases in motive power in the form of coal, oil or electricity and a number of them require large amounts of coal as a raw material. The synthetic oil industry demands at least four tons of coal for each ton of oil produced while the iron and steel and the chemical industries use large amounts of coal in the form of coke, gases and coal tar products. If a country has abundant supplies of coal but possesses neither petroleum nor hydro-electric sites, it is possible to develop thermo-electric power and to obtain liquid fuel from coal. All of the countries in the Yen Bloc possess coal and water power sites in relative abundance, but they are poor in petroleum and are attempting to make good this deficiency by obtaining oil from shale and coal; North China is especially rich in coal and Japan in water power possibilities. The problem, therefore, is one of increasing coal production, of developing means of cheap transportation, and of perfecting methods of synthetic oil production which are not too costly.

The Japanese Four Year Plan and the Manchukuo Five Year Plan are interrelated to such an extent that the realizing of the former is very much dependent on the successful completion of the latter. The period has been officially extended to seven years for

MINERAL RESOURCES OF JAPAN AND MANCHUKUO   419

many industries; private observers believe that it will require ten, fifteen or even twenty years for some of the more ambitious projects under existing political conditions. The Japanese program outlined by the president of the Planning Board (page 274) early in 1939 covered output in the Japanese Empire, Manchukuo and North China. It was expressed not in terms of the ultimate tonnages expected but in terms of the percentage increase to be achieved between the fiscal year 1938–39 and the fiscal year 1942–43.[51] For the more important mineral products these percentages were as follows:

PRODUCT	PERCENTAGE INCREASE	PRODUCT	PERCENTAGE INCREASE
Ordinary Steel.........	60	Copper..............	80
High Speed Steel.......	200	Lead................	90
Steel Ingots...........	60	Zinc................	70
Pig Iron..............	200	Tin.................	100
Iron Ore..............	250	Natural Gasoline......	30
Aluminum.............	Several Hundred	Natural Heavy Oil.....	40
Magnesium............	1,000	Synthetic Gasoline.....	3,000
Coal.................	30	Synthetic Heavy Oil....	900

Unfortunately we have no production figures for the year 1938–39. The latest official figures for mineral production in Japan are for 1936 (Tables 68–91) and for the first half of 1937. We are not entirely without guidance, however, for the period after July, 1937; there are fairly reliable private estimates; there are details about new plant construction and capacity; there are the trade statistics of other countries; and finally there are the monthly production *indices* of the Japanese Ministry of Industry and Commerce.

The output of the principal minerals in Japan increased very substantially in 1937, appreciably in 1938, and to a much smaller extent in 1939 when shortages of labor, materials, machinery, and of hydro-electric power began to assume serious proportions. The great increase in 1937 was due primarily to plans for expanding industrial capacity because it was not until the last quarter of the year that it became apparent that the war in China would not be confined to the north but would spread and become a major conflict. Japan participated in the world wide boom in raw materials at the end of 1936 and early in 1937; moreover, this movement was

[51] The fiscal year ends on March 31.

420 THE INDUSTRIALIZATION OF JAPAN AND MANCHUKUO

accentuated by the plans of the military to expand armament expenditures and to make Japan more nearly self-sufficient in essential industries. When the Konoye Cabinet assumed office in June, 1937, it announced that the three important principles of its fiscal policy would be the balancing of international payments, the regulation of commodity supply and demand, and the expansion of productive capacity. It was well recognized before the outbreak of the war that the desired expansion of the heavy industries could be accomplished without foreign borrowing only if there were very careful planning which implied increasing government control and regulation. Before July, 1937, there was considerable opposition to more government regulation and to increased government expenditure, but the opposition has naturally become much weaker under war-time conditions. This situation is not peculiar to Japan; in all countries, government control over economic life becomes intensified in time of war. Then the problem arises at the end of any great war as to whether it is possible to restore industry to its former position without a complete collapse or a very difficult transition period.

The China War simply accentuated the development of the heavy industries which had been marked in Japan since 1933. Mineral output and metal, chemical and machinery production were encouraged in every way at the expense of industries producing consumers' goods except in so far as the latter were for export.[52] The essential industries were given preferential treatment as to capital expansion and the supply of materials and were allowed to import materials and equipment without payment of duty. A number of national policy companies were formed to encourage gold, synthetic fuel, and general mineral production with the government contributing half the capital and exercising considerable control. The companies were usually exempted from income, excess profits and local taxes for a term of years; the government might grant subsidies, or permit the issue of bonds up to several times the paid-up capital with principal and interest guaranteed. On the other hand, the government controlled organization, output, distribution and prices in varying degrees.

[52] For a description of government control and industrial production in the war period, see Conclusion.

MINERAL RESOURCES OF JAPAN AND MANCHUKUO 421

The monthly production figures compiled and published by the Ministry of Commerce and Industry [53] showed substantial gains in the early months of 1937. The percentage increases in the first half of 1937, as compared with the first half of 1936, were 14 per cent for gold and silver, 8 per cent for copper, 11 per cent for coal, 6 per cent for crude petroleum, 40 per cent for sulphur, 16 per cent for pig iron and 17 per cent for steel. It is generally acknowledged that the output of pig iron, steel, coal, aluminum and gold in Japan Proper rose considerably in 1937 and 1938. The Ministry of Commerce and Industry no longer publishes output figures but has continued to compile index numbers which the *Oriental Economist* combines with other materials in a volume index of industrial production and in various group indices.[54] This index has confirmed impressions which were the result of information from other sources.

Oriental Economist INDEX OF THE VOLUME OF INDUSTRIAL PRODUCTION

(1931–1933 = 100)

	CONSUMERS' GOODS	PRODUCERS' GOODS	CHEMICAL PRODUCTS	IRON, STEEL AND MACHINERY	ELECTRICITY AND GAS	MINERAL PRODUCTS
Average 1936...	125.3	171.5	192.5	209.5	140.4	137.8
Average 1937...	136.5	197.9	220.5	251.9	153.0	150.0
Average 1938...	125.1	220.4	227.5	295.0	167.5	159.5
Average 1939...	121.4	239.7	225.1	293.4	144.4	164.5
August 1938....	125.1	224.0	230.9	299.0	170.4	165.5
August 1939....	124.3	254.2	244.6	365.7	180.4	165.9

The statistics of electricity generated in the first eleven months of 1938 registered a gain of 19.4 per cent over the corresponding period in 1936, whereas the index for electricity and gas rose from 140.4 in 1936 to 167.5 in 1938 or a little more than 19 per cent. The index for mineral products rose by 16 per cent from 137.8 in 1936 to 159.5 in 1938. This index is dominated by coal and copper which have weights of 37 and 10 out of 54 for the whole mineral group.[55] It has been estimated that coal production rose from just under 42 million tons in 1936 to 50 million tons in 1938 or about

[53] Available in the English edition of the *Oriental Economist*.

[54] For a description of this index, see the *Oriental Economist* for August, 1938, pp. 498–501. After September, 1939, electricity is grouped with iron, steel and machinery. The 1939 indices for the two groups affected are not comparable with earlier years.

[55] Other weights are gold (3), silver (1), sulphur (1) and petroleum (2).

422 THE INDUSTRIALIZATION OF JAPAN AND MANCHUKUO

19 per cent. The index for mineral products advanced slightly in the first half of 1939 but it is generally conceded that there was a decline in many lines during the last quarter of 1939 and the first quarter of 1940 because of an acute shortage of coal and electric power.

The program of industrial expansion is dependent not only on adequate supplies of labor and equipment but also on sufficient coal, oil, and electricity for motive power and transportation. It is natural, therefore, that hydro-electric power which conserves coal and oil should have been so widely developed in Japan and that it is being extended in Korea and Manchukuo.[56] In an average year about 80 per cent of the total power generated is water power, but it is necessary to have large reserves of steam power in certain areas, at certain seasons of the year and for such emergencies as severe droughts or floods which may interrupt or reduce the supply of hydro-electricity. There is usually a rise in the amount of steam power during the winter months.[57] In the winter of 1939–40 a prolonged drought reduced the supply of water power and accentuated the usual seasonal demand for steam power. The Japan Electric Power Generating and Transmission Company in its first year of operation rather badly underestimated its coal requirements and does not seem to have accumulated any reserve stocks of coal for

---

[56] These developments have been described in Chapter X and in sections (2) and (4) of this chapter.

[57] Rainfall is usually abundant in Japan from April to September and less so from October to March. Though the seasonal movement is somewhat obscured by the sharply rising trend, the influence of rainfall on the output of hydro and steam power is shown by the quarterly output figures for 1936 and 1937 as given in the *Monthly Trade Report, Japan*, February, 1938, p. 20.

ELECTRIC POWER OUTPUT — JAPAN PROPER

(in million KWH)

1936	Hydro	Steam	Total
1st Quarter...............	3,887	1,764	5,651
2nd "	5,255	745	6,000
3rd "	5,164	810	5,974
4th "	5,194	1,324	6,518
Total................	19,500	4,643	24,143
1937			
1st Quarter...............	4,982	1,353	6,334
2nd "	5,571	1,087	6,658
3rd "	5,392	1,139	6,531
4th "	5,705	1,339	7,045
Total..................	21,650	4,918	26,568

MINERAL RESOURCES OF JAPAN AND MANCHUKUO   423

the production of steam power. As a consequence of the universal shortage of coal then prevailing in Japan, the company was obliged first to curtail power supplied and finally to suspend it entirely in certain districts for a few days during February, 1940. Normal service was not restored until the end of March, 1940. This meant the suspension of all industrial activity including the manufacture of armaments and ammunition for a short time and sharply curtailed operations during the entire first quarter. About 100,000 tons of coal were imported from abroad at a cost nearly three times as great as for the domestic product. The fixing of coal prices in Japan at a comparatively low level in September, 1938, may have been responsible in part for the failure of coal output to expand during 1939. Subsidies will be provided to stimulate output during 1940–41 without raising prices.

Before the China Incident, Japan was nearly self-sufficient in coal though some anthracite and some coking coal were imported from the colonies, Manchukuo, China and French Indo-China. Domestic production rose from 28 million tons in 1932 to 42 million tons in 1936 and 50 million tons (estimated) in 1938. The net imports from foreign countries were just about three million tons each year from 1934 to 1939.[58] The foreign countries which supplied the coal were Manchukuo, China and French Indo-China. Manchukuo supplied more than two million tons in each of the years 1933 to 1937 but with increased consumption of coal at home and delays in the output expansion program the imports from this region dropped to 1,440,000 tons in 1938 and to 752,000 tons in 1939. It must be remembered in this connection that the Japanese coal producers had opposed Manchurian imports before the war and were therefore somewhat responsible for the undeveloped state of the Manchurian mines. Imports from North China on the other hand have increased from about half a million tons in 1934 and 1935 to 1,621,000 tons in 1938 and 2,434,000 tons in 1939. Imports from French Indo-China have declined from 869,000 tons in 1936 to 604,000 tons in 1939. The traffic in coal within the Yen Bloc is rather confusing. Japan not only imports coal from her colonies and the adjacent foreign countries but also exports coal to them. To some extent this is due to differences in the kind of coal pro-

[58] Tables 88–90.

424 THE INDUSTRIALIZATION OF JAPAN AND MANCHUKUO

duced, but it also seems to be due to the fact that water carriage is cheaper and more convenient than overland transportation. The situation with respect to supply and demand within the Japanese Empire from 1932 to 1936 is summarized below.

COAL IN THE JAPANESE EMPIRE, 1932–36 [59]

(in thousand metric tons)

	1932	1933	1934	1935	1936
Japan Proper					
Production...........................	28,053	32,524	35,925	37,762	41,803
Imports from Foreign Countries.........	2,716	3,496	4,060	4,049	4,419
Imports from Japanese Territories.......	510	776	1,012	1,164	1,760
Exports to Foreign Countries...........	1,388	1,560	1,087	1,019	1,112
Exports to Japanese Territories.........	459	568	589	746	896
Total Supply [60]......................	*29,876*	*35,498*	*38,884*	*41,375*	*46,211*
Percentage Production to Supply........	94	92	92	91	90
Japanese Empire					
Production — Japan..................	28,053	32,524	35,925	37,762	41,803
Korea..................	1,077	1,307	1,689	1,999	2,282
Formosa...............	1,355	1,533	1,521	1,597	1,744
Saghalien..............	677	889	1,197	1,516	2,075
Total..................	*31,163*	*36,252*	*40,331*	*42,874*	*47,904*
Imports from Foreign Countries.........	3,162	4,020	4,696	4,664	5,098
Exports to Foreign Countries...........	1,560	1,753	1,267	1,197	1,283
Percentage Production to Supply........	95	94	91	92	92

Coal production within the Japanese Empire increased by more than 50 per cent between 1932 and 1936 and by at least another 20 per cent from 1936 to 1938. Nevertheless, consumption outstripped production. Some years ago the coal reserves in Japan Proper were estimated at 16,691 million tons, Korea at 1,000 million metric tons, South Saghalien 1,998 million tons and Formosa 400 million tons.[61] The latest estimate for Manchukuo is 15,000 million tons. The coal deposits of China, on the other hand, have been estimated at the huge sum of 239,059 million tons of which 132,817 million tons or 55 per cent of the total are to be found in the five provinces of North China. The deposits in Japan Proper are divided largely between Kyushu and Hokkaido with the mines in Kyushu much more thoroughly exploited than those in Hokkaido. The

[59] Data originally published by the Ministry of Commerce and Industry and reproduced in the *Mitsubishi Monthly Circular*, February, 1939, p. 15.
[60] Adjusted for stocks on hand at the beginning and end of year.
[61] By the Bureau of Mines of the Ministry of Commerce and Industry in 1932.

MINERAL RESOURCES OF JAPAN AND MANCHUKUO   425

increase in production in recent years has been most rapid in Hok-kaido, Korea and South Saghalien where many promising new mines have been opened up and developed. The Governor of Saghalien stated in the Diet on March 13, 1940, that coal production in Saghalien would be increased from 5 million tons in 1939–40 to 6.1 million tons in 1940–41. This compares with 2 million tons in 1936.[62]

If plans for the expansion of the heavy industries, for coal lique-faction and for electric power are carried out as scheduled, Japan alone will soon require from 70 to 80 million tons of coal a year, of which 50 to 60 million tons may be produced in Japan and the remainder imported from the colonies, Manchukuo and North China. The three largest individual consumers will be the Imperial Railways, the Japan Iron Manufacturing Company and the Japan Electric Power and Transmission Company. The coal liquefaction industry will consume from 9 to 10 million tons a year while the Electric Power Company plans to increase its consumption from 6.7 million tons in 1940 to 10 million tons within a few years. The heavy industries and the chemical industry have been the largest consumers of coal in recent years; between them they used 25.9 per cent of the total in 1934, 26.8 per cent in 1935, 30.1 per cent in 1936 and 33.7 per cent in 1937. The proportional consumption of electric power by these industries was even greater. The appor-tionment of coal among various types of consumers in 1934 and 1937 was as follows:

JAPANESE COAL CONSUMPTION CLASSIFIED BY INDUSTRIES [63]

	Per Cent of Total Consumption	
	1934	1937
Heavy Industries	15.6	19.5
Chemical Industry	9.3	14.2
Steamships	11.4	8.8
Railways	10.0	9.6
Textiles and Dyeing	9.6	8.9
Ceramic Industry	8.7	8.7
Electricity	6.8	8.0
Gas and Coke	6.0	5.0
Foodstuffs	5.6	4.9
Household, Offices, etc.	17.0	11.9
Total	100.0	100.0

[62] *Japan Weekly Chronicle*, March 21, 1940, p. 66.
[63] *Mitsubishi Monthly Circular*, February, 1939, p. 16. *Contemporary Opinions,* August 3, 1939, pp. 5–6.

426 THE INDUSTRIALIZATION OF JAPAN AND MANCHUKUO

There seem to have been several reasons for the shortage of coal in Japan in the winter of 1939–40. First of all, the demand for coal rose rapidly as a consequence of the expansion of the heavy industries and the necessity for substituting steam power for water power. Output was well above the pre-Incident level but had not advanced as rapidly as the demand for coal. A corresponding increase in demand in Manchukuo had reduced exports from that country to Japan. The price control policy of the government, which fixed prices at a stable level though costs were rising, probably discouraged the extension of coal mining operations. In September, 1938, the government ordered a 10 per cent reduction in prices and has since maintained prices at the new level. Two joint committees, made up of administrative officials and business men, controlled production and distribution on the basis of official regulations during 1939. There was a plan for a semi-official monopolistic concern, to be called the Japan Coal Sales Company, which should buy and distribute all coal mined in the country, and although this did not meet with the approval of mine owners or dealers, it was finally provided for in the Coal Distribution Control Bill passed by the Diet in March, 1940. There seems to have been a certain amount of demoralization in the industry itself as a consequence of the shortage of skilled labor, equipment and transportation facilities, and of poor organization. It is alleged, for example, that there was plenty of coal stored in the mines in Kyushu which could not be transported quickly to the industrial cities of Osaka and Nagoya over the stormy winter seas. It is also frequently alleged that the wages of coal miners are now so high by Japanese standards that the miners will not work long hours and actually absent themselves from work from time to time. The miner's wage was said to average "¥10.37 per day so that a family of miners . . . is able to draw nearly ¥600 a month." [64] The government is reluctant to raise coal prices and has compromised on subsidies for increased output and for new tunneling operations. It is intended to increase coal production by 5.5 million tons in Japan Proper in 1940–41. A subsidy of ¥4 per ton to be paid on the *increase* in output will amount to ¥22 million. In addition the sum of ¥22.4 million will be paid as a compensation to high cost producers and ¥3.73 million for the exca-

[64] *Japan Weekly Chronicle*, February 8, 1940.

MINERAL RESOURCES OF JAPAN AND MANCHUKUO   427

vation of new pits. The government will invest ¥6.25 million in the Japan Coal Sales Company which will purchase and sell all coal produced and consumed in Japan. There is also the possibility of improving transportation and of using more Korean labor in the mines. The fact that there is a coal shortage is likely to make observers overlook the fact that the increase in coal production in Japan, Korea and Southern Saghalien during the first two years of the China Incident was truly remarkable. But now, it is to North China that the Yen Bloc must look for large additional supplies of cheap coal.

Japan, Korea, South Saghalien and Manchukuo are all reasonably well endowed with coal, but the estimated deposits in North China and Inner Mongolia are many times those of all these other regions combined.[65] The producing fields are centered in the provinces of Hopei, Shantung, Shansi and Hunan but the largest deposits are in the parts of Shansi and Shensi which are difficult to exploit because of lack of capital and transportation facilities. It has already been pointed out that exports of coal from North China to Japan rose steadily from 550,000 tons in 1935 to 2,434,000 tons in 1939. It is hoped that from 4.5 to 5 million tons will be exported to Japan in 1940. The bulk of this coal is now coming from the British owned Kailan Mining Administration and from the Tatung mine in North Shansi. Early in 1938, the Kailan Administration which formerly shipped most of its coal to Hongkong, Shanghai and other places in Central and South China, promised to ship 1.7 million tons of coal to Japan in 1938–39 for the use of the Japan Iron Manufacturing Company. At the same time it announced that it would increase its output from 5 to 8 million tons a year. The Tatung Coal Mine in North Shansi was taken over by the Japanese Army in October, 1937. The output of the mine was 876,129 tons in the next fifteen months rising from 10,000 tons a month to 100,000 tons in December, 1938. The estimated deposits have been revised from 12 billion tons to 40 billion tons. This coal is suitable for liquefaction and some of it is good coking coal. There is an ambitious ten year plan which calls for an output of one million tons in 1939, 10 million tons in 1942 and 30 million tons in 1947. A letter

[65] The total coal deposits of China are estimated at 233 billion tons of which 215 billion tons are supposedly in North China and Inner Mongolia. *Mitsubishi Monthly Circular*, February, 1938, p. 18.

428 THE INDUSTRIALIZATION OF JAPAN AND MANCHUKUO

in the *Oriental Economist* pointed out that such plans were foolish dreams in that they ignored the fact that China was a very large country with inadequate transportation facilities. The coal of Tatung must be transported by rail a distance of 600 kilometers from Tatung to Tientsin.[66] The harbors of North China and the shipping facilities of Japan are now being fully utilized and would require a very great expansion to handle 30 million tons of coal a year.

There are two main problems in connection with the exploitation of these North China coal fields; one is the political situation and the other is the problem of transportation. Enough has been written about recent developments in Japan, Korea and Manchukuo to show that there is a real possibility that heavy industries could be established in these regions to serve all of East Asia as far as cheap and heavy equipment is concerned. The coal of North China would be a tremendous asset to the heavy industries of the Yen Bloc under conditions of genuine cooperation between China and Japan. If, however, a Japanese army has to keep the mines running, the cost in the long run will be prohibitive. Similarly real cooperation between the Chinese and the Japanese might lead to the same improvement in transportation facilities as has recently taken place in Manchukuo, but an attempt to accomplish this under conditions of military occupation will be extremely difficult. The real interests of China and Japan will be served best if China will abandon her obstructionist tactics of many years' standing and if Japan will realize the futility of extensive military operations. In the meantime, under existing difficulties, North China coal is actually being mined and shipped to Japan to an increasing extent.

There have been no significant discoveries of natural petroleum resources within the Yen Bloc and it is for this reason that oil shale and coal for liquefaction play an important part in current plans. The small domestic supply of petroleum is undoubtedly Japan's greatest strategic weakness. Just before the China Incident, Japan and Manchukuo consumed from 3.5 to 4 million [67] tons of petroleum products annually and the consumption is now higher because of military and naval requirements, despite strict rationing of gasoline for ordinary use, the compulsory mixing of alcohol with gasoline,

[66] *Oriental Economist,* January, 1940, p. 31.
[67] This estimate is higher than those usually given which apparently do not include gasoline and fuel oil consumed by the Army and the Navy.

MINERAL RESOURCES OF JAPAN AND MANCHUKUO   429

and the use of charcoal gas engines in buses and even in motor cars. Japan produced at home and in Formosa about 10 per cent of the petroleum consumed and another 5 per cent in its concessions in Russian Saghalien while Manchukuo produced somewhat more than 100,000 tons of oil from shale. Crude oil and refined products were imported from the United States, the Netherlands Indies and British Borneo. The United States supplied about 75 per cent of the crude and heavy oil imported and the Netherlands Indies about 65 per cent of the kerosene and gasoline imported. Japanese tariff policy favored the importation of crude oil and the growth of refining in Japan so that there was a tendency for imports of crude and heavy oil to increase much faster than imports of refined products. In 1935 Japanese refineries supplied 50 per cent of the gasoline, 50 per cent of the kerosene, 94 per cent of the lubricating oil, and 12.5 per cent of the fuel oil used in Japan; [68] in 1939, these percentages were much higher.

Professor Penrose discussed the supply of crude and heavy oil in Japan in Chapter VIII and presented statistics for domestic crude production and imports by countries of origin in Table 92. He did not present statistics showing imports of kerosene, gasoline and other refined products. A comparison is made below between imports of crude and refined petroleum according to quantity and value. The figures were compiled from the Japanese trade statistics which are given in units of 100 gallons (1 barrel = 42 U. S. gallons). From 1927 to 1931 the imports of refined mineral oil were of approximately the same value as the imports of crude and heavy oil, but from 1932 the latter rose rapidly. In 1936 imports of crude petroleum were five times as great as those of refined petroleum in quantity and two and one-half times as great in value. This indicated a considerable increase in refining capacity in Japan.

The Japanese import statistics put "crude" and "heavy" oil together in the same category because there is in practice no sharp distinction between them. Some heavy crudes from California and Borneo are burned directly as a fuel without refining whereas fuel oil and crude oil of any gravity may be used in a modern cracking plant in the manufacture of gasoline and other refined products.[69]

[68] *Petroleum in the Far East,* Supplement to International Petroleum Trade, U. S Bureau of Mines, April 27, 1937, p. 5.
[69] *Petroleum in the Far East,* p. 6.

430 THE INDUSTRIALIZATION OF JAPAN AND MANCHUKUO

IMPORTS OF MINERAL OIL INTO JAPAN [70]

YEAR	QUANTITY			VALUE (in 1,000 yen)	
	Crude and Heavy (100,000 gallons)	Refined		Crude and Heavy	Refined
		(100,000 gallons)	(metric tons)		
1927	1,627	535	20,040	23,993	31,298
1928	3,806	847	23,954	45,163	44,772
1929	4,198	1,068	20,938	46,603	46,324
1930	4,264	1,189	20,188	44,796	44,772
1931	4,538	1,275	17,229	44,064	41,724
1932	5,687	1,396	15,902	54,887	43,701
1933	6,130	1,415	8,193	68,347	40,513
1934	7,440	1,752	13,243	82,483	41,544
1935	9,187	1,924	13,499	106,826	45,821
1936	10,336	2,058	13,293	129,688	53,082

In 1935 and 1936 the United States supplied just under 75 per cent of the imports of crude and heavy oil, the Netherlands East Indies about 12 per cent and British Borneo about 7 per cent (Table 92). The output from the Japanese concessions in Russian Saghalien was used by the Imperial Navy and does not appear in these import statistics. In these same years, the Netherlands East Indies supplied 65 per cent of the *imported* gasoline and kerosene and the United States 19 per cent.

No official Japanese statistics on mineral oils have been published since 1936, but we have United States statistics of exports to Japan and we may assume that any increased demand has been met largely from American sources in view of the low prices prevailing in California. The American statistics are usually quoted in barrels whereas the Japanese statistics may be quoted in gallons, liters, kiloliters or metric tons. There is little or no difficulty in converting from one volume measure to another—that is from gallons or liters to barrels.[71] In attempting to convert from a volume measure to a weight measure—from kiloliters or barrels to metric tons—we have to face the fact that there is no uniform rate of conversion because different kinds of crude petroleum and different refined products have specific gravities which vary considerably. The approximate number of barrels per metric ton of crude petro-

[70] *Monthly Return of the Foreign Trade of Japan*, December, 1936, and earlier years.
[71] 1 liter = .264 U. S. gallons; 42 U. S. gallons = 1 barrel; 1 kiloliter = 6.29 barrels; 1 metric ton petroleum = 7 to 7.5 barrels; 1 metric ton gasoline = 8.5 barrels.

MINERAL RESOURCES OF JAPAN AND MANCHUKUO   431

leum varies from 6.75 for Venezuela oil to 7.39 for United States oil; the average specific gravities used for conversion purposes in the Statistical Year-Book of the League of Nations [72] are: natural gasoline 0.680; motor spirit 0.735; aviation spirit 0.790; kerosene 0.810; gas oil 0.860; Diesel oil 0.870; fuel oil 0.930; lubricating oils 0.900. The rates of conversion chosen in the interests of simplification are 7 to 7.5 barrels of crude petroleum and 8.5 barrels of gasoline per metric ton. An estimate of the principal mineral oils consumed in Japan for the years 1930–35 is presented below: [73]

MINERAL OILS CONSUMED IN JAPAN, 1930–35
(in thousand barrels)

YEAR	APPARENT CONSUMPTION FOR CIVILIAN USE						IMPORTED FOR JAPANESE GOVERNMENT [74]
	Gasoline	Kerosene	Gas Oil Solar Oil Neutral Oil	Fuel Oil	Lubri- cating Oil	Total	
1930	3,473	891	1,440	6,763	1,306	13,873	1,979
1931	4,324	772	1,242	7,270	1,254	14,862	1,579
1932	5,117	883	1,395	8,623	1,190	17,208	1,843
1933	5,380	833	1,238	9,046	1,289	17,786	2,142
1934	6,473	1,100	1,256	11,581	1,544	21,954	2,069
1935	7,433	1,137	1,132	14,257	1,617	25,576	4,011

These estimates of consumption include imports of refined products and mineral oil refined in Japan from both domestic and imported crude. The total above is for civilian consumption only; the report from which these estimates were taken states that the Japanese Government imported considerable quantities of fuel and other oil from foreign countries and that the Army and Navy have their own cracking plants in which fuel oil and other refined products are produced. Since no statistics for these purchases were issued, the estimate for government imports was obtained by comparing the export statistics of the United States, the Netherlands East Indies and the Soviet Union with Japanese import statistics. Export statistics for the United States from 1934 to 1939 are given on the following page.

It is at once obvious that the United States supplied much of the fuel oil but little of the gasoline and kerosene used in Japan. These

[72] 1938–39, p. 11 and 136.
[73] *Petroleum in the Far East*, p. 2.
[74] Difference between shipments from exporting countries and imports stated in Japanese statistics.

432 THE INDUSTRIALIZATION OF JAPAN AND MANCHUKUO

EXPORTS OF PETROLEUM AND PETROLEUM PRODUCTS, 1934–39
FROM THE UNITED STATES TO JAPAN [75]
(in thousand barrels)

	1934	1935	1936	1937	1938	1939
Crude Petroleum........	6,693	10,483	10,381	15,995	21,272	16,086
Gasoline and Other .. Motor Fuels..........	1,079	699	1,013	1,093	1,059	1,198
Gas and Fuel Oil........	3,433	5,129	4,990	6,308	5,297	6,020
Residual Fuel Oil........	4,484	4,163	4,265	4,045	3,030	3,889
Lubricating Oil.........	254	280	308	444	307	514
Total above items.....	15,943	20,754	20,957	27,885	30,965	27,707

were refined in Japan from United States crude petroleum or were imported from the Netherlands East Indies. The export of gasoline hardly rose at all during the war period. It is claimed that Japan now produces airplane gasoline and it is known that the industry in the Netherlands East Indies was constructing at least 3 airplane gasoline refineries in early 1940. Between 1934 and 1939, there was a small increase in exports of fuel oil and a very large increase in exports of crude petroleum. Crude petroleum made up 42 per cent of America's exports of mineral oils to Japan in 1934, and 58 per cent in 1939. Contrary to popular impressions gasoline constituted only 5 per cent of Japan's mineral oil imports from the United States. There must have been a considerable increase in Japanese refining and storage capacity since the last publication of official information on these points. It is claimed that storage capacity was much increased in 1937 and 1938. Exports from the United States to Japan were about one million tons or 30 per cent higher in 1937 and 1939 than in 1935 and 1936. It is possible, therefore, that Japan has been consuming about 5 million tons of mineral oil annually since 1937.

The great dependence on foreign countries for so essential and strategic a material has very much influenced Japanese fuel policy. Among other things the government has promoted the growth of refining capacity; controlled the import, distribution and storage of petroleum products; encouraged better utilization and economy in fuel consumption; urged the intensive exploitation of natural oil

[75] Figures for 1937–39 from U. S. Department of Commerce *Reports on Trade with Japan, China, Hong Kong and Kwantung.* Figures for 1934–36 from *National Petroleum News,* July 19, 1939, p. 21. Include exports to Japan, Korea and Formosa.

MINERAL RESOURCES OF JAPAN AND MANCHUKUO   433

resources; and has promoted actively the development of the synthetic oil industry. Japanese tariff policy encouraged the importation of crude petroleum and the growth of a Japanese refining industry which has evidently expanded very rapidly since 1936. This
means that Japan can buy crude petroleum from Mexico and various South American countries if the problem of transportation can
be solved. Both the government and private interests have paid
much attention to the expansion and improvement of the tanker
fleet and other transport facilities.

The Petroleum Industry Law of 1934 subjected the production,
importation, refining and sale of mineral oil in Japan, Korea and
Formosa to strict government control. The government determined
maximum prices and the amounts to be imported and refined. Importers and refiners were licensed and were required to keep on
hand at all times a six months' supply of mineral oil; refiners were
required to construct plants according to government specifications.
The foreign companies protested against constructing storage facilities at their own expense.

There were two large foreign importing companies and four
major Japanese refining companies: the Rising Sun Petroleum Company (Royal Dutch-Shell), the Socony-Vacuum Corporation
(Standard Oil of New York), the Japan Petroleum Company, the
Ogura Oil Company, the Mitsui Bussan Kaisha, and the Mitsubishi
Oil Company. A company was formed to divide the officially determined quota among refiners and importers. The dispute with the
foreign companies about compulsory storage was settled in the
middle of 1936 when Mitsui Bussan Kaisha agreed to construct the
storage equipment and lease it to the foreign companies. In addition to whatever oil was stored by the military, there was on hand
in Japan at the outbreak of the war with China at least six months'
supply of crude and refined petroleum. It has been frequently stated
that storage facilities were much increased during 1938 when there
was a very large import of crude oil from the United States. The
quantity in storage would be a matter of the utmost importance in
the event of oil sanctions.

The government introduced a number of bills concerned with
the national fuel policy at the last session of the Diet before the
war and in June, 1937 established the Fuel Bureau under the

434 THE INDUSTRIALIZATION OF JAPAN AND MANCHUKUO

Ministry of Commerce and Industry to carry out the national fuel policy. The Fuel Bureau was to encourage the exploitation of fuel resources, execute the Petroleum Industry Law, encourage the synthetic oil industry, and promote the better utilization of fuel. The seventieth session of the Diet passed the Petrol Excise Law, which exempted all synthetic oil from the tax, and the Alcohol Monopoly and Compulsory Alcohol Admixture bills. The production of alcohol was made a government monopoly and the mixing of alcohol with gasoline to the extent of 5 per cent was required. This was subsequently raised to 10 per cent. At the same time the production of alcohol from sweet potatoes and from sugar cane refuse in Formosa was encouraged.

The Synthetic Petroleum Production Law and the Imperial Fuel Development Company Law were passed at the seventy-first session of the Diet, a special session held in July and August, 1937, after the outbreak of hostilities, and the Petroleum Resources Exploitation Law was passed by the seventy-third Diet in March, 1938. The Synthetic Petroleum Production Law made the manufacture of synthetic oil and gasoline a licensed industry subject to government permission, supervision and control. The government may give subsidies and permits the free import of necessary materials and equipment for 7 years. Japanese subjects must control more than half the capital stock and constitute more than half of the directors in any company established under this law. Additional duties were placed on the importation of heavy oil and gasoline while synthetic petroleum was put on the free list. A national policy concern, the Imperial Fuel Development Company, was established to help carry out a seven year plan to produce 2 million tons of artificial oil at an estimated capital expenditure of ¥770 million. The government was to provide half of the authorized capital of ¥100 million and the company was permitted to issue debentures up to three times its paid-up capital. The Petroleum Resources Exploitation Law represents part of a five year plan for the intensive exploitation of natural petroleum resources. This law provided for government supervision and control of drilling operations, compulsory co-operation between owners of mining rights, and government subsidies for drilling to the extent of ¥5.6 million over five years for 240 new wells. The producers of oil from subsidized wells

MINERAL RESOURCES OF JAPAN AND MANCHUKUO   435

may be required to pay to the government 2 per cent of the annual value of the oil for 5 years. Moreover, the Finance and Overseas Ministries, in co-operation, are attempting to develop the petroleum resources of Saghalien and Formosa.

The possibility of increasing the supply of natural liquid fuel in Japanese controlled territory does not appear to be promising with the possible exception of shale oil production in Manchukuo. The exploitation of the Japanese concessions in Russian Saghalien has been very much hampered by the Soviet Government since the conclusion of the Anti-Comintern Pact. The Japanese had participated in the allied invasion of Siberia after the Great War and occupied North Saghalien in the process. Eventually the Japanese withdrew from the Russian Territory, but by the Treaty of Moscow in 1925, they acquired prospecting rights for 11 years and mining rights for 45 years in alternate squares over 272,000 acres of land. The prospecting concession was extended by another 5 years to 1941. The North Saghalien Petroleum Company attempted to explore and develop these resources with the assistance of subsidies from the Japanese government. This company in 1936 produced about 180,000 tons of oil which was supplied to the Imperial Navy. Formerly the Soviet production in this region was also sold to Japan, but now it is shipped to a Soviet refinery at Khabarovsk on the Amur River. As part of the national fuel policy, the government granted additional subsidies for prospecting and it was planned to raise production considerably in the five years 1937–41. This plan has met with some success but it is not likely that the goal of 500,000 tons a year will be attained. Even if this should happen eventually, it will still be necessary to depend on synthetic oil and gasoline to a large extent if Japan wishes to decrease her dependence on foreign countries.

The synthetic fuel industry was actually started in Japan, Korea and Manchukuo in 1936 after many years of experiment but there was no production on a commercial scale until 1939. At least three different methods are being employed: 1) the direct liquefaction of coal or the hydrogenation process, 2) the Fischer-Tropsch synthetic method, and 3) the low temperature carbonization method. The direct liquefaction process was developed in Japan by the Navy Fuel Depot with the assistance of the South Manchuria Railway Com-

436 THE INDUSTRIALIZATION OF JAPAN AND MANCHUKUO

pany and the Korea Nitrogen Fertilizer Company. It differs from the Bergius hydrogenation process in significant details but also combines hydrogen with coal under great pressure at a very high temperature with the aid of a catalyst. The method of catalytic hydrogenation produces a gasoline of relative high octane value; one type of process yields a gasoline of 70-octane value and another a gasoline of 80- to 82-octane value *without lead*. The use of tetraethyl lead can raise a gasoline of 70-octane rating to 87-octane rating. The Mitsui Mining Company purchased the right to use the Fischer-Tropsch process which synthesizes gases with the aid of a catalyst. The gasoline produced by the synthetic method has a very low octane value and must be cracked to produce good motor fuel. The direct liquefaction and the synthetic method are considered more promising than the low temperature carbonization method.

In 1936, the Korea Coal Industry Company (a subsidiary of Korea Nitrogen) began the construction of a 50,000 ton plant at Agochi, Korea and the South Manchuria Railway Company started a 20,000 ton plant at Fushun. Both were to use the direct liquefaction method. In the same year, the Mitsui Bussan Kaisha sent several experts to Germany, purchased machinery for the Fischer synthetic method, and commenced work on a 30,000 ton plant at the Miike coal field in Omuda, Kyushu. A number of firms producing iron and steel, gas, and synthetic nitrates also engaged in the manufacture of synthetic oil by means of the low temperature carbonization of coal. The Korea Nitrogen Company had a plant at Eian in Korea and the Ube Nitrogen Company one at Ube in Japan. The Japan Iron Manufacturing Company produced synthetic oil at its Wanishi Iron Works and the Mitsubishi Coal Liquefaction Company at Uchiharo in South Saghalien. These enterprises were all under construction by 1936 and had started operations by the spring of 1939. It is impossible to be very definite about the scale of operations; often the plants start with a capacity of only 10,000 or 20,000 tons a year with the purpose of expanding rapidly after the experimental stage.

The Synthetic Petroleum Production Law, the Imperial Fuel Development Company and the seven year plan for synthetic oil production were all launched at the special seventy-first session of

MINERAL RESOURCES OF JAPAN AND MANCHUKUO 437

the Diet in August, 1937. The seven year plan provided for the production of one million tons of synthetic fuel oil and one million tons of synthetic gasoline in Japan and Manchukuo. This was soon replaced by a five year plan which called for a total output of 3.7 million tons of which 2 million tons were to be produced in Japan, Korea and Formosa and 1.7 million tons in Manchukuo. The Manchurian plan has already been discussed. According to the original plan, half of the liquid fuel requirements of Japan and Manchukuo were to be met by means of domestic resources of natural and synthetic petroleum. For the production of 2 million tons of synthetic oil, it was estimated that 8.9 million tons of coal will be needed for oil production and another million tons for the production of hydrogen from steam or about 10 million tons in all.

Since 1937 a number of large companies employing either the direct liquefaction or the synthetic process have been established with the assistance of the Imperial Fuel Development Company, the Manchukuo government, the Mitsui Bussan Kaisha and the Noguchi interests. In general these are larger and much more ambitious undertakings than the earlier ones. Mitsui has a large interest in the Manchuria Synthetic Fuel Company which is erecting a plant at Fuhsin in Manchukuo and in the Hokkaido Artificial Oil Company which is building three large plants in Hokkaido. These plants will use the Fischer-Tropsch synthetic process. The direct liquefaction or hydrogenation process will be used at the Ssupingkai plant of the Manchuria Coal Liquefaction Company and at the Kirin (Manchukuo) plant of the Kirin Artificial Oil Company. The latter is a Noguchi project which plans to produce 300,000 tons of oil a year and to begin operations in 1941. Much of the equipment to be used is of Japanese design but has been ordered in Germany and the United States. There will be difficulties and delays in obtaining it. Nevertheless Japan has passed the experimental stage and has actually produced oil from coal. This has been accomplished by giving synthetic fuel all kinds of preferential treatment in tax and tariff exemptions and by means of government subsidies and other financial assistance. The subsidies would not be considered large by western standards. It is possible that in a few years the threat of oil sanctions will no longer be feared. The United Kingdom produced 170,000 tons of synthetic gasoline in 1938 and the German

438 THE INDUSTRIALIZATION OF JAPAN AND MANCHUKUO

production, estimated at nearly one million tons in 1937,[76] has risen rapidly since that year. The Japanese have spent many years in patient experimentation and they now seem to be determined to carry their experiments to a successful conclusion whatever may be the cost.

In view of the abrogation by the United States of its commercial treaty with Japan and the possibility of an embargo on shipments to Japan of oil, scrap and metals, the question rises as to what would be the consequence of such an action. The United States has been supplying Japan with something like 60 per cent of her total mineral oil requirements, mostly in the form of crude and heavy oil. In such an event Japan would stretch her own small resources of natural and synthetic oil to the uttermost, draw upon the large supplies in storage, make larger purchases from the Netherlands East Indies and perhaps make some arrangement with Mexico. The production of petroleum in the Netherlands East Indies has risen steadily from 4,698,000 tons in 1931 to 7,263,000 tons in 1937. Early in 1940 three new refineries for aviation gasoline were being constructed in the Netherlands East Indies. Mexico exported 22,000,000 barrels or 3 million tons a year before the expropriation. Japan's war time consumption may be in the vicinity of 5 million tons a year. In 1936 Japan and Manchukuo produced about 600,000 tons of petroleum and shale oil; in 1940 the two countries will produce at least one million tons of crude petroleum, shale oil and synthetic oil and probably rather more than this. Mexico, on bad terms with the United States and unable to sell petroleum to Germany because of the British blockade, would be glad to find a market for her petroleum. The first important contract for the delivery of Mexican oil to Japan provided for the delivery of 2,402,000 barrels within one year after May 1, 1940, at prices averaging 30 cents below the world market to compensate for the cost of transportation through the Panama Canal in Japanese tankers.[77] The difficulty with Mexican oil at present is that there is no cheap way to transport it from the Atlantic to the Pacific Coast. It is reported from time to time that Mexico would like to improve the railroad across the narrow Isthmus of Tehuantepec or

[76] *Statistical Year-Book*, League of Nations, 1938–39, p. 134.
[77] Wireless to the *New York Times* from Mexico City, April 2, 1940.

even to build a pipe line across the Isthmus to the port of Salina Cruz on the Pacific Coast. It has also been suggested that the pipe line from the rich Poza Rica oil field to Mexico City might be extended some two hundred miles to Acapulco on the Pacific Coast. If Japan were cut off from cheap California crude oil, she might well assist in some such undertaking. It is by no means certain that an embargo on oil shipments by the United States would have the effect desired.

[28]

5

чо

JAPAN'S
INSTITUTIONS
AND
PRACTICES

In its policies toward the acquisition of raw materials during the past thirty years, Japan has differed from the United States in one critical respect. There have been struggles and debates inside the country over its policies, as well as occasional false starts and outright errors. But the policies that have been selected have followed a coherent line and have been more or less responsive to the country's needs. At first, Japan's emphasis was on securing its raw materials at the lowest possible prices. In the 1970s, security of supply became a major consideration, especially with regard to oil. In the 1980s, in response to the country's improving procurement capabilities, Japan has begun to balance security with efficiency in an effort to respond to both objectives.

During most of Japan's modern history, the country's concern about the availability of key industrial materials has been understandable enough. With few raw materials of its own, it has always had to rely heavily on foreign sources. As a latecomer to the rank of industrialized nations, it has had to confront the entrenched positions abroad of enterprises from other countries. Besides, in viewing the likely behavior of these foreign-owned enterprises, the Japanese have typically assumed that there was a high degree of concordance and collaboration between the enterprises and their respective governments, a perception that has heightened Japan's sense of exposure to foreign political pressures.

Japan's policies and practices with regard to industrial raw materials, however, were not simply the result of its perceptions of high risk. Whether because of the country's distinctive position as a have-not latecomer or because of cultural factors that had their roots elsewhere, Japan has formulated and executed its policies through a set of institutuions different in critical respects from those of the United States.

The Japanese System

Over the past few decades, a hoard of analysts have exposed and dissected the political, social, and economic structure of Japan, hoping to understand the process that has produced the country's phenomenal economic performance.[1] For once, the studies of the academic community have shown considerable agreement, albeit with a few important differences in interpretation yet to be resolved.

A system of governance. Japan, like the United States, is a practicing democracy, in which political power is well dispersed. Although the country has been governed by only one party since the peace treaty following World War II, that party is actually a coalition of various rival factions, whose competitive strength within the party rests on their ability to command the popular vote. And although the minority parties have been unable to take power, they have not been wholly without influence upon governmental policy.[2] An independent press and an autonomous judiciary fill out the picture of a practicing democracy.[3]

There is another fundamental respect in which Japan and the United States present striking similarities. Competitive marketing plays a very considerable role in the economies of both countries. Although the Japanese government engages in price control more readily than its U.S. counterpart, price competition among Japanese producers is endemic.[4] Advertising, too, plays a vital role in domestic marketing.[5] And as in the United States, the formation of new business ventures and the bankruptcy of existing ventures are commonplace.[6]

Yet despite these basic similarities, Japan's culture and system of governance represent in numerous fundamental ways the antithesis of their American counterparts. Those differences, extensive and deep-rooted, produce differences in style and method that sharply distinguish the strategy and operations of the two countries.

Perhaps the most important difference lies in the fact that industry organizations and governmental agencies play a much more direct role in the Japanese economy than in the economy of the United States.[7]

84 TWO HUNGRY GIANTS

These organizations introduce a measure of coordination and control in Japan that is critical in the country's relations with foreigners. The concept of "administrative guidance" by the government, a concept offensive to the U.S. culture, is a firmly established part of Japan's economic environment.[8] Without involving the authority of any explicit law, the Japanese government in August 1979 suddenly imposed "guidelines" on its trading companies that prevented them from completing lucrative deals for the importation of spot oil.[9] In another manifestation of its power, the government compelled the giant Mitsui interests to retain a foothold in a vast Iranian petrochemicals enterprise long after the firm was eager to withdraw.[10]

This aspect of the Japanese economy has been grossly parodied in the American and European press, creating the basis for the notorious Japan Incorporated metaphor. Japanese firms on occasion can be fractious and willful, bitterly resisting the suggestions of government and striking out on an independent course. Nevertheless, those episodes are less common with respect to foreign issues than domestic ones; and they are carried out by the public and private disputants in a spirit which suggests that each side recognizes its need for the other over the long run.

For various reasons, the inherent capacity of Japan's government to guide its enterprises on a sustained basis is far greater than that of the U.S. government. One of the more obvious reasons is the fact that Japan is a parliamentary democracy, hence a democracy that has greater similarities to Great Britain or France than to the United States. The power to govern the domestic economy lies much more firmly in the executive branch and its bureaucracy than in the case of the United States. The Japanese parliament and courts have nothing like the capacity of the U.S. Congress and courts to duplicate the executive's authority or to veto the executive's actions.

The power, however, is in the executive branch and its bureaucracy as a whole, not in the person of the prime minister. One factor that limits the power of the prime minister and other members of the cabinet is the competence and cohesiveness of the bureaucracy. This is no "government of strangers," such as the United States produces, periodically dismantled and reconstituted in a vast house-cleaning of key positions, as political leaders come and go. It is a professional bureaucracy, operated on the usual Japanese principles of recruitment by merit and of lifetime tenure in a single ministry or agency. Its members normally take their posts on the basis of a long weeding-out process that begins in middle school, a process that channels the most promising aspirants through a few prestigious universities into government service.[11] In each ministry, the entering group in any year is indoctrinated and socialized as a class, retaining its group identity throughout the professional lives of its members. Ministers rely upon these professionals to a degree that is only infrequently matched in the United States.[12] In American terms, the Japanese have unequivocally chosen the Hamiltonian tradition over the Jacksonian.

Although the Japanese bureaucracy exercises considerable power, it is restrained by a potent factor that has no counterpart in the U.S. bureaucratic process. This is the pronounced tendency of Japanese society, much advertised and widely documented, to reach decisions by building a national consensus.[13] That generalization, however, can easily be misunderstood and misinterpreted. Some observers insist, for instance, that the consensus which is so commonly identified with the Japanese political process is usually an agreement among elites, rather than agreement at the grass roots. Moreover, the agreement is not achieved without bitter struggles in the system.[14] Indeed, decision making inside the Japanese government shares many characteristics with the chaotic process that has been so well described for the United States.[15] The rivalries, animosities, and alliances that are the bread and butter of Washington bureaucratic politics have fairly close counterparts in Tokyo, but with one profound difference: whereas the common strategy of the strangers who make up the U.S. government is to try to avoid and circumvent the opposition, the Japanese approach is to find a process of decision making in which all the affected parties have participated. That approach may prolong the decision-making process endlessly. If eventual consensus is ever achieved, it may be the result of wearing down the opposition or adopting a compromise that seems extraordinarily ambiguous to outsiders; but it is ordinarily indispensable for Japanese action.[16] In this sense, one might say that the Japanese government behaves rather like the highly socialized U.S. Senate, whose members are aware that they must live with one another over the long pull, and not in the least like the U.S. government as a whole.

The difference between the Japanese and American governments in this aspect of their decision making is consistent and pervasive. It is

86   TWO HUNGRY GIANTS

found not only in the relations of the executive to other branches of the government, but also in relations between the different parts of the executive branch, and among the various divisions within ministries or agencies. The same characteristic is found within individual business firms in Japan.[17] In all likelihood, that trait is linked inseparably to the other characteristic that distinguishes Japanese from U.S. processes — namely, the much greater stability in the positions of institutions and individuals in Japanese structures. With stability of the various participants assured, none can as readily afford to win an isolated decision through evasive action.

Business and government. The nature of the interactions between Japan's government agencies and the country's business institutions has been influenced by more than the general style of Japan's system of governance. Economic historians are almost certainly right in attributing the close ties between business and government in part to the latecomer status of Japan as an industrializing power.[18] By the time Japan was ready to launch modern industries, the technology was already in the hands of other countries; by the time her firms were searching abroad for secure sources of oil and minerals, the enterprises of the United States and Europe had already staked out claims to the most obvious sources in Asia, Africa, and Latin America. It seemed almost inevitable, therefore, that Japanese business should summon up the help of government in overcoming its latecomer status.

That late start was probably instrumental also in helping to give the Japanese enterprise a distinctive strategy as it attempted to penetrate foreign markets and foreign sources of materials. Unlike the Americans, Japanese firms until quite recently had made few direct investments in raw materials in foreign countries; and even when they invested, they rarely sought to manage the foreign properties in which they had a financial stake. On the other hand, free of the restraints imposed by antitrust statutes, the Japanese have commonly organized their buying in any country through joint arrangements with other Japanese firms, including consortia, trading houses, and chosen lead firms. And they have frequently been assisted in such joint buying arrangements by initiatives from the government side.

The strategies of Japanese firms in acquiring overseas sources of raw materials have also been affected by the Japanese government's central role in the financing of Japanese business. By U.S. standards, big business in Japan is burdened with a remarkably high level of debt, of which an unusually large proportion is either official in origin or is subject to official guidance. In the 1975–1979 period, for instance, a little over 40 percent of the funds of Japanese corporations came from bank credit, including credit extended by official banking institutions or by private banks. Such credit, whether from public or private banking sources, was much influenced by governmental policy such as the Bank of Japan's practice of "window guidance" — that is, its practice of suggesting to lending banks where their added loans should be directed.[19] In the United States, in the same period, corporations drew about 25 percent of their funds from bank borrowing and bonds, of which hardly any were governmental.[20]

More narrowly, the evidence indicates that the capital-intensive raw materials industries are especially affected by the differences. One study covering the middle 1970s compared the capital structure of eight Japanese nonferrous metal firms with five U.S. firms in the same industries. In the case of the Japanese firms, about 90 percent of the capital came from debt, whereas the comparable figure for the U.S. firms was in the neighborhood of 50 percent.[21]

The government's influence on business policy does not depend on the banking channel alone. The process is helped by the private sector's respect for the position and capacity of the governmental bureaucracy. (The fact that the movement of former government officials to business is referred to as *amakudari* — literally, descending from heaven — is a telling sign of the relationship.) It is helped as well by a highly articulated set of institutions. On the government side, the much celebrated Ministry of International Trade and Investment (MITI) has been the key entity; on the business side, the almost equally well-known Federation of Economic Organizations, the Keidanren, has been the pivotal organization.

The Keidanren functions as the supreme coordinating body of big business in Japan. Although it is an organization for private business, the Keidanren's corporate membership also includes public and quasi-public corporations such as the Japan National Railways, the Japan Development Bank, and the Bank of Japan. Its elaborate staff is buttressed by an impressive array of several hundred prominent corporation executives, mostly presidents and board chairmen, who serve as directors. Its activities run a wide gamut, but consultation with the government constitutes the central function.[22]

88 TWO HUNGRY GIANTS

Formal manifestations of some of the results of this consultation process have appeared periodically in the reports of so-called deliberation councils, bodies made up of prestigious senior figures from private industry, government enterprise, trade associations, and universities. Councils of this sort have been responsible for producing a series of reports, defining the goals to be achieved and the programs to be pursued in their achievement.[23]

As was noted earlier, similar reports have been produced sporadically by prestigious commissions in the United States, but there has been a critical difference in the role that such reports have played in the two societies. The U.S. reports have been largely hortatory and educational, whereas the Japanese reports have defined a framework in which Japanese business and government have been expected to act. The framework has legitimated the subsequent behavior of Japanese government agencies and credit institutions in selecting specific projects and choosing specific firms for special support.

The fact still remains that powerful and strong-willed business executives in Japan can sometimes resist the pressures of the bureaucracy to conform to official views. In the 1960s the resistance of Japan's automobile industry to MITI's attempts to force mergers was resolute and successful; so, too, was the resistance of Japan's mainframe computer producers to similar MITI attempts in the 1970s.[24] But as the managing director of Nippon Oil Company recently observed, "We cannot ignore what MITI has to say."[25]

The element of cooperation has characteristically been even stronger on issues in which foreign economies are to be confronted. The cooperation between government and enterprise in foreign trade and investment manifests itself in numerous ways. Where a special entrepreneurial push from the government has seemed useful, MITI has had no great difficulty in securing the needed authority to create a new publicly controlled enterprise. Accordingly, various public organizations that have no counterpart in the United States—some owned by the state, some ambiguously endowed with responsibility for serving the public interest—have acted to coordinate private actions with public objectives.[26] In addition, specialized official lending institutions, operating on a very large scale, have funneled credit to the private sector on a highly selective basis for closely targeted purposes.[27] In the field of industrial raw materials, the distinctive institutions and practices have produced a set of policies and programs that are starkly different from those of the United States.

The Case of Oil

To understand how the Japanese have approached the problem of access to oil in recent years, one needs to know something of the overwhelmingly vital role that oil has played at critical points in Japan's modern history. The fact that Japan imports practically all of that basic commodity only begins to tell the story. The fact that until very recently most of that oil has been imported under the control of foreign companies suggests a little more. What has to be recalled in addition is that throughout most of the country's modern history, Japan's efforts to gain direct access to foreign oil were blocked by the commanding position of U.S. and British companies, a fact that hobbled Japan in its efforts to expand into Asia in the 1930s and that greatly increased the country's difficulties during World War II. Oil, from the Japanese viewpoint, was not just another basic commodity; it was the country's historic Achilles' heel.

Origins of the policy. Japan's dependence on foreign oil goes back to the nineteenth century, when Standard Oil of New York (later Socony Vacuum, later still Mobil) began exporting to Japan from the United States and the Dutch East Indies.[28] By 1928 the principal international oil companies of the world — none of them Japanese — had developed a set of alliances through which they effectively controlled the world trade in oil. By that time, Exxon (then the Standard Oil Company of New Jersey) and Mobil, together with the British-Dutch combination of Royal Dutch Shell, were securely in control of the principal sources of crude oil and the principal refineries in Japan's part of the world. From the time Japan seized Manchuria in 1931 until it attacked Pearl Harbor ten years later, the country was engaged in a continuous effort to gain some measure of control over the refineries and oil supplies on which its national economy so heavily depended.

For the most part, Japan's efforts were thwarted. As late as 1939, Japanese interests controlled only a tiny fraction of the oil that the country consumed; and practically all of the country's imports of crude oil and oil products came from the Dutch East Indies or from the west coast of the United States. To make matters worse, there were signs

90   TWO HUNGRY GIANTS

from time to time during these difficult decades that the international oil companies were working hand in glove with their respective governments to frustrate Japan's objectives. When in 1934 Japan sought to monopolize the refining and distribution of oil and oil products in its puppet state of Manchukuo, the Japanese government was faced with "rhetorical thunder" from London and Washington.[29] At about the same time, Japan began to impose regulations on its home territory in order to generate an indigenous capacity for oil refining and a national oil stockpile; in reaction, the country had to reckon with the oil companies' hints of a retaliatory embargo and with sporadic diplomatic protests from the United States and Britain.

The tension that this dependence created can easily be imagined. Traditionally, the naval strategic planning of Japan tended to identify the United States as the principal hypothetical enemy.[30] After Japan seized Manchuria in 1931 and from time to time in the decade that followed, discussions in the West of the possibility of embargoing oil to Japan seemed to confirm Japan's vulnerability.[31]

The work of scholars since that time strongly suggests that the seeming teamwork of the U.S. oil companies and the U.S. Department of State during the middle 1930s was mainly the result of different interests that sometimes offered the opportunity for joint action. The diplomats were consumed with the importance of the Open Door principle, whereas the oil companies had their eyes mainly on the processing and selling of oil products. Because of the differences in perspective, the oil companies could not always count on diplomatic support when they felt they needed it; such support turned out to be sporadic and episodic, its timing, tone, and content being influenced by larger developments in world politics.

There were other signs at the time that, in facing the United States, Japan was not exactly confronting a monolith. In 1934 when Stanvac, Texas Oil, and Shell Oil threatened to pull their subsidiaries out of Manchuria in reaction to pressures from the Manchurian monopoly, Standard Oil of California and Union Oil — two companies regarded in the 1930s as "independents" — offered to fill their shoes.[32] But even if the Japanese were aware of the less-than-total cohesion of the U.S. companies and the U.S. government, the recognition probably offered only cold comfort.

Besides, as prewar tensions built up in the latter 1930s, the oil companies and their respective governments moved closer together. By that time, the main concern of the United States and its European allies was to avoid goading Japan into an attack on the Dutch East Indies. To put off such an attack, the common strategy of the companies and the U.S. government was to provide Japan with enough oil to keep the country from feeling cornered—but not with so much oil as to allow the military to build up its stockpiles. Some sources attribute the timing of the Japanese attack on Pearl Harbor and the Dutch East Indies in 1941 to the failure of the U.S. government faithfully to execute its chosen strategy.[33]

In any event, Japan's experiences after seizing the oil fields and refineries of Sumatra and Singapore simply confirmed once again the dangers of having to rely upon foreign-owned sources of crude oil and foreign-owned oil refineries. The careful demolition plans of the foreigners actually had worked in many key installations. Japan was a full year in bringing the Sumatran fields up to 60 percent of their prewar production levels, and the related refineries up to 40 percent of their prewar levels. Even that achievement is said to have required close to 70 percent of the trained personnel available in Japan.[34]

The occupation years that followed the war had various profound effects on the Japanese, contributing to the guardian-ward relationship with the United States. One consequence of that relationship was to temporarily alleviate the anxiety of the Japanese over the security of their access to crude oil. Instead, for about a decade, the country's policy makers turned their minds to methods for securing crude oil at the lowest possible price.[35]

Japan's decision to concentrate on procuring its energy cheaply was altogether consistent with U.S. preferences at the time. During the occupation, the personnel on the Supreme Commander's staff who were responsible for policy toward Japan's oil industry included a number of individuals borrowed from the U.S.-based international oil companies.[36] Their preference, inevitably, was to have the Japanese return to the prewar situation in which foreign firms provided the crude oil and dominated the refining and distribution system of Japan. In the short run, that arrangement also appeared to the Japanese government to be the least costly way by which the country could obtain its needed supplies of crude oil.

The pattern that emerged proved only a shade more complicated. The enterprises of the prewar era did return, joined by one or two newcomers. At the same time, however, the Japanese firms that had gained a foothold in the refining and distribution of petroleum and its products during the war went back into business as well. The upshot was a series of joint ventures. Between 1949 and 1952, using their access to world oil as their principal bargaining counter, Stanvac, Caltex, Union Oil, Shell, and one or two others reentered the Japanese market as the partners of domestic oil firms. By the middle of the decade, the foreign firms and their Japanese partners dominated Japan's oil market.[37] Once again the oil industry was reestablished in Japan as the exceptional case — as the major industry in which foreign interests were dominant.

Shaking off foreign domination. Throughout the 1950s, Japanese policy makers pushed aside various proposals to reduce the degree of foreign domination over the country's domestic oil refining and oil distribution industries, concentrating instead on the acquisition of cheap energy sources.

In the early part of that period, the effort to throw off foreign domination was hobbled in any case by the fact that the Japanese government was determined to rebuild a refinery industry and badly lacked the capital to perform the job. For Japan, the need for refineries was abnormally large because of the country's general policies with respect to the processing of industrial raw materials. There was a determination in all fields to avoid the importation of processed products and to limit imports to materials in their unprocessed state. This meant that a huge refinery industry had to be put in place — a need that seemingly offered foreign firms an opportunity to acquire even greater control of the Japanese petroleum industry.

Although Japan's policy makers were prepared, for the time being, to treat the oil industry as an exceptional case that justified maintaining a high degree of foreign ownership, they could not allow the foreign oil companies to take over the industry altogether. Some degree of independence was being urged by respected national leaders who had been identified with Japan's prewar oil industry.[38] Accordingly, MITI took some measures to hold down the acquisition of new equity by foreigners. Moreover, MITI used its allocation powers to reduce the majors' share of the Japanese market,[39] and it supported one or two projects to develop Japanese oil sources outside the control of the majors.[40] But these were minor achievements, exceptions to its general policy during the 1950s of relying on the foreign-owned international oil companies to supply Japan's oil.

It was not very long, however, before some of the drawbacks of such a policy became apparent. During the 1950s, MITI found itself approving a series of deals between refinery companies that were partly or wholly owned by Japanese interests and individual foreign-owned (mainly U.S.-owned) crude oil suppliers, entailing loans tied to crude oil purchase commitments. Between 1951 and 1961, in fact, twenty-one such loans involving $139 million were authorized, involving nine Japanese borrowers and eight foreign lender-suppliers.[41]

From the viewpoint of achieving an independent Japanese industry, loans were better than equity, particularly as their terms were commonly limited to the five-to-ten-year range. But tying Japan's economy to specified foreign-owned sources had inhibiting consequences for Japan's ability to manage its affairs. For better or worse, this fixed the sources to which Japan could turn in periods of shortage. And it reduced Japan's capacity to shop for bargains in periods of surplus. The inhibitions on Japan's capacity to shop proved especially important in the latter 1950s and early 1960s. Apart from some brief periods of trauma such as the closing of the Suez Canal in 1956, these were years of easy oil supply, in which spot bargains were not uncommon. With tied purchases reaching 80 percent of Japan's oil imports by 1962,[42] the problem began to take on serious proportions in the eyes of the Japanese government.

Nevertheless, larger developments in the world oil markets were beginning to create the conditions by which Japan could recapture control of its domestic industry. By 1962, despite the obstacles, Japan had managed to establish a fairly substantial group of Japanese refiners that were free of equity ties to the majors. Indeed, four such companies — Idemitsu, Maruzen, Daikyo, and Nihon Kogyo — had come to account for nearly 45 percent of Japan's total refining capacity.[43] At the same time, new sources were offering their crude oil to Japanese refiners. The international oil cartel, dominated by six leading firms from 1928 on, had been dissolved in 1948, freeing Gulf, Shell, and Compagnie Française de Pétroles to bid for some of the Japanese market. Moreover, during the 1950s, half a dozen new international firms — most of them American in origin — had developed independent sources of crude oil from North Africa and the Middle East; relative newcomers, such as Union Oil, Standard Oil Company of Indiana, and the American Independent Oil Company (a consortium of ten so-called independent U.S. oil companies), were offering crude oil for sale in Japan.

94 TWO HUNGRY GIANTS

In 1961, therefore, the Japanese government in effect served notice on the foreign-owned oil companies that it intended to develop new tools to guide the growth of the Japanese market. At that stage, Japan began to repeat its regulatory history of the 1930s. A Petroleum Industry Law was passed in 1962 that assigned to MITI a permanent supervisory role over the development of the industry, including the licensing of refineries, the approval of financial arrangements, the approval of production plans and crude oil acquisition plans, and so on. With new powers of this sort, MITI hoped to be able to reduce Japan's tied oil sales from 80 percent of its purchases to 30 percent.[44]

Looking back at this period, these various steps could easily be interpreted by foreigners as confirmation of the existence of a Japan Incorporated juggernaut, which enlisted the unquestioned support of all sectors of the Japanese economy and proceeded singlemindedly to overcome the foreigners. In fact, each such step encountered plenty of domestic opposition. During the 1950s, individual Japanese firms constantly jockeyed for position in the domestic market, using the resources of their respective foreign partners whenever they could be used to advantage. When MITI first proposed its Petroleum Industry Law in 1961, both the electric power and the steel industry expressed opposition. The ease with which the law was eventually passed is explained in part by the fact that such an open-ended grant of authority for the regulation of an industry was in no way offensive to the fundamental ideology of the country—indeed, was wholly in harmony with the ideology. Despite some selective opposition, the law easily garnered the support of small business organizations, the Petroleum Producers' Association, and the small cluster of special oil companies that were already assuming the role of Japan's national champions in the development of an independent oil industry.[45]

The willingness of industry to countenance a delegation of power to government depended in part, of course, on its expectation that it would have a hand in the exercise of that power. In the case of Japan, there were strong reasons for the expectation. To begin with, the industry's trade association, the Petroleum Association of Japan, was accustomed to acting as MITI's implementing arm, carrying out MITI's production regulation plans under the general guidelines laid down by the ministry. But the strong test of Japanese practice was provided by MITI's handling of disputes with the oil companies.

The importance of national style in the handling of disagreements between government and industry was illustrated in numerous ways. In the first place, the 1962 act contained no overt sanctions of a powerful sort — a fact that led the U.S.-based *Oil and Gas Journal* to assume erroneously that the bill might prove unimportant.[46] After the law's adoption, when a bitter dispute arose between Idemitsu and MITI, fundamentally threatening to the existence of the control system, it took six months of elaborate negotiation to bring Idemitsu back into the fold, during which each side occasionally lost its temper. But by and large, the language of battle was one that emphasized persuasion, cooperation, and the national welfare, and the outcome was one that involved concessions on both sides.[47]

With the adoption of the 1962 petroleum act, the process that would eventually bring a considerable part of Japan's petroleum industry back under the control of Japanese nationals was fairly well launched. Subsequent developments, however, could be attributed only partly to the existence of the appropriate law; more important was the declining power during the 1960s of the guardian-ward relationship between Japan and the United States. By 1967 a Comprehensive Energy Advisory Committee — a typical consensus-building committee of prestigious leaders — was calling for the promotion of independent sources of oil for Japan.[48] But a critical link still had to be created if the Japanese strategy was to work, this link being a direct tie between Japan's refineries and its crude oil sources.

Securing crude oil. Although a considerable proportion of Japan's refinery industry was under the control of Japanese nationals by the early 1970s, nearly 80 percent of the country's crude oil imports still went through the vertical channels of the big multinational oil companies. Most of that total went to supply the refineries and distribution networks in which these foreign companies had an equity interest; the rest went to nationally owned entities. MITI therefore was still far from the national objective of controlling some of the channels by which the country imported its crude oil.

To that end, well before the 1973 embargo, MITI was already encouraging a number of different initiatives. In 1967 the Petroleum Development Corporation was created, charged with subsidizing some of the overseas exploration activities of Japanese firms and with assisting in the financing of their development activities. By 1973 the corporation was expending a little more than $100 million on loans and investments. Between 1969 and 1973 the Mitsui, Mitsubishi, and Sumi-

96   TWO HUNGRY GIANTS

tomo groups each created their own petroleum development corporations as vehicles for promoting the groups' overseas activities in crude
oil and petroleum refining. In the same period, the trading firms of C.
Itoh and Marubeni undertook major initiatives of a similar sort. The
results were apparent in the rapid growth of Japan's overseas exploration. Between 1968 and 1973 the number of Japanese firms engaged in
such exploration rose from 8 to 49, the number of wells drilled rose
from 44 to 180, and expenditures on exploration and development rose
from $44 million to $488 million.

Although Japan fared comparatively well at the hands of the majors
during the 1973 oil embargo,[49] the episode accelerated Japan's search
for independent sources of crude oil. Japan's new efforts were based
upon the assumption that the guardian-ward relation was ended —
that in a pinch the country would get no help from the United States or
from other industrialized countries with which Japan was associated
through the Organization for Economic Cooperation and Development.[50] An agreement among most of the OECD countries to share
their oil resources in a period of scarcity, it was assumed, would be ineffectual in an emergency. With Japan's pervasive sense of isolation
and deprivation, it was not surprising that this should be the country's
basic planning assumption.

To get its new approach off the ground, the government in 1974
followed its customary pratice of mobilizing all sectors of the economy
to the new public objective. MITI formed an Advisory Committee for
Energy, which was charged to develop a series of national goals. In the
years subsequent, that body and others repeatedly proposed quantitative goals and the policies by which they might be reached.[51]

Meanwhile, the government pressed ahead with new efforts to secure
its own sources of foreign oil. In October 1973, 120 Japanese companies
from assorted industries created a Japan Cooperation Center for the
Middle East, intended to lubricate the communication process with the
area. In 1974 those efforts blossomed into a full-fledged plan that
would engage oil-producing countries in "cooperative economic
resource diplomacy." The program envisaged several interrelated
elements, most of which could be found to some extent in the national
programs of other governments: government-to-government agreements would provide a long-term framework for the conduct of large-
scale investment and trading activities; individual Japanese firms,
operating in partnership with one another and with the government-

owned enterprises, would provide technology and capital for development projects; and refineries in Japan would provide the markets for
the exporters' crude oil.

The Japanese plans differed from those of most other governments,
however, in one critical respect: despite bitter squabbling among its
various national interests, and despite charges of incompetence and
rigidity on the part of the Japanese bureaucracy, Japan succeeded in
implementing its plans to a degree that other governments found
difficult to achieve.[52] Once the formal plan was adopted, Japan set
about expanding its loans to the area through various channels, including the country's Export-Import Bank and its Overseas Economic
Cooperation Fund. By the end of 1976, Japan had signed economic and
technical cooperation agreements with Iraq, Saudi Arabia, Iran, and
Qatar.

In terms of the immediate objective of securing independent sources
of crude oil, results were a little slow in coming. By 1978 crude oil imports arranged through governments or by direct deals between
Japanese importers and state exporters came to only 19.4 percent of
Japan's total crude oil imports. Even that limited performance depended largely on Iraq's stepped up exports, which were linked to a $1
billion loan by Japan to that country. When added to other crude oil
imports arranged outside the networks of the multinational oil companies, these supplies did little to improve Japan's position of
independence.

But the Japanese government persisted. And in 1978, when Iran's
revolution and its war with Iraq again created an international oil
crisis, its efforts were intensified. By 1980 it was evident that Japan's
long-run program for freeing itself from multinational sources was
beginning to bear fruit. By that time, Iran, Abu Dhabi, Qatar, Saudi
Arabia, and Kuwait had been added to the list of Japan's heavy suppliers, and direct deals of various sorts were generating 45 percent of
Japan's crude oil imports.[53] By that year, too, the supplies provided by
the multinational enterprises had been cut back to about 45 percent of
Japan's crude oil requirements.

If there were unique elements in Japan's program for the acquisition
of independent sources of crude oil, however, they were associated
with the way in which the partnerships, consortia, and trading companies of the country performed to implement the national campaign.
Consortia of this sort drew their strength from various features: their

direct sponsorship by the Japanese government as chosen instruments for the execution of government-to-government deals; their direct linkage, through some of their participants, to official sources of equity investment, credit, and guarantees; and a capacity, especially through the big trading houses, to accept payment in the form of commodities, as well as a capacity to offer a wide range of technical services and capital equipment in integrated deals. In Saudi Arabia, for instance, this set of capabilities was evident in two such groups, both headed by Mitsubishi; by 1980 one group had brought eleven years of planning to a successful close with a commitment for a 450,000-ton ethylene plant, while the other had undertaken to build and operate a 730,000-ton methanol plant.[54]

Despite these efforts at diversification and linkage, Japan's economy still seemed to face considerable uncertainties in the early 1980s. With very few vertical links back to their sources of crude oil supply, the Japanese refiners and distributors faced high financial risks. Their import costs were being determined by two prices, both disconcertingly volatile: the dollar price for oil demanded by the exporters, and the dollar-yen exchange rate. Sometimes the two rates worked in opposite directions, stabilizing their costs; at other times the two rates moved in a common direction, exposing the industry to large losses.[55] Questions of security obviously remained much on the minds of Japanese officials and businessmen. But at least the country had achieved its first objective — that of getting some of the tools of oil policy out of the control of foreigners and back into its own hands.

The Basic Metals

In the basic metals, during the three or four decades following the end of World War II, the Japanese economy managed to get even closer to achieving a national sense of security of supply, despite the economy's heavy reliance on foreign sources. Some profound changes in the supply structure of the metallic ores were critical in helping the Japanese move so swiftly toward their goal.

Developing supplies. At the beginning of the period the dependent situation of Japan was almost as pronounced in the case of metallic ores as it had been in oil. The option of developing some domestic sources of supply for metallic ores existed in Japan only with respect to copper, lead, and zinc. And as Japan's economy mushroomed and its needs grew, such sources were obviously too limited to supply any substantial part of the country's needs.

The metal industries differed from oil, however, in one important respect: their domestic processing facilities were always owned by Japanese interests. Accordingly, the country's strategy could be much more straightforward. From the first, MITI's objective was to develop secure foreign sources for the unprocessed ores while building up the home processing industry. In the 1950s, immediately following the end of the military occupation, the problems presented for the Japanese economy by the principal metals industries were part of a much larger problem — that of an inadequate supply of foreign exchange. Within the limits imposed by foreign exchange availabilities, the Japanese bought their foreign requirements largely on the spot market. In the decades that followed, the swift growth of their economy and the gradual depletion of their limited domestic sources of ore required the Japanese to launch a much more aggressive approach for developing foreign sources of raw materials.

In 1963 MITI established a subsidiary, the Metal Mining Agency of Japan. In the first few years of its life, the agency concentrated on domestic exploration, mainly of copper and lead, paying out a steady stream of subsidies on a modest scale — on the order of 3 billion yen annually.[56] By 1968, however, the agency was promoting loans for exploration and development in foreign locations, and by 1973 these expenditures were being made at a rate of 2 billion yen annually.[57] That support was used as seed money to help foreign mine operators develop new sources of supply for Japanese markets. Japan's willingness — indeed, in many cases, its eagerness — to enter into long-term contracts for the output of the mines gave the mine owners an improved basis for borrowing in international markets. Lending banks in Europe and the United States could comfort themselves with the hope that in times of glut Japanese buyers would favor the sources with which they held such contracts.[58]

An additional element in Japan's strategy was to organize its principal users of metal ores into buying groups, with a designated leader who conducted the negotiations for the group in any given country; Nippon Steel, for instance, handled all of the Japanese steel industry's major iron ore and coal purchases in Australia. The power of such buying groups was considerable from the first, inasmuch as many of the exporting countries found themselves relying on the Japanese market as

100 TWO HUNGRY GIANTS

their principal buyers. By the latter 1970s, Australia was selling over three-quarters of its exports of both iron ore and copper ore to Japan. India, too, was exporting about three-quarters of its iron ore exports to Japan, while Brazil was relying upon the Japanese market for the sale of one-third of its exports of ore.[59] These buying strategies were reinforced by Japan's tariff policies, which closely paralleled those traditionally used by the United States. Whereas ores were typically admitted without duty, processed metals usually bore significant duties[60]

A very early version of Japan's policies could be seen in the case of copper, a product in which the perils of instability seemed especially marked for Japan. Japanese firms were obliged to buy their foreign copper ore on the basis of prices that were greatly influenced by the copper quotations of the London Metals Exchange, quotations that were notoriously unstable. It was probably no coincidence, therefore, that the Japanese government allowed its copper-refining firms to make investments in foreign copper mines earlier and on a larger scale than was the case for other metal-processing industries. As early as 1953, for instance, when Japan was in a difficult balance-of-payments situation, it was already providing financial assistance to a copper mine in the Philippines.[61] In subsequent years, Japan extended loans and guarantees to copper mines in Canada, Papua New Guinea, Indonesia, and Malaysia.[62] By the latter 1960s, the Japanese were not only lending to foreign copper mines but also taking equity interests in such mines, including operations in Zaire, Malaysia, Canada, Peru, and Chile.[63] By 1973 the nation's Overseas Development Guarantee Fund had reached about $95 million.

It was evident by the mid-1970s that Japan was making the most of the fortuitous discoveries of vast quantities of ores in Australia. The payoff was enlarged not only by Japan's practice of pooling its national buying through a single agent but also by the country's systematic efforts to reduce shipping costs. As a matter of national policy, Japan took the lead in developing large ore-carrying ships. In 1953 Japan had no ore vessels that exceeded 20,000 tons. But by the 1970s Japan had acquired 150 such vessels, with a total ore-carrying capacity of over 5.6 million tons; and by 1980 it had 206 such vessels, with a capacity of 10.2 million tons.[64] The consequence was a sharp reduction in the cost of Japan's ocean freight.[65]

By almost any measure, the performance of Japanese industry in securing its ores during the 1960s could be counted as an extraordinary success. It was helped, to be sure, by a great stroke of luck—the fact that nearby Australia was so rich in the needed resources. But Japanese policies seemed to be making the most of the god-given opportunities.

The uncertainties of long-term contracts. By the end of the 1960s, Japanese imports of metallic ores rested mainly on the efficacy of long-term loans or other long-term financial assistance from the government, coupled with long-term contracts and coordinated national buying.[66] Despite the seeming success of Japan's policies during the 1960s, however, the Japanese may have thought of themselves as pursuing a second-best strategy in this period. This was a time in which American firms—and European ones only a little less so—were relying heavily on vertical integration for the security of their foreign supplies of bauxite, copper ore, and iron ore.

Of course, in the 1960s Japan would have had great difficulty in pursuing a strategy of actual ownership on a broad scale. Some Japanese investors were being allowed to take small equity positions in foreign copper mines. But generalizing that policy to all important minerals would have required vast quantities of capital. Besides, it would have placed latecomer Japanese firms in direct competition with well established U.S. and European firms for mining concessions in third countries, a competition that the Japanese were not yet prepared to face. Finally, Japan would have had to overcome the latent or active hostility of many developing countries to any foreign investments in raw materials, a hostility that would come to a head in the early 1970s in a great rash of nationalizations. Long-term investments of a less massive and less intrusive sort may have been seen as a safer course for trying to reduce the uncertainties of supply.

But the policy of relying solely on long-term contracts seemed to entail high risks. The first Australian call for renegotiation of long-term iron ore contracts came in 1966, before the ink on the contracts had dried, and it became clear very early that such contracts would not be providing the degree of stability of supply and price that Japan constantly sought.[67] The various Australian states showed little disposition or ability to pool their bargaining power effectively.[68] But threatening noises in that direction were sufficiently frequent to keep the Japanese on edge.

In the 1970s, therefore, the Japanese responded to the obvious instability of their situation by increasing their equity holdings in overseas mines. Having already invested extensively in copper mines, they began to move at this stage into other types of ore. In iron ore,

102   TWO HUNGRY GIANTS

such equity investments appeared in Brazil, Peru, and Australia; by 1980 Japanese interests held equity in four of Australia's eight mammoth iron ore mines.[69] And in aluminum, Japan acquired equity interests in a string of smelters and bauxite mines spread throughout New Zealand, Venezuela, Canada, Indonesia, Brazil, Australia, and the United States.[70] These investments rarely entailed actual management commitments on the part of the Japanese, but they did entail a less transitory involvement.

Apart from increasing Japan's right to call on the output of specified mines, Japan's increased emphasis on equity investment also had another purpose. As the fragility of long-term contracts grew evident, banks proved less willing to finance new mines on the basis of such contracts alone. Equity investment thus came to substitute for the banking role that long-term contracts had served in the past. It was widely assumed in financial circles that in times of glut the Japanese would treat mines in which they held some equity more favorably than other mines, thereby reducing the lending risk; and there is some evidence that the assumption was justified.[71]

By the early 1980s, the Japanese practice of taking equity interests in overseas mining facilities had been well established. As a rule the size of the interest was not much over 10 percent. But by that time, about half of the country's supplies of iron ore were coming from foreign mines in which Japanese had an equity interest, and similar tendencies were visible in the other ores. How far Japan would go in that direction in an effort to bolster its sense of security was not yet clear.

The country's efforts to improve its access to foreign sources of ore and metal extended also to some of the policies it was following at home. The stockpile policy of the Japanese government, undertaken in earnest in the 1970s, was a logical extension of its policy of trying to increase its security of supplies through long-term contracts. The drawback of such contracts is that they usually commit the buyer over a long period of time to some minimum quantity of purchases, irrespective of the buyer's needs. That restraint had embarrassed Japanese metal-ore buyers during the 1960s and 1970s, whenever demand temporarily fell. In response to that problem, it appears that in the early 1970s the steel companies had already created a stockpile whose function was to take up their surplus steel production. Finally, in 1976, the Japanese government helped set up a number of such stockpiles, by lending funds to the stockpile associations at preferential credit rates.

Here again, the difference between Japan's policies and those of the United States are worth noting. In the U.S. case, stockpiles for various metals and ores had been created in the 1940s ostensibly in response to a strategic need, not as an economic device for the stabilization of markets; justifying their existence by viewing them as stabilizing devices would have been offensive to American ideology. Nevertheless, without a coherent long-term policy, the American stockpiles were used from time to time as stabilizing devices, in response to short-term pressures that built up in the U.S. economy. In contrast, the Japanese government, unencumbered by ideological considerations to the contrary, maintained its stockpiles explicitly for stabilizing purposes.[72] Accordingly, having acquired about 72,000 metric tons of copper in 1976 and 1977, the government fed out 64,000 tons from 1978 to 1980; and having acquired 22,000 tons of aluminum from 1976 to 1978, it sold its holdings in 1979, only to buy again heavily in 1981.[73]

Transactions of this sort eased the burden of Japanese processors in fulfilling their long-term commitments to buy foreign ores. But they also served another important purpose. During the 1970s it became clear that Japan's handicaps as a result of the high cost of energy and the limited availability of space for industry would present formidable difficulties for Japanese metal-processing industries. Besides, some developing countries with which Japan was eager for firmer economic relations had the energy, the space, and the capital to expand those very industries. The government, therefore, set about trying to persuade Japanese firms in some of these industries that their future in Japan was insecure. By 1974 this perception was being built into the agreed-upon views of government and industry, and was being reflected in MITI projections of the economy. And by the early 1980s specific plans were on the way to implementation.

The decline of uncertainty. By the early 1980s, Japan could look back on several decades of remarkable success in the procurement of its basic needs for key industrial materials. With good luck and careful planning, the country had managed to acquire its needed materials on adequate terms. Indeed, in iron ore and bauxite it had managed to better its terms over the years by comparison with those available to U.S. importers, and in copper ores it had managed to keep abreast of the United States (see Figures 5.1, 5.2, and 5.3). With such a record, the

104   TWO HUNGRY GIANTS

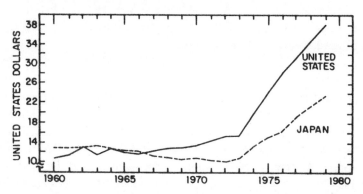

Figure 5.1. Price of iron ore used in steelmaking, c.i.f. price per metric ton, 1960–1979.

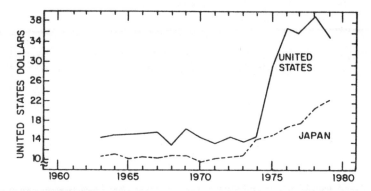

Figure 5.2. Price of bauxite, c.i.f. price per metric ton. 1960–1979.

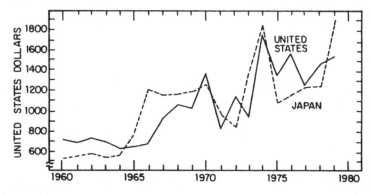

Figure 5.3. Price of copper ores and concentrates, c.i.f. price per metric ton of copper content, 1960–1979.

country's confidence in its ability to procure critically needed products from abroad could not fail to grow.

The apparent growth in Japan's confidence with respect to its mineral supplies appears to be part of a broader change in the country's perception of itself as a have-not nation. This critical shift is suggested by Japan's plans for adjusting to the high cost of energy. The 1970s had impressed two critical facts on Japanese policy makers: first, that the country's scarce land and acute environmental needs limited the extent to which industries such as metal processing could be placed on Japanese territory; and, second, that Japan ran the risk of being a high-cost user of energy. Confronting these factors, Japan has resolutely determined to shrink some of its energy-using industries.

Japan's plans to cut back its aluminum industry in an effort to reduce its uses of high-cost energy represent a particularly striking manifestation of the country's increased confidence in its capacity to procure key materials from abroad.[74] The demand for aluminum in Japan is expected to grow rapidly during the 1980s. But according to MITI's plans, all of the increase will be supplied from foreign production. On the other hand, Japan has no intention of leaving its needs to the

---

Sources: FIGURE 5.1: Robert W. Crandall, *The U.S. Steel Industry in Recurrent Crisis* (Washington, D.C.: Brookings Institution, 1981), p. 21; 1977–79 figures from United Nations, *World Trade Annual 1977, 1978, and 1979*, vol. 1 (New York: Walker and Company, 1979, 1980, and 1981); U.S. 1977–79 figures adjusted by the freight index in World Bank, *Commodity Trade and Price Trends* (Baltimore: Johns Hopkins University Press, 1980), p. 34. FIGURE 5.2: For the United States: Leonard L. Fischman, project director, *World Mineral Trends and U.S. Supply Problems*, Research Paper R-20 (Washington, D.C.: Resources for the Future, 1980), p. 370. For Japan: United Nations, *World Trade Annual*, vol. 1 (New York, 1966–1980); idem, *Yearbook of International Trade Statistics* (New York, 1960–1965). FIGURE 5.3: For the United States: Fischman, *World Mineral Trends*, p. 392, adjusted by rates on pp. 394–395 to arrive at c.i.f. figures; Metal Bulletin, *Metal Bulletin Handbook* (Surrey, England, 1981). For Japan: United Nations, *World Trade Annual*, vol. 1 (New York, 1966–1980); idem, *Yearbook of International Trade Statistics* (New York, 1960–1965); Mia de Kuijper, "The International Copper Industry," Program on U.S.-Japan Relations, Center for International Affairs, Harvard University, May 1981, appendix VI.18; W. Gluschke et al., *Copper: The Next Fifteen Years* (Dordrecht, Holland: D. Reidel, 1979), pp. 156–157.

Note: C.i.f. = cost, insurance, and freight included in price.

106 TWO HUNGRY GIANTS

vagaries of the international market: the largest part is to come from
the carefully diversified sources in which Japan has accumulated its
equity interests.

The Japanese approach to the petroleum-refining industry was still
being formulated in 1982, but it also appeared to involve a freeze on
the growth of that industry in Japan.[75] At the same time, the Japanese
were encouraging their petrochemicals producers to develop joint ventures with producers in other countries, in a pattern described as
"horizontal specialization." The pattern implied a certain amount of
cross-hauling of products between affiliates, suggesting once again that
Japan was prepared to accept some of the risks of relying on foreign
sources for part of its vital supplies.[76] In the same spirit, Japan has even
been showing signs of a willingness to rely on foreign sources for a
minuscule portion of its steel supplies. A few of Japan's complex deals
for importing Brazilian iron ore, for instance, have entailed importing
steel as well.[77]

In light of Japan's long history of concern over its basic materials, its
decision to rely upon some importation of these vital supplies is quite
extraordinary. It suggests that Japan is at last capable of confronting its
import vulnerabilities with a certain equanimity. That equanimity is
not based, however, on serendipity, but rests on a strategy that calls for
the diversification of sources and the use of long-term organic ties to
suppliers. Rational responses of that sort can be expected to continue in
the future.

For notes to accompany this chapter please see page 676.

650 - 72

[29]

Excerpt from Nobutoshi Akao (ed.), *Japan's Economic Security: Resources as a Factor in Foreign Policy*, 145–67.

[1983]

7 Non-fuel mineral procurement policies

PHILLIP CROWSON

Japan
HS7
L7²
F14

Government policies for the procurement and utilisation of mineral raw materials evolve over an extended period in response to changing circumstances. No major industrial country, with the possible exception of France, has a coherent and planned set of policies. Most countries, and Japan is no exception, have introduced successive *ad hoc* measures to meet differing needs, and have tended to retain them long after their original justification has passed. Although countries do copy measures introduced elsewhere, most are essentially home grown. Differing historical experiences, industrial needs and structures have shaped varying responses to similar problems.

Like most Western economies Japan has relied mainly on market mechanisms and on private industry to ensure adequate supplies of mineral materials at acceptable prices. Nonetheless, it has occasionally needed to lubricate these mechanisms with guarantees or incentives. These have been applied both to encourage internal Japanese developments and also to facilitate procurement from overseas. Inevitably, foreign policy has sometimes been influenced by Japan's heavy reliance on imported raw materials. This chapter focuses primarily on the non-ferrous metals, but it also refers to iron ore and to uranium. Many of the measures that are used to ensure adequate supplies of the latter have their genesis in the non-ferrous sector, and in turn influence new policies in that sector.

*　　　　　*　　　　　*

145

The context of policy

In the initial post-war years, Japan's main objective was to rebuild its shattered domestic industrial base. Its domestic resources of many major mineral raw materials, such as copper, lead, zinc, and even iron and coal, were adequate for its needs, and smelting and refining centres were based on indigenous ores. It imported raw materials for aluminium, nickel and tin, and many of the minor metals. Its consumption of metals, even in the mid-1950s, formed a relatively insignificant share of total world demand. By the early 1960s, however, the situation was changing. Domestic demand for metals had in most cases outstripped the production capabilities of Japanese mines, and import dependence had increased. With a strong primary processing base, however, and many mining companies, the tendency was to import ores and concentrates rather than refined metal. This policy, which evolved almost without conscious planning, ensured that most of the value added in metal production remained in Japan. The sources of supply of most ores and concentrates were, however, fairly restricted. The historical tendency had been for resource-rich countries to process ores and concentrates locally, at least to the primary metal. In 1955, for example, the eight leading copper-mining countries outside Europe accounted for 88% of the Western world's mine production, and the same share of smelter production (with a lower 70% share of the output of refined copper). Japanese imports of primary metal did increase during the 1960s, but the protection that was afforded to domestic production encouraged a search for overseas producers prepared to supply ores and concentrates. The rapid growth of Japanese demand forced Japanese industry to develop new sources of supply, often outside the established channels. By 1974 the eleven leading non-European mining countries controlled 89% of mine production, but only 74% of smelter output, and 63% of refining production. Japanese purchase of concentrates explains most of the difference between mine and smelter output. A different cause of pressure was the build-up to Japanese accession to the OECD in 1964 and the accompanying foreign requests for greater import liberalisation. Japan feared that without tariffs and quotas its domestic mines and smelters would be unable to compete with North American and European suppliers.

Table 7.1 brings out the increase of Japanese production and consumption of major metals during the 1960s. During the decade consumption of primary aluminium, for example, increased sixfold, steel output quadrupled, zinc consumption more than tripled, and demand for lead doubled. This growth continued during the early 1970s, to reach a peak during the 1973–4 boom. Part of this latter rise represented a concealed build-up of inventories throughout the production

146

Table 7.1

Trends in Japanese production and consumption:
major metals 1955–80
(thousand tonnes except for steel)

	1955	1960	1965	1970	1975	1980
Aluminium						
Primary production	57	133	294	728	1013	1091
Primary consumption	49	150	288	911	1171	1671
Total consumption (incl. scrap)	–	–	–	1178	1484	2379
Copper						
Mine production	71	89	107	120	85	53
Production of refined	113	248	366	705	819	1014
Consumption of refined	108	304	428	821	827	1325
Lead						
Mine production	26	39	55	64	51	45
Metal production	37	74	108	209	194	221(1979)[a]
Metal consumption	42	100	147	210	189	267(1979)[a]
Nickel						
Metal production	10	19	26	90	87	110
Consumption	5	18	27	99	83	115
Steel						
Crude production (million tonnes)	9.4	22.1	41.2	93.3	102.3	111.4
Tin						
Mine production	0.7	0.9	0.9	0.8	0.7	0.6
Metal production	0.9	1.7	1.6	1.4	1.2	1.2
Metal consumption	6.0	14.6	17.0	28.6	28.1	31.1
Zinc						
Mine production	108	157	221	280	254	238
Metal production	112	180	368	681	698	739
Metal consumption	115	189	329	623	547	756

[a] Statistics on lead have recently been revised and 1980 figures are not comparable with those of earlier years.
Sources: Metallgesellschaft, *Metal Statistics*; *UN Statistical Bulletins*; and World Bureau of Metal Statistics (WBMS).

pipeline, and consumption fell off dramatically in 1975. In some instances, such as steel, zinc and aluminium production, the peak of the early 1970s has never been regained. In the case of aluminium, domestic output has been hit by burgeoning energy costs, and the share of imported metal in total consumption has increased, but in other metals the slackening of production has reflected a slower growth of consumption.

The years of rapid growth up to the early 1970s saw a sharp rise in Japan's share of world consumption of metals. By 1970 Japan consumed a much greater proportion of world mineral production than its share of gross domestic product (8¼% of the market economies' total, according to United Nations statistics). Japan's shares of consumption of some metals rose during the 1970s, but in other cases they fell, and by 1980 its shares were more in line with its proportion of the market economies' GNP. The details are shown in Table 7.2. Because much of the Japanese consumption of primary metals is incorporated in exported products, undue emphasis should not be placed on the proportions in the table. Nonetheless, it does clearly demonstrate the substantial, and growing, Japanese demands on world mineral resources during the 1970s, demands that have had inevitable repercussions on foreign policy.

Table 7.2

Japanese shares of world consumption
of major non-ferrous metals
(percentages)

	1955		1970		1980	
	Total world	Western world	Total world	Western world	Total world	Western world
Aluminium[a]	1.6	1.9	11.3	14.2	10.8	13.8
Copper	2.4	2.8	11.3	14.1	13.9	18.2
Lead	1.9	2.3	5.4	7.2	7.5	10.4
Nickel	2.5	3.1	17.2	22.0	16.4	22.4
Tin	3.5	4.1	12.7	15.8	13.6	18.3
Zinc	4.3	5.1	12.5	16.0	12.4	17.1

[a] Primary only.

Sources: Metallgesellschaft and WBMS.

148

Table 7.3

Japanese net import reliance of selected minerals and metals
as a percentage of consumption in 1978
(Net imports as % of apparent consumption.[a] E denotes exports)

	%	Major foreign sources (1978)[b]
Bauxite	100	Australia, Indonesia, Malaysia
Alumina	27	Australia
Aluminium	28	Canada, New Zealand, Bahrain
Antimony	100	Bolivia, China, Thailand
Asbestos	97	Canada, South Africa
Barium	20	China
Cadmium	E5	—
Chromium	99	USA, West Germany, South Africa
Cobalt	100	Belgium, Zaire, Canada
Columbium	100	Canada
Copper	91	Canada, Philippines, Zambia
Fluorine	100	China, Thailand, South Africa
Gold	95	Switzerland, UK
Gypsum	2	Morocco
Iron ore	99	Australia, Brazil, India
Lead	76	North Korea, Mexico, Australia
Manganese	95	South Africa, India, Australia
Mercury	—	
Mica (all forms)	100	India, Malaysia
Molybdenum	100	USA, Canada
Nickel	100	New Caledonia, Indonesia
Phosphates	100	USA, Morocco
Platinum group metals	98	USSR, South Africa, UK
Potash	100	—
Salt	86	Australia, Mexico
Selenium	E123	—
Silver	60	Peru, Mexico
Sulphur	E41	—
Tantalum	100	USA, Malaysia, Australia
Tin	98	Malaysia, Indonesia, Thailand
Titanium (ilmenite)	100	Australia, Malaysia
Tungsten	51	South Korea, Canada, Peru
Vanadium	100	South Africa
Zinc	61	Canada, Peru, Australia

[a] Net imports = imports − exports.
  Apparent consumption = domestic primary production + secondary production + net imports.
[b] Sources shown are points of shipment to Japan, and are not necessarily the initial sources of the material.

Source: US Bureau of Mines, March 1980.

149

Table 7.4

Major suppliers of metallic materials to Japan
(percentages of Japan's total imports of each commodity
1979/80 averages)

DEVELOPED COUNTRIES

Australia

Bauxite	67
Alumina	98
Aluminium	4
Copper	3
Lead	8
Zinc	28
Nickel	16
Iron ore	44
Manganese ore	34
Titanium ores	17

New Zealand

Aluminium	12

Canada

Aluminium	12
Copper	19
Lead	65
Zinc	32
Nickel	3
Iron ore	4
Titanium ores	20

United States

Aluminium	24
Copper	6
Nickel	1
Ferrochrome	3
Phosphates	59

South Africa

Copper	3
Lead	2
Nickel	1
Iron ore	5
Manganese ore	42
Chrome ore	44
Ferrochrome	80
Titanium ores	8

Norway

Aluminium	2
Nickel	2

Sweden

Ferrochrome	2

European Community

Alumina	2
Aluminium	1

CENTRALLY PLANNED ECONOMIES
(USSR, China, North Korea)

Aluminium	12
Zinc	12
Nickel	3
Tin metal	1

LESS DEVELOPED COUNTRIES:
AFRICA

Morocco

Phosphates	24

Zaire

Copper	3

Zambia

Copper	13

LESS DEVELOPED COUNTRIES:
ASIA & OCEANIA

India

Iron ore	12
Chrome ore	17
Titanium ores	13

150

Continued overleaf

Indonesia

Bauxite	21
Copper	4
Nickel	27
Tin metal	21

Malaysia

Bauxite	9
Copper	2
Tin metal	59
Titanium ores	35

Papua New Guinea

Copper	8

Philippines

Copper	20
Zinc	2
Nickel	11
Chrome ore	20

Sri Lanka

Titanium ores	7

Thailand

Tin metal	20

New Caledonia

Nickel	31

LATIN AMERICA

Brazil

Iron ore	21
Manganese ore	9
Ferrochrome	10

Chile

Copper	9
Iron ore	5

Mexico

Copper	1
Zinc	1
Manganese ore	4

Peru

Copper	7
Lead	18
Zinc	22
Iron ore	3

Venezuela

Aluminium	15

Note: The percentages for copper, lead, zinc and nickel cover the metal content of all forms imported up to and including unwrought metal.

Source: Phillip Crowson, *Minerals Handbook 1982/83* (London, Macmillan, 1982).

Table 7.3, which is based on a somewhat eccentric analysis by the US Bureau of Mines, shows Japan's net import dependence for each major mineral and metal, and the major foreign sources. The analysis is eccentric, partly because the original list omitted products such as molybdenum and phosphate in which the United States is self-sufficient, but mainly because it ignores the ultimate source of either domestic production or imports. Thus Japan's apparent export surpluses of cadmium, selenium and sulphur are based on the processing of imported base metal ores of which these materials are by-products. Domestic production of alumina and primary aluminium is ultimately derived from imported bauxite. The points of shipment to Japan, particularly of the minor metals, are often far removed from the sources of the original ores. Neither West Germany nor the United States, for example, has a domestic chromium-mining industry, and both rely mainly on ores from southern Africa.

For all its imperfections, Table 7.3 demonstrates Japan's heavy dependence on imports of most major minerals. Several countries recur frequently in the list of Japanese suppliers, and this is brought out further by the analysis of Table 7.4. This table shows the geographical origin of the main minerals imported into Japan as a percentage of total Japanese imports of each mineral. For the major non-ferrous metals, separate breakdowns are given for ores and concentrates and for primary metal. Again the immediate sources, rather than the ultimate suppliers, are sometimes given. Not all the suppliers of each material are shown, and some of the countries included supply small percentages of the listed minerals (New Zealand, for example, ships small tonnages of iron ore). It does, nonetheless, bring out the important role of a few mineral-producing countries, such as Australia, Canada, Peru and, perhaps surprisingly, India, as suppliers to Japan.

Methods of supply

The existence of a domestic smelting and refining industry encouraged an aggressive search for minerals from overseas when domestic mine production proved incapable of meeting growing demand. Like the mainland European countries, Japan began to cast envious glances during the late 1960s at the possible opportunities for profitable investment in mineral prospects overseas. It was assumed that the British and North American mining companies provided the United Kingdom and the United States with a security of mineral supplies denied to importing countries that were dependent on arm's-length negotiations. A range of policies has been developed in Japan to encourage the estab-

152

lishment of overseas mines and processing facilities owned and managed by Japanese companies. Similar policy objectives exist in France,
and to a lesser extent West Germany. It is argued that such national
ownership best ensures that raw materials are available when needed,
in the desired quantities, and on competitive terms. Contentious
negotiations over prices, such as have characterised Japanese purchases
of iron ore from Australia, are minimised where a smelter owns the
overseas mine. Yet to the extent that host governments are involved,
as they are in the Japanese overseas copper mines, the prices paid may
be set well above world averages. In order to safeguard their investment, the Japanese investors may have to condone continued uneconomic operations even in periods of weak market conditions. The host
government shareholders may be more concerned to increase local
employment, or export receipts, than to produce metal in the most
efficient and competitive fashion. Some Japanese commentators argue
that an intense desire for overseas mineral investments led Japanese
companies to develop relatively unattractive high-cost ore bodies which
other private investors had spurned.

The main targets of direct overseas investment have been copper
and uranium. Even here, Japanese-owned mines have provided only a
small portion of total import requirements. A more effective mechanism has been the signature of long-term purchase contracts, often tied
to the provision of loan finance. Table 7.5 provides some perspective
for copper and zinc in 1978.

Table 7.5

Sources of Japanese copper and zinc supplies 1978
(percentages)

	Copper	Zinc
Domestic mine production	7	29
Domestic scrap	9	...
Imports of ores and concentrates		
Japanese-developed mines	6	5
Japanese-assisted mines[a]	30	—
Term contracts (3-5 years)	14	63
Spot purchases	13	
Imports of blister	3	—
Imports of refined metal under annual contracts	12	3
Imports of refined metal — spot	6	

[a] Long-term loans, etc.

Source: MMAJ.

153

Domestic mine production of copper has been declining, and imports of metal have been increasing. The latter reflects the tensions between Japanese fabricators, who favour imports, and the smelters. Of the 63% of supplies imported as ores and concentrates, nearly half, or 30% of the total, is under long-term contracts from mines such as Ertsberg in Indonesia, Atlas in the Philippines, Bougainville in Papua New Guinea or Lornex in Canada, which were developed with the assistance of Japanese loans. Japanese-owned mines provide a relatively small, but growing, portion of the total. In zinc, where selling methods differ, nearly all of the imported concentrate is under evergreen contracts of 3−5 years' duration. Imports of metal are relatively insignificant, but there is a large domestic mining industry. Most other minerals, except uranium (in the future at least), are nearer the zinc than the copper pattern.

The provision of loan finance against long-term sales contracts, a device also used by German metal processors, has given Japan access to low-cost and efficient sources of minerals. In many instances, the loans have been partially tied to the export of Japanese equipment as well as to mineral supplies. Japanese industry has been able to combine the advantages of secure long-term access to raw materials with the technical and managerial skills of the international mining companies. In some instances Japanese companies have additionally taken small equity stakes. Table 7.6 shows the major Japanese investments in operating non-ferrous metal mines (including one uranium mine), both through equity and through the provision of loan finance. This investment developed in the late 1960s, and has subsequently followed the movements of the international business cycle.

Figure 7.1 shows the movement of overseas expenditure on exploration and development by Japanese mining companies since 1960. Canada and Australia were important destinations in the early 1970s and again in 1979, but most of the spending has been in developing countries. Cumulatively to 1979 expenditure had moved as shown in Table 7.7 (the figures include Japanese loan finance).

The annual level of spending during the late 1970s, at some $110 million in 1980 terms, compares with well over $150 million per annum by Chile's Codelco in its five large copper mines. Although this comparison places the Japanese spending in perspective, it does belittle its importance as a catalyst in mining projects. This catalytic role is also noticeable in Japanese involvement in iron ore and coking coal projects, which is summarised in Table 7.8.

Although the pattern is changing rapidly, the past tendency was to take relatively small equity stakes in significant projects, but to provide loans against contracts. This approach enabled Japan to develop new sources of supply and gain a foothold in international raw materials trade in competition with established trading channels.

154

Table 7.6

Major Japanese overseas investments in non-ferrous metals, late 1960s to late 1970s
(million US$)

		Overall cost	Japanese Share				Japanese % share of overall cost
			Equity	Cash loan	Equipment loan	Total	
Copper							
Bougainville Copper	: Papua New Guinea	405.7	–	30.0	20.3	50.3	12
Gunpowder Copper	: Australia	26.0	–	4.1	–	4.1	16
Toledo	: Philippines	32.5	0.6	17.6	14.3	32.5	100
Mamut	: Malaysia	122.3	–	88.5	33.8	122.3	100
Ertsberg	: Indonesia	n.a.	–	24.0	–	24.0	< 100
Katanga	: Peru	n.a.	(?)	...	4.4	4.4	n.a.
Qaleh Zari	: Iran	n.a.	...	7.3	–	7.3	n.a.
Musoshi	: Zaire	193.6	6.0	143.6	44.0	193.6	100
Copper/Lead/Zinc							
Huanzala	: Peru	15.0	2.3	10.3	2.4	15.0	100
Nickel							
Inco Indonesia Soroako	: Indonesia	840.0	11.3	36.0	–	47.3	6
Rio Tuba	: Philippines	27.7	0.9	24.2	–	25.1	91
Uranium							
Akouta	: Niger	n.a.	3.9	37.0	–	40.9	< 50

Source: MITI.

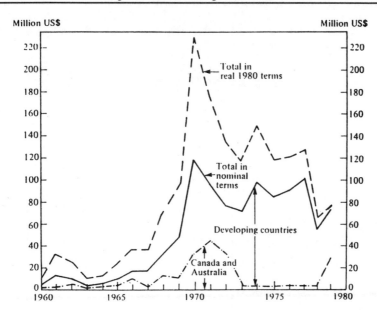

Figure 7.1 Overseas expenditure on exploration and development by Japanese mining companies since 1960: copper, lead, zinc, nickel, bauxite, chrome, uranium and manganese nodules (yen converted to US dollars at annual average exchange rates)

Note: The annual totals include loans from Japan.

Source: MMAJ.

Table 7.7

Total Japanese exploration and development spending overseas 1953–79:
Copper, lead, zinc, nickel, bauxite, chrome, uranium and manganese nodules

| | Exploration | | Development | |
	No. of projects	Total spending 1953–79 '000 million yen	No. of mines	Total spending 1953–79 '000 million yen
Australia	29	2.8	5	25.9
Canada	57	8.2	11	29.4
Bolivia	5	1.1	2	2.7
Chile	11	3.1	3	18.6
Malaysia	2	1.1	1	32.7
Peru	15	4.0	8	11.9
Philippines	28	2.6	6	21.9
Zaire	4	9.8	1	60.1
Others (incl. sea-bed)	73	39.0	10	40.8
Total	224	71.7	47	244.0

Source: RTZ Japan.

157

Table 7.8
Japanese participation in coking coal and iron ore projects up to 1981

Coking Coal			
Australia:	Mitsubishi	12%	Central Queensland Coal Associates
	Mitsui	20%	Kianga Coal Company Pty Ltd
		20%	Thiess-Dampier Mitsui
	Marubeni	4% ⎱	Hail Creek Project
	Sumitomo	2% ⎰	
	Marubeni	10%	Yarrabee Project
Iron Ore			
Australia:	Mitsui	30% ⎱	Robe River
	Other trading companies	5% ⎰	
	Mitsui ⎱ C. Itoh ⎰	10%	Mt. Newman
	Steel companies & trading companies	6.2%	Hamersley (bought out by CRA 1981)
	Mitsubishi ⎱ Sumitomo ⎰	49%	S. River Tasmania
Brazil:	Steel companies & trading companies	20%	Minas Aguas Claras
Chile:	Japanese loans		El Algarroba

Source: Ecole Nationale Supérieure des Mines de Paris, 1981 Seminar Papers.

158

Government policies

Private industry has had the main responsibility for securing Japanese raw material needs, under the guidance of MITI. The latter's involvement in most mining matters is delegated through the Metal Mining Agency of Japan (MMAJ), which was established in 1963. The original motive for its creation was concern about the competitiveness of the Japanese industry within the OECD.

Domestic exploration and mining

A comprehensive national exploration programme on three levels began in the early 1960s. First, basic regional geological survey work, carried out by contractors, is funded entirely by central government through the MMAJ. Some 11–15 areas have been surveyed annually since 1966, at a cost rising from around 130 million yen in 1966 to 864 million yen in 1980. Next, the regional surveys are followed up by detailed exploration of promising areas. Some 48 potentially promising districts were selected in the 1960s. The government contributes two-thirds of the cost, prefectural governments two-fifteenths, and the remaining 20% is paid by the mining companies which own the concessions. There were about eight projects per year in the 1970s, and the annual government subsidy is now just over one billion yen. At least three new mines have been found and some 75 million tons of copper/lead/zinc ore confirmed. The third stage of the domestic programme is the provision of subsidised loans to the larger companies (those with a paid-up capital exceeding ¥100 million or over 1,000 employees) and outright subsidies to smaller firms (which may be subsidiaries of larger companies) for detailed prospecting of individual projects in thirteen metallic minerals, including copper, lead, zinc, manganese, gold and molybdenum. Funds are provided only to Japanese nationals or mining companies. Figure 7.2 compares the available funds with the annual take-up. In 1979 some 2.5 billion yen were available from that year's budget and from funds unspent in previous years. Demand has fluctuated with metal prices, somewhat to MITI's concern. Copper has been the main target. In the 1963–79 period the MMAJ's loans accounted for about 55% of total domestic exploration spending by mining companies. The terms of the loans have been periodically changed. At present up to 70% of the cost of individual projects can normally be covered, with a grace period of up to two years and a repayment period of seven years. In previously unexplored areas, 80% of the exploration cost can be covered, the grace period is three years and the repayment terms are twelve years. Interest rates are normally one or two points below commercial rates. The programme has successfully led to the proving and partial ex-

159

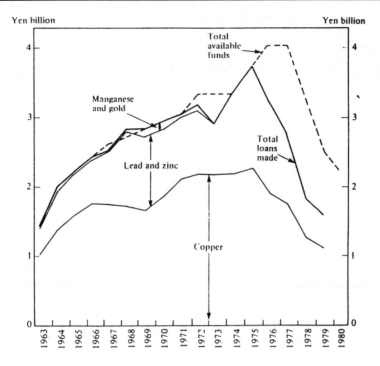

Figure 7.2   Japanese loans for domestic exploration (nominal terms)

Source: MMAJ.

160

ploitation of almost 110 million tonnes of new copper reserves, 35 million tonnes of lead/zinc, and additional manganese and gold/silver deposits. Applications for assistance are filed with local MITI offices and are collated centrally. Theoretically, the outright subsidies to the smaller companies (for which ¥1.5 billion was budgeted in fiscal 1980) cover 50% of the cost of exploration. In practice, because of inflation, they cover only around 40% of the cost.

Exploration to develop new mines would be nullified if old mines were meantime closing down. In late 1978 an emergency scheme was introduced for the 1978–80 period to bail out copper and zinc mines that had been weakened by the post-1975 recession in metal prices. The production of Japanese copper mines had fallen from a peak of around 120,000 tonnes in 1969–70 to 73,000 tonnes in 1978 (to barely 50,000 tonnes in 1983), and mine output of zinc had weakened from 1971's 294,000 tonnes, although not to the same extent. Soft loans at very low interest rates were available when market prices dropped below defined floors. A recovery in prices in 1979 meant that the take-up of loans was restricted to rather under three-fifths of the £56 million allocated for fiscal 1978. Mines were expected to contribute when metal prices exceeded given levels. As with most Japanese schemes for loan support, the government's commitment was limited to guaranteeing the MMAJ's borrowings from commercial banks, and to making up the difference between the MMAJ's commercial borrowing rate and its subsidised lending rate. The weakening of prices in 1980, and a steady rise in production costs, have caused MITI to extend its emergency loan scheme in fiscal 1981, but with higher floor prices.

Mounting concern with environmental protection during recent years has endangered the continued viability of many Japanese mining and smelting facilities. Since 1973 the MMAJ has provided both subsidised loans and guarantees for commercial borrowings to companies that are required to carry out anti-pollution works, and restore polluted farmland, or compensate farmers as a condition of continued production. The prevention of heavy metal contamination is an urgent social priority in Japan, and the assistance is mainly directed towards this end. The loans provided amount to up to 80% of the cost of approved schemes, with the balance covered by guarantees. Loans are available for up to fifteen years with very low interest rates, which vary with the size of company.

Mining companies generally pay normal corporate taxes, but some incentive is provided towards exploration for metallic minerals, oil, coal and limestone. Part of high profits earned in one year can be set aside for spending on exploration over the next three years.

Overseas exploration

As with domestic schemes, there are several levels of support for overseas exploration and a mixture of subsidies and loans. The former are available for general survey work up to half the cost of initial drilling and two-thirds of other work. Subsidies have been granted on some ten projects a year in recent years, and their total annual expense, including the companies' share, has been around one billion yen. Detailed follow-up exploration is assisted through low-interest-bearing loans, financed by annual government subventions. Up to half the cost of approved projects (including the Japanese share of consortium ventures) in copper, lead, zinc, manganese, nickel, bauxite and chromite ores is covered, or 70% in special cases. Loans are repayable over ten years after a five-year grace period. In the case of uranium, the repayment period is greatly extended, and loans are repaid only from successful projects. Figure 7.3 shows the development of the loan programme since its inception. The annual fund available was fully utilised only in the early years. Copper was then the main interest. More recently there has been a sizeable investment in work on manganese nodules, and since 1974 the MMAJ has been able to invest its exploration funds in the work of the Overseas Mineral Resources Development Company (OMRD). The latter's funds are derived from the MMAJ, the Japanese aid programme (Overseas Economic Cooperation Fund) and the mining and smelting companies who own 50% of the shares. Its authorised capital is 7 billion yen, of which 5.8 billion yen, or £14 million, has been issued. The MMAJ's annual investment in the OMRD is held as shares, which are sold to private stockholders at a reasonable price when a project reaches the development stage. If exploration prospects prove unsuccessful, the MMAJ shares will be cancelled. The OMRD's present major exploration interests are in the Frieda River consortium in Papua New Guinea and the Coroccohuayco copper prospect in Peru. Its one completed mine to date is the Mamut copper project in Sabah, Malaysia, and it has also carried out surveys in Indonesia, Chile, Ecuador and Mexico.

Overseas mine development

The support of exploration would be of limited use if mining companies were unable to raise sufficient finance to develop their discoveries. The MMAJ has long recognised this. Since 1968 it has guaranteed the liabilities of Japanese mining companies which borrow from Japanese commercial banks to develop copper, lead, zinc, manganese, uranium, nickel, bauxite or chromite mines abroad. The maximum guarantee is 80% of the total borrowings, and a guarantee fee of 0.4% per annum is charged. The MMAJ's guarantee fund is accumulated

162

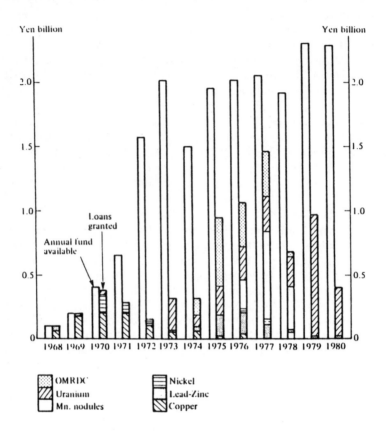

Figure 7.3   Japanese loan support for overseas exploration (nominal
              terms)

Source: MMAJ.

163

by government investments, and its guarantee limit stood at 55.5 billion yen at the end of 1980. Its outstanding guarantees at nearly 35 billion yen covered seven development projects — three in copper (Musoshi in Zaire, Sagasca in Chile and Mamut in Malaysia), two in nickel (the Rio Tuba project in the Philippines and the Soroaco project in Indonesia), one chromite mine (the Serjana project in Brazil), and a lead/zinc development (Huanzala in Peru). Aside from this commercial guarantee fund there is an official scheme to insure against non-commercial — i.e. political — risks. It provides cover only against 'safe' countries, and has an annual limit on the investments that can be covered. Like their European counterparts, Japanese companies have pressed for an extended scheme, but so far unsuccessfully. Companies that undertake to sell their output to Japan, whether or not Japanese-owned, can obtain loans on relatively favourable terms from the Japanese Export—Import Bank.

Some problems

Japanese industry was totally unprepared for the first oil crisis of 1973–4, and the slower rate of overall growth that has subsequently ensued. Mine development has lengthy lead-times, and it is necessary to sign long-term purchase contracts with planned mines well before material is needed. Furthermore, it is costly and difficult to halt mine construction once it has started. Japanese smelters and steel mills have been committed during the past few years to raw-material purchase contracts substantially in excess of their actual needs. In some instances, such as iron ore, the overhang of purchase commitments based on frustrated expectations of demand still exists. In other minerals, however, Japanese production has attained new peaks, and raw material supplies have again loomed as potential bottlenecks. In copper, for example, the development of competitive smelters elsewhere in the Pacific Basin has put pressure on raw material supplies to Japanese smelters, a pressure temporarily eased by the purchase of US concentrates as a result of US plant closures. The pressure arises for two reasons. First, newly industrialising countries, such as South Korea and Taiwan, are following behind Japan and establishing their own smelting and refining industries behind tariff barriers rather than relying on imports of metal. Second, most countries that export ores and concentrates sooner or later decide to upgrade their output in order to raise the value added locally. This inevitably means the installation of smelters and refineries. Unless mine output expands, supplies of concentrate for export diminish. In copper, the Philippines is building a smelter with the assistance of Japanese trading companies, and the Malaysian government has

164

actively contemplated one.

Japan's need to tailor purchases to actual usage of mineral raw materials since 1974 has shaped its mineral policies. The tensions created with supplying nations have, moreover, influenced its foreign policies. Most steel mills were able to reduce their purchases of iron ore under flexible purchase contracts, but contracts for copper and zinc were less flexible. Many suppliers of copper concentrate are less-developed economies, heavily dependent on the Japanese market. They would have been seriously harmed by reduced Japanese purchases. Japan's gross imports of copper ores and concentrates fell from 3.12 million tonnes in 1974 to 2.59 million tonnes in 1976, a 17% decline, which compares with its 31% drop in consumption of refined metal between 1973 and 1975. Partly to cushion the reduction in demand, the MMAJ assisted in the creation of a stockpiling scheme in 1976 to stabilise the import of base metal ores and concentrates, under long-term contracts during the recession. Two private stockpiling associations were set up — one for copper, lead and zinc, and one for aluminium — which purchased metal from the smelters with subsidised loans from the MMAJ (it borrowed from commercial banks at 9% and lent at 6.05%). These loans were to be repaid, and the stockpiles liquidated within three years, but small tonnages remained in the stockpiles at the end of 1980. These stockpile arrangements were complemented in copper by a temporary ban on exports of refined copper metal that persisted until the late 1970s. This was imposed at the request of Zaire, on the grounds that Japanese sales on the London Metal Exchange were weakening market prices. There was an implicit threat that Japan's failure to introduce such a ban would lead Zaire to nationalise Japanese investments in Zaire.

Concern about its relationships with mineral-exporting countries complicated Japanese attitudes towards the UNCTAD discussions about the Common Fund and individual commodity agreements. On the one hand, Japan philosophically favoured a free-market approach and maintenance of the *status quo*. At the most it countenanced commodity study groups analogous to the International Lead and Zinc Study Group. On the other hand, its dependence on some less developed countries has on occasion prevented it from adhering closely to the US line (which has admittedly seldom been totally coherent or consistent). It has sometimes appeared that Japanese policy towards the UNCTAD commodity discussions has been so torn between conflicting objectives that Japan has failed to play a role commensurate with its importance as a mineral importer.

The stockpile arrangements of the mid-1970s were designed as strictly temporary responses to specific problems. Japan has had no permanent strategic stockpiling arrangements comparable to those now widely discussed in Europe and the United States. The Japanese

165

steel mining companies used to run a private scheme for stocking nickel, cobalt, tungsten, molybdenum and chrome. The last two were never stocked, and although a little nickel remains in stock, the scheme has not been used since the early 1970s. MITI has argued for government-backed arrangements for stocking those minerals supplied mainly by South Africa. MITI's Agency of Natural Resources and Energy has agreed to contribute substantially towards the interest costs of a privately organised stockpile of 'rare' metals (defined as nickel, cobalt, chrome, tungsten and molybdenum) from July 1982. The scheme is similar in operation to those described above for the non-ferrous metals, but is designed specifically as a strategic stockpile. Under the fiscal 1983 budget, drafted in December 1982, a scheme was approved for the strategic stockpiling of the above five metals as well as manganese and vanadium, with the financial burden to be shared by the private sector and the government.

The southern African dimension is the most obvious, but in the longer term, perhaps, not the most important form of import dependence. The post-1973 rise in oil prices greatly reduced the viability of energy-intensive metal processes within Japan, and prompted new attitudes to overseas processing. Growing concern about pollution and environmental damage have reinforced this change. In aluminium, MITI encouraged a freezing of Japanese smelting capacity from 1973's peak of 1.64 million tonnes to 1.1 million tonnes until 1983. The 1979–80 oil price rises forced smelters to reduce their aluminium output to well under 1.0 million tonnes, a voluntary movement that MITI aims to reinforce. A restructuring plan sponsored by MITI in 1981 envisages a domestic smelter production of no more than 0.7 million tonnes by the mid-1980s. The plan includes temporary alleviation of Japan's high energy costs. Through the encouragement of joint smelting ventures overseas, MITI aims to raise the share of imported aluminium ingots produced by Japan/foreign joint ventures to over 40% by 1990. In consequence, Japan is investing in new processing facilities in resource- or energy-rich countries such as Australia, Indonesia, Brazil, Malaysia, the Philippines and the Middle East. Imports of oil and other primary energy are being replaced by purchases of energy-intensive products. This replaces Japan's direct dependence on imported primary energy by an indirect dependence – a move that involves potential strategic costs. At present Japanese industry has very flexible import arrangements. It can draw ores and concentrates from a wide variety of sources to feed its domestic processing plants and can simultaneously import processed materials. To the extent that processing plants are closed in Japan and set up near raw material supplies, this flexibility is greatly diminished. A similar trend is apparent in the supply of ferro-alloys to North America and Europe. South African mines with relatively cheap coal-based energy have

166

undercut traditional producers and forced their closure on economic grounds. The strategic implications of the past decade's dramatic switch in cost structures, and their effects on industrial locations, have not yet been fully considered.

Notes to Chapters 2 and 28

2. The World Oil Market in Transition

1. John Blair, *The Control of Oil* (New York: Pantheon, 1976), pp. 159–164; Federal Trade Commission, *The International Petroleum Cartel*, U.S. Senate, Select Committee on Small Business, 82nd Cong., 2nd Sess. (Washington, D.C.: Government Printing Office, 1952), rpt. Arno Press, 1976, pp. 163–190.

2. Blair, *The Control of Oil*, pp. 63–71.

3. Elements of the structure went back even earlier. See Edith T. Penrose, *The Large International Firm in Developing Countries* (London: Allen and Unwin, 1968), pp. 178–185.

4. But see Federal Trade Commission, *The International Petroleum Cartel*, pp. 352–370; Wayne A. Leeman, *The Price of Middle East Oil* (Ithaca, N.Y.: Cornell University Press, 1962), pp. 84–115; Helmut J. Frank, *Crude Oil Prices in the Middle East* (New York: Praeger, 1966), pp. 7–115.

5. Federal Trade Commission, *The International Petroleum Cartel*, pp. 275–346.

6. See, for instance, Benjamin Shwadran, *The Middle East, Oil and the Great Powers* (New York: Halsted Press, 1973), p. 539.

7. J. E. Hartshorn, *Politics and World Oil Economics* (New York: Praeger, 1962), p. 107.

8. See, for instance, O. E. Williamson, *Markets and Hierarchies: Analysis and Antitrust Implications* (New York: Free Press, 1975), pp. 82–131; D. L. Kaserman, "Theories of Vertical Integration: Implications for Antitrust Policy," *Antitrust Bulletin* 23, no. 3 (Fall 1978): 483–510.

9. For the role of vertical integration in the international oil industry, see M. A. Adelman, *The World Petroleum Industry* (Baltimore: Johns Hopkins University Press, 1972), pp. 89–100; D. J. Teece, "Vertical Integration in the U.S. Oil Industry," in E. J. Mitchell, ed., *Vertical Integration in the Oil Industry* (Washington, D.C.: American Enterprise Institute, 1976), pp. 83–89, 116–117; Penrose, *The Large International Firm in Developing Countries*, pp. 150–172; and Brian Levy, "World Oil Marketing in Transition," *International Organization* 36, no. 1 (Winter 1982): 113–134.

10. For a sampling of views, see, for instance, D. A. Rustow and J. F. Mugno, *OPEC: Success and Prospects* (New York: New York University Press, 1976), esp. pp. 1–32; A. D. Johany, *The Myth of the OPEC Cartel: The Role of Saudi Arabia* (New York: Wiley, 1980), pp. 33–53; Ian Seymour, *OPEC: Instrument of Change* (New York: St. Martin's, 1981); and Raymond Vernon, ed., *The Oil Crisis* (New York: Norton, 1976), p. 6, introduction. An extremely well-balanced and informed description of OPEC's role appears in J. E. Hartshorn, "Two Crises Compared: OPEC Pricing in 1973–1975 amd 1978–1980," in Ragaei el Mallakh, *OPEC: Twenty Years and Beyond* (Boulder, Colo: Westview Press, 1982), pp. 17–32.

11. R. C. Weisberg, *The Politics of Crude Oil Pricing in the Middle East, 1970–1975* (Berkeley: Institute of International Studies, 1977), pp. 37–51.

12. Rustow and Mugno, *OPEC: Success and Prospects*, pp. 130–131.

13. Fariborz Ghadar, *The Evolution of OPEC Strategy* (Lexington, Mass.: Lexington Books, 1977), pp. 35–46.

14. The events are well chronicled in J. E. Hartshorn, "Two Crises Compared," pp. 18–26.

15. See, for instance, "First Split in OPEC Pricing Unity," *Petroleum Economist* 44, no. 1 (January 1977): 2; "Competition Cuts 1978 OPEC Output," *Petroleum Economist* 46, no. 1 (January 1979): 5; "Widening OPEC Differentials," *Petroleum Economist* 46, no. 2 (February 1979): 65. For 1981–82, see "Market Trends," *Petroleum Economist* 49, no. 4 (April 1982): 160; and "OPEC Moves to Defend Prices," ibid., p. 122. Although sponsored by OPEC itself, Ian Seymour's *OPEC: Instrument of Change* contains a fairly dispassionate

recapitulation of OPEC decisions; his evaluations of OPEC's role, however, differ from mine.

16. See, for instance, "OPEC Agonistes," *The Economist*, January 23, 1982, p. 59.

17. Estimated from Petroleum Economics, Ltd., *Oil Industry Development* (London: January-February 1978 to May-June 1980).

18. Estimated from published sources by Exxon International, photocopy, February 11, 1980.

19. For Venezuela, see Alirio A. Parra, "The New Role of National Oil Companies," *Middle East Economic Survey* 23, no. 47 (September 8, 1980): 5; for Nigeria, Øystein Noreng, "State Trading and the Politics of Oil," in M. M. Kostecki, ed., *State Trading in International Markets* (London: Macmillan, 1982), p. 112.

20. "Denmark—State Oil Company," *Oil Industry Developments*, January-February 1980, p. 48.

21. *The Economist*, January 23, 1982, p. 34 advertisement.

22. George W. Grayson, *The Politics of Mexican Oil* (Pittsburgh: University of Pittsburgh, 1980), pp. 177–179.

23. George W. Grayson, "Oil and Politics in Mexico," *Current History* 80 no. 469 (November 1981): 382.

24. This development is a central theme in M. A. Conant, *The Oil Factor in U.S. Policy, 1980–1990* (Lexington, Mass.: D. C. Heath, 1982), pp. 91–92.

25. *Shell Polymers* 6, no. 1 (1982): 3–4.

26. The behavior of such stocks since 1973 is hard to interpret, probably reflecting such ambivalence. On U.S. inventory data, see *Twentieth Century Petroleum Statistics* (Dallas: De Golyer and MacNaughton, November 1981), pp. 57, 65.

27. "Saudi Arabia Buys a Japanese Maccano Set," *The Economist*, April 22, 1981, p. 53; "European Petrochemicals: End of an Era," *The Economist*, December 19, 1981, p. 64; and "Oil Refining: A Scrap Metal Business," ibid., p. 65.

28. See, for instance, "A New Chemical Triangle Takes Shape in Arabia," *The Economist*, February 7, 1981, p. 71.

29. "Kuwait to Buy Santa Fe for $2.5 Billion," *Oil and Gas Journal*, October 12, 1981, pp. 56–57.

5. Japan's Institutions and Practices

1. T. J. Pempel, "Japanese Foreign Economic Policy," in P. J. Katzenstein, ed., *Between Power and Plenty* (Madison: University of Wisconsin Press, 1978), pp. 139–190; Hugh Patrick and Henry Rosovsky, eds., *Asia's New Giant* (Washington, D.C.: Brookings Institution, 1976); E. F. Denison and W. K. Chung, *How Japan's Economy Grew So Fast: The Sources of Postwar Expansion* (Washington, D.C.: Brookings Institution, 1976); Herman Kahn, *The Emerging Japanese Superstate* (Englewood Cliffs, N.J.: Prentice-Hall, 1970); G. C. Allen, *Japan's Economic Policy* (New York: Holmes and Meier, 1980); Jiro Yao, ed., *Monetary Factors in Japanese Economic Growth* (Kobe, Japan: Research Institute for Economics and Business Administration, Kobe University, 1979); James

Abegglen, ed., *Business Strategies for Japan* (Tokyo: Sophia University, 1970); Kazushi Ohkawa and Miyohei Shinohara, eds., *Patterns of Japanese Economic Development: A Quantitative Appraisal* (New Haven: Yale University Press, 1979); Richard Caves and Masu Uekusa, *Industrial Organization in Japan* (Washington, D.C.: Brookings Institution, 1976); Kazushi Ohkawa and Henry Rosovsky, *Japanese Growth: Trend Acceleration in the Twentieth Century* (Stanford: Stanford University Press, 1973); Wilbur Monro and Eisuke Sakakibara, *The Japanese Industrial Society: Its Organizational, Cultural, and Economic Underpinnings* (Austin: Bureau of Business Research, University of Texas at Austin, 1977); Ezra Vogel, *Japan as Number One: Lessons for America* (Cambridge, Mass.: Harvard University Press, 1979).

2. For information concerning Japanese politics in general, and the anatomy of the Liberal Democratic Party in particular, see Edwin O. Reischauer, *The Japanese* (Cambridge, Mass.: Harvard University Press, 1977), pp. 234–331. See also Hans Baerwald, "Parties, Factions, and the Diet," in Murakami Hyoe and Johannes Hirschmeier, eds., *Politics and Economics in Contemporary Japan* (Tokyo: Japan Culture Institute, 1979), pp. 21–63: and I. M. Destler et al., *Managing an Alliance: The Politics of U.S.–Japanese Relations* (Washington, D.C.: Brookings Institution, 1976), pp. 49–60.

3. Sueyoshi Ohtani, *Who Is to Be Tried* (Los Angeles: ITS Information Co., 1978), p. 227; Reischauer, *The Japanese*, pp. 263–265.

4. See M. Y. Yoshino, *The Japanese Marketing System* (Cambridge, Mass.: MIT Press, 1971), pp. 131–137. Yoshino, who is thoroughly familiar with both U.S. and Japanese merchandising methods, is presently of the view that Japanese distributors resort to price competition more readily than their U.S. counterparts.

5. For information reflecting the importance of advertising in Japan, see Toshio Naito, "How Advertising Works in Japan: The Market and the People," *Dentsu's Japan Marketing/Advertising*, no. 14 (January 1979): 40.

6. On bankruptcies, see, for instance, MITI, Chusho Kigyo Hakusho (Tokyo, 1980), pp. 53–57.

7. Caves and Uekusa, *Industrial Organization in Japan*, pp. 47–87, 141–154; Vogel, *Japan as Number One*, pp. 65–84; Abegglen, *Business Strategies for Japan*, pp. 71–82; and Eugene Kaplan, *Japan: The Government–Business Relationship* (Washington, D.C.: Department of Commerce, 1972).

8. For a general description of administrative guidance and its use in Japan, see Gardner Ackley and Hiromitsu Ishi, "Fiscal, Monetary, and Related Policies," in Patrick and Rosovsky, eds., *Asia's New Giant*, pp. 236–239; and Vogel, *Japan as Number One*, pp. 75–76.

9. *Petroleum Intelligence Weekly* 18, no. 35 (August 27, 1979): 4; ibid. 18, no. 52 (December 24, 1979): 7; "Costly Spot Oil 'Shopping' Is Going to Be Penalized," *Japan Economic Journal*, December 4, 1979, p. 1; and "Gov't Will Curb Buying of High-Priced Iranian Oil," ibid., December 18, 1979, p. 1.

10. "Pessimism Strengthens over Iran Petrochemical Project," *Japan Economic Journal*, September 8, 1981, p. 16; Martha Ann Caldwell, "The Dilemma of Japan's Oil Dependency," in R. A. Morse, ed., *The Politics of Japan's Energy Strategy* (Berkeley: University of California Press, 1981), pp. 72–74.

11. See Taketsugu Tsurutani, *Political Change in Japan: Response to Postindustrial Challenge* (New York: D. McKay, 1977), p. 27; also Ryutaro Komiya and Kozo Yamamoto, "Japan: The Officer in Charge of Economic Affairs," *History of Political Economy* 13, no. 3 (Fall 1981): 600–628.

12. See, for instance, Vogel, *Japan as Number One*, pp. 36–40, 60–61; Albert Craig, "Functional and Dysfunctional Aspects of Government Bureaucracy," in E. F. Vogel, ed., *Modern Japanese Organization and Decision-Making* (Berkeley: University of California Press, 1975), pp. 20–28; and Tracy Dahlby, "Anatomy of Japan, Part One: The Bureaucrats," *Far Eastern Economic Review* 111, no. 13 (March 20, 1981): 34–40.

13. Reischauer, *The Japanese*, pp. 286–297; Kanji Haitani, *The Japanese Economic System: An Institutional Overview* (Lexington, Mass.: D. C. Heath, 1976), pp. 87–92; Nobutaka Ike, *Japanese Politics: Patron-Client Democracy* (New York: Knopf, 1972), pp. 16–17, 72–73; Takeshi Ishida, *Japanese Society* (New York: Random House, 1971), pp. 37–40.

14. An outstanding analysis that documents both these points appears in Martha Ann Caldwell, "Petroleum Politics in Japan: State and Industry in a Changing Context," diss., University of Wisconsin, 1981, reproduced by University Microfilms, Ann Arbor, Michigan, 1982.

15. For information that brings out the conflicting nature of Japanese bureaucratic politics, see I. C. Magaziner and Thomas Hout, *Japanese Industrial Policy* (Berkeley: Policy Studies Institute, 1980), pp. 53–54; Chalmers Johnson, "MITI and Japanese International Economic Policy," in Robert Scalapino, ed., *The Foreign Policy of Modern Japan* (Berkeley: University of California Press, 1977), pp. 230–244; and Pempel, "Japanese Foreign Economic Policy," p. 155.

16. The struggle among government agencies and power companies over the shape of the Japanese nuclear power industry, for instance, reflects all these elements. See R. W. Gale, "Tokyo Electric Power Company," in Morse, *The Politics of Japan's Energy Strategy*, pp. 89–100.

17. See Rodney Clark, *The Japanese Company* (New Haven: Yale University Press, 1979), pp. 125–134; Kazuo Noda, "Big Business Organization," in Vogel, ed., *Modern Japanese Organization and Decision-Making*, pp. 120–129, 144–145; and M. Y. Yoshino, "Emerging Japanese Multinational Enterprises," ibid., pp. 158–166, Also see Thomas Rohlen, *For Harmony and Strength: Japanese White Collar Organization in Anthropological Perspective* (Berkeley: University of California Press, 1974), pp. 107–108, 114–115.

18. The connection in general is explored in Alexander Gerschenkron, *Economic Backwardness in Historical Perspective* (Cambridge, Mass.: Harvard University Press, 1962), pp. 44, 354–355, 358.

19. Ackley and Ishi, "Fiscal, Monetary, and Related Policies," pp. 202–204; Yoshio Suzuki, *Money and Banking in Contemporary Japan* (New Haven: Yale University Press, 1980), p. 166.

20. Japan Economic Institute, *JEI Report*, October 9, 1981.

21. Translated into English from *Mining Handbook*, 1978 and 1980 editions, published in 1979 and 1981 respectively in Tokyo by the Japan Agency for

Natural Resources and Development, and reproduced in Economic Consulting Services, "Nonfuel Mineral Policies of Six Industrialized Countries: Final Report" (Washington, D.C., September 1981; prepared for the U.S. Department of Commerce), Table VI-20.

22. See, for instance, Gerald Curtis, "Big Business and Political Influence," in Vogel, ed., *Modern Japanese Organization and Decision-Making*, pp. 33–70; and Tracy Dahlby, "Anatomy of Japan, Part Three: The Businessmen," in *Far Eastern Economic Review* 112, no. 18 (April 24, 1981): 76–80.

23. For a summary of some major reports of this kind bearing on energy policy, see Akira Mastuzawa and Akinobu Tsumura, "Evolution of Japanese Energy Policy," *Journal of Petroleum Technology* 32, no. 10 (October 1980): 1691–94.

24. Magaziner and Hout, *Japanese Industrial Policy*, p. 38.

25. Quoted in "Japanese Adjust to Oil Supply Changes," *Oil and Gas Journal*, January 26, 1981, p. 96.

26. Chalmers Johnson, *Japan's Public Policy Companies* (Washington, D.C.: American Enterprise Institute, 1978), pp. 25–60.

27. Haitani, *The Japanese Economic System*, pp. 156–158; "Japan's Gentle Persuaders," *The Economist*, January 17–23, 1981, pp. 70–71; Eisuke Sakakibara, Robert Feldman, and Yuzo Harada, "Japanese Financial System in Comparative Perspective," U.S.-Japan Program, Center for International Affairs, Harvard University, 1981, pp. 52–61.

28. One of the best accounts of the period up to World War II is contained in I. H. Anderson, Jr., *The Standard-Vacuum Oil Company and United States East Asian Policy, 1933–1941* (Princeton: Princeton University Press, 1975). The source includes an exhaustive bibliography.

29. Anderson, *The Standard-Vacuum Oil Company*, p. 64.

30. Asado Sadao, "The Japanese Navy and the United States," in Dorothy Borg and Shumpei Okatomo, eds., *Pearl Harbor as History: Japanese-American Relations, 1931–1941* (New York: Columbia University Press, 1973), p. 237.

31. Compare Anderson, *The Standard-Vacuum Oil Company*, p. 57.

32. Ibid., p. 62.

33. Ibid., pp. 171–192.

34. J. B. Cohen, *Japan's Economy in War and Reconstruction* (Minneapolis: University of Minnesota Press, 1949), p. 140.

35. Yoshi Tsurumi, "Japan," in Raymond Vernon, ed., *The Oil Crisis* (New York: Norton, 1976), p. 115; Caldwell, "Petroleum Politics in Japan," p. 43.

36. Caldwell, "Petroleum Politics in Japan," p. 49.

37. The various sources disagree somewhat on the precise amount under foreign control, perhaps because of definitional problems; the lowest estimate is 50 percent, the highest 75 percent. The sources include Tosuke Iguchi Gendai Nihon Sangyo Hattatsushi [Developmental History of Modern Japanese Industry], vol. 2 (Tokyo: Gendai Nihon Sangyo Hattatsushi, 1964), p. 464; "Japan's Import Rules Trim Majors' Markets," *Oil and Gas Journal* 58, no. 30 (July 25, 1960); "Kurusania genyu kyokyu," *Nihon Keizai Shinbun*, March 25, 1960, p. 4.

38. "Do naru yokkaichi mondai," *Ekonomisuto*, May 1, 1952, p. 10.

39. See "Japan's Big Independent Planning to Double Everything," *Oil and Gas Journal*, Oct. 17, 1960, p. 82; Tosuke Iguchi, *Sekiyu*, vol. 2 of Gendai

Nihon Sangyo Hattatsushi, p. 464; Japan's Import Rules Trim Majors' Markets,"
Oil and Gas Journal, July 25, 1960, p. 141; and "Kurusania genyu kyokyu,
karutekkusu, gogatsu tsumi kara nisseki ni," *Nihon Keizai Shinbun*, March 25,
1960, p. 4.

40. "Nanasha ga chosadan o haken: Indoneshia yuden kaihatsu," *Nihon
Keizai Shinbun*, September 14, 1958, p. 3; "8Oman Ton Ijo no 40% o Nihon e
. . . . ," ibid., October 7, 1959, p. 3; "Gutaika no dankai ni hairu: Kita-
sumatora yuden kaihatsu," ibid., October 16, 1959, p. 4.

41. Tosuke Iguchi, *Sekiyu* (Tokyo: Gendai Nihon Sangyo Hattatsushi
Kenkyukai, 1964), p. 509.

42. "Gaishi shakkan ni ittei kijun," *Nihon Keizai Shinbun*, March 13, 1962,
p. 4.

43. Yoshi Tsurumi, "Japan," in Vernon, ed., *The Oil Crisis*, p. 115.

44. "Gaishi shakkan ni ittei kijun," *Nihon Keizai Shinbun*, March 13, 1962,
p. 4.

45. "Seisei ote: Sekiyu gyohoan ni hantai . . . ," *Nihon Keizai Shinbun*,
August 25, 1961; "Enerugii seisaku no arikata: Denryoku gyokai ga toitsu kenkai
. . . ," ibid., December 20, 1961, p. 4; "Sekiyu gyoho ni hantai: Tekko gyokai
. . . ," ibid., January 28, 1962, p. 4; "Sekiyu gyohoan ni sansei: Sekiyu kogyoren
rijikai . . . ," ibid., January 19, 1962, p. 4.

46. See "Sekiyu gyoho," in *Tsushosangyo Roppo* (Tokyo, published annually),
Law 128, May 2, 1962; "New Japanese Oil Law Stirs Uneasiness," *Oil and Gas
Journal*, June 25, 1962, p. 92.

47. "Daikyo sekiyu: Genyu shori o zenmen teishi . . . ," *Nihon Keizai Shinbun*, September 29, 1963, p. 4; "Idemitsu kosan, tsuyoi fuman; Shacho dan,"
ibid., October 5, 1963, p. 4; Idemitsu, keiei ohaba ni akka," ibid., October 6,
1963, p. 5; "Muhai seishiki kettei: Idemitsu kosan," ibid., October 26, 1963, p. 5;
"Kaki seisan chosei tsuzukeru, sekiyu renmei kinkyuri . . . ," ibid., December 4,
1963, p. 4; "'Idemitsu taisaku' shincho ni, sekiyu renmei . . . ," ibid., December
6, 1963, p. 5; "Settoku ni ojinai, idemitsu shacho wa kataru," ibid., December 12,
1963, p. 5; "Japanese Juggle Refinery Runs Formula," *Oil and Gas Journal*,
March 9, 1964, p. 64; "Idemitsu mondai kaketsu no kizashi, konshuchu ni
assenan," *Nihon Keizai Shinbun*, January 19, 1964, p. 5; "Idemitsu mondai ga
kaiketsu, tsusansho assenan o ryosho," ibid., January 25, evening, 1964, p. 1;
"Zosetsubun chosei ni shinkijun, tsusansho, hatsugenken tsuyomeru," ibid.,
January 26, 1964, p. 3.

48. Caldwell, "Petroleum Politics in Japan," p. 123.

49. Robert B. Stobaugh, "The Oil Companies in the Crisis," in Vernon, ed.,
The Oil Crisis, pp. 192–193.

50. R. A. Morse, "Energy and Japan's National Security Strategy," in Morse,
The Politics of Japan's Energy Strategy, p. 40.

51. See, for instance, Agency of Natural Resources and Energy, *Energy in
Japan: Facts and Figures* (Tokyo: Ministry of International Trade and Industry,
1980), pp. 18–24; *The Vision of MITI Policies in 1980s* (Tokyo: Ministry of International Trade and Industry, 1980), pp. 11–13; *White Paper on the International Trade* (Tokyo: Ministry of International Trade and Industry, 1980), pp.
92–97.

52. See especially Caldwell, "Petroleum Politics in Japan," pp. 274–370.

53. Jeffrey Segal, "The Rise of the 'Sogo Shosha,'" *Petroleum Economist* 48, no. 5 (May, 1981): 201–204.

54. David Watts, "Export Drive," *November 1979 Middle East Economic Digest Special Report: Japan and the Middle East*, November 1979, p. 51; Edmund O'Sullivan, "Saudi Arabia: A Deal—Technical Expertise For Oil," *December 1980 Middle East Economic Digest Special Report: Japan and the Middle East*, December 1980, p. 63.

55. Hiroshi Yokokawa, "Japanese Oil Industry and Oil Policies," U.S.-Japan Program, Center for International Affairs, Harvard University, Working Paper, April 1982.

56. Economic Consulting Services, "Nonfuel Mineral Policies," Table IV-17.

57. Economic Consulting Services, "Nonfuel Mineral Policies," Table VI-12, derived from *Kinzaku Kogyo Jigyodan no Gaiyo* [Metal Mining Agency Overview] (Tokyo: Metal Mining Agency of Japan, 1980); Kiyohiko Nanao, "Minerals Policy in Japan," in *Mineral Society*, vol. 3 (New York: Pergamon, 1979).

58. See, for instance, Y. Okawara, "Japanese Minerals Policy: A New Dimension," *Mining Review*, October 1978 (Canberra, Australia), p. 4.

59. MITI, *White Paper on International Trade 1980* (Tokyo: September 1980), p. 94, Table 4-1.

60. By 1981 these duties had been reduced to 5–10 percent; earlier, they were much higher. *Customs Tariff Schedule of Japan, 1981* (Tokyo: Japan Tariff Association, 1981).

61. A. K. Young, *The Sogo Shosha: Japan's Multinational Trading Companies* (Boulder, Colo.: Westview Press, 1979), pp. 148–149.

62. Wolfgang Gluschke et al., *Copper: The Next Fifteen Years* (Dordrecht, Holland: D. Reidel, 1979), p. 130; also Economic Consulting Services, "Nonfuel Mineral Policies," Table VI-14.

63. Economic Consulting Services, "Nonfuel Mineral Policies," Table VI-14.

64. Lloyd's *Register of Shipping Statistical Tables*, London, various dates.

65. R. O. Goss and C. E. Jones, "The Economics of Size in Dry Bulk Carriers," in R. O. Goss, ed., *Advances in Maritime Economics* (Cambridge: Cambridge University Press, 1977), pp. 90–123, reports that overall costs per ton when shipping ore in a 120,000-ton carrier amounted to about one-third of the costs in a 15,000-ton vessel.

66. Terutomo Ozawa, "Japan's Resource Dependency and Overseas Investment," *Journal of World Trade Law* 11, no. 1 (January-February 1977): 64.

67. "Australia's Iron Boom Comes Down to Earth," *Business Week*, no. 1928 (August 13, 1966): 99–100.

68. E. Gough Whitlam, *A Pacific Community* (Cambridge, Mass.: Harvard University Press, 1981), pp. 82–83.

69. Australian Department of Trade and Resources, *Australia's Mineral Resources* (Canberra, 1980), p. 5.

70. Australia/Japan Joint Study Group on Raw Materials Processing, *Australian and Japanese Aluminum Smelting Industries: Future Development and Relationships* (Canberra: Australian Government Publishing Service, 1980), pp. 6–8.

71. Y. Okawara, "Japanese Mineral Policy," p. 4; "Japanese Electricity: The Coal Rush Continues," *The Economist*, April 22, 1981, p. 59. For Japan's acquisition practices in coal, see Joseph D'Cruz, "Quasi Integration in Raw Material Markets: The Overseas Procurement of Coking Coal by the Japanese Steel Industry," diss., Harvard Business School, 1979, esp. pp. 178–192.

72. For an official summary of Japan's stockpiling policies, see MITI, *White Paper on International Trade, 1981* (Tokyo: MITI Information Office, 1981), pp. 132–133.

73. ECS report, Table VI-16, based on data from *Mining Handbook 1980* (Tokyo: Japanese Agency for Natural Resources and Energy, 1981).

74. The program is described in "Tariff Quota May Be Used to Aid Aluminum Industry," *Japan Economic Journal*, October 13, 1981, p. 3; "Japanese Ministry's Plan to End Tariffs in Some Aluminum Draws U.S. Criticism," *Wall Street Journal*, October 1981, p. 31.

75. "Japan Brings the Curtain Down on the Stars of Yesteryear," *The Economist*, September 26, 1981, p. 67; "Natural Resource and Energy Agency Is Asked to Take Up Excessive Oil Refining," *Japan Economic Journal*, January 12, 1982, p. 6.

76. Stuart Kirby, "Japan's Role in the 1980s," Economist Intelligence Unit Report 81, London, June 1980, pp. 8, 11.

77. "Brazil's Steelnut," *The Economist*, June 12, 1982, p. 78.

Name Index

Aarons, L. 155
Aikawa 580, 582
Aitken, Hugh 477, 489
Alessandri, Jorge 496, 503, 504, 515
Allende, Salvador 491, 492, 519, 520, 521
Anderson, George 317
Anderson, Roy S. 464, 465
Antunes, Augusto T. de A. 554, 555, 557
Antunes, Paulo C. de A. 556
Archbold, J.D. 289, 290
Arenberg, Prince d'Ernest 98
Ashmead, Edward 398
Ashton, Hubert 542
Atlee, Clement 543

Baillieu, W.L. 158, 172, 179
Bain, H. Foster 588
Bancroft, J.A. 185
Barnato, B. 408
Barrett, David 389
Beatty, A. Chester 187, 188, 205
Becquey, Louis 102
Bedford, A.C. 445
Beit 408
Bemis, William E. 456, 464–9, 471, 474, 475
Benard, M. 445
Bennett, W.A.C. 389
Berle 559
Berwind, E.J. 306
Betancourt 62
Blainey, G. 135–7, 151, 155
Blake, Charles H. 464
Blum, Léon 332
Body, J.B. 441, 444
Bogle, Walter S. 314, 317
Bonaparte, Napoleon 103, 286
Borkin, Joseph 237
Bostwick, J.A. 289
Boulton 81, 84, 87–92
Bowker, James 535, 538
Boyle, E.H. Jr 16
Bradfield, J.R. 486
Brandegee, Frank 314
Brewster, Benjamin 289
Bryan, William J. 466
Burnham 559
Butler, R.A. 545

Callbreath, James 314, 315, 317
Callot, F.G. 6
Carden, Sir Lionel 442
Carey, Rupert 531–4, 536–8, 541, 547
Cassel, Ernest 408
Castelbajac, Viscount 103
Castro, Fidel 54
Chadborne, Humphrey 486
Chandler, Alfred 113, 126–8, 131
Chapman, Stanley 395, 413
Chaptal, Count Jean-Antoine 100, 101
Chou Tzu-ch'i 466, 467, 469, 470, 472, 474, 475
Churchill, Winston 545
Clapp, Moses 314
Cochrane, Peter 156
Cohen, Waley 444
Coltman, Robert, Jr 461
Connell, R.W. 156
Courbold, W.H. 156
Cowdray, Lord 442, 444, 445, 446
Crouzol, Count Chabrol de 100
Crowson, Phillip 18
Cummins, Albert 314

Dalton, W.H. 438
Daly, Marcus 123, 124
Davies, Robert 150
Davis, Sir Edmund 187, 188, 205
Davis, L. 397
Denoon, Donald 135–8
Désandrouin, Jacques 98
Deterding, Henri 444
Diaz, President 460
Dodd, S.C.T. 285, 288
Drysdale 537
Dunkelsbuhler, Anton 558
Dupin, Charles 96
Duran 495
Dutra, President 554
Duval 389

Eckstein, F. 142
Eckstein, Hermann 146, 408
Edelstein 397
Eden, Anthony 545
Edwards, Humphrey 105